# JUDGE AND JURY

# JUDGE AND JURY:
## The Life and Times of
## Judge Kenesaw Mountain Landis

### David Pietrusza

Foreword by Gov. Dick Thornburgh

Diamond Communications, Inc.
South Bend, Indiana
1998

**JUDGE AND JURY:**
**The Life and Times of Judge Kenesaw Mountain Landis**
Copyright © 1998 by David Pietrusza

*10 9 8 7 6 5 4 3 2 1*

Manufactured in the United States of America

Diamond Communications, Inc.
Post Office Box 88
South Bend, Indiana 46624-0088
(219) 299-9278
FAX (219) 299-9296
Website: http://www.diamondbooks.com

Library of Congress Cataloging-in-Publication Data

Pietrusza, David, 1949-
    Judge and jury : the life and times of Judge Kenesaw Mountain
Landis / David Pietrusza : foreword by Gov. Dick Thornburgh.
        p.   cm.
    Includes bibliographical references (p.  ) and  index.
    ISBN 1-888698-09-8
    1. Landis, Kenesaw Mountain, 1866-1944.  2. Baseball
commissioners--United States--Biography.  3. Judges--United
States--Biography.  I. Title.
GV865.L3P54   1998
796.357'092--dc21
[B]                                                          98-13938
                                                                CIP

# CONTENTS

# FOREWORD

Baseball fans should be grateful for this comprehensive biography of one of the game's most towering and dominating figures.

Those of us who cut our baseball teeth during what we perceived to be the golden days of the 1930s and 1940s have an indelible image of the man who personified the national game to us. The Czar. Judge Kenesaw Mountain Landis. The craggy-faced, white-thatched, God-like figure whose chin seemed to be perpetually perched on a box seat railing at a World Series, All-Star Game, or other contest of baseball significance.

Behind that sober image, however, lay a vastly more complicated reality as David Pietrusza tells us in this work. The image was a carefully cultivated one, shrewdly promoted by one of the master showmen of his era. Landis' czardom was based, in large part, on symbolism. The banning for life of the eight criminally-acquitted "Black Sox" defendants was the master stroke in his effort to save baseball from public disgrace at its hour of maximum peril. The author points out how this dramatic move saved baseball from joining boxing as a perpetually discredited enterprise. And it was followed by others throughout his lengthy tenure.

The waxing and waning of Judge Landis' wrath was carefully tailored to the public's temperature. Seemingly inconsistent approaches were taken, from time to time, by baseball's "Judge and Jury" in what appeared to be similar cases. No compulsion seemed to exist to "treat like cases alike" as the varied responses to alleged wrongdoing in the Joe Gedeon and Rube Benton cases illustrate.

Self-promotion, which began during Landis' tenure on the federal bench, was a hallmark of his commissionership as well. Although he studiously eschewed judicial robes, he was never one to overlook an opportunity to catch the public eye, no matter what the cause. His judicial forays against Standard Oil and John D. Rockefeller, embellished by a $29 million fine (later reversed), were matched by his patriotic zeal in cases involving Socialist Party leaders and IWW chieftain "Big Bill" Haywood.

Yet can there be any doubt that Judge Landis truly "saved" professional baseball in the aftermath of the scandals which led up to the notorious 1919 World Series? Or that his stewardship established an image of the game as unsullied and truly worthy of its designation as "the national pastime" throughout his 24-year tenure? Since his time, baseball—owners, players, and fans—have searched for his like to preserve and perpetuate that status. And, by and large, they have failed.

There are many peculiarities of the man and his mission set forth in this instructive work. Landis' persistent effort to retain both his federal judgeship and the baseball commissionership, almost leading to his impeachment from the judiciary, bespeaks streaks of both stubbornness and avarice that are difficult for us to justify. His eventual resignation from his bench, on the other hand, illustrates Landis' capacity to know just how far he could push the limits of his personal agenda. The farcical feud with *The Sporting News* head J. G. Taylor Spink over the publishing of an *official* baseball guide from 1942 to 1945 is another puzzling episode of pique over what was but a minor challenge to the czar's domain.

But Landis' sense of limits served him well in his treatment of allegations made against two of the game's giants, Ty Cobb and Tris Speaker, for alleged pre-1919 betting on their clubs' games. Landis chose to ease these two stars, in the twilight of their respective careers, quietly off the stage rather than pillory them for practices that were not viewed as seriously prior to his own iron-handed rule.

On the other hand, his feuds with Ban Johnson, Babe Ruth, Rogers Hornsby, and Branch Rickey were battles to the bitter end, with little quarter shown. Moreover, Landis' opposition to gamblers of all stripes and to those associated with horse racing and his support of Prohibition were legendary. His hard line on pre-1919 fixers and post-1919 ballplayer bettors like Shufflin' Phil Douglas and the Cozy Dolan-Jimmy O'Connell duo provided the game with a genuine deterrent capability as to those subsequently tempted.

Sadly, the Judge chose to walk too precarious a tight rope on the issue of breaking the color line in baseball. He responded to the temper of the times and the recalcitrance of most owners when it came to question of major league contracts for African-American ballplayers. That development would have to await Landis' death and the path-finding action of the Dodgers' Branch Rickey in signing Jackie Robinson in 1946. But what an opportunity was missed by Landis truly to underscore baseball's status as a "national pastime" by taking an earlier lead role on this battlefield of racial progress.

It was, however, Landis' pragmatism that had helped to thrust him forward as the leading candidate for the commissioner's job in the first place. In 1915, the Federal League had sued the existing major leagues for anti-trust violations, bringing into question the validity of the reserve clause and other restrictive provisions of baseball's player contracts. The case was assigned to Landis who, after hearing the evidence, stalled in making a decision until the upstart league collapsed of its own weight and settled out of court. It was not to be the last time that the Judge was credited with "saving" baseball, but in this instance, it also advanced the cause for his eventually being tapped for the com-missioner's position.

A major contribution of this work is the examination of Landis' pre-commissioner contacts with the world of politics. His first full-time job was a patronage position in the office of the Indiana Secretary of State for whose election he had campaigned. Later, after a brief stint in law practice, the 26-year-old Landis went to Washington as a personal aide to Charles Gresham, a Republican-turned-Democrat who was appointed secretary of state in the administration of President Grover Cleveland ("the favorite Democrat of many Republicans"). Upon Gresham's death in 1895, Landis declined Cleveland's offer to become minister to Venezuela and returned to Chicago to practice law and rejoin the progressive wing of the Republican Party. By then, his older brother, Charles, had been elected a Republican congressman from Indiana, soon to be followed by brother Frederick in another Hoosier house of representatives seat. Both brothers unseated GOP incumbents and neither was to have a lengthy stint in office. Ultimately it was as a Teddy Roosevelt Republican that Landis himself gained appointment to the federal bench. Thereafter he was to flirt with the notion of seeking higher office—as Chicago mayor, governor of Illinois, and even, in flights of fancy, the presidency and vice presidency—but never made a leap into the maelstrom of elective politics.

Despite his resisting a yen for elective politics, his popularity within the constituency which counted remained high during his tenure.

Years following Judge Landis' death, former American League pitcher Elden Auker is quoted in this work as noting:

> "He was ... the best thing that happened to baseball. I wish we had him today."

I sense that a residue of that feeling persists, but it is a minority view. In 1993 I was among those asked to meet with the baseball owners' search committee appointed to recommend a new commissioner following the untimely death of my friend, Bart Giamatti, and the brief and unhappy reign of Fay Vincent. After an exchange of pleasantries at our Chicago hotel get-together, I asked the assembled executives:

"Are you folks really sure you want a commissioner?"

I had in mind, obviously, my model of a Judge Kenesaw Mountain Landis, empowered to act against anything, "detrimental to the best interests ... of baseball" as he saw it. It was evident then, and remains so this day, that they were not, in fact, looking, for such a person. And baseball remains the poorer for such an attitude.

*Dick Thornburgh*
*April 1998*

# ACKNOWLEDGMENTS

Thanks are due to the following institutions: the Albany (NY) Public Library, the Cass County Historical Society, the Chicago Historical Society, the Chicago Public Library, the Cleveland Public Library, the Hofstra University Library, the Indiana Historical Society, the Indiana State Archives, the National Baseball Library, the New York Public Library, the New York State League Library, North Central Michigan College, the Petoskey (MI) Public Library, the Omni Ambassador East Hotel, the Schenectady County Community College Library, the Schenectady (NY) Public Library, the Society for American Baseball Research, *The Sporting News,* the Union College Library, and the University of Albany Library.

Thanks also are due to the following individuals who assisted me in my research: Jeff Angus, Heather Cunningham, Rob Edelman, Steve Gietschier, Chuck Hershberger, W. Lloyd Johnson, David Jordan, Audrey Kupferberg, Len Levin, Ted Hathaway, Lily M. Kuo, Jerry Malloy, John Miller, Paul Morgan, Herb Moss, Archie Motley, James Overmyer, Doug Pappas, Violet M. Owen, Fred Schuld, Dennis Stegman, John Thorn, and Barbara Schull Wolfe.

The following individuals were gracious enough to grant interviews regarding Judge Landis: Elden Auker, Bob Broeg, Susanne Landis Huddleson, Bob Feller, Howard Green, Keehn Landis, Lincoln Landis, Nancy Landis Smith Lucas, Carl Lundquist, William McCarthy, Jo-Jo Moore, James A. Riley, and Robert Wood. I am especially indebted to the members of the Landis family for their assistance.

Thanks also to Jill and Jim Langford of Diamond Communications for believing in this project, to Jeremy Langford for stepping into the breech, and to Jack Kavanagh who graciously assisted in the editing of this work.

I am honored that Dick Thornburgh, former United States Attorney General and governor of Pennsylvania, graciously agreed to provide the book's foreword. I thank him for his good words and support.

And special thanks goes to my wife Patty who patiently waited for me to finish a medium-sized project that turned into a very large one.

*Dedicated to*
*Patricia Basford Pietrusza*

# INTRODUCTION

For more than a third of a century, I have followed the game that Kenesaw Mountain Landis once so autocratically ruled. For the better part of a decade I have had the honor to write professionally about our national pastime.

In that time, I have been barely able to escape Mr. Landis. First and foremost, he, of course, materializes in any historical perspective of baseball's commissionership. When we discuss that office, when we envision an all-powerful czar acting in the best interests of the game, our mind's eye does not envision a Ford Frick or a Fay Vincent, it conjures up only one individual—a scowling, little, white-haired man named Kenesaw Mountain Landis.

It is simply impossible to discuss the office, to envision or debate it, without at least subconsciously thinking of its dictatorial first occupant. For good or ill, he is the model against whom all his successors are compared.

And it is not merely in regard with the commissionership that we continue meeting Kenesaw Landis. He appears in any discussion of baseball gambling. We debate his banning of Joe Jackson and Buck Weaver. And increasingly—not decreasingly—he is a central figure in discussions of baseball's race relations and its once long-standing Jim Crow tradition.

Yet, we know Landis—and we do *not* know him. While everyone remembers the unique name of Kenesaw Mountain Landis and has a vague picture of the man who dominated Organized Baseball for a quarter century, that is about it. Too often we can barely see beyond the caricatures that first he—and later others—created.

Increasingly we have lost more of the detail and texture of this extraordinary figure. Remarkably, only one biography of Landis—J. G. Taylor Spink's *Judge Landis and Twenty-Five Years of Baseball*—has previously been published. That was in 1947, barely three years after the Judge's death. And although we routinely greet numerous biographies of all sorts of baseball luminaries (can one explain why not too long ago two studies of Honus Wagner appeared in a single year? Or two of Dizzy Dean?), no full-scale portrait has since been written of baseball's most powerful individual.

And so, until *Judge and Jury* no Landis biography has featured new perspectives on such topics as the Byzantine plotting surrounding his appointment; the Judge's handling of the Black Sox scandal; his banishment of numerous other players, such as Bennie Kauff or Phil Douglas; his power struggles with Babe Ruth, Branch Rickey, and American League president Ban Johnson; or his attitudes and actions on racial segregation.

That is bad enough. But *Judge Landis and Twenty-Five Years of Baseball* was by no means a true biography. The volume's title is instructive, although to be absolutely accurate it should have more properly read *Judge Landis' Twenty-Five Years of Baseball*. The reason: Taylor Spink's seminal book explains almost nothing about the Kenesaw Mountain Landis that existed before its central character's involvement with the national pastime. A mere 28 pages are devoted to the more than 50 years Kenesaw Landis lived before baseball turned to him. Hence, when one gets down to brass tacks, *Judge and Jury* is not the second but the *first* full biography of this remarkable figure.

The years of Landis' life that Spink ignored are important years, fascinating years. If we do not know what Kenesaw Landis accomplished in that time period, we will not fully understand what compelled baseball to turn to this man, why it rejected so many other viable candidates, and chose as its savior someone who otherwise would now be a largely long-forgotten midwestern federal judge.

The judge baseball picked was, of course, a fan of the national pastime (as he showed in the Federal League case of 1915). But any number of mere fans—or judges or politicians—could have been selected. Baseball's magnates anointed Landis because he had established himself as a remarkable national figure. We remember him today as the "grandstanding" jurist who in 1907 fined the Standard Oil company a record $29 million (a fine later overturned), but Landis' judicial career was far more than a single high-profile case nearly a decade and a half before his commissionership.

By overlooking Landis' pre-baseball career, we not only fail to understand why he was chosen, we also deprive ourselves of the pleasure of viewing numerous fascinating slices of American history—a peak inside the State Department of the 1890s; instances of murder, vice, and corruption in pre-Prohibition but still wide-open Chicago; Landis' often-harsh and often-controversial (but oddly enough frequently humane) treatment of anti-war activists during the First World War; an unsuccessful bomb plot against him; and the bleeding-heart progressivism that cause a United States senator to call for his impeachment.

Beyond amassing a piquant resumé, Judge Landis accumulated something else on the federal bench—the public's trust. The man in the street did not feel that way about most judges, and certainly not about most federal jurists. His decisions and his populist manner (he never wore judicial robes) attracted attention. He could, in fact, temper justice with extreme leniency and sentiment. Yet conversely, the Judge could also impose the harshest of sentences and, for good measure, announce them with massive doses of sarcasm and vitriol. Often the same case revealed both sides of the Landis personality. The quiver of his judicial style had many arrows, and Kenesaw Landis chose each carefully as he masterfully cultivated public opinion.

In dealing with Landis' pre-baseball life and career we approach this biography in the standard chronological format. But in dealing with his baseball career a different approach is often mandated. There are certain episodes—the machinations that surrounded his appointment; the Judge's confrontation with Babe Ruth; the Cobb-Speaker imbroglio; the banning of Jimmy O'Connell and Cozy Dolan—that we rightfully devote entire chapters to. To interrupt them with other incidents, or to switch back-and-forth between topics such as his policing of the farm system; gambling in baseball; his overall style; his little-known personal life; or his racial attitudes would soon prove counterproductive. Accordingly, we have reserved a good number of chapters to topical treatments of those issues.

Of those subjects, we hear most today of Landis and baseball's segregation. Increasingly, modern observers have created the image of Kenesaw Landis as the George Wallace of baseball, standing in the doorway of every ballpark in the country, an unyielding racist who prevented the game's integration.

It's a convenient image. Unfortunately, it oversimplifies the issue and—by shifting all or most of the blame to Landis—exculpates the rest of baseball for its actions, inactions, and attitudes. If truth be told, few in baseball wished to integrate, a fact revealed by the many teams that did not hire even token blacks until years following Landis' death.

Much of the discussion of Landis and the issue of race has centered on the Judge's supposed quashing of Bill Veeck's 1942 plan to purchase the threadbare Philadelphia Phillies and restock the team with star Negro Leaguers. Veeck's actions would have shattered baseball's color line.

It's a good story—and clearly establishes Landis as a prime villain in the drama of baseball's racial integration. Good stories, however, are not necesarily *true* stories. Recent scholarship (virtually unreported in the mainstream media) has done much to debunk Veeck's contentions. "I think most people today," historian Jules Tygiel summarizes, "believe that [Veeck's story] was never the case."

And just as it is significant to reexamine Landis' role in Bill Veeck's allegations, it is important to further probe his role in the rest of the story of baseball's color bar. Landis is certainly not a hero in the drama, bit it makes little sense to overestimate his perfidy — and to do so on such slim evidence. There is enough blame to go around. The creation of demon-figures may make for good theater. It does not make for good history.

It used to be the common wisdom that Judge Landis stepped up to the plate in 1920 and saved baseball from the consequences of the Black Sox scandal. That was somewhat simplistic — but it was largely true. His forceful actions, coupled with his carefully cultivated public persona of forceful honesty, did help to restore baseball's good name. We take it for granted that baseball is honest, that we can count on it being free from gamblers and corruption. We take it for granted *because* of Kenesaw Landis. Before his advent fans had a naive faith in the game. He changed that naive belief into a reality. In 1920 baseball shared the sporting public's favor with just one other professional sport. It was not football, not basketball, certainly not hockey or soccer. It was boxing. The gentlemanly art of self-defense has since traveled the road baseball could have traveled, a road of fan suspicion, of wondering if each contest was fixed, if each hero was a puppet on the strings of outside interests. Landis' often harsh methods — most significantly in the Buck Weaver case — prevented the game from becoming the tawdry business boxing soon descended to.

All in all, this diminutive judge remains as big a part of the baseball firmament as much — if not more — than almost anyone who has played the game. If one were to sculpt baseball's version of Mount Rushmore, it would contain Babe Ruth, Ty Cobb, Jackie Robinson, and — learning over a granite rail, peering across the prairies at some far distant ballgame — Kenesaw Mountain Landis. A half century after his death, the Judge's game is still honest. That is his legacy, and it is no small accomplishment.

*David Pietrusza*
*February 1998*

CHAPTER 1

# "I Had an Ambition to Become the Head of Something"

Physically Kenesaw Mountain Landis was not a mountain. But he was named for one.

In November of 1862, Dr. Abraham Hoch Landis, the father of the future lord of baseball, left his home in Millville, Ohio, 25 miles north of Cincinnati, as an assistant surgeon with the 35th Ohio Infantry Regiment. The Civil War would eventually take the 41-year-old Dr. Landis to northern Georgia and provide his son with an unusual given name.

The war was not at all kind to this country doctor. Landis saw much of death and human suffering. Chickamauga, for example, was a disaster for the Union. Fought in northern Georgia in September 1863, over 16,000 Northern troops were either killed, wounded, or taken captive. The 35th Ohio lost half its men. Dr. Landis himself was taken prisoner and, along with 46 other surgeons, was sent by way of Atlanta to Richmond's infamous Libby prison. His fellow prisoners' suffering shocked the doctor. "The mere appearance of their faces told us starvation and exposure were closing the work of death ..." he noted.[1]

Released in an exchange of prisoners, he returned to the 35th Ohio and was one of 100,000 men who moved from Tennessee into Georgia as William Tecumseh Sherman struck deeper into a dying South. Sherman, however, found himself confronted by General Joseph Johnston's tenacious and skillful retreat. Normally, Sherman would have tried outflanking Johnston. But horrifically muddy roads made that impossible. Waiting out the rebels also seemed out of the question, as Union soldiers grew ever more restive from their slow pace. Finally in late June 1864, Sherman flung 16,000 troops

1

into a desperate frontal assault on Johnston's well dug-in 18,000-man force, just 20 miles northwest of Atlanta.

The result was the Battle of Kennesaw Mountain, one of the worst Union defeats of the entire war. The Confederates lost just 800 men, while federal casualties amounted to 2,500. Most famous among the wounded was Ambrose Bierce, the future acerbic humorist, but the most significant for Abraham Landis was a teen-aged infantryman being treated at Landis' surgical headquarters. "A 12-pound cannonball, apparently spent, was bounding toward the group," Kenesaw once recounted. "Nobody paid any attention to it. But it struck my father's left leg, just below the knee, and shattered it horribly.... He had to keep his fellow surgeons off with a gun, in order to keep them from amputating it."[2]

In August the 35th Ohio was mustered out of service, and the crippled Landis returned to Millville.[3] Badly mangled, he was unable to immediately resume the practice of medicine. "When I was six years old," recalled Kenesaw, "eight years after that battle, I remember distinctly how he was still going through special exercises, trying to regain more use of the injured leg."[4]

So the Battle of Kennesaw Mountain was never far from Dr. Landis' mind—not even on November 20, 1866 when his wife, Mary Kumler Landis, gave birth to their sixth child and fourth son.

Actually Dr. Landis' morbid fascination with the site of his personal disaster might have been a positive development, for the Landises were involved both in a general domestic dispute over what to name the newcomer and a specific debate over Abraham's suggestion to name the child after himself. "For months after I was born," Kenesaw later recalled, "my folks couldn't agree on a name for me. I lay there in a basket and my aunts and uncles would come in every night and argue with my mother and father about what I should be called. It got to be a community problem. The blacksmith thought I ought to be named Abraham, for my father, but my mother vowed she wouldn't have a son of hers shackled with a name like that."[5]

Indeed, Mary Landis must have truly hated the name Abraham—not to mention all the other proposals—for when her husband finally suggested, "Let us call him Kenesaw Mountain," she agreed.[6]

The name must not have always gone over well among young Landis' often cruel contemporaries. "They called me every damn thing they could think of," contended Kenesaw.[7]

As queer as this nomenclature may seem to modern ears, it was not nearly so foreign to 19th-century ones. Civil War veterans often named children after engagements in which they had fought. One child found himself christened Malvern Hill Barnum. In Boston, the legend went, two brothers were named "Sixth Corps" and "Army of the Potomac."[8]

With that in mind, we—and he—may consider ourselves lucky that baseball's first commissioner was Kenesaw Mountain Landis and not Libby Prison Landis or 35th Ohio Regiment Landis.

The spelling of the name provides some interesting history. The child was named "Kenesaw Mountain," but we have recorded the battle as being "Kennesaw Mountain" — and in fact that is the modern spelling of the battle and the location. Most historians have explained the difference as a mere misspelling, but this is an oversimplification. Actually, there were two spellings of the name—*Kennesaw and Kenesaw*. In the 19th and early 20th centuries, Kenesaw was as acceptable as the now-standard Kennesaw. Abraham Landis was not guilty of a misspelling, he simply paid his money and took his choice. He chose Kenesaw.[9]

To understand Kenesaw Mountain Landis one must comprehend his family—and how highly visible, idea-oriented, and flamboyant it was. No one ever accused Kenesaw Landis of being shy. Most saw him as a hopeless ham, whose flair for the dramatic often outshone his legal or judicial acumen. Staring down from his judge's bench or glaring across his commissioner's desk at club owners, Landis possessed a stage presence that many actors would have given their Screen Actors Guild card to possess. He never hesitated to employ it.

Ultimately Kenesaw Landis would establish a reputation as a religious skeptic —perhaps even an atheist, but he sprang from highly religious roots. The Landises were originally Swiss Mennonites. Distant ancestor Hans Landis was beheaded at Geneva in September 1614 for his faith. Authorities later imprisoned Hans' son Felix and so mistreated him he died from jail's ill effects. Soon afterword, the Landises left Switzerland, relocating most likely in the Germanic Alsatian region near Strasbourg. These Catholic lands were, however, only marginally more hospitable, and shortly before the American Revolution eight Landis brothers sailed for the New World, settling in Pennsylvania. One, Frederick, was Kenesaw Mountain Landis' great-grandfather.[10]

Frederick's son Phillip and his second wife Elizabeth Hoch were among the earliest settlers of Butler County, Ohio, where, their youngest son, Abraham Landis, was born at Hickory Flats, Ohio, on February 14, 1821. Educated in a log cabin schoolhouse, Abraham later studied medicine under a Dr. Rigdon of Hamilton, Ohio, and graduated from Cincinnati's Ohio Medical College in 1849.[11] In Millville on September 17, 1850, he took Mary Kumler as his bride. Shortly thereafter they moved back to Millville, living in a humble three-room brick cottage constructed atop a hillside overlooking Indian Creek.[12] It would later serve as Kenesaw's birthplace.[13]

Abraham Landis was not marrying down. The Kumlers were a distinguished clan, particularly in matters of religion. Mary Kumler's grandfather, Henry Kumler, Sr., had come from a family of "some means." Raised in the German Reformed Church, in 1815 he converted to the United Brethren in Christ and devoted himself to the propagation of its faith. He circuit rode long distances for the "U B of C" (as Kenesaw would later flippantly refer to the sect) and became a church bishop in 1825. Sixteen years later, one of his 12 children, Henry Jr., followed in his footsteps as a church bishop. In January 1855 Henry Jr., his brother Dr. D. C. Kumler (Mary Kumler's father), and Daniel Kumler Flickinger (a grandson of Henry Sr. by his daughter Hannah)[14] were the first three United Brethren missionaries to visit Africa. Another of Henry Sr.'s grandsons (by his daughter Susannah), Franklin Abia Zeller Kumler, distinguished himself, as president of two colleges and won election to the Society of Science, Letters and Arts of London, England. The Kumlers were clearly not a family to be trifled with.[15]

Five children had already been born to Abraham and Mary Kumler Landis prior to Kenesaw's arrival: Catherine Jeannette (born August 15, 1851), Sarah Frances Q. (December 28, 1853), Walter (April 15, 1856), Charles Beary (July 9, 1858), and John Howard (October 10, 1860). Another son, Frederick Daniel (August 18, 1872), would follow Kenesaw.

On his mother's side, Landis was descended from Bible-believing clergymen. While he failed to inherit his ancestors' religious zeal, Kenesaw did inherit their I-am-speaking-from-Holy-Writ mein. But evangelism was not the only family strain influencing Kenesaw.

Landis' four brothers all dabbled successfully in a pair of very public avocations: journalism and politics. Two of his brothers ultimately won election to Congress. Both interests they inherited from Abraham Landis. Originally a Whig, Dr. Landis became a lifelong and staunch Republican. He also had a flair for writing, sending back numerous dispatches of his wartime experiences to various Northern newspapers and periodicals. The combination of those two pursuits with evangelism would eventually give physically small Kenesaw Mountain Landis the presence to cow criminals, industrial monopolists, or baseball owners—in fact, just about anybody he came in contact with.[16]

Kenesaw's oldest brother, Walter Kumler "Happy Jack" Landis, set the journalistic pattern for his younger siblings, starting in that profession with the *Logansport Journal* and continuing on with the *Marion Chronicle*, the *Indianapolis Journal & Sentinel*, and the *Cincinnati Commercial Tribune*.[17]

Walter, a lifelong bachelor, was not beyond employing every journalistic trick required to obtain a story. Once at the *Commercial Tribune* he and Gid Thompson, a reporter at the rival *Enquirer*, rushed out independently of each other to the rail yards to interview a woman, Della Shellabarger, about a suspected murder. When Thompson arrived, Shellabarger informed him that a police detective named Kratz had warned her against speaking to anyone else about the case. Kratz, she added, was in the railroad car's drawing room. Thompson demanded to see him—and discovered "Kratz" was actually Landis. From then Walter Landis' fellow journalists knew him as "Detective Kratz."[18]

Charles Beary Landis, the stockiest of the five brothers, graduated from Wabash College. In 1883 he followed Walter into journalism, also with the *Logansport Journal*—a paper then owned by Daniel P. Baldwin, who had served as Indiana's attorney general from 1880 through1882. There Charles held the grand title of city editor, although in actuality he was the paper's solitary employee. An active Republican in an era when newspapers were openly and proudly partisan, Charles tackled opponents mercilessly. In 1884, for example, a local Democrat, H. J. Roach, picked a fight with the young journalist for remarks Charles had made in the *Logansport Journal* impugning Roach's moral integrity. Bystanders had to separate the pair. On the urging of *Journal* editor W. D. Pratt, Charles became his own boss in 1887, purchasing the *Delphi* (Indiana) *Journal*. From 1894 through 1896 he served as president of the Indiana Republican Editorial Association.

Some around Logansport considered John Howard Landis to have possessed an "intellectual superiority" over his brothers and to have been more "thorough and painstaking." He lacked, however, their flair and one observer thought him "less showy."[19]

John also harbored journalistic ambitions, but his enthusiasm began to decline after his participation in a December 1878 Logansport High School Literary Society debate. He took the negative in the question, "Resolved, that the Pen is Mightier than the Sword"—and lost.

At one point he wrote a novel. But when he sent the manuscript to a friend for "candid" review, she found it totally lacking "the element of love." Not only did he not publish the work, he also never contacted her again.[20]

Graduating from high school in 1879, John spent the next decade drifting from position to position. In 1885 he entered the railway postal service, passing his entrance exam (which relied on accuracy in sorting 1661 cards) with only 12 mistakes, a grade of 99.5 percent (90 percent was passing). The following February, however, he contracted malaria. When he recovered, he moved to Minneapolis where he became an accountant in a plumbing firm operated by an old Logansport school chum. Finally John entered the medical profession, graduating in 1890 from his father's alma mater, the Ohio Medical College. Remaining in Cincinnati, he began his practice in that city in 1891.[21]

Frederick "Buckskin" Landis was the youngest of the seven Landis children —and perhaps the most dramatic, outstripping even Kenesaw in that regard.

Frederick held the "Buckskin" nickname since age 10 when he had delivered papers from atop his father's aged horse "Buckskin." His next career move was even less propitious. Dropping out of high school after his freshman year, he went to work clerking in a local drugstore. Frederick quickly tired of "sweeping out cigar stubs and washing bottles," however, and returned to school. In 1893 he obtained a law degree from the University of Michigan and that September began practicing in Logansport. But he focused more on politics than law, and when the *Logansport Journal*'s W. D. Pratt convinced him that journalism was a convenient political stepping stone, he quickly joined the *Journal*'s staff.[22]

And what of the two Landis sisters, Kate and Sarah? In an era when few women worked outside the home, the teaching profession was a rare avenue open to women—particularly unmarried women. In 1872 Sarah Frances (usually known as Frances, and to family members as "Frank" or even "Q") moved back to Seven Mile, Ohio, to take up that spinsteresque profession. In 1880 she took up teaching in Logansport, eventually accepting a position as first grade teacher at that city's Southside school. The other sister, Kate, attended Ohio's Otterbein College and regularly won ribbons at the Cass County Horticultural and Mechanical Association for such entries as sweet preserves, catsup, comb honey, and wax flowers. But lest we underestimate her, she is one of the first of the Landises to be recorded in political activity. In October 1884 she served on the Fifth Ward's Floral Committee in welcoming GOP presidential candidate James G. Blaine to Logansport.

In the decade following the Civil War, Abraham Landis was on the move. In 1869 he relocated the family to Seven Mile, Ohio, where Frederick Landis was born, and then moved to northern Indiana in 1875, settling in the small town of Logansport.[23]

When in the early 1870s Abraham Landis was considering his move to Logansport, he also pondered such alternatives as Omaha and Chicago. He had even picked out a particular block-sized parcel in the Windy City, but finally decided that Logansport had a greater future as a railroad hub and opted to become a Hoosier.

Years later, after Kenesaw had moved to Chicago and established a law practice in the city, Abraham Landis visited him. One day, Kenesaw, a great walker, and his father went hiking about the city when Abraham spied the parcel he had once considered purchasing. It had become the site of the LaSalle Street rail station. Had Dr. Landis acquired the land he would have become a wealthy man.

"Sir," Kenesaw jokingly reproved his father, "if it hadn't been for your bad judgement, I would now be one of those young blades driving down Michigan Avenue in a carriage, instead of spending my youth cooped up in a law office."[24]

In Logansport, Dr. Landis served on the board of the Logansport State Hospital for the Insane.[25] He also augmented his medical income with a $17-per-month Civil War pension and practiced farming. In October 1878 the doctor even took second place at the Cass County Fair for his half bushel of sweet potatoes. Life was satifying but not easy. Each of the Landis children was expected to pitch in and help with the chores. The work was hard, but years later Kenesaw—never really known for his interest in physical labor—professed not to mind. In 1907 he reminisced to a reporter about his Indiana farm days:

Did you ever cradle wheat? If you haven't, you don't know what work is. It is the one thing, besides mowing hay at the back side of a big hay mow on a hot day, calculated to make one lose confidence in Providence.

Nowadays farmers are regular dudes and sit on a spring seat under an umbrella, while a self-binding machine does the work. Now they read Shakespeare and reap their harvests at the same time.

Those were the happiest days of my life. We raised corn mostly, with a little wheat and such, plowing with Bob and Liz. Liz was a lovely character, one of the sweetest mules in the world. Both are dead in their graves—Bob and Liz, too, but it was not until long after did we five boys realize that we had been working just to keep Bob and Liz supplied with enough to eat.[26]

Eventually Abraham Landis gave up country life, moving to the Logansport outskirts, buying the city block bounded by Seventeenth, Eighteenth, Market, and Broadway and constructing a two-story frame house at 1706 E. Market Street for his large family. It was a huge house, which even after the neighborhood built up around it, stood out in its grandeur.

"We had a big house...," Kenesaw's nephew Lincoln Landis recalled, "with a parlor, high ceilings, large living room, sitting room and probably six or seven or eight bedrooms, when I lived in it. We had a coal furnace in the basement and a very large yard."[27]

Yet the Landises (or "the Landii" as some called them) were by no means settled financially and reacted accordingly. "This splendid American family," wrote one contemporary, "practiced thrift from their very youth and did it in the most charming manner. Nobody ever heard a Landis complain. It was thought wonderful that the Landises...should walk clear down town from Twenty-sixth street when a street car was running right along beside them. But they did."[28]

It was, to be sure, a talented and ambitious family, but even then Kenesaw stood out. There was just *something* about him, a lord-of-the-manor air, a bearing that marked him as, well, different. His siblings respectfully nicknamed him the "Squire" for his lordly manner—and in the family, at least, the nickname stuck for the rest of his life.

Whoever named him had not mistaken his intentions. "I do remember," he once remarked, "that when I was a youngster, I had an ambition to become the head of something. I mean the man who was responsible to nothing except his own conscience."[29]

It was not surprising that someone with such a keen sense of self also had a keen sense of history. It was Kenesaw's favorite subject in school, with a particular interest in another Hoosier schoolboy, Abraham Lincoln. But Kenesaw's curiosity clearly failed to extend to things mathematical, specifically to matters of algebra.

When Kenesaw reached algebra class, he reached the end of his secondary education. Algebra so frustrated him, that in 1882 the 15-year-old dropped out of high school. His previous work experience had been as a paperboy for $1 per week. For this worldly sum he arose before each sunrise to load up "like a pack mule"[30] and peddle the *Logansport Morning Journal,*[31] the city's official Republican paper.[32]

But a single dollar per week was nothing to be satisfied with, and Kenesaw secured a full-time, $3-per-week junior clerk's position at Logansport's principal grocery store.

The oddest thing about Kenesaw's decision to leave school was his father's ignorance of it for six full months. When Dr. Landis (by now sporting a long white beard and looking strangely like abolitionist John Brown) finally found out, he was aghast. But try as he might he could not persuade his son to return to his studies.

Kenesaw, however, needed little persuading to leave the confines of the general store. Even in the early 1880s $3 per week did not go far, and any young man who strove to be "responsible to nothing except his own conscience" could hardly be satisfied sweeping sawdust or stocking soda crackers and calico.

In the next few years Kenesaw would bounce from job to job, slowly increasing his responsibilities and rapidly expanding his ambitions.

He left his budding mercantile career for a $5-per-week job as errand boy in the dispatcher's office of the Vandalia Railroad. Before long he requested a transfer—to the post of brakeman.

"Well," Kenesaw explained to the Vandalia's local superintendent, "I am kind of tired of Logansport and I want to see something of the world. If I was a brakeman why I would probably get as far as Delphi, Indiana, and maybe even to Indianapolis."

Taking a withering look at the puny young man (Landis never grew to be taller than 5'6" with an adult weight at little more than 130 pounds), the superintendent turned to another employee, and snarlingly barked: "Look at the little squirt who wants to be a brakeman."[33]

Then turning back to Landis he pronounced, "You will be no brakeman on this line or any other, if I can prevent it. If you have got to break your fool neck, you can do it easier in some other way."[34]

Landis now saw that the railroader's life was not for him and went to work for his brother Charles at the *Logansport Journal*. The young Squire's work at the *Journal* sometimes required him to cover proceedings at Cass County's old Greek Revival courthouse, where the newfangled art of shorthand court reporting caught his eye.

Here was a job with a future, or at least a present. Landis cajoled incumbent court reporter John J. O'Connor to instruct a small class of local lads in the subject and before long was good enough to land the position of official circuit court reporter in Indiana's Lake County, serving there from 1883 to 1886. "I may not have been much of a judge, nor baseball official," he once wrote, "but I do pride myself on having been a real shorthand reporter."[35]

But to think the ambitious, hyperkinetic Landis was all work and no play would be a substantial mistake. Kenesaw was quite the local athlete, making up for his small stature with an unusual dexterity. Despite his height he played first base for the Goosetown semipro club. "Our favorite enemy was the New Jerusalem team," he once recalled. "It was an endless feud between us. However, we licked them no oftener than we were licked." He supposedly declined a chance to turn pro, arguing that he played "merely for sport and the love of the game." At age 17 he even became the team's manager.[36]

Kenesaw also took to a new sport that was sweeping America, racing on the old high-wheeled or "ordinary" (so named because the later lower models were thought to be "extraordinary") bicycle. Riding these unstable contraptions high above the treacherous unpaved roads of the time, on unforgiving solid rubber tires (the pneumatic tire had not yet been invented), was not for the faint of heart. "Only the very athletic and committed set out on long rides," noted one historian of the sport, "and long-distance records were hailed in the newspapers as great achievements."[37] Indiana was a cycling hotbed and Landis competed at numerous county fairs. He sought every advantage. Prior to one key competition in another town, he purchased 20 racing medals from a curio dealer and ostentatiously wore them upon his chest. The display cowed the local competition and helped give him an edge.

Knowing how to compete against sparse competition was also helpful. "There were three contestants in the bicycle race at Delphi last Friday," noted the *Logansport Sunday Critic* in July 1884, "Sam Patterson, Squire Landis and Emil Keller; therefore, S. P., S. L., and E. K. won the prizes. Lucky boys!"[38]

But even on Indiana's flat terrain, Landis couldn't race in the winter, so he invested what small savings he had in another 19th-century fad: roller skating. It was not the Squire's first brush with the "entertainment" industry; earlier he had ushered for free at the local opera house, so he might see such popular acts as minstrel George Primrose. In November 1886 he and an associate, Eugene Mulholland, converted a Logansport meeting hall into the Broadway Rink. The venture, proved a financial failure (the fad for roller skating had already largely passed), and Landis found his enterprise padlocked for non-payment of rent.

The Squire had other options. That same year he made his first known foray into Republican politics, supporting a friend, Charles F. Griffin, for the post of Indiana secretary of state. Griffin won, and Landis' reward was a "prominent position" in that department. The appointment, noted the *Logansport Sunday Critic*, was "highly pleasing to the young Republicans in this city, and secures to Mr. Griffin a worthy and competent assistant." While in that patronage job on July 13, 1889, he took advantage of then-current Indiana law to secure admission to the bar. After two years Kenesaw left the secretary of state's office to read law with the firm of Custer and Stevenson in Marion, Indiana, where brother Walter had already set himself up as editor of the local *Chronicle*.[39]

"Attorney" certainly *sounded* better than store clerk, errand boy, bicyclist, roller-rink entrepreneur, or shorthand reporter—but in 19th century Indiana it required little more preparation or qualification. Years later the *Logansport Leader* explained that Landis had "obtained for himself a certificate of admission to the Indiana bar, under the constitutional provision which did not require an examination."[40]

Landis had few pretensions about his admission to the bar. "All a man needed," he would later admit, "was to prove that he was twenty-one and had a good moral character."[41]

His clients—or rather, his prospective clients, also had few illusions about Landis' qualifications. They stayed away in droves. After a year of less-than-lucrative practice in Marion, Kenesaw realized that being a self-taught lawyer would take him only so far and en-rolled in Cincinnati's YMCA Law School.

Landis performed well enough in his studies (the practice of law does not require discipline in mathematics), but he failed to mix into the school's fraternity-dominated social life. The reasons were obvious enough. He was not a college graduate; he was not even a high school graduate. And if that were not bad enough, he worked at playing the rube, the hayseed from small town Indiana. Some might have found his act charming, but his more polished classmates did not and blackballed him from the existing fraternity system. Incensed, Landis organized his fellow outcasts, creating a political machine that captured the school elections.[42]

That sense of ostracism never quite left him. "Because I'm a law-yer, persons naturally think I'm a college graduate," he once told *Cincinnati Post* sportswriter Tom Swope. "But I'm not, and I'm proud of it. I don't go around shouting that I never went to college; I just keep my mouth shut about where I acquired my knowledge of the law."[43]

Landis took his senior year not in Cincinnati but at Chicago's Union Law School (now part of Northwestern University). His legal work was not entirely uniform. "I was very weak on 'pleading and real property,'" he once admitted, "and when the time for my examination approached I knew that I would have to show my hand. So I went to Judge Booth, in whose department those branches of law were taught and confessed that I was not very strong in them.

" 'Young man,' said the Judge grimly, 'am I to understand that you are under the impression that you are imparting to me any exclusive information?' "[44]

Nonetheless, in June 1891 Landis was one of 60 graduates from Union Law in a ceremony held at the city's Central Music Hall. He was admitted to the Illinois bar that same year, and despite his flaws in "pleading and real property" his grasp of the law was sound enough that he was soon asked to serve as an assistant on the Union faculty.

The Squire also established a reputation as a reformer. In 1893, along with Clarence C. Darrow and William Bross Lloyd, Kenesaw took the lead in forming the liberal and nonpartisan Chicago Civic Centre Club designed to reform local government.[45]

Chicago needed reforming. The young attorney's Chicago was already a wide-open, often violent city. Its earthier districts featured not only the home of the original Mickey Finn (yes, his invention really did incapacitate his customers), but directories touting the charms of the city's many sporting houses. It was a city of immigration and quick fortunes and violent strikes, with the McCormick Reaper strike and the Pullman strike soon to be etched in citizens' minds.

But Landis' career would soon lead him to a faraway—and rather unexpected—detour.

# CHAPTER 2

# "THE ONLY NATURAL-BORN LAWYER CONNECTED WITH THIS ADMINISTRATION"

Walter Quinton Gresham was an old family friend of the Landises, but no ordinary family friend—and no ordinary man. Almost forgotten today, in the decades following the Civil War, Gresham was among the most influential and popular figures on the national scene—a man who served in three separate cabinet posts and was considered presidential timber. He would play a significant role in the political life of Kenesaw Mountain Landis.

Gresham had been born to politics. His father had been a backwoods county sheriff and even before his admission to the bar at age 22 he held two appointive political posts. Originally a Whig, Gresham once ran for minor political office as a "Know-Nothing" before joining the infant Republican Party in 1856. Four years later he won election to the Indiana legislature from a normally Democratic district. Gresham soon left the state capital, however, to enlist as a private in the Union Army, quickly winning promotion to the lieutenant colonelcy of his regiment and then to command of a division.

Abraham Landis came under Gresham's command during Sherman's advance through Tennessee and Georgia. But they also shared a far more personal war experience. As his regiment moved toward Atlanta Gresham was wounded in the left knee by a rebel sharpshooter. Like Dr. Landis, he was left lame for life. Gresham left the active service but in April 1866 was brevetted a major general of volunteers and commanded the occupation of the Tennessee port city of Natchez.

After returning home, Gresham twice ran for Congress, losing both times. Never again nominated for elective office, his political

14

star rose nonetheless. In 1869 President Grant appointed Gresham a district judge for Indiana, and in 1882 Chester Arthur designated him postmaster general. While in the Post Office Gresham accomplished a task modern observers would find impossible: reducing the rate for a first-class stamp from three cents to two cents. A year later he became secretary of the treasury, but left just four months later to accept another federal judgeship, this time with the Seventh District in Chicago.

Gresham was somewhat of a reformer, and albeit modestly, a bit of a Gilded Age Renaissance Man. *The National Cyclopaedia* described him as "tolerant of the opinion of others, . . . genial and humorous, widely read in classical literature, a skillful rifle shot, and a learned botanist."

On the bench Gresham earned the reputation as a foe of railway greed, particularly when he cracked down on shady Wall Street financier Jay Gould's manipulations of the Wabash rail line. Gresham was so highly regarded that in both 1884 and 1888 he was a credible dark horse candidate for the Republican presidential nomination, losing first to James G. Blaine and then to fellow Hoosier Benjamin Harrison.

Harrison and Gresham had long hated each other. In the 1870s Harrison had appeared as a defense attorney before Gresham. After the prosecuting attorney had presented his evidence, Gresham decided to instruct the jury that the case was so pitifully weak that Harrison's client should go free.

Before Gresham could begin, however, Harrison bolted up to present his case. Gresham ordered him back down —"My mind is made up . . . and I am ready to instruct the jury without further hearing."

Harrison, not knowing the reason from Gresham's comments, grew increasingly agitated and demanded his say. Again, Gresham ordered him to sit down, but Harrison—still oblivious to Gresham's motivation—insisted on speaking. Finally, Gresham succeeded in silencing Harrison —and in freeing his client.[1]

The relationship between the two men never recovered from the incident, and Harrison, firmly in control of the Indiana Republican Party, used his influence to hamper Gresham's political career. But Benjamin Harrison was hardly the only problem Gresham had with the GOP. The Republican Party was the high tariff party—making it popular among protected industrialists and the workers who toiled in their mills but unpopular among many farmers. The GOP's stand on the tariff bothered Gresham, and he became increasingly disaffected from other Republicans.

In the Midwest, many farmers opposed to the power of the railroads and the magnates of industry banded together to form the Populist Party. In 1892 the nascent party came close to nominating Gresham for president, but he declined that honor. In the final days of the campaign, however, Gresham threw his support to Democrat Grover Cleveland, helping push him over the top.

From a purely theoretical viewpoint Gresham's decision made little sense. He was leaning increasingly to the left, at one point telling the Populists: "With the exception of your sub-treasury scheme...there is no difference [between us], unless it be that many entertain a stronger hope than I do that we are to escape a bloody revolution before this plutocracy of wealth surrenders its hold." In endorsing Cleveland, Gresham supported one of the most conservative of presidents. Yet Gresham considered Cleveland "an honest, courageous, patriotic man" and appreciated the nominee's traditionally Democratic low-tariff position. Obviously Cleveland stood the only chance of defeating Benjamin Harrison and that certainly played a large part in Gresham's decision. Republicans branded their former Cabinet secretary an "ingrate" and a "traitor."[2]

Cleveland, however, appreciated Gresham's move and in March 1893 after his first two choices for secretary of state turned him down, named Gresham to the office. Turning his back even further on the GOP made Gresham uneasy. "I have committed political suicide," he wrote to a friend. "Some people are unable to understand that a man can deliberately do that."[3]

Of course, not only Republicans were vexed by Gresham's appointment. Democrats were similarly flummoxed. Cleveland "enraged his followers," by appointing the Republican Gresham, noted Republican congressman James E. Watson. "I never saw a more exultant crowd or witnessed more uproarious enthusiasm than on the day of Cleveland's inauguration," Watson would write in his autobiography, "nor saw such a bedraggled and dumfounded, thoroughly mad, exasperated, fierce, and raging lot of people as those same ones were [when Gresham was appointed] on the sixth of March." Watson— probably correctly—thought that Gresham's place in the Cabinet played a major role in ultimately destroying Cleveland's base of support within the patronage-hungry Democratic Party. "The 'unwashed and unterrified Democracy' wanted their own people in public positions," concluded Watson, himself a firm believer in party regularity, "and no renegade Republicans; and in that they were dead right."[4]

As Gresham prepared to return to Washington, he had to select a personal secretary to accompany him. His choice was Kenesaw Mountain Landis—a 26-year-old Chicago attorney with no knowledge of foreign affairs or any experience abroad with the exception of having a few African missionaries in the family.

Some biographers have seen Kenesaw's appointment as a mere favor to Gresham's old comrade-in-arms, Abraham Landis. That would be a mistake.

For a good portion of his young political life Kenesaw had supported Gresham. In June 1888 he had even braved Benjamin Harrison's wrath and joined with other Indiana Republican "Young Turks" in traveling to Chicago for the party's national convention to support Gresham's presidential bid.[5]

After graduation from law school, Landis had practiced in Gresham's court (one source even credits Gresham with urging Landis to take up the law in the first place). He had also spent a great deal of time in Gresham's chambers. Unable to afford a law library of his own, Landis availed himself of Gresham's. The judge not only tolerated Kenesaw's presence, but the more he saw of Landis the more the young man's intelligence and attitude impressed him. Beyond that, Kenesaw's skill at shorthand made him a doubly valuable employee, particularly for a personal secretary.[6]

And there was Gresham's peculiar situation to consider. He was returning to the Cabinet as a turncoat, a renegade. Republicans saw him as a traitor. Democrats wondered how many of his old loyalties he retained. Gresham needed someone near him he could *trust*, someone who owed his loyalties first to Gresham and not to either party. That man—however young or inexperienced he might be—was Landis.

Why Landis turned his back on his party was another question. His career was not at an end; it was barely beginning. He had served under Republican secretary of state Charles F. Griffin (1887-1891) at Indianapolis. His brothers were active in the party of Lincoln. Was it merely the question of a regular income—$2,000 per year at federal expense? Or had the Squire, who shared Gresham's feelings on the tariff question, meant to permanently turn Democrat? Or did he merely view this as a once-in-a-lifetime opportunity despite the risk of becoming a young man without a party? Most likely it was the latter. Returning to good Republican graces might just not be as big a problem as some feared.

The State Department Landis entered was full of promise—and pitfalls. Gresham's tenure as America's foreign policy chief was an often-nervous prelude to an era of United States imperialism. Gresham, like Cleveland, desired an expansion of American commercial interests and fueling stations abroad. But neither coveted an overseas empire. "A free government cannot pursue an imperial policy," Gresham believed. "We acquire territory with the sole expectation of bringing it into the Union as a State."

Accordingly, one of Gresham's first acts was to derail Benjamin Harrison's planned grab of the former Kingdom of Hawaii, recalling a treaty of annexation from the Senate. In Cuba, the administration supported a policy of maintaining Spanish rule but at the same time increasing native autonomy.

But the nonexpansionist Gresham was hardly a weakling in foreign policy. Gresham's Department of State tenure saw the United States actively assert the Monroe Doctrine, confronting both Germany and Great Britain. He successfully maneuvered Britain out of its interests in Nicaragua. In Brazil his opposition toward a British-backed monarchist revolt helped ensure its downfall, and just before his death in May 1895 Gresham was preparing to resist London in its boundary dispute with Venezuela.[7]

Presumably, Landis shared Gresham's policies, but more importantly the duo shared populist personal styles. "The thing that most impressed me about Mr. Gresham," Landis once recalled, "was ... he made the doorman sit over in the corner, threw open the doors to the public, and ran a democratic open house. The office heretofore had been a closed door office. It became a place where the entire public might come at will, and they might come in as often as they pleased, in as many numbers and without the slightest discrimination or distinction. That idea fitted my views. It made the place one of the American people and not apart of the American people."[8]

Despite such statements, Landis could nonetheless be a jealous guardian of Gresham's privacy, since part of his job was to shield the judge—a man in increasingly failing health—from unwanted and annoying visitors. Once he snarled at a pack of aggressive reporters, "I said you can't see Secretary Gresham today, and damn it, I mean you can't see him."[9]

On another occasion, however, Landis used reverse psychology on an overeager—and overbearing—journalist. This individual, a Princeton graduate known to history only as "Evergreen," came bounding into Landis' office, officiously demanding to learn Gresham's whereabouts. Landis despised the man. He barely looked up, muttering, "In the other room."

Whereupon Evergreen burst through the door into Gresham's inner office. Seconds later he reappeared, in even faster fashion—if that were possible—than his entrance. After gingerly shutting the door behind him he chided Landis, "Why the British ambassador, Sir Julian, and the Chinese ambassador are with the judge!"

"I know that," snarled Landis. "They're trying to fix up the Chinese treaty; but I supposed of course the judge would stop to see you."

With that, the correspondent left, thoroughly embarrassed by his adventure.

Twenty minutes later Gresham emerged from the session. With a slight smile, he asked Landis, "You were trying to play some joke on that young man?"

"He's too fresh," the Squire responded, "I thought I'd let him blunder into a coal-hole or two. It'll teach him to go a little slower."

"I know," admitted Gresham, "but it cut him up badly. I could see that he felt much ashamed."

"That won't hurt him any," Landis shot back. "If there's anyone in Washington who is thoroughly fitted by nature to cope with mere shame, Evergreen's the individual."[10]

"Evergreen," however, was an exception to Landis' general policy of currying favor with the working press. It was a skill at which he was a master—and one which would serve throughout his life. "I had heard of young Landis as altogether a 'friendly Indian,'" noted Alfred Henry Lewis, then a *Chicago Times* correspondent, concerning his first meeting with Landis. "I found him neither hard to meet nor difficult of acquaintance, and after a talk of 10 minutes felt as though I had known him as many years."[11]

Landis endeared himself to most members of the press, to Gresham, and to an influential circle of friends, but the young assistant's outspoken ways still outraged many of his more established and conventional State Department colleagues. Gresham's more affected underlings spoke of their department as the "Foreign Office," paraded about in cutaway coats, and looked down their noses at the employees of less lofty branches of the government. This high school dropout son of a midwestern surgeon-farmer would have none of the pretense and snobbery of some of his associates. "He tried to treat a poor man with all the respect he did a rich one," noted one firsthand observer.

And as he did at the YMCA Law School, Landis went out of his way to alienate the swells. In response to their cutaways, he wore baggy pants and a beat-up hat.[12] While they spoke of the "Foreign Office," he mouthed homespun aphorisms on the value of diligence: "Necessity is a great teacher," was one of his favorite sayings. Yet while he would develop into a great performer in his favorite role— as Kenesaw Mountain Landis—he seemed to be somewhat overplaying the part. "He was a plain man whose lack of ostentation was ostentatious," noted journalist Henry Pringle.[13]

The story is told that one day Gresham was engaged in private conversation with British ambassador Sir Julian Pauncefote. Landis, in receipt of a message from President Cleveland summoning Gresham to the White House, burst into Gresham's study and snapped, "Cut that story out!" and ordered his boss to see the president.

The startled Pauncefote waited for Landis to dart back out of the room, then inquired, "Who is that officious young man?"

Gresham informed Pauncefote that he was Kenesaw Mountain Landis and that "he is the only natural-born lawyer connected with this administration, and I have to mind him. I couldn't hold my job if it wasn't for Landis."[14]

That was far from the only time the Squire flaunted the influence he held over Gresham. Often he would wait for some departmental underling for whom he had formed a dislike, to appear before Gresham. He would then saunter into the secretary's office and begin interrogating his mentor about something Landis had wanted done.

Whatever the secretary's response, Kenesaw huffed and puffed about some detail and threatened to return to the Midwest if matters didn't improve. After a few more muttered harrumphs, he'd storm from the room.

Oddly enough, the entire scenario was played out with Gresham's eager cooperation. Sharp observers could even detect a slight smile on the judge's lips as Landis went through his paces.

Clearly, the relationship was not the usual one between employer and employee. "Secretary Gresham loved Landis," summed up Alfred Henry Lewis, "and trusted him as a father loves and trusts a favorite son."[15]

Actually, neither Landis nor Gresham had much use for the British ambassador, whose manner was marred by the worst of aristocratic pretensions. Once, Sir Julian had asked for an appointment with Gresham and when he received one, languidly called to a lackey, "Put that down. I'm quite sure I shan't remember it."

The attitude rankled Landis. The next day Pauncefote turned to him, saying, "Let me see. I've an appointment for Thursday at three, haven't I?"

"I'm quite sure I can't remember," drawled Landis as he glared at Pauncefote. "You might better ask your secretary."[16]

Once again Landis' seemingly rash actions were not taken without some calculation, for Gresham's own opinions of Pauncefote were equally low. "He lied to the judge once," Landis recalled, "and from that time, we opened on him with a line of Wabash Bottom diplomacy that rubbed his British fur the wrong way" — or putting it another way the secretary of state would respond to Pauncefote's every suggestion with the same four words, "Put it in writing."[17]

Landis may have been referring to an incident involving an abortive attempt to restore the Brazilian monarchy. When the coup failed, the Brazilian government learned that one of its key leaders, an Admiral Da Gama, would be given asylum by the British. They informed Gresham of this, and when the secretary confronted Pauncefote with this rumor, Sir Julian gave his assurances this would not be the case.

Nevertheless, at midnight Gresham received a telegram from the Brazilian authorities reporting that Da Gama was aboard a British warship. "Get a carriage, Landis," Gresham barked. "We must go and see Sir Julian."

They arrived at 2 AM and Pauncefote naturally wished to know the nature of this unexpected visit. "Sir Julian," Gresham responded, "I have word from Brazil that your flagship has taken Da Gama aboard. Of course that is not true. You and I know it is not true, but I must be able to tell the president and the Cabinet when we meet this morning it is not true." By the time Gresham and Landis met with Cleveland at 11 AM, Pauncefote had phoned Gresham to inform him Da Gama was back upon his own flagship.[18]

It should not, however, be assumed that Landis was the *bête noire* of all foreign representatives — just those guilty of untrustworthy behavior or of putting on airs. With other diplomats — most notably the Chinese minister Yang Hu and the Korean representative Ye

Sung Soo—Landis developed "fast" friendships. His relations were downright diplomatic.[19]

But Grover Cleveland was not too confident Gresham had made the proper choice in a private secretary. One day he sharply inquired of Gresham regarding Landis "where in heaven he found him."

Gresham informed Cleveland that his protegé was one of the best young attorneys around. To which Cleveland, not noted for his sense of humor, responded with a laugh. It was not a good sign. Gresham, however, was not cowed and continued, "And some day when you and I are forgotten he will be known as one of the great men of all time."[20]

Grover Cleveland may never have warmed to Landis *that* much, but he nonetheless did warm to him. And for his part Landis developed a true loyalty to Cleveland, the favorite Democrat of many Republicans. "He was never meant to be a Democrat,"[21] Landis in later years would often approvingly state of the chief executive.

Landis was definitely an *acquired* taste for the president. During the administration's re-tooling of the nation's Hawaiian policy as it backed away from the imperialism of the Harrison administration, word leaked out to the press that the United States was attempting to return Queen Liliuokalani to the throne and wanted the Hawaiian minister to go to Washington, Lorrin M. Thurston recalled.

The Squire had already formed the habit of associating with reporters, and Cleveland assumed it was he who had leaked the story. He demanded Gresham fire his protegé. The judge refused saying if Landis went so would he. Cleveland relented, eventually discovering that Landis was indeed innocent of the accusation.[22]

Cleveland eventually not only tolerated Landis, he grew to admire him. And finally Landis, never shy about taking advantage of a situation, decided the time had arrived to manipulate not only the secretary of state, but the president himself.

One of Landis' friends had been tendered a consular appointment by Cleveland, but he found it not to his liking and, as much as he wanted a diplomatic post, reluctantly determined to decline it. Traveling to Washington, he informed Landis about the situation. Landis told him he might be able to come up with something better, and approached Gresham.

Gresham was not encouraging, telling his secretary "that was not likely to occur."

Landis was beside himself. "It's got to occur," he insisted, "I haven't asked anything from the administration, but I want you to do this for me now."

The following day, the Squire brought his friend to meet Gresham. "Judge," Landis said his superior, "will you go out to the White House with [the individual in question] and introduce him to the President?"

Gresham protested he did not think Cleveland would be at his office at that hour.

"He is in," Landis stated matter-of-factly. "I have arranged for him to be in. He is waiting for you now."

Gresham, accompanied by Landis and his friend, meekly trotted over to the White House. Once the prospective appointee had been introduced to the president, he informed Cleveland he could not take the post that he had been offered. He wrote out something to that effect on a corner of the chief executive's desk.

"The Senate is not in session," Cleveland responded, "but I will make a recess appointment—the best I have left."[23]

All in a day's work for a former high school dropout.

Another of Landis' White House activities involved Cleveland's private secretary, former Detroit attorney Henry T. Thurber. Periodically, when the Squire became bored with his diplomatic duties, he would pay a visit to the nervous, quietly self-important Thurber.[24]

"Mr. Thurber, may I see you alone," Landis often began.

Once sequestered, Landis—the picture of gravest concern—would warn Thurber "he was killing himself" with hard work.

"Yes!" Landis would exclaim. "I know how you feel! Duty!—your duty to the public!—that is your cry! And so you go on sacrificing yourself. I tell you, Thurber, it's wrong. You've a duty to the public—yes! But you've also a duty to yourself. You've no right of self-destruction—no right to work yourself into a grave for a public or any other interest; And I felt it my duty to come and say so to you."

Or he might vary his routine by asking to see Thurber's family Bible—the Holy Writ upon which this dedicated public servant had taken his oath of office. Landis would then marvel at it, and expound in mock awe of how Thurber's descendants would forever treasure the very book which ushered in their noble ancestor's service to a president.

Thurber never caught on.

In fact, he was so dense in such matters that President Cleveland himself decided to have a little fun with his private secretary. On his return from a hunting trip, the president presented Thurber with an ancient—and no doubt gristly—swan.

Loyalty had its limits, and Thurber confided in Landis that he had no intention of eating the tough old bird. Ah, but that was a mistake, rebutted Landis, a severe breach of etiquette.

"Roast it as you would a turkey," Landis advised. "I'll come and help you eat it."

Into the oven with the swan. Out came a bird that Thurber could not cut with a hacksaw. At the table sat an innocent-looking Landis— who had no doubt made arrangments to take his *real* meal elsewhere.

But it would be a mistake to view Landis as merely some youthful Washington wiseacre, Roy Cohn crossed with Will Rogers. He also had streaks of common sense and savvy discretion, which served Gresham in quite good stead.

On one occasion, the Chicago press had printed an interview with a certain politician by the name of Springer, in which he raked Gresham over the coals. An infuriated Gresham promptly composed a scathing letter in response and was about to post it when Landis stopped him. "Don't send it," Landis warned. "I've read the interview, and I know as well as I know I'm alive, that it's a fake. Springer hasn't got poison enough in him to frame up such a talk. If you send him that letter, and it should turn out he isn't really guilty, you're going to feel tremendously ashamed, Judge."

Gresham pulled in his horns and never sent the letter. Events later proved Landis was precisely right, and Gresham saw his faith in his unorthodox young associate confirmed. "Now, there!" he exclaimed. "There you see how lucky it is to have someone about you who knows more than you do."[25]

Two decades later, Gresham's widow—despite misgivings "about some of Landis' judicial judgments"—would write approvingly of her late husband's protegé, revealing that his "energy and ability to work and mix was prodigious." She was, however, quick to add that it was only with Gresham's guidance that he made "no mistakes."[26]

Matilda Gresham had not exaggerated Landis' ability to maintain a killer schedule—a regimen also kept by her husband. At 8 AM Landis and Gresham would leave the Arlington Hotel and walk to the State Department's headquarters in the old State, War, and Navy Office Building. Once at Gresham's ornate office the duo would meet with a dizzying array of diplomats, reporters, departmental personnel, and office-seekers, until approximately 2 PM. Meetings of a more structured sort followed until 4 PM (a brief lunch and perhaps a meeting with the president would also have been squeezed in by then). From 4 until 6 Gresham and his secretary slaved away on paperwork. At that point they would bundle up more papers and return home to the Arlington—for dinner and for more work far into each night. Gresham, Landis noted, "never rested." He might as well have been talking of himself.

For as long as Gresham remained secretary of state, the two men proved inseparable. Even when Gresham escorted Cleveland and a host of other top dignitaries to the World's Columbian Exposition back in Chicago in May 1893,[27] Landis went along.[28]

Of the many foreign policy questions vexing Cleveland and Gresham—Hawaii, Venezuela, Brazil, Cuba—Cuba was most significant. Despite increasing pro-Cuban sentiment on the part of the American public, the president insisted on a policy of strict neutrality regarding the Spanish colony. The *Allianca* incident of March 1895 put the administration's strategy to its most difficult test yet.

Somewhere off Cuba's Cape Maisi, a Spanish *guardacosta* gunboat chased and then boarded an American passenger vessel, the USS *Allianca*, on suspicion that it carried arms bound for Cuban rebels. The *Allianca*'s captain maintained that his craft had been six miles off the Cuban coast—in international waters. The Spanish ship's captain contended that the *Allianca* was well within the three-mile limit when his 25-mile chase of the American ship began.[29]

American public opinion took the *Allianca*'s side and demanded action. Frustrated patriots wanted to know "Is there an American in the State Department?" There probably was, but there was no secretary of state. Gresham was too ill to come to his office, and President Cleveland—out hunting again ("We killed fifty brant, three geese, and fourteen snipe"[30])—could not be reached for guidance. Under Secretary of State Edwin H. Uhl took responsibility and signed a telegram (drafted by Second Assistant Secretary Alvey Adee) to American Minister to Madrid Hannis Taylor instructing Taylor to demand "prompt disavowal of the unauthorized act and due expression of regret" from the royal Spanish government.

Before the telegram was transmitted, however, Landis—ever loyal to Gresham—spied the document and carried it to his ailing mentor. Landis, who thought the document a fine one, had just one change to suggest to Gresham—scratch out the signature, "Uhl, acting" and substitute Gresham's own. Gresham did so, and when news of the telegram reached the jingoistic public; he became a national hero.

Gresham did not, however, attain heroic status with Grover Cleveland, who thought the State Department's handling of the matter was overwrought. He again demanded Gresham fire Landis, but Gresham (who upon his own reflection also thought the telegram had "gone too far") stoutly refused. If Landis left, so would he.[31]

Gresham did not restrict himself to mere foreign affairs. Landis and Gresham were also on the scene for matters of domestic import. On race relations of the day, Gresham was described as "opposed to unlimited Negro suffrage [but] demanded equal protection for the Negro under the law." In this latter regard he was highly influential in preventing Southerners from repealing key sections of Reconstruction Era civil rights statutes.[32]

The Judge also threw himself into the fierce battle over whether hard-money gold or inflationary silver should be the basis of the nation's coinage, supporting Cleveland's successful effort to repeal the Sherman Silver Purchase Act of 1890 — and to place the gold standard on a firmer footing. And Landis found himself at the White House when discussions took place regarding the Pullman Strike of 1894, in which the infant American Railway Union struck the Pullman railway car company, a strike broken when Cleveland called out federal troops. "He [Landis] was in the office when the President called out the troops down in Chicago . . . ," his granddaughter Nancy Landis Smith Lucas recalls, "and I remember him telling me that, that he was sitting in the office when they called out the militia." Gresham thought Cleveland's use of federal force illegal. It is likely Landis shared that opinion.[33]

Judge Gresham's effectiveness in office, however, was seriously hampered by an illness which ultimately took his life. "Judge Gresham was not well when he was in Washington and granddaddy got pulled into a lot more things because of that," says Nancy Landis Smith Lucas. In Gresham's absence Landis often represented the State Department at Cabinet meetings. That a mere personal secretary, rather than an under secretary of state, would represent the department was extraordinary. "Gresham did not like to go to Cabinet meetings," contends Landis grandson Keehn Landis, "in fact, he didn't like to go to a lot of things. My grandfather would represent him, and that is how he helped expand his knowledge of the Cleveland administration's social circle."[34]

But Gresham was not merely sick. Unlike Mr. Thurber, Gresham actually *was* working himself to death. Immersed in settling the boundary dispute between Venezuela and Great Britain, Gresham made frequent evening visits to the president's Woodley, New Jersey, home. In the process he contracted pneumonia and died in late May 1895. By then Cleveland had come to treasure Gresham professionally and even personally. He was overcome with grief. Along with the Cabinet, he accompanied Gresham's body back to Chicago. At one point during the train ride he requested a cabinet member accompany him back to the car in which the casket was kept. On arriving, the president asked to go in alone. When he was not seen again for over an hour, some concern arose. Two Cabinet members went into the car and found Cleveland kneeling before Gresham's bier, sobbing and oblivious to the passage of time.[35]

With such devotion to Gresham's memory, it should not be too surprising that Cleveland offered Gresham's young protegé the post of minister to Venezuela at an annual salary of $7,500. The tendering of that position, however, was no mere hollow honor. With tension growing between Britain and Venezuela, even before Gresham's death, Cleveland had written to an associate that he "ought to send someone there of a much higher grade than is usually thought good enough for such a situation." Landis seemed to be the man for the job, but he missed the legal profession. "Every hour I spend here is an hour wasted," he exclaimed and declined Cleveland's offer.[36]

It was not the first time Landis had expressed such sentiments. He just didn't feel the diplomatic corps was worth his effort—or the effort the entire government was putting into it.

When Gresham was still living, Kenesaw shared with him the contents of a letter Abraham Landis had written home. In the letter Dr. Landis told Kenesaw of how he had failed miserably at an attempt to hitch up a pair of mares to help him fill in a mire of swampy land behind the family barn.

Evidently, the turf was sheer quicksand and the two mares suffocated before they could be pulled out. "Morgan mares they were and worth every splinter of five hundred dollars," moaned young Landis. "Gone at a gulp—both of 'em!"

Gresham muttered his regrets, but Landis cut him short. This was not just an epistle from home—it was a parable.

"You miss the point," Landis chided. "It wasn't the sympathy end I was thinking of, Judge. But doesn't this whole business remind you of the State Department?—filling up a fifty-cent hole with a five-hundred dollar team. Between us, it strikes me as vastly resembling our position on the Alaska seal question."[37]

But Landis had yet another reason for leaving Washington: matrimony.

# CHAPTER 3

# "ROOSEVELT HAD HIS LITTLE JOKE"

And so Kenesaw Mountain Landis returned to Chicago and re-sumed the private practice of law. J. G. Taylor Spink in his *Judge Landis and Twenty-Five Years of Baseball* hints that the still-youth-ful attorney's new practice was of limited importance, but this is far from true. For a man still not yet 30, Kenesaw Landis resided at the center of a web of political connections that featured extremely use-ful ties to both parties. Ultimately, he would use them to win a fed-eral judgeship.

Settling once more in Chicago, Kenesaw had formed a partner-ship, Uhl, Jones & Landis, with two former Washington associates: Under Secretary of State (former ambassador to Germany) James Uhl and former assistant postmaster general Frank James. Uhl, one of the most eloquent attorneys of his age, no doubt influenced Landis' growing sense of theatricality—although one might observe that further inspiration was unnecessary. In tandem with his new part-ners, Landis built up a flourishing Cook County practice that even-tually included such well-paying clients as the Grand Trunk and the Calumet railroads, at a yearly retainer of $2,500 per year, among several other large corporations.

But being a successful corporate attorney bestowed on Landis no more respect for titles and authority than had his role as private sec-retary to the secretary of state. At the turn of the century, Chicago's federal judiciary included Peter Stenger Grosscup, James Jenkins, and Christian C. Kohlsaat. One day, Kohlsaat—jealous of his pre-rogatives and of the very title of judge—archly inquired of attorney Landis: "I understand that you refer to me as 'Chris' Kohlsaat."

Kohlsaat's line of inquiry failed to impress Landis. "I bet I know who told you," he countered. "It was either 'Pete' Grosscup or 'Jim' Jenkins."[1]

Landis had a similar lack of respect for James Uhl and Frank Jones and soon parted ways with them. "How did you happen to retire?" he was once asked about his decision to leave the firm. "Oh," he breezily responded, "I just called in Jones and Uhl and discharged them."[23]

Uhl and Jones, however, were far from the only highly placed Cleveland appointees Landis met in Washington. Another was Comptroller of the Currency James H. Eckels. Landis' acquaintance with Eckels would have the longest and most lasting effect upon him.

Eckels had come to Washington in a storm of controversy. A still-youthful practicing attorney in rural Ottawa, Illinois, he had already been long active in the Democratic Party, but otherwise he possessed no qualifications whatsoever to hold the post of comptroller of the currency. His critics gleefully reported that he had never even *read* the current National Banking Act. Republicans in the United States Senate were in an uproar, and at least one Democratic senator went to Cleveland, begging him to withdraw the nomination. He refused, and the nomination squeaked through.

No sooner had Eckels taken office than a great panic struck the nation's economy. The banking system virtually collapsed. One hundred and sixty-five banks failed—compared to just 212 in the entire three previous decades. Eckels' predecessors had been content to let such unsound institutions die. Eckels, however, broke from extreme laissez-faire doctrine and labored strenuously not only to keep more banks from collapsing but also to reopen those that had already failed. Thanks to his efforts 115 reopened, of which a full 100 remained permanently in business. Through his intervention, still more banks on the verge of collapse pulled back from the brink. By the time Eckels left office in 1897 to become president of a prominent Chicago bank, the man who came to Washington widely derided as an unqualified hack had won universal acclaim as a financial genius. He "never made a mistake," praised one prominent financier.[4]

What has this to do with Landis? Everything. In 1887 Eckels had married Fannie Lisette Reed, daughter of Ottawa, Illinois, postmaster John H. Reed. After Eckels joined the Cleveland administration, Fannie's sister, Winifred, visited Washington to see Fannie and while there was introduced to eligible bachelor Kenesaw Mountain Landis. The two became smitten. When Winifred returned home, Landis commuted to Illinois as often as he could to be with her.[5]

In fact, one reason Landis had refused Cleveland's offer to be minister to Venezuela was Miss Reed. Cleveland had argued that Landis was missing a splendid opportunity by refusing the diplomatic post, but Landis countered, "maybe you think so, Mr. President, but there's a girl . . . who thinks otherwise."[6]

The 28-year-old Kenesaw and the 23-year-old Winifred were married at Ottawa's First Presbyterian Church on the evening of July 25, 1895. The *Chicago Evening Post* reported "a number of prominent society people of Chicago and other cities of Illinois" had graced the ceremony. Kenesaw's ushers included his brothers Walter and Frederick and a fellow up-and-coming Chicago attorney named Frank Lowden. The couple honeymooned in the northern lakes and back east.[7]

Kenesaw and Winifred's union produced three children. A son was born on July 17 of the following year and named in Walter Gresham's honor, Reed Gresham Landis. A year later a daughter, Susanne, arrived. A third child, Winifred, born in November 1901, died almost immediately after birth.

Despite Landis' service in the Cleveland administration and his partnership with two active Democrats, on returning to Chicago he had rejoined the Republican Party, the majority party in Illinois.

Landis had certainly jumped the Democratic ship while the jumping was good. The GOP had recaptured Congress in 1894 and the White House in 1896. Depression-era president Cleveland—try as he might—could not even regain his party's nomination and was so alienated from William Jennings Bryan and the Democrats' new free silver (and anti-gold standard) leadership that he and most of his cabinet members supported a presidential ticket of "Gold Democrats." It garnered few votes that November.

Meanwhile back in Indiana that year, Charles Beary Landis won election to Congress from Indiana's Ninth District, defeating a one-term Republican incumbent, James Franklin Hanly. Just three days later Abraham Landis died from nephritis and heart disease.

Described by the *New York Tribune* as "one of those vigorous capable young Republicans who are likely to make an impression in the House," Congressman-elect Landis had enough nerve to visit President-elect McKinley and proffer advice on whom to appoint as secretaries of state and treasury. By 1900 Charles was toying with the idea of a run for governor of Indiana.

He was also an accomplished enough public speaker to be invited to New York for a dinner honoring the memory of Ulysses S. Grant, where perhaps carried away by the occasion he not only praised the Civil War hero as a fine general but also a "great President." In an age of florid stump-speeches Charles' favorite oratorical topic was "Optimism," which he often used as a springboard to illustrate the healing of the divisions of the Civil War. The latter topic was one of passion with him. In 1898 he informed an audience that the war with Spain presented a laudable example of progress for Americans, "Instead of being arrayed against one another, the blue and gray are now camping in the same tent, under a united flag and dying for the same cause—their union and to free oppressed humanity."[8]

When Charles won election to the House, he took Frederick Landis to Washington with him. For a while Frederick worked in the nation's capital—first as his congressman brother's private secretary then as a journalist with a number of papers including the *Washington Post*. Eventually, he returned home to Logansport. On leaving Washington he was asked when he was returning.

"Not until I am elected to Congress," he brazenly replied.[9]

He made good on his boast in 1902, being elected from Indiana's Eleventh District. "Business was rather poor, and as there appeared to be nothing of importance in sight, for a time at least, I thought I would come to Congress," he explained a year later. "Idleness, you know, is said to lead to mischief, and as it had a hand in urging me into politics, I am not prepared to refute the statement without a more extended experience."[10]

Such an explanation modestly glosses the real reason for Frederick's political rise: his dazzling oratorical skills. In 1899 he was attending a local Lincoln League banquet at which the state Republican chairman was present. Frederick responded to a toast the state official had made to "The Army and the Navy" with such moving eloquence that Booker T. Washington, who was also attending the dinner, sat there with tears streaming down his cheeks.

The state chairman realized he had just heard from a young man of rare talent. He tapped him to make campaign speeches for the GOP—118 in the election of 1900 alone. In that capacity he met vice-presidential candidate Theodore Roosevelt, beginning a fast friendship between the two men. Frederick's reputation had now grown so large that the following year Ohio Republicans invited him to crisscross their state to orate on their behalf.[11]

When Frederick gained election to Congress, he, like Charles, unseated a Republican incumbent, the eight-term Major George W.

Steele. Steele was no pushover. A former Benjamin Harrison loyalist, the first governor of the Oklahoma Territory, and the favorite of the "old soldier" element in the party, Steele was known as "a consummate master in the intrigues of practical politics." Primaries were then unknown and the battle was settled in May 1902 at a hotly contested party district convention held at Wabash under a huge circus tent. Thousands come to witness the outcome. Two other candidates, Calvin Cowgill of Wabash and C. H. Good of Huntington, also challenged Steele, but earlier Frederick had received a major boost when at the state GOP convention at Indianapolis, United States senator Albert Beveridge made a point to introduce him to the crowd. It was believed Beveridge, who in 1899 had outmaneuvered Steele to gain his Senate nomination, had been working hard in favor of Landis.

At Wabash a deadlock quickly developed. Balloting dragged on until three in the morning, then resumed eight hours later. All the while a terrific storm threatened to topple the massive tent, but the tumult outside could not slow down the tumult inside. Balloting continued, and at 5 PM Cowgill, Good, and Landis—all determined to retire Steele—agreed to support the strongest amongst them in order to achieve their common purpose. Frederick Landis emerged as the prime contender and captured the nomination on the 1,012th ballot. In years to come Frederick would mock the difficulty he had in winning the nomination, usually remarking, "After they offered me the nomination 1,012 times I finally accepted."[12]

In the course of his campaign, one stop brought him to the Erie Railway's yard at Huntington, Indiana. At the yards pit wipers were preparing a train, and one offered the candidate a chaw of "scrap" tobacco from a particularly grease smeared pouch.

"That's all right," Frederick replied. "I always chew whatever kind the other fellow's got."

The remark so amused his audience, that the workmen organized a Landis marching club that followed Landis in politics for the rest of his career.[13]

At the time of his nomination Fred was not yet 30 but looked even younger and still lived at home with his widowed mother. He turned 30 by election day, but still was youthful enough that one prospective voter called out as he went to the polls, "Hey, boy, does your mother know you're out?"

"Yes," he cheekily replied, "and when the votes are counted tonight, she'll know I'm in."[14] He was absolutely correct.

Other Landises were also on the move. In 1904 sister "Frank" had finally left the teaching profession and become a special agent for a Logansport insurance company. Shortly after the war with Spain, Theodore Roosevelt named Walter Landis as the first director general of posts in Puerto Rico. In that capacity he visited a nearby island shortly after it had totally destroyed by a volcano. But his journalistic inclinations were not yet dead and he filed a graphic— and highly popular—newspaper account of the devastation. In Puerto Rico he also owned a plantation, growing grapefruit, coconuts, and pineapples. He died in November 1917.[15]

With two brothers in the Republican House caucus in the first decade of the century, another in a lucrative federal appointment, there was every reason for Kenesaw—including disaffection with Democrats' position on free silver—to merrily skip back to the Republican Party. And he wasted little time in so doing.

Kenesaw's rediscovery of the Republican Party, however, had little impression on his new bride. Winifred Reed's family was strongly Democratic, so much so that it was even rumored they were related to General Robert E. Lee. "It was a family joke that when they went to the polls, they always canceled each other out," recalled grandson Keehn Landis. "She always voted Democratic."[16]

While J. G. Taylor Spink contended that Landis "was always a staunch Republican, even while working for Cleveland, and found the Democrats too 'radical,' " his affiliation with the GOP was hardly based on rock-ribbed conservatism. In Chicago, Landis aligned himself with the party's progressive wing.[17]

Illinois, though solidly Republican, had long flirted with the party's growing reform faction. As far back as 1872 Illinois governor John M. Palmer and United States senator Lyman Trumball bolted the national GOP to throw in their forces with the breakaway Liberal Republican Party. As the decades progressed the populist agrarian Granger movement also fueled the Illinois GOP's flourishing reformist wing.

Nationally, progressive Republicans gained new ground when, on William McKinley's assassination in September 1901, Theodore Roosevelt (TR) became president. Previously shunted off to the vice presidency, "that damned cowboy," as Ohio senator Mark Hanna referred to him, was now in the White House. Tentatively in substance—but flamboyantly in style—TR began attacking the growing power of corporate wealth. Soon a series of progressive measures were fighting their way through the conservative United States Senate: the Elkins Act ending railway rebates; the Hepburn Act strengthening the Interstate Commerce Commission; the Pure Food and Drug Act; the Meat Inspection Act; and the Aldrich-Vreeland Act, setting the stage for the Federal Reserve System. Starting with the prosecution of the Northern Securities case, Roosevelt gave impetus to more aggressive prosecution of business monopolies or "trusts."

In *The Era of Theodore Roosevelt*, historian George Mowry outlined a profile of the typical progressive. Landis matched uncannily. He was from a middle class background, from old American stock, college (or at least law school) educated, an attorney, and relatively youthful. The majority of progressives, Mowry pointed out, had come not from populist but rather conservative political backgrounds. Most Republican progressives had dutifully supported McKinley in 1896; most Democrat progressives had supported either the Gold Democrat ticket that same year or remained mum. Landis clearly fit that mold.

Most progressives also believed in the cult of great men and of strong leaders. "The world," wrote Frank Norris, "wants men, strong, harsh, brutal men—men who let nothing, nothing stand in their way." Decades later the world would find no shortage of such strong, dictatorial leaders whose every word was law— Hitler, Stalin, Mussolini. Since men could not govern themselves, wrote Walter Lippman in 1912, they constantly sought some sort of "benevolent guardian." Landis, on both the federal bench and as baseball's first commissioner, would become that benevolent—if somewhat blustery—guardian.[18]

And so Landis fit rather nicely into the progressive movement. The story is told that soon after Roosevelt assumed the presidency, he visited Chicago and was given the honor of a parade down Michigan Avenue. Kenesaw Landis was among the spectators, and as Roosevelt approached, the prodigal Republican could no longer contain himself, rushing at TR and enthusiastically waving an American flag almost in his face.[19]

In 1902 rumors floated of a Landis congressional bid. It came to nothing, but it did generate a revealing piece of correspondence. An old Washington associate, newsman Joseph G. Gannon, with the *New York American & Journal*, wrote the Squire urging him on. "You know," Gannon advanced, "that you'd have all the newspaper correspondents with you by way of liquidating past obligations as well as by reason of your personal [sic] popularity with them."[20]

Instead, Landis managed the campaign for governor of fellow Chicago attorney Frank Orren Lowden in 1904. Lowden and Landis, both Republicans of the TR stripe, had first met in 1892 and would remain lifelong friends and allies.

Of course, not everyone *knew* that Kenesaw Mountain Landis was a Republican. Many assumed that this youthful veteran of the Cleveland administration must logically be a loyal Democrat. Such was the case of a man in Washington who asked Charles Landis what his brother was now doing and was shocked to learn he was assisting Lowden's campaign. "But Lowden is a Republican and Kenesaw is a Democrat," came the response.

"Oh, no," Charles retorted, "Kenesaw has been a lifelong Republican—since 1896."[21]

Landis and Lowden had more in common than mere politics. Both were farmboys of modest means, graduates of the Union School of Law (Lowden had been class valedictorian), and were now embarking on successful corporate law careers. Lowden brought Landis into his circle of friends which included such men of substance as Frederick A. Delano, a superintendent of the Burlington railroad and the uncle and namesake of Franklin Delano Roosevelt.

Lowden, however, had one advantage Landis did not: *extremely* wealthy in-laws. In 1895 Lowden had served as an usher at Landis' wedding. In 1896 Lowden topped Kenesaw's catch of Winifred Reed when he married Florence Pullman, daughter of *the* George Mortimer Pullman, inventor of the Pullman sleeping car and president of an elevated railway line in New York City. The match left Lowden financially set for life, and he quickly turned to the challenge of the electoral arena. In the same year as his marriage he made his first entrance into national politics, campaigning heavily for William McKinley's successful presidential bids.

Landis also flirted with Republican politics, and, as noted earlier, by 1902 was toying with the idea of a congressional race. A real campaign would, however, have to wait until 1904.

In that year Illinois' Republican incumbent governor, Richard Yates, was up for re-election. But Yates was hardly a dominating figure and his most significant political patron, Cook County Republican chief, Congressman William Lorimer, was shopping for another horse to back.

Lorimer, the English-born "Blond Boss" of the stockyards district of Southwest Chicago, had worked himself up from being apprenticed at age 10 in the sign painting trade to election to the House of Representatives at age 33. While industrious and ambitious, he was, however, hardly the paragon of rectitude, and many observers considered him among the worst of all of Chicago's questionable politicians. The "Boss of the Stockyards" would throw his support to high society's Frank Lowden.

With Lorimer's support, purportedly came Theodore Roosevelt's. Some said that TR had agreed to quietly support Lowden in return for Lorimer dropping his support of Mark Hanna's rumored renomination challenge to the "damned cowboy."[22]

Lowden was not the only vulture circling above Yates' rapidly decomposing political corpse. Other candidates were in the field, most prominently the state's attorney for Cook County, Charles S. Deneen, a prosecutor with a national reputation. Deneen would prove to be a formidable opponent for both Yates and Lowden.

Shortly after declaring his candidacy Lowden announced that Landis would be running his key Cook County headquarters. Landis operated out of Chicago's Great Northern Hotel. He prepared Lowden leaflets (eventually over 200,000 were mailed from the site) and buttons. He organized neighborhood Lowden clubs such as the Business Men's Lowden Campaign Committee of Cook County, which applauded Lowden's support for a charter for the city of Chicago and warned against "all the wild schemes and vagaries of the socialistic, communistic and impractical theories" allegedly being hatched at Springfield.[23]

But in comparison to Deneen, who had strong support on the north and northwest sides as well as in his own South Side neighborhood, Landis' efforts on behalf of Lowden seemed anemic. The *Tribune*, the *News*, and the *Record-Herald*—disgusted by Lorimer's support of Lowden—vigorously supported Deneen. Virtually every day from April 27 through May 7 each paper ran a front-page cartoon attacking Lorimer, and by implication—and often by more than implication—Lowden.[24]

It would, however, be a mistake to see Deneen as a modern-style reformer. He was not. "I am not a civil service reformer or civil service agitator," Deneen stated flat out. "Not at all. I believe that positions ought to be held out as inducements for political work."[25]

Landis meanwhile was busy estimating that Lowden would

capture 300 to 325 of Cook County's 529 delegates to the state convention. He was living in a dream world. Even Lowden's wife knew her husband would be lucky to get 35 to 40 percent of the total. When Chicago's votes were in, Lowden could count on the support of between 195 and 200 delegates, carrying just five of the city's 35 wards. In the disaster, Boss Lorimer lost control of the Cook County Republican organization for the first time in eight years.

Yet when results poured in from downstate, there remained a flicker of hope. Yates was strongest there; Deneen weakest, and Lowden emerged with over a hundred downstate delegates. With 1,752 delegates necessary to win, no candidate was poised to claim victory. If a deadlock did develop at the Republican state convention in Springfield, Lowden might still claim the nomination.

That gathering has been rightly described as "one of the historic political battles of the state."[26] It was not unusual for balloting at such sessions to proceed for two or three days, but the 1904 convention rumbled on for two full weeks.

As the balloting dragged on, tourists descended on Springfield to gawk at the proceedings. It was a circus reeking of cigar smoke and deal-making. At one point a free-for-all nearly erupted over the positioning of a Yates banner. Only the intervention of sheriff's deputies prevented a riot. And if the politics were not enough to drive one crazy, three brass bands stood at the ready to increase the level of chaos. Landis watched from the hall's huge rostrum which could accommodate several hundred favored guests.

Finally, in an effort to break the impasse, each candidate released his delegates. Lowden surged upward, on the 67th through 73rd ballots when he peaked at $631\frac{1}{2}$ votes. But he could go no further and began to decline. On the 79th ballot, to the accompaniment of spectacular thunder and lightning outside, Yates and most of the minor candidates threw their support to Deneen. Most of Lowden's delegates held out to the end, but it was all over.

Lowden, worn out from the struggle, advanced to the platform and sanguinely told the convention, "So, cheer up, because we will all meet again in a very short time, fighting shoulder to shoulder, for a common cause."[27] Lowden could afford to be a good loser. He had no financial worries. His disappointed backers, such as Landis, had different thoughts. They knew that Deneen and Yates would carve up the state's patronage, particularly at the expense of the Lowdenites and Lorimerites. They bitterly charged that an unholy deal had nominated Deneen and the rest of the ticket.

The Deneen-Yates combine had reason to be polite to Lowden but nothing more. The Lowden faction's political fortune was saved by the fact that this was also a presidential election year. The 1904 GOP national convention was held in Chicago, and Lowden attended as a delegate. He had hoped that the powerful congressman from his home district, Robert L. Hitt, would be chosen as TR's running mate, thus opening up the seat for himself. The convention, however, stampeded for Indiana's conservative senator, Charles Fairbanks. Lowden and by extension Landis, appeared shut out even further of the political game, but suddenly a new opportunity opened up as Lowden won a surprise appointment from the state GOP organization to the Republican National Committee, thus not only providing him with the chance to make new contacts in Washington—but also to mend fences with Deneen, going out of his way to be photographed literally arm-in-arm with his former rival.

After Roosevelt cruised to an easy victory, Lowden was in position to cash in his chips. As 1905 opened, a new judgeship for the United States District Court for the Northern District of Illinois was created.

Theoretically TR was looking to place solid progressive allies in the judiciary, but politics was always paramount in his mind. Lowden filled the progressive bill. But obviously not needing a federal judge's $7,500 salary, he declined the position and pressed Landis for the post—even attending Roosevelt's inaugural with that goal partially in mind. Lorimer [28] and United States senator Albert J. Hopkins, both influential in the Illinois GOP's so-called federal crowd, also argued for Landis' cause.

Many, however, thought that Landis' two brothers—and not Lowden—had maneuvered the appointment.

"I had nothing to do with his appointment . . . ," Charles Beary Landis would later contend, giving all credit to Lowden and Hopkins, "At that time . . . Roosevelt sent for us—Fred and myself—and we went to the White House. When we approached the president he assumed a very dignified and serious appearance.

" 'I have sent for you,' he said in great dignity, 'because I want to confer with you about the appointment of a federal judge out in Illinois. A number of men have been recommended, but there is one—Kenesaw Mountain Landis, I believe his name is—who has been very highly recommended. I did not feel that I should make the appointment, however, until I consulted you. What do you think of it?' Well, Kenesaw was appointed. Roosevelt had his little joke, and I don't believe the country has ever regretted it."[29]

Yet in point of fact Charles *had* conferred with Vice President Fairbanks regarding Kenesaw's appointment. The Squire too had corresponded with Fairbanks on the subject, and while the new vice president informed Kenesaw that he had no claims on patronage, he also told him of a meeting he had with Illinois senators Shelby Cullom and Albert Hopkins to lobby for the appointment.

Hopkins, wrote Fairbanks, was "most positive and earnest in your behalf. You were and are his last ditch candidate. While I said what I could in your behalf—it was not necessary for his mind was well made up when I mentioned the matter."[30]

Two days after Fairbanks wrote to Kenesaw, Fairbanks, Cullom, and House Speaker Joe Cannon visited the White House to press for TR to fill the Northern District of Illinois' judicial vacancies. Landis' name was among those presented, and Roosevelt sent the suggested slate to the Senate. That very same day all his nominations breezed through the Senate, not even having to detour through the Judiciary Committee. Within an hour of Kenesaw's confirmation his widowed mother found out about it and wired him: "Always be a just judge."

Landis claimed never to forget the words. "Do you blame me for taking a great pride in that message?" he once told a reporter. "It is what a great statesman might say, but had I sent a telegram to a brother of mine similarly honored I would have said: 'Bully, old man,' or something like that. But she looked into the future, when there would be things to do."[31]

Many thought former corporation attorney lawyer Landis would—despite his progressive leanings—prove to be a pliant tool of business. One of his business friends must have thought that as he appeared in his courtroom one day. Still sporting his topcoat, he joked to the new jurist, "I suppose that I oughtn't to wear an overcoat in your presence."

"You wait till I get my court running," Landis grinned back, "and I'll make you take off your shoes."[32]

It *seemed* like Landis was joking. He wasn't.

Landis' new kingdom could be found in Room 627 of Chicago's new Federal Building, a $2 million, 16-story Beaux Arts jewel set in the heart of the city's loop. Landis' courtroom was an equally imposing two-story mahogany and marble chamber, festooned with polished brass. On one side wall was a mural of King John at Runnymede, conceding to his barons the Magna Carta. Opposite it was Moses returning from Mount Sinai and about to smash the tablets of the Ten Commandments. Such a chamber was just the spot for Landis' sense of the theatrical. In it he would hold court for nearly the next decade and a half.[33]

Landis' first major decision involving corporate regulation concerned the Allis-Chalmers Company's illegal importing of foreign laborers under contract. He could have—and probably should have—recused himself from the case because James Eckels served on the board of Allis-Chalmers. However, instead of going easy on the corporation, he slapped the maximum fine, $4,000, upon it.[34]

His second significant decree involving corporate power concerned the Street's Western Stable Car Line case. The Interstate Commerce Commission (ICC) wanted to know if the company, which owned 9,000 railway cars, had paid illegal rebates to various rail lines. Rebates—the practice of returning discounts to large freight users and forcing smaller users to pay the full rate—were an important tool in maintaining the monopoly status of such industries as Street's Western Stable Car Line and Standard Oil. Street's Western Stable Car Line vice president, a Mr. Reichmann, refused to answer that question, claiming the ICC was without authority on the matter because he said, a payment by a car company to a railroad was not a "rebate" as defined by the relevant statute.

Landis ruled otherwise and instructed Reichmann to testify. In doing so he significantly expanded the scope of antirebate legislation.[35]

Landis' stand moved United States Attorney General William H. Moody to write Charles Beary Landis. "I have just received a copy of Judge Landis' opinion in the case of the Interstate Commerce Commission v. Reichmann and read it. Get a copy and read it. Apart from the decision in the opinion, it is a long time since I have seen an opinion where the reasoning was stronger or more lucidly expressed. Evidently we made no mistake in his appointment as judge."

Charles conveyed the contents to Kenesaw, retaining the originals because he was, as he put it "so devilishly selfish."

"By George!" Charles exclaimed. "Old boy, I am proud of you!"

Soon even a higher commendation was on its way. In March 1906, Theodore Roosevelt dashed off the following to Charles Landis:

My dear Mr. Landis:

Just a line to say how glad I am at the admirable reports I hear of your brother's work as judge. It is delightful to have been instrumental in getting him on the bench.

Faithfully yours,

Theodore Roosevelt[36]

While official Washington took notice of such cases, the general public was more interested in such high-profile episodes as that of the German-born bluebeard Johann Hoch.

Hoch had been married 39 times. He usually married 40-ish women who were concerned about menopause. He convinced them that he knew of a "cure"—but the treatment consisted of fatal injections of arsenic.

William Randolph Hearst's *Chicago American* had first broken the Hoch story. The afternoon paper had tremendous influence with Chicago's Democratic politicians—so much influence, in fact, that it actually caused executions to be moved up from the traditional sunrise venue to a four-hour window of 10 AM to 2 PM so that Hearst could scoop his rivals who published earlier editions than his paper did.

After delaying matters for nearly a year, Hoch's execution was scheduled for February 23, 1906. The *American* determined to milk the story for all it was worth, printing up an additional 200,000 copies, rushing them to the farthest points of its circulation.

Such an operation, however, had to be set in motion before the actual execution. Over 75,000 copies of the *American* were printed—but not yet released—as Sheriff Thomas E. Barrett led Hoch from his cell to the gallows. Communications from inside the Cook County jail were halted on execution days. An *American* reporter secreted inside the jail would wave a blue handkerchief when that procession started. When the execution was complete a red one would flash.

Just after 10 AM on February 23, 1906, word reached *American* city editor Moe Koenigsberg that the death march had started. He issued word for the "Hoch Hangs" papers to hit the streets—and for more copies—at the rate of 130,000 per hour—to be printed. But at 10:30 a question crossed his mind: "What happened to the red handkerchief?"

He soon found out: Hoch's two attorneys and a United States marshal had appeared in the jail with a writ of habeas corpus ordering the condemned man to be taken immediately to the court of Kenesaw Mountain Landis.

Koenigsberg was beside himself. If Landis overturned Hoch's sentence or even delayed matters until after 2 PM the *American* would look foolish. Koenigsberg phoned Levy Mayer, one of Chicago's top lawyers, for advice. Mayer provided him with little guidance, beyond warning him that any attempt to influence Landis would probably backfire. "None of us knows what path Landis will choose and some of us don't recognize it after he has chosen it," Mayer told Koenigsberg, "Don't make book on him following the law, no matter how clearly it seems written. He calls them as his conscience sees them."

Koenigsberg decided to go ahead. He ordered additional thousands of copies of the *American* to  roll off the presses prematurely proclaiming Hoch's now hardly assured demise.

Meanwhile, Hoch and his attorneys were standing before Judge Landis, who may very well have taken a little extra interest in the case because of the Hochs in his own family tree (the Squire's maternal grandmother was a Hoch). Hoch had fled from Illinois to New York when the *American* had first exposed him. His lawyers had claimed that his constitutional rights had been violated. He had been extradited from the Empire State on charges of bigamy—but he had been tried by Illinois authorities on charges of murder.

Landis admitted the above might be correct, but, nonetheless, justice was being meted out. He denied Hoch's motion for an injunction. The execution would proceed as originally ordered. The clock was ticking on whether Hoch would still be hung that day. Sheriff's deputies grabbed Hoch and shoved him in a hackney cab for return to the Cook County jail. They made it in time. At 1:34 Hoch fell through the gallow's trap door. Hundreds of thousands of additional copies of the *Chicago American* rolled off the presses. Moe Koenigsberg breathed a sigh of relief. Johann Hoch had not been spared—but Koenigsberg's job had been.[37]

Of less drama but more significance was the John Alexander Dowie case of July 1906.

Little remembered today, at the turn of the century the messianic Dowie was a phenomenon of the religious world whose notoriety was exceeded by only that of the polygamous Mormons.

Dowie had begun innocently enough as a Congregationalist minister in his native Scotland. He immigrated to Australia but met with little success until 1878 when he turned to evangelism and faith healing. In 1889 Dowie determined to relocate to England but stopped to settle in San Francisco. Soon driven out of the city, he moved to Chicago where his flock grew rapidly as did the controversy surrounding it.

Dowie, "rough, uncouth, and dictatorial in manner," provoked hostility wherever he went. From South Chicago and the northern suburb of Evanston he and his followers fled to nearby Pullman. In 1895 he was arrested over a hundred times. Dowie's religion, now called the Christian Catholic Apostolic Church, excoriated alcohol, tobacco, and medicinal drugs. Dowie proclaimed himself Elijah III (to Dowie "Elijah II" was John the Baptist) and the "first apostle" and "general overseer" of his creed. He was fundamentalist in the extreme and waged a virtual war against modern science, contending the earth was flat and that medical treatment was to be avoided. Not only did Dowie urge followers to forego doctors, he led them into battle as they invaded drug stores and smashed medicines.

By 1900 Dowie had founded his own flat version of heaven on earth 40 miles north of Chicago. His disciples swarmed over the area, almost instantly building up a theocratic municipality, which they named Zion City. Within seven years this religious commune had reached a population of 10,000 boasted both a 6,000-seat auditorium and the Zion Conservatory of Music; and featured numerous industries, most principally lacemaking. Overall Zion City's property was valued at $21 million.

Dowie, however, was not satisfied with lording over a single small midwestern town. He wanted to convert the world. So in 1903, at a cost of $300,000, he herded 3,000 of his disciples onto trains, shipping them to New York for a religious assault on the metropolis. For two full weeks his oratory filled Madison Square Garden and Carnegie Hall, but the invasion failed. New York remained round. A planned colonization in Mexico also fizzled. On his way south of the border in October 1905, Dowie suffered a debilitating stroke at Chicago's Union Station.[38]

By now Dowie's empire was crumbling. In February 1906 he summoned from Australia a young former Christian Connection minister named Wilbur Glen Voliva to serve as Zion City's deputy overseer and gave him power of attorney. Voliva saw the operation was quickly collapsing from inept business practices. Along with another Dowieite named Alexander Granger, Voliva engineered a coup against Dowie. In March 1906 Voliva conveyed all of the sect's property to Granger who in turn overthrew Dowie as head of the church, replacing him with Voliva. Dowie loyalists were similarly purged and threatened with expulsion from the "Fellowship."

Dowie, through a Kentucky follower, sued to overturn Voliva's coup. The case thus went to federal court and into Landis' jurisdiction. In July 1906 Landis, descendant of numerous acolytes of less flamboyant religions, issued his decision in the case, seeking to untangle this theocratic power struggle.

As Landis read his lengthy decision he hunched down lower and lower in his chair. Finally his head hung just six inches above the Judge's bench. Of everything about Dowie and Zion City what incensed him most was the oath the First Overseer had imposed upon his followers binding them to obey all of his "rightful orders issued by him, and that all family ties and obligations, and all human government shall be held subordinate to this vow."

Though Landis would eventually be thought of as a similar despot, he was a strong family man and ardent patriot and had little stomach for such a religion.

"It is not my duty to express my contempt," he stormed, "for the man that could exact or take such an oath. But I am not obliged to repose confidence in a man so constituted that living in this republic, he could serenely vow his readiness at all times to abandon his family and betray his country. I will not appoint Alexander Granger receiver. And in this connection, while I make no pretense to technical learning in respect of what is good policy for this church organization, I suggest that whoever ultimately prevails in the ecclesiastical controversy give prompt and serious consideration to the question whether or not such an oath tends to give respectability to the church, and whether such prevailing faction may justly expect a court of the United States to long continue to foster an estate for the use of a religious organization whose conscience and intelligence does not cause an unconditional disavowal of this obligation of dishonesty."

The crowd, composed mainly of Dowieites, gasped at Landis' blasphemy. An uproar arose. Women cried out. Landis gaveled furiously and threatened to clear the courtroom if order was not restored.[38]

Yet the Squire was also careful to steer a middle course between the two factions, exhibiting equal contempt for both. His first decision was that Dowie did not "own" and had never "owned" Zion City, that in "overseeing" its property he had been merely a trustee for members of the congregation. "It is just, as if a contributor sitting in a church pew had placed the funds on the collection plate passed to him by a deacon," wrote Landis. "Surely in such case the court would not decree that the parson might put the money in his [own] pocket..." Beyond that he found Voliva and Granger had violated the trust placed in them by Dowie and had affronted "common decency" by their purge of Dowie's followers "for their refusal to desert their leader."

Landis' remedy was three-fold: to compensate Dowie for the work he had done in creating Zion City (Voliva had thrown him virtually out into the street), to appoint a competent business person as receiver for Zion City, and to order elections to settle the issue of church leadership by "all male and female members of that church ... in accordance with the laws of the state of Illinois, under what is known as the 'Australian System.' " Landis had interposed state power into a religion sect as few men had ever dared to do under the American system.

"If the decree of Judge Landis stands, the Christian Catholic Apostolic Church of Zion is uprooted," complained a Dowie spokesman. "The church is founded on the theory of a theocracy and how then can an election under the laws of Cook County, Illinois [sic] proclaim who shall be leader of the hosts?"[40]

But Landis' decision did stand. That September Voliva won the Landis-sponsored election to succeed Dowie. Dowie, a broken man, held to his religious beliefs and refused medical care, dying in March 1907. His remaining followers predicted he would return to earth in 1,000 years, but a few hours after his death, John Hately, Zion City's Landis-appointed receiver, seized his home and his furnishings.[41]

Landis had exercised his authority over Elijah III, but he was just warming up for bigger game—John D. Rockefeller I.

# CHAPTER 4

# FIFTY-EIGHT FREIGHT CARS OF SILVER

In turn-of-the-century America, monopolistic capital's nearly unbridled power loomed as the day's great issue, as immense "trusts" ruthlessly stifled competition and propelled prices and profits well beyond fair market levels. To combat these monsters Congress in 1890 passed the Sherman Anti-Trust Act, but until September 1903 when Theodore Roosevelt entered the White House, little was done to enforce it. The "Trust Buster" instituted over 40 lawsuits aimed either at such giant monopolies as the Northern Securities Company, Swift and Company, the American Tobacco Company, the Du Pont Corporation, the New Haven Railroad or against such obscure combines as the "fish trust" or the "licorice trust." The signal went out: a new political and economic era was beginning.

The greatest monopoly of all was John D. Rockefeller's Standard Oil Company. At its peak Standard Oil controlled 85 percent of the nation's refined oil. To gauge this combine's immense scope, consider what became of its component parts: Standard Oil of New York became Mobil; Standard Oil of New Jersey, Exxon; Standard Oil of Ohio, Sohio; Standard Oil of Indiana, Amoco; and Standard Oil of California, Chevron. Atlantic Richfield and Continental Oil also owe their origins to the cartel. It is as if Ford, Chrysler, and General Motors all traced their ancestry back to some huge—and predatory— ancient progenitor. Standard Oil was not just big, it was fantastically lucrative. In the century's first decade it regularly returned at least 40 percent annually on aggregate investment.

Two key philosophies guided the monopoly's prosperity. First, bring other refiners into the combine in exchange for stock. Second, exact handsome rebates from the railroads, and as a special twist, double—or even triple—the standard rail freight fares for

47

competitors who were not as well situated. These unfortunates quickly saw the futility of competition and sold out for whatever they could get.[1]

Another significant factor in any trust's success was the pliability (either from strict constructionist conviction or from outright bribery) of state and federal courts. While public outrage occasionally manifested itself in corrective legislation against these monopolists, sympathetic judges could usually be relied on to discover—or invent—convenient technicalities. For example, once when a subpoena was issued against Rockefeller as president of Standard Oil of New Jersey and served upon him at Forest Hills, his Cleveland estate, a state court ruled that he was in Ohio for private purposes and not on business, and, therefore, could not be legally served.

On another occasion, again in Ohio, the state's Court of Appeals invalidated a conviction against the oil cartel. Its reason: a corporate report of Standard Oil of New Jersey upon which the conviction was based had been certified with the New Jersey secretary of state's seal and not with the state's Great Seal.[2]

Such slick practices virtually guaranteed immunity from prosecution—as well as huge profits—but also generated bitter hostility on the part of those not in on the scam. Resentment from those paying high prices to the cartels, or worse, those run to ground by them, fueled the Populist and Progressive movements. From William Jennings Bryan to Teddy Roosevelt to Robert La Follette to Woodrow Wilson, politicians could be found to flay the increasingly unpopular monopolies. Each day William Randolph Hearst's *New York American* ran the motto "Congress Must Control the Trusts." Cartoonists such as Frederick Burr Opper (creator of "Happy Hooligan" and "Alphonse and Gaston") portrayed President McKinley in a series known as "Willie and His Papa" as an obedient small boy taking orders from his "papa," the trusts. And muckraking writers such as Lincoln Steffens, David Graham Phillips, and Ida Tarbell provided further grist for the mill. Wrote Tarbell, "If business is to be treated as warfare and not as a peaceful pursuit, as they have persisted in treating it, they cannot expect the men they are fighting to lie down and give up without a struggle."[3]

In Kentucky irate tobacco growers took Miss Tarbell's words literally. "Night riders," struggling to force crop prices up, burned villages and destroyed American Tobacco Company property. Others worked for legal redress. Individual states attempted to ban monopo-

lies and rebates but more often than not had been stymied by a
probusiness federal judiciary.

Not until passage of the Elkins Act in February 1903 would Congress finally ban railroad rebates. On May 4, 1906, Commissioner of
Corporations James R. Garfield, son of the late president, submitted
a report to President Roosevelt, alleging widespread rebating of
Standard Oil shipments. Federal prosecutors zeroed in on the firm in
a series of cases—in the Indian Territory (i.e., Oklahoma), Kansas,
Tennessee, Texas, Louisiana, Missouri, New York, Minnesota, Ohio,
and, most significantly, Illinois, with indictments returned in the
latter state on June 28, 1906.[4]  The Illinois case centered on shipments on the Chicago & Alton Railroad from Whiting, Indiana, to St.
Louis, Missouri, made between September 1, 1903, and March 1,
1905. Standard Oil of Indiana had accepted a rate of six cents per 100
pounds of oil when the official rate was 18 cents. The violations involved 6,428 car loads of oil, and the government designated each
shipment as a separate count in the indictment.

The case would come before Landis.

Standard Oil might have thought it was relatively safe. The
Squire had been a prominent corporate attorney, even representing
such large railroads as the Grand Trunk and the Calumet. "If there
ever was a corporate lawyer anywhere in Chicago," noted the *Saturday Evening Post*, "it was Kenesaw Mountain Landis." In any case,
federal courts in general—and Landis' seventh district specifically—
had shown little interest in cutting any trust down to size.

But in his Allis-Chalmers and Western Stable Car decisions the
diminutive jurist had dealt firmly with erring corporations. Now,
with the national spotlight upon him, he would be put to the test.[5]

Before Standard Oil's trial began, its attorneys attempted to toss
out, on a variety of grounds, all indictments. Landis quashed two for
technical reasons, but affirmed eight others. Now Standard Oil faced
a mere 1,903 counts, but still refused to dignify the proceedings with
a plea. Landis tersely ordered his court clerk to enter a "not guilty"
plea for them.[67]

Proceedings in *United States v. Standard Oil Company of Indiana* began on March 4, 1907. Although a quarter of the 100-member
jury panel failed to even appear, a jury was chosen with little or no
difficulty. One prospective juror boldly stated that the government
had no more right to dictate to a corporation than to himself. Landis

ordered him to stand aside. Another bore an unusually striking re-
semblance to John D. Rockefeller but was seated anyway.[8]

By contemporary standards the trial was monumental in scope,
costing the government $200,000 and the defense $100,000. The
original indictment weighed a world's record 53 pounds and mea-
sured 13 inches high. The prosecution called 143 witnesses; Standard Oil just seven.[9]

There was little controversy regarding the actual fact of a rebate.
That was readily admitted. The crux of the trial revolved around
whether Standard Oil had in fact *known* what the posted tariff was
and how obligated it—or any other shipper—was to determine the
true rate.

In late February the United States Supreme Court had ruled
regarding the posting of rate sheets and the culpability of shippers.
The following month Landis cited those decisions in denying additional Standard Oil motions. Rumors floated out of Washington that
the trust had calculated its chances, decided to cut losses, and plead
guilty not only in *Standard Oil of Indiana* but in the seven other
cases it faced nationwide.[10]

It was a false report, and neither Standard Oil lawyers nor employees showed any inclination to cooperate with the government, as
witnessed by this colloquy between Chicago district attorney Edwin
W. Sims and a Standard Oil employee named Edward Grady:

> *Sims:* What does C. & A. mean?
> *Grady:* C. & A.
> *Sims:* Well, what is it?
> *Grady:* A C. & A. order.
> *Sims:* Chicago and Alton railway order?
> *Grady:* I suppose so.
> *Sims:* Don't you know?
> *Grady:* Yes.
> *Sims:* What does P.L.O. mean?
> *Grady:* P.L. oil.
> *Sims:* What kind?
> *Grady:* Lubricating.
> *Sims:* What does L. mean?
> *Grady:* Lubricating.
> *Sims:* What does P. mean?
> *Grady:* Petroleum.

*Sims:* Now what does P. L. mean?

*Grady:* Petroleum lubricating.

The exchange infuriated Landis. He leaned over his bench and sneered, "Mr. Witness, you have no other business on earth but to answer questions. I don't want any more delays or instructions in the ABCs. Tell me what a thing means when you are asked about it if you know. If you don't know, say so."[11]

Still, a not guilty verdict remained a possibility. Much depended on how Landis charged the jury regarding Standard Oil's knowledge of the actual rate—and how much ignorance could be used as an excuse. "The question as presented to my mind," noted Landis as the trial drew to a close:

> shows that the defense may make any showing of the facts to excuse the shipper, it being shown that the defendant applied to the carrier for rates and was induced to believe that the 6-cent rate was lawful.
>
> The question is where the shipper must go to procure rates. Bearing in mind that the Inter-State Commerce law was not passed to obstruct the commerce of the country, but to emancipate it, I hold that the shipper need not go to the Inter-State Commerce Commission for rates. There is no escape from that conclusion unless commerce is to be tied up and shippers driven to Washington for the lawful rates.[12]

Landis' decision threw the prosecution on the defensive. Yet when the Judge charged the jury, his position had veered back toward one more favorable to the government:

> The indictment alleges that the defendant accepted a concession knowingly. To sustain this averment the proofs need not be established that the defendant had actual knowledge of the lawful rate. It was the duty of the defendant diligently to endeavor in good faith to get from the Chicago & Alton . . . the lawful rate by applying to one of the railway company's officials. In making this endeavor, the defendant is presumed to have known that the railway company would be guilty of a misdemeanor if it gave the defendant a rate... which was not set down on paper and a copy of the schedule filed with the Inter-State Commerce Commission.[13]

Landis presented his charge to the jury at 6 PM on April 13. They reached their first decision quickly enough: to go to dinner. Their second was achieved nearly as briskly. At 9 PM after just one ballot, they sent out word they had reached a verdict. Returning at 9:45 they first affirmed a technicality, that Standard Oil was indeed not guilty of the 440 counts Landis had thrown out during the course of the trial. Next came the real verdict, on the remaining 1,903 counts: "We, the jury, find the defendant, the Standard Oil Company, guilty in the manner and form charged in the indictment."

"Is that your verdict, gentlemen?" inquired Landis.

"It is," they—even the juror who looked so much like Mr. Rockefeller—responded. Landis rejected a Standard Oil motion for a new trial.[14]

The following morning saw the Squire dealing with a personal problem. At Union Station, he boarded a train for Logansport. Along with United States Steel chairman Elbert H. Gary, Kenesaw and Winifred had been invited to a small "breakfast party" or brunch at James Eckels' Chicago home, but Landis, either fearing association with a monopolist like Gary or more likely simply avoiding his in-laws, begged off. The breakfast never took place. After Eckels' sister-in-law tried unsuccessfully to phone him, a butler went to wake him. He found Eckels with a Bible by his side, dead in his sleep of a heart attack.

A messenger bounded onto Landis' train and brought the news to him. By now it was moving down the tracks, but a conductor pulled the emergency cord. Landis rushed off and within minutes—even before the coroner's office had arrived—had reached Eckels' home, dealing with the necessary arrangements.[15]

The Standard Oil jury had moved against the nation's largest trust, but bold steps against cartels had been taken many times before, only to be undone by pliable judges. Now, it remained for Landis to determine an appropriate penalty. The punishment provided for each count ranged from a minimum of $1,000 to a maximum of $20,000, technically making Standard Oil liable for $29,240,000 in damages. In the public debate few—if any—doubted the legality of the maximum offense. The only question was: would Landis choose *or dare* to impose it.

The fundamental issue was whose assets should Landis consider in determining the fine: those of Standard Oil of Indiana or rather those of its giant parent company, Standard Oil of New Jersey? Ever since 1899 the New Jersey firm had been the cartel's key to control of its petroleum empire. Through it, Rockefeller and his small group of associates directly commanded 69 corporations and indirectly guided another 114. Of Standard Oil of Indiana's $1 million in capital stock all but four $100 shares were held by the Rockefeller trust.[16]

Only after the cartel brazenly stonewalled Landis on supplying information on its finances did Landis finally subpoena the company's top men to testify, including the biggest Standard Oil man of all, indeed the biggest capitalist of all, John D. Rockefeller. Though Rockefeller still carried the title of Standard Oil president and owned over 25 percent of Standard Oil stock, there was either an element of monumental grandstanding in summoning Rockefeller to Landis' court—or a more calculated attempt to hold the oil tycoon as a virtual "hostage" to compel compliance with Landis' request for information. The nearly 68-year-old Rockefeller had not been involved in the cartel's day-to-day affairs since 1897, but he was the biggest game of all. Bringing him to the bar of justice would serve notice that *nobody* was bigger than the law, no one was bigger than Kenesaw Mountain Landis.

Rockefeller, however, had no interest in testifying before anyone, having successfully dodged *any* court appearance since 1888. As his spokesmen argued it would be a "hardship" for this "old man" to travel in his private railway car to Chicago,[17] the richest individual in America would play hide-and-seek with process servers in a comic opera attempt to dodge Landis.[18]

While Rockefeller went underground, his attorneys attempted to cut a deal, trying to buy Landis off with promises that their client would submit to being deposed on the subject. Landis refused, reiterating, "This court is no respecter of wealth or other claims of immunity."

"John D. Rockefeller will be found if he is in this country," vowed one of Landis' court officers. "If it is necessary to send subpoenas to every district marshal's office in the United States and to send out fifty men from each office to look for the oil magnate, it will be done."[19]

That wasn't quite necessary, but Rockefeller's whereabouts nonetheless remained a mystery. Some said he had boarded a steamer for Europe. Others claimed he was variously at a Lakewood, New Jersey, golf course; at Forest Hill near Cleveland; at his 5,000-acre Pocantico Hills estate outside Tarrytown, New York; or at son-in-law E. Parmalee Prentice's Taconic Farm, outside Pittsfield, Massachusetts.

Deputy United States marshals swooped down on the homes of Rockefeller's friends on the chance he might be at one of them. Even his pastor's house was "under espionage."

Armed guards reportedly patrolled each Rockefeller mansion to keep marshals and process servers at arm's length. At Forest Hill, Rockefeller's gatekeeper refused entrance to Special United States Marshal B.A. Fish, who responded by climbing over the estate's huge iron fence and fording a creek. Other lawmen followed, scouring the entire grounds. At Rockefeller's Lakewood, New Jersey, home a process server similarly failed to locate the oil magnate. A half dozen more process servers futilely camped out around-the-clock about Pocantico Hills.[20]

But the real game was afoot in Pittsfield. Printed reports had Rockefeller and his private secretary arriving at Prentice's lakefront 250-acre estate, Taconic Farm, in a closed carriage on Thursday night, June 27. E. Parmalee Prentice, a Chicago attorney, had married the second of Rockefeller's three daughters, Alta. After the wedding Prentice moved to New York City where he founded the firm of Milbank, Tweed and ostensibly oversaw Rockefeller's legal matters. As the years passed, however, Prentice fled New York's pressure, spending most of his time at Taconic Farm, practicing "scientific agriculture" and amusing himself by translating such works as *Treasure Island* into Latin.[21]

Friday, June 28, was golf day for those on the case. Landis, an avid if not particularly talented golfer, was enjoying a day on the Logansport links. District Attorney Sims played at Chicago's Midlothian Club, while Rockefeller—an avid golfer known to have servants clear snow off a course for winter play—plied Taconic Farm's private fairways. That evening he boarded a sleeper car for New York.

On Saturday afternoon Prentice rode into Pittsfield and publicly offered $50,000 to anyone who could prove Rockefeller was in town—although he soon was denying the offer. If, however, Rockefeller was still not at Prentice's estate, rumors of elaborate measures made observers suspicious. Farm hands patrolled the grounds. Armed guards appeared. Fantastic stories circulated of searchlights sweeping Onota Lake and boats being warned not to approach too near the shore. Equally dubious tales were told of a prize bull being killed for fear it might get loose and injure Rockefeller as he strolled about the grounds.

On Tuesday night, July 2, Deputy United States Marshal Charles L. Frink arrived from nearby North Adams and was met at Pittsfield's Hotel Wendell by Deputy Marshal James Ruhl of Boston. Neither had bothered to secure a search warrant. The next morning the two men, followed by a swarm of reporters, rented a carriage and drove out to Taconic Farm. Prentice interrupted his breakfast and jovially met them on the south veranda, making a great show of throwing open the blinds to reveal his family—minus father-in-law—having breakfast. However, he did not invite anyone into the house. "Really, I have nothing to say," he blandly told Frink and Ruhl, "Please pay no attention to the newspaper stories."

Frink and Ruhl reacted with a meek retreat, returning to their hotel and checking out. Despite receiving a telegram from their superior back in Boston, Marshal Charles K. Darling, ordering them to "keep on the ground," the duo displayed a lack of tenacity unusual even for government bureaucrats. Ruhl boarded a train for Boston and Frink took the trolley back to North Adams, 25 miles north of Pittsfield.

Back home the mutton-chopped Frink, a member of the city council, reflected on the day's events and realized he had been had. He discounted a report that Rockefeller was at an estate in nearby Great Barrington and resolved to return to Taconic Farm. Again he hired a carriage, arriving back at Prentice's villa at 3 PM. The grounds were heavily wooded, and Frink's drive down the roadway to the house was hidden until he had virtually reached it.

As Frink approached the end of the drive he saw Rockefeller and Prentice on rocking chairs on the veranda. Prentice bolted, but Rockefeller could not move fast enough to avoid service. The 6'3" Frink shoved the subpoena into the oil magnate's wizened hand, and the chase was over. "I had hoped to avoid a trip to Chicago just now," Rockefeller explained, "but I suppose I shall have to go. I have avoided the marshals, as I hoped my attorneys would secure a modification of the order compelling me to appear in Chicago, but . . ."

Rockefeller paused and managed an odd smile. "I see you are not a marshal to be avoided," he added, then shook hands with Frink and asked him to have a seat. Prentice handed the deputy a cigar. Later he would be left to sheepishly explain to reporters why he had offered $50,000 to anyone who could prove Rockefeller was in Pittsfield—and more to the point why he was not about to pay it.

Rockefeller still tried to avoid going to Chicago and wired Landis there, but the judge was visiting an old acquaintance, a Dr. Carr, at tiny Green Bush, Wisconsin, about 20 miles north of Sheboygan. Rockefeller fired off another telegram, this time of some length, again volunteering to make a deposition before a United States Commissioner in Pittsfield. Landis, however, still couldn't be reached, and Standard Oil attorneys made the same offer to District Attorney Sims. Sims refused.[22]

Rockefeller lingered in Pittsfield to assist with Fourth of July fireworks but that evening finally left aboard his private railroad car, arriving in Chicago simultaneously with Landis on Friday afternoon, July 5. While he traveled, his Standard Oil propaganda machine went to work. Company vice president John D. Archbold issued the bold-faced lie that his employer had never dodged any subpoenas and, in fact, had telegraphed Marshal Darling that he had been available at Pittsfield to receive any issued for him.

Rockefeller, who would later repeat such nonsense, wired Landis: "I understand that a subpoena has been issued for my appearance in Chicago on Saturday. No subpoena is necessary. I will be there."

Landis ignored the message.[23]

In Chicago, Rockefeller stayed with his second daughter, Edith,[24] who had returned from her Lake Forest, Illinois, summer home for that purpose. Crowds of reporters and curiosity-seekers stood guard outside the gray granite mansion's wrought-iron gates in hopes of catching a glimpse of the great man.[25]

Landis scheduled Rockefeller's court appearance for 10 AM on Saturday, July 6. Security precautions had been taken to preserve Rockefeller and his fellow oil company officials from harm not just from "fanatics" or "anarchists," but more dangerously from process servers in civil suits. The usual Federal Building staff was augmented not only by Secret Service agents but by five specially engaged Pinkerton Agency private detectives. Twenty Chicago police were engaged to clear a path for Rockefeller and his brother William to enter the building, and every single one was needed. Two women fainted. Nearly 20 men—including one alderman—felt the sting of policemen's billyclubs. Despite Rockefeller's reputation as the very embodiment of avarice, the crowd displayed greater curiosity than hostility, focusing more upon his obvious gray wig than on his alleged criminal behavior.

Once inside further security precautions were taken as the Rockefeller brothers were led into a darkened elevator and taken to the sixth floor. Riding alongside Rockefeller was a reporter who commented he was "a hard man to get to."

"Why, bless you my boy," Rockefeller jovially exclaimed. "I like the newspaper men. I have many friends among them, and if you ever come down to Ohio I will play golf with you."

For an hour before court began the low-ceilinged corridors outside Landis' chambers had been choked with persons excitedly pushing and shoving in anticipation of the magnate's entrance. Those jammed against the walls shouted for help. United States Marshal L. T. Hoy and his men were responsible for maintaining order but instead were forcibly swept about by the crowd's elemental force. And while spectators were technically admitted to the courtroom only by displaying specially printed cards, many forced their way in without them. A few men passed themselves off as reporters; one woman claimed to be a court stenographer. None of these ruses worked.[26]

Surrounded by a crowd, anxious, even desperate, to catch sight of him, Rockefeller moved through the packed corridor and into the courtroom itself. "Take your hat off, John," cried one onlooker. "Let's see that wig." Rockefeller seemed unaffected by the crush, but his exasperated brother remarked, "An outrage. I never heard of such treatment." Once both were in the courtroom, however, it got worse. The crowd in the hallway burst out of control, and Marshal Hoy called for reinforcements.

Rockefeller took a chair to the left of the judge's bench and like everyone else awaited the bailiff's announcement of Landis' presence, at one point calmly looking up at a reporter and puckishly mimicking his note taking. Hoy wished to know if he was comfortable, and he replied he was fine. When Landis' arrival was finally boomed out, the judge moved quickly to his seat, adjusted his glasses, settled in and announced court was indeed in session.

A visible air of excitement filled the packed courtroom, but neither Landis nor any other court official paid any discernible notice to their prominent, and hitherto reluctant, visitor. "If all men are not equal before the law," noted a *Chicago Tribune* reporter, "there was a surprising amount of surface indication in Judge Landis' court that they are." What no one ignored, however, was the terrific heat generated in a chamber jammed to twice its normal capacity. Electric fans made little difference, merely moving the hot, damp July air about from person to person. Stiff celluloid collars wilted. The crowd rumbled as if it revolted against its discomfort, but Landis threatened to clear the room if perfect silence was not adhered to.[27]

It was.

The Standard Oil case was fourth on the docket, and Rockefeller would have to sit through the preceding actions. The first concerned Patrick J. Brown, an 18-year-old bank post office messenger, sentenced for stealing letters. The second was that of 37-year-old George Smith, who had reversed the usual practice of taking the alias of Smith, operating under the pseudonym of Brady. Authorities charged him with stealing not just letters but an entire mail wagon in front of the Chicago stock market.

Next came yet another case involving the mails. This concerned a Czech immigrant named George Konda. Konda's attorney pled for mercy, arguing that his client was penniless, and that, although he was a man of "culture and education," he had violated the laws "in ignorance." Rockefeller looked on in rapt attention, but as sentencing came it was clear the defense had overplayed his hand.

"The court finds it hard to put the burden of justice on the innocent," Landis intoned as he removed his glasses and peered down at the defendant, "but in the case of a man of education the crime has additional offensiveness. The sentence is a year in the house of corrections."

Rockefeller stiffened slightly, drawing in his breath as the clerk wasted no time in announcing the next case: "The United States against the Standard Oil Company."[28]

Three witnesses preceded Rockefeller to the stand. Landis had one hand on a cut-glass water pitcher and nervously fingered a pencil in the other as he finally called, "John D. Rockefeller." The room erupted in a great rustle of sound. "Order!" shouted a marshal, gaveling furiously. "Order! Order!"

Landis' interrogation of Rockefeller was pure anticlimax. In between objections from Standard Oil attorneys, he asked 19 questions but elicited almost no information from Rockefeller, who, despite holding the title of president, contended that for the last "eight or ten" years he had "not been rendering any service whatsoever" to the company. Before answering each question Rockefeller would pause slightly and glance at his attorneys to see if they had any objections. Only if they had none — would he proceed. The witness spoke, one reporter observed, "in a tone so softly modulated and with an air so mildly careless that money, temporarily, lost all value in that courtroom."

True, Rockefeller had a rough idea of the outstanding capital of Standard Oil stock ($100 million), but claimed he did not even know where its refineries were and professed he could barely state what his firm's occupation was beyond the "production, the refining, and the sale of oil." He claimed he could not tell Landis what Standard Oil dividends were for 1903, 1904, or 1905, although he did think he would name an official who could, Charles M. Pratt, company secretary.

"Then call Mr. Pratt," responded Landis. "That is all for the present, Mr. Rockefeller."[29]

A Standard Oil attorney tried to lead Rockefeller out of the courtroom but went through the wrong door—the entrance to Landis' chambers. On the other side someone slammed the door in their faces. With Landis glaring down at them, they sheepishly returned to their seats, remaining until Pratt and three more witnesses had been heard. By 11:25, the proceedings were over.[30]

As Rockefeller left the courthouse he was besieged by reporters, and amused them with such homespun wisdom as "The way to happiness is to be good." He dodged questions regarding the judge who had summoned him half way across a continent. "Judge Landis is an energetic and enterprising jurist," was all he would comment. "I wouldn't say anything against him if I could, and I couldn't say anything nice about him for fear people would accuse me of trying to curry favor with him."[31]

Unlike Pratt and Archbold, Rockefeller foreswore the $90 in travel expenses due him for testifying. He wasted little time in leaving for Cleveland by train. On board he met a brakeman who informed him that his name was also Rockefeller. "Young man," replied the millionaire, "I'm sorry for you. You ought to have it changed at once."

"Do you think you could beat Judge Landis in a game of golf?" reporters asked Rockefeller on his arrival in Cleveland.

All they got out of him was a broad smile.

Rockefeller's attorneys weren't smiling. They stayed behind to reiterate the company's formal refusal to furnish information and to snipe at Landis, hinting he had been swayed by the "gossip of the street and charges of the mob."

The nation, of course, was transfixed by the spectacle of this modern Croesus being subjected to this leveling treatment. Some, however, advocated even more intensive familiarity with the legal system: jail. Speaking in Warsaw, Indiana, William Jennings Bryan thundered, "Send John D. Rockefeller and a dozen trust magnates to prison for a long term of years and one of the most vital questions before the people of this country will have been solved." [32] He groused that any fine levied against Standard Oil would only be passed on to consumers. [33]

Having had the immense fun of watching John D. Rockefeller squirm, Landis, in what would prove to be a lifelong habit, took his time about rendering an actual decision, announcing it would not be forthcoming until Saturday, August 3.

His time, of course, was still occupied with other judicial affairs, and with the spotlight remaining on his court, he wasted little time in exhibiting what the Landis legal style was all about.

The following Tuesday, he disposed of the George Brady (a.k.a. Smith) case, one of those heard just before Rockefeller's testimony. It was Brady's second conviction, and he pled for mercy, arguing that he had attempted to go straight but it was difficult in a "cold" world.

"I realize," Landis replied in sentencing him to five years and eight months in Leavenworth, "what a man in your position is up against, and if I can help one under those conditions I am with him. If you'll write to me and have shown yourself to be well-behaved prisoner I'll get you a job and I'll see that you have dignified employment, too." [34]

A second defendant appearing that day was Samuel Bergh, a 19-year-old employee at the Chicago Musical College, who had been found guilty of forging a $6 money order.

Bergh's father, a minister, tearfully begged for his son's freedom. "I don't believe he was responsible," cried the father. "I'm sure he must have been in the hand of the devil. He has always been a good son."

The Squire wasn't buying any theological arguments, but he was moved by the father's concern. "Now, young man," he lectured, "it is the judgment . . . of this court that you pay a fine of $200. You may pay $2 a week to the clerk . . . until the whole fine is paid. And there is just one thing more. Don't you get it into your head that the devil was responsible for your predicament. It was your fault and not the devil's, so don't shift the blame off onto the devil. That is all."

Then Landis had a second thought, asking the boy how much he earned each week. On learning that it was just $7 of which he paid $3 to his parents for room and board, Landis turned to the father and ordered, "Mr. Bergh, you reduce the boy's board to $2 a week." The reverend had no problem with that.[35]

The third case was that of 25-year-old letter carrier John McCaffrey. He had opened a piece of mail, stolen some cash from it, and been found out. After hearing McCaffrey's pleading that his wife was ill and needed his care, Landis sentenced him to the minimum sentence, a year in Bridewell prison. But instead of ordering him immediately carted off to his punishment, Landis gave the defendant two months to get his affairs in order. When McCaffrey promised he would appear at Bridewell at 10 AM sharp two months hence, he walked out of court a temporarily free man unencumbered by either bail or parole — at liberty merely on his word of honor.[36]

At 10 o'clock on the morning of August 3, 1907, however, Landis entered the packed courtroom to hand down his sentence on Standard Oil. He had just returned from Logansport and was dressed in a pale blue shirt and a light gray suit, festooned with a white carnation. Over his bench was a surprise: a life-size portrait of Walter Q. Gresham. It had been hung there just the previous day. The Judge was quite pleased by the gesture.

Six hundred persons packed the chamber. Spectators ignored the rule against standing as the overflow crowd stood two and three deep against each wall. An odd silence and an almost motionlessness stillness hung in the air as Landis proceeded with his decision.

Before Landis began, defense attorney Merritt Starr interrupted him, offering some comments on the yet-unannounced sentence, "If the court please," said Starr, "on behalf of the defendant . . . I desire to make a suggestion or two in the case before . . ."

"Doesn't it strike you," Landis shot back, shaking his manuscript at Starr, "that it would be well to wait until I have finished with this document? Then I will hear what you have to say."[37]

All told it took Landis 55 minutes to deliver his 7,500-word decision, a document that aside from citing the statutes involved quoted but one other legal document, a textbook on evidence. He began slowly but soon picked up the pace, at times rattling on so fast that he put the stenographers' skills to the limit. Through it all he spoke loudly enough to be heard to the room's furthest corner.

Sometimes he would deliver a particularly stinging comment, and the room erupted in raucous hilarity, compelling bailiffs to gavel loudly for order. When Landis confessed he could not see this case as the giant corporation's "virgin offense," the audience first smiled, then burst into embarrassed laughter, and then finally into thunderous applause. Even before the bailiffs could restore order, Landis, maintaining an air of intense gravity, rapped his hand on the bench. The room was stilled.[38]

After stating the case's basic facts, Landis arrived at the first serious issue before him, upholding the constitutionality of the Elkins Act and of the provisions of the Interstate Commerce Act of 1887. He derided Standard Oil's contention that it had every right to make a "private contract" with whomever they chose for whatever rate was mutually agreeable to them. He held that neither the railroad nor the oil company had any right to create a "secret" rate on a "public functionary," i.e., a railroad, that exists "for the benefit of the public; not part of the public, but all of the public."

Waxing indignant, Landis argued "there is no more reason for the claim of natural right to private contract for the exercise by a railway company of the public power with which it is endowed than there would be for the claim of similar right to private contract with the collector of customs or tax assessor for a secret valuation of property."

Obviously still smarting over defense counsel's remarks that he had been swayed by "the gossip of the street or the charges of the mob," Landis railed against the "studied insolence" of that intimation and of the cartel's contention that because no other oil was hauled on the Alton line no one had been injured. Landis found such logic insulting, pointing out that, of course, no other oil was shipped on the line, since it would cost three times as much as what Standard Oil had paid. "It requires no great wisdom," Landis observed, "to understand that if other men of capital, genius, and integrity should embark in the oil business . . . , the methods unveiling in this proceeding would force them out."

By now Landis had reached his most singular point: "We might as well look at this situation squarely. The men who thus deliberately violate this law wound society more deeply than does he who counterfeits the coin or steals letters from the mails."

He was now speaking for the frustrations of a nation. "Throughout the reading," noted the *Chicago Tribune,* "Judge Landis seemed to the spectators in general no more a court tribunal than the embodiment of the crystallized sentiment of the country against the ignoring or the cunning violation of laws by great corporations by means of which they have destroyed weaker competitors."[39]

Next came the issue of the amount of the fine. Noting that Rockefeller's trust held all but a handful of shares of Standard Oil of Indiana's $1 million of capital stock, Landis announced: "The nominal defendant is the Standard Oil Company of Indiana, a million dollar corporation. The Standard Oil Company of New Jersey, whose capital is $100,000,000 is the real defendant."

And with that he decided to hit Standard Oil, a defendant whose wealth had been matched only by its arrogance, with the maximum financial penalty, a $20,000 fine for each of the 1,462 counts—for a total of $29,240,000. It was the largest fine ever imposed by an American court.

Landis would have preferred a stiffer penalty: imprisonment. The current law allowed for that punishment, but the original Elkins Act permitted only monetary penalties, and Landis employed this as a rationale for imposing the maximum fine: "For the law to take from one of its corporate creatures as a penalty for a dividend producing crime less than one-third of its net revenues accrued during the period of violation falls far short of the imposition of an excessive fine, and surely to do this would not be the exercise of as much real power as is employed when a sentence is imposed taking from a human being one day of his liberty."[40]

*Now*, Landis was willing to hear Starr's suggestions. What the defense attorney wanted was a delay in the judgment's execution so Standard Oil could file an appeal. "The court is as anxious to have this taken to the Court of Appeals as anybody," Landis replied in granting Starr 60 days for that purpose.[41]

Spectators were jubilant at Landis' verdict; the prosecution was ecstatic; much of the nation could hardly believe a federal judge had finally cracked down on a trust—and cracked down *hard*. "What is the matter with running Judge Landis for president?" asked one of the lawyers in the case. "Surely that opinion was Rooseveltian enough?"[42]

The *Chicago Tribune* attempted to place the fine in some perspective. Twenty-nine million dollars was six times the national budget of Venezuela; the annual salary of 48,730 street laborers; slightly more than half the money coined annually by the United States Mint, the cost of five battleships; and, most pointedly for John D. Rockefeller, 29 times the entire capital stock of Standard Oil of Indiana.

The rival *Record-Herald* put the matter in more physical terms. Twenty-nine million silver dollars would weigh 980 tons and require 58 freight cars for its transport.[43]

# CHAPTER 5

# "THE MAN OF THE HOUR"

Landis' decision electrified the nation. To increasingly anxious conservatives the courts were "the sheet anchor of the Republic." But frustrated progressives saw it differently. They had long believed that the judiciary stood athwart of the reform process. The courts had struck down scores of progressive measures and by use of both injunctions and contempt citations hobbled the formation of organized labor. Prominent progressive journalist William Allen White damned the judiciary as "one of the most ruthless checks on democracy permitted by any civilized people." Law professor (and later dean of Harvard Law School) Roscoe Pound fumed that the judiciary "do nothing and obstruct everything."[1]

Now that had changed. One honest judge had at last been found. Someone had *finally* brought the trusts to their knees. Landis was what two decades of reformers had hoped for. He was, in the breathless words of the William Randolph Hearst's *Chicago Examiner*, "The Man Who Came At Last."[2]

He was showered with lavish praise. Former federal circuit court judge John A. Blevins of St. Louis appraised his decision as a "masterful one [with] no parallel in Anglo-Saxon jurisprudence, neither in literary quality, or force." The attorneys general of Texas, Utah, Florida, Arkansas, and Wyoming also were quick with approval. The *New York World* editorialized that Landis' action would "prove a sharp rebuke to much incendiary talk about the federal courts as a shield for corporation oppression." It was, they gushed, "a great event in American political and financial history." The *Chicago Tribune* expressed the belief that "no judicial act will be more popular." The *St. Louis Globe-Democrat* acclaimed it as "magnificent." The *Albany Argus* saw it as "calm and judicial throughout."

The *New York Press*, which advocated Standard Oil's dissolution, thought that Landis' opinion would "rank with the memorable utterances of American statesmanship." It reminded readers to "never cease to be grateful" to him. A wire service report lauded Landis as "the man of the hour" who had "brought the cause of honest commercialism from degradation into light and gives independent operators hope of freedom of competition."

From Iowa City, William Jennings Bryan grandly postulated that "this penalty may be large enough to teach [the trusts] some respect for the law," although Iowa governor Albert Cummins thought it "too bad" the fine "were not bigger." James R. Garfield, now secretary of the interior, had no doubt that the $29 million would be collected and revealed that he was preparing 10,000 more counts against Standard Oil. Attorney General Charles J. Bonaparte felt the massive fine's example would forever end the practice of rebates.

The *Pittsburgh Post*, however, was among the many who thought the fine was "most salutary" but that the public would end up paying it. Princeton University president Woodrow Wilson, however, declared that "one really responsible man in jail" was better than any fine.

Out in Indianapolis, the manager of the local Tiona Oil Company also expressed pleasure at the decision. He himself had brought charges against Standard Oil before the State Railroad Commission, but he had another more personal reason for satisfaction. "Judge Landis is my cousin," J. V. Zartman told reporters. "When we were boys the Landis family lived in Logansport and ours lived in the country, ten miles distant. Kenesaw and I used to go swimming and fishing together and were great chums. Of course, we did all the mean things that boys usually do, but Kenesaw seems to have outgrown it. I tell you, I am proud of that boy!"[3]

Not everyone was Kenesaw's cousin. The *Pittsburgh Gazette-Times* thought the fines were "beyond all reason." The *New York Times*, clearly dumbstruck, wondered if he had attempted to render the law "ridiculous" by carrying out enforcement to "its unconscionable rigor."

"No theory of law or justice," it maintained, "sustains such a thumping penalty as Judge Landis has pronounced."

The *Times*' Republican rival, the *Tribune*, was more balanced. Although it admitted that "so startling a penalty," even if overturned, would awaken those running great corporations "to the danger of taking chances in evading or overriding the laws," it also declared that "no public interest will be promoted by stage thunder in a proceeding of this kind."

The *Wall Street Journal*, while conceding that Standard Oil had long gouged the public, argued that "two wrongs do not make one right" and felt that Landis' "severe" and "confiscatory" decision might very well create sympathy for the avaricious cartel.

The *North American Review* soberly warned investors that the Elkins Act "makes it possible for a court to confiscate the entire property of a company in which they are investors as a penalty for the failure of a railroad company to properly file its tariff schedules at Washington."[4]

John D. Rockefeller struck a public pose of equanimity. While golfing in Cleveland, Landis' nemesis had just hit a drive for 160 yards, when a messenger tracked him down, dismounted from his bicycle, and handed him a yellow envelope. Rockefeller read the message, folded it over, and slowly placed it in his pocket. Present were two newspaper reporters, who knowing Landis' verdict was imminent, were too reticent to speak.

"Well, gentlemen, shall we proceed?" Rockefeller finally said as he began to play through.

"How much was the fine?" someone finally dared ask.

"Twenty-nine millions," Rockefeller pronounced calmly, and then, despite topping a ball just 75 yards on the second hole ("The power of the press to spoil any sort of a drive is wonderful") proceeded to shoot a 53 for nine holes, his best score ever. After golf, he headed for services at Cleveland's Euclid Avenue Baptist Church. Later he sneered, "Judge Landis will be dead a long time before this fine is paid."[5]

It seemed that everyone had something to say — except for one man. Theodore Roosevelt was pleased enough with the decision. "That is the reason why I appointed Landis," he privately crowed to his advisors. "I knew that the Standard Oil gang did not own him." But publicly TR said nothing.[6]

Roosevelt eventually did speak out in angry, determined detail. In the wake of the decision, rumors of a business panic swept the nation. On August 20 TR traveled to Provincetown to dedicate a monument to the Pilgrims. There he scored "certain malefactors of great wealth" for stirring up talk of a panic in hopes of cooling the Square Deal's trust-busting activity "so that they may enjoy unmolested the fruits of their own evil doing." The Roosevelt administration was not about to back down.[7]

While the nation went back and forth on the wisdom of Landis' actions, the Squire had little time to bask in his newfound fame. On

August 5 he was back in court, first deciding on the fate of the Zion City Lace Company, on the auction block to pay off $245,000 in mortgages. Then, before hurrying to preside over federal court in Indianapolis—a convenient way of getting back to Logansport—he struck down yet another trust, this time issuing a permanent injunction against the "Prudential Club," a cartel encompassing the American Seating Company and 13 other furniture firms. Each month this trust formally convened to gouge higher prices out of schools and churches. Unlike Standard Oil, this cartel went quietly. Only three of its firms even bothered to send representation, and no objections were entered against Landis' decree, which included a $43,000 fine.[8]

"I should think," Landis had angrily observed in May, "that between resorting to [such practices] for the purpose of getting a country church or a country school board to believe that these gentlemen were there in good faith bidding for their job, that any man with any self-respect would prefer to dig a ditch at $1.50 a day, which is unquestionably the more dignified occupation of the two."[9]

Meanwhile, Standard Oil prepared its counterattack. Its attorneys and officers professed shock at Landis' fine, comparing it to the values involved in the original crime, pointing out that the rebates had been worth a mere $223,000 and the oil transported just $650,000. "For each car of oil, valued at $450," they huffily pointed out, "we have been fined $20,000."[10]

Their strategy may not have always been quite so gentlemanly. From Indiana came a report that the company had men tailing their antagonist. A Logansport paper reported that as far back as June, Standard Oil had sent an agent to Landis' hometown to "quietly sound . . . everybody supposed to know much about the Landis family." He aroused little if any suspicion, but was recalled when two other agents began trailing Landis on his post-verdict visit to Indiana. When the Squire left for Indianapolis, they followed him. When he returned to Logansport, they returned and were joined by another man. "I guess I can stand inspection," Landis nonchalantly remarked, but the incident bothered him.[11]

For their part the company denied all. "The Directors of the Standard Oil Company," came the official denial, "wish to brand as false in every particular the statement made in a widely published telegram from Logansport, Ind., in to-day's papers, to the effect that the Standard Oil company has been employing or is employing any spies, detectives, or secret agents to dog or report upon the movements of Judge K. M. Landis."[12]

Standard Oil's earnings were not a matter of public record, but during the proceedings Landis had forced a figure of $100 million in capitalization from John D. Rockefeller, and secured an admission from Standard Oil secretary Pratt that the firm earned dividends of 44, 36, and 40 percent on its investment in 1903, 1904, and 1905 respectively. Landis' supposedly fabulous $29 million fine, noted a news report in the normally unsympathetic *New York Times*, "might have been paid out of the amount paid in dividends in any of those years and would have still left enough to pay the stockholders anywhere from 6 to 14 per cent on . . . capital." Within a week of Landis' decision United States Commissioner of Corporations Herbert Knox Smith confirmed Pratt's figures and added that they were not even Standard's Oil's historic high. In both 1900 and 1901 the firm yielded a hefty 48 percent in dividends.[13]

As startling to the business establishment as Landis' fines had been, equally disconcerting was his call for a special grand jury to be impaneled on August 14 to investigate a possible conspiracy between Standard Oil of Indiana and the Chicago & Alton, a probe that could result in jail terms for both firms' highest officials. In this move Landis and the Justice Department sharply parted company, with the government calling his actions "ill advised" and "unfortunate." Thus began a month-long, rarely skillful dance in which each party would artlessly dodge responsibility for letting the railroad off the hook.[14]

At first rumors swirled as to which oil and rail officials would be personally prosecuted, with Standard Oil traffic agent Edward Bogardus being among the most prominent. But within a week word leaked out regarding the Justice Department's reluctance to prosecute the rail line: they had granted it immunity in exchange for testifying against the oil cartel.

But the issue had even wider implications. In the seven other rebate cases pending against the Standard Oil, similar "immunity baths" had been granted. If Alton officials were prosecuted, other lines would be extremely reluctant to cooperate further with the Justice Department. Landis' actions could crash not only every other rebate case extant against Rockefeller but every rebate case period.[15]

Why then had Landis acted as he had? First, the government had not bothered to inform him of any agreement, and it would be unlikely for Landis to presume one. While grants of immunity were even then common in state courts, they were rarely employed by federal prosecutors. Instead cooperative witnesses were subjected to a trial, found guilty, and then pardoned by the president. Secondly, grand jury proceedings were by law not the Justice Department's responsibility, but rather that of the United States Attorney's Office. During the trial Alton officials had proved to be less than forthcoming. Press accounts described them as "evasive" and "hostile." In United States Attorney Sims' summation to the trial jury he had bitterly complained of their recalcitrance. After Landis' call for a grand jury Sims commented that he could have secured the needed evidence from the railroad "by force" and was "under no special obligation" to grant immunity. Thus, he could "proceed accordingly."[16]

As word of the controversy leaked out, no one knew how Landis would resolve the crisis he had created. A Logansport paper quoted him as saying he "would not be a party to any such [immunity] agreement." The Chicago press had him saying, "I don't want to be mysterious, but anything I have to say on this subject I will say from the bench."[17]

What Landis said from the bench on August 14 was that he was dumping the matter squarely back in the lap of Attorney General Charles Bonaparte.

Bonaparte, a grandnephew of Napoleon Bonaparte and the grandson of King Jerome of Westphalia, held impeccable progressive credentials, having helped found a number of good government groups, including the National Civil Service Reform League and the National Municipal League. He had served with distinction on both the United States Civil Service Commission and the Board of Indian Commissioners before being appointed secretary of the Navy in 1905. As attorney general he followed a vigorous anti-trust policy, speaking out strongly for "the imprisonment of individual defendants" and against immunity in rebating cases. Now, however, he would have to eat those words.[18]

As the grand jury convened, Landis conceded that not even the "meanest criminal" should be able to "truthfully charge" the government with "bad faith"—but he was obviously skeptical that Chicago & Alton officials had lived up to their portion of the bargain, hinting they had endeavored to "deceive and mislead the jury." In what the *New York Times* deemed a "master stroke," he successfully threw the entire matter back in Bonaparte's lap, ordering him to review whatever agreement had been made to ascertain whether it did indeed cover such unsatisfactory testimony.[19]

Complicating matters was the fact that none of the current prosecutors had been a party to any grant of immunity. When the case began neither Bonaparte nor United States Attorney Sims had been in office. Bonaparte's predecessor, William Henry Moody (who had won fame as the unsuccessful prosecutor in the Lizzie Borden case), had departed the Justice Department in December 1906 when Roosevelt nominated him for the United States Supreme Court, an appointment that alarmed monopolists. United States Attorney Sims' predecessor, Charles B. Morrison, had similarly left office in the interim. They had, as was the current custom, made oral agreements on immunity—leaving nothing behind in writing.[20]

Morrison, Sims, Bonaparte, and Moody conferred and determined that immunity had indeed been granted and why. In June 1906 Congress amended the Elkins Act, mandating not only fines but imprisonment for violations. There was a fear, however, that the new law might erase the penalties for prosecution under the original act. Prosecutors rushed indictments, fearing that if they were not filed quickly they could never be made. Complicating the situation was a new bookkeeping system railroads across the nation were then instituting, resulting in the destruction of literally carloads of old records—data critically necessary to prove cases. Moody, and even Sims, felt that without the Alton's cooperation no more than 150 counts could have been delivered against the oil cartel. As it was, the government had to keep 21 clerks working feverishly on the paperwork necessary to meet its August 1906 deadline for indictments.[21]

Meanwhile rumors flew that Landis had suffered a nervous breakdown. Presiding over a session at Quincy, Illinois, Landis took pains to deny the gossip, and the denial looked genuine. "At the time and on the day which I was reported as being a nervous weck," he fumed, "I traveled the Tippecanoe river, near my brother's farm in Delphi, Ind., in sometimes as much as four feet of water, in search of bass. Do you think I could have done anything like this if I had been in the condition in which I was reported?"[22]

The press concluded that when Landis' court reconvened on September 3, the grand jury would be dismissed. It was not. Sims still felt snookered by the railway's behavior at the trial. Like Landis, he was particularly incensed at the testimony of Alton chief rate clerk F. S. Hollands, whose uncooperative testimony nearly sunk the government's case. And Bonaparte, despite, or perhaps because of, his tough talk on rebaters, did not want responsibility for letting the Alton officials go free. Despite the attorney general's written assurance that he supported immunity, he reported to Landis that Sims had discovered "certain new, and in his judgment, material facts" and recommended a three-week delay. It was widely rumored, however, that if Landis did not drop his plans for prosecution, Bonaparte would publicly cross swords with him on the issue.[23]

Reporters wanted to know if Landis knew the exact reason for the continuance and if he had spoken privately with either Bonaparte or Sims. "The lawyers practicing in this court, have learned by this time, I think, that any communication they may have to make to me on the business of the court must be made when I am on the bench," he responded. "I'm going back to the Tippecanoe River tonight and resume fishing."[24]

But if Landis went fishing in Indiana he caught his limit in record time, for the very next morning he arrived in New York and saw two friends off on a steamer to Europe. From there he journeyed to Princeton for a visit with Grover Cleveland, ostensibly for advice on fishing equipment from the former president, an avid outdoorsman. From Princeton, Landis returned to New York, where he stayed incognito at the Hotel Gotham and whiled away his time on such diversions as a trip on an excursion boat and a pilgrimage to Grant's Tomb.

Finally reporters caught up with him, and he did his best to divert the subject from either Standard Oil or immunity. "It's a trip well worth while," he prattled on about his sightseeing tour. "It's glorious. Grant's Tomb is a place where too few New Yorkers go. I visit it every time I come here, and that averages twice a year. It is a place every American should love.[25]

"If there hadn't happened to be some litigation in my court I could come here and never be noticed," he concluded. "I wish it were so now. I have a deep conviction of the duty of my office; it is the position and not its occupant that should mean most to the public, and if you have to write anything I wish you would make it as short as possible."[26]

The newsmen, however, had not divined the real purpose of Landis' trip—to visit Theodore Roosevelt at Sagamore Hill. On September 5 Landis lunched with TR. Unfortunately no details are known of the Squire's visit to his political idol.[27]

From New York, Landis traveled by boat to Albany, continuing by train to Detroit and thence to rural, wooded northern Michigan. There, he toured an abandoned lumber town and went bass fishing with District Attorney Sims. At Bay City the local newspaper, while finding him to be "one of the most companionable fellows who ever walked the earth," nonetheless dismissed him as the "Glad Hand Judge."[28]

After Michigan, Landis left for Cincinnati. Staying with his brother John, he visited his boyhood home in Millville, still dodged questions about Standard Oil, and, along with his brother Charles, addressed a reunion of their father's Civil War regiment. In Cap Anson's distinguished company he took time out to attend a Reds-Cubs game at rickety old Palace of the Fans. He chatted with Cubs owner Charles P. Taft, wealthy brother of William Howard Taft, but rooted for Cincinnati "for the good of the game" because, as he put it, the pennant-winning Chicagoans "don't need any more games."[29]

Even at the ballpark the press dogged Landis for comments on his $29 million case, but he pretended not to hear them. One correspondent asked for his thoughts on the organization of corporations.

"Now, take the attitude of the people of Detroit, for instance," he responded in almost Stenglesque fashion, "they positively refuse to discuss the base ball situation upon any basis which contemplates even as remotely possible that the Tigers will fail to land on top of the American League heap. I see that the Detroit club is just a little over a game behind the leaders and that if Detroit wins to-day and Philadelphia loses, they'll be practically tied for first place."

The reporters still wanted a new slant on Standard Oil, but the Squire would not accommodate them, continuing, "What is the matter with the Cincinnati club? I understand they are up as batters and are all right in the field. I can't understand why they should be in sixth place. Cincinnati is a great base ball town, I have heard, but you ought to see Detroit. They talk nothing but base ball and what they are going to do after the Tigers have foreclosed their air-tight cinch on the American League pennant and destroyed the Cubs in the world's championship series."[30]

From Cincinnati he visited his maternal aunts and cousins in Dayton, which he praised as "the most beautiful city in North America" and still prattled on about the national pastime.

"What game requires more skill, agility, accuracy, the exercise of physical and mental faculties? Can you name one? No, it is the greatest of all. I attend the games in Chicago pretty regularly. I don't 'holler,' because I can't." [31]

He stopped in Indianapolis to hear a few cases before returning home in late September, to finally settle the Chicago & Alton affair. On September 20 Bonaparte instructed Sims to request Landis to dismiss the grand jury. "Although some parts of the evidence are undeniably open to adverse criticism," Bonaparte noted, "the most perfect good faith requires the Government of the United States to accord to the Chicago and Alton railroad company the privileges granted an accomplice who becomes a witness for the prosecution"— immunity. Four days later, Landis informed grand jurors they now had no duties to perform. The "criminal classes," as he pointedly phrased it, had escaped prosecution by cutting a deal. The insult must have galled the Alton officials present, but they had the satisfaction of knowing they were getting off scot-free.[32]

But as Landis settled the immunity issue he staged another trick to remain in the public eye. With the grand jury—and the press—still in his courtroom, Landis drew notice to a small defense of Standard Oil of Indiana's actions published by its president, James A. Moffett, for distribution to company employees and stockholders. In it Moffett ventured beyond a mere justification, insinuating the government had "a purpose in selecting the Standard as a victim" and contending that numerous other Chicago shippers had regularly violated the Elkins Act, an allegation hinted at during the trial but never fully advanced. Moffett's charges incensed Landis, and he subpoenaed the New York-based executive to appear in Chicago, challenging him to prove his charges.

"I hope, I need not say to you, gentlemen," Landis tartly remarked concerning Moffett's insinuation of "purpose," "that the highest ambition I have as a judge on this bench is so to administer the authority which the law confers upon this court as that no man may truthfully allege what I have read to you."

In regard to selective prosecution, he snapped, "I can best answer his criticism by directing the prosecution of all other offenders he points out." Moffett, like Rockefeller, would grudgingly appear in Landis' courtroom, but his visit would be far less pleasant. Commissioner of Corporations Smith would brand his testimony as riddled with "evasions" and would further accuse his firm of falsifying accounts to hide the fact that rebates had indeed taken place.[33]

All the while a modest Landis-for-president boomlet grew. With Teddy Roosevelt publicly committed to stepping down in 1908, the field was wide open, and Landis was, after all, "the man of the hour." Newspapers trumpeted his virtues. The *Zanesville News* called him a "logical candidate." The *Boerne Texas Star* remarked that "the people of this country will find very much like sending Judge Landis to the White House."[34]

Telegrams and congratulatory letters flooded in. The Park Republican Club of New York City wired: "In expressing to you the great satisfaction that your masterful opinion in the Standard Oil case has given all Americans we hope you will see no impropriety. Legislators may fail and executives waver but the hope of the country is ever in its great jurists. You have the personal satisfaction of knowing you are right. The country has the satisfaction of knowing that in the right time and the right place and for a just purpose there was a right man.[35]

And not just Republicans favored his candidacy. A rumor floated that, while in Princeton, Landis had conferred with Grover Cleveland over the possibility of securing the Democratic nomination in the event of a deadlocked convention. To the conservative Cleveland, the Republican Landis as his party's nominee would be far preferable than the radical Bryan.[36]

Landis discouraged such thoughts, and he pooh-poohed a gubernatorial boomlet launched by the *Springfield Evening News*, a paper financially (but not editorially) controlled by Frank Lowden. From Washington came the *Herald*'s opinion that he would make a fine vice-presidential candidate. And from New York arrived an offer arrived of a salary of $25,000 per year to become general secretary of a 200-union labor federation.[37]

Newspapers and magazines such as the *Saturday Evening Post*, *Review of Reviews*, *Appleton's Magazine*, *American Mercury*, and *Outlook* ran worshipful articles. *Human Life* featured him on its cover. Details of his childhood, of his family life, of his days in Washington, of his thoughts on farm life and baseball and dandelions, were provided to an eager public.[38]

The headlines were adulatory:

JUDGE LANDIS HAS BACKBONE
Only Federal Jurist Who Has Had Courage To Hale
Oil King Into Court Man of Iron Will[39]

Judge Landis Unawed By Standard Oil
Has Been Noted for His De-termination Throughout His
Career of Distinction[40]

### JUDGE WHO ORDERS JOHN D. TO BAR
### FEARLESS CHAMPION OF JUSTICE[41]

One paper called him the most talked about man in the world. For a week that might have been right.

Publicly and privately Landis' thoughts were virtually identical. To the press he announced: "To think that I would accept political preferment as a reward for what I have done on the bench is to impeach my integrity as a judge and my honor as a man."[42]

"Presidential candidate? Me?" he said to a reporter at his brother Fred's home. Then he let out a hearty laugh.[43]

Landis collected the clippings mentioning a presidential bid and carefully pasted them in his scrapbook. But he knew it was not meant to be. To Lowden he wrote, "I have the best position in the world. I would not give up the judicial work for three times Mr. John D. Rockefeller's money. This is my estimate of the place you got for me, old fellow."[44]

Landis continued on with his life, with court, and despite the fact that a Landis candidacy never materialized, with politics. June 1908 was a particularly eventful month. The Republican National Convention met in Chicago to nominate William Howard Taft, and Landis was on hand, meeting with, among others, Charles P. Taft.[45]

That same month saw Landis interject himself into one of Chicago's most lurid murder cases, that of Czech-immigrant fortune teller and con man Herman Billick.

The Billick saga began when 22-year-old Mary Vrzal visited "The Great Billick, Card-Reader and Seer" for a potion to restore a neighborhood butcher's affections for her sister Emma. Billick soon ingratiated himself with the Vrzal family, particularly with mother Rosa. Before long Rosa and Billick were allegedly lovers, hatching a grisly murder-for-insurance-money scheme of poisoning Billick's wife and mother along with most of the Vrzal family, including Rosa's milk dealer husband, Martin, and four of their children, including Mary Vrzal. Twelve-year-old Ella Vrzal's insurance policy paid off in the amount of just $105.

"Billick and my mother sat at a table in the corner," young Jerry Vrzal would testify, "and Billick said, 'You know, in a few days your

husband will be dead.' He turned to me and said that in a few days
my father would be dead, and others also. If I was all right they
would take me with them, he said. Otherwise he would kill me too."

Instead of poisoning his own wife and mother and marrying
Rosa, Billick did neither. Instead, he spent all the insurance money,
leaving Rosa destitute. Desperately, she begged Billick not just for
money but to murder his own family. With police closing in on Rosa
in December 1906, Billick—according to Jerry Vrzal—hypnotized her
into committing suicide. That did not save the fortune teller from
prosecution for the five murders, although he was convicted only for
Mary Vrzal's death. Sentenced to death, an appeal to a higher state
court resulted only in a stay of execution.[46]

With the time thus gained, Billick's lawyer succeeded in stirring
up popular opinion on the case, particularly when Jerry Vrzal suddenly repudiated his testimony. Billick not only denied any part in
the Vrzals' wholesale poisoning but of any "sinful relations" with
Rosa. Segments of the daily press beat the drums for reopening the
case. Adding to the mix was an energetic Paulist priest, Father P. J.
O'Callaghan, and a nun, Sister Rose of the Order of the Sacred
Heart, who frantically organized support in Chicago's huge immigrant community for Billick. Twenty thousand citizens signed a petition urging the Board of Pardons to grant clemency. Inside the Cook
County Jail, its 400 inmates fell to their knees in prayer to beg God
to spare their popular fellow prisoner. After the emotional gathering,
the convicts presented floral bouquets to Father O'Callaghan, Sister
Rose—and even to the warden.[47]

An appeals court had set Friday, June 12, 1908, as the new date
for Billick's hanging. The day before Landis denied Billick a writ of
habeas corpus, and it appeared the execution would proceed on schedule. Churches were jammed with parishioners organized by Father
O'Callaghan to pray for Billick's safety. Thousands of other people,
either sympathetic or merely curious, gathered in the streets outside
the Cook County jail. Inside, tension and agitation pervaded the
grounds. Gallows had been erected, and prisoners were confined to
their cells as they normally would be on days a hanging was planned.

Overnight Landis poured over his law books. He discovered an
1895 United States Supreme Court opinion mandating an appeal
from his ruling. The next morning he shook his finger at the prosecution and chided them for not discovering it on their own.

"Gentlemen," Landis railed, "in this proceeding you have looked up a good deal of law, but I am surprised that in studying the law governing appeals in the federal courts you have not discovered that there are certain cases, of which the one at the bar is typical, in which when the petitioner raises a question of the construction of the federal constitution it is not discretionary with the court but mandatory upon it, to grant the appeal. How you left it out of your arguments and compelled me to stumble upon the most important law on this question is a puzzle to me."

As adamant as Landis professed to be regarding Billick's rights, he was hardly convinced of his innocence. "If I had the power to deny the appeal I would deny it," he stated. "However, it is not a question of merit, it is a question of right—whether I have the right to stand between this man and a reconsideration of his plea. I cannot find that I have any authority to do that."[48]

News of Landis' decision reached the jail just 20 minutes before Billick was to be hung. A priest assisting Father O'Callaghan stepped outside the jailhouse doors and waved his panama hat to the mob, exclaiming, "Billick is saved! Judge Landis has reprieved him!" The crowd became hysterical, shouting loudly and frantically tossing headgear and handkerchiefs in the air. Their frenzy made the guards nervous, and they kept their billy clubs at the ready. Inside prisoners heard the racket and started their own demonstration, which swelled in volume and swept from tier to tier. It took the guards a full half-hour to quiet the din.[49]

Landis had indeed saved this foul creature from the hangman's noose. In January 1909 Governor Deneen, acting on the recommendation of the Board of Pardons, commuted Billick's sentence to life imprisonment. In January 1917, however, Billick became a free man—via a pardon from Governor Edward F. Dunne.[50]

One last major case came before Landis' purview that month, and it involved rebates. A Chicago wholesale fish dealer had been found guilty of forcing concessions from the Nickel Plate and Lehigh Valley railroads. The maximum penalty was nowhere near $29 million—just $10,000. District Attorney Sims said that amount would be just as bracing a penalty as that given Standard Oil, but the firm had already gone into bankruptcy, and Landis let its receivers off easy—with a mere $1,000 penalty.[51]

It was a larger fine than Standard Oil would ever pay.

# CHAPTER 6

# "THE JUDGE IS ABOVE THE LAW"

While Landis busied himself extending mercy to murderers and fish peddlers, the fate of his $29 million verdict fell to the hands of the three-judge Seventh Circuit Court of Appeals.

Presiding over that panel was Peter Stenger Grosscup, a jurist of national—albeit controversial—reputation.

Lean-faced, with oddly full lips, an ice-cold gaze, and a pince-nez balanced upon his nose, Grosscup resembled a particularly malevolent version of Woodrow Wilson. Like Landis, he was Ohio born. Unlike Landis, he remained there long enough to obtain a law degree and to set himself up as a city solicitor. Twice Grosscup sought—and lost—election to Congress. First he was beaten by a Democrat, then he was reapportioned into a district with a Republican incumbent in favor of whom he eventually withdrew.

In the second instance, many said his deference was based less on strategy than on dishonorable reasons. Some contended he had been bought off. Others pointed to the rumors swirling about his personal life. Grosscup, they said, was a noted philanderer and had stolen his wife away from her tinsmith first husband. That is not, however, why he left Ohio. Matrimony had failed to cool Grosscup's lusts, and, while dallying with yet another man's wife, her husband, a Lutheran minister, arrived on the scene. The clergyman must have anticipated such a scenario, for he carried a pistol and a willingness to use it. Grosscup escaped with his life only through "adroit dodging and [his] ability as a sprinter."[1]

Shortly thereafter—critics said he was aided by funds provided in exchange for withdrawing from the congressional race—Grosscup moved to Chicago. There he joined several exclusive clubs and entered into partnership with one of Abraham Lincoln's old law partners and quickly established himself as one of the city's premier attorneys. When a federal judgeship opened up during Benjamin Harrison's administration, Grosscup, along with a former United States senator, was one of two finalists for the post. Grosscup, however, had the backing of George S. Pullman who had contributed $75,000 to Harrison's campaign. What finally sealed the appointment though was Grosscup's promise to name his rival as his court clerk. He gained his judgeship in December 1892, but three years passed before he honored his pledge. Skeptics said he feared letting the incumbent go, lest he divulge details of Grosscup's lurid past life.[2]

Almost immediately Grosscup made a national name for himself when the United States Supreme Court upheld his minority opinion that Chicago's World Columbian Exposition could remain open on Sundays. He followed that up, however, with a series of reactionary pro-business decisions, leading to charges of "government by injunction."

In 1894 he repaid his debt to Pullman. Eugene V. Debs' American Railway Union (ARU) had struck his sleeping car company. When the strike failed to bring Pullman to his knees, sympathetic railroad workers refused to service his cars, disrupting rail service all the way to the Pacific Coast. Grosscup, who the year before had thundered that "the growth of labor unions must be checked by law," and fellow judge William A. Woods, notorious for his acceptance of "important favors" from the various railroads, issued an injunction against the ARU, not just prohibiting participation in the boycott but violating its free speech and basically shutting it down as a union. When the ARU ignored the injunction, Grosscup ordered Debs jailed. Still, the strike continued. Rioting and bloodshed increased. On the pretext of protecting the mails—but actually to break the union—Grosscup and Williams went over the head of Illinois governor Altgeld, calling on President Cleveland to dispatch federal troops to get the railroads moving again.

Meanwhile Debs, whom Judge Williams had sentenced to six months for violating the injunction, was also indicted on more serious charges of conspiracy to block a mail train. Grosscup heard the case, and his actions added to his controversial reputation. When defense lawyers called George Pullman as a witness, the magnate ignored the subpoena. Grosscup did nothing to punish him. The prosecution had no proof of Debs' guilt, and with its case all but lost, Grosscup adjourned the trial. Despite Debs' repeated protests, Grosscup never brought the case back for conclusion.[3]

The strike and the union soon collapsed, but at a terrible cost. Not only Altgeld but the governors of Kansas, Texas, Oregon, and Colorado protested Cleveland's unilateral use of troops. Never before had states' rights been so egregiously trampled. Never before had the federal government so blatantly intervened in favor of an employer. American workingmen felt betrayed and grew increasingly radicalized. So did Debs. Formerly a Democrat, he soon emerged as a leader in the growing Socialist Party.

In 1898 Grosscup was elevated to the United States Court of Appeals (by the former Ohio congressman he had stepped aside for, now President William McKinley) and in 1905 to its chief judgeship. Still he went out of his way to invite controversy. A skilled polemicist, one of his 1896 speeches was reprinted in the amount of 100,000 copies. Similarly, his 1898 debate with Carl Schurz on the subject of territorial expansion — Grosscup took the affirmative — attracted national attention.

Grosscup was most voluble on the topic of corporations, standing athwart the rising tide of trust-busting and advocating what he called the "peopleizing" of corporations, i.e., the selling of stock shares to as wide a segment as possible of the public as a bulwark against socialist sentiments. But despite "peopleizing," and vague public rumblings about the growing power of corporations ("something is wrong . . .," he wrote, "there is a disturbing, even sinister look") Grosscup had by now earned a reputation as a tool of the corporations and an erratic jurist.

His views on corporate regulation may be gauged from remarks he made as the verdict was coming down in *United States v. Standard Oil of Indiana*:

> In many State Legislatures bills have been introduced regulating local railroad matters. . . . With a few exceptions these bills are not the result of inquiry into the cost of service; are not founded on considerations of place or circumstance; are not founded on any judgement of the legislators other than the general judgment of the legislators that the thing done is a popular thing to do.[4]

Adding to Grosscup's growing unpopularity was a series of controversial episodes. Most notable was his tortuous handling of the Chicago Union Traction Company bankruptcy. Even if no improprieties had been involved, Grosscup's incredibly slow, 10-year-long, settling of the case would have caused criticism. But that was the least of his problems. The first was the appointment of his close friend, business partner, and court clerk, Marshall H. Sampsell, as receiver of the line.[5] Grosscup saw that Sampsell, whose clerk salary was just $3,500 per year, received a princely $18,000 salary as receiver. Some felt even more was sticking to Sampsell's fingers. Additional charges circulated that Sampsell had illegally used Union Traction funds for political purposes.[6]

The second major issue was Grosscup's financial interest in the Chicago Street Railway Co., ultimately the sole bidder for what was left of Union Traction. In January 1908, as the case finally drew to a close, the U. S. Supreme Court ignored conflict of interest charges against Grosscup. If they had acted, Congressional impeachment would have been in order.[7]

Such missteps took their toll. Grosscup had long coveted a Supreme Court post, but the United Traction controversy caused Theodore Roosevelt to kill any such appointment.[8] This then was the judge who would decide the fate of Landis' historic Standard Oil decision—virtually the prototype of the individual who created massive public distrust of the federal judiciary.

But there was even more to the Grosscup story. The judge also served as a director and chief stockholder of the Mattoon and Charleston Interurban Railway (M & C). In August 1907 a jam-packed M & C trolley car was speeding along a curve on the way to a county fair. It collided with a heavily loaded freight car, causing horrific carnage. Fifteen persons, included two eight-year-old boys and a six-year-old, were killed. Fifty-two people were seriously injured. The motorman deserted the dead and dying. Both radio telephones were ruined in the wreck, and survivors had to walk a mile before finding help. While waiting to be rescued, the injured suffered additionally from the blazing August heat. The carnage moved rescuers to tears.[9]

In operation for just three years, the Mattoon and Charleston had already compiled a terrible safety record. This was its third major accident. In the first, 15 were injured. In the second, a motorman died and a woman lost both legs.[10] A grand jury indicted Grosscup and Sampsell, the line's vice president, for manslaughter. Charges were eventually quashed, but Grosscup's shabby reputation was further soiled.[11]

Just as the indictments were being handed down, Grosscup

managed to further anger President Roosevelt. At a formal dinner in Indianapolis, he bragged how Roosevelt had asked him to select a blue ribbon commission to draft legislation providing for the federal incorporation of firms engaged in interstate commerce. Roosevelt had in fact advocated such action in his Provincetown speech but quickly and angrily denied Grosscup would play such a role. Soon the embarrassed jurist was disavowing his boast, although at least two credible witnesses testified they had overheard it.[12]

In December 1907, with the Standard Oil case still under appeal, Landis and Grosscup butted heads over the issue of judicial oratory. Landis had refused an invitation to appear at a banquet in Kansas City. Ironically, in view of his past, and certainly future, reputation for public eloquence, he went on to criticize jurists who traipsed about the country delivering speeches, saying that "a judge may with propriety limit his activities to his judicial work."

Grosscup, noted orator and pundit as he was, took this as a personal affront. "I do not believe because I am a judge, I lose my rights as a citizen," he exploded. "I say what I durn please in public." Bad blood was obviously growing in the Federal Building. As one newspaper would soon observe, Grosscup bore "no love for Judge Landis who reached his present exalted position by merit and whose indifference to corporations is as pronounced as is Judge Grosscup's subservience."[13]

In early June 1908 Grosscup made headlines again. William Randolph Hearst's *Chicago Examiner* reported that when it came to railroads Grosscup's hand was always extended outward—for free passes. The paper blasted his close ties to rail lines and hinted he would soon leave the bench to accept a lucrative post as a corporate lawyer, a rumor Grosscup did little to squelch.[14]

But how would Grosscup rule in the Standard Oil case? His initial public reaction to Landis' $29,240,000 fine had come within days of its announcement. Speaking at a Chicago area country club, he again attacked state attempts at regulation, ominously commenting that "the Federal courts will retain their authority over interstate commerce and their right to regulate and control it, in spite of the frantic efforts in several parts of the country by state authorities to deprive them of the right."[15]

Yet, on the day of Grosscup's decision, the morning editions of the *Tribune*, the *American,* and *Inter-Ocean* predicted Landis would be upheld two-to-one, with Grosscup in the majority. After all, back in

January 1907 in affirming the bulk of the indictments against Standard Oil, Landis had even cited a Grosscup opinion in support.[16]

At noon on Wednesday, July 22, 1908, in a Chicago courtroom packed with attorneys and reporters, Grosscup announced the appeals court's decision. Unlike Landis, Grosscup would not read out his entire decision. Instead, like a thunderclap he released a brief statement. In the harshest of terms he not only overturned the $29 million fine and ordered a new trial for Standard Oil, but in unusually strident terms condemned Landis as an "arbitrary" despot who had clearly abused his "judicial discretion."

From pillar to post Grosscup ripped Landis apart. He ridiculed the government's contention that each rebated carload constituted a separate offense. Choosing to interpret each carload as a separate count, he contended, "was wholly arbitrary—had no basis in any intention or fixed rule discoverable in the statute." Nor did Grosscup concede that Standard Oil's 500 separate shipments were separate counts. Instead, he construed the statute as narrowly as possible, by designating only the 36 separate days, or "settlements," oil was shipped as counts. That translated into a minimum fine of just $36,000 and a maximum of $720,000.

Grosscup also severely took Landis to task for considering the assets of Standard Oil of Indiana's parent company, the $100 million Standard Oil of New Jersey, in assessing the penalty. Grosscup asked:

> Can a court without abuse of judicial discretion wipe out all of the property of the defendant . . . and all the assets . . . in an effort to reach and punish a party that is not before the court—a party . . . that is not even indicted? Can an American Judge without abuse of judicial discretion condemn any one who has not had his day in court?
>
> That, to our mind is strange doctrine in Anglo-Saxon jurisprudence. . . . Can that rightfully be done here on no other basis than the Judge's personal belief that the party marked by him for punishment deserves punishment? If so, it is because the man who happens to be the Judge is above the law.

He hammered Landis on the contention that ignorance of the law was no excuse: "The cases cited by the government, such as those requiring liquor sellers, at their peril, to know whether the person to whom a drink is sold, is a minor, . . . are not controlling, nor very persuasive."

Grosscup even questioned whether it was permissible to fine a defendant in an amount larger than the value of the goods in question, or to fine him an amount large enough to wreck him or his creditors.

Couching his argument in pseudo-populist terms, he asked, "Are the creditors to be thus punished? Would a cab driver, convicted of violating the city law against excessive cab fares, be sentenced to pay a fine that would take his horse and cab, and then leave him bankrupt many times over, unable to pay anything but the least proportion of his debts to his other creditors?"

And with that Grosscup, with Judges Baker and Seaman concurring, unanimously reversed Landis' decision and remanded the case with instructions that a new trial be granted.[17]

Each part of Grosscup's reasoning sparked new controversy. He had charged that Landis had excluded from the jury Indiana Standard Oil manager Edward Bogardus' testimony that he was unaware that the standard rate was 18 cents and that Standard Oil was receiving a significant rebate. Critics rightly pointed out that the trial record revealed just the opposite.[18]

In another instance, Grosscup inferred that Landis had overstepped his bounds because the Supreme Court had ruled in *Armour Packing Company v. United States* that "shippers who pay a rate under the honest belief that it is a lawful published rate when in fact it is not" are not culpable. What the Supreme Court had actually said was that the issue was "a question not decided." Hence, Landis had not overstepped his authority.[19]

Front-page cartoons by the *Chicago Tribune*'s John T. McCutcheon—a personal friend of Landis who had been among those invited to James Eckels' ill-fated breakfast party—had particular fun with Grosscup's argument that assessing a corporation in excess of the value of the actual goods involved in the crime was illegal and unconscionable. One McCutcheon drawing depicted a stereotypical "darky" being fined $5 for habitual "chicken embezzlement." The defendant argued: "Yo' honah, yaint gunna fine me $5.00 foh a 30 cent chicken? That's more than I can afford."

Another—labeled "when rebates are punished by the train load instead of the car load"—showed a farmer cooling his heels at a railroad crossing ("Wall, I swan [swain]. I reckon I'll haf to wait a spell"), while a train of seemingly unending length, passed by.[20]

On a more refined level, articles defending Landis' position appeared in both the *Illinois Law Review* and the *Central Law Review*.

"Let us drop this rather timeworn appeal to the sacred rights of free Anglo-Saxons as an answer to every attempt to adjust to new conditions," argued Northwestern University law professor Charles D. Little. "No one today, much less, Judge Landis, would attempt to punish without trial either a natural person or one corporation entirely dissociated from another."[21]

William Jennings Bryan was—for once in his life—struck virtually speechless. The *Chicago Tribune* condemned as bad law the reasoning that Standard Oil of New Jersey was beyond the law's reach. The socialist daily, the *New York Call*, reminded readers it had predicted Landis' fine would never be collected but expressed puzzlement that the capitalist class had not waited until after the 1908 election to scuttle it. Federal officials in Chicago received a series of letters detailing "scurrilous" information on Grosscup.

Theodore Roosevelt, whose opinion of the federal judiciary had already been soured earlier in the year by its invalidation of the Employers' Liability Act of 1906, was at his Oyster Bay, Long Island, home. At first he reserved comment. But with mosquitoes infesting the place his mood must have been foul. It was no doubt worsened when off Newport his yacht crashed into a lumber schooner. TR soon denounced the decision as a "gross miscarriage of justice," to which Grosscup retorted that the president's words meant no more to him than those of any other "citizen." Roosevelt refrained from further public comment but that November he would write to William Allen White: "It is an outrage that a creature like Grosscup should be permitted to sit on the bench."[22]

Not everyone was outraged. The *New York Times* happily noted that "if it may ever be assumed that reversal is rebuke, that assumption may be made in this instance." The *New York Sun* remarked that Grosscup's decision reaffirmed the "equal and impartial protection" of property and was a rebuke not only of Landis but of Rooseveltian bluster. The *New York Tribune* obtusely called Grosscup "one of the most outspoken and determined enemies of corporation abuses on or off the bench."

"No outcry," its editorial continued, "can be raised against him for entertaining opinions too friendly to the corporations."

John D. Rockefeller had no comment.[23]

Rumors again floated of Grosscup's resignation. He denied them, cavalierly saying that if he did step down he would feel free to work for any individual or corporation he chose. "The corporation is here to stay," he proclaimed:

> It already embodies more than one-third of the property of the entire country. One-half of the people of the country get their bread and butter out of it. It is the form in which the largest proportion of the property of the future will be carried.
>
> My position is this: That the corporation should be made so secure, as a form of holding property, that the corporate domain of the country will invite investment by the people, just as the farms of the country are distributed among the people, and this will be done if we go about the work of corporate reconstruction wisely and constructively.[24]

While all this transpired publicly, behind closed doors even more interesting events were taking place. In August 1907, a very edgy Standard Oil vice president, John Archbold, had proposed a compromise to Attorney General Bonaparte, in which his company would admit guilt and settle the fines in the amount of $508,950 in both the Standard Oil of Indiana case and a later anti-trust case. Bonaparte rejected Archbold's offer, but, nonetheless, contacted the Bureau of Corporations for advice. As Landis had, the bureau damned the company as a "habitual offender," and believed it held evidence of Standard Oil crimes totaling penalties of $195,280,000—a sum that made Landis' $29 million fine seem like a slap on the wrist.

In May 1908 Bonaparte informed Archbold that he would not compromise on Landis' $29 million fine, but that he would settle the anti-trust suit if the company pled guilty to one count in five and paid another fine of $1,744,000.

On June 4, Standard Oil "accepted" the deal but wanted a grant of immunity, a halt to further anti-trust prosecution and further negotiation on Landis' fine. Archbold personally visited Roosevelt at the White House to lobby for such an agreement, but Bonaparte argued against undercutting Landis' authority.

On Thursday, July 16, however, Standard Oil stock prices began a steady rise and rumors of a "leak" of Grosscup's decision filtered through Wall Street. Negotiations continued through Monday, July 20—just two days before the Appeals Court decision. It was obvious Standard Oil had been tipped. "Archbold must have known in advance what the Grosscup decision would be," Roosevelt wrote to Bonaparte on July 25. His suspicions could only be further aroused as rumors flew regarding Grosscup's activities. Following his decision he reportedly traveled east with Standard Oil attorney John S. Miller, meeting with Miller and another Rockefeller attorney, Moritz Rosenthal, at a New York City hotel; all denied the reports. Various papers also claimed that T. Parmalee Prentice had thrown a party in honor of Grosscup who was beginning a two-month New England vacation. Prentice was also alleged to have invited Bonaparte, who coincidentally was summering in nearby Lenox. Yet reports of Bonaparte's presence at the Prentice dinner, though widely circulated, were, as the attorney general put them, "a figment of a lively imagination." Prentice was not even in Pittsfield, having sailed for Europe.[25]

Simultaneous with Grosscup's decision, Standard Oil announced a slight recalculation of its capitalization. It seemed that the $100 million figure extracted from John D. Rockefeller did not include the true valuation of its plants. Thus the corporation's actual worth lay between $500 million and $600 million and Landis' $29 million fine was hardly the crippling blow its critics alleged it to be.[26]

In that year of 1908 John D. Rockefeller's personal philanthropies, mostly church related, had amounted to $15 million. One wit contended that wizened old John D. had split his savings on the Landis fine right down the middle with the Lord.[27] In responding to Grosscup's decision, the Justice Department enjoyed limited alternatives. The Elkins Act provided appeals to the United States Supreme Court for only civil—not criminal—violations of the Interstate Commerce Act. *United States v. Standard Oil of Indiana* was a criminal case, and, therefore, not appealable beyond Grosscup's court. Bonaparte asked for a rehearing of the case. He accused Grosscup of misquoting the trial record, committing an "injustice" against Landis, and creating an entirely new doctrine of law by ruling that a defendant cannot be fined more than he has. That approach failed. Bonaparte then asked the Supreme Court to hear the case, filing a *writ of certiorari* with them. In January 1909 Chief Justice Melville Fuller, a Cleveland appointee, rejected it without comment or explanation. [28]

Landis had to be disappointed in the Supreme Court's action but, as usual, dodged attributable comments. "I have heard nothing official . . . ," he told reporters in his chambers. "I was just going out to buy my daughter a birthday present, and I guess I will do that anyway."[29]

Now there was but a single option left: retrial in the original court of jurisdiction—with a maximum fine of only $720,000. In February 1909 United States Attorney Sims commenced a retrial. But Landis was no longer involved. He could have presided over the case but chose not to, arguing that his original decision had prejudiced him. Judge Sol H. Bethea wanted no part of the case either, frankly saying he "didn't want to get mixed up in it." Landis let honors go to Judge Albert B. Anderson of Indianapolis. In some ways Anderson was a Landis clone. They had been boyhood friends in Indiana, studied law together, and even entered politics together. It was Anderson who introduced Landis to Burt Lake, Michigan, where Landis maintained a summer home for over four decades. Both men had been appointed to the bench by Roosevelt. There the similarities ended. In little over a week Anderson, contending there was insufficient proof that any 18-cent rate ever existed, tossed out most of the indictments. "The evidence," Anderson said in his charge to jurors, "does not support the charge." The jury affirmed his judgement.[30]

Reporters rushed to Landis for comment. "It wouldn't be quite proper for me to make any comment at this time," he remarked. "I finished my part in the Standard Oil case some months ago and just now I am deeply interested in the hearing of a suit brought by a boy who lost four fingers in an accident. I also am interested in knowing who took a package of tobacco from my chambers yesterday, but as for Standard Oil [at that he tossed up his hands] I can only repeat I have nothing to say."[31]

The government tossed up its hands as well. Newly elected President William Howard Taft (presidency 1909-1913) had replaced Bonaparte with George Woodward Wickersham, a highly successful corporate attorney who once had represented the Chicago Railways Co. in the Union Traction case. Despite his background, Wickersham developed into a highly effective, if not particularly colorful, trust buster. He would institute indictments against 43 trusts and in 1911 even secured dissolution of the Standard Oil monopoly. But there would be no further action on *United States v. Standard Oil of Indiana*.

The case was simply dead.[32]

Landis and Grosscup, however, clashed again in January 1909 when Grosscup's Appeals Court reviewed Landis' handling of a case involving an Elgin, Illinois, marriage broker, or as the then-current parlance put it, an "affinity agent." After 28 ballots, the jury acquitted Marian Grey on two counts of using the mails to defraud clients but convicted her of a third. She faced 18 months in prison; Landis gave her one year.

Miss Grey's attorney, Elijah N. Zoline, went before Grosscup's court and excoriated Landis' conduct during her trial, calling him a "prosecutor from the bench," charging him with "gross errors" in regard to evidence, and accusing him of "poisoning the minds" of the jury, whom he pictured as a bunch of easily led farmers, despite the fact that they had split six-six on their first ballot.

"I have not found," continued Zoline, "a parallel in the legal books for the conduct of the court in this case. His conduct was undignified, to say the least, for a judge in the Federal Court, and I think this court should take notice of it so that no judge in the Northern District will in the future so conduct himself."[33]

The trial had indeed been a circus, largely due to Miss Grey, but not without Landis' help. Often she broke into tears. At one point she physically attacked a former employee who had testified against her. On another occasion she flirted with the jury. During the jury's deliberations she went so far as to faint. Nervous to the point of exhaustion she refused to leave the courthouse while the jurors deliberated. For his part, Landis fumed that the advertising for her "mercenary matchmaking" was "rot" and "contemptible," and he had as little use for most of her clients, terming them in his sentence, as stamped with "congenital inferiority, people without intellect, people absolutely incompetent to protect themselves from a woman of the defendant's type."[34]

But in his charge, Landis urged jurors to give full consideration to the defendant, although he did it in the most backhanded and insulting manner imaginable:

> I ask you gentlemen not to allow yourselves to become nauseated at this mass of correspondence in this contemptuous business. I also ask you not to allow your abhorrence to arouse you to an expression of it by returning a verdict of guilty.
>
> Such a verdict can be given only if you believe beyond all reasonable doubt that the defendant conducted the business for the purpose and with the intent to defraud. . . .
>
> The act itself may be taken as showing the intent of the defendant, as well as her testimony on the witness stand. If her intent was good, she is not guilty. If it was bad, she is guilty.[35]

To no one's surprise, Grosscup's court reversed the verdict.

A few weeks later, Landis had regained enough composure to comment obliquely on the Grosscup and Anderson decisions—and to junk his previous thoughts on speechifying by judges. In Milwaukee to address Marquette University law students, his topic was public criticism of the judiciary system.[36]

At the time, public objections to judicial decisions were often regarded as subversive of the sanctity of the judicial process. "Remember that anything that is entitled to public confidence will have it"; Landis told his audience, "that honest, intelligent service on the bench as in another sphere, will be accorded the full measure of merited respect; that no official act of any functionary is, or ought to be, above investigation, and that no wrong on this earth is too sacred to be condemned."[37]

It is hard to believe that he was merely speaking theoretically.

While Grosscup had bested Landis in both the Standard Oil and Marian Grey cases, fate was not kind to him. Contention haunted him as his old missteps followed him about and new lapses were committed with regularity. Even his social occasions gave cause for comment. In December 1909 his opulent ball featuring the scandalous dancing of 22-year-old Ruth St. Denis shocked many and led to spirited public criticism.[38]

The following month Eugene V. Debs, a man who had never gotten over his treatment at Grosscup's hands, finally had his revenge, printing a scathing series of articles in the Socialist Party organ, *An Appeal To Reason*. The articles dredged up every known piece of dirt on Grosscup: his political deals, his corporate friendships. To this they added allegations that President Taft had investigated Grosscup for possible impeachment and printed a laundry list of additional Grosscup sexual peccadilloes, including the supposed rape of a Boston chambermaid.

No names were supplied, but the author flung this challenge: "If Judge Grosscup, however, desires to test the knowledge of the writer regarding these transactions, he can bring suit for criminal libel and the whole matter can be heard in court."[39] Grosscup never did.

In March 1910 the American Federation of Labor, outraged over Grosscup's decisions in a series of labor cases, had Chicago Democratic congressman Adolf Sabath issue a call for his impeachment, but nothing came of the matter.[40]

In September 1911 Grosscup at last announced he would be

leaving the bench. He said he wished to enjoy "more freedom," particularly in regard to the 1912 presidential and congressional elections in which he predicted a Democratic sweep. Some even believed he would turn Democrat and seek the seat of veteran United States senator Shelby M. Collum—who back in 1892 had temporarily blocked his judicial appointment. A political career was not to be, however. Instantly, reports circulated regarding the *real* reason for his retirement.[41]

An extensive private investigation into Grosscup's professional and personal life had been underway for two full years, under the direction of crack former secret service agent Lawrence Ritchie.[42] Ritchie was not only examining Grosscup's handling of the Union Traction Co. and his appointment of Marshall Sampsell but also other cases involving trolleys and rail lines. He peered into rumors that Grosscup and his friends had profited from the Standard Oil reversal. He looked into his acquisition of property, what Grosscup paid for it, and when it was bought. Grosscup's "private life," dramatically noted the *New York Call*, "has been watched by lynx-eyed men."[43]

That was interesting enough, but the incident soon took on bizarre cloak-and-dagger aspects. It was rumored that *Everyone's Magazine* had bankrolled Ritchie, spending $100,000 on the inquiry. Grosscup reported that on a foreign vacation he had been tailed across Egypt and Europe. Detectives had watched his meals, his sightseeing, his every move. George Shoaf, author of the *Appeal to Reason*'s exposés on Grosscup, had mysteriously disappeared in Los Angeles, and a blackjack was found outside his door. Marshall Sampsell claimed his office had been broken into, reportedly in a search for incriminating financial records—"that I deposited money not accruing from earnings."[44]

"I am not a rich man," Grosscup said in his defense. But newspapers spoke of his $20,000, 10-acre lakefront suburban "villa"; his interests in various businesses, such as the Mattoon and Charleston trolley line, and his lengthy and luxurious vacations. If he were not rich, he certainly was not poor. On leaving the bench, his new residence, New York's Waldorf-Astoria Hotel, hardly spoke of modest circumstances.[45]

Two days after announcing his resignation an angry Grosscup withdrew it, challenging critics to prove him guilty of any malfeasance in office. "I have known of this espionage for years," declared Grosscup. "I have not yet tendered my resignation, and if there is any intimation by a reputable man or magazine that there has been any act in my official life that will not bear the closest scrutiny, I will never send in my resignation. I will force my enemies to prefer charges against me, and meet them in the open."[46]

But Grosscup was bluffing and within a month handed in his resignation to President Taft.[47]

Rumors flew that he would join the Chicago law firm of Mayer, Meyer, Austrian & Platt, which would then represent Standard Oil. Landis was a logical candidate to replace Grosscup, but he had long indicated that, except for the issue of salary, he didn't consider the position better than what he already had.[48]

On leaving office Grosscup's behavior continued to be an embarrassment. In October 1912, perhaps still bitter over Taft's handling of his ouster, he bolted the Republicans to support Teddy Roosevelt's Progressives—once more proving the axiom of politics making strange bedfellows. With the beginning of World War I Grosscup and TR parted company once more, with the half-German (some said his family name was originally "Grosskopf"), half-Dutch Grosscup blaming Russia for starting the war, attacking Britain for un-neutral actions in protecting Belgium's neutrality, and writing in the German-language *Staats Zeitung*. Following the *Lusitania*'s sinking, he gave an interview to the *Washington Post* urging "the separation of passengers crossing the ocean from ammunition-bearing ships," an implied criticism of British naval policy. By December 1918 he was named in testimony before the Senate Judiciary Committee as having appearing on a suspicious list of "important" German sympathizers found in enemy documents. He promptly denied receiving "any compensation" for pro-German writings or speeches.[49]

With enemies like Grosscup, there is little mystery why Landis' reputation grew no matter how many reversals his decisions suffered.

"Out of all this," exclaimed the *Fort Wayne Labor Times-Herald*, "comes just Landis, the fearless Judge, the incorruptible man encircled by a halo which all the Grosscups and Bakers and Seamans in the universe cannot disturb and never reach."[50]

# CHAPTER 7

# "DIRECT AND FORCEFUL METHODS"

John D. Rockefeller's victory over Landis was short-lived. In November 1909 a federal district court in Missouri unanimously ruled to dissolve the Standard Oil trust. When the cartel appealed to the United States Supreme Court, Chief Justice Edward White delivered a 20,000-word opinion finding the trust in violation of the restraint of trade provisions of the Sherman Act. He affirmed its dissolution.

Landis was in some sense vindicated. But John D. Rockefeller cried all the way the bank. Placed on the New York Stock Exchange for the first time, Standard Oil stock soared. Standard Oil of New Jersey shares skyrocketed from $260 to $580; Standard Oil of Indiana shares rose from $3,500 to $9,500. A year later a rueful Teddy Roosevelt would comment: "No wonder that Wall Street's prayer is: 'Oh Merciful Providence, give us another dissolution.' "[1]

In 1952 the last act of Rockefeller versus Landis played out. Continental Oil, one of Standard Oil's myriad descendants, purchased the Landis home in Logansport, tore it down—and constructed a gas station.

By and large after *Standard Oil* Landis retreated from the national stage but still generated reams of local publicity, at times proving he could generate public notice almost out of whole cloth. In September 1910 a case regarding the mislabeling of a baldness cure came before him. The product promised to "produce hair on bald heads," and Landis asked an assistant district attorney for directions—and to play straight man.

"Rub briskly on the hair three times a day," came the prosecutor's response.

"How can a bald-headed man do that?" Landis mused as he wrinkled his brow and decided on a continuance.[2]

In January 1909 the Squire presided over the trial of a "white slaver," (or pimp), one Matthew Aronson. A jury found Aronson guilty, and as Landis sentenced him to the House of Corrections he noticed something.

"Aronson," he snapped, "where's your overcoat?"

"Your Honor," Aronson responded, "I ain't got none. That was one of the first things I soaked when I came to Chicago."

"Bailiff," ordered Landis, "get mine and give it to him."

Later that day, as Landis walked home *sans* topcoat in the freezing cold a friend called out, "Hi there, Judge, where's your overcoat?"

Landis cryptically replied: "I used it to light a fire."

"Used it to light a fire?"

"Yes," the Squire explained, "I used it to light a fire to keep warm inside of me the spirit of charity that life in a great city like Chicago tends to freeze."[3]

In March 1911 Landis visited Cleveland to help dedicate a new federal building. Once again he demonstrated the ability to generate headlines by saying virtually nothing. Somehow the topic of the recall of federal judges arose. Landis expressed limited but practical approval.

"I might favor the recall of judges generally," said Landis, "but I do not favor any law that will apply to me."[4]

Landis' fame (and photogenic qualities) even qualified him for a role—as a judge—in what has been called the federal government's first motion picture. *The Immigrant* was directed by the appropriately named (but otherwise obscure) Edwin L. Hollywood and featured character actor Warren Cook, who would go on to star with Mary Pickford in the 1917 movie *Pride of the Clan*.[5]

Some matters before Landis, however, were more serious. In 1911 he presided over the trial of an early Chicago "Black Hand" named Gianni Alongi who had been charged with sending threatening letters to a woman.

Landis received his own letter. "You discharge Alongi," it read, "or we will kill you."

The Squire pointedly included the letter's contents in his charge to the jury. "The man who is influenced the fraction of a hair's breadth by having received a threat is as guilty of corruption as though he had taken a money bribe," he commented. "And nowhere in the whole wide world is there room for a man corrupted."[6]

Yet while threats could not budge Landis off the federal bench, nonetheless in 1909 Landis came very close to vacating his judge-ship. The circumstances involved Frank Lowden.

Back in 1906 Lowden decided to run for a seat in Congress. The millionaire, however, took too much for granted in the race (shortly after filing for office he and Landis adjourned for a two-week vaca-tion in Hot Springs, Arkansas) and barely squeaked through to vic-tory that November. Once in Washington he expanded on the Landis connection, becoming close friends with Charles Landis and to a lesser extent with Frederick, occasionally even corresponding with him. "Any time I get a little money," he wrote the youngest Landis brother in March 1907, "I buy a farm adjoining mine somewhere and turn myself loose upon it." On winning re-election in 1908 Lowden ("tired, nervous and with a bad cold") and Kenesaw (but without Mrs. Lowden who later joined them) promptly headed for Atlantic City for a few more weeks of vacation.[7]

By 1909 Lowden had positioned himself to replace Albert Hopkins as United States senator. "If it shall finally appear," he wrote Landis in February 1909, "that Hopkins cannot be elected, there may be an opportunity; if so we ought to seize it."[8] Landis cher-ished his judgeship above nearly all things. But he valued his friend-ship with Lowden more. He offered to step down from the bench to work for Lowden's election—United States senators still being cho-sen by state legislatures. But Lowden had promised Hopkins he would not actively oppose him and so procrastinated. When the state House of Representative's minority Democrats joined with anti-Hopkins Republicans to elect a speaker, Landis knew Hopkins' chances were quickly evaporating and wrote Lowden urging action. "This means that 'hell has broken loose' . . . ," he warned, "everybody seems to regard Hopkins's election as seriously jeopardized. I am not advising you to get into it now, but the situation should be closely watched."[9] Lowden, however, kept out of the fray and Landis re-tained his judgeship.[10]

In December 1910, with Chief Justice Melville W. Fuller, and Associate Justices William H. Moody and David J. Brewer all leaving the United States Supreme Court virtually at once, Landis' friends and supporters launched a campaign for his appointment to the high court. Landis said nothing.[11]

But there was little chance of President Taft appointing him. While the Landis family and Theodore Roosevelt formed a virtual mutual admiration society, Taft had little love for the Squire, once telling journalists Landis was "an obscure demagogue of a judge." The appointments instead went to Wyoming's Willis Vanderventer, Georgia's Joseph Lamar, and New York's Charles Evans Hughes.[12]

Landis remained in his circuit court, but one by one other members of the Landis clan were leaving their federal positions.

Frederick Landis had won re-election to the House in 1904 by a healthy 7,000-vote margin. Following the tradition that freshmen congressmen were seen and not heard, he waited until midway through his second term before delivering his maiden speech. Filled with proper progressive vigor, the address alarmed conservatives, even provoking the Democratic—but still quite conservative—*New York Times* to a lengthy editorial, dripping with sarcasm and ill-disguised contempt.

The subject of Landis' talk was the insurance industry and the need for federal regulation. "Subject these corporations to National supervision," said Landis, "and the eagle will keep the vulture from picking the bones of the dead." The *Times*, noting that the power to regulate insurance was found nowhere in the Constitution, sarcastically observed that "no member of the House . . . gives promise of a career that will stamp his name deeper upon the tablets of history than Mr. Fred Landis of Indiana."[13]

Others must have shared their opinion. In 1906 Democrats swept Indiana, and Frederick was one of the casualties. Not helping matters were GOP dissidents ("Bull Frogs") who turned against him, helping elect Democrat George C. Rauch. Frederick, still just 34 years old, returned home to Logansport to follow brother Walter's footsteps, becoming editor of the *Logansport Journal*. But Frederick could also earn a dollar through sheer oratory. His vote-getting skills may have deserted him, but his speaking skills had not. Fellow Hoosier George Ade (a close friend of Kenesaw) called Frederick "one of the most amusing, entertaining and forceful speakers who ever faced an audience." Author Booth Tarkington contended he "would walk ten miles through the snow to hear Frederick Landis make a speech and I am not particularly fond of walking or of snow."[14]

Frederick also turned his hand to popular fiction. Two of his efforts appeared in 1910, *Angel of the Lonesome Hill: A Story of a President* and *Glory of His Country*. The first, actually more a short story than a novel, combined the maudlin tale of an aged couple who seek a pardon for their unjustly convicted son along with unvarnished praise of Theodore Roosevelt. On its publication Roosevelt wrote

Frederick that "nothing could touch me more than to appear just as you make me appear in your stories. I especially value the volume because it came from you."[15]

*Glory of His Country* involved another god in the Republican pantheon, Abraham Lincoln, and received decidedly mixed reviews, with criticism centering on the author's rather undisciplined and too exuberant style. But less demanding critics liked it. "The story," noted the *Literary Digest*, "is not only interesting, but clean."[16]

Charles Beary Landis followed Frederick out of office just two years after his younger brother's defeat. Charles had carved out a solid career in the House, emerging as a Republican spokesman on issues ranging from the tariff to congressional ethics to the American presence in the Philippines, but perhaps his proudest accomplishment occurred in 1905—the shuttering of the United States Capitol's two saloons.

Fellow Indiana congressman (and future Senate majority leader) James E. Watson termed him "brilliant," but Charles could be as cynical as the next politician. Once Maine's Charles E. Littlefield had delivered a particularly impassioned and skillful speech on the House floor. When Littlefield finished, he approached Landis and Watson. "Boys," he wanted to know, "what do you think of my speech?"

"Well, Charley," Landis responded, "you convinced my judgement, but not my vote."[17]

In 1908, Charles was defeated for re-election, one of the few incumbent Republicans to lose as William Howard Taft swept to the White House. But it was not entirely his fault. Indiana had shifted dramatically Democratic. William Bryan Jennings defeated Taft for the state's electoral votes; Thomas R. Marshall bested Watson for governor; a Republican lost his Senate seat; Democrats captured the state House of Representatives; and only two of 13 Indiana United States House seats remained in GOP hands.

Charles briefly returned to journalism in Delphi but soon took up a position with the du Pont Powder Company, later becoming vice president of the du Pont Engine Company and manager of the E. I. du Pont de Nemours Co. offices in Washington.[18]

In 1910 John Landis temporarily reversed the family's political fortunes, becoming Cincinnati's health commissioner; he radically improved sanitary conditions in Cincinnati, mandating the inspection of restaurants, groceries, and dairies. After a typhoid epidemic hit that city, John mandated the pasteurization of milk supplies entering his jurisdiction. His efforts earned him a national reputation in the field of public health.[19]

In 1910 Kenesaw again found himself in a major anti-trust case, one of national import—and controversy. In 1903 Peter Grosscup had issued an injunction against the nation's leading meat packers for violating the anti-trust actions—a conspiracy that squeezed not only consumers but also agricultural producers of meat. For five years the case bumbled along with nothing really happening to break the "Beef Trust's" monopoly. In 1908 a new grand jury investigation was undertaken but was discontinued before charges were brought.

In January 1910 the Squire decided to take action and empaneled his own grand jury. His decision embroiled him in a bitter battle with the Taft administration, which felt upstaged by his actions. With the new Payne-Aldrich Tariff raising food prices generally, being able to strike at the packers would clearly aid Taft's declining political fortunes. But Landis had beaten them to the punch.

The administration, nonetheless, refused to be outmaneuvered and began leaking information about the case, particularly regarding who the government was targeting in the matter. This infuriated Landis. "Such a thing is unheard of," one of the Squire's friends complained. "The fact is that the government does not know whom it can indict or whether it can indict anyone. It is outrageous to subject these men to public suspicion."

When Landis issued his charge to the Beef Trust grand jury on January 24, 1910, the atmosphere between him and United States Attorney Edwin Sims was tense. He decried the government leaks and insisted that "every degree of decency and honor" require discretion on everyone's part.[20]

The grand jury returned indictments on March 21. Not surprisingly the defense moved to have them dismissed. More surprisingly, Landis did just that, ruling on June 23, 1910, that the indictment contained a significant—and fatal—defect—it never mentioned that the defendants had been engaged in interstate commerce:

> The most painstaking search of this indictment fails to disclose the presence of a charge that during the statutory period the defendants have been engaged in or had anything to do with interstate commerce, or that they have done anything having an effect upon

such commerce, and the court is not clothed with authority to supply, entirely by inference, the complete omission of such a fundamental element of the offense.

The general averment that the defendants engaged in a combination in restraint of interstate trade is, of course, a mere conclusion, and therefore insufficient. The demurrer must be sustained.[21]

He immediately convened another grand jury. On September 12, new indictments were handed down against each of the 10 meat packing executives.[*22] As Woodrow Wilson noted in his *History of the American Nation*, "extra pains were taken in the drafting of these papers to make them error proof." Error proof or not, the four-month-long packers' trial of December 1911-March 1912 saw all 10 acquitted.

For Landis the upshot of the case was worsening relations with the Justice Department, particularly with his old friend Sims. When Sims' reappointment came due in the summer of 1911, Landis wrote Attorney General George Wickersham blasting Sims' conduct, alleging "undue restraint was exerted by the district attorney to prevent the indictment of individuals" during grand jury procedures not only in the Beef Trust case but in another matter involving oleo margarine manufacturers. The Squire was so perturbed at Sims he threatened to appoint a "special attorney to protect the interests of the United States." Only after Assistant Attorney General William S. Kenyon promised to "carry through [the investigations] in good faith" did Landis back off from his threat. Sims, for his part, denied Landis' allegations.[23]

Nineteen twelve was not a good year for the Landis family. It began with Landis again displaying his lenient streak, but in a way not normally designed to curry public favor. On January 4 he sentenced convicted white slaver Coleman Heitler to just 30 days in the Cook County jail and fined him a mere $10. The uproar was so great Attorney General Wickersham felt morally obligated to write Landis to inquire what motivated him.[24]

In March the Judge revealed himself to be somewhat naive in terms of assessing character. He had recommended one Emil Schulze for employment as a custodian of bankruptcy funds at the Department of Interior at Washington. Schulze disappeared when his accounts were found to be short $179, and Landis felt compelled to write a personal check to cover the amount. "It seems to me that I have been a pretty good thing," he fumed to reporters as he signed the check. "I am tired of this court being used for a good thing—an easy mark.

"I will also appropriate a like amount if you gentlemen will please find this man," he went on. "It seems that I am a pretty good thing. It was only a few days since a young man came to me from Indianapolis, presented credentials and letters from persons I know in the Hoosier State, and asked me to cash his personal check. I did. I now have this document as a souvenir. It was returned by the bank without being paid."[25]

That October 26, back in Logansport Mary Kumler Landis died at age of 80. She divided her real property among her daughters and provided Kate Landis with an additional $1,000. The Landis brothers received nothing. "I do this," she noted, "with the full knowledge that I have other children but upon due reflection esteeming this my highest duty, my other children being sons and able to make their own way in the world."[26]

And in national politics, the Landis clan's loyalty to Teddy Roosevelt was landing them in increasing difficulties. Roosevelt had long been feuding with his hand-picked successor, William Howard Taft, and by February 25 of that year "threw his hat in the ring" to seek the Republican presidential nomination.

Despite the backing of the great majority of Republican primary voters, the nomination went to the more conservative Taft. That August Roosevelt's supporters met at Chicago's Orchestra Hall to organize a new political party, the Progressives, and to run TR as their presidential candidate.

The Landis brothers were among the Republicans joining the Rough Rider. Charles seconded the nomination of Roosevelt's vice-presidential candidate, California's Hiram Johnson. Frederick himself ran unsuccessfully as Progressive Party candidate for Indiana lieutenant governor. When Roosevelt campaigned in Indiana he made sure he appeared on the stump at Logansport with his admirer. In retaliation, the vengeful Taft dismissed Walter from his position as postmaster in Puerto Rico.[27][28]

Even after 1912 Frederick remained with the Progressives. Two years later, in a "fiery and brilliant speech," he placed former senator Albert Beveridge's name in nomination for United States senator from Indiana.[29][30] By 1916, however, the Progressive Party was virtually finished, and so were the political fortunes of the Landis brothers. Only Kenesaw survived, and only by benefit of his lifetime appointment.[31]

Frederick was now a pariah in Indiana Republican politics, but luckily his writing skills kept him more than afloat. He continued as an author, his works including such titles as *Days Gone Dry* (1919). He even wrote several plays, the best known of which were "The Water Wagon," and "Montana." In 1918 *Glory of His Times* became the smash Broadway hit *The Copperhead* featuring Lionel Barrymore.[32]

Meanwhile, Kenesaw continued grinding out decisions. One of his more piquantly named rulings came in May 1916. *United States v. 1,950 Boxes of Macaroni* concerned itself with the addition of a dangerous coal tar dye, "martius yellow," to commercially produced pasta. Landis found the dye "serve[d] no purpose other than to change [the macaroni's] color, and is a poison which will kill."

The defense argued the amount of "martius yellow" included in the product was not necessarily enough to cause injury. Landis thought otherwise. "With a portion of our population macaroni is a staple of food," he ruled, "and under the evidence here the cumulative effect of the poison in the substance under examination would be injurious to health." He ordered the affected inventory destroyed.[33]

In 1916 Landis branched out into an investigation of Chicago organized crime. While most Americans link the topic of Chicago gangsterism to the Roaring Twenties, the Windy City roared *long* before that. For decades the city's Levee had been wide open, riddled with gambling and prostitution. "Chicago is unique," pronounced Alderman Charles E. Merriam, a political science professor at the University of Chicago, "it is the only completely corrupt city in America."[34]

Landis' investigation centered on Chicago's gambling king, Jacob "Mont" Tennes. Tennes had begun as a bartender, purchasing his own North Side establishment in 1898, a combination saloon and billiard hall that became a popular hangout for gamblers. He soon challenged other Chicago gamblers such as the South Side's James O'Leary and John O'Malley and the West Side's Bud White and Harry Perry. Tennes' assault started in fairly low-key fashion. In those days in Chicago private constables were empowered to make arrests. Tennes, feeling no sense of hypocrisy, cheerfully swore out complaints of gambling violations against his rivals.

By 1907, however, Tennes launched a full-scale gang war against O'Malley, White, and Perry. White, Perry, and fellow gambler "Social"

Smith had aggravated Tennes by operating a floating poolhall and gambling emporium named "The City of Traverse." But far more annoying was the trio's attempt to break Tennes's "racing wire" monopoly, which fed horse racing information to local pool halls, saloons, and bookmakers. The war saw 32 establishments bombed. Miraculously, no one was killed. Only the intervention of First Ward alderman Michael "Hinky-Dink" Kenna, a front man for early Chicago vice lord "Big Jim" Colisimo, settled the struggle.[35]

The war ended with Tennes' total triumph. "The City of Traverse" ceased operation; Tennes' gambling wire monopoly was validated, and his opponents ceased operation. Flushed with success, in 1910 Tennes spread his wings beyond Chicago, founding the General News Bureau to compete with Cincinnati's Payne Telegraph Service. After a new campaign of bombings and arson (including the bombing of Payne's Cincinnati headquarters), Tennes quickly drove Payne out of business. He now dominated horse race gambling nationwide.[36]

The following year Tennes moved into the protection racket. Downtown Chicago hotels that featured gambling (and most did) paid Tennes the following exorbitant fees:

> Poolrooms—40 to 50% of the win.
> Roulette—40% of the win.
> Faro—50% of the win.
> Craps—60% of the win.
> Poker and other games—50% of the house take.[37]

Landis had virtually stumbled into investigating Tennes. His probe grew out of the issue of straw bonds provided as bail for an alleged blackmailer named George Irwin. Irwin's bond had been raised by gamblers affiliated with the General News Bureau.[38]

Representing Tennes was an attorney known to history more for his defense of civil liberties than of Chicago hoodlums—Clarence C. Darrow. Darrow had initially distinguished himself as a labor attorney but his career took a sharp downward turn in 1912 when he was charged with bribing a policeman in the *Los Angeles Times* bombing case. Darrow was acquitted, but his reputation suffered. Many former friends shunned him (Landis for one refused to appear as a character witness) and he found himself reduced to largely taking purely criminal cases.[39] [40]

At one point during Landis' probe, Tennes commented he would pay Darrow from $12,000 Tennes had stashed away in the First National Bank, a sum he admitted he had won on racing. "Don't do it," Landis snapped. "Don't give Mr. Darrow that money covered with dirt and slime, with the blood which has come from a lot of young fellows about this town who are being made criminals. See if you can't get some clean money."

"I've real estate, too, Your Honor," Tennes responded, "or I might pay expenses out of General News Bureau funds."

"Better not," snarled Landis. "Better give Mr. Darrow his money from your eye remedy company funds. It might be cleaner."

"I don't care if he doesn't pay me at all," Darrow interjected.[41]

This interrogation was in keeping with Landis' aggressive style throughout the investigation. The *Chicago Herald*'s Jack Lait described the atmosphere. "Two assistant United States attorneys sat below," wrote Lait. "But they were spectators, just as all of us were. The court did the prosecuting, the defending, the questioning. . . . To get [information] he led, he cajoled, he bullied when necessary."[42][43]

At one point Landis badgered a Tennes partner, H. T. Argo, regarding his family — and what they knew about how he made his money.

"Have you any children, Mr. Argo."

"One."

"Boy or girl[?]"

"Girl."

"How old is she?"

"Eighteen."

"Did you ever tell her what your business is?"

"What business?"

"You know what business I mean."

Argo mumbled an inarticulate response, but Landis bore on: "Did you ever tell her how you make your money, Mr. Argo?"

Argo still stalled and wanted the question repeated.

"You know what business I mean," Landis responded. "I'm talking about the gambling business you're carrying on. You get money from the working people, an element that can't afford to lose it on gambling. I'm talking about this school for criminals you're engaged in. Don't you think it's too bad you're in a business you can't talk to your children about? You wear a Knight Templar charm. Did you ever tell a lodge of brother Masons about the business you're in?"[44]

Shame was a finely honed arrow in Landis' quiver. Having little actual power to get what he wanted, he shamed the police to raids. He even shamed the phone company into ripping out Tennes' phones. Just before the investigation ended, Landis summoned to his court-room S. W. Tracy, a vice president of the Illinois Telephone & Tele-gram Company (ITT). He wanted to know if ITT instruments served gambling establishments. When Tracy responded that he had "no definite information as to the character of those places," a surprised Landis leaned over the bench and asked Tracy to please send for his attorney at once.

When Tracy's counsel, Daniel J. Schuyler, appeared, he lectured him: "I have no power to order [the phones] out, but I want to know that you, as attorney for the company, have personal knowledge of the situation."

After Schuyler indicated agreement, Landis continued, "I don't suppose there is any law in the State of Illinois that will force a pub-lic service corporation to cooperate with a gambling organization, is there?"

"No," smiled Schuyler, "I guess there isn't, Your Honor."

"If there was you'd know it," pressed Landis, "wouldn't you?"

"Yes."

"Now here are the proofs," Landis went on as he handed a sheaf of documents to the attorney, "and I want to be sure that you and the vice president have personal knowledge of the list; that is all."

Such tactics hardly endeared Landis to Chicago's emerging gangland culture. During the investigation he received threatening calls at his home. In response he peered down at F. W. Sells, who had helped ignite the investigation, inquiring, "You haven't been sending me belligerent telephone messages have you?"

"No, sir."

"You wouldn't think that would make me any better, would you?" Landis, totally in control, grinned.

"No, sir," Sells responded, "I'd think that would make you worse."[45]

Landis' unorthodox investigation not only triggered huge amounts of unwanted publicity on Chicago vice and revealed the names of dozens of Tennes' henchmen and the locations of their es-tablishments, it triggered police raids and promises of further federal and local investigations.

The work earned Landis a rest, and he took one. "I'm going down to my old home in Indiana," he said as he adjourned court for a week-and-a-half. "It's my first vacation in two years, and I'm going to have more fun than any man ever had. Going to play golf and m-m-boy! How I will slam that ball."[46]

Once Landis had finished with Tennes, however, the fireworks were over. Chicago mayor Big Bill Thompson was hardly about to clean house. The police raided a few of Tennes' establishments, but the matter was soon dropped. Tennes' gambling empire flourished. Rumors even swirled that it had fixed the 1920 Kentucky Derby. Not until 1923 did a new Chicago mayor, William E. Dever, make a con-certed—and successful—effort to drive Tennes from business. Tennes, who never was convicted or even arrested in his long career, finally sold his holdings in 1927 to brutish one-time Hearst circulation man-ager, Moses Annenberg, future owner of the *Philadelphia Inquirer.*[47]

As ultimately unsuccessful as Landis might have been in his fight against the Tennes crime octopus, the case further cemented his reputation as the one judge the public could believe in. That Decem-ber he received a postcard. On the front was a hand-drawn cartoon showing him sentencing a well-heeled criminal to prison. On the back was the message:

> In a city, even a big one, like Chicago there's a feeling akin to safety where the citizens can count among them a jurist such as you.
>
> Every Decent Chicagoan[48]

"Judge Landis, to rigid legalistic minds," the *Chicago Herald* editorialized, "may occasionally seem to skirt on the thin edge of ju-risdiction and authority. Possibly [noted English jurists Sir William] Blackstone and [Sir Edward] Coke might have been inclined to raise a warning finger against some of his direct and forceful methods. What of it? He goes to the root of things, he pulls out the truth that lies at the core of frauds ..."[49]

The big winner in the case, however, was probably Darrow. His advice to Tennes to invoke the Fifth Amendment—and keep on in-voking as often as necessary—was universally credited with frus-trating Landis' inquiry—and provided Darrow with an entree into the lucrative profession of defending Chicago's gangland figures.[50]

In November 1916 the Judge's old comrade Frank Lowden finally captured the governorship. The next spring both men would be involved in an extremely confusing court case involving railroad rates and state versus federal powers.

The Illinois Public Utility Commission had mandated a rate of two cents per mile for all passenger rail travel originating and ending within its borders. Following that, however, the Interstate Commerce Commission had approved a 2.4 cent-per-mile rate. The railroads retained the two cent rate for intra-Illinois travel but implemented the higher rate for trips between Illinois and other states.

This, however, caused complaints from commercial interests in Missouri and Iowa. It was now cheaper for, say, some Missouri travelers to reach Chicago than to reach St. Louis or for some Iowa travellers to reach Chicago as opposed to Keokuk, and businessmen in those cities complained to Washington. The ICC ordered carriers to standardize rates beginning in January 1917.

The railroads raised their intrastate rates to 2.4 cent per mile, and thinking ahead, went to Landis to prevent Illinois authorities from prosecuting them for violating the Illinois Public Utility Commission's rate structure.

Lowden, protecting Illinois consumers and Chicago mercantile interests, argued that the ICC had no right to overrule a state's rights regarding intra-state traffic. Landis, while not buying Lowden's reasoning, ruled that the ICC's ruling was too vague to be enforced and ordered the state rate to stand.

Shortly thereafter, however, in St. Louis another federal judge, D. P. Dyer was ruling exactly oppositely. The railroads—not surprisingly, since it would bring them a higher fare—decided to honor Dyer's decision. In response Lowden ordered the railroads to ignore Dyer. Dyer, who termed Landis' decision "preposterous," retaliated by threatening to imprison railroad officials if they did not institute the 2.4 cents per mile fare.

In January 1918 the case went to the United States Supreme Court which unanimously supported Landis. The ICC's ruling, it determined "should not be given as precedence over a state rate statute otherwise valid, unless, and except as far as, it conforms to a high degree of certainty."[51]

Landis felt vindicated, but his mind had already turned from purely domestic matters to thoughts of an America at war.

# CHAPTER 8

# "DAMN THE KAISER, AND HIS SONS"

With the exception of Teddy Roosevelt's charge up San Juan Hill, America had known peace since just after Abraham Landis had been hit with a cannonball at Kennesaw Mountain in 1864—but that was changing rapidly.

After Europe plunged into war in August 1914, America managed to avoid joining into the conflict. Even as late as the presidential election of 1916 the issue was not how to avoid entering the carnage—but how prepared we should be *just in case*. Woodrow Wilson, trumpeting the slogan "He Kept Us Out of War," defeated Republican Charles Evans Hughes. Barely six months later, however, the nation declared war on Germany—and embarked on a patriotic binge unlike any it had known before.

Woodrow Wilson should have known better. "Once lead this people into war and they'll forget there ever was such a thing as tolerance," Wilson had commented in his "He Kept Us Out of War" phase, adding, "To fight you must be brutal and ruthless, and the spirit of ruthless brutality will enter into the very fibre of our national life, infecting Congress, the courts, the policeman on the beat, the man in the street. Conformity would be the only virtue, and every man who refused to conform would have to pay the penalty."

Now Wilson would not only lead Americans into war on Germany, he would lead Americans into a war against those still opposed to that war—German-Americans, Irish-Americans, socialists, anarchists, pacifists, and radical unionists such as the International Workers of the World (IWW).

Patriotic antipathy to those either anti-war in principle—or to those just plain disloyal—translated itself into wide-ranging legislation. The Espionage Act of 1917 forbade persons to "convey false reports or false statements with intent to interfere with the operation or success of the military or naval forces of the United States or to promote the success of its enemies . . . or attempt to cause insubordination, disloyalty, mutiny, or refusal of duty, in the military or naval forces of the United States, or . . . willfully obstruct recruiting or enlistment service. . . ."[1]

The Sedition Act of 1918 forbade anyone to "utter, print, write, or publish any disloyal, profane, scurrilous, or abusive language about the form of government of the United States, or the Constitution of the United States, or the uniform of the Army or Navy of the United States, or any language intended to . . . encourage resistance to the United States, or to promote the cause of its enemies."[2] Maximum penalty: a $10,000 fine and 20 years in prison.[3]

Authorities closed the mails to pro-German or radical publications. Crackdown followed crackdown. Arrest followed arrest, and if Woodrow Wilson could respond with such zeal, imagine the response of someone like Theodore Roosevelt or of his followers such as Kenesaw Mountain Landis.

Landis' generation never had a chance to match the Civil War exploits of its fathers. It was also a generation that saw America reach true world-power status. Landis shared the country's nationalism, and—in 1917-18—its rabid jingoism. He craved not only American victory but he also wanted its enemies ground into the dust. And he wanted to play his own part in their humiliation. "Damn the Kaiser, and his sons," he once exclaimed. On another occasion he attempted to subpoena Wilhelm II for his role in the sinking of the *Lusitania* and advocated shooting him, his six sons, and the 5,000 leading German militarists "in justice to the world and Germany."

The reverse of the coin was the tremendous concern he displayed for German victims. When his court found Fred Sill, a tubercular former coal stoker on a torpedoed freighter, guilty of writing a threatening letter to a government official to recover a $24 debt, Landis not only failed to pack him off to prison, he got Sill admitted to a hospital and saw that he received his $24.[4]

Motivating Landis most during the war was concern for his son Reed. "There are only three things Landis really cares about," an associate once observed. "They are fishing, baseball and his son Reed."

Reed had begun his military service even before America entered the European conflict. In June 1916 Reed saw his old high school classmates enlisting in the Illinois National Guard so as to be a part of General "Black Jack" Pershing's pursuit of Mexican revolutionary Pancho Villa. Reed decided he wanted a part of the action and at breakfast one morning broached the idea to his father. The Squire responded first with stunned silence, then grunted a few words of approval.

By the time Reed actually enlisted as a private with the Illinois National Guard's First Illinois Cavalry, the Judge was crowing about his son's enlistment. "He would have cuffed the boy," the *Chicago Tribune* later noted, "if he hadn't been eager to go . . . . He swore by him and of him—swore in real he-man language."[5]

Reed's Mexican adventures consisted of little more than grooming officers' horses and got him no further than Brownsville, Texas. When the expedition ingloriously ended, Reed was mustered out.[6]

But in April 1917 a real war came to America. The following month Reed Landis enrolled in Fort Sheridan's Officer Candidate School; his father admitted he was the "happiest man alive."[7]

Before long Reed had earned his pilots wings. As America had nothing like a real air force he had received his training from a British pilot, Major A. Cushman Rice. Beginning in September 1917 Reed saw service with Britain's Twenty-Fifth Zero Squadron at Toul, France.

In his first flight young Landis saw a German plane advancing upon him. The German didn't fire. Reed, thinking his enemy was out of ammunition, gallantly refrained from firing on what he thought was a helpless opponent. Suddenly, the German swung at him, coming up under his tail and firing all the way. Reed's plane was completely riddled with bullets. "It was the worst shooting up I ever saw," Major Rice admitted, "but the strange part of it was the young Landis didn't have a scratch. You can bet he didn't wait for the other fellow to start the fun now."[8]

Other close calls followed. In April 1918 Reed battled a German Albatross at point-blank range. To make matters worse nine enemy triplanes flew above Reed and his opponent. Only the intervention of Reed's fellow Allied pilots kept the Germans from swooping down upon him. He hadn't seen the triplanes and he didn't know how close he had come to death. On landing he discovered his fuel tank and engine had been sprayed by enemy bullets and that no oil or water remained in his plane.

Within the space of two weeks in August 1918 Reed, flying solo, shot down two German aircraft and one enemy balloon. On another occasion he attacked five enemy planes, destroying two and forcing the others to flee. The activity earned him the Distinguished Flying Cross.[9]

By that October young Landis, now ranked third behind Eddie Rickenbacker and Elliot Spring among living American aces, transferred from the British to the American front. Promoted to captain, he was given command of the 20-plane, 164-man American Aero Squadron 25. His father refused comment to reporters, but his broad smile made words superfluous.

While flying under the American flag, Reed notched just one flight over German lines. By war's end he had shot down nine German planes and one balloon, thus qualifying him for ace status.[10] "If you lived long enough," he said decades later, "that happened."[11]

But while the Squire promised not to comment on his son, he had not pledged to refrain from generating his own publicity from the conflict. He trumped Reed when his own image appeared in the *Chicago Evening American* alongside that of Major Rice, now in the Windy City on invalid furlough. Rice, who had been gassed, promised to pilot Landis from Chicago to New York—if a United States mail plane could be secured.[12]

The Squire was not bluffing about going above the clouds. He took several flights during and immediately after the war—both in airplanes and even in a balloon. At 3 PM on the afternoon of November 31, 1918, he and a Lieutenant William Bretting took off from Chicago's Grant Park. While Bretting piloted his flimsy plane through a stiff gale, Landis leaned out—at 3,000 feet—and tossed handfuls of war bond literature down upon the city. Bretting did not make the trip any easier. "I tried a couple of stunts then," he admitted. "I did everything but a loop." Forty-five minutes after takeoff the duo landed at the South Shore Country Club. "That was a bully trip," Landis crowed to reporters. "I'll give all of you fellows a ride when I get my own machine." This from a man who never really learned how to drive a car.[13]

The Squire even toyed with the idea of his own enlistment. After watching aviators train at Rantoul, Illinois ("the finest of the fine, whose only fear is that something will come between them and service"), he told an audience of downstate attorneys, "I felt ashamed of myself to see those boys of twenty and twenty-one doing tasks I ought to be doing myself. The age limit in these camps should be raised from thirty-three to fifty-four."[14]

In late 1917 the Squire even wrote Secretary of War Newton D. Baker requesting Baker take him into the service and send him to France in some capacity.[15] Baker urged him to remain on the homefront and to serve on the banquet circuit.[16]

"I never knew until now the penalties of old age," the Judge complained, "which keep me here, when I want to be over there. But you may meet my boy over there."[17]

He did, however, follow Baker's advice, stumping for the war, selling bonds, and loudly decrying traitors and slackers. A favorite Landis laugh-getter was the topic of "slacker bridegrooms," young single men who suddenly got the urge to marry when Uncle Sam suddenly got the urge to draft young single men. To Wisconsin and Iowa audiences Landis claimed that back in Chicago the number of marriage licenses issued per month jumped from 50 to more than 1,200, with lines snaking outside City Hall.

"I wish you could have seen the men and women in line," he informed audiences. "I studied them over and over for quite a while, and there was something out of the ordinary in the looks of nine out of ten. At first I thought I pitied the men most. Then I decided I was sorrier for the women, but at last I made up my mind I most pitied the men for marrying women who would marry that kind of man."[18]

But Landis cracked more than jokes; he cracked dissenters. His first big sedition case came in July 1917 and earned him the title "the scourge of the disloyal" when he lashed out at a group of foreign-born Socialists and IWW members ("whining and belly-aching puppies") accused of failure to register for the draft and for rioting in Rockford, Illinois, that June.[19]

When journalist Henry Pringle wrote of Landis: "Few men have been as zealous in the suppression of minorities, and his charges to juries were dangerously similar to patriotic addresses," he may have had the Rockford case in mind.[20]

The circumstances were as follows. A small number of draft resistors were being held at the Rockford jail. One hundred and fifty protesters marched on the place, demanding the sheriff arrest them himself. He did so, but that hardly solved his problems. Once inside, protesters ripped the jail apart, destroying even its plumbing and heating systems.

At Rockford, Landis, as was his habit, took over the interrogation of each defendant. He demanded to know the accused's age, his national origin, how long he had been in America, whether he was undergoing naturalization, what anticonscription organizations he belonged to, why he had neglected to register for the draft, and would he register now. But Landis often went beyond his basic line of questioning and was frequently brutal in his remarks.

Defendant Nels Larsen, who testified he had left Sweden nine years before to avoid conscription and had failed to take out United States naturalization papers, particularly annoyed Landis.

"So you dodged military service in the country of your birth," he stormed, "and now when the country in which you have been earning for the last nine years calls upon you to help it out, you deliberately do the same thing.

"One year in the house of correction," the Squire snapped, "and take this man out of here."

Another Swede who incensed Landis was Swen Lingren, who told the court he objected to participation in all warfare.

"Do you belong to any party or organization?" Landis wanted to know.

"I am a member of the Socialist Party."

Landis turned to defense attorney Seymour Stedman to deride Lingren. "This," said Landis, "is the type that has damned the Socialist Party."

"It's probably a matter of conscience with him," Stedman responded.

"Why," exclaimed Landis, "if this man experienced a spasm of conscience he would have an epileptic fit."

For their part in the riot, Landis sentenced 117 of the slackers (including 62 aliens) to the maximum sentence of one year and a day in a Chicago House of Correction. To three others he gave a lesser sentence: he directed all to register for the draft. Thirty-seven more he ordered deported (for "moral turpitude")—after serving their sentences.[21]

The wartime cases kept coming. Two days after the Rockford trial concluded Landis began a trial in which a number of alleged German agents, including the Imperial Government's former consul in Chicago, were accused of plotting to overthrow British rule in India.[22]

Another wartime case involved the Reverend David Gerdes, a pacifist, who, along with his brother, was accused of opposing the sale of Liberty Bonds. At one point in their trial Landis inquired of them: "What would you do if a Hun were to attack the honor of your daughter?"

The brothers responded they would refrain from violence, beg the Germans for mercy, and pray for their souls.

This infuriated Landis, who snapped, "These men hold their measly little shriveled souls of more importance than the honor of their mother, wife, or daughter." He sentenced Gerdes to 10 years in Leavenworth, a penalty later commuted to a year and a day.[23]

Landis also found an antagonist in Chicago mayor Big Bill Thompson.

Yale-educated Thompson was the son of a successful Chicago real estate developer. Not particularly bright, he was nevertheless energetic and possesed a certain skill in attracting votes. A former protegé of William J. "The Blond Boss" Lorimer, he was elected to the city council where he sponsored legislation creating the first municipal playground in America. In 1915, and with Frank Lowden's assistance, he was elected mayor.

When war came, however, Thompson and Lowden[24]—and Landis—parted company. Chicago was a hotbed of anti-interventionist ethnic groups, Irish, Germans ("the sixth German city in the world" as Thompson put it[25]), Poles, and Hungarians. With the support of the city's two Hearst newspapers (but against the opposition of the *Tribune*), Thompson became fiercely isolationist. Dubbed "Kaiser Bill" by opponents, he opposed the draft and the supplying of food to America's new allies. When France's Marshal Joseph Joffre visited Chicago, Thompson refused to extend him an official welcome. "Are these foreign visitors coming here to encourage the doings of things to make our people suffer further or have they some other purpose?" asked Thompson. The city council condemned his actions and the local Rotary Club voted to expel him. When Thompson allowed an anti-war group, the People's Council for Democracy and Terms of Peace, to meet in Chicago, Lowden dispatched the militia.[26]

Thompson's attitude was simply too much for Landis. At a July 1917 speech to the city's Hamilton Club he blasted the mayor's opposition to feeding our allies as "disloyal." He followed that with another scathing address to the downstate Sangamon County Bar Association. "I wish the mayor of my home city would do one— ONE—patriotic thing," he told his audience. "If the mayor would act I would not be kept apologizing for him wherever I go."[27]

The mayor responded that he regretted, "Judge Landis feels that I am unpatriotic because I want to feed our own country first and export only our surplus and prepare our country for our defense against the world if necessary."[28] In 1918 Thompson unsuccessfully sought the Republican nomination for United States Senate. Despite overseeing a corrupt administration that turned a $3 million surplus into a $4.5 million deficit, he would be re-elected mayor the following year.[29]

Tied into the nation's anti-German feelings was its growing Prohibitionist sentiments. Most of the nation's brewers were German-Americans, and their enthusiasm for the war was forced at best. The nation reacted by turning against both the brewers and their products. "Kaiserism abroad and booze at home must go," warned Anti-Saloon League head Wayne Wheeler. The feeling was mutual. "In order to gain for the Germans of America that place in the sun which has hitherto been denied them," read an article in one German-American publication, "it is absolutely necessary that they enjoy personal liberty, and that this shall not be whittled away by the attacks of the prohibitionists and the persecutors of the foreign-born."[30]

In 1918 Landis would take part in the growing crackdown against the saloon. That year a scandal enveloped the city government of East St. Louis, Illinois, just across the Mississippi River from St. Louis, Missouri. Illinois blue laws (so-named because the nation's first Sabbatarian laws were drawn up on blue paper) prohibited saloons from staying open on Sundays, but East St. Louis authorities were all too eager to wink at the practice. The practice brought $175,000 each year into East St. Louis' treasury and not incidentally helped line the pockets of crooked police and politicians. Landis investigated the situation and grilled an official of the Anheuser-Busch Brewery, forcing him to admit that his company owned 32 saloons in East St. Louis and had illegally kept them open each Sunday for the past decade.

Just the day before, however, Anheuser-Busch's August A. Busch, Sr., had condemned lawbreaking saloons, pontificating that they only fueled the rise in Prohibitionist thinking. Landis gleefully dispatched a copy of his employee's embarrassing testimony to Busch. The beer baron quickly backpedalled, denying any knowledge of events.[31]

But Germanic beer barons were a mere warm-up to the anti-war forces Landis would next encounter: the Industrial Workers of the World.

# CHAPTER 9

# "THE FACE OF ANDREW JACKSON THREE YEARS DEAD"

The political lineup of the Progressive Era consisted not merely of stand-put Republicans or Democrats and Rooseveltian and Wilsonian progressives.

Standing on the fringe was an active—and sizable—anti-capitalist contingent. Socialists garnered votes. Anarchists threw bombs and committed assassinations. And in the union arena stood William Dudley "Big Bill" Haywood's Industrial Workers of the World.

Before World War I concluded, Landis would clash head-on with these impetuous radicals.

Haywood's IWW was no mere union. While Samuel Gompers' American Federation of Labor (AFL) battled for simple wage and working condition improvements, the IWW pledged itself to the "abolition of the wage system" and to wholesale overthrow of the capitalist system.

Unlike the AFL, the IWW (or "Wobblies") consisted mostly of unskilled workers, farmers, lumbermen, and longshoremen. Largely restricted to the West, the IWW occasionally did venture east, its most famous forays being the Lawrence textile strike of 1912 and the Patterson silk strike of 1913.

As the "Wobblies" were no ordinary union, they were no ordinary group of radicals. Their predilections for inflammatory rhetoric—and sabotage—attracted the most romantic of characters, including the martyred organizer-songwriter Joe Hill. In November 1915 when Hill stood before a Utah firing squad after being convicted of murder, he wrote: "Don't waste any time in mourning. Organize."

It was to IWW boss Big Bill Haywood that he addressed those words.

Haywood personified the IWW. "His gigantic frame and one eye gave him the appearance of a sinister Cyclops," noted fellow radical Elizabeth Gurley Flynn, "but his face lit up with kindliness in talking to workers."

Big Bill had no such warm feelings for capitalists or those who defended capitalism. With an omnipresent huge black Stetson hat and a vocabulary of unusual invective, Haywood, the son of a Pony Express rider, was the Wild West leader of a Wild West union. He was no stranger to the sort of backbreaking work most Wobblies pursued, having himself gone down into the mines at age nine. But he quickly rose out of it. Joining the Western Federation of Miners (WFM) in 1896, he became its leader just four years later. In 1902 he enrolled in the Socialist Party (SP), and at Chicago in 1905 he joined fellow SP members Eugene V. Debs and Mother Jones in creating the IWW, a combination formed from 40 different labor organizations—the "One Big Union."

Haywood was also no stranger to violence—or accusations of violence. In 1906 Idaho authorities arrested Haywood and several other labor leaders for the December 1905 murder of former governor Frank R. Steunenberg whom a bomb had blown to bits as he opened his front gate. After the actual bomber implicated several WFM leaders, Haywood was arrested in a Denver brothel. The trial generated national interest[1] with future United States senator William Borah leading the prosecution and Clarence Darrow heading the defense. In 1907 jurors found Haywood not guilty after concluding the prosecution's case rested solely on mere "inference and suspicion."[2]

By now Haywood was on a collision course not only with the capitalistic bosses, but also with more moderate elements within the Socialist movement. In 1908 Socialist leader Daniel DeLeon denounced Haywood's Wobblies as "bums, anarchists, and physical force destroyers." That same year the WFM, increasingly wary of the Wobblies' often violent tactics, withdrew from the IWW. Haywood did little to calm fears of IWW fanaticism. In one memorable December 1911 speech at New York's Cooper Union, he thundered, "I am not a law-abiding citizen, and more than that, no Socialist can be a law abiding citizen. . . . It is our purpose to overthrow the capitalist system by forcible means if necessary." Such rhetoric caused the Socialist Party to expel him from its national committee in February 1913.[3]

The pre-war Wobblies probably peaked in 1912, with a membership of just 10,000, but the World War gave the union a new lease on life. Membership spurted from under 30,000 in 1915 to over 100,000 in 1917. Part of this explosive growth was based on labor shortages created by war in Europe. But a large portion came from the union's anti-war stance. Haywood and his fellow Wobblies opposed United States military involvement, both before and after America's declaration of war in April 1917. According to the IWW, "of all the idiotic and perverted ideas accepted by the workers from that class who live upon their misery, patriotism is the worst."

Yet, it would be a mistake to regard the union as classically anti-war. "The Industrial Workers of the World were not 'pacifists,'" admitted one-time member Helen Gurley Flynn. "They were opposed to a 'rich man's war.'"[4]

Even before the United States entered the World War, IWW activity—and strikes—had increased. Wobblies organized the wheat fields, copper mines, lumber mills, and logging camps of the Pacific Northwest. In 1916 they organized copper miners at Bisbee, Arizona. Authorities retaliated by packing 1,162 Wobblies into cattle cars and dropping them off at a desert prison camp.

By the summer of 1917 IWW strikes and sabotage had shuttered 85 percent of the nation's logging camps and sawmills. Spikes were hidden in logs, trains derailed, and mills burned. The results imperiled the nation's wartime shipbuilding program. "This is a Capitalist war," Haywood thundered. "If the Capitalists want lumber, then let them give us bigger pay and the eight-hour day."

"In 1917," historian William Preston, Jr., noted, "the apparent success of the IWW's dramatic organizing campaign, was a frightening reality in several sections of the United States."

After Montana's Speculator mine disaster of June 1917 cost 164 lives, massive strikes plagued that state's copper industry. IWW hooligans dynamited a WFM union hall. At Butte in August 1918 vigilantes beat crippled IWW leader Frank Little, dragged him from a moving automobile, and lynched him from a railroad trestle. Federal authorities dispatched troops to maintain order. They would need to remain until January 1921.[5]

The IWW's activities galled not only industrialists and wartime production officials, but also ordinary patriots, of whom there was no shortage in 1917. It would be unreasonable to think that no reaction would occur—particularly when the Wobblies added insult to injury, carrying on a vociferous anti-war program.

Posters distributed by the IWW read: "Don't Be a Soldier, Be a

Man." Their propaganda declared "already the war is being conducted on the skins of the poor—Refuse to Join the Army . . . Refuse
to Go to War."[6]

After the U.S. declared war, the union's newspaper, the *Industrial Worker*, printed the following:

> I love my flag, I do, I do,
> Which floats above the breeze,
> I also love my arms and legs,
> And neck, and nose and knees.
> One little shell might spoil them all
> Or give them such a twist,
> They would be of no use to me;
>     I guess I won't enlist.
>
> I love my country, yes I do
> I hope her folks do well.
> Without our arms, and legs and things,
> I think we'd look like hell.
> Young men with faces half shot off
> Are unfit to be kissed,
> I've read in books it spoils their looks,
>     I guess I won't enlist.[7]

Such attitudes were hardly to be tolerated in the era of super-
heated patriotism of an America at war. Theodore Roosevelt de-
cried the IWW as a "criminal organization." Arizona senator Henry
F. Ashurst jibed that the organization's initials stood for "Imperial
Wilhelm's Warriors." Others thought they simply meant "I Won't
Work."[8]

On September 5, 1917, federal authorities raided 48 IWW halls
nationwide, including the union's national headquarters in Chicago.
They seized five tons of IWW documents, correspondence, newspapers, and pamphlets. United States Attorney Maclay Hoyne followed
that up on September 28 with indictments of 166 IWW leaders. Not
all would face trial. Forty were never found, and charges against 10
defendants were dropped. Ultimately 113 defendants would face
trial, the largest number of persons tried in any United States criminal case.

They would appear before Kenesaw Landis.[9]

The indictment in *The United States of America v. William D. Haywood, et al* consisted of five separate counts. The first charged the union with conspiring to "hinder, delay and prevent by force" the implementation of the declaration of war against the Central Powers. The second charged that IWW members had received compensation from employers while nonetheless fostering a "conspiracy to injure, intimidate and oppress" those supplying materials to the war effort and "to render inefficient service, and to purposely assist in producing bad and unmarketable products and intentionally to retard, slacken and reduce produce whenever employed, and intentionally to restrict and decrease the profits of said employers and interfere with and injure their trade and business, and secretly and covertly to injure, break up and destroy the property of said employers; and that they would teach, incite, indict, aid and abet others to do so"— i.e., industrial sabotage. The third count implicated the IWW in conspiring to hinder registration for the draft. The fourth accused the defendants with plotting "insubordination, refusal of duty and disloyalty" within the armed forces themselves. The fifth and final count charged Haywood *et al.* with violation of the postal laws in furtherance of the first four counts.[10]

The trial began on April 1, 1918. Almost immediately Landis dismissed charges against a dozen defendants including the improbably named A. C. Christ, who had shown up for his sedition trial equally improbably dressed in his new doughboy's uniform—he had just joined the service. Jury selection took a month. Complicating the process were prosecution charges of jury tampering by the defense. "This does not appear to be other than a systematic campaign," Landis announced, "and I don't like it. I don't want a jury of this kind. It is perfectly proper for the litigant [sic] to make an investigation of the jurors, but this is beyond the limit. For an agent of the defendant to approach the juror, directly or indirectly, is the same as the defendant himself trying to influence the juror."

He dismissed what jurors had already been chosen, issued a warrant for the arrest of IWW supporter L. C. Russell,[11] and the process started all over again. When it did, the Squire mandated unprecedented security. Five deputy marshals guarded the jurymen. Jurors entered and left the Federal Building through a cordon of city police. Even a section of seats nearest the jury box was kept empty.[12]

The trial itself would last five months and create 30,000 pages of transcripts. All in all, 7.5 million words were uttered or inserted into the official record. Special Assistant United States Attorney Frank K. Nebeker, a former counsel for western copper mining companies, headed the prosecution. Haywood found him to be "a smooth individual, a slimy creature, even more foxy than he tried to prove to me." Assisting Nebeker were Claude R. Porter, the Democrat candidate for governor of Iowa, and Chicago district attorney Charles F. Clyne.[13]

The IWW first tried to obtain Clarence Darrow's services, but when he declined, it tapped Seattle attorney George Francis Vanderveer. Like his clients, Vanderveer bubbled with confidence, even arrogance, regarding the odds for acquittal. "I have not the slightest doubt," he wrote to a sympathizer, "about our ability to make the position the government has outlined in the indictment look ridiculous." Working with Vanderveer were Fred H. Moore and Miss Caroline A. Lowe, who had assisted him in the famed Everett case, and local attorney Otto Christensen. A late addition to Vanderveer's team was William B. Cleary of Bisbee, Arizona.[14]

The American Federation of Labor, which had helped defend Haywood in Idaho, now stood clear of the union. So did most of the Socialist Party, which was facing its own problems with government prosecution. Yet the IWW retained its share of high-profile supporters. Intellectuals Roger Baldwin, Helen Keller, John Dewey, and Thorstein Veblen signed an ad in the *New Republic* appealing for defense funds. "It is," they argued, "for American liberals to make it financially possible for the defense to present fully the industrial evils underlying the IWW revolt against intolerable conditions of labor."

Former Socialist Party member Carl Sandburg, then with the *Chicago Daily News*, came to interview Haywood and wrote with admiration of how Haywood voiced the "defiance of the [union] to its enemies and captors."

And in Yakima, Washington, William O. Douglas "waited for hours" to see the train carrying the indicted Wobblies pass by on its way to Chicago. "I walked home with tears in my eyes," the future Supreme Court Justice would write in his memoirs, "I thought of all the pompous members of the Establishment in Yakima who should have been in those cars."

When in early August Haywood took the stand, a galaxy of radicals witnessed the event, among them Eugene V. Debs and New York congressman Scott Nearing. Also present was Mother Jones, now 88 years old. Landis allowed Jones to sit at the defense attorneys' table, and she was seen wiping away a tear at the sight of the accused. But the Irish-born radical recovered her spunk to sniff at "social cats" — settlement house workers who left comfortable backgrounds to work among the poor. Adolph Germer, national secretary of the Socialist Party, also dropped in.[15]

Another key IWW supporter was William Bross Lloyd, decades earlier a co-founder with Landis of the Chicago Civic Centre Club. Lloyd, now known as the "millionaire socialist"[16] put up the bulk of Haywood's $15,000 bail (finally reduced by Landis from an original figure of $25,000) and the revolutionary leader went free on February 12.

Writer John Reed had just returned from reporting on the Russian Revolution. In late June he and cartoonist Art Young arrived in Chicago to cover the trial for *The Liberator*. There was no question in Reed's mind who was in the right. And if Reed had any uncertainty, his Windy City host would set him straight — Reed was rooming at Bill Haywood's apartment. "I doubt if ever in history there has been a sight just like them," Reed proclaimed. "One hundred and one lumberjacks, harvest hands, miners, editors . . . who believe the wealth of the world belongs to him who creates it . . . the outdoor men, rock-hard blasters, tree-fellers, wheat-binders, longshoremen, the boys who do the strong work of the world. . . . The IWW trial looked like a meeting of the Central Executive Committee of the All-Russian Soviets of Workers' Deputies in Petrograd! . . . like the Bolshevik Revolutionary Tribunal."[17]

The prosecution no doubt would have agreed with his description.

Reed also turned his fine descriptive powers on Landis. "Small on the huge bench," he noted, "sits a wasted man with untidy white hair, an emaciated face in which two burning eyes are set like jewels, parchment-like skin split by a crack for a mouth; the face of Andrew Jackson three years dead."

Yet, Reed could also be appreciative of Landis' unusual courtroom manner — a style often benefiting the defendants. "Upon this man," Reed noted, "has devolved the historic role of trying the Social Revolution. He is doing it like a gentleman."[18]

"In many ways a most unusual trial," Reed continued,

When the judge enters the court-room after recess no one rises — he himself has abolished the pompous formality. He sits without robes, in an ordinary business suit, and often leaves the bench to come down and perch on the step of the jury box. By his personal order, spittoons are placed beside the prisoners' seats, so they can while away the day with a chaw; and as for the prisoners themselves, they are permitted to take off their coats, move around, read newspapers.

It takes some human understanding for a Judge to fly in the face of judicial ritual as much as that. . . .[19]

Not only radicals visited the Landis courtroom. In June Senator William S. Kenyon of Iowa, a friend of Landis', dropped in.[20] One day in early July actor (and rabid baseball fan) Louis Mann, then locally trodding the boards in the play "Friendly Enemies," arrived. The Squire invited him to sit with him on the bench and pointed out the trial's various luminaries to the thespian.

As the prosecution began the presentation of its case, Landis' court received another distinguished visitor—evangelist Billy Sunday. Sunday, a former major league outfielder, was in the midst of a highly publicized Chicago crusade. Entering the court he exclaimed "Why, you codger, Judge."

"Billy, you son of a gun!" Landis shot back. "What on earth are you doing here?"

Sunday ducked the question and began examining the Squire's crow feet. "You're looking old Kenesaw," he jibed. "I'm not a juvenile, Billy, but you're no kid yourself," Landis rejoined. All the while the two men grabbed each other about the shoulders and laughed uproariously. "My hair may be whiter," the Judge taunted the preacher, "but you haven't got enough left to be white."[21]

The proletariat must have wondered about the sanity about the ruling class.

One July morning, Ben Fletcher, the only black defendant, did not appear in court. Defense counsel could not explain his absence so Landis sent a deputy marshal to Fletcher's lodgings (Fletcher was out on bail). While the lawman was absent, rumors spread that Fletcher had been felled by appendicitis. When, an hour later, the marshal returned, he reported Fletcher's problem had more to do with the huge breakfast he had consumed that morning: buckwheat pancakes, pork, roast beef, onions, lettuce, baked beans, asparagus, kippered herring, and ice cream!

Landis returned to his bench and informed the court that

Fletcher's malady was a belly ache and not appendicitis and dismissed the court for the day.

"We don't want to lose Ben," commented a relieved Bill Haywood, "he is one of the whitest men we've got."[22]

Remarkably as the trial progressed, observers of Landis—"the scourge of the disloyal"—witnessed him displaying a remarkable tolerance for the defendants. David Karsner sat through the entire trial, covering it for *The Call Magazine*, a New York City Socialist organ. Karsner was absolutely bewildered by Landis, whom he termed an "enigma" unable to fit in "any human category." Karsner had arrived expecting the defendants could never receive a fair trial under a capitalist judge. And while Karsner was eventually shocked by the severity of sentences Landis handed down and found in them evidence of either some intellectual or moral weakness, he could not help but admit that the Squire "gave the IWW the fairest trial it was possible to get under the capitalist system."[23]

He was hardly alone in his opinion. Haywood biographer Professor Melvyn Dubofsky declared that Landis "exercised judicial objectivity and restraint for five long months . . ." Baseball historian Harold Seymour, otherwise no fan of Landis' judicial style, conceded that "on the whole Landis conducted the trial with restraint, despite his reputation as a foe of all radical groups." Henry Pringle, another tough critic, admitted that the Judge "felt sorry for some of them [the IWW defendants], admitted them to bail, and did what he could to make their lot easier. He felt that at their worst, they were ineffectual and rather absurd."[24] Even the IWW's *Trial Bulletin* had to applaud Landis' decision to provide cuspidors to the defendants. "Evidently, his Honor appreciates the feelings of men accustomed to chewing," it observed. "It is possible that he likes a chew himself now and then."[25]

Landis' solicitude went beyond spittoons. When one-armed 80 year-old defendant Harry Trotter took the stand, he could barely answer the questions posed to him. The Squire looked on with real concern, his face screwing up in pain. Finally he had enough and summoned prosecutor Nebeker and defense attorney Cleary to the bench. After a whispered conversation he announced charges against Trotter were dropped. The old man was free to go. "Nine o'clock tomorrow morning," Landis then blurted out. With a wave of his hand he bounded off the bench and into his chambers.

Defendant John Pancher had not been able to make bail. Nonetheless, in early July he got married. Landis released him on his own recognizance—and for good measure on the same day let five more men free on the same terms.[26]

One day defendant Norval Marlatt, a Hammond, Indiana, locomotive fireman, approached the bench. Landis was leaning forward, his chin resting on his folded arms as if he were at Comiskey Park.

"Judge," Marlatt began, "I would like to have back $50 of my bail money to pay interest on the mortgage on my house. If I can't meet the payment, I stand to lose it."

"Well," Landis drawled, "I don't want to see a man lose his house just because he is accused of a crime, when he may not be guilty. See me at four o'clock about that, Marlatt."

At four, Marlatt raised the issue again. "Sully," Landis told court clerk Joseph O'Sullivan, "Marlatt wants $50 for some personal usage. Give him an order for a hundred."[27]

At first only a handful of the defendants secured bail, and it was something they dearly wanted. Conditions at the Cook County jail were wretched, with three or four men crowded into each dark, dank cell. One prisoner, Henry Myer, went insane and hung himself. The facility's food was equally abominable. When one defendant, Ted Fraser, showed the Judge a piece of prison bread containing a cockroach, Landis allowed the prisoners to take their meals in the courthouse, where the food would be significantly better. Later the defendants petitioned Landis to also take their suppers in the courthouse. Again, he assented.

A defendant who had secured bail was a Finnish anti-war organizer from the Mesabi copper range named Charles Jacobson. After a while Jacobson approached Landis, asking if he could transfer his bail to another defendant, a much older man. Jacobson was willing to sit each night in the Cook County jail so that elderly gentleman might have some taste of freedom.

Landis refused. Instead, very shortly thereafter he began releasing many of the 70 incarcerated prisoners on their own recognizance.[28][29]

At another point in the trial Jacobson received a telegram which caused him to weep visibly. Another defendant took the wire from the slumping Jacobson's hand. IWW attorney Caroline Lowe spoke to Jacobson and learned that his sister had died back home in Virginia, Minnesota. Meanwhile Landis had seen what was happening and called associate defense counsel Cleary to the bench to learn what was bothering Jacobson. Lowe also approached Landis, asking if Jacobson might return home for the funeral.

"That's asking a whole lot, Miss Lowe," the Squire responded. "I don't know about that. See me later." At four that afternoon she asked again. This time Landis relented: "I guess we might stretch the point a bit and let Jacobson go home with a deputy." Remarkably, Jacobson refused to go unless he went on his own recognizance. Equally remarkably, Landis agreed. "Well, you people don't want much do you?" he replied. "All right, if you want to perpetrate a fraud on this court, the court won't know it."

Jacobson signed papers waiving his rights as a defendant in his absence and off he went. In a week he returned—right on time.[30]

One afternoon the trial's youngest defendant, Ray Fleming, a 19-year-old Harvard sophomore who was assisting defense counsel Vanderveer, was not on time. He arrived 10 minutes late from lunch, thus delaying the proceedings. Landis hated tardiness and just glared at him.

"What's the matter with you?" he wanted to know. "Where have you been? Don't you know what time we begin this matinee?" Fleming thought he *was* on time but on examining his pocketwatch found it was slow.

"Let me see that watch," Landis barked.

Landis perused the timepiece and then handed over to an assistant. "Mr. Bailiff," he ordered, "take this watch over to — — — [a local jeweler] and tell him to fix it, charge it to me and return it at 9 o'clock tomorrow morning."[31]

After that Fleming made sure he was on time.

Landis even publicly defended the Wobblies after the *Chicago Tribune* had reported that he and Nebeker had both received death threats in the mail. Landis read the entire *Tribune* story to the jury. When he finished, Landis turned to glare at the press table. "Gentlemen of the jury," he continued, "that is a lie. I have received no death letter, nor has Mr. Nebeker. Moreover, this is a deliberate attempt to prejudice the public against these defendants. The IWW had nothing to do with this, gentlemen of the jury. This is a concoction of the *Tribune*. They are only cowards who send death letters, and I say the IWW had nothing to do with this."

Landis then summoned the working press to step before his bench and proceeded to berate them in unmerciful terms—particularly the *Tribune*'s representative—concluding that he "wanted it understood by you gentlemen of the Chicago press, and you gentlemen of the two news services, that you are to print nothing about this lawsuit [ie., trial], except that which occurs in this courtroom. There is a good story here, and you don't have to invent one in your offices. If you do, I shall close this court to the press."[32]

All the while prosecution and defense attorneys were dealing with the central issues of case: Was the IWW disloyal? Had it fomented strikes to injure the war effort? Had it discouraged conscription?

The defense claimed that once war had been declared the IWW had never taken an official stand against it. They pointed out that many IWW members worked without incident in munitions factories and in loading munitions onto ships bound for Europe. They took pains to note how the IWW had avoided causing troubles at the key port of Philadelphia, in which 80 percent of all traffic was war-related. They drew attention to sons of IWW members serving in the armed forces and derided the government's prosecution as part of a "general reign of terror" designed "to enslave the working class with the interest of a profit-mad coterie of industrial pirates."

The defense also attempted to place capitalism on trial, attacking the modern industrial system for harsh working conditions, low wages, and long hours. Landis disallowed such evidence but nonetheless permitted Nebeker to elicit such material from witnesses he called to the stand.[33] Some of the testimony was clearly effective and even heartrending;[34] other material was merely humorous—such as when defendant Edward Hamilton revealed why he had joined the Wobblies: "Broken dishes." Hamilton, a Chicago waiter, had been fined so much for dropped china that he sometimes came home with no pay in his envelope.

The sum of such testimony certainly had as a basic motive the creation of a propaganda trial against capitalism. The IWW had clearly instructed Vanderveer to use this trial to attack the existing system. But it was also sound practical strategy: an attempt to prove that the IWW's wartime strikes were not designed to injure the war effort—but were caused by a pattern of low wages, long hours, and intolerable working conditions.

The Wobblies' testimony had its effect. Finally Nebeker submitted an affidavit, conceding many of the defense's key points:

> 1. The prosecution admits the evil social and economic conditions that obtained in the lumber industry prior to the IWW strike last summer.

2. The prosecution admits that there are several hundred lumber mills in the northwest and they showed only two evidences of sabotage in two mills. . . .

3. The prosecution admits evil mining conditions in Butte which caused the Speculator fire costing the lives of 178 miners.

4. The prosecution admits the deportation of striking copper miners from their homes in Arizona.

5. The prosecution admits that farmers of the Dakotas organized in the Non-Partisan League were pleased with the labor of IWW harvesters.[35]

But the prosecution also had its moments. The IWW *was,* after all, composed of radicals—and they had not shrunk from violent talk. As late as July 15, 1917, the union's official paper, *Solidarity,* was running such inflammatory statements as the following: "In Russia they did not wait for democracy to come to their rescue. They took matters into their own hands and with quick action overthrew the Government. The same thing can be done in America through the IWW."[36]

That was certainly grist for the prosecution mill, as was a letter from defendant James M. Slovick, secretary of the Marine Transport Union, to Haywood. In it Slovick dreamed of a great disloyal coalition. "Like little brooks streaming into one great channel our organization would swell into one great river," he mused. "All in all, we could muster quite an army. There are in this country Germans, Austrians, Hungarians, Bulgarians, and some Irish, who, for patriotic reasons, if you please, will be willing to fight this government."

Much of the material the prosecution presented had predated America's declaration of war, and the defense and pro-IWW journalists ridiculed the idea that it had any relevance to the case. But historian William Preston, Jr., pointed out the connection in his *Aliens and Dissenters: Federal Suppression of Radicals, 1903-1933.* The IWW had clearly conducted strikes during wartime. No one denied that. At issue was the union's *intent.* Were the strikes designed merely for economic conditions? If they were, they were legal. If, however, they intended to attack the capitalist government or slow the war effort, they were illegal. "In its interpretation of intent," noted Preston, "the government simply turned the IWW propaganda of the pre-war years upon itself."[37]

And not all IWW statements predated America's declaration of war. "The Wobblies had no possible defense for their record and their pamphlets offered proof beyond all doubt," noted Vanderveer's biographer Lowell Stillwell Hawley, "The only course open to them had to be an unflinching agreement: 'If this be treason, make the most of it!' "[38]

Perhaps the worst witness along those lines was defendant Charles L. Lambert, a member of the IWW's executive committee. Lambert told Nebeker he would gladly blow up Folsom Prison to free two fellow Wobblies.[39]

Not all defendants were so graceless. John T. "Red" Doran held the stand for five hours as the Squire permitted him to present examples of his famous "chalk talks." "Judge Landis' courtroom," noted the *New York Call*, "was transformed into an I.W.W. hall with the witness stand as a soap box."

When Doran concluded, "It is customary to throw our meetings open to questions and make a collection," the room erupted in laughter. Two jurymen positively convulsed themselves with hysterics. Even Landis grinned and chuckled.[40] "Under the circumstances," Doran backtracked, "we will dispense with the collection."[41]

The trial, as momentous as it may have been, did not prevent Landis from conducting other judicial business. One day in early August he dealt with a whole slew of war-related cases. He sentenced two women—Mrs. Ethel Durham and her niece Mayme Plowden—who had smuggled flasks of liquor into Camp Grant in Rockford, Illinois—to four months each (including the three months they had already served).

A soldier, separated from his wife, was given a year for having his mistress represent herself as his spouse in a sworn statement. But the heaviest sentence went to one Steve Rubick who had impersonated an Army officer. Landis fined him $800 and sentenced him to three years in Leavenworth. The sentences, the Judge said, represented "an effort to protect the heroes over there from the cowards over here."[42]

Haywood, of course, was Vanderveer's star witness.[43] The long-awaited appearance of the IWW "Swivel Chair King" energized the trials. Reporters, sketch artists, and spectators filled the courtroom. Jurors regained their attention. Bailiffs and marshals paid particular heed. Landis leant forward on one elbow and listened with rapt interest. On the first day of Haywood's testimony Landis kept the trial in session for an hour past his usual four o'clock deadline. Had he not been reminded of the time he might have kept court in session even longer.

For three days Haywood attacked "wage slavery" and told often lurid tales of capitalist oppression. In the South, he claimed, lumber bosses gave heroin and cocaine to black workers. "They knew," Haywood alleged, "that when they became addicted to the drugs, that they were sure to return to their jobs. It was the strongest method of holding them—stronger even than the chains of chattel slavery or the whips of the turpentine bosses.

"In many cases," Haywood explained, "the chattel slave was better off than the wage slave is today.

"Take the black man of the South before the civil war. He enjoyed better conditions than he does at this time. He was a slave of the master, it is true. But the slaves' souls were free, and they were housed and clothed and given medical attention. And you can recall the songs they sang. They are no more, those songs—'The Suwanee River' and 'My Old Kentucky Home' "—songs, the press pointed out, were actually written by white men.[44][45]

And he flayed the rich, their ostentation, their Palm Beach and Newport mansions and lavish parties. "At Newport they give monkey dinners," he recounted, "and such things for the unemployable. . . . what I want to tell you about was this dog wedding which Mrs. Penrose, Mrs. Frank Heath, and Mrs. McNeil attended with all the formalities of high society—the wedding of two poodle dogs! That is the kind of stuff we don't want them to do. We want them to do something more useful, the same as we do."

And if the prosecution could dredge up pre-war oratory, so could Haywood. The employers had no sympathy for their workers he contended, quoting an early 1890s *Chicago Tribune* editorial regarding feeding the unemployed. "Give them bread," it allegedly read, "and put strychnine in it."

Haywood denied attempting to injure the war effort, noting quite accurately that the IWW's executive board had never formally urged draft dodging.[46] He also attempted to turn the tables on the issue of sabotage. "The boss is the real saboteur," he charged—the manufacturers of adulterated food and shoddy cloth, the packers whose "rotten meat" had killed more American soldiers in the Spanish-American War than had enemy bullets—and were "doing it yet."

But he was not always successful. On cross-examination

Nebeker introduced the following Haywoodisms (in the defendant's own handwriting):

• Join the Army and Navy. Confess. Be prepared to die.
• It is better to be a traitor to a country than a traitor to your class.
• Why be a soldier? Be a man. Join the IWW and fight on the job for yourself and your class.
• A policeman is a pimple; a soldier a boil on the body politic; both the result of a diseased system.

Haywood admitted he had written those words, but contended he had done so in 1916, i.e., before America entered the war. He could not however deny writing: Nothing has been left undone to help out the boys arrested for evading registration.[47]

And there was this embarrassing exchange:

*Nebeker:* "Is not the keynote of your attitude and the whole IWW proposition that every time a man is induced to join in the organization of industrial labor a nail is driven in the coffin of military preparedness?"
*Haywood* (after being pressed for a direct answer): "Yes, that is true."
*Nebeker:* "Members [of the IWW] had read the organization was on record for a general strike in case of war and were in favor of it in event of war. Isn't that so?"
*Haywood:* "Yes, that is true."[48]

The trial ended suddenly on August 17, 1918. Just the day before, Landis had turned the first spade of dirt at a re-creation of No Man's Land (the most dangerous part of the front-line in France) at Chicago's Grant Park. After the trial's two last witnesses, and minor ones at that, had testified in the morning, the prosecution and the defense agreed to limit their summations to just two hours each, but after United States Attorney Nebeker had spoken for 45 minutes, defense counsel Vanderveer interrupted to announce he would make no closing statement. "I want to thank you for your patient consideration," he told the court, "and ask your honest Christian judgement."

Landis was simply dumbfounded. "I am taken a little bit by surprise here," he slowly said as he recessed the proceedings and headed back to his chambers to prepare a charge to the jury.[49]

"Honest Christian" feelings, however, were in somewhat short supply. While Landis worked, a fist fight broke out in his court between a Department of Justice attorney and a defense stenographer.

The court adjourned to 2 PM. Half an hour later Landis began reading his charge to the jury. To prevent any disturbance a veritable army of lawmen had been called out—200 city policemen, a dozen United States marshals, and eight federal agents. Each prisoner was searched before re-entering the courtroom.

In his charge Landis threw out the fifth count of the indictment, conspiracy to violate the postal laws. The IWW's hopes were now raised higher than ever. But they were soon to receive even more cause for optimism. "Mere passive knowledge of the criminal activities of other persons is not sufficient to establish a conspiracy," Landis told the jurors. "Some participation, cooperation, must be shown to establish the connection of any defendant, and by evidence of fact and circumstances independent of the declarations of other people—that is, by evidence of the defendants own acts. . . ."[50]

Yet Landis tempered his remarks with, "You do not need to decide whether a conspiracy was completely successful. For instance, it is not necessary that anyone had been induced to refuse to register, that anyone had been made impotent to furnish supplies, or that any other ultimate act has been accomplished. It is enough to show that a conspiracy was formed and that some of the defendants committed one of the overt acts.[51]

"Organized labor is not on trial. Working men have a right to organize to improve their conditions as to wages, health or other welfare, and the right is theirs in time of war as well as in time of peace.

"The only limit is that they must not by their organization violate the laws of the land. And if in organizing for a lawful purpose they effect the organization by unlawful means or accomplish knowingly an unlawful act, they are guilty of conspiracy to violate the laws."

In the course of Landis' charge, Vanderveer objected several times, attempting to secure instructions to the jurors he had previous requested but which Landis had neglected to insert. Haywood had far less of a problem with Landis' instructions. "Fair enough charge," he admitted. [52] [53]

At 4:05 the jury began its deliberations, and the prisoners started on their evening meal. At just 5:10 PM the jury sent back word that they were returning, a development that totally confused the defendants. Could a verdict have been reached already? Or was the panel merely returning for more instructions or a clarification? By 5:15—although none of their counsel had yet returned—the Wobblies had been assembled to hear the verdict. Ten minutes later the jury—and defense counsel Christensen—entered the courtroom. "We, the jury, find the defendants . . . ," began foreman F. W. Brayton. Then before he could get to an actual verdict he was forced to read out the names of all the remaining 100 defendants. That litany took 10 minutes, 10 minutes of excruciating suspense for the accused. Finally, came the words—"guilty as charged."

Almost as one, the defendants let out a low moan of disappointment. Haywood fell backwards in his chair but quickly caught himself and resumed his iron-man pose. Vanderveer had now rushed into the room and learned he had suffered the first major loss of his career. With fists clenched and tears streaming down his cheeks, he turned his back toward the defendants. He had thought some of his clients could be found guilty, he told reporters, "but that all of them should be is astounding."[54]

"That we should be convicted so quickly is the surprise of my life," said a shocked Haywood.[55]

After the verdict had been pronounced, reporters rushed to Haywood for a comment. Haywood, who had slumped down in his chair, came back to life. "I believe Judge Landis' instructions pointed clearly to an acquittal. Very well—we can only make the best of it."

Out in the lobby a band struck up "Hail, Columbia!"[56]

Landis took almost two weeks before handing out sentences. He spent all day on August 29 listening to each man plead his case. Big Bill Haywood toughed it out, displaying no remorse whatsoever. Declaring the verdict was "one of the greatest miscarriages ever perpetrated in a court of justice," Haywood contended that "no member of the IWW is guilty of anything," and that if he was released he would "do nothing but continue to uphold the IWW constitution . . ."

Landis made no response to Haywood but was "visibly affected" by some of the men's remarks. However, when one defendant, Anson Soper, begged that fellow defendant Norval Marlatt's sentence be added to his and that Marlatt be set free, Landis was unswayed.[57]

On the day of sentencing the Squire spoke for two hours, mostly in reviewing the evidence and the reasons why the jury had no choice but to find the defendants guilty:

When the country is at peace it is a legal right of free speech to oppose going to war and to oppose preparation for war. But when once war is declared that right ceases. After war is declared and before the law was passed to raise the army, it was the legal right of free speech to oppose the adoption of a compulsory military service law. But once the law was passed, free speech did not authorize a man to oppose or resist that law.

The question before the jury in the sixteen or seventeen weeks of the trial was whether or not there was a conspiracy as charged. I am obliged to say that the jury was left, in my opinion, no avenue of escape from its verdict. The express declarations of the leaders of the organization, the correspondence of its district officers, everything on the subject of the frame of mind of the organization, and its purposes with respect to war, cannot be treated as mere abstractions; all point to one ultimate object.[58]

Then came the actual sentencing. First, Landis summoned two defendants who had been minor employees at IWW headquarters. On these he imposed 10 days in the Cook County jail. The other prisoners saw this as a sign of hope—that Landis might go easy upon the lot of them.

Next he called a dozen men to stand before the bench. On these he imposed sentences of a year and a day—and fines of $25,000 each. Then 26 more names were read.[59] As this group stood before the bench, Landis meted out five-year sentences with $30,000 in fines apiece. The defendants no longer retained any illusions about light punishment. Next came a group of 33.[60] Each of these men received 10 years in jail and fines of $30,000. Then came a group of seven more. On these Landis gave only five years in Leavenworth and $20,000 in fines.

Only the IWW's 15 top leaders remained. Bill Haywood arose first to receive Landis' judgment. The room, which had been marked by the sound of weeping women, suddenly hushed as Haywood advanced toward the bench. But it was but a momentary lull. A mild wave of applause swept the courtroom, but bailiffs quickly silenced it. All the while Landis paid no attention to either silence or noise. Next came George Andreytchine, a radical Russian poet, exiled from his homeland for plotting revolution there. "His eyes," as John Reed wrote, were "full of Slav storm." As Andreytchine advanced toward Landis he blew a kiss to his attractive young wife, who for her part waved a handkerchief toward her husband. Haywood, Andreytchine, and the 13 others each received the maximum: 20 years in Leavenworth and $30,000 in fines.

All totaled Landis had meted out prison sentences amounting to 807 years and 20 days. To this he added fines amounting to $2.3 million.[61]

With sentences pronounced, the defendants were chained together and led away through a jeering crowd to Chicago's Dearborn Street Station where they would remain until being transported to Leavenworth. As police and soldiers led them away, they sang "Solidarity Forever, for the Union Makes Us Strong."

The nation, still swept up in the enthusiasm of war, applauded Landis' sentencing. The *New York Times* editorialized that the IWW was "yellow clear through"[62] and commended him for conducting the trial in "absolute fairness." Commented Senator Kenyon: "If we had more judges like him it would be well for the country."

At least one radical still expressed grudging admiration for Landis. As the trial was winding down, David Karsner had written with some prescience in the *New York Call*, "Judge Landis will not hesitate, in my opinion, to sentence the IWW's to the limit. But before the verdict is returned, the judge is more than willing to temper justice with mercy, to gear the law's machinery so that it will not torture men needlessly. By view of this fact, the fates did well in placing the Indiana lawyer in a United States court."[63]

Landis gave the defendants 90 days to appeal and seven days to petition for bail. On an early September afternoon a massive explosion rocked the Federal Building's entrance. The blast occurred just after Bill Haywood had returned from lunch. Haywood and the IWW claimed the bomb had been planted by the government. Most Americans thought otherwise.[64]

While waiting to be transported to Leavenworth on September 7, the convicted Wobblies busied themselves in a variety of ways, but it was clear Landis was on every mind. Some amused themselves by holding a mock court, with Benjamin Fletcher doing his imitation of the Judge. Haywood wrote a letter describing the genesis of his antiwar position, closing it in the hope that some day when the world had grown more peaceful "even a man like Judge Landis will know the meaning of the words of one great martyr: 'The world is my country. Man is my brother, to do good is my creed.'"[65]

Within just a few weeks the war would be over. In France, Reed
Landis was pondering what it all meant. At 11 AM on November 11,
1918 as the Armistice took effect, he turned to a fellow officer and
muttered: "The war's over and I'm alive. I haven't a right to be. I
should have been killed a dozen times. But I fooled 'em. Now I'm going home and get married and begin raising exemptions for the next
war."[66]

Back in the States neither his father nor Bill Haywood was exhibiting such a let-live attitude. In July 1919 Haywood obtained bail
and appealed his case all the way to the Supreme Court. Back on the
streets he continued working for the movement, organizing, and delivering impassioned speeches against the hated bosses. One such
Haywood address was scheduled for Detroit's Auto Workers' Hall in
December 1921. The local American Legion begged Landis to bar him
from speaking. "It is the outrage of the century that these men should
be permitted to go around making speeches," Landis replied, but he
declined to take any action. "The United States Circuit Court of
Appeals released them, though, and there is nothing I can do."[67]

In April 1921 the appeals court refused to hear Haywood's (and 79
other IWW members') motion. Faced with 20 years in Leavenworth,
Haywood would take any chances. Even before the court's turndown,
he sailed for Russia.

In some ways the news was hardly a surprise. When Lenin had
overthrown Kerensky's government in November 1917, the Wobblies
had cheered the event from their cells, taunting their captors with
threats that they too would soon seize power. In September 1919 a
duly impressed Haywood had been present at the founding of the
American Communist Party. "Here is what we have been dreaming
about," he told one fellow Wobbly. "Here is the IWW all feathered out."

Now the Communists were his last chance to stay out of jail—at
age 60 a life sentence. "You've had your back turned on me for too
long," Haywood crowed as he watched the Statue of Liberty ("the old
hag," as he derisively called her) recede into the distance. "I am going
to the land of freedom." In Lenin's Russia he would be given a minor
position disseminating Bolshevik propaganda.[68]

The American Civil Liberties Union, which had aided in the
IWW's defense, was "at a loss to explain" why Haywood would have
left the country under the circumstances, but expressed full confidence that he would soon return to serve out his sentence. The *New
York Times*, on the other hand, editorialized that "if his followers who

happen to be out of jail would follow his example, it would be the best disposition they could make of themselves." Haywood's closest supporters were left holding the bag, and had to raise money to pay his bond. The experience left many of them bitter toward the man.[69]

Haywood remained in Russia, where his new superiors confidently announced that "openly and undisguised he will return to America; but the time and manner of his coming will be determined by the requirements of the revolutionary class struggle and not by the decrees of the capitalist courts."

The real story of Big Bill Haywood's life in Russia was far less heroic. As early as that July he was already itching to get back and his lawyers proposed a deal: he would return if his bail would not be forfeited. The United States government wasn't interested in getting him back: in federal prison Haywood was a martyr; in Russia he was simply a traitor.

In fading health (he was diabetic), unwilling to learn Russian, and with virtually no responsibilities, Haywood spent his last years in a vodka-filled haze, longing to return to America. "Do you think that guy Coolidge would let me pass through?" he anxiously asked one visitor. Calvin Coolidge commuted the sentences of the last of the imprisoned Wobblies (30 in all) in December 1923, but Haywood was not among them.[70] Big Bill died in Moscow in May 1928 and, along with John Reed, is the only American buried in the Kremlin walls.[71][72]

Big Bill Haywood's life was filled with constant surprises. But no sight was as startling as the one that greeted visitors to his Moscow apartment. On its walls gently hung a framed portrait—that of Kenesaw Mountain Landis.[73]

# CHAPTER 10

# "DID THE JUDGE GET A BOMB
# IN THE MAIL THIS MORNING?"

The Wobblies would not be the last to be charged with sedition in a Landis courtroom. Woodrow Wilson's anti-war dragnet targeted more than Wobblies. As federal agents raided the IWW's national headquarters in Chicago in September 1917, just a few blocks away other lawmen swooped down on offices of the Socialist Party.

If the Socialist Party was a fringe party on the American political scene, it could at least boast of being a very wide fringe. Socialist presidential candidate Eugene V. Debs polled 901,255 votes in 1912 (out of just over 26 million votes cast). The party boasted 100,000 members, 12 state legislators, and 1,000 local elected officials. Milwaukee and Schenectady elected Socialist mayors.

But that was in peacetime. When war erupted in Europe, American Socialists opposed national military preparation. In 1915 their party went so far as to overwhelmingly amend its constitution mandating that any member holding public office "who shall in any way vote to appropriate moneys for military or naval purposes, or war, shall be expelled from the Party." In 1917, as America moved closer to hostilities, the SP called a national convention in St. Louis to deal with the issue. The date it chose was April 7—the same day Congress would declare war.

The party, however, did not back down. "We brand the declaration of war by our government as a crime against the nations of the world," read the convention's majority report.

The government did not back down either. It arrested Debs ("Do not worry over the charge of treason to your masters"), indicting him in June 1918 on 10 counts of Espionage Act violation.[1] Numerous other Socialists also faced Espionage Act charges.[2]

The SP almost fell apart as a consequence of its division over the war. True, it enjoyed some successes in the 1917 elections. In New

York State it elected 10 members of the state assembly and seven New York City aldermen. But by and large it was about to plunge over the edge. Hundreds of its members were tried and found guilty of violating the Espionage Act.[3] Postal authorities barred its publications from the mails. Socialists lost much—if not all—of their influence in the American Federation of Labor (AFL). The Socialist Party of Oklahoma—after leading an abortive "Green Corn Rebellion" against federal authorities—simply disintegrated. Approximately 1,500 of the national party's 5,000 local units dissolved.[4]

In February 1918 Milwaukee party leader Victor Luitpold Berger joined those indicted for Espionage Act violation. "The war of the United States against Germany can not be justified," he would proclaim. "The blood of American boys," he contended, is "being coined into swollen profits for American plutocrats."[5]

Eugene Debs enjoyed national publicity and is the best remembered of the early Socialists, but it was Berger and New York's Morris Hillquit who were the real powers within the party. Born in Austria-Hungary in 1860, Berger immigrated to America in 1878. He began his newspaper career in Milwaukee in 1892 and supported both the People's (Populist) Party in 1896 and the early versions of the Socialist Party. It was Berger, in fact, who had brought Debs his first copy of *Capital*. But Berger was more politician and organizer than ideologue. He led Wisconsin's A. F. of L. and built the Socialist Party up into a power in the city of Milwaukee. Elected as a Milwaukee alderman-at-large, in 1910 Berger became the SP's first member of Congress, serving for one term.[6]

Despite his indictment he campaigned for the United States Senate that spring of 1918, narrowly losing a special election to pro-war progressive Republican Irvine L. Lenroot. Undaunted, that fall he ran an openly anti-war campaign for Congress in the Milwaukee-based Wisconsin Fifth District. Despite being indicted once again that October, he won, becoming the only Socialist elected to the Sixty-Sixth Congress.

For his part Berger claimed persecution because of his socialist beliefs. To a rally of 10,000 at Chicago's Coliseum in November 1918—just six days after the Armistice—he asserted: "I can show four indictments of about sixty counts. I was not indicted because I had committed any crime—I was indicted because I stood for Socialism."[7]

The government had indicted four other Socialist leaders along with Berger: the Reverend Irwin St. John Tucker, a lecturer and writer and the former rector of a Chicago Episcopal parish, who was also active in the anti-war People's Council for Democracy and Terms of Peace;[8] East Prussian-born Adolf Germer, national executive secretary of the Socialist Party and former vice president of the United Mine Workers of America for the Illinois district; 27-year-old William F. Kruse, secretary of the Young People's Socialist League (YPSL) and editor of the Young Socialist; and J. Louis Engdahl, a former editor of the *American Socialist* (a journal shut down by the government) and, at the time of the trial, head of the National Socialist Press Service.[9]

All five Socialists would be tried before Kenesaw Landis.

It took months, however, before the case came to trial. In October 1918 defense counsel Seymour Stedman (defense attorney in the Rockford trial and a member of the Socialist Party's National Executive Committee) moved for a dismissal. Landis denied his motion. On November 12 Stedman moved for a change of venue, charging Landis with prejudice against his clients because of their German ancestry.[10] On November 1, the Squire had allegedly commented, "If anybody has said anything about the Germans that is worse than I have said, I would like to hear it so I could use it myself."[11] [12]

Landis had been responding to German-American August Weisenfel who had been found guilty of violating the Espionage Act. "Germany," Weisenfel had bragged, "has the money and plenty of men and wait and see what she is going to do to the United States." An infuriated Landis, Stedman charged, retorted:

> One must have a very judicial mind, indeed, not to be prejudiced against the German-Americans in this country. Their hearts are reeking with disloyalty. This defendant is the kind of man that spreads this kind of propaganda and it has been spread until it has affected practically all the Germans in this country. This same kind of excuse of the defendant offering to protect the German people is the same kind of excuse offered by pacifists in this country, who are against the United States and have the interest of the enemy at heart by defending that thing they call the Kaiser and his darling people. You are the same kind of man that comes over to this country from Germany to get away from the Kaiser and war. You have become a citizen of this country and lived here as such, and now when this country is at war with Germany you seek to undermine the country that gave you protection. You are of the same mind that

practically all German-Americans are in this country, and you call yourself German-Americans. Your hearts are reeking with disloyalty. I know a safe blower, he is a friend of mine, who is making a good soldier in France. He was a bank robber for nine years, that was his business in peace time, and now he is a good soldier, and as between him and this defendant, I prefer the safe blower.[13]

Landis, however, examined his transcript of the Weisenfel case and found the defendants' affidavit to be a "perjurious document." In some sense, it would be puzzling if he had uttered the above statements. The Landises were German-Swiss. The Squire's genealogy was riddled with such names as Hoch and Kumler and Flickinger. Even Winifred Reed Landis had Germanic antecedents, Reed being originally a German name. If Landis was indeed violently opposed to *all* German-Americans, he was exhibiting a sense of self-hatred.[14]

He denied the motion, and a jury was impaneled on December 9, 1918. Both sides sparred over its composition. The defense weeded out prospective jurors who had been involved in defense bond sales, active in antisedition organizations, or had sons in the service. For its part the prosecution bounced a Geneva, Wisconsin restaurateur for being of German parentage and a frequent visitor to Milwaukee. While the jury was being chosen, Berger was again reindicted, this time for 16 counts of Espionage Act violations committed during his unsuccessful senatorial campaign.[15]

At one point the defense charged jury tampering. Stedman produced an affidavit from juror Thomas C. Nixon (who gave his occupation as "inventor") alleging that bailiff W. H. Streeter (charged with guarding the jury) had made derogatory statements about the defendants in their presence. Stedman demanded a mistrial. Landis grilled Nixon regarding his assertions and learned that he made them only after being approached by defense counsel and told that several other jurors had made similar allegations. This was not so, as every other juror denied hearing Streeter utter such statements. Nixon also admitted he had not read his affidavit before signing it. When Landis inquired of him as to whether the document did indeed "speak the truth," Nixon pled the Fifth Amendment. Landis allowed the trial to continue.[16]

The prosecution's case largely rested upon the stacks of Socialist Party literature and correspondence it had seized on September 5, 1917, but both sides presented witnesses to buttress their arguments.

Berger was the last of the defendants to take the stand. German accent aside, he was not a good witness. He claimed he had only voted for the majority report at the St. Louis convention because he feared something more radical might otherwise pass, but dodged questions on whether he attempted to deny Socialist Milwaukee mayor Daniel W. Hoan renomination for not endorsing that platform.

The prosecution set a number of traps for Berger—and he fell into them with a thud. "Ever advocated violence?" United States Attorney Charles F. Clyne asked, to which Berger responded that he never had. But he soon admitted to writing in the *Social Democratic Herald* in July 1909 that Socialist voters and supporters should "have a good rifle and the necessary rounds of ammunition in his home and be prepared to back up his ballot with his bullets if necessary."

The next trap had to do with the Congressman-elect's sympathies for the IWW Berger ("I suppose the IWW hates me more than any other man in the country") declared he had "never been in sympathy" with that organization, but found himself confronted with May 1916 correspondence in which he "gladly admit[ted] that the IWW has stood the test of being a class organization infinitely better than the trade unions." The prosecution even produced a $10 donation Berger had written to the Wobblies.

Berger's credibility suffered further hits when the prosecution produced evidence contradicting his claim that Socialists opposed all wars. In 1916 he had advocated war with Mexico.[17]

On the afternoon of January 7, Assistant United States Attorney Joseph B. Fleming took four hours to wrap up his case. Then it was up to Landis to deliver his charge to the jury. At the request of the jurors he adjourned the court until the next morning.

In anticipation of Landis' charge, great throngs of onlookers packed his courtroom and the corridors leading to it. He took the bench at 10 PM, giving a stiff nod of his head to the opposing attorneys, to the jury, and, of course, to the working press. It was still somewhat dark in the great marble room, and Landis reached across the bench to switch on a light. When he did, his great shock of white hair came quite close to the lamp and shone with an unusual intensity. His eyes assumed what one observer termed a "fiercer glow."

His instructions lasted just short of an hour. He emphasized the secretive nature of conspiracies. "Rarely, if ever," he commented,

are conspiracies proved by direct testimony. When such a crime is about to be committed by a group of individuals they do not act openly. Guilt generally must be proved by circumstantial evidence...

If two or more persons agree to cause insubordination in the military forces or willfully obstruct the recruiting or enlistment service of the United States, and any or more of such persons does not act in furtherance of the common design they are guilty of the offense of conspiracy.

If you find that a conspiracy was formed and any one of the overt acts was committed the case is made out against the defendants: it is not being necessary to prove all of the acts alleged.

It is not necessary that two or more persons should actually meet together or directly in words or writing state what the unlawful scheme to be or the means by which the unlawful combination is to be made effective. It is sufficient if two or more persons come to a mutual understanding to accomplish an unlawful design.

Common design is the essence of the crime. In determining the question of the existence of a conspiracy you will take into consideration the relations of the parties one to another in their personal and business associations and all the facts that tend to show what transpired between them during the time of the alleged combination.

In delivering his charge Landis was at his kinetic best, lifting his gold-rimmed glasses over his forehead, pointing a bony finger at the jury box, piercingly emphasizing such points as "the country was then at war." At one point he bolted out of his seat, swirled it around, and sat on its arm. Another time he lay fully prone upon the bench.

"Landis," marveled socialist writer David Karsner, "would have been a great tragedian. He has a natural sense of the dramatic, a splendid sense of humor, a severity that has been called brutal, and a sense of right and justice and morality splendidly and consistently in keeping with the conventions of the time."[18]

When Landis concluded, he asked counsel if they had any comments to make upon his charge. The prosecution had none. Defense counsel Stedman, however, took exception to Landis' instructions regarding conspiracy. All during the trial Stedman had hammered away at the point that there was no "meeting of minds or conspiracy." Still, optimism ran high among the defendants. Tucker, Germer, Engdahl, and Kruse expected a hung jury. Berger held out hope for acquittal. "The jury cannot convict me of this charge," he assured listeners.[19]

Helping the Socialists' mood was Landis' rather subdued performance during the trial. While he seemed to lack the warmth he had shown IWW defendants, he had done nothing untoward during the course of the Socialists' trial. As Karsner recorded in *The Call Magazine,* he heard "not a word of criticism of Judge Landis' conduct" from the defendants.[20]

Jurors deliberated not in the jury room but within the courtroom itself. On the first ballot, it stood 10-2 for conviction. Outside in the corridors a full 500 persons congregated in small groups. Each defendant gathered little knots of supporters around him. At 11:45 deputy marshalls ordered everyone to remove their hats for a full five minutes in memory of Theodore Roosevelt, who had died just two days before. Not all the defendants and their supporters were inclined to obey. One marshall came upon Berger talking to some women on the stairway. "Oh yes, Roosevelt he's dead," Berger responded unenthusiastically but nonetheless promptly doffed his hat.

At one o'clock the jury broke for lunch. Four bailiffs and two detectives escorted them to a nearby restaurant, where they dined at a large table at the establishment's rear. Shortly thereafter, Berger, Engdahl, and their wives; Stedman; two other Socialist attorneys; and a few supporters entered the same restaurant. The two parties properly did not join one another, but neither were they bothered by the other's presence. Surreally both groups laughed and joked as if they had not a care in the world.

Back in the federal court house, jurors continued their deliberations, while  defendants and their wives adjourned into a small room adjoining the courtroom and proceeded to engage in a five-handed game of "pitch." On a second ballot the vote was now 11-1 to convict. Then came a third ballot. At three o'clock a verdict was announced. Landis ordered the jury's foreman, Waukegan fruit dealer A. L. Hendee, to gave the verdict: all five defendants were guilty as charged. Landis made no comment, uttering nothing more than his thanks to the jury.

Berger folded his hands over his lap on being pronounced guilty. Some thought he looked bored. Tucker responded with a smile. Germer gaped at the jury dumbstruck. Engdahl looked nervously at his young wife, while Tucker stared morosely at the grand. Seymour Stedman, face flushed with anger, leapt to his feet and demanded a poll of the jury. It did him little good.

Slowly the defendants regained their wits. "You men have sat through this trial and you know I am not guilty," Berger swore to newsmen, as he placed his arms around two of them. "If I must go to prison for something I have not done it is all right."

Adolph Germer now almost seemed to take the matter as a joke. "Well," he said, grinning broadly, "it's all right if we do have to go to prison. Better men than we have gone and we can ... if we have to, but I don't think we will have to go."[21]

The jury had given particular weight to written material generated by the defendants. "We paid more attention to the documentary evidence than to the testimony," declared jury foreman Hendee, "We were unanimous in declaring the 'proclamation and war programme' of the socialist party, passed at St. Louis, to be a traitorous document." Editorials in Berger's *Milwaukee Leader* and St. John Tucker's pamphlets "The Price We Pay" and "Why We Should Fight" also played a part in their decision.

"After hearing the evidence," observed the jury's youngest member Seldon Wakem, a Chicago insurance agent, "I couldn't understand why they wanted a trial by an American jury."[22]

Landis did not pronounce sentence until February 20. Prior to sentencing he extended to the defendants the right to address the court. They took full advantage of the privilege—going on for five hours. "They berated the judge and jury," noted the *New York Times*, "used the same utterances which led to their convictions and flatly declared that no power would ever seal their lips." St. John Tucker compared his travail to that of Christ. Berger concluded his oration by saying that he asked for no mercy. But his appearance belied his words. His face was flushed. Tears streamed down his eyes. "He was not a heroic figure," the *Times* noted.

In his sentence Landis quoted liberally from the Socialists' own printed material. "The speeches and writings of the defendants ... ," he concluded,

> all exhibiting a consistent, persistent, campaign throughout the whole period to discredit the cause of the United States and to obstruct its effort to win the war. So far as I can recall, no single word or act of any one of the defendants was apparently intended by any of the defendants to help this country win the war ... In the view of the Court the conceded writings, declarations, and activities of the defendants, giving their language its ordinary, every-day meaning

(without considering any other evidence) clearly established a conscious, purposeful, continuing occupation to discourage, obstruct and prevent enlistment and recruiting, and to cause insubordination, disloyalty, mutiny and refusal of duty in the forces. If this was not in the contemplation of the defendants, the whole enterprise was aimless and purposeless. What has been said here today by the five defendants appears to have been in justification of what the defendants seemed to assume was a policy and attitude of opposition and obstruction.[23]

He sentenced each defendant to 20 years in Leavenworth.

Quickly defense counsel moved for a new trial, a stay of execution, and for bail. Their grounds: Landis' failure to grant a change of venue, his allowance of defendants' statements made before the war, and the issue of double jeopardy (Germer had been previously acquitted on charges of draft obstruction). Just as quickly, Landis denied each motion but permitted the filing of a writ of error.

Almost instantly the defendants now stood before Appeals Court judge Samuel Alschuler. Alschuler offered the defendants bail—but on condition of silence. "While the minorities have rights," Alschuler warned, "the majorities also have rights which must not even seemingly be transgressed.... They must refrain absolutely from doing those things for which they have been convicted. If their promise is not kept ... their ... bail will terminate. Their lawyers will be responsible for their action."[24]

The defendants took the deal. With jail staring them in the face they bartered their silence for their freedom, and Alschuler ordered Berger released on $25,000 bail.

During the IWW trial Landis had received stacks of threatening and abusive correspondence. "I didn't pay any attention to them," he once recalled. "One was particularly uncomplimentary. I don't think such letters should be given any consideration.[25] But prose did not explode. Bombs did. As noted earlier, a few weeks after the conclusion of the Wobbly trial a bomb was flung against the Federal Building's north entrance. Several men were killed, but Landis, upstairs in his office, was unharmed.[26]

Political violence was in fashion. In January 1919 a bomb wrecked the home of California governor William Stephens. A month later authorities uncovered an alleged IWW plot to assassinate

Woodrow Wilson while he traveled through Spain. In Paris an anarchist wounded France's aged premier George Clemenceau.

May Day 1919 saw the uncovering of a massive bomb plot. Unknown persons mailed 36 explosive devices to some of America's most prominent citizens, including John D. Rockefeller, J. P. Morgan, Supreme Court Justice Oliver Wendell Holmes, Attorney General A. Mitchell Palmer, Postmaster General Albert S. Burleson, Secretary of Labor William B. Wilson, United States Commissioner of Immigration Anthony Caminetti, Mayors John F. Hylan of New York and Ole Hansen of Seattle, United States senators Lee Overman (D-NC) and William H. King (D-UT), former senator Thomas W. Hardwick (D-GA), IWW prosecutor Frank K. Nebeker, and Kenesaw Landis.[27]

Each bomb had been dispatched from New York's General Post Office in white boxes, two inches by seven inches, and marked with the return address "Gimbel Brothers, Thirty-third St. and Broadway, New York City." Red seals closed each parcel's ends. The bombers must have had a sense of humor. To each package they attached a label reading "Novelty."

The first two bombs were addressed to Mayor Hansen and Senator Hardwick. Hansen's bomb failed to go off and no damage was done, but the bomb addressed to former Senator Hardwick injured his wife and blew both hands off their black maid. "My regret is I could not have borne the brunt of it," he commented, "instead of my wife and a helpless negro being the sufferers."[28]

The alert was now on for packages bearing the Gimbel's sticker. Back in the New York General Post Office an employee remembered seeing 16 such packages. Remarkably, they had all lacked postage and he had put them aside. Authorities took control of them and widened the alert for the others.

Even more remarkably, a *17th* bomb had lacked postage. Addressed to Senator Reed Smoot (R-UT), it traveled all the way to Utah before being returned to New York for insufficient postage. In Manhattan a postal employee opened the package and examined the contents. He saw a vial of acid and percussion caps—but thought they were part of some "joke." He rewrapped the parcel, put postage on it, and sent it *back* to Senator Smoot. Luckily, more alert postal authorities intercepted the explosive before it got there.[29]

Landis' bomb was not among the 16 that never made it out of New York. He was in Rockford when his parcel reached his office.

When news of the bomb plot reached Chicago, the Federal

Building's press room buzzed with speculation. "New York, Atlanta, Seattle," commented one reporter. "That's both coasts. They'll be hitting Chicago with these bombs soon."

"If they do, it'll be Judge Landis who'll get the first bomb," someone theorized.

"Maybe he's got one now," advanced one newsman.

Nobody thought much of that idea, but its author decided to hike up to Landis' chamber and find out for himself. Having nothing better to do, the others followed from the press room.

"Did the Judge get a bomb in the mail this morning?" he breezily asked Landis' secretary, Miss Hilda Krekel.

The question didn't faze her. "The judge is liable to get anything," she smiled and replied, "A batch of mail just came in."

With that she pointed at that morning's delivery just over on the Judge's desk. Bomb or no bomb, the reporters could not resist the temptation to paw through a public official's mail.

The *Chicago Evening American*'s Albert Baenzinger (immortalized as the effeminate reporter, "Bensinger," in Ben Hecht and Charlie MacArthur's classic *The Front Page*) picked up a small package and suddenly exclaimed, "It's a bomb!"

The others weren't sure if he was kidding or not, but based upon the excitement in his voice, weren't ruling anything out. They rushed toward him. The package bore all the earmarks of the bombers' handiwork, both in size and shape and in the "Gimbel Brothers" address.[30]

Baenziger put the parcel put aside. When the Judge returned he demanded to see it.

"It was sent to me in the mail, so it is my property," he fumed.

Cooler heads prevailed, and Landis turned the package over to police. It *was* a bomb, and Landis was on hand when police exploded it. The force of the explosion shook his bravado. "I would have opened it," he said ashenly, "had I been in town when it first was received."[31]

This, however, would not be the last bomb meant for Landis. Within the month another plot was in the works, and an explosive device had been sent from Boston to Chicago with Landis as its most likely target. On May 29 a police raid on an anarchist meeting broke up the conspiracy.[32]

Meanwhile, the issue remained of Berger's Congressional seat. When Berger presented himself for swearing in, a storm of controversy erupted. In November 1919 the full House, with only one dissenting vote, barred Berger from taking office. Wisconsin's governor ordered a special election for December 19, and Berger ran once more. Determined to block his election, local Republicans and Democrats united on a single candidate, but the strategy failed as Berger again swept to victory, this time by a 25,802–19,800 margin.

The results startled the nation. "The sooner Berger and his sympathizers follow Emma Goldman and [Alexander] Berkman out of the United States," editorialized the *Boston Evening Transcript* in a typical response, "the sooner the United States will be a better place to live in."

Landis was equally incensed. "It was my great disappointment to give Berger only 20 years in Leavenworth," he roared in a speech to the Chicago Advertising Men's Post of the American Legion. "I believe the law should have enabled me to have him lined up against the wall and shot. . . ."[33]

"The districts that voted to re-elect Berger ought to get out of this democracy and back in their monarchy. Berger's platform was that he was 100 percent German, and on that basis he was re-elected. Watch the vote in Congress for his re-instatement and let those fellows who upheld him know how we feel about it."[34]

On January 10, 1920, the House voted again. By a 330–6 margin, it once more barred Berger from membership. This time the governor refused to call a special election. In November 1920, Berger ran again. This time, with Republican Warren Harding sweeping the nation, he finally met defeat.[35]

Landis was also participating in the election of 1920. In Indianapolis that October to address a convention of 3,000 school teachers, he found a threatening note hurled into his automobile. "For the last time," it read, "you are warned to keep your damned mouth shut concerning charges that you have made against radical movements in Chicago and other cities in which you have spoken." Not only did he ignore this warning by again attacking the Socialist Party's antiwar stance, he also claimed the SP had aided the enemy and was "responsible for the fact that the bodies of thousands of American soldiers are now in France." For good measure, he criticized Harding and Democrat presidential candidate James M. Cox for insufficient support of the Eighteenth Amendment.[36]

Also on that November's presidential ballot was Eugene V. Debs, now serving a 10-year sentence at Atlanta. The incarcerated Debs received 919,799 votes, the highest total ever recorded by an American Socialist.

Meanwhile Victor Berger's appeal was proceeding apace. By June 1920 the Circuit Court of Appeals had sent his case to the United States Supreme Court to decide if Landis should indeed have recused himself as Seymour Stedman had requested in November 1918.[37] On January 31, 1921—the same day Woodrow Wilson was rejecting a plea to commute Debs' sentence—the Supreme Court overturned the Socialists' conviction and ordered a new trial. Ruling for Berger and against Landis were Chief Justice Edward White and Associate Justices Joseph McKenna, Oliver Wendell Holmes, John H. Clarke, Willis Van Devanter, and Louis D. Brandeis. Dissenting were Justices James C. McReynolds, William R. Day, and Mahlon Pitney.

The court's majority, led by Associate Justice McKenna found that the case turned on three issues:

1. Is the aforesaid affidavit of prejudice sufficient to invoke the operation of this act which provides for filing of an affidavit of prejudice of a judge?
2. Did Landis have a right to pass upon the sufficiency of the said affidavit of his prejudice or upon any question arising out of the filing of said affidavit?
3. Upon the filing of the said affidavit of his prejudice or upon any question arising out of the filing of said indictment?

It responded to those issues as follows:

To the first question we answer, yes, that is, that the affidavit of prejudice is sufficient to invoke the operation of the act.

To the second we answer to the extent that we have indicated Judge Landis had a lawful right to pass upon the sufficiency of the affidavit.

To the third we answer no; that is that Judge Landis had no lawful right to preside as judge on the trial of the defendants upon the indictment.

We are of the opinion that an affidavit upon information and belief satisfies the section, and that upon its filing if it shows the objectionable inclination or disposition of the judge, which we have said is an essential condition, it is his duty to proceed no further in the case.

And in this there is no serious detriment to the administration of justice nor inconvenience worthy of mention, for of what concern is it to a judge to preside in a particular case; of what concern to other parties to have him so preside, and any serious delay of trial is avoided by the requirement that the affidavit must be filed not less than ten days before the commencement of the term.

In other words, once the defense had filed an affidavit alleging prejudice, Landis—because of the 1913 federal statute—had no real choice but to turn the case over to another judge. Justice McReynolds,[38] in his dissent, disagreed wholeheartedly. "It was not the purpose of Congress," he argued, "to empower an unscrupulous defendant seeking escape from merited punishment to remove a Judge solely because he had emphatically condemned domestic enemies in time of national danger."[39]

McReynolds, who questioned the "accuracy" of the defendant's original affidavit of Landis' prejudice, continued: "Intense dislike of a class does not render the Judge incapable of administering complete justice to one of its members. A public officer who entertained no aversion toward disloyal German immigrants during the late war was simply unfit for his place. And while 'an overspeaking judge is no well-tuned cymbal,' neither is an amorphous dummy unspotted by human emotions a becoming receptacle for judicial power."[40]

William R. Day wrote his own more moderate dissent, in which Associate Justice Mahlon Pitney concurred. Regarding Landis' berating of August Weisenfel, Day noted:[41]

> The judge, in speaking of the convicted defendant, said he was of the type of man who branded almost the whole German-American population, and that one German-American such as the defendant talking such stuff did more damage to his people than thousands of them could overcome by being good and loyal citizens; and that he, the defendant, was an illustration of the occasional American of German birth whose conduct had done so much to damn the whole 10,000,000 in America.
>
> There is nothing in this language firmly establishing that the judge directed his observances to the German people in general. It does not appear the judge had any such bias or prejudice as would prevent him from fairly conducting the trial. . . .
>
> It does not appear that the trial judge had any acquaintance with any of the defendants, only one of whom was of German birth, or that he had any such bias or prejudice against any of them as

would prevent him from fairly and impartially conducting the trial. The opinion of the court places the Federal courts at the mercy of defendants who are willing to make affidavits as to what took place at previous trials in a court which the knowledge of the judge and the uncontradicted test of an official show to be untrue, and in many districts may greatly retard the trial of criminal cases.[42]

In Milwaukee Victor Berger was overjoyed. "The conspiracy has failed," he announced, "and I have nothing to retract from anything I have written or said about the war or about those who pushed us into this war."[43]

In Chicago, Kenesaw Landis refused to comment. "I decline to discuss the matter at all," he tersely responded as he walked away from reporters.[44]

The *New York Times* applauded the High Court's decision as "a signal triumph of public justice," demonstrating that the state was bending over to be fair beyond the "smallest cloud of doubt." Yet the *Times* admitted that "on the record and the face of the proceedings" nothing would "indicate to the layman that the defendants didn't have an absolutely fair trial nor is there any reason to suppose that the trial would have been different with a different judge."[45]

Another paper contended, the High Court's reason for granting a new trial was "more of a compliment" to Landis than to the defendants."

"We should say," it editorialized, "the Court had principally merely cinched Judge Landis' credentials as a red-blooded, he-American." The *Chicago Tribune* took pains to point out that the Supreme Court had not criticized Landis' behavior during the trial. "The trial before Judge Landis," it contended, "was more than ... liberal in its admission of all proper or plausible defense."[46]

A new trial was expected, but the government was now in the business of letting dissidents out of prison—not bringing more in. At Christmastime 1921 Harding commuted Eugene Debs' sentence and received him at the White House. "Well," said Harding, extending his hand, "I have heard so damned much about you, Mr. Debs, that now I am very glad to meet you personally."[47]

In 1922 all federal charges against Berger and the other Socialists were dropped.

# CHAPTER 11

# "I HAVEN'T TOLD MRS. LANDIS YET"

Few of Landis' fervors could match his patriotic passion, but one was certainly for baseball. He had played the game as a youth and vociferously rooted for teams in Chicago, his adopted hometown. He'd been booed for his Cubs partisanship during the 1906 World Series, but against outsiders could turn into a loyal White Sox fan. During the 1917 World Series he telegraphed the Sox to congratulate them on their triumph over New York. "Well, we did a good day's work today," he crowed. "We disposed of the Giants."

Even Bill Haywood noticed the depth of the Squire's attachment to the national pastime. During the IWW trial, Haywood would write, Landis' "time was much preoccupied and he could not go to as many ballgames as had previously been his custom."[1]

It was that element of fandom that led him into Organized Baseball in the first place.

In 1914 the upstart Federal League challenged major league hegemony, placing franchises in such cities as Chicago, Brooklyn, Indianapolis, Buffalo, Kansas City, Baltimore, Pittsburgh, and St. Louis. Big leaguers such as Joe Tinker, Hal Chase, Mordecai Brown, and Dutch Zwilling defected to the Feds. Others, such as Walter Johnson, were tempted to jump. A combination of higher salary offers and threats, however, kept most quality players in check.

But when those tactics failed, baseball moved into the courts. The Cincinnati Reds served a summons on righthander George "Chief" Johnson who had jumped to the Feds' Kansas City Packers. The Reds also went to court to retrieve Cuban-born outfielder Armando Marsans. The Giants successfully secured the return of star southpaw "Rube" Marquard from the Brooklyn Feds. The White Sox' Charles Comiskey was less successful when he sought first baseman Hal Chase's return from Buffalo's Federal League club. New York

State Supreme Court judge Herbert Bissell refused to cooperate. Bissell condemned Organized Baseball's reserve clause as "peonage" and "the domination of a benevolent despotism through the operation of the monopoly established by the National Agreement."

Such activity goaded the Feds into counteraction. Infuriated by the loss of such talent as Marsans, Chase, and Walter Johnson, on January 5, 1916 the Federal League brought suit in Landis' court, alleging Organized Baseball had violated the Clayton Anti-Trust Act, a 1914 strengthening of the Sherman Act.[2]

In one of the most fateful (and mistaken) decisions in baseball history the Feds chose Landis' venue to hear their case. On the surface their decision seemed logical. Most basically, his United States District Court for the Northern District of Illinois held forth in Chicago, headquarters of both the American and Federal leagues. Further, Landis had certainly earned a reputation as a "trust-buster" of the highest order. And he had been scrupulously impartial regarding Chicago's competing baseball franchises. "The Judge," noted *The Sporting News*, "at least came into court with 'clean hands,' for last season [1914] he refused to accept passes for the Cubs, White Sox and Chifeds. When he went to the game he paid his way in."[3]

Federal League magnates expected Landis to deal a knock-out blow to Organized Baseball's monopoly. They knew baseball's legal standing was built on sand; Organized Baseball's lawyers knew it; and Judge Landis knew it. But the Federal League had not counted on how much Landis feared doing harm to the game he loved.

American League president Byron Bancroft "Ban" Johnson, baseball's most powerful figure, was in New York, overseeing the transfer of the AL's New York franchise from its original owners, gambling kingpin Frank Farrell and former NYC police chief William Devery, to brewer Colonel Jacob Ruppert and his fellow millionaire, engineer Captain T. L. Huston. "I understand that they want to arrest me in Chicago in this action," Johnson blustered. "Well, just as soon as I finish my business here tomorrow, I will go to Chicago and they can have me.

"I consider this action by the Federal League as a scheme to get a lot of publicity because organized baseball has been getting all the attention in the papers, and the outlaw league has been getting little.

"The American League is not a trust nor is organized baseball a restraint of trade. I think that fact has been well established."[4]

The Federal League's complaint ran to 92 legal pages and contained 11 prayers for relief, the most important of which were the first six:

1. That the national agreement and the rules of the National Commission be declared illegal and the defendants enjoined from operating under them.
2. That the defendants be declared to constitute a combination, conspiracy, and monopoly in contravention of the anti-trust statutes, and that they be enjoined from further doing business as a part of said monopoly.
3. That the defendants be declared to have conspired to injure and destroy the plaintiff's business and enjoined from continuing their conspiracy, particularly from saying the plaintiffs are financially irresponsible and from threatening with "black list" any players under Federal contract.
4. That all contracts with players heretofore be made by the defendants under the national agreement be declared as to the plaintiffs, "null, void and of no effect" and that the defendants be enjoined from seeking to enforce such contracts against players later signed by the Federals.
5. That the defendants be ordered to dismiss the various actions now pending against players.
6. That they be restrained from seeking by injunctions, threats or promises to prevent other players from performing their several contracts.[5]

For its part, Organized Baseball held that the labor of a human being was neither a commodity nor an article of commerce and endeavored to compare the labor of ballplayers with that of entertainers, citing the opinion in *Hammerstein v. Metropolitan Grand Opera Company* which held that theatrical exhibits were not commerce. National League counsel George Wharton Pepper explained: "Their grievance is not that we prevent them from finding young ball players on the 'lot' and developing them through training in the various minor leagues as we do; they want to attain in one bound the advantage we have gained through ten years of labor; they want to profit from the skill developed by our money."[6]

When proceedings opened on January 20, 1916, over 650 fans jammed Landis' courtroom. Without a scorecard, however, fans had difficulty in identifying their heroes. National League president John K. Tener, a former pitcher, was frequently mistaken for a police officer. Walter Johnson, dressed in low-key fashion in cap and sweater, was often ignored.

When Landis' bailiff banged his gavel and called for order, one spectator yelled, "Hey, boy, gimme a bag of peanuts!"

That was *not* regarded as amusing. Other bailiffs scoured the court but found no suspects. A warning went out that such behavior would not be tolerated.[7]

As the proceedings opened, Federal League counsel Keene Addington hammered away at Organized Baseball's draft and waiver rules, arguing they substantially hamstrung a player's freedom of movement. To this end he introduced an affidavit from former Cubs righthander, Mordecai "Three Finger" Brown, a particular Landis favorite. In his deposition Brown recounted how Minneapolis manager Pongo Joe Cantillon had once traded a player for a bird dog. Landis listened with rapt attention and wanted that portion of Brown's account reread.

Some players testified in person. Another Landis favorite, Joe Tinker, now manager of the Feds' Chicago entry, delivered a scathing attack on baseball's 10-day clause. Baltfed manager Otto Knabe objected to the take-it-or-leave-it nature of the standard National and American League contracts.[8]

As far as baseball playing was concerned, it was clear Landis' frame of reference remained on the sandlots of 1870s Indiana. At one point, Pepper commented on ballplaying as "labor." Landis archly responded, "As a result of thirty years of observation, I am shocked because you call baseball 'labor.' "[9]

On January 23, as Organized Baseball wrapped up its defense, Landis sent out decidedly mixed messages. At one point American League attorney George W. Miller leaned toward Landis and exclaimed with much emotion, "You know, Your Honor, I love Baseball."

"But we have to keep love and affection out of this case," Landis snapped.

Later as Pepper urged the Judge "to save the great sport for the fans," the Judge responded: "You all understand—both sides—that a blow to the game of baseball will be regarded by this court as a blow to one of our national institutions." The audience erupted in applause. Even Federal League officials joined in the general enthusiasm.[10]

Perhaps most significantly, Landis wanted to know from the liti-

gants: did he really have jurisdiction in the case? It was not a frivolous question. At the time most would have agreed the answer was
no. Even Judge Bissell's ringing condemnation of the reserve clause
held that baseball was not interstate commerce.[11]

At the end of four days of testimony, Landis' vexation became
obvious. "I have gone just about far enough in this case," he snarled at
Federal League attorney Edward E. Gates. "The time has come when
I should ask you gentlemen just what you want me to do. . . . Do you
want me to stop the teams from going on spring training trips? Do you
want me to break up the clubs or what do you want me to do? . . .

"Do you realize that a decision in this case may tear down the
very foundations of this game, so loved by thousands, and do you
realize that the decision must also seriously affect both parties?"[12]

Nonetheless, Federal League president "Fighting Jim" Gilmore
thought the matter could be handled quickly enough. "As far as I can
see," Gilmore observed, "there is nothing which might drag matters
over any extended period. We are ready now, and there is no reason
the other side should want any delay. The sooner this fight is over the
better it will be for the game."

Gilmore soon discovered just how wrong he was. The 1915 season
began and ended. More players—including Eddie Plank, Chief
Bender, Ed Konetchy, Hooks Wiltse, Lee Magee, and "Germany"
Schaefer—jumped to the Feds. But Landis issued no decision. Recog-
nizing that if he ruled in favor of Organized Baseball he would be
reversed on appeal, Landis simply stalled. Month after month
passed, and he issued no verdict. While he delayed, owners on both
sides tired of the struggle. Not helping Federal League fortunes was
the death of Brookfed owner Robert B. Ward, a key league backer.

In December 1915 Organized Baseball basically bought out its
faltering rivals. In return for $600,000 the established major league
clubs received a promise that the Federal League would drop its litigation. The last move in the drama now was Landis'. Only he had the
power to dismiss the Feds' suit. He had delayed for a full year to
avoid ruling in the case; he wasted no time in dismissing it.[13]

Due in large part to Landis' strategic inaction, Organized Baseball was saved—temporarily. Baseball's profitability returned in 1916
and 1917. But with America in a world war, baseball seemed of marginal importance to a nation enmeshed in patriotic fervor. Baseball,
however, thought it could conduct business as usual. Ban Johnson
even suggested exempting 18 men on each major league roster from

the military draft. But in May 1918 the government issued a "work or fight" order, designed to force all able-bodied adult males into either a uniform or an essential occupation. Baseball clearly was not considered "essential." Worse than that, attendance was falling like a rock—from 5,219,994 in 1917 to 3,080,126 in 1918. Even taking account the game's retrenchment to a 140-game schedule, it was a dramatic drop. Only one minor league finished the season. Players, upset over a new division of post-season spoils, threatened to strike during the Cubs-Red Sox World Series. Baseball itself threatened to vanish by 1919.

Yet, when the war ended, the National Pastime bounced back splendidly. Even with its 140-game schedule in place, major league clubs attracted 6,532,439 fans in 1919. Fifteen minor leagues opened the season, and only one failed to finish the campaign. That fall's World Series—now expanded to a best-of-nine format—promised to be as popular as any in history.[14]

Instead, baseball received a blow that threatened to destroy its future—the 1919 Black Sox scandal. The game had never been entirely free from gambling influences, but the "work or fight" order had an unusual impact on the National Pastime. In 1918 the Wilson administration had kept ballparks open but shuttered the nation's racetracks. Gamblers flocked to ballparks, refocusing their activity on baseball. Their interest would remain long after Armistice Day, resulting in a dramatic increase not only in wagering but in fixed games.[15]

In the 1919 World Series the White Sox were heavily favored to beat the National League's Cincinnati Reds but instead played sloppily and fell to the Reds in eight games. Suspicions of a "fix" circulated almost immediately, but when Chicago sportswriter Hugh Fullerton hinted of such a possibility, baseball's power structure responded with vitriol. *The Sporting News* fumed: "Because a lot of dirty, long-nosed, thick-lipped, and strong-smelling gamblers butted into the World Series . . . and some of them got crossed, stories were peddled that there was something wrong with the games. . . . [Sox owner Charles] Comiskey has met that by offering $10,000 for any sort of a clue that will bear out such a charge. . . . [but] there will be no takers, because there is no such evidence, except in the mucky minds of the stinkers who—because they are crooked—think all the rest of the world can't play straight."[16]

Landis meanwhile busied himself with yet another high-profile case. Impressed by the huge profits of the Ford Motor Co., in 1916 a failed insurance man, Samuel Conner Pandolfo, had created the Pan Motor Company out of whole cloth and went to great lengths to fool gullible investors into thinking he could actually produce motor vehicles. But Pandolfo had no intention of building autos—renderings of the Pan auto were actually cut-and-paste jobs composed of photos of a Mercer and an Oldsmobile. It was all a massive fraud, and to fool investors and investigators Pandolfo even went so far as to spend $350,000 to construct and "operate" a bogus auto plant at St. Cloud, Minnesota. The phony Pan complex encompassed 50 acres, with one building stretching for 600 feet. His scheme eventually collapsed but not before heavy advertising attracted $4.8 million from 70,000 investors. During Pandolfo's trial Landis exhibited contempt for the "get-rich-quick" artist. At one point he warned Pandolfo's lawyers to "make a close investigation of [him] and go on guard for your good name. I don't know where he was schooled or what his environment has been, and I warn you."[17]

In December 1919 the jury found Pandolfo guilty of mail fraud, and Landis took pleasure in sentencing him to 10 years in Leavenworth, which was newsworthy enough. But the Squire created his own headlines when he took a broad swipe at the newly powerful advertising industry. "It is a matter of common knowledge, not only to me as a judge," he pronounced, "but to the layman as well, that an advertising man does not reproduce a thing as it is. If he did he would lose his job."

For once Landis may have gone too far. Not every newspaper editorialist thought his comment appropriate—a turn of events that should have hardly surprised the Squire, considering how much advertising money found itself into newspaper coffers.[18]

All the while whispers about the 1919 World Series slowly receded. Then on September 4, 1920, the *Chicago Herald and Examiner* reported that an August 31 Cubs-Phillies game had been fixed in favor of the last-place Phils. Cubs management, the paper revealed, had received six telegrams and two phone calls warning of a fix. To prevent his players from hippodroming the game, Cubs manager Fred Mitchell substituted Grover Cleveland Alexander for suspect starting pitcher Claude Hendrix. Hendrix supposedly had sent a telegram to Kansas City gambler Frog Thompson, placing a bet against the Cubs.[19]

On September 7, 1920, District Attorney Maclay Hoyne and Chief

Justice of the Criminal Court, Judge Charles McDonald, impaneled a grand jury to investigate not only the tainted Cubs' game but the entire issue of baseball gambling. Hearings began on September 22. Witnesses included Comiskey and Ban Johnson, and under oath they revealed their suspicions. Then Giant pitcher Rube Benton and Cub infielder Buck Herzog reported details of other plots. Former ChiFed owner Charles Weeghman testified that back in August 1919 Mont Tennes had told him that the Series would be fixed.[20]

But the biggest news came from Philadelphia where gambler Billy Maharg provided firsthand testimony regarding the Series fix. Maharg claimed he and former major league southpaw Sleepy Bill Burns had worked with ex-featherweight world champion Abe Attell and New York gambling kingpin Arnold Rothstein to throw the Fall Classic. A day later righthander Eddie Cicotte and hard-hitting outfielder Shoeless Joe Jackson confessed to their role in the scheme and implicated six of their Sox teammates: first baseman Chick Gandil, shortstop Swede Risberg, third baseman Buck Weaver, center fielder Oscar "Happy" Felsch, pitcher Claude "Lefty" Williams, and reserve infielder Fred McMullin. Soon Williams and Felsch were also spilling their guts. On October 22 the grand jury indicted all eight players plus a number of gamblers including Burns and Attell. Rothstein— the big man—was not charged.

The news jolted baseball, its fans—and major league owners. They began to see the need for strong new leadership to cleanse the game and restore public confidence.[21]

Since Ban Johnson had transformed the American League into a major league at the turn of the century, baseball had been ruled by a three-man National Commission, composed of the National and American League presidents and a neutral third party. That third party was Cincinnati owner Garry Herrmann, and, although Herrmann was a National Leaguer, he was, nonetheless, Johnson's pliant tool, making the American League president virtual ruler of baseball.

For nearly two decades Johnson reigned. He backed his umpires and controlled the roughhousing which demeaned baseball in the 1890s. He made the American League a success and forced the once-proud National League to take a position subservient to it. But within Ban Johnson were the seeds of his own destruction. Overbearing in nature, he was given to blubbering and sentimental boasting about his "American League—the greatest institution in the country;

the greatest institution in the world." But above all he drank, and was usually at his embarrassing worst in highly public situations.

In 1910 Johnson won a new 20-year term as American League president, but his power soon began to slowly unravel. In 1913 his old friend and ally Charles Comiskey turned upon him. Within a few years Harry Frazee of Boston and the Ruppert-Huston tandem in New York would also become his bitter enemies, leaving him a bare 5-3 majority within the AL itself. Within the NL he enjoyed virtually no support. When the Federal League war exploded, he had little grip on the reality of the situation and believed Landis would rule in favor of Organized Baseball. American and National league owners thought otherwise. "Thus," noted historian David Q. Voigt, "instead of siding with Johnson who called Landis a 'showboat,' most magnates considered the judge their champion and Johnson a blundering fool."

Meanwhile, the National Commission was tottering. After its clubs lost a series of controversial decisions, the NL refused to acquiesce in Garry Herrmann's reappointment. On January 8, 1920, he resigned. Thus, as the Black Sox scandal erupted that fall, Organized Baseball's governing body was hopelessly deadlocked. The time had come for a dramatic change in leadership—and leadership styles.

"The club owners were willing enough to have rules and regulations made to control the players but they were not so ready to set their own houses in order," National League attorney George Wharton Pepper later observed. "The situation called for a sporting dictatorship..."[22]

Landis had been mentioned as that dictator as early as September 1919—and rumors of his replacing Herrmann dated back to November 1916. In January 1920, months before the Black Sox scandal broke, *Chicago Daily News* sportswriter Oscar Reichow, *The Sporting News'* Chicago correspondent, trumpeted the Judge as a person "who would go a long way to devising some method to wipe out completely the gambling evil that threatens to wipe out the game." Reichow, however, admitted that Ban Johnson would not support the Judge as he considered him "too radical." Numerous newspapers even reported Landis had the backing of all eight NL clubs and the three anti-Johnson AL franchises and that he would accept the job if offered.[23]

Of course, Landis was not the only candidate being considered. Ban Johnson angled for former Milwaukee and Boston stockholder Henry Killelea to replace Herrmann. Some National League interests reportedly favored two New York City attorneys—"Big Bill" Edwards (the collector for the Second Internal Revenue District and a former Princeton football star) and John Conway Toole (who would become International League president in 1921). None seemed viable choices. "This," summed up the *Chicago Evening Post*'s Al Spink, "leaves Judge Landis as the only man named who is really the untrammeled candidate." Yet, officially, all three remained in the race and were soon joined by New York state senator James J. Walker (the father of Sunday baseball in New York) and *Chicago Tribune* sports editor Harvey Woodruff. All five were supposedly acceptable to both Johnson and National League president John Heydler.[24]

Cubs minority stockholder Albert D. Lasker, a prominent Chicago advertising executive and the assistant chairman of the Republican National Committee, attempted to break the deadlock. A year earlier, when AL clubs and Ban Johnson tangled over the sale of Red Sox pitcher Carl Mays to the Yankees, Lasker had proposed that the commission be turned over part-and-parcel to non-baseball men.

The German-born Lasker now modified his plan. Immediately, a whole raft of non-baseball luminaries found their names mentioned for chairmanship of the revitalized commission: former president William Howard Taft, General John J. Pershing, United States senator Hiram Johnson (R-CA), presidential contender General Leonard Wood, former treasury secretary (and Woodrow Wilson's son-in-law) William Gibbs McAdoo — and, that most perennial of candidates, Judge Kenesaw Mountain Landis.[25]

Eventually ownership would settle on Landis, but they would not have Ban Johnson's support. His choice was the hero of the Black Sox grand jury, Judge Charles A. McDonald.

McDonald and Landis shared similar backgrounds. Both were midwestern farmboys; both had aspired to work on the railroads, McDonald had even toiled for six years as a brakeman. Both then returned to school, with McDonald obtaining his law degree from Kent Law College as valedictorian of the class of 1897, after which he went to Chicago to practice law. He became a member of the Superior Court in 1910, eventually working his way up to Chief Justice.[26]

In point of fact, it was no coincidence that McDonald oversaw the grand jury. McDonald and Johnson had known each other since at least 1912 when they had been joined by such notables as Garry Herrmann, White Sox manager Jim Callahan, and Red Sox co-owners Jake Stahl and Jimmy McAleer in a hunting expedition to Comiskey's private hunting lodge in northern Wisconsin.

But the Johnson-McDonald relationship went far beyond hunting parties. According to information found in White Sox official Harry Grabiner's diaries (and discovered by Bill Veeck, Jr., during his tenure as Sox owner), during the key period of 1920-21, Grabiner and Charles Comiskey were fed information from inside the Johnson camp, with their source being Chicago coal merchant Edward Fleming. Fleming revealed that Johnson, along with Browns owner Phil Ball, planned to use the Black Sox scandal to wreck the White Sox franchise.[27] If the Black Sox were exposed, they would be barred from Organized Baseball and Comiskey's once-lucrative ballclub would be ruined. Then the franchise would be handed over to a mysterious Johnson ally named Patterson.

The anti-Comiskey plot, Fleming alleged, was concocted in June 1920 "at a party at the Wayside Inn at which Patterson, Ball, [and] Johnson remarked that Comiskey has a wonderful plant and a great money-maker but after we get through wrecking it we will be able to buy it at our own price."[28] Albert Lasker quickly confirmed Fleming's account.

Veeck, however, missed the real point of Johnson's machinations. Johnson possessed no need for a governmental investigation of the Black Sox Scandal. He maintained all the investigative authority he needed as league president, and from that position could have *easily* wrecked Comiskey and the White Sox single-handedly. Johnson was playing for *far* higher stakes than simply supplanting Comiskey. He planned to create a public image for McDonald as a tireless guardian of baseball virtue. "Johnson's confidence in the judge was perfectly understandable," argued Bill Veeck, whose father, Cubs executive William Veeck, Sr., was a personal friend of Landis and one of the Judge's original backers for the commissionership. "He was merely promising to make Judge McDonald the head of the new Commission."

McDonald was perhaps Johnson's only chance to recover control of that body—and of baseball. Without the Black Sox investigation in his resumé, there was little hope for McDonald, a mere police court judge, to assume the chief commissionership.[29][30]

Timing was everything, and almost equally important was the creation of a deft excuse for probing the Black Sox scandal. Johnson had been sitting on knowledge of the Series fix for months but was waiting for McDonald to assume the chief judgeship before he created a situation that could demand a grand jury probe.

The situation was the Cubs-Phillies fix, and it had been leaked by Johnson. Once telegrams had been sent to warn of that scheme, everything began unfolding at breakneck speed. On the very day that news reports of the fix appeared on September 4, 1920, McDonald called Johnson and National League president John Heydler to meet him at Chicago's Edgewater Golf Course.[31][32]

At the Edgewater, McDonald significantly asked Johnson, rather than Heydler, as to whether the allegations warranted further investigation. "Most decidedly . . ." Johnson responded.[33] Within days McDonald convinced State's Attorney Maclay Hoyne to bring the matter before the Cook County grand jury. The matter of the fixed Cubs-Phillies game (of which nothing was ever actually proved) was instantly forgotten, and the grand jury focused instead on the Black Sox scandal. As soon as the grand jury was sworn in, it was again McDonald who had recommended that its focus also include the possibility of a World Series fix.

McDonald continued to be a dynamo in unearthing the Black Sox scandal. Author Eliot Asinof notes that Johnson met with McDonald on September 20, 1920 and laid out the scenario of the fix. Five days earlier, District Attorney Hoyne had been defeated in a Democratic primary. In disgust, he left Chicago for New York, leaving his assistant, Hartley Repogle, to conduct the investigation. McDonald and Repogle now went full speed ahead. McDonald played a crucial role in obtaining confessions from Ed Cicotte, Joe Jackson, and Lefty Williams. He fought Hoyne's efforts to delay completing the investigation. And when the confessions mysteriously disappeared from the State's Attorney's office, it was McDonald who granted a badly needed extension for the prosecution to gather new evidence.

McDonald might have made an excellent candidate to lead baseball except for one small matter: he was Ban Johnson's candidate, and Johnson's influence was fast slipping away. Johnson's support was clearly the kiss of death.

On October 7 the National League adopted the Lasker Plan and invited American League clubs to participate in a joint session on October 18. Johnson ignored their call, but his three rebel clubs, the Yankees, Red Sox, and White Sox, attended anyway.

After meeting for a full nine hours, the 11 anti-Johnson insurgents abrogated the old National Agreement and agreed to appoint a six-member committee to implement the Lasker Plan. To staff Lasker's new blue-ribbon commission they authorized a $20,000 salary for its chairman and $10,000 apiece for its remaining two members. Capping their work was an ultimatum. If Johnson's "Loyal Five" failed to ratify the Lasker Plan, a new 12-club major league would be created. It would consist of the 11 Laskerite clubs plus a new franchise to be created later—most likely in the same city as one of the "Loyal Five."[34]

Johnson still wanted no part of their plan.

October 21 was a key date in the process. Comiskey's attorney Albert Austrian informed Grabiner that Veeck now controlled six National League votes for Landis, being unsure only of Cincinnati and Brooklyn. More significantly Austrian confided that he had already spoken with Landis concerning the commissionership and that Landis would "take the matter up with his family" and get back to Austrian later in the month. Austrian, however, did not think Landis would agree to take the job, unless offered a salary in the $50,000 range.[35]

On November 1, the day before the 1920 presidential election, a bump developed in the Landis-for-Commissioner road. At a meeting at Albert Austrian's law office between Austrian, Grabiner, Lasker, and Veeck, Austrian confided to his fellow Landisites that Chairman of the Republican National Committee Will Hays "intimated that he did not feel as though the Federal Bench should be tampered with and he wished to use his good offices in behalf of MacDonald [sic]."[36]

Nonetheless, the plan moved on. After all the only viable alternative to Landis was another judge—and what was the real difference between "tampering" with one level of justice and not another? On Wednesday, November 3 Heydler invited Johnson's "Loyal Five" to meet with the other 11 clubs to reorganize the game. Johnson still wasn't interested. He continued pushing for a nine-member committee to name any new commission. And beyond that, he launched a heavy-duty plot against his erstwhile New York franchise, contacting New York Giants owner Charles Stoneham. The Yankees were still tenants at Stoneham's Polo Grounds. Johnson wanted that lease from Stoneham. In return, he offered Stoneham not only the right to select the new Yankee ownership but also his choice for the third member of the new national commission.

It was an offer Stoneham not only could refuse; he did refuse and informed Lasker of it. Lasker decided to have Stoneham report this to Ruppert face-to-face at their upcoming meeting.

On the morning of Monday, November 8, the "Eleven" met at

Chicago's Congress Hotel. Conferring separately in the same establishment were the "Loyal Five." Crossing the no-man's land from one group to the next was Washington's Clark Griffith. The Eleven sent Griffith (with Ruppert in tow) back to the "Loyal Five" inviting them to meet at once with the Eleven. No stenographers or league presidents would be present.

Arguing vehemently against this was American League attorney George Miller, who repeated the Johnson line in favor of a nine-member committee. For over an hour he harangued Griffith and Ruppert. But as he spoke the clock was running out. The Eleven had issued an ultimatum: agree to the Lasker Plan by four o'clock that afternoon or face baseball war.

Four o'clock came and went, and the "Eleven" wasted no time, unanimously electing Landis their new High Commissioner at $50,000 per year. Then came far more radical action. The Yankees, Red Sox, and White Sox resigned from the American League and the National League dissolved itself while a 12-club new National League formed. Whichever member of the "Loyal Five" that defected first would be admitted to the new circuit to fill out the vacant 12th slot. If none did, a new franchise would be placed in either Detroit or Cleveland.

The "Eleven" then appointed a six-member committee—Veeck, Austrian, Philadelphia's William F. Baker, Herrmann, Ebbets, and Ruppert—to call upon Landis and offer him chairmanship of baseball's new governing body. The latter three were less sure of their path. Their inclusion was designed to tie them further to the majority agenda.[37]

Landis gave no reply but told the owners he would take the matter under advisement. Nonetheless, they went away confident he would accept the job.

The press soon learned of the meeting. A reporter wanted to know Landis' response. As usual he ducked the issue. "A thing of that kind is something that I cannot decide in a hurry," he said. "It is a big thing. It is a big job. I deeply appreciate the honor these gentlemen have conferred upon me in offering me the chairmanship, but I told them I would have to give my answer later."

But he was nonetheless leaning toward it—and being quite obvious about it. When the reporter inquired if he had provided the delegation with any impression he would turn them down, the Judge fairly jumped out of his skin. "By no means!" he exploded. "Emphatically no; I just can't give an answer of that kind in a hurry, that's all."

Then he turned the tables on the reporter, asking, "Deep down in your belly, what do you think of it?"

The reporter responded he thought it was a "regular job" and that Landis was "the right man for it."

"Thank you!" the Judge exclaimed with some relief. "I—well, all I can say now is that I am a fan and love the game and admire clean sport, and that I would do everything in my power to help make baseball worthy of the name it has borne all these years as the cleanest sport we have.

"My decision will be announced later."[38]

On Tuesday, November 9, the owners assembled at Kansas City's Hotel Muehlebach, where the National Association would meet the following day.

Johnson remained as belligerent as ever. Not only were his "Loyal Five" threatening to go their own way, but rumors circulated that pro-Johnson forces were scheming to oust National Association secretary John H. Ferrell and replace him with a friendlier individual. Addressing the minor league convention for the first time in his career, Johnson laughed at the threat of conflict and called war "the best cleanser." He attacked "undesirable owners" who tolerated gambling in their parks and declared that only his "Loyal Five" had aided him in any meaningful sense in battling the gaming scourge. Albert Lasker, he sniffed, was "one who has not shed his swaddling clothes in baseball." The National Association, Johnson warned, should steer clear of the new league and Lasker's plan.[39]

Aside from such bluster, the Johnson forces did manage to present their own version of baseball's future. George W. Miller proposed an unwieldy nine-member commission, composed of three members named by the National League, three by the American, and three by the National Association.[40]

The minor league delegates had seemed impressed by Johnson's enthusiastic rhetoric, but while he had been orating his major league allies wavered. In a Hotel Muehlebach corridor, Barney Dreyfuss, Bob Quinn (Phil Ball's general manager), Clark Griffith, and Garry Herrmann assembled. "If my two boys wanted to fight over anything so silly," Quinn sadly observed over the coming baseball war, "I would spank them both." The Johnsonites concurred, and it was agreed that

Griffith and Quinn, representing the "Loyal Fives" interests, would sit in on a meeting with the "Eleven."

At that session Herrmann raised the issue: "Judge Landis has been chosen as head of the new Commission at a salary of $50,000.00 a year. It is now proposed that his two associates be selected at a salary of $25,000.00. It seems to me that considerable trouble will result unless we pay these associates as much as Judge Landis. They will naturally be prominent men who will consider themselves as competent as the Judge and deserving of as much salary."

Quinn advanced an entirely new issue. "Personally," he stated, "I see no necessity for having three commissioners. In my mind one would do as well. A man like Judge Landis who is a Federal Judge and accustomed to handling large business interests can certainly be trusted to administer any business Organized Baseball may give him."

Herrmann interrupted. He wanted to know if Quinn spoke for himself or for Ball. "I have not consulted Mr. Ball on this matter," Quinn admitted, "but I will say that he has never failed to back me up in any reasonable measure. I consider this measure reasonable. I am sure that the St. Louis Browns would never be involved in any difficulties they would not trust to the hands of Judge Landis."

The proposal failed to meet with any enthusiasm. Shortly thereafter, when Clark Griffith proposed a six-member joint committee (three members from each faction), the session nearly collapsed. But when the owners reconvened, Herrmann endorsed Quinn's one-commissioner proposal. In the interim every owner had swung around to Ball's thinking.[41]

Navin and Herrmann each spoke to the National Association convention the next morning. As Herrmann addressed the minor leaguers, he was handed a note. He stunned the gathering with its contents. His fellow owners had agreed to meet the next day in Chicago. No attorneys, no stenographers, and, most significantly, no league presidents would be present.[42]

The *Kansas City Journal* headlined "Moguls Leave Determined to Fight It Out," but it was wrong. It was all over for Johnson. His loyalists had realized the futility of a new baseball war. Before the next Opening Day, they would have had to create three new franchises and staff them. If they tried to place new clubs in Boston, New York, and Chicago, they would have to have to locate not only new owners but new ballparks. In New York that would be virtually impossible. In bidding for talent they would compete against such millionaires as Ruppert and Stoneham. They knew resistance would be folly.

On the morning of November 12 the 11 pro-Landis owners, presided over by Baker, met at Austrian's office at the Congress Hotel "to agree on a plan of procedure." Even Albert Lasker, who had been scheduled to visit Panama in the company of President-elect Harding, was there. Harding told him the baseball meeting was more important.[43]

At noon they were joined by the "Loyal Five." Again Baker chaired the session, but soon after it began, he received word his wife was ill, and he left for Philadelphia. William Veeck replaced him. Only one incident marred the proceedings. Comiskey called Phil Ball a "crook" and Ball stormed out, leaving Bob Quinn behind. Quinn cast the Browns' vote for Landis, making his election unanimous.

Not included in the official minutes of the session, but recorded in Harry Grabiner's notes, was this item: "It was finally agreed that if acceptable to Landis, no associate members would be selected but Landis to be sole judge."[44] Thus while most observers have concluded that it was Landis who junked the Lasker Plan's other two commissioners, it was in fact ownership which originally proposed the idea.[45] Veeck theorized that Johnson himself was behind it (supporting this theory is the fact that it was Bob Quinn, front man for Phil Ball, who had proposed the idea originally). "It is . . . possible," Veeck contended, "that Ban Johnson, having been eliminated from the job in the new ground rules, exacted this one small concession to keep himself as close as possible to the seat of power. If so, he made a final mistake. By the time Landis got through interpreting his powers . . . there was nothing left over for Johnson or anyone else." If Johnson now acted on the belief that he would have a better chance of influencing Landis by eliminating middle men, he had double-crossed McDonald, for McDonald's chances of being chosen for one of the other two slots were still considered excellent.[46]

In any case, a joint American-National League committee consisting of Comiskey, Ruppert, Griffith, Mack, Dunn, and Quinn from the American League and Veeck, Ebbets, Herrmann, Dreyfuss, and Breadon from the National traveled across town by taxi to the Federal Building where Landis was trying an income tax case involving a $15,000 bribe. Later they would be joined by every other owner save for the recalcitrant Ball.

They most likely expected Landis to recess his court and to welcome them and the huge salary they were bringing. He did nothing of the sort, and while waiting they began to talk among themselves in the back of the courtroom.

Landis soon established what sort of commissioner he would be. "There'll be less noise in this courtroom," he barked, "or I will order it cleared."[47]

Only when the bribery case finished—45 minutes after the magnates had first arrived—did Landis finally acknowledge his visitors' presence. "Will you gentlemen wait for me in my chambers?" he asked.

It was only appropriate that Chicago owners Veeck and Comiskey spoke for the group. "It will make us very happy if you will accept and serve us," they said.

Landis had been expecting this moment for weeks, if not months. It moved him visibly, yet one thing held him back. He truly gloried in his judgeship. He could not bear to give it up. He was almost about to say no. "I love my work here as judge," he told his visitors, "and I am doing important work in the community and the nation."

"Why not keep your position on the bench and accept our offer, too?" one owner asked.

Landis silently pondered his options. "The work will not call for much time," another offered.

Landis thought aloud that he had a few free days each month he could offer to the commissionership. And to himself, he must have noted that all federal courts shut down from June to mid-September, a very convenient recess for the baseball season.[48]

That was enough. He was back in the fold—if he had indeed ever left it. "Gentlemen," he pronounced, "we need go no further with this thing. I accept. But if I am to remain on the bench I desire to deduct my federal salary from the original amount you offer me." In this Landis was less altruistic than he appeared, for he immediately regained the $7,500 he had so cheerfully surrendered by requiring a $7,500 expense account on which, of course, he would pay no income taxes. Since steep wartime rates had not yet been repealed, this was not a negligible factor.[49]

In any case, Landis had said yes, and the owners let out a whoop. As they did—and as if by prearranged signal—reporters and photographers massing outside burst into the Squire's chambers. Among them were men from the newsreels. For their benefit Harry Frazee, theatrical producer that he was, pumped the new High Commissioner's hand, striking up an animated stage conversation. The cameramen wanted the other owners to join in, and they did. All that is, except Connie Mack, who was heard to mutter about the silliness of the whole process.

A beaming Landis went out of his way to point out his son Reed's propeller hung suspended from a corner of his chamber (Reed had recently provided the Judge with his first grandchild, a daughter Nancy. When Reed called him long distance to tell him the news, Landis responded, "Oh, well, we can't all have boys.") "That drove the airplane which carried my boy back from the German lines more than one hundred times," the Squire boasted. "Isn't that a splendid memento to have?

"He served on the British front," he revealed, as his eyes fairly gleamed with pride. "The British war report gives him credit for bringing down twelve airplanes and a balloon, while the American report credits him with nine airplanes. He was ready to go and he was a fine soldier."[50]

The Judge continued, "Don't you know, gentlemen, that my son is a bug on baseball and he has been writing me about four letters a week with all kinds of reasons why I should take the job if it was offered. Why, during the world series at Brooklyn he and I sat beside each other and he pointed to the vast crowd and said: 'Dad, there are millions of little kids who get just as much fun and are made just as happy by clean baseball as those folks do in this crowd of men and women. Oughtn't something be done to keep the good old game from being taken away from them? Should they be robbed of the game?' [51]

"Well," Landis declared, "while you gentlemen were talking to me I saw the propeller from Reed's old Army plane up there on the wall, and I remembered what he said." He paused dramatically before concluding, "Griff, we've got to keep baseball on a high standard for the kids. That's why I took the job, because I want to help."[52]

And what of Winifred Landis' reaction? "I haven't told Mrs. Landis yet," the Judge admitted, "but she will learn it before I get home, I guess. And, gentlemen, I'm going over to New York in a few days and tell my new, little granddaughter the news."[53]

To the press he made the following statement: "I have accepted the chairmanship of baseball on the invitation of the 16 major league clubs. At their request and in accordance with my own earnest wishes I am to remain on the bench and continue my work here. The opportunities for real service are limitless. It is a matter to which I have been devoted for nearly 40 years. On the question of policy, all I have to say is this: 'The only thing in anybody's mind now is to keep baseball what the millions of fans throughout the United States want it to be.'"[54]

Having finished his statement that the only thing that mattered was the fans' opinions, he turned to his new bosses for approval. "Is that all right, boys?" he asked. They said it was fine. Little did they know, it was the last time he would be concerned with their approval.[55]

In another Chicago courtroom sat Charles McDonald. The newspapers still carried reports he would be part of the new three-person National Commission. But Ban Johnson must have informed him that no appointment would be coming his way. As Landis received baseball's ownership, McDonald greeted another delegation, of 12 South Side boy scouts. They stood at stiff attention, while one presented McDonald with a resolution saluting his "good turn" for "maintaining the ideals of our national game."

It would be the last recognition he would receive for having helped expose baseball's greatest scandal.[56]

That evening Ban Johnson visited the Congress Hotel to learn firsthand of what had transpired. As disappointing as the outcome was, the battle was over—for now at least. He looked more relaxed than he had in months, and even managed a smile as he told reporters, "It is very satisfactory to me."[57]

Johnson continued, "I am for Judge Landis and I think these club owners have acted wisely. Baseball will be placed on the highest possible standard now, and there will be no more fights. I am well satisfied ..."[58]

Then he dictated a congratulatory letter to Landis and, in Phil Ball's company, left for New Orleans and a badly needed hunting trip.

One especially jubilant onlooker to Landis' appointment was a Chicago bootlegger who jumped to the conclusion Landis would now be leaving the federal bench.

"Congratulations, Judge, congratulations," he beamed. "Great news indeed. Greatest thing ever happened to sport. Just the man they needed. Only thing about it is that it takes you away from the bench. . . . Too bad you got to quit. . . ."

"I don't have to quit the bench," Landis set him straight, "I'm not going to quit."

The rum runner's face drained. He could not even speak at first, then muttered, "Aw, hell."[59]

# CHAPTER 12

# "REGARDLESS OF THE VERDICT OF JURIES..."

Almost universally positive reaction greeted Landis' appointment. Bolstering that popularity was his no-nonsense stance toward the eight accused Black Sox. "There is absolutely no chance for any of them to creep back into Organized Baseball," he proclaimed two weeks after his selection. "They will be and remain outlaws. .... It is sure that the guilt of some at least will be proved."[1]

He also took pains to discover the *hidden* background of the Black Sox scandal—and how its behind-the-scenes scheming might impact him. On December 1 Landis phoned Charles Comiskey's spy, Edward Fleming, and set up an appointment for the following day. At that meeting Fleming revealed all of Johnson's machinations in placing the scandal before Judge McDonald's grand jury. An infuriated Landis pledged to investigate further, specifically to track down whatever telegrams had been sent by Johnson and his allies. According to Harry Grabiner's diaries, Landis "said it was a hell of a state of affairs when a judge on the bench could be secured to work with a matter of this kind ..." Johnson, he determined, was a "sonofobitch."[2]

But while Landis plotted against Johnson, Johnson schemed against Landis.

Later that month American League and National League representatives met in New York to draw up a new National Agreement. Major league owners, previously stiff-necked with pride, were still frightened that the public might turn against their now-sullied game. Accordingly they agreed to be "bound" by Landis' decisions and even to refrain from challenging them in courts. A key section of the new agreement provided the Squire with the power "to investigate, either upon complaint or upon his own initiative, any act, transaction, or practice ... suspected to be detrimental to the best interests of the national game of baseball" and to take action based on his investigation. It was a grant of unprecedented power over the game.

Johnson, however, moved to substitute the words "recommend action " for "take action," thus making Landis essentially powerless. Barney Dreyfuss had warned the Judge of Johnson's actions. As the new agreement's text was read, Landis was ready and barked his protest. "You have told the world that my powers are to be absolute," he complained. "I wouldn't take this job for all the gold in the world unless I knew my hands were free." He would leave the room, he coldly informed the owners, so they might discuss the matter among themselves, but he knew what their answer would be. Having gone this far, they could not afford to have their savior walk away at the last minute. Even Ban Johnson realized that. When Landis returned, it was Johnson himself who moved that "recommend" be amended to read "take."[3]

Beyond this huge grant of power, the owners also vowed never to publicly criticize Landis' rule, signing this unprecedented oath of fealty:

> We, the undersigned, earnestly desirous of insuring to the public wholesome and high class baseball, and believing that we ourselves should set for the Players an example of sportsmanship which accepts the umpire's decision without complaint, hereby pledge ourselves loyally to support the Commissioner in his important and difficult task; and we assure him that each of us will acquiesce in his decisions even when we believe them mistaken and that we will not discredit the sport by public criticism of him and of one another.[4]

Landis was now dictator of baseball, and his rule would set the pattern for the rule of other industries under fire. When the film industry came in for criticism, they turned to Will Hays to be their Landis. To magnates wishing to regain favor while avoiding federal regulation it seemed like a good bargain.

In January 1921 the Judge conferred with White Sox secretary Harry Grabiner, wanting to know about the worst of the game's dark underside. He, no doubt, probably met with others on this topic but this is the only such session we know about. Grabiner provided him with a list of 27 suspected players. Of these only three names are known to history: Grover Cleveland Alexander, Rabbit Maranville, and Gene Packard, whom Grabiner noted as "1918 Series fixer."

It is through Bill Veeck that we know of the contents of Harry Grabiner's diaries, and in revealing this episode Veeck provides us perhaps the most rational explanation for at least some of the "inconsistency" in Landis' baseball decisions—an inconsistency that has puzzled every student of the game. Why did Landis punish some— such as Buck Weaver—with such finality but deal with other players so easily?

Veeck explained that the problem is one of perception—our perception of Landis' actions are woefully skewed. We expect him to be flamboyant and to overreact—and when he does not do so we are flummoxed. But, as Veeck points out:"Instead of setting out to be the knight on white horseback, which is exactly what his critics have always accused him of doing, he did no more than the bare minimum that was necessary."

*The bare minimum that was necessary.* In other words, from the very beginning of his tenure, Landis could have exiled two or three dozen crooked players. In doing so, however, he would have tied the game up in legal red tape and sunk it in the morass of scandal. Instead, he banned players who were outwardly scandalous and discreetly packed a few other crooks off to oblivion. Just as Charles Comiskey realized that exposure would wreck his ballclub, Landis realized that too much exposure could wreck what was now *his* sport. He was not about to voluntarily put himself out of business any more than Comiskey was. Only Ban Johnson saw it differently—and he would pay a terrible price for his single-mindedness. "As for the rest of it," as Veeck summed up, "[Landis] simply drew a line between the present and the past, granting an amnesty—if not necessarily immunity—to all who had sinned under the previous regime."[5]

Such a policy had immediate benefits. Despite dire predictions of the game's demise, attendance remained reasonably strong during 1921.[6] The turnaround in public perception from the darkest days of the scandal had been singularly quick. "Unusually large crowds at all of the major league games indicate that the public's confidence has been restored," John Heydler boasted in early June, i.e., *even before* the Black Sox trial had started. "The sport has been made clean through the efforts of Judge Landis and no further trouble is expected."[7]

Landis' first major decision did not involve the Black Sox; their time would come later. He had to choose an assistant—and one he could trust.

He received no shortage of suggestions. Harry Grabiner tried cajoling Landis into appointing Tip O'Neill, a White Sox official, as his secretary. Landis, however, wanted no assistant with other loyalties. In Grabiner's words, the Squire would not accept "anyone who has ever had any baseball affiliation or connections with any one side."[8]

At one point Landis offered the job to John H. Farrell, secretary-treasurer of the National Association since its founding in 1901, but Farrell turned him down. John Heydler then recommended *Spalding Guide* editor John B. Foster. "A number of men were suggested to me," Landis later recalled, "but after Farrell rejected the job, I didn't want anyone representing some particular faction in baseball, I wanted a Landis man, and I got such a man in O'Connor."[9]

That was Leslie O'Connor, a talented, 31-year-old Chicago attorney.[10] "I picked Attorney O'Connor," Landis revealed, "not only for his personal character but also because I know he is not interested in baseball except as a sport and a recreation. He has no financial interest in the game, but has the qualifications that I think are needed to handle the job." O'Connor would remain with Landis throughout his entire commissionership, often writing many of the Judge's decisions, but never overstepping his authority.[11]

Landis' first case did not concern the Black Sox, but it did involve two men who would become two of his most implacable foes: the Browns' Phil Ball and the Cardinals' Branch Rickey. At issue was first baseman Phil Todt, signed in 1919 by Rickey when he was just 17 years old and then "covered up" for two seasons with Sherman of the Class D Western Association and Houston of the Texas League.

In 1920 Todt signed a Browns' contract, but the Cardinals fought the deal. On February 22, 1921, Landis awarded Todt to the Browns. The case had been pending before the old National Commission since March of the previous year. "Todt," Landis ruled, "was a free agent when signed by the St. Louis American League club in whom clear title was invested."

"Legally Judge Landis is correct," Rickey admitted. But he still argued his club should have Todt on "moral grounds," perhaps the last instance until the Jackie Robinson signing when Rickey approached a personnel transaction on that basis.[12]

Meanwhile, the Black Sox case was slouching toward trial. On February 14, 1921, the eight accused White Sox players were arraigned before Judge William Dever. Now, the trio of Cicotte, Jackson, and Williams did an about-face and denied ever admitting to fixing games or conspiring to fix them. Ban Johnson was becoming increasingly nervous about the chances of breaking the case wide open. In March his attorney George F. Barrett entered Dever's court. He demanded a six-month adjournment. Dever refused to grant it; the trial was to begin on March 14.

Nonetheless, the case was going nowhere fast and the baseball season was about to begin. Landis had originally taken the position he would not act while the matter remained in court: "Don't you think," he observed, "it would be an injustice to players who are facing trial on criminal charges for the baseball commission to take any action in the matter in the place where the jurors who are to try the case will be chosen?"

But the fact that the White Sox—who he knew full well to be guilty—might play in the upcoming season caused him to change his tune. "I deeply regret the postponement of these cases," he announced on March 13, the day before the trial was to begin. "However, baseball is not powerless to protect itself. All the indicted players have today been placed on the ineligible list." Suddenly it occurred to Charles Comiskey that Landis might prove as dangerous to his fortune as Ban Johnson—and there would be even less he could do about it. The realization provoked Comiskey into a fit of one-upmanship. The White Sox owner now announced he was granting the Black Sox their unconditional release.[13]

Just after suspending the Black Sox, Landis struck again, banning Phillies first baseman Eugene Paulette for life. In 1919 Paulette, a light-hitting but versatile journeyman, had been with the Cardinals. In St. Louis he kept company with local gamblers Carl Zork (a gambler connected with 1919 Series fix) and Elmer Farrar. From Farrar Paulette borrowed an undisclosed amount of money but never bothered to repay the "loan." At that point Farrar and Zork approached the first baseman about throwing games. Instead of informing his superiors, Paulette wrote Farrar asking for more cash and naming two players (unknown to this day) whom he thought would cooperate in fixing Cardinal contests.

Supposedly, no games were thrown and no further "loans" came Paulette's way. In July St. Louis traded him to the Phils. Paulette's letter to Farrar somehow fell into official hands. At first Philadelphia Club president William F. Baker took Paulette at his word that no games had actually been fixed, but he remained uneasy about his new player. Now that Landis was in office, Baker, a former New York

City police commissioner, turned Paulette's incriminating letter over to him.[14]

The Judge summoned Paulette to Chicago for a March 7 hearing on the matter. Paulette denied associating with any "corrupting influences" but refused Landis' request for another meeting. On March 24 the Squire issued a terse decision, concluding "Paulette denies he had ever thrown a ball game and asserts that during the last playing season he held himself aloof from corrupting associations; but the fact remains that he offered to betray his team and that he put himself in the vicious power of Farrar and Zork. He will go on the ineligible list.

"My only regret," Landis explained to reporters, "is that the real culprits, the gamblers, cannot be reached by this office."[15]

Landis followed up the Paulette ruling with perhaps his least-popular decision—the banishment of Cincinnati righthander Ray Fisher. Fisher had compiled a mere 10-11 record in 1920, and the parsimonious Reds mailed him a contract cutting his annual salary by $1,000 to just $4,500. Fisher didn't like the terms but signed anyway.

Shortly afterward, the University of Michigan offered him a coaching job at $5,000 annually, and he was inclined to take it. Garry Herrmann now offered the pitcher a raise, but Fisher raised the ante, demanding a two-year contract. Herrmann refused, and Fisher took the coaching job. Herrmann allegedly promised to place him on the voluntarily retired list, which was reported in the daily press.

Shortly thereafter, the situation grew even more complicated. Cardinals manager Branch Rickey offered Fisher a job as pitching coach and spot reliever for St. Louis when the college baseball season closed—contingent, of course, on Cincinnati granting Fisher his unconditional release.

Fisher was certainly in demand that spring. At virtually the same time Rickey tendered his offer, an outlaw club in Franklin, Pennsylvania, approached Fisher. Franklin, part of an obscure two-team "league," employed several blacklisted players. They offered him $750 per month.

Fisher wrote Herrmann, requesting his release, but Herrmann refused to cooperate. He had as yet taken no action on placing the righthander on the voluntary retired list. Instead, he relegated him to the ineligible list. Not only had Fisher violated a signed contract, Herrmann pointed out, he had not even provided the Reds with 10 days' notice that he was leaving.

Fisher truculently wrote Herrmann: "Do not for one minute think I am begging of you to give me a position this summer. I simply want to know if you wish my services. If so, I am very willing to work for you. If not, I wish you [would] let me know so I can accept other propositions."

Herrmann did not bother with a response, and Fisher took no further action until May 21. On that day his University of Michigan team was in Chicago to play the University of Chicago. By coincidence Michigan was staying at the Auditorium Hotel, where Landis still maintained temporary offices. Without benefit of appointment, Fisher dropped in on Landis. The Judge was in the process of moving to his permanent quarters in the People's Gas Building but took time out to listen.

He listened—but made no commitment beyond saying he would investigate the matter. A week and a half later, Fisher phoned Landis from Ann Arbor. The Judge responded that he had been informed that Fisher was to play for the Franklin outlaw club. Fisher admitted that Franklin had called him. He concluded with the veiled threat, "Baseball's my livelihood and if you blacklist me, I'm going to have to play somewhere."

Landis then contacted Reds manager Pat Moran for information. Moran responded that despite Fisher's testimony to the contrary Moran had never given him permission to visit Ann Arbor. That was all Landis needed. He fired off a brief telegram to Fisher informing him he was permanently ineligible. Fisher responded by calling Franklin: he would report to the outlaws immediately.[16]

The Fisher ruling is Landis' most unpopular among baseball historians. Lee Allen called it "one of his inexplicable decisions"; Daniel Ginsburg termed it an "injustice"; Harold Seymour found it "incomprehensible."

Yet while Seymour found it "incomprehensible," he was able to postulate a reason for Landis' action. "Apparently," wrote Seymour, "Fisher's crime was his independent attitude in exercising a choice of employment outside baseball." Seymour's theory coincided with economist Richard Nardinelli's belief that the case was an early example of Landis preventing players from using the leverage of outside employment to gain better wages. Landis, the old "trust-buster," was now in charge of preserving America's favorite cartel.

Nardinelli's theory may be true, but other factors were at work. First off, Landis had no use for players who would perform with or against blacklisted players, as Dickey Kerr and Hippo Vaughn would also soon discover. He also had no use for liars. In this case, the Judge took Pat Moran's word over Ray Fisher's. *Ipso facto*, in Landis' mind, Fisher was a liar.

As it was, Landis never reinstated Fisher, although Fisher believed that had he formally reapplied he would have won reinstatement. In this he was most likely correct. In early 1921 southpaw Phil Weinert jumped the Phillies, causing Landis to suspend him for five years (raising of course the question of why Fisher earned a *lifetime* penalty, which in Seymour's eyes is the "incomprehensible" part). In 1922 Weinert applied for reinstatement, and his request was promptly granted.[17]

In the first year of his commissionership, Landis also had his hands full with the New York Giants. During the 1921 season he would repeatedly have to deal with John McGraw's team, in the process setting all sorts of precedents—and not all of them consistent.

The first involved New York outfielder Benny Kauff, the erstwhile "Ty Cobb of the Federal League."

Kauff was no shrinking violet. He sported gaudy, expensive suits and extravagant diamond jewelry and was known to carry $6,000 on his person, a sum equivalent to his annual salary.

After the Federal League folded, Kauff landed with the Giants, and while no one ever called him the "Ty Cobb of the National League," twice he managed to hit better than .300.

Kauff had other interests than baseball, however. The diminutive southpaw loved automobiles. He drove "a big ninety horse power car" and in partnership with Giants pitcher Jesse Barnes went into the tire business on New York's Columbus Avenue. Kauff may, however, have been involved in other automotive transactions—and with less savory associates. In February 1920 New York City police arrested Kauff for auto theft.

Two Kauff employees, both ex-convicts, told of dining with him on Broadway on the evening of December 8, 1919 and how he informed them of an "order" he had for a late model Cadillac. When the trio finished eating, they went outside, finding a Cadillac on West End Avenue. They made off with it, changed its tires and repainted it before selling it for $1,800—a sum they allegedly split three ways.[18]

Soon new charges arose against Kauff. Ban Johnson told the *Chicago Tribune* that Arnold Rothstein had informed him that Kauff and a Rhode Island gambler named Henderson had sought $50,000 from Rothstein to fix the 1919 World Series. That was not the first time Kauff had been linked to the fix. Billy Maharg had told the Black Sox grand jury that Kauff had been involved in throwing the Series.

And there was more. An already banned player, former Giant catcher Heinie Zimmerman, the goat of the 1917 World Series, boasted to Landis in an affidavit that he had successfully bribed Kauff and pitchers Rube Benton and Fred Toney to throw the last game of the 1919 season. Toney denied being in on the fix, although he did admit that Zimmerman had attempted to give him $200 to throw the game in question. McGraw, perhaps trying to protect Kauff, also dismissed Zimmerman's account. "I have no time to waste," he scoffed, "on a statement made by a confessed crook."[19]

Kauff played the entire 1920 season under indictment for auto theft, and went south to San Antonio, Texas, with the Giants the following spring. At that point Landis summoned Kauff to Chicago for a hearing to give his version of events. Two weeks later he placed Kauff on the ineligible list. While conceding that an indictment "does not imply guilt," he, nonetheless, found that "an indictment charging felonious misconduct by a player certainly charges conduct detrimental to the good repute of baseball." *The Sporting News*, perhaps taking its cue from Johnson, applauded the Judge's ruling as "refreshing evidence of the new moral consciousness in Organized Baseball."

What seemed to anger Landis more than the accusation itself was the 13-month stall in bringing the case to trial—a delay caused in part by Kauff, a tactic which had enabled him to play the entire 1920 season. Landis clearly had had enough.[20]

Coincidentally or not with Landis' suspension, justice now accelerated as Kauff's attorneys (who included former New York City magistrate and future Braves owner Emil Fuchs) argued to the court that without any baseball income, further delay would "seriously menace the player's means of livelihood." Kauff's case now magically appeared on the court's "preferred" calendar. In May 1922 the case went to trial in General Sessions. Kauff's former employees testified that he had assisted them in auto theft. Nonetheless, the jury seemed more impressed with Kauff's list of character witnesses, which included McGraw, Jesse Barnes (who nonetheless testified he received and later resold another car from Kauff which proved to be stolen), former National League president John K. Tener, and star Giants outfielder George Burns. Kauff, who claimed he had a legitimate bill of sale for the Cadillac, had his wife testify that she had dinner with him on the night in question. On Friday, May 13, 1921, after deliberating for less than an hour, the jury acquitted Kauff of all charges.[21]

Acquittal did not translate into reinstatement. Despite Kauff's protests he remained out of the game. Landis simply wasn't impressed by Kauff's trial.[22] On August 25, 1921, he wrote Kauff: "the evidence in the Bronx County case disclosed a state of affairs that more than seriously compromises your character and reputation.

"The reasonable and necessary result of this is that your mere presence in the line-up would inevitably burden patrons of the game with grave apprehension as to its integrity."[23]

To sportswriter Fred Lieb he was only slightly more blunt. "I read every line of testimony," he fumed, "and the acquittal smells to high heaven. That acquittal was one of the worst miscarriages of justice that ever came under my observation."[24]

In September Kauff obtained an injunction from Supreme Court judge Isadore Wasservogel against Landis, the Giants, and the National League, requiring them to reinstate the player.

"I say I am every inch as much a gentleman, and have as high a sense of ethics and character as this man Landis," Kauff told reporters, "who has no standing as far as I am concerned, and who has maliciously and cunningly conspired to further his position at my expense without regard to conscience, standing or duty."[25]

Landis and his fellow defendants appealed, arguing that Kauff had no grounds to obtain reinstatement but should instead sue for breach of contract and back wages. In January 1922, a New York appeals court overturned Judge Wasservogel's injunction. "An apparent injustice has been done the plaintiff," ruled Supreme Court Judge Edward G. Whitaker, but "this court is without proper power to grant him the relief he asks, there being at this time no contract between him and the defendant."[26]

*The Sporting News* was again pleased. "The grounds for the decision may be technical," it editorialized, "but they satisfy."[27]

The following September Kauff dropped his suit. In view of comments made before Judge Whitaker it can only be assumed the defendants settled with Kauff for his lost 1921 wages.[28]

With Kauff out of the lineup as the 1921 season opened, the Giants needed to beef up their lineup. In Cincinnati a very talented player had become available.

That spring outfielder Edd Roush (a future Hall-of-Famer) and third baseman Heinie Groh (largely known today for his "bottle bat" but in his day a star player) both staged holdouts from the Reds. Roush soon capitulated, but Groh's walkout continued as the season opened, and 10 days following Opening Day he automatically landed on Landis' ineligible list. The third baseman had wanted a raise of $2,000 to $12,000 but informed Herrmann he was sick of playing in Cincinnati and would accept $10,000 if he were traded elsewhere. "This demand," ominously noted *Baseball Magazine*, "struck to the very heart of the reserve clause and entered into the dark and dubious field of mid-season player deals." Garry Herrmann began shopping his recalcitrant player around. The Pirates seemed interested in Groh's services, but in early June Herrmann received an acceptable offer from the Giants—$100,000 and three players for his recalcitrant third baseman. Only then did Groh sign his contract.[29]

He remained, however, on the ineligible list. Neither Groh nor Herrmann had counted on Landis obstructing the deal in this way. Players forcing trades from their old clubs were a long part of baseball tradition. A recent, controversial example had occurred in late 1919 when pitcher Carl Mays went from the Red Sox to the contending Yankees. Ban Johnson, acting from another long-standing baseball tradition—antipathy to deals bolstering contenders—attempted to block the deal. He not only failed to do so as both the Boston and New York clubs went to court [30] but in the process also made unyielding enemies of the two franchises in question.[31]

Landis and Johnson eventually disagreed on almost everything. But on the issue of players forcing trades through holdouts they were in concert. "Of course, this arrangement cannot be carried out," Landis ruled. "The suggestion that by the hold-out process a situation may be created disqualifying a player from giving his best service to a public that for years has generously supported that player and his team, is an idea that will receive no hospitality here. It is at war with the ABCs of sportsmanship and impugns the integrity of the game itself."[32]

Landis, nonetheless, approved Groh's reinstatement, but *only* "on the express condition . . . that Groh joins the Cincinnati team immediately and remains with it throughout the season."[33]

This enraged Groh. "I signed my contract with the Reds," he fumed to Cincinnati reporters, "with the distinct understanding that I was to be traded. What's more, August Herrmann gave me his word of honor I would be traded.

"By what right does Judge Landis presume to cancel such an

agreement? What right has Judge Landis to make me play where I don't want to play and to make me accept a salary I don't want to take?

"I won't play ball in this league. Not till Judge Landis gives a square decision. That isn't one sided and unjust.... Tell Judge Landis what I think about the whole affair."[34]

Herrmann admitted he had indeed promised Groh he would be traded, but neither the Giants nor the Reds, having just invested absolute power in their new employee, were about to challenge him. Groh saw the handwriting on the wall. Just two days after his outburst he was back at third with the Reds. He would have to wait until season's end to join New York, who had managed to win a World Championship without him—although his unavailability did cause them to go out and trade for an aging Casey Stengel ("Wake up muscles! we're in New York now"[35]). With Groh at third in 1922, '23, and '24, the Giants, who had surrendered George Burns and Mike Gonzales and $150,000 for Groh, captured three more pennants.[36][37]

Landis had succeeded in blocking trades of such holdouts where the once all-powerful Ban Johnson had failed—and the taboo continued as long as he was commissioner. The *Reach Guide* viewed Landis' ruling to be "unexpected and radical" but "on the whole satisfactory." The *New York Times* applauded the crackdown on personnel with "real or fancied grievances" and warned that Landis "might have gone even further" against recalcitrant players.

"It was charged by some of those opposing his election...." the *Times* noted, "that Judge Landis lacked the knowledge of baseball matters which would be needed for such a post, but his actions to date have not justified the contention. Going a bit farther than his predecessors in reaching sensible conclusions has been the story of Judge Landis ever since he has assumed charge of the sport."[38]

*Baseball Magazine* melodramatically intoned that "the strong hand of the high Commissioner has been laid with crushing force on a practice which has long menaced Major League baseball. Mid-season deals for cash are questionable under most circumstances. They are intolerable when dictated by the personal prejudice of the player."

Even Ty Cobb thought the decision was "just right."[39]

Meanwhile Landis was also taking direct aim at Giants club ownership. Following the 1919 season John McGraw and new Giants owner Charles Stoneham purchased Havana's Oriental Park racetrack and the Cuban American Jockey Club and Casino from Texas racetrack entrepreneur H. D. "Curly" Brown, who was cleaning up his affairs in anticipation of doing jail time for shooting a Cuban politician.

One of Landis' first official acts had been to order Stoneham and McGraw to divest themselves of their Havana holdings within the next six months. "It will have to be one or the other," the Judge informed the Giants' brain trust. "It can't be both."

McGraw should have been glad to rid himself of the operation. A passionate but woefully unsuccessful gambler, he managed to lose money even at his own track. Of McGraw, Frank Graham had written, "No man in a position to get inside information, much of it sound, ever made less use of that position."

Landis had his way. On July 13, 1921 Stoneham and McGraw sold their Havana gambling holdings to fellow New Yorker Thomas V. Monahan.

Soon afterward, however, Landis chastised Stoneham again—this time after the Giants' owner had entertained Arnold Rothstein in his private Polo Grounds box. Stoneham promised not to do it again.[40]

In August, Landis and the Giants tangled once more. This time he finally went easy on the club. Perhaps the issue wasn't clear-cut. Perhaps, like a bad umpire, Landis had decided to "even up" on his calls.

The case involved the July 25, 1921 trade of talented Phillies outfielder Emil "Irish" Meusel to the New York Giants for three marginal players and $30,000. Phillies owner William F. Baker claimed he could "no longer endure the sight of Meusel" whom he accused of malingering, and that he had suspended him for several days before the trade.

In-season trades to contenders were, of course, in popular disfavor, but the Meusel trade created a particularly bad taste in the public's mouth. Already that season—in trading Stengel—the penurious Baker, still a New York City resident, had aided the Giants. And there was more to pique Landis' interest. Shortly after the Meusel trade, Baker fired Phils manager Wild Bill Donovan, implying that Donovan, who had testified at the Black Sox trial, was unduly friendly with gamblers. With the Phillies posting a 25-62 record under Donovan, Baker hardly needed to make aspersions about gamblers.

Donovan, however, had a one-year contract and expected to be paid for the remainder of the season. He complained to Landis, who sent Leslie O'Connor to Philadelphia to investigate. During the course of the interview Donovan revealed that he had never reported

Meusel to Baker for "indifferent" play and that the player was never suspended.

Baker had clearly lied about why he had traded Meusel. His story was simply a cover for a trade designed to aid a contender. Landis was tempted to void the trade but thought better of the idea. He did, however, see that Donovan, whom he admired from his days as a White Sox pitcher, received payment for the balance of his contract.

The incident not only created a breach between Landis and Baker but between the Judge and Pittsburgh's Barney Dreyfuss, one of the earliest backers of his candidacy. Meusel had helped sink Pirates' pennant hopes as the Giants swept the Bucs in a five-game series, helping to obliterate their seven-and-a-half-game lead. Dreyfuss, confident of a pennant, had constructed new stands at Forbes Field to accommodate World Series crowds. He remained bitter about the Meusel trade for years.[41]

All the while the Black Sox case was proceeding. On March 14 a bombshell exploded when Assistant State's Attorney George Gorman announced that the confessions of Jackson, Cicotte, and Williams were missing. Ban Johnson charged that Arnold Rothstein had paid $10,000 for the missing papers, and he was no doubt right. Nonetheless, Rothstein threatened to sue Johnson for $100,000. "I hope he sues," Johnson smirked. "Then I can get him into court, and learn a few things I want to learn." Rothstein thought better of the idea.

Judge Dever tossed out the original indictments, and Gorman secured new ones (this time Fred McMullin was not among those charged). Criminal Court Chief Justice Charles McDonald now assigned the case to a young, Czech-born jurist named Hugo Friend.[42] Meanwhile, Johnson redoubled his efforts on the case, hiring detectives to secure new evidence and witnesses. He even tracked down Sleepy Bill Burns in Texas and cajoled him to travel to Chicago to testify. For his part, Landis maintained a discreet public silence. Privately, he was doing much the same thing. When Johnson demanded to know what he proposed to do about the case, the Squire responded, "Nothing," but as later events would prove he only meant nothing *for now*.

On Monday, June 27, 1921, the Black Sox trial finally began. Now not only the players' confessions were missing, so was Abe Attell. Once Attell had been itching to testify against Rothstein, but the "Big Bankroll" had gotten to him and even provided his own attorney, William "The Great Mouthpiece" Fallon, to keep Attell from being extradited from New York. Attell would never appear at the proceedings.

During the trial some of the intrigue surrounding the case was revealed. Who was paying for the players' high-priced 12-man defense crew? Was it Rothstein? Was it Comiskey? Both had their reasons for wanting the case to die. Even more suspiciously, four of the defense's battery of 12 lawyers had switched sides from the prosecution. Fingers were now pointed in all directions. An attorney for the gamblers on trial pointed to collusion between Rothstein and Albert Austrian. Austrian had joined Rothstein's legal team and even escorted the gambler to the original grand jury proceedings. Counsel for the players even contended it was Johnson who had maneuvered to leave Rothstein out of the indictment. Once Johnson had wrecked Comiskey, it was alleged, he had no interest in touching the real guilty parties.[43]

This sordid trial finally came to a close at 7:52 PM on Tuesday, August 2. In his charge to the jury, Friend pointed out that in order to find the defendants guilty, the jury must be convinced that their intent was not merely to throw games but to defraud the public. With such instruction it took the jury only two hours and 45 minutes to find the defendants not guilty. A crowd of 500 enthusiastically cheered this miscarriage of justice. Even the bailiffs joined in—as the *Reach Guide* pointed out, "without being checked by Judge Friend." Then both the defendants and their lawyers and the jury adjourned separately to a nearby Italian restaurant. Once there all parties celebrated as one big happy family.[44]

If the baseball public had not previously suspected the power of gamblers, they now were all too familiar with it. Into the breach stepped Landis. "Regardless of the verdict of juries," he announced, "no player that throws a ball game; no player that undertakes or promises to throw a ball game; no player that sits in a conference with a bunch of crooked players and gamblers where the ways and means of throwing games are planned and discussed and does not promptly tell his club about it, will ever play professional baseball.

"Of course, I don't know that any of these men will apply for reinstatement, but if they do, the above are at least a few of the rules that will be enforced. Just keep in mind, regardless of the verdict of juries, baseball is entirely competent to protect itself against crooks, both inside and outside the game."[45]

Landis' terse two paragraphs did for him what "There is no right to strike against the public safety by anybody, anytime, anywhere" had done for Calvin Coolidge just two years earlier. Landis became a national hero, the guardian of public virtue, a man the public could trust to do the right thing. Players might fail, owners might fail, juries might fail, but Landis had finally brought justice—and closure—to the matter.

And he had shown once more that he would stand independent of any owner. Comiskey had been one of his original backers. Now, he had wrecked Comiskey's club far more neatly and decisively and on better grounds than Ban Johnson had ever dared to do. And, of course, Comiskey was just the latest magnate to feel Landis' lash. Charles Stoneham had backed Landis' candidacy—Landis had stripped him of a racetrack, a casino, and (for a while anyway) Heinie Groh. Barney Dreyfuss was the first owner to back the Lasker plan— Landis let the Meusel trade go through. Another early backer was William Baker—Landis sided with Bill Donovan. Here was a commissioner bigger than any owner.

The *New York Times'* reaction to Landis' Black Sox verdict was typical. It editorialized approvingly: "the new High Commissioner is not much troubled by that respect for quibbles and technicalities which is the Western idea of justice. He goes straight to the essential rights and wrongs in the good old Oriental manner—the manner of Haroun-Al-Raschid."[46]

Decades later, even Branch Rickey—never a Landis fan—would have to admit: "At no point did he temper justice with mercy. And today who is there to say that he did not act wisely?"[47]

Rickey may not have realized what truth he spoke. Landis' Black Sox decision was the most important of his commissionership. In 1920 professional football and basketball barely existed—let alone were powerful enough to challenge baseball's supremacy. But another sport *did* rival the sport in popularity—boxing. In the years that followed, baseball maintained, even *increased*, its popularity largely because it maintained (or more accurately *recovered*) its good name. Boxing, on the other hand, went down another road toward shady deals and fixed bouts. It became a sport that could not be trusted. Where once boxing matches were seen on a regular basis— not only in every big city but in most small towns as well—eventually the squared circle found refuge in a strange and unhealthy dichotomy of grimy inner city clubs and multi-million-dollar matches in Las Vegas.

Baseball could have gone down a similar road. In the flash of Landis' Black Sox decision, it did not.

Just after the Black Sox suspension, Landis struck again against a Chicago player, but this time his target was a Cub, and the case had little to do with gambling.

The Cubs' 6'4" Jim "Hippo" Vaughn was one of the finest south-paws of his era. In five different seasons, he won 20 or more games. His lifetime ERA sparkled at 2.49. In 1920 Vaughn's record stood at just 19-16, but his ERA remained strong at 1.79.

The following summer was not as productive—a 3-11 mark with an abysmal 6.01 ERA. Cubs manager Johnny "The Crab" Evers sus-pended Vaughn for breaking training during a trip east. During his suspension Vaughn, under an assumed name, pitched a game for a Kenosha semi-pro club. The Squire responded by branding him ineli-gible for contract violation. On hearing of Landis' action, Vaughn promptly signed a three-year deal at $6,900 per year with another out-law team, the Fairbanks Morse team of Beloit, Wisconsin (a.k.a. the Beloit Fairies), a club that normally employed ineligible personnel.

Cubs general manager William L. Veeck, probably glad to be rid of a rapidly failing pitcher, took no issue with Landis' decision. "While we are sorry to lose the services of Vaughn, whose work we could use . . . handily," Veeck contended, "Judge Landis is the boss and whatever he says goes."

Nonetheless, not everyone approved. In the *Chicago Tribune*'s "In the Wake of the News" column, the Judge was blasted as "ap-pointed and paid by the owners."

"Vaughn," it was alleged, "would do what every liberty loving American would do in like circumstances."

The pitcher continued in the semi-pro ranks, with Chicago's crack Logan Squares and Mills teams, until he was well over 40. Only then did he apply to Landis for reinstatement. The Judge, no doubt amused that someone of Vaughn's age wanted reinstatement, replied that the same rule applied to Vaughn as to anyone: he must first cease playing on teams employing or playing ineligible players for a full season before applying. Vaughn did, and in November 1930, Landis finally reinstated the 43-year-old southpaw.[48]

Landis was a busy man during the spring and summer of 1921, busier than most modern baseball fans could guess. Not only was he creating the commissionership, while retaining his federal judge-ship, he was spreading himself even thinner with other endeavors.

The early 1920s were a time of great economic readjustment, with deflation slashing wages in industry after industry. Chicago packing house workers saw their wages cut by 19 percent. United States Steel slashed salaries 40 percent. Road crews received a 45 percent decrease. Throughout the country unskilled labor saw pay envelopes lighten by between 22 and 52 percent.

In Chicago, contractors had tried imposing a 20 percent wage cut on workers. When unions balked, employers on May 1 locked out workers. To resolve the deadlock both sides agreed to submit differences to an "umpire with full power and authority to act and decide all questions involved."

On Friday, June 11, after the Chicago Building Trades Council rejected a list of 10 names submitted by the Building Construction Employers' Association of Chicago—and vice versa—both sides turned to Landis. The Judge was out of town when the announcement was made, at Crawfordsville, Indiana. He caught the first train back home, detrained at Chicago's Englewood Station, and headed for his apartment at the Chicago Beach Hotel where he met with union and management officials. He accepted the task, and between 20,000 and 25,000 workmen returned to work the following Monday.

Landis faced not only the issue of construction workers' wages but a host of other vexing problems, from jurisdictional disputes to arcane and unproductive work rules. Chicago's construction industry was sick, operating well below pre-war levels. Building costs and rents were high; families could not afford homes.

Landis issued his report on September 7. He cut wages an average of 12.5 percent and flayed the general state of the construction industry:

> It is the violation of no confidence to say that building construc-
> tion had gotten into bad repute in this community. There was a gen-
> eral disposition to keep away from it as a thing diseased. Capital
> avoided it. The wise dollar preferred almost any other form of activ-
> ity or no activity. And this applied to the whole range of building
> construction, from the cottage to the skyscraper.
>
> The attitude of the public, added to the profound commercial
> and industrial depression generally existent, resulted in a virtual
> famine in housing accommodations and brought about the idleness
> of many thousands of men willing to work.

But Landis recognized that an inflated cost of labor was not the only problem dogging the local construction trade:

> This loss of public confidence was not due entirely to the wage question. . . . The real malady lurked in a maze of conditions artificially created to give the parties a monopoly and in rules designed to produce waste for the mere sake of waste, all combining to bring about an insufferable situation, not the least burdensome element of which was the jurisdictional dispute between trade members of the same parent organization.

Accordingly he ended restrictions on labor-saving machinery and materials, standardized overtime rates, and curbed jurisdictional disputes. The unions carped ("Landis Soaks Workers"), but the decision had nationwide influence and was credited with helping revive the American construction industry. "It reads like an Emancipation Proclamation," exclaimed one Boston editor. "The average worker," noted the *Chicago Journal*, "can once more aspire toward the ownership of a home."[49]

In October 1921 Landis again attacked "gentlemen's agreements" and the already widespread covering-up of minor league players without proper paperwork. Striking at the Tigers, the Robins, and the Braves, the Judge declared six players free agents, including 20-year-old Heinie Manush, who had battled .321 with Edmonton in the Western Canada League. Manush was freed from the Tigers but resigned with them.[50]

After the 1921 World Series Landis nailed the baseball coffin shut on one more figure in the Black Sox scandal, former Browns second baseman Joe Gedeon. In 1920 Gedeon, a lifetime .244 batter, achieved his finest season, hitting .292. But Gedeon not only had knowledge of the Series fix, he sat in on a meeting with gamblers to discuss the plot. After Gedeon testified before the Black Sox grand jury, the Browns released him. No other club would touch him, and he spent the 1921 season outside the game.

Following the season, however, he began playing winter ball in California, performing against several Coast League players and at least one major leaguer. In late October PCL president William H. McCarthy learned that Gedeon would perform against such competition again on November 11. He wired Landis asking if Gedeon was ineligible or not.

On November 3 Landis banned Gedeon for life. Barred from the game, a bitter Gedeon turned to running a speakeasy near the Sacramento ballpark—until he lost his share after cutting cards. He moved to San Francisco where he worked tending bar. "I have the greatest job in San Francisco," he told a reporter. "They pay me $5 a day, I steal $5 a day and I drink $5 a day."

He died of liver disease at age 47.[51]

In early December 1921, Landis had an unlikely visitor to his office: Buck Weaver. By invitation Weaver had come to ask for reinstatement. Landis, as was his habit, was mannerly. "He was a funny man," Weaver told James T. Farrell years later. "He'd say, 'Sit down, sit down.'" He had that big box on his desk full of tobacco. He knew I chewed tobacco, too." He offered Weaver a chaw.

The presence of a court stenographer, however, indicated that Landis was not all friendliness and hospitality. Weaver informed the Squire that although he had needed money to open a drugstore with his brother, he had never taken any of the $10,000 bribe offered him and never done anything to throw down a game. Landis wanted to know why he hadn't told anyone of the plot. Weaver replied that informing just wasn't in him, and that since nothing had been said after the original offer,[52] he wasn't sure what was happening and who actually was involved. "I couldn't bring myself to tell on them, even had I known for certain," Weaver explained. "I decided to keep quiet and play my best."[53]

Landis gave no answer but said he'd respond by letter. Weaver's visit had occurred in secret, but a week later word of the session leaked out—most likely through Weaver. Landis, who had been laid up at home with a bad cold, still had not written back. Shortly thereafter, however, he released a statement to the press: "Birds of a feather flock together. Men associating with gamblers and crooks could expect no leniency."

Weaver was incensed. Landis, he later fumed, "didn't have the guts to tell me to my face." But years later when 14,000 Chicago and northern Illinois Masons petitioned Landis to reinstate their fraternal brother, the Commissioner provided his version of the session.

"I had Weaver in this office," he informed the visiting Freemasons. "I asked him 'Buck, did you sit in on any meeting to throw the 1919 World Series?' He replied, 'Yes, Judge, I attended two such meetings [a statement consistent with Harry Grabiner's evidence], but I took no money and played the best ball I am capable of.'

"So I told him anyone who sat in on such a meeting and did not report it was as guilty as any of the others. 'Buck, you can't play with us again.' That too, is my answer to you gentlemen."[54]

A year after Weaver's visit, Landis issued a formal report on the Weaver case:

> Indictments were returned against certain members of the team, including Weaver. On the trial of this case, a witness for the prosecution gave what he claimed was a detailed account of his meeting with the indicted men and arranging with them for the throwing of the world's series games.
>
> The report showed that Weaver was present in court during the testimony of this witness, who most specifically stated that Weaver was present at the conference, and yet the case went to the jury without any denial from Weaver from the witness stand.
>
> If the incriminating evidence was false, the baseball public had a right to Weaver's denial under oath. Of course, it is true that a verdict of not guilty was rendered in Weaver's favor. It was also likewise true that the same jury returned the same verdict in favor of Cicotte, Claude Williams and Joe Jackson.
>
> Weaver denies he had anything to do with the conspiracy as alleged in the confessions, which were introduced at the trial. However, his own admissions forbid his reinstatement.[55]

Often treated as a sentimental footnote to the larger Black Sox scandal, Landis' treatment of Buck Weaver ranks as important as any baseball decision he, or anyone else, ever issued.

The game was not "saved" when Landis banished obvious crooks like Gandil and Risberg and Cicotte. Nor did it become simon-pure because the dim-witted Joe Jackson was bounced for taking $10,000. Landis' most important action in the Black Sox case was his most controversial: banning Weaver.

Unlike Jackson, Weaver took no cash from gamblers. From all accounts it appears that he took no action to purposely throw the Series. Nor did he give his assent in any manner to the plot.

Landis knew all that. When he wrote that "no player that sits in a conference with a bunch of crooked players and gamblers where the ways and means of throwing games are planned and discussed and does not promptly tell his club about it, will ever play professional baseball" he was referring to the hapless Weaver.

Banning personnel who had thrown games was hardly groundbreaking. Ever since professional baseball had begun, players had known that crooked play would earn them a one-way ticket out of the game. Sometimes that had dissuaded hippodroming; sometimes it had not.

What Landis did in banning Weaver was to *ex post facto* place guilty knowledge of crooked play on the same level as the deed itself.

Landis ratcheted baseball's moral code up several notches, making it akin to West Point's Code of Honor.[56] If a player was found to simply *know* of a bribe attempt or conspiracy and did not report it he was finished. "It was rough justice . . . ," George Will, no particular fan of the Judge, once observed of his decision. "But roughness can make justice effective."[57]

Before 1920 if one player approached another player to throw a contest, there was a very good chance he would not be informed upon. Now, there was an excellent chance he *would* be turned in. No honest player wanted to meet the same fate as Buck Weaver. The Weaver decision had a great chilling effect on dishonest play—and *talk* of dishonest play. After Landis took control of baseball, only two new attempts at game-fixing took place at the major league level: the Shufflin' Phil Douglas case of 1922 and the O'Connell-Dolan affair of 1924. In both cases players approached to throw games almost instantly turned in their would-be seducers.

When Cardinals outfielder Les Mann informed on the pathetic drunk Douglas and when the Phils' Heinie Sand did the same to naive Jimmy O'Connell, the shadow of Buck Weaver was not only in evidence, it was lengthening to cover—and protect—all of baseball. Without the forbidding example of Buck Weaver to haunt them, it is unlikely Mann and Sand would have snitched on their fellow players. After Landis' unforgiving treatment of the popular and basically honest Weaver they dared not to. And once prospectively crooked players knew that honest players would no longer shield them, *the scandals stopped.*

# CHAPTER 13

# "THE MOST BOLSHEVIK DOCTRINE I EVER HEARD"

On Wednesday, February 2, 1921, Kenesaw Landis threw open the doors to the headquarters of his new commissionership, an office suite at Michigan Avenue's Auditorium Hotel.

On that same day, a chain of events began that threatened the credibility of his new position.

It concerned Landis' decision to remain on the federal bench. The issue had already ignited a flurry of criticism, dogging the new commissioner from the very beginning of his tenure. Instead of taking the matter seriously Landis ignored the issue. He was simply blind or pretended to be blind regarding the conflict of holding a $7,500 federal judgeship and the new $50,000 commissionership.

"If there's an impropriety here I haven't seen it . . . ," the Squire pointedly informed the Missouri Bar Association on December 4, 1920, while virtually daring Congress to remove him by saying, "There is a method by which a federal judge may be removed from office if he is unsatisfactory, and that is by impeachment. But they will never impeach me. If both houses of Congress by a majority vote pass a resolution expressing disappointment at my attempt to benefit 10,000,000 persons who have a whole hearted interest in baseball, I will send my resignation as a federal judge to Washington by telegram."[1]

The statement reeked of arrogance, but not everyone believed his position was based on insolence. Some saw it stemming from insecurity. He had entered a hornet's nest in taking the commissionership. He was not sure how badly he would be stung. "The Judge, in the beginning," Ban Johnson's confidential secretary Earl Obershain once noted, "was not so sure he could go along with the sort of magnates he had taken under his care, so that he kept an anchor to windward and held on to his job as judge . . ."[2]

There was some truth to that. Even the veteran baseball man

Cap Anson had warned that Landis' commissionership would not last "any great length of time." Ban Johnson, having lorded over baseball for nearly two decades, was not about to cede power quietly. His January 12 attempt to dilute the Squire's authority had failed— but it, nevertheless, had been made. Landis, despite his flinty exterior, may have been as beset by fears as any other man.[3]

Trouble was soon brewing. On January 15, 1921, Chicago attorney Thomas J. Sutherland petitioned the congressional delegation of Illinois, objecting to Landis' dual-position. It was not a quiet protest. Additionally, he wrote each Chicago newspaper warning of the Squire's "attempt to mulct the Government and also to set an example of vicious infidelity to public service."

Sutherland charged Landis with violating the spirit of federal statutes barring government employees from engaging in outside activities for pay:

> Judge Landis by his contract with the league [sic] has attempted to barter away what belongs to the Government and all the people, to an organization of a special few and to receive therefrom an office of profit in direct violation of the mandates of the Constitution and laws.
>
> Unfortunately, it has been done publicly and ostentatiously with all its vicious and demoralizing influences; and if his conduct is to remain unchallenged by Congress it will become an incentive to lawyers of a certain class to seek appointments to the federal bench with the purpose partly of doing precisely what he has done, to its degradation.[4]

Some theorized Sutherland acted on behalf of Ban Johnson. The *New York Globe*'s Harry Schumacher wrote that his colleagues saw the "fine Italian—or perhaps we should say the course Bulgarian—hand of Byron Bancroft Johnson" in the affair. They thought it suspicious Sutherland had acted only after Johnson's attempts to trim Landis' authority had failed.[5]

Landis maintained a nonchalant air, replying he had "looked into things well before accepting this baseball work" and that he felt he "did right in accepting the place offered me."[6] No petition or letter to the editor would scare Kenesaw Landis off the federal bench. But *impeachment* might.

No one from Illinois' congressional delegation paid much attention to Sutherland's missive, but on February 2, Ohio congressman Benjamin Franklin Welty introduced a resolution demanding an investigation of Landis' dual functioning as federal judge and "arbitrator of organized baseball."

Welty was a lame-duck Democrat backbencher. Elected in 1916 and defeated in the massive Harding landslide of 1920, he had not yet left office. Initially his action stirred little public interest, rating just a single paragraph buried on an inside page of the *New York Times*.[7]

Welty also queried Attorney General A. Mitchell Palmer concerning the legality of Landis' holding both jobs. Palmer replied on February 11, 1921, unequivocally upholding the Squire's right to moonlight from the federal bench. While the action might appear— and be—patently illegal by modern standards, in 1921 no one had yet bothered to pass a law to that effect.

Wrote Palmer:

> It is not a crime, either misdemeanor or felony. While it might be true that the Judge's duty as arbitrator[8] would take so much of his time as to interfere with the performance of his judicial duties, this, of course, would be a matter to be disposed of when such interference had actually occurred, and would probably be an objection only on that ground only. . .
>
> There seems to be nothing as a matter of general law which would prohibit a district judge from receiving additional compensation for other than strictly judicial service, such as acting as arbitrator or commissioner.
>
> The fact that the judge's acts as arbitrator might come up collaterally in the court of which he is a member, but does not affect his right to hold the position or perform the functions though it might make it improper for him to sit in the federal court in some particular case.

If Landis' actions *weren't* illegal, Welty would try to *make* them illegal. He must have anticipated Palmer's ruling, for on the same day he received the attorney general's answer he introduced legislation barring federal judges from accepting outside salaries. Welty also charged Landis with neglect of his judicial duties. "I received a telegram today from District Attorney Clyne at Chicago in which he states that there are approximately 1,230 cases in Judge Landis' docket," he noted to reporters. "At the same time I have received several complaints from attorneys who tell me their cases have been postponed."[9]

Reached for comment, Landis smugly replied that he "was not in the least bit interested" in the congressman or his actions. "I did notice that Attorney General Palmer said I wasn't a lawbreaker," he twanged, "but I have too many other things to do to bother about Mr. Welty."[10]

Landis appeared to have largely dodged Welty's bullet but on that same Friday, April 11, he stepped in front of an exploding shell. In Landis' court Francis J. Carey, a 19-year-old receiving teller with the National City Bank of Ottawa, Illinois, pled guilty to embezzling $96,500. Carey, the sole support of his mother and two sisters, earned just $90 a month from the bank. "I was troubled about the folks," he explained to the Judge. "I gave my mother my pay every month. I bought things for my two sisters, and to keep up the house it took all I made. At night when I was working overtime I got to wishing I had more money. Suddenly I thought how easy it would be to open the safe and escape before the bank officials arrived the following morning.

"I began to get scared as soon as I had opened the safe. The sight of so much money frightened me. Finally, I picked up all I could and wrote a note telling the officials I would not have taken the money if I had been better paid. Next day I realized what I had done and what it meant to my mother. I gave myself up."

Landis professed amazement at the lad's tale, took pity on him, and proceeded to excoriate the president of the National City Bank for underpaying him. "You should be in a position to pay this man more," he scolded. "I frankly criticize the bank. It placed temptation in this boy's path. Much of the responsibility is on the bank directors. I don't wish to send this boy to Leavenworth. I could not send him there today." Instead he ordered Carey to go home with his mother.[11]

Landis had pronounced an opinion at least once before in court. The previous April a postal clerk had pled guilty to stealing from the mail diamonds valued at $1,100. "Look at this man," Landis proclaimed. "He has two children to support. He works from 5:30 o'clock in the afternoon until 3 or 4 o'clock in the morning, and all he is paid by the government is $1,200 a year.

"I suppose I will have to send him to prison, but he has been working like a slave and getting only half of what he would get as private secretary to a hod carrier."[12]

In April no one noticed Landis' words, but in the Carey case they set off new congressional criticism—this time in the Senate. In the upper house Landis' primary accuser was South Carolina's Nathaniel Barkdale Dial, wealthy both from manufacturing and (most significantly) from banking, being president of two banks, the Enterprise National Bank and the Home Trust Company. "Any man who utters that kind of statement," Dial charged, "is not worthy of public confidence and should be impeached . . . .

"This is the most Bolshevik doctrine I ever heard in my life. If this goes unchallenged, it is an invitation to every employee in the United States who handles other peoples' money, if not satisfied with his salary, to takes what he wants."

It was, he noted, "anarchistic" and "revolutionary."[13]

Dial received support from Senator Charles S. Thomas, a 71-year-old Colorado Democrat who termed Landis "the most conspicuous crank now holding high position." He added it was probably Landis' new $50,000 income that fostered his contempt for the bank's low payscale.[14]

Thomas had crossed swords with Landis once before. Shortly after Armistice Day, the Judge had observed that most of the lawyers who appeared before him wearing wristwatches (a new-fangled and slightly effeminate innovation in many minds) had not seen service in the Great War.

"Have all these wrist-watch lawyers file a statement what branch of service they were in," Landis barked to his clerk.

Thomas, having heard of the remark, demanded even then that Landis be impeached. Landis was unimpressed by either Thomas or Dial. "Doesn't it beat the devil what some Senators will do to pass the time away?" he asked reporters.[15]

But Welty, Dial, and Thomas were not alone.[16] Many agreed with the *New York Post* that Carey was an odd recipient of Landis' sympathy, that he had gone far beyond mere stealing to support his family. "When Victor Hugo wished to show how society weighs down on the unfortunate he depicted Jean Valjean as spending half a lifetime in prison for stealing a loaf of bread for his sister's hungry children," it said in an editorial entitled "Wild Words From The Bench." "Between a loaf of bread and $96,500 there is a difference."[17]

Of course, not everyone disapproved of Landis' handling of the Carey matter. *The Sporting News* contended the Judge had received scores of messages and visitors urging him not to give in. He has, it noted, "more friends as a result of the attacks on him—even among conservatives who do not approve of his theories as he expresses them from the bench . . . than he had before." A Chicago Baptist Ministers conference passed a resolution of full support and contended that attacks on him resulted from his "fearless, rigorous and impartial application of the law."[18]

Landis also found support from the man on the street. One day on the way to the train station, he was stopped by a passerby.

"I want to shake hands with you for the way you handled that young bank thief Carey," said the man, who by his appearance was a common laborer. "We are proud of you in Chicago."

"I will try to see that you are not disappointed in the future," the Squire replied.

Turning to the reporter accompanying him, Landis exclaimed, "Great Lord! And they tell me that there is nothing in the approval of these people! Why, I would rather have the people of that man's type looking upon me as a man who would protect the public interest than have all the money in the world. I tell you that the greatest position any man can achieve is the one upon which his fellow man looks with approval. The meanest man in the world is the man who destroys the faith of any human being in anything."[19]

Lost in all the controversy was the fact that Landis had not actually sentenced Carey. Accordingly, Chicago attorney Edward Mayer pointed out that it was "highly improper" for Dial "to try to influence a court's judgment while a case is under advisement. But no lawyer who knows Judge Landis will believe he can be influenced in any manner." A former head of the Illinois Bar Association even warned Dial that except for his senatorial immunity he could be found guilty of contempt of court. "It hardly seems proper that when a judge has a sentence under consideration," noted Harry Standidge, "he should be subjected to possible intimidation by anything said by a United States senator, either on or off the floor."[20]

Landis was unusually eager to battle Dial—and not just to battle him, but to slash his jugular. The Squire launched his first attack at an American Legion convention in Des Moines, Iowa, on Saturday, February 12, attempting to turn the tables on the conflict-of-interest charges raised against him. "I think [Dial] had better get out of the banking business," he demanded, "or else get out of the Senate."[21]

He poured it on the next day at Chicago's Studebaker Theater where he addressed the Lincoln-Kosciuzko celebration of the Polish National Alliance. This time he accused Dial of exploiting child labor:

> Senator Dial has hundreds of little girls as young as 11 working for him. What is he paying the fellows in his banks and those children in his cotton mills? He could not stand an investigation of wage conditions in the institutions he owns. He is an owner of an industry in South Carolina, and it was this particular industry in South Carolina which caused repeal of the federal child-labor law.
>
> I don't condone stealing. The rub is that this Ottawa boy was getting only about half of what a carpenter or a section hand on the railroad is able to make. Senator Dial objects to my plain statement of the case. And remember, he is a United States Senator who will soon pass on his own taxes, those of the industry in which he competes in business.
>
> The Senator has seen fit to turn the spotlight on me. He attacks me for going slow in imposing a sentence upon a $90 a month clerk handling thousands of dollars daily.
>
> Now, I'd like to turn the spotlight on the Senator. He's a banker. I'll wager it would be cold meat for anybody investigating Senator Dial's pay-roll. The cotton mills of the south are notorious for the way they have underpaid their help. I would like to know what he pays his little girl employees.[22]

To the *Literary Digest* he continued his goading of Dial. "Pish-tush," he exclaimed. "Dial and Welty . . . demonstrate that I have a positive genius in the selection of enemies.

"As for Senator Dial, I have succeeded in performing the Herculean feat of dragging him from airtight obscurity."[23]

The Squire's broadsides incensed Dial. On February 14, 1921, he took the Senate floor to counterattack. He derided Landis as a "self-advertised crank and a freak" and again denounced his "most Bolshevik doctrine." He repeated Welty's charge that Landis had a huge backlog of cases, a backlog that would take two years to clear. But on at least one point Landis clearly had him on the defensive. "He tries to abuse the people of South Carolina for working children in cotton mills . . . ," Dial sputtered. The senator may also have lost ground when he let slip he had not "a very high regard for this professional baseball . . ."[24]

But the firestorm had only begun for Dial. Its next blast arrived on February 16, singeing not only him but his immediate family. On that date the nation learned (how the information was disclosed was not revealed) that the senator's own son had been the beneficiary of the sort of unrestrained mercy that Landis had hinted at in the Carey case.

In 1909, Naval authorities charged Dial's son, Lieutenant (junior grade) Haskell Dial, an officer in the supply corps, with financial irregularities. Dial Sr. used his influence, however, particularly with South Carolina's United States senator "Pitchfork Ben" Tillman (then the ranking Democrat on the Senate Naval affairs Committee). Dial's pull worked. On January 21, 1910 the Navy allowed Haskell Dial to resign "for the good of the service."

Senator Dial protested this had nothing to do with the Landis-Carey matter, and that he had no comment except that "nothing to the detriment of either father or son is involved in the matter."[25]

Meanwhile Welty moved toward actual impeachment. On February 14, 1921 he told the House:

> On March 3, 1917, the Sixty-Fifth Congress passed an act which, in part, provides, that:
>
> "No government official or employee shall receive any salary in connection with his services as such official or employee from any source other than the government of the United States . . ."
>
> I therefore impeach said Kenesaw M. Landis for high crimes and misdemeanors as follows:
>
> First. For neglecting his official duties for another gainful occupation not connected therewith.
>
> Second. For using his office as district judge of the United States to settle disputes which might come into his court, as provided by the laws of the United States.
>
> Third. For lobbying before the legislatures of the several states of the Union to procure the passage of state laws to prevent gambling in baseball, instead of discharging his duties as district judge of the United States.
>
> Fourth. For accepting the position of chief arbiter of the disputes in base ball associations at the salary of $42,500 per annum, while attempting to discharge the duties as a district judge of the United States, which tend to nullify the effect of the judgment of the Supreme Court of the District of Columbia and the baseball gambling indictments pending in the criminal courts of Cook County, Ill.

Fifth. For injuring the national sport of baseball by permitting the use of his office as district judge of the United States because the impression will prevail that gambling and other illegal acts in baseball will not be punished in the open forum, as in other cases.[26]

On February 21, 1921, before a Judiciary Committee subcommittee Missouri's William Igoe, another Democrat defeated in the 1920 landslide, inquired of Welty, "Have you any proof that Judge Landis has neglected the duties of his court?"

"I have not," Welty replied. "But I know he cannot give full time to his court, as required by law, and attend to his work under the contract with the baseball players." He claimed that major league players had bought off Landis: "I want to prove that these baseball players were guilty of bribing Judge Landis. You are not required to have a statutory law to try and convict Judge Landis of high crimes and misdemeanors. He is appointed during good behavior under the constitution and he can be removed for misbehavior."

Welty went on to provide evidence that one could remove a Federal judge even though he had committed no statutory offense, offering examples of a judge found drunk upon the bench in 1806, another in 1862 who went over to the Confederacy, another for "riding on a railroad without paying his fare" in 1904, and one in 1912 for "commercializing" his position.

James Ambrose Gallivan, a Boston Democrat who had taken James M. Curley's seat in Congress, announced that he had appeared to defend Landis, but seemed to have wasted his time "because there is no case presented against the judge."

Welty's charges received their first official consideration at a hearing of the House Judiciary Committee. Welty and Committee Chairman Andrew J. Volstead, the Minnesota Republican who authored Prohibition's enabling legislation, sparred over a report from the Chicago District Attorney's Office regarding cases before Judge Landis. How productive—or rather unproductive—the session may have been can be surmised from the following Volstead-Welty exchange:

*Volstead:* "How many were tried last year?"
*Welty:* "If you want to know you can find out."
*Volstead:* "I'm not going to be insulted by you."[27]

*Welty:* "I am going to show that these baseball players are guilty of bribing Judge Landis."[28]

Despite Volstead's attitude, a Judiciary Committee subcommittee composed of three Republicans and two Democrats reported the case to the full 25-member committee. It unanimously determined that holding of the commissionership was inconsistent with retention of a federal judgeship.

Acting on the subcommittee's recommendation, on March 2 the full Judiciary Committee voted 24-1 to endorse a full House investigation of Welty's allegations. Only Volstead dissented. He termed Welty's charges "entirely unjustified" and contended that not one member of the committee would actually vote for impeachment based on the evidence Welty had presented.[29]

Volstead's support of Landis may have stemmed from Landis' vigorous upholding of the act named for him. In the Chicago of Big Bill Thompson, Big Jim Colosimo, and Al Capone, Kenesaw Mountain Landis seemed to be one of the few public officials taking Prohibition seriously. Others besides Volstead may have been influenced by Landis' anti-alcohol stance. Some in fact thought it may have instigated the entire matter.

*The Sporting News* mysteriously hinted of a conspiracy in regard to the Welty-Dial efforts. Within baseball, the paper stated, it was believed that their efforts could be "traced" to those who "would feel much easier" if the Judge were not on the bench to try "certain cases." A decade later Ban Johnson's former confidential secretary Earl Obershain repeated the same story in a series for *Collyer's Eye*.[30]

The Landises had long been ardent prohibitionists. Charles had boasted of helping shutter the House of Representatives' two saloons. And on February 17, 1917, Frederick gave this rousing defense of the Noble Experiment entitled "Good-bye America" before a convention of the National Retail Dry Goods Association:

> A great calamity confronts our country. It doesn't come from abroad, but from within. It is prohibition. The corkscrew is losing its 'pull,' and it's good-bye America. Think of the straight-jacket made obsolete; padded cells empty; insane asylum and prison forces thrown out of work! Shall we strike at the divorce lawyer, and shall we confiscate tuberculosis?
>
> Then too, universal prohibition would put our steel industry

out of business with no demand for handcuffs, jimmies, blackjacks, prison bars, and the like. And what of the glass industry? What of the embattled hosts and of gamblers, reduced not only to want, but to work? Even southern hospitality would fade away. Think of the change on Saturday night when the head of the family comes home on his feet, instead of drifting in on the tide, and think of the sitting room of the future, nobody throwing anything or upsetting the lamp. Then again, think of watching the Old Year out, and the New Year in, sober. This is a situation to engage your earnest attention.[31]

Even before federal Prohibition took effect on January 16, 1920, Kenesaw Landis had distinguished himself as one of the few federal judges seriously interested in shutting down the alcohol traffic. In October 1919 when Wisconsin brewers attempted to ship beer into Illinois, Zion City law officers seized their trucks. The breweries went into Federal Court—Landis' court—demanding return of their property. Not only did Landis refuse their request, he found them to have violated federal statutes limiting beer to just 2.75 percent alcohol. Landis further issued subpoenas for over 200 saloonkeepers and more than 20 other brewers. "He completely broke up the Wisconsin-Illinois beer running enterprise," noted one sympathetic press report.

Once Prohibition went into effect, he maintained the pressure, winning the admiration of "drys" everywhere.[32] Hundreds of Chicago bootleggers felt his sting. In January 1921 the Judge issued a temporary injunction to prevent four Chicago breweries from making "real" beer. That same month he sentenced two café owners, J. and W. McGovern, to two years in prison for violating prohibition. The following month he closed a Chicago drugstore for violating Prohibition (by June 1921, 300,000 Chicago physicians has written approximately 300,000 questionable prescriptions for alcohol) and issued injunctions against bootleggers in Hurley, Wisconsin, from selling intoxicants.[33]

In one case involving a West Madison Street saloonkeeper Landis made headlines by his grilling of a Prohibition investigator. His method of certifying evidence would certainly have speeded up the O. J. Simpson trial.

"How much did you pay [for a glass of whiskey]?" Landis wanted to know.

"Fifty cents."

"Was it real whiskey."

"Yes."

"How do you know it was real whiskey?"

Here the defense protested that the witness had no actual proof that the beverage was alcoholic and that after stopping off at many such establishments his senses may have been dulled.

"That all depends on the drinker's experience," Landis contended. Turning to the witness he inquired, "And you been drinking for how long?"

"Four years."

"Did you have as many as four or five drinks every year?"

"Yes," the investigator responded, fighting back a smile, "at least that many."

"That's enough," ruled the Judge, "I hold that a man with these qualifications need qualify no further."[34]

Meanwhile criticism of Landis grew. The *New York World* was among those calling for him to step down, adding that Landis "has an appetite for cheap notoriety that might pass without comment in a Police Court Judge. On the Federal bench other standards of conduct are not usual."[35]

Some said he might have left the bench had it not been for the controversy. The hours were grueling but now Landis dug in his heels and refused to leave under fire. "The Judge really would have resigned earlier but for those Congressional critics," Leslie O'Connor once revealed. "He waited until one of those Washington storms blew over—so that it wouldn't look like he quit under fire and then quietly resigned."[36] He now, however, declined further comment on the matter except to say that he stood by his remarks at the Missouri Bar Association in December.[37]

In the Senate, Dial now had also introduced a bill barring outside employment by federal judges. On March 2, 1921, the Senate Judiciary Committee reported it to the full Senate, but with the Sixty-Sixth Congress fast expiring, no action was taken. On July 18, 1921, a vote was finally taken on the measure, but failed on a tie vote.[38]

While Landis' congressional adversaries were inching closer and closer to his removal, another attack was launched at him from within the ranks of his own profession. On September 1, 1921, the American Bar Association formally censured the Judge, heaping their "unqualified condemnation" upon him and damning his dual role "derogatory to the dignity of the bench." The resolution had been sponsored by Hampton L. Carlson, former attorney general of Pennsylvania, who condemned the Squire for "soiling the ermine by yielding to temptation of avarice and private gain."[39]

Resolutions of censure hurt, but they had no force. Still the pounding must have been getting to Landis. In November, the Squire received word from Yankee co-owner T. L. Huston that Ban Johnson might have been playing a continuing role in the imbroglio:

November 15, 1921

Judge K. M. Landis, Commissioner of Baseball
People's Gas Building
Chicago, Illinois

My dear Judge,

Further inquiry develop [sic] the facts that the bright mind behind the Bar Association attack is Paul Howland, of Cleveland, Ohio, a former member of the United States House of Representatives.[40] He was a candidate for president of the Bar Association. We understand that he induced Cason to father the resolutions. Probably the action is through Jim Dunn, president of the Cleveland club, who is pretty close to Governor Davis of Ohio, former mayor of Cleveland.

Did you get the significance of the fact that the draft of these resolutions was put in the hands of the Associated Press representative in Cincinnati, by John E. Bruce, chairman of the meeting, at 5:30 in the afternoon and they were not adopted until ten o'clock that night?

I am told that the Bar Association is pretty well impregnated with politics and that the lawyers representing the utilities and the other corporations strongly supported Mr. Severns, the newly elected president of the Association. I feel quite confident that the people who are working on this for us will get to the nigger in the woodpile in due time.

I would feel a delicacy in working on this matter while the Ruth case [see Chapter 16] is up before you for adjudication did I not know that it would not influence you in the slightest degree and did I not feel sure that you would know that I would not think otherwise.

I want you to know that you are placed under no obligation whatever. I am working from purely selfish incentives. If it can be established that the attack was from sordid motives, I believe that your mind will be relieved and that you will see your way clear to stand pat. You are very important to the life of baseball.

With kind regards, I am

Yours very truly,

(signed) T. L. Huston[41]

Landis was hearing from others regarding the motivation of his enemies. Cincinnati attorney J. W. Heintzman cryptically wrote him, "I have heard it stated from friends of his that the same persons who interested Congressman Welty in the introduction of his resolution in the last Congress were the ones behind this matter." Whether that was bootleggers or Ban Johnson or just persons who thought Landis' dual position was a bad idea we will probably never know.[42]

But as the new year rolled around, the controversy was dying down. Landis finally felt he could jump—without looking like he was pushed.

At 10:15 in the morning of February 18, 1922, he called reporters into his chambers. He had an odd grin on his face, and the men of the press knew he had some sort of a joke in mind, but they couldn't figure out what it was. The Judge shook hands all around, then announced, "I have a little news item for you boys. It's not very big, but I thought you might be interested." To each he handed a slip of paper on which he had written in pencil:

There are not hours enough in the day for all these activities, therefore I have forwarded my resignation to the President, effective March 1.

The reporters had a thousand questions, but Landis wouldn't answer any. Still grinning broadly, he told them, "That's all gentlemen. I'm not going to discuss this any further. I have business to attend to."

With that he moved to his bench and started the day's proceedings. While he conducted court, the report of his resignation flashed through the building. Even when the day's session had concluded, however, he had little to say regarding his decision. He refused comment on whether he had been pushed off the bench and denied reports that his physician had ordered a vacation for him. "That's all there is to it," he remarked. "There isn't time enough to do everything. I've worked hard. I've been getting up at five o'clock in the morning. I've had to go without lunch for two weeks." He realized the situation could not continue. It was just plain wearing him out. "A fellow," he observed, "is in a bad way when he wants to stay in bed in the day time."[43]

On hearing the news former Congressman Welty fired off a letter to President Harding, demanding that he *not* accept Landis' resignation. Harding ignored him.

The Squire's last day on the bench was a typical Landis performance, in a courtroom packed to its green and gold walls with those who had come to bid him farewell.

Not surprisingly one case involved bootlegging. "Your Honor," the defendant's attorney pled, "the owner of this building didn't know there was a saloon in it and besides he won a distinguished service medal in the war and . . ."

The lawyer was obviously aware of Landis' often sympathetic support for veterans. Once the Squire had even wept as he sentenced a veteran to prison. What this attorney had discounted was the fact that the weeping Landis *had* sentenced the man to prison.

And so Landis interrupted: "When you start citing war records you evidentally are afraid to try your case on its merits and why didn't he know it was a saloon? He went in there twice a month to collect rent."

Another lawyer claimed that his client didn't know any saloon was in his building.

"Why that place had swinging doors, sawdust on the floor, a footrail and spittoons that no one ever hit," the Judge shot back. "Of course he knew it was a saloon.

"The only difference from the well known good old days was that this fellow charged 75 cents a drink instead of 10 cents. Motion denied."

Still another alcohol-related case saw the defense attorney plead: "Your Honor, the case here is the alleged sale of two glasses of whiskey . . . "

"You mean the pretended sale of two glasses of alleged whiskey," Landis interrupted. "One year and $1,000 fine for the alleged matter."[44]

The last case involved sentencing the two owners of the Empire

Theatre on West Madison. Abraham Paley and Jacob Grossman had been found guilty of evading the federal amusement tax.

Here was Landis' last chance to put on a show in this grand old room. He would not miss the opportunity.

He sprung from his chair, setting his jaw as solid as he could. With eyes blazing he strode toward Paley, pointing a bony finger at him and barked: "For you, the sentence will be a fine of . . ." And then he paused for effect, ". . . one cent. You tried to do right!"

Then he turned upon Grossman: "But for you—it will be $5,000."

The verdict was pure Landis. Paley had attempted to make restitution. Grossman had refused. The Judge would teach Grossman—and all of Chicago—the value of a repentant attitude.

When the last of the 10 items on the docket had been disposed of, Landis turned to clerk Joseph O'Sullivan and asked, "Mr. Bailiff, are there any more cases?'

"None, Your Honor."

"Court," he began and then stopped cold for a few seconds, "is adjourned."

With that, he bounced wordlessly off the bench and into his chambers, where a group of reporters greeted him. His flinty reserve was melting fast and as he shook hands with each, tears welled up in his eyes. He wiped them away with his sleeve.

One of the reporters spoke for the group and presented him with a placard that read:

> JUDGE LANDIS: For newspapermen the federal building will not be the same place after you have gone. You will take the life of the joint with you. The good opinion of newspaper reporters is seldom sought, but few men can say as you can that their departure made the pressroom blue.
>
> We've known you for a long time and we'll miss you for a longer time. Not just because there is copy in your forthright way of doing things but because we think you are an honest-to-God man and a judge with the right kind of backbone.
>
> Good luck.

Landis was seated in his swivel chair as the words were read. Emotion filled him and he could not respond. His head slumped downward. Then he swung around, his back to the crowd, staring out the window at the snow flakes gently falling upon Chicago. For at least two minutes—some said five—he could not speak. Tears rolled down his cheeks, and the only sound heard in the room was the hissing of the old steam radiator.[45]

"Boys, I am sure sorry to leave you all," he finally told them, "I sure will miss you. I want to tell you, and I hope everybody hears it, that there are no finer lot of gentlemen in the world than the members of the Fourth Estate. . . .

"Oh, hell! What can I say to you fellows? These people come in and say I'm a great man. But I know you fellows made me. You printed stuff about me and that's the reason I've got a $50,000 job now. I don't kid myself."

With that, there was little to do except watch movers cart away his law books and mementos. As they took his son Reed's propeller off the wall, he mused, "That little piece of wood served to bring my son back from behind the German lines on lots of occasions. I can't let it get away."

More photographers and friends caught up with him in the corridor. There, talking with Reed, he sat atop a packing box. Photographers asked him to return to the bench for a few more photos. For once Landis refused the chance to perform for the camera.

"I shall never return to the bench." he vowed. "If you want to photograph me, do it here."

The crowd bidding him farewell represented a cross-section of Chicago society. There were bank presidents (who presumably had forgiven him for the Carey embezzlement case) and wounded veterans, businessmen and "negro elevator men," attorneys and criminals whom Landis had once sentenced.

The last to say farewell was Landis' first bailiff, Joe Buckner. Buckner, ill with pneumonia, had left a sickbed to see the Judge off.

"Why, Joe, Joe," Landis exclaimed, "what are you doing here?"

"I just had to come to tell you goodbye Judge."

"Why, I was just going to see you," Landis responded. "I wouldn't leave without telling you goodbye. Now you put this muffler on and go back to bed."

With that he took off his own scarf and handed it to Buckner, ordering him to return home as soon as possible.

Now it was time to walk across the street to the simple lunch counter where he had eaten lunch nearly every day for 17 years. As Landis walked in the door the waitress didn't even wait for instruction before yelling out an order for him.

"Swiss on rye and milk the cow for the government."

And with that ex-Federal Judge Landis sat down at his usual high stool and had his cheese sandwich and glass of milk.[46]

Landis went on to a commissionership of nearly a quarter century. What happened to his congressional accusers and defenders?

Andrew Volstead lost his House seat in the 1922 election.

In the 1924 South Carolina primary, Nathaniel Dial also suffered defeat after charges were made he was under investigation by a Senate Committee for speculating in oil stocks and cotton futures.[47]

Landis' friends in the American Legion triggered an investigation of Benjamin Franklin Welty. They charged he had violated a federal law limiting a lawyer's fee to 10 percent of whatever veterans benefits they had obtained for a client. Welty, nonetheless, had received $1,274 for securing a $3,700 benefit (plus an $80 pension) for a Lima, Ohio, veteran. Landis' tormenter received a term of one year in the Dayton workhouse and a $500 fine. In Congress Welty had fought for passage of the law. On trial, he argued it was unconstitutional.[48]

# CHAPTER 14

# "I WISH I WERE PRESIDENT OF THE UNITED STATES"

One might assume that when Kenesaw Landis resigned his federal judgeship he immersed himself in baseball and left his old political world behind.

That assumption would be wrong.

After all, one could not easily envision Ford Frick pontificating on the Job Corps or Peter Ueberroth analyzing supply side economics while holding baseball's highest job.

But they were not Kenesaw Mountain Landis.

Beyond the not inconsequential consideration of the Squire's own unique personality, when Landis assumed that commissionership in 1921, one simply did not *know* what the job of baseball commissioner was supposed to be, what he was supposed to comment on—or not comment on. The position had never before existed. It would exist as whatever Landis made of it. And for his first few years in office Landis would not be shy. He would expound on whatever he thought he could get away with—Prohibition, Socialism, the veterans' bonus, the duties of citizenship. The Judge seemed almost as interested in political topics as he did in baseball, and the general public seemed as interested in his opinions on those far-flung subjects as it did on diamond-related topics. After all, was this not the man who had whacked Standard Oil on the nose, sentenced Big Bill Haywood to 20 years in Leavenworth, and been the target of radical bombs? Asking a man of Judge Landis' caliber to limit himself to sporting matters seemed a downright waste of talent.

But there might have been more to Landis' volubility on matters political than mere vanity. When he sat upon the bench, and reporters wished to know how he stood on a certain case, he talked instead of baseball. He talked instead of dandelions. He talked of *anything* but the case before him in federal court.

Now his business was baseball—and he often talked of anything but.

Prohibition was certainly a matter of national concern and in the early '20s it still retained a modicum of popularity. Landis was not yet about to hop off its bandwagon. To Evanston, Illinois, Presbyterians in January 1921 he orated on a variety of topics—disabled veterans, gambling, and, above all, the nation's Noble Experiment.

The Eighteenth Amendment, he claimed, was "negligently misunderstood and maliciously maligned in quarters where it should receive the warmest reception." He denied that it had been put over on the nation while millions of voters were overseas in the armed forces. "It has been my privilege to know quite a few of these boys," he told the congregation at the local First Presbyterian Church, "and sound out their sentiments. Let me tell you right now, I would be willing to take the Eighteenth Amendment and submit it to the returned soldiers for a vote and abide by their decision."

He further denied that Prohibition was responsible for an increase in crime, but in the same breath hinted something was amiss. "I wish I were the President of the United States," he said, warming to his topic. "I wish I might be both houses of Congress and the Supreme Court as well. Then I would pass a law, sign it, hold it constitutional and enforce it, that would strike a blow at these corrupt drug stores and doctors who make the Eighteenth Amendment a source of profit and would put out of business these politicians who gumshoe their way to the offices of those in authority and whisper, 'Lay off of Mike McCarty, he's a nice fellow and I don't want him bothered.'

"I know these things are going on. I didn't come to Evanston today prepared to give a list of names and addresses but if luck is with me I hope to be able to do so in the near future."[1]

A month after he preached the dry gospel in Evanston, the Squire—still ensconced on the federal bench— imposed a $1,000 fine and a year in jail upon Chicago saloonkeeper Phillip L. Grossman for violating an injunction barring alcohol sales at his establishment.

Ordinarily, the fate of one Chicago bootlegger was hardly enough to warrant national attention—even when Kenesaw Mountain Landis was center stage. But three years later the case would garner Congress's attention as part and parcel of the flurry of scandals surrounding the Harding administration.

In 1920 Warren Harding had won a landslide victory to the presidency, and while his cabinet contained such "best minds" as Herbert

Hoover, Andrew Mellon, and Charles Evans Hughes, it also contained such obvious scalawags as Attorney General Harry Daugherty and Interior Secretary Albert F. Fall. Soon their misdeeds would become public knowledge.

First came revelations of Fall's granting of questionable oil leases at Elk Hills, Wyoming, and California's Teapot Dome. Then came allegations of massive theft at the Veterans Bureau as its director, Charles R. Forbes, fled to Europe. Suspicions already existed about Daugherty—particularly after his influence-peddling henchman Jesse Smith committed suicide the previous Memorial Day. On March 1, 1924, a Senate "Extraordinary Investigation Committee" was appointed to investigate Daugherty's Justice Department.

Harding had twice refused to pardon Phillip Grossman. Minnesota congressman Oscar Keller had accused Daugherty of securing pardons for favored individuals and, while Harding stood by his old crony, he refused to issue any pardon unless the accused had first served some prison time—"no matter what the situation was." When Harding died in August 1923, Calvin Coolidge succeeded to the presidency. He had even less confidence in Daugherty than Harding had (at one point Silent Cal had Chief Justice Taft drop in on Daugherty and hint he should resign), but nonetheless he kept Daugherty on—and in December 1923 carried through on Justice Department recommendations to pardon Grossman.[2]

That pardon would fall within the scope of the Senate investigation.

An extraordinary array of large Republican fish had interceded on Grossman's behalf —Fred W. Upham, treasurer of the Republican National Committee; Homer K. Gilpin, chairman of the Cook County GOP Committee (Grossman was a Republican precinct captain in Gilpin's ward); Illinois' United States senators Medill McCormick (brother of *Chicago Tribune* publisher Robert McCormick) and William B. McKinley; Illinois attorney general E. J. Brundage; and Assistant Attorney General Augustus T. Seymour.

First-term Iowa senator Smith Wildman Brookhart headed the "Extraordinary Investigation Committee" and, while a Republican, he was more than sufficiently progressive to enjoy ripping Daugherty apart—on this or any other grounds. He called to the stand a witness any committee would relish—Kenesaw Mountain Landis.

When the Squire entered Brookhart's hearing room on May 2, 1924, there was no doubt of his celebrity status. Clad in his most

Landiseque outfit—a stark black suit, a high collar, and four-in-hand tie—he made all heads turn on his approach. When he shook hands with Brookhart, the crowd burst into applause. The Landis scowl turned into a smile. This would be his show today.

Landis, not surprisingly, disapproved of Coolidge's pardon. "Just why," he had publicly fumed, "may we expect $1,800 a year prohibition agents to stand up four square for law enforcement with the President of the United States granting a pardon under such circumstances. It is a gross misfortune that with the announcement is carried the statement of two political gentlemen in Grossman's behalf? Political power has just as much right to influence executive action after conviction as it has to influence judicial action before conviction."[3]

He named Gilpin, Upham, and a Judge Barrett as those active in pressing for Grossman's freedom. "These gentlemen are all friends of mine," Landis testified, "but I would be suspicious of the merits of the application for pardon if they were in it."[4]

But soon his testimony veered from specifics of the Grossman case to the more interesting topics of Prohibition in general and his own attitude toward demon rum and to the laws of hospitality and discretion. "You cannot go to a dinner party now," Landis informed Montana Democrat Burton K. Wheeler, "if you are sitting at the table for three hours, two hours and ten minutes is taken up about the Volstead law and fifty minutes about bobbed hair. That is the atmosphere of the modern dinner party."

"And those dinner parties are all violating the law?" Senator Brookhart wanted to know.

"Now you are asking me to violate the laws of hospitality, sir," Landis smilingly responded. "I am coming out to Iowa and I may come to your house to dinner, and I don't want anybody asking me what I had for dinner."

"Well," Brookhart shot back, "I have been accused of being a bolshevist, but I think the Constitution is a bigger law than the law of hospitality."

"Well, I will tell you this, Senator," said Landis, "although I was after a short service on the bench converted to the doctrine of Prohibition, from what I saw disclosed in a number of criminal cases, I must confess to you, sir, in response to your inquiry, that I have never been a total abstainer. Now, if I should be invited to your house—"

"You would be a total abstainer then," Brookhart, no doubt mindful of his dry constituents, interjected.

Landis continued, "And I say this not for the purpose of enabling you to prepare for my reception, sir—if being at your house you should let me in on your pre-war stock,[5] if there were any—which I know there is not—I should probably, having a recollection of that provision of the Volstead law which allows you to have it at your family table and dispense it to me—I might fall for it."

"Yes; but the pre-war stock, considering the general thirst of the country, had probably been expended long ago."

"Oh, yes. The funny thing about it is . . . "

"These dinner parties that are being held now, these high toned parties, are violations of the law, are they not?"

"I cannot say they are."

"Where they have liquor in violation of the law?"

"I cannot say they are," Landis, growing a bit edgy, replied, "I agree with you as to the wonderfully lasting possibilities of the pre-war supply, but the uniform statement of the host is, in all confidence and with every assurance of honesty. 'This is a little pre-war stuff.' "

The colloquy then turned to Landis' reputation as a "severe" enforcer of the Prohibition statutes—a characterization he denied.

"I do not like that word 'severe,' " he explained, "I will tell you what the fact was, and then you may characterize it. I never imposed a day's penalty or imprisonment upon a man who brewed a little democratic felicity for his own fireside. I never put him in jail for a day. But I had the conviction that the way to enforce this law was to put the commercial violator in jail.

"And, as far as I know, I never failed to do that. Now, Grossman ran a regular saloon, in a part of town where they bred and developed criminals; and he just kept running it, while this supersedeas was in effect, down to the day of the pardon. This is just hearsay, as I was not in it; but it is a matter of universal acceptance in Chicago that after the penalty was imposed that place was operated down to the day Grossman was pardoned. Now, whether he quit when he was pardoned or not I do not know. But that was not a severe penalty."

Representing Harry Daugherty's interests at the proceedings was attorney L. Paul Howland. Howland thought he might back Landis into a corner by appealing to either his party loyalty or his respect for authority.

He guessed wrong.

"With the knowledge or absence of knowledge you have,"

Howland wanted to know, "you would not want to be placed in the position of criticizing the executive, would you?"

Landis, fumbling with his cigar, thought about it a second. "If you call it criticism," he responded matter-of-factly, "I guess I will have to let it stand."

The audience burst into applause.[6]

Some of Grossman's supposed defenders had quickly backed away from him; some had not. Senator McKinley denied he had ever written in Grossman's behalf—and in fact he had been at sea on an Army transport ship when he had supposedly signed a letter supporting the alleged saloonkeeper. Upham and Gilpin also denied any connection to the case.

A week after Landis testified, the Brookhart Committee received an unexpected visitor. Assistant Attorney General C. W. Middlekauff stormed into its hearing room and was sworn to testify. He charged Landis with "untruthful and unwarranted and misleading" statements. He disputed Landis on the number of witnesses who had testified against Grossman (and of the reliability of those who indisputably did testify against him), denied that it was well known that Grossman was still selling alcohol, and called Coolidge's action "the most righteous pardon ever granted by any President."

Middlekauff recounted how he had gone to Landis with information discrediting anti-Grossman witnesses (one had supposedly padded his expense account). "Judge Landis looked down at me with one of those prima donna smiles of his," Middlekauff recounted, "and said, 'Those Washington fellows would like to have my name on an application for a pardon so they could bawl me out.' I said, 'I have the nerve to do it if it is the right thing to do.' And if I had it to do over again I would do the same today as I did then."

"I have no doubt of that," Brookhart sarcastically shot back.[7]

Soon afterward Landis' stand was temporarily vindicated, when federal judges James H. Wilkerson and George A. Carpenter ruled that Coolidge had exceeded his authority in pardoning Grossman. Landis, it will be remembered, had not actually sentenced Grossman for selling liquor. He sentenced the saloonkeeper for *violating an injunction* prohibiting that act.

Thus Grossman was in contempt of court. Judge Carpenter found that presidential pardoning powers did not extend to contempt charges. "It was well said that the power to tax is the power to destroy; it is just as true that the power to pardon for contempt is the power to destroy judicial authority."

Grossman, however, appealed to the Supreme Court—and won. "Our Constitution confers this discretion on the highest officer in the nation in confidence that he will not abuse it," wrote Chief Justice Taft. "An abuse in pardoning contempts would certainly embarrass courts, but it is questionable how much more it would lessen their effectiveness than a wholesale pardon of other offenses." In March 1925 Philip Grossman went free. [8]

With each passing year some newspaper editor or interested citizen would view Landis as just perfect for some elective office or other—mayor of Chicago, governor of Illinois, or even president. The speculation was always for an executive position. Perhaps, it was all too apparent that Landis—"the first successful American dictator"— would have been temperamentally unsuited for the frustrations of a legislative post.

With Woodrow Wilson a spent political force, the 1920 presidential election loomed as a great Republican opportunity. The party's main suitors included Congressional Medal of Honor winner General Leonard Wood; progressive California senator Hiram Johnson; humanitarian Herbert Hoover; Massachusetts favorite son, Governor Coolidge and, of course, that distinct dark-horse, Ohio senator Warren G. Harding.

But a few scattered sources saw Landis as presidential timber. Arthur Vandenberg's *Grand Rapids Herald* advocated a presidential ticket of Landis ("even more than Leonard Wood ... the 'Roosevelt of America' today") and Seattle mayor Ole Hanson ("the living embodiment of effective anti-Bolshevism"). Longtime Landis friend and ardent prohibitionist Iowa senator William S. Kenyon (whose middle name actually *was* "Squire") felt much the same way.[9]

But Landis was smart enough to know that he could not muster enough support to sustain a national candidacy. A Fort Atkinson, Wisconsin, editor, touting Landis, received this somewhat skeptical response from his prospective candidate:

> Dear Mr. Hoard:—Much obliged for that letter and enclosure. "They don't all talk that way."
>
> Yours truly,
> Kenesaw M. Landis[10]

A more significant reason for Landis' reticence involved Frank Lowden. After winning the governorship in 1916 Lowden had put together a popular reform record, including antiracial and antireligious discrimination statutes.

Not particularly favored by the party powerhouses, he was, nonetheless, a favorite of the farm vote and of much of the "Regular Republican" element. By 1920 he had emerged as a solid presidential contender. The national convention was on Lowden's home turf, at the Chicago Coliseum, and he proved to be Leonard Wood's prime opponent in a hopelessly deadlocked convention. Delegates were on edge. It was only June but Chicago sweltered. On the first few ballots Wood led, but on the fifth Lowden took the lead, with 303 of the 493 votes needed for nomination. Ballot followed ballot, but while neither Wood nor Lowden could attain the two-thirds majority necessary, Harding began moving up. From his headquarters at the Blackstone Hotel, Lowden, bitter over his battle with Wood and sensing a Harding victory, threw his support to the Ohio solon. On the 10th ballot the convention nominated Harding.[11]

In the spring of 1921 rumors circulated that Landis might be a candidate for mayor while retaining his judgeship *and* the commissionership. It was a fantastic proposition, but considering the fetid state of Chicago politics with Big Bill Thompson as mayor it was not one to be *totally* rejected. "If Chicago takes over but one third of [Landis]," noted the *Cincinnati Tribune*, "she will have made a distinct gain over her present Mayoralty possession." Later that summer a downstate Illinois paper boomed the Squire for governor.[12]

When he finally resigned from the bench in early 1922 the rumor mills were back in business. The Chief Justice of Chicago's Criminal Courts urged Landis to take the mayoralty, saying "He would sweep Chicago from one end to the other." The *Chicago Tribune* sent its "Inquiring Reporter" out on the street in February 1922 wanting to know if passerbys believed the Judge would be a "good mayor" for the city. All five respondents replied in only the most glowing terms.[13]

In July 1922 Arthur Vandenberg was again pumping Landis (whom he trumpeted as "a unique genius with merited respect of all straight thinking people") for public office, this time for governor of Illinois. Landis remained in no mood for electoral politics. He wrote Vandenberg, professing not the "slightest interest" in running for office. Nonetheless, he confessed, "that I am human enough to like what you said. On this I am reminded of what Lincoln said about gingerbread, namely, that he reckoned nobody ever quite liked it as much as he, and got so little of it."[14]

With a presidential election coming up in 1924, Landis was about to get a few more tastes of gingerbread. By December 1923 a modest Landis presidential boomlet was in full swing, with paid advertisements appearing in Battle Creek, Michigan, newspapers touting him as: "One Man the People Believe In" and "The Sunshine Upon the Political Horizon."

The ads were the work of one Roy W. H. Crabb, a Battle Creek candy manufacturer, and they quickly attracted the attention of various politicians and Legionnaires who thought the idea a good one.

Crabb, a former Bull Moose Republican, had bolted the party because of President Coolidge's opposition to the bonus and now proclaimed himself a "Bonus Democrat." His idea was that Landis should follow him into the Democratic Party. By March 1924 Crabb was preparing to accelerate his campaign and place ads in several Chicago papers.

Landis now had enough and wrote Crabb that March 4. While the Squire professed to be flattered than anyone would be "so friendly inclined" towards him, he informed his admirer that "any suggestion of political ambition" might "discredit" his work for the bonus.

When Calvin Coolidge succeeded to the presidency in August 1923, it left the vice presidency vacant. Some Chicagoans believed they knew who should fill that slot. In May 1924 a sign appeared on a building on North Michigan Avenue reading:

FOR VICE-PRESIDENT JUDGE LANDIS
SOLDIERS' FRIEND WITH LANDIS
**COOLIDGE CAN WIN**

The billboard was the brainchild of Chicago attorney John H. Lally, who claimed to be the campaign manager for the draft, and Hadrian Baker, secretary of an association of Chicago attorneys calling itself the American Tribunal. Among Tribunal members supposedly backing Landis were former solicitor general Charles H. Aldrich, Landis' erstwhile ally, ex-United States attorney Edwin Sims, and, perhaps most surprisingly, Clarence Darrow.

On May 18 Baker had written a rather fulsome and sloppily typed letter to Landis urging him to take the vice presidency. "Give

Americans the chance to nominate you," Baker concluded, "and bea-
con fires will flame from the cascades to San Diego—from the Statue
of Liberty to the Straits of San Juan de Fuca—from the lighthouse on
Cape Flattery to the palm trees of Florida—from the Chicago Tribune Tower to the pampas of the Southern States."[15]

There is no record of Landis responding to Baker's overheated
peroration but shortly thereafter Lally wrote William Wrigley, asking the chewing gum magnate to bankroll the Landis candidacy to
the tune of $1,000 of his own money and the remainder ($6,500 to
$9,000) to be raised by him and other baseball owners by devoting 10
percent of their Memorial Day receipts to the cause.[16]

Again there is no record of any response but we do know that
Wrigley passed the correspondence on to Landis.

Lally then dispatched a flurry of telegrams to Illinois Republican
delegates urging them to place the Judge in nomination. "Landis
alone can carry the soldiers and postal workers [Coolidge had vetoed
measures aiding both groups]," he contended. "His voting ability is
right now the equal of any 10 other men in United States combined
. . . . The delegate who introduces the name of Landis to the Convention will make the name glorious in the pages of history."

The delegation's head promptly wired Landis for direction. The
Squire fired back:

> I have just received what purports to be copy of telegram ad-
> dressed to you and other delegates by a so-called quote Manager,
> Landis campaign for Vice President unquote last night. Not only
> was this done without my knowledge or authority, but in no con-
> ceivable circumstance would I have anything to do with that nomi-
> nation. If the suggestion comes from any quarter, hit it hard.

The idea of organizing a Landis draft movement was hardly as
impractical as it seems to modern ears. Calvin Coolidge (who himself
had won the vice-presidential nomination when the 1920 GOP Convention stampeded in his favor) had left the matter open to the  Convention, and no particular favorite had emerged before Republicans
met that summer in Cleveland. When nominations opened, the Arizona delegation surprised everyone by offering Frank Lowden's
name. On the second ballot Lowden was rolling to a majority, when
suddenly—as startled listeners on the newfangled medium of radio
heard—a letter arrived from Lowden.

He didn't want the nomination.

The convention adjourned in confusion. When it reconvened, it nominated yet another Landis friend, Chicago financier Charles G. Dawes.[17] Nominating the commissioner of baseball to the vice presidency might not have been proven less seemly. On his inauguration Dawes shocked the nation with a fist-pounding attack on Senate institutions. One of his first "acts" as vice president was to be asleep at the Hotel Willard while the Senate voted on the nomination of Attorney General-designate Charles B. Warren. The Senate deadlocked, and Dawes should have broken the tie. Instead he was fast asleep. By the time Dawes returned to the Capitol, a vote had switched and Warren went down in defeat.[18]

By the mid-1920s, Landis, once a progressive, was now solidly conservative. He stood firmly against recognition of the Bolshevik regime in Russia and aligned himself closely with the new American Legion, for whom his son Reed now worked. It was not surprising that Landis' last non-baseball pet project would be the veterans' bonus, although God help you if you called it a "bonus" to his face. To Landis it was "adjusted compensation."[19]

In January 1924 he received a letter from a Mr. R. P. Martin, an Evanston farmer and an antibonus veteran who thought the American Legion was disgracing itself in "clamoring always for money, more money" and was as mercenary as the hired-soldier German Hessians in the Revolutionary War.

Landis, noted for his terse correspondence, fired back a single-spaced, two-and-a-half-page letter to Martin point-by-point refuting the farmer's arguments and peppering him with question after question to demonstrate the falsity of antibonus "sophistries" and "vile propaganda."[20]

A few weeks later a more friendly missive arrived from young Miss Gladys Brown. She wanted information on the probonus argument for a debate against another high school. Landis was only marginally more restrained in his reply. After first correcting her for using the term "bonus" he provided her with a brief exposition of pro-"adjusted compensation" reasoning, ending with the remarks, "There are many, many arguments in favor of this obviously just measure and there is not one against it that I have heard that would feel at home outside the asylum or penitentiary."

Landis was so pleased with his response he carefully pasted it into one of his scrapbooks.[21]

Landis also went on the road for a series of probonus speeches. Occasionally, he took his message into hostile territory, as in late January 1924 when he addressed the Philadelphia Real Estate Board in the ballroom of that city's Bellevue-Stratford Hotel. His speech was broadcast over Philadelphia radio station WFI, but the 1,700 diners were more interested in California senator Samuel M. Shortridge's call for restricting immigration by radicals and Orientals (not that the latter was a big problem in Philadelphia), than in Landis' thoughts on the bonus. It was "apparent in the faces" of the audience that many opposed Landis, as he shakily admitted the bonus was less popular in the East than the Midwest. No doubt the real estate men and their elegantly begowned ladies would have much preferred an evening of baseball anecdotes.[22]

A week later Landis was on the stump again to another mixed audience. Booked to address the Ohio Society of Chicago on "The Care of Wounded Soldiers," he contended the listing of that topic was a "mistake" and launched into yet another impassioned plea for "adjusted compensation," citing Lincoln, Grant, and Lee's acceptance of land bounties for their service in the Black Hawk and Mexican wars as precedent.

As for arguments that if a bonus were provided "to the men, they will only squander it," Landis shouted, "That's not a reason! That's an excuse—and it's a—poor one. . . . It's none of your business what a man does with the money you pay him to clear up a debt. It's his money, and it's his right to do as he pleases with it.

"Be against it if you must . . . ," he told his audience. "But don't let the fellows [the veterans] believe you are against it in protection of the war fortunes rolled up while they were fighting for $30 a month."[23]

On Monday, February 19, 1924, however, Landis arrived at Cleveland's Public Hall to address a far more receptive audience, an American Legion-sponsored mass rally of veterans and their families. It was a classic Landis performance, filled with sarcasm, vituperation, and stinging invective.

Not all of his vitriol was aimed at bonus opponents. The program began at 8:00 PM with a musical program and was followed with an interminable introduction by Brig. General John R. McQuigg, a former state Legion commander. McQuigg droned ever onward, whining about a media blackout of bonus advocates and making many points Landis hoped to make in his own address, including the ones he had made in Chicago about Lincoln, Grant, and Lee. Landis, his disposition (as well as his appearance) aggravated by a large painful boil on his nose, sat there fuming. When he finally reached the podium at 9:30, his first target was not antibonus Treasury Secretary Andrew Mellon but McQuigg.

The Squire admitted he had never regretted leaving his judgeship until that very evening. "If I were only back on the federal bench now I'd administer a little impartial justice for your purloining of my speech."

But, in fact, the Judge did have some salient points to make.

"I came here tonight to nail a few lies," he began, "Adjusted compensation has been called a bonus. It is misbranded. A bonus is a gift, something not due, not earned.

"This is not a bonus. It is America's debt to the 4,800,000 who served at $30 a month while the white wings in Cleveland were getting $5 a day....

"Adjusted compensation is not a 'treasury raid.' It is only giving opportunity to a hundred million people to go through the motions of adjusting that unfairness."

Then he turned his guns on the United States Chamber of Commerce, which had been conducting an aggressive campaign in favor of a projected Mellon-sponsored income tax cut and against the bonus. It had recently been revealed that a New York insurance firm, the Aeolian Company, had forced its employees to write their congressmen and senators to adopt the tax cut and defeat the bonus. An Aeolian vice president was made to resign. "It is a powerful organization," Landis said of the Chamber. "When it strikes, the blow is felt all over the country. It has been working three shifts a day, seven days a week to defeat compensation."

By now Landis was just getting started, pacing the platform, waving his arms about in the air and punctuating remarks by pointing his finger at the crowd. In the glare of the spotlights, his white mane fairly glistened.

"One of the [bonus'] hottest opponents is a man who has been president of that chamber," he continued. "During the war, his son applied for exemption from the draft. The draft board turned down his claim. Then something happened. He was made a second lieutenant.

"But in justice to that soldier, I must say he was one of the most ferocious warriors who ever set spurs to varnish."

Treasury Secretary Mellon had argued that the bonus would prevent implementation of a series of Coolidge administration-backed tax cuts. Landis derided the idea as "the most colossal bribe ever offered the American people and the crowning infamy in America's treatment of her ex-service men."

"We paid claims of war contractors amounting to billions of dollars," he thundered. "Nobody said, 'Reduce taxes and don't pay these claims.' That argument was postponed until adjusted compensation came up.

"Adjusted compensation merely is a step to enable 100,000,000 people to feel they have gone through the motions, at least, of paying the debt they owe to the 4,000,000 who fought for them.

"It is those 4,000,000 we have to thank that we are here tonight in Cleveland, Ohio, U.S.A., instead of in an imperial German colony."[24]

In August, the Landis presidential boomlet was long dead, and Landis' preoccupation with the bonus was also fading fast. Now he hopped aboard new hobby horses—the God-given right to vote and the refighting of his homefront battles of the Great War.

That fall the Squire appeared before 3,000 adulatory Texas American Legionnaires at a state convention at Galveston's City Auditorium. He may have been at his oratorical best that night. If he wasn't, he at least never received a better reception; never was he more at one with an audience.

Even before he started he received a standing ovation and had to raise both hands to quiet the din. He began by explaining why America had gone to war with Germany, and, to much applause, how once war was declared the Democrat Wilson was the Republican Landis' president. Throughout the address he moved about the dais, in what one reporter called a modified Billy Sunday-like style of elocution. When he spoke of war profiteers, standing on the sidelines while our boys marched off to war, he crouched down low, with both hands on his knees, like a catcher. The only sensation these profiteers knew, he jibed, was "an itching of the palms."

The aggregation exploded in laughter.

"The Socialist Party opposed the government in war," Landis continued. Then he bent over the platform, nearly reaching the floor of the podium, before bellowing out, "I have yet to learn that a criminal conspiracy becomes legal by calling itself a political party."

That brought down the house, with the Legionnaires nearly blowing the roof off the place.

When the cheering finally subsided he continued. "A few of these gentlemen," he said very quietly before stopping to take a sip of water, "got into jail. Only a few." Now he picked up the volume, "Too few."

The throng went wild once more.

"Now," Landis explained, "if a private soldier, tired out from a day of hard labor, went to sleep at his post on guard duty, the rules of war say that the penalty is death.

"I maintain that a 20-year sentence for those fellows who fought the government of the United States in war was inadequate, to be mild about it.

"Some of them are being let out now, after only five years. All I say is that I don't think that's right."

Winding up his oration, Landis provided the Legionnaires with a vivid description of the type of pro-German and pro-Austrian politicians he had encountered during the war—a clear reference to 1924 third-party presidential candidate "Fighting Bob" La Follette.

"If a politician of that sort ever comes to Texas seeking office, tho it be the presidency itself he is after . . ."

At that he leaned out toward the audience and stage-whispered, "Just paste him one for me."

The crowd went simply nuts.[25]

That October, with the Coolidge-Davis-La Follette presidential election on tap, Landis turned to endorsing the Legion's get-out-the-vote program. He started his salvo with a relatively straightforward telegram of support to Middletown, Ohio, Legion post in support of their efforts, but hit his stride with a speech later that month at Chicago's Drake Hotel to a joint session of the Audit Bureau of Circulation and the American Association of Advertising Agencies.

He created front-page headlines as he demanded jail for so-called "vote slackers."

"Now," Landis told his audience, "we find both parties going about on election day with big limousines, to get his majesty the voter out and carry him to the polls and both parties spend vast sums to do that.

"The remedy? I would substitute the Black Maria [a police van] for those limousines and cart them off to jail."

He seemed to be stuck in a Great War frame of mind, and likened his idea to conscription.

"There were a good many who didn't want to go to war then," he fairly screamed, "and so we put conscription on the books. There are a good many who don't want to go to the polls now, and it is the same thing. We should make them go to the polls and vote or send them to jail just as we sent men to jail who refused to obey the law and go in the army."[26]

His words would soon boomerang on him. "I cannot agree with my friend, Judge Landis," remarked Charles E. Merriam, head of the Department of Political Science at the University of Chicago, "that obligatory voting is advisory."

But that was not the worst of it. Merriam pointed out that in the previous mayoralty election—a contest in which Big Bill Thompson was finally ousted from City Hall—*Landis* himself had not voted.[27]

Another presidential campaign approached in 1928. No one was considering Landis a candidate for *any* office, but Frank Lowden was still seen as a possible GOP nominee, and Landis was busily plotting pro-Lowden strategy with minor league czar William G. Bramham, another long-active Republican. Landis viewed Lowden weak in the "extreme east" but strong everywhere else. "My own guess is, when the gang gets together in June," he wrote Bramham, "and looks over the map of the United States, they will be obliged to conclude that they will have to nominate Lowden in order to get enough electoral votes to elect the nominee of the convention."

But Lowden's effort was far too half-hearted to overtake favorite Herbert Hoover. Accused of campaign irregularities back in 1920, Lowden seemed afraid to vigorously pursue delegates in 1928. His candidacy went nowhere.[28]

By the end of the '20s Landis no longer spoke out on non-baseball issues. With the exception of the bonus, most of his old issues were either dead or, in the case of Prohibition, increasingly unpopular. By 1930 he was writing to his old friend Captain Lew Wallace, Jr., turning down a Florida speaking engagement and bluntly and wearily explaining why.

"The trouble is, Cap," he wrote, "I have no stomach for this talking business, mainly for the reason that I have been making speeches for fifty years to a public that is so damned stupid that today it is going along just about as it did when I commenced to talk, so I have concluded to quit and let it go to hell, as it seems determined to do—contrary to my instructions.

"On the question of throwing any light on anything else, directly or indirectly to publish or propaganda, certainly I will do nothing to stimulate that sort of activity, either on the air or by billboard method. There is too much of it already."[29]

# CHAPTER 15

# "WHO THE HELL DOES THAT BIG APE THINK HE IS?"

Two schools of thought exist regarding the question of who saved baseball following the Black Sox scandal—if indeed any one person could singly claim credit. Legalists chose Landis, crediting his stern justice with restoring public faith in the game's integrity. But others opted for slugger Babe Ruth, the greatest star the game would ever know. Almost coincidentally with Landis' arrival, Ruth revolutionized the art of batting and did so with a style that caused America to fall in love with the moon-faced Yankee incorrigible.

Traded from the Red Sox to the Yankees in December 1919 by financially strapped Boston owner Harry Frazee, with New York Ruth completed his transition from star pitcher to slugger of unprecedented, even mythic, proportions. In 1920 he ripped the cover off the ball, clubbing a then-record 54 homers and smashing the old record of 29 (set the previous year by Ruth himself); driving in 127 runs and recording the all-time slugging mark of .847. It was a stunning performance, but the following year Ruth surpassed it—59 homers, 171 RBI, a .376 average, and an .846 slugging percentage.

And, of course, Ruth not only hit, he hit with swagger and authority and color. America took the Babe to its heart. But as it did, the star-making process went to Ruth's head—literally as well as figuratively. On the last day of the 1921 World Series, Yankee manager Miller Huggins placed a crown manufactured from $600 worth of silver atop the Bambino's head. It bore the inscription, "King Ruth," and it told the 26-year-old ex-orphanage inmate that no one in—or out of—baseball would ever again tell him what to do.

Ruth loved to spend money—and he loved to earn it. One of the easiest ways was through post-season exhibitions, but since 1911 baseball had banned players on World Series teams from participating. Back in 1916 Ruth and several teammates from the world champion

Red Sox had engaged in a post-Series game at New Haven. The National Commission fined each $100, but even then this was hardly a crippling penalty.

In January 1921 baseball reiterated that ban:

> Both teams that contest in the World Series are required to disband immediately after its close and the members are forbidden to participate as individuals or as a team in exhibition games during the year in which that world's championship was decided.[1]

Ruth's Yankees captured the 1921 American League pennant, losing the World Series to John McGraw's Giants in eight games. Rule or no rule, Ruth, who in 1920 had legally earned an estimated $40,000 in exhibitions, was not ready to forego the cash bonanza that post-season 1921 should have provided. On the last day of the regular season, Landis stopped in the Yankee clubhouse to congratulate the club on their pennant. Ruth looked at him and asked, "Judge, what's all this talk about our being forbidden to barnstorm after the Series?"

Landis repeated what the rule was and said it would be strictly enforced.

"Well," Ruth shot back, "I'm notifying you that I am going to violate the rule and I don't care what you do about it."

Landis could not ignore such a direct challenge to his authority and remain an effective commissioner. He would have to *make* Ruth care about just what he could do it about it.

Ruth, for his part, was adamant because he had already signed a package deal with vaudeville magnate E. F. Albee to play ball from October 16 through November 1 for $1,000 per game in a series of contests scheduled in upstate New York, Pennsylvania, and Oklahoma. He would then perform in Albee's vaudeville circuit for $3,000 a week.[2]

Adding to the brewing storm between Ruth and baseball's establishment was Ruth's absence from part of the World Series. While stealing third in Game Two, Ruth ripped open his right elbow. In Game Three he aggravated the injury while stealing second, leaving the contest in the eighth inning. After Game Five doctors ordered Ruth to skip the rest of the Series. That he was *now* able to perform for the "Babe Ruth All Stars" opened him up for merciless second-guessing. "I heal quick," the Babe explained. "I always heal quick,"[3] but not everyone bought his answer. Observers wondered: if an injured Ruth wasn't able to appear in the World Series, how could he perform just three days later in meaningless—albeit—lucrative exhibitions?

Originally, Ruth had asked permission of Yankee general manager Ed Barrow to barnstorm. Barrow, knowing the rule, told Ruth he had no personal objection but that the Babe would need Landis' approval.

Ruth later pleaded ignorance as to the consequences of his defying baseball authority, but most observers dispute that. Two decades later Taylor Spink of *The Sporting News* wrote:

> It frequently was said that the Babe was ill advised and that if the club could have gotten to him in time, [Yankee owners Jacob] Ruppert and [T. L.] Huston would have prevented him from making this foolhardy move. However, I can say that Ruth knew exactly what he was doing when he defied Landis . . .; he was willing to back his own popularity and well-known drawing powers against the Judge.[4]

Huston and Ruppert even offered to compensate Ruth if he would cancel the tour, but he bullheadedly refused. "The game has been advertised," said the Bambino. "We have to fulfill our commitments."[5]

Ruth, moreover, dragged his feet on contacting Landis, failing to keep an appointment with him on Saturday, October 15, just one day before the first exhibition. "He gets away with a lot in the American League," fumed Landis, "but in this office, he's just another player."[6]

On the same day, baseball's advisory council, consisting of all major league owners, voted to back Landis in whatever action was taken against Ruth. The Judge ordered all clubs in Organized Baseball to bar Ruth's tour from their parks. That evening, with Landis' noose tightening around his neck, Ruth placed a call to a now barely civil commissioner at his suite in Manhattan's Commodore Hotel.

Landis ordered the Babe to appear before him, but Ruth stupidly begged off, saying he had another engagement. At that Landis grew still testier. Ruth then blithely informed the Judge he was leaving that night for Buffalo to perform the following day in the first of the scheduled exhibitions.

"I absolutely refuse to give you and your companions permission to make that trip," Landis roared as he slammed the receiver back on its hook. Swearing profusely, he exclaimed "Who the hell does that big ape think he is? That blankety-blank! If he goes on that trip it will be one of the sorriest things he has ever done."[7]

In Landis' suite was New York sportswriter Fred Lieb, who hurried over to Huston's room at the nearby Martinique Hotel. Huston had been violating the Volstead Act with Harry Frazee and both were out cold, snoring loudly. Lieb grabbed Huston and shook him awake, shouting, "You've got to stop Babe from going to Buffalo. Landis will throw the book at him. He may throw him out of baseball."[8]

In one version Huston, who knew Ruth was on his way to Grand Central Station, realized there was nothing he could physically do to stop Ruth from leaving New York. But according to another account Huston tracked Ruth down, getting nowhere with his star. "What has that long-haired old goat got to do with me?" Ruth supposedly asked Huston.

"Go on this trip and you'll find out," Huston responded.[9]

Ruth only grew angrier as the conversation progressed, finally snarling, "Aw, tell the old guy to jump in a lake."[10]

That evening Landis gave out a statement to the press, clearly indicating that squashing Ruth would be part of his consolidation of power. The man who summoned John D. Rockefeller to the witness stand would not be cowed by any mere sultan of swat. "If Ruth breaks the rule against world's series players engaging in such contests," Landis told reporters, "then it will resolve itself into an issue between the player and myself. I have no interest in the matter one way or the other, but as long as it is a rule I must enforce it or see that those violating it pay the penalty. Whether or not the rule is fair or unfair to the player is not the question. It was adopted for good reasons, I presume, and was in the code before I came into baseball. My duty concerns its enforcement or penalizing its violation."[11]

Ruth wasn't the only one risking Landis' wrath. Joining the Babe on his junket were three other Yankees, outfielder Bob Meusel and pitchers Bill Piercy and Tom Sheehan, with the rest of the roster filled out by New York area semipros. Sheehan, although a Yankee, was called up very late in the season and was ineligible for World Series play—and thus legally available for the Ruth tour. Yankee pitcher Carl Mays and catcher Wally Schang were originally to have been a part of Ruth's roster but on the afternoon of the October 15 met with Landis. Also visiting the Judge that day was Giants catcher Mike Gonzales who sought permission to play in his native Cuba.

Landis told Mays, Schang, and Gonzales that he had no personal objections to their actions, but he was bound to enforce the existing rule. All three decided against barnstorming.

On Sunday, October 16 the Babe Ruth All-Stars played their first game. Per Landis' orders Buffalo's International League park had been barred to them, so they instead performed at the city's Velodrome Park, defeating the local Polish Nationals, 4-2, with Ruth and Meusel each homering for their cause. Fifteen thousand attended, but crowds soon dwindled. At Elmira the next day only 1,500 turned out to see Ruth and Meusel each homer twice as the All-Stars triumphed, 6-0. Ruth nonetheless remained defiant, telling reporters:

> We are going to play exhibition baseball until November 1, and Judge Landis is not going to stop us. I am not in any fight to see who is the greatest man in baseball. Meusel, Piercy and I think we are doing something that is in the interest of baseball. I do not see why we are singled out when other big players, members of second and third place clubs in the world's series money, are permitted to play post-season games. I am out to earn an honest dollar, and at the same time give baseball fans an opportunity to see the big players in action.[12]

Ruth further played the role of clubhouse lawyer, contending that since his Yankee contract had expired on October 2 (the last day of the regular season), he was now free to pursue any activity he wished.

The next day Ruth's barnstormers traveled to Jamestown, New York, where, Piercy played center, Ruth first, and Meusel pitched in the All-Stars' 14-10 victory. Crowds continued to be small, but Ruth maintained his composure, stating, "I don't care if my case comes up tomorrow. I am not worrying."[13]

Landis, as was his habit, bided his time and said little, preferring to banter with reporters about the wonders of New York City and the marvels of the recent Fall Classic, although there was no question he would *not* back down. Just before leaving New York, he snapped to reporters, "If [Ruth] insists on making this a personal issue with me, then he will find every satisfaction. He cannot expect to get off with a light fine, as was the customary discipline, I am told, under the old National Commission." On the afternoon of the October 16 he left for Chicago aboard the Twentieth Century Limited, spending most of his time on the way to Albany in the cab, playing railway engineer. He reached home the following morning but still said little, using as his excuse the large pile of papers he had brought with him on the case, saying he had to study them before rendering an opinion. He did comment in none-too-subtle fashion, "In the meantime, law-abiding baseball men have no fear that the laws of the game will not be enforced. The law of gravitation is still in force and what goes up must come down."[14]

Landis was stewing on remarks Ruth had made to the press that the Judge had hung up on him. This, for some reason, incensed Landis, who insisted on denying his action. Cryptically he said his upcoming decision would show "what kind of a gentleman Ruth was."[15] Then he added in equally cryptic but more pointed form that he had not "the slightest regard for the size of the hat the gentleman in question wears."[16]

The Judge was sampling public opinion: would it support Landis if he threw the book at the wildly popular Ruth? Or would it turn on Landis, who needed all the help he could get as he consolidated his control over baseball?

The public supported Landis. Even those who thought the rule was unfair or whose self-interest demanded leniency for Ruth supported punishing the Sultan of Swat.

Typical were the thoughts of *New York Herald* columnist W. J. MacBeth who floridly editorialized that there could be "no sympathy" for Ruth, who after all was defying Kenesaw Mountain Landis— "baseball's supreme authority—the man who saved baseball's good name . . .; the only man who possibly could have saved the fair name of the game."[17]

Also chiming in was former star ballplayer John Montgomery Ward, who back in 1890 had organized a wholesale player revolt against management. "The rule is unfair," Ward, now an attorney, commented. "Ruth is justly entitled to make as much money as possible out of baseball. He can't play the game forever and now he has the chance of a lifetime."

But Ward continued, "There is no excuse for his attitude toward Judge Landis. . . . The Commissioner's position in the matter is unassailable, of course, and he ought to be sustained by the leagues, the press and the public."[18]

Yankee owners Huston and Ruppert also fell in line. While decrying the barnstorming rule, they admitted that it had been violated "so defiantly . . . that Judge Landis has no alternative but to meet the situation firmly. . . . As long as it exists it should be obeyed." All the while, they were so nervous about losing Ruth and Meusel for at least the beginning of the 1922 season, they conferred with the White Sox about acquiring veteran Harry Hooper to bolster what they assumed would be their decimated outfield.[19]

As Ruth's tour continued the weather was rainy, and crowds continued to be sparse. Some said gate receipts totaled just $1,000 per day, barely enough to pay Ruth's salary—but nothing more. The noose was clearly tightening around Ruth.

Leslie O'Connor had remained behind in New York, but before he left for Chicago on October 18 he informed reporters that his boss had not been as adamant on the rule's enforcement as he appeared: "He was planning for some sort of a modification until Ruth made his defiant stand. All he could do then was to stand firm and see that the rule was enforced. . . .

"The club owners and the judge were all in New York and Ruth could easily have appealed to them for some alteration of the rule which he considered unfair."[20]

Meanwhile, Colonel Huston told the press he was leaving New York on Thursday, October 20, for a week's vacation at his Dover Hall, Georgia, hunting lodge. Instead, he headed straight for Scranton, Pennsylvania, to rendezvous with his wayward star.

On Friday in Scranton, October 21, Ruth's team suffered an 8-6 defeat at the hands of local competition. The tour had now turned into both an artistic and financial liability. Each day it continued chances grew that Landis would impose even more severe penalties. Some now said that Landis might suspend Ruth, Meusel, and Piercy for all of 1922. Ruth, however, held one powerful advantage. Rumors flew that movie and theatrical interests, encouraged by the $900,000 gate at the recent World Series, were forming a third major league, with teams in the Baltimore, Brooklyn, the Bronx, Cincinnati, Cleveland, Detroit, Pittsburgh, and Washington.[21] Ruth informed Huston that he had been offered $100,000 to play "outlaw" ball in the upcoming season, and that figure was only *half* what other reports held.

Nonetheless, the Babe was clearly in a conciliatory mood, eager to forego barnstorming and crawl back to the Yankees in 1922. The story given out to the press was that Huston had convinced Ruth that all he had accomplished was to damage the ballclub (and the owners) who had done so much for him. The tale, however was a mere face-saving device for Ruth.[22]

Ruth's change of heart actually stemmed from more coldly financial factors. Facing declining gate receipts, Ruth and E. F. Albee were simply bought out by Huston and Ruppert. Said the Babe in his autobiography: "It was reported that the trip then was abandoned because of lack of interest, but what really happened was Huston paid off the promoters and the players involved. . . ."[23] Ownership furthermore promised Ruth a huge salary increase for 1922.

A gleeful Huston assured reporters that Ruth would personally travel to Landis' Chicago office to beg for forgiveness. Some felt that once Ruth exhibited proper contrition, the Judge would let him off with a public tongue-lashing, a heavy fine—and, at worst, a brief suspension. The *New York Times* editorialized, "It is hard to believe that there would be one dissenting voice among the fans, club owners or other players if Ruth were let off with a fine and no suspension. The majority agree it is a bad rule, and that the punishment for an infraction of such a rule might well not be made too severe."[24] Even *The Sporting News*, no fan of the "spoiled" Ruth, chimed in that while he "may be a rule breaker, [and] anything but a hero . . . but he is not to be classified a baseball criminal." The "Bible of Baseball" also argued against any suspension approaching a "considerable part" of the upcoming season.[25]

Huston urged leniency:

> Ruth has had a change of heart and feels that he was badly advised . . . in face of a rule which Judge Landis . . . , was bound to enforce. I...consider the rule a bad one, and unfair to players like Ruth. In talking with him at Scranton, I promised to use my best efforts to have the rule rescinded. I also promised to intercede...with Judge Landis to have the punishment as light as possible, in view of the fact that he feels now that he made a mistake. Ruth expressed regret to me that he had not given more consideration to the New York Club, which he admitted had always treated him with utmost fairness. I was glad to see him take this attitude and naturally urged him to give up the barnstorming trip in the hope that Judge Landis would not feel the necessity for imposing a long suspension.[26]

Yet Ruth seemed incapable of facing Landis. Instead of heading for Chicago, he departed for a hunting trip with pitcher Bob Shawkey. Any chance for leniency was now destroyed. A panic-stricken Yankee ownership dispatched to Chicago an individual identified only by the *New York Times* as "a well-known sporting writer from this city,"[27] as well as club general manager Ed Barrow.

Landis was in no mood to let Ruth off the hook. "Well, what do *you* want?" he sneered in his best theatrical manner as Barrow entered his office.

"I guess you know what I want."

"Yes, I do. It's about those lawbreakers. Come in here, Ed."

"See those kids," Landis added as he led Barrow over to his window, pointing to two small boys across Michigan Avenue. "I suppose they're saying to each other, 'That big white-haired so-and-so in that office up there is the one who's keeping Babe Ruth out of the ball game.' "

Barrow seemed amused by Landis' remark. The Squire continued, throwing the question back at his visitor: "But tell me: what would you do?"

The question surprised Barrow who meekly answered, "I'd do the same as you've done."[28]

When Ruth had terminated his tour, Landis promised a decision within two weeks. Again, he went into a stall.

Landis let the Babe twist slowly in the wind. There was little to study in the case, but the Judge gave himself still another pretext for delay, by requesting questionnaires from Ruth, Meusel, and Piercy explaining their rationale for barnstorming.

Only Ruth bothered to respond.

All the while, however, Landis was on particularly intimate terms with Yankee ownership, as they were quietly assisting him in getting to bottom of impeachment talk against him. In his November 15, 1921 letter to Landis, Colonel Huston alluded to how uncomfortable this made him:

> I would feel a delicacy in working on this matter while the Ruth case is up before you for adjudication did I not know that it would not influence you in the slightest degree and did I not feel sure that you would know that I would not think otherwise.
>
> I want you to know that you are placed under no obligation whatever. I am working from purely selfish incentives. If it can be established that the attack was from sordid motives, I believe that

your mind will be relieved and that you will see your way clear to stand pat. You are very important to the life of baseball.[29]

Landis timed his announcement to coincide with that year's minor league meetings in Buffalo. When word reached that session, it spread like wildfire.

Landis had fined Ruth, Meusel, and Piercy the entire amount ($3,302.26 each) of their 1921 World Series shares and suspended them through May 20 of the 1922 season. Yankee management was actually relieved; they had feared worse.

Landis' ruling read:

> These players were members of the New York American League team, a contestant for the world championship in 1921. Immediately after that series, willfully and defiantly, they violated the rule forbidding their participation in exhibition games during the year in which that world championship was decided.
>
> This rule was enacted in 1911, only after repeated acts of misconduct by world series participants made its adoption imperative for the protection of the good name of the game. The rule was known to all players, and particularly to these men, upon one of whom a fine was imposed in 1916, for a violation.
>
> This situation involves not merely rule violation, but a mutinous defiance intended by players to present the question: Which is the bigger—base ball, or any individual in base ball?
>
> There will be an order forfeiting their share of the World Series funds and suspending them until May 20, 1922, on which date and within ten days thereafter they will be eligible for reinstatement.[30]

Unclear from the above was the issue of spring training. Would the crowd-drawing Ruth be banned from grapefruit league play? If he were, Yankees exhibition attendance would suffer precipitously, and, more to the point, Ruth would be free to perform several additional weeks on the vaudeville circuit. He might even *make* money from his suspension.

Landis allowed him to play.[31]

While the *Reach Guide* editorialized that Landis' decision "could be criticized for its extreme leniency,"[32] Yankee management—their relief that Ruth would not be banned for the entire season quickly turning to resentment that he would be suspended at all—publicly contended they were being unfairly punished for Ruth's transgressions. It sent lawyers to Chicago to argue the point. Thousands of fans petitioned Landis for their hero's speedy return. Landis stood firm.

Ruth, however, continued to live in his dream world. When he heard the news of his suspension, he was in a Washington hotel suite, on tour with his vaudeville troupe. "Leave Judge Landis make the next move," he told reporters. Ruth's next move was simpler, as he ordered the hotel room service waiter to "bring lotsa potatoes with the steak."[33] In St. Louis, a few days later he hinted to the press that once he saw Landis "there may be something big for the boys" to report.[34]

But Ruth never visited Landis in the off-season. He and Meusel did not see the Judge until the spring, when the Judge visited the Yankees' New Orleans training base. They wanted their sentence commuted; what they got was a two-hour lecture on the value of authority. "He sure can talk," the chastened Ruth remarked.[35]

The following August baseball amended the rule on barnstorming to allow Series participants wishing to barnstorm to petition Landis for permission. Exhibitions could last only through the end of October (a date later extended through November 10), and each touring squad was limited to three World Series players.[36] The Yankees won the pennant again in 1922, but this time both Ruth and Meusel barnstormed together legally.[37]

Landis also displayed some flexibility in interpreting the old rule, choosing to define "the year in which that world's championship was decided" as the calendar year. That allowed Bob Meusel, along with his brother, New York Giant outfielder Emil "Irish" Meusel, and Emil's teammates, second baseman Johnny Rawlings and 1921 NL home run champion first baseman George "Highpockets" Kelly, to tour the Pacific Coast immediately following New Year's Day 1922. *The Sporting News* was livid, contending that the year involved should be the "baseball" year, and sullenly commented: "Thus Babe Ruth et al were subject to fine and suspension—and they got it a plenty—for playing exhibition games in the East in October, but the Meusel brothers, Rawlings and Kelly can play without being subject to penalty a series of games against a bunch of negroes in California after January 1, without being impaired."[38]

On March 6, 1922, Ruth signed a three-year contract at $52,000 per annum, the highest salary ever paid a ballplayer and an estimated 40 percent of the Yankees total payroll. But the 1922 season began without Ruth, Meusel, or Piercy. As Ruth sat home, the Browns' Ken Williams piled up the home runs. The *St. Louis Post-Dispatch's* L. C. Davis jibed:

> The King of swat is sitting in a box
> And makes note of Kenny's four ply knocks
> "Barnstorming stunts may be all right," said he
> "But they are not what they are cracked up to be
>
> I thought I was bigger than the game
> And that the Judge would tremble at my name
> But now I have the wide world informed
> No barns by me in future will be stormed[39]

On Saturday, May 20, the Yankees wired Landis requesting reinstatement of the offending trio. The Judge immediately gave assent. In his first game back Ruth went 0-for-4 and was roundly booed by a Polo Grounds crowd of 38,000. Within five days he threw dirt on an umpire and received a day's suspension and a $500 fine from Ban Johnson. Landis calmly declared it a league affair and outside his jurisdiction.

In exiling Ruth for a full six weeks, however, Landis had gone far beyond banishing petty crooks, usurping powers from league presidents and bending recalcitrant owners to his will. He had stared down a national idol, the biggest star in baseball or any other sport. It was a major step in achieving autocratic control over the national game. Always a politician, there was one boss Landis did fear: public opinion. He had no guarantee at the outset of the Ruth controversy that the public and press would back him to the hilt as he assumed unprecedented powers over baseball.

Now, he knew they would.

# CHAPTER 16

# "I'M AS INNOCENT AS A CHILD"

The Black Sox—Eugene Paulette, Benny Kauff, and Joe Gedeon— were among the first players Landis would banish. They would not, however, be the last, as hard-drinking spitballer Shufflin' Phil Douglas soon discovered.

Douglas had emerged from Georgia's mines and turpentine mills to excel in his region's semipro leagues. At first he caught, but after he threw out 12 runners in a single game, someone finally converted him into a pitcher. After just two years in the minors, he reached the majors with the 1912 White Sox. There Hall-of-Famer Big Ed Walsh taught him the spitter.

But the new pitch could not keep Douglas from sinking back to the minors not once but four times. True, he possessed a good-sized talent but with it came a larger-sized thirst. Punctuating each season were week-long boozing bouts, which Douglas termed "vacations." The 6'3" righthander wasn't a mean drunk, but managers quickly tired of wondering what condition he'd be in on any given afternoon. And even when sober Douglas was no genius. The *Reach Guide* dismissed him as a "physical giant . . . with the mentality of a child."[1]

For the 1917 Cubs Douglas lost 20 games, but the next year he helped Chicago to the pennant. In the fourth game of the 1918 Fall Classic he unleashed an eighth-inning wild pitch that cost the Cubs the game.

Wild pitches were a way of life for spitballers. On August 16, 1920, however, one spitball was *far* too wild. On that date one of Carl Mays' wet offerings skulled Cleveland shortstop Ray Chapman, killing him. New practitioners of the delivery were now outlawed, although Mays, Douglas, and 14 other big leaguers employing the pitch were allowed to continue throwing it.

By then, however, Douglas had once more worn out his welcome in Chicago. In July 1919 the Cubs shipped him to the Giants, where he became yet another of John McGraw's many reclamation projects.

Douglas wasn't the worst drunk McGraw ever managed. That honor probably went to righthander Bugs Raymond. In 1909 McGraw had made an 18-game winner out of Raymond, but by 1912 Bugs was out of baseball and dead from wounds suffered in a Chicago street brawl. Such failure did little to discourage McGraw, whose motives were partly charitable—the Little Napoleon was famous for helping down-on-their-luck ballplayers—and partly calculated. Douglas was, after all, a talent whose services were available on the cheap.

McGraw promptly learned why so many clubs had already dispensed with Douglas' services. In short order Douglas took not one but two "vacations." McGraw ordered the spitballer home for the rest of the 1919 season but didn't give up on him, hiring a series of detectives to shadow the pitcher and keep him sober. "He was watched continuously," Douglas' daughter recalled decades later.[2]

Douglas resented being tailed, but rather liked a new "keeper" McGraw hired in midsummer 1921, Chicago gumshoe James O'Brien. Douglas and O'Brien quickly became drinking buddies, discreetly whiling away the hours in various illicit speakeasies and saloons. In part to avoid embarrassing O'Brien ("that fellow who goes around with me") Douglas now avoided serious benders.[3]

McGraw wasn't the only one who kept a tight rein on Douglas. Douglas' wife didn't resort to hiring detectives, but she retained the power of the purse strings. The Giants sent Phil's paychecks directly to her, and when he left home for each game, she parceled out to him only carfare plus 20 cents. Douglas' benders came to depend on the kindness of friends and accommodating fans.[4]

Jim O'Brien's methods were hardly a textbook style of handling alcoholism, but they worked. In 1920 Douglas enjoyed his best season yet, going 14-10. In 1921 he improved to 15-10, helping the Giants to their first pennant since 1917. In that October's eight-game World Series Douglas started three times against the Yankees' Carl Mays, losing the opener, 3-0, but coming back to win Game Four, 4-2, and Game Seven, 2-1.

Douglas was clearly John McGraw's ace as the Pirates and Cardinals battled New York for the 1922 pennant. But in late June word finally reached McGraw that Douglas and O'Brien were drinking together. Adding to McGraw's chagrin was his fear that the duo was imbibing on the club's expense account. Enraged, he suspended Douglas and fired O'Brien.

Replacing O'Brien was coach Jesse "The Crab" Burkett. The diminutive Burkett had been a great hitter in his day, three times batting over .400, but that fact cut little ice with Douglas. After all, one thing Burkett was crabby about was alcohol; he hated it and was determined that Douglas abstain. As catcher Frank Snyder recalled, the two Giants "probably drank more ice-cream sodas together than any two men in history."[5] Douglas, who had previously liked Burkett, now intensely resented him.

Adding to Douglas' angst was McGraw, a tough man to please. Against the Cardinals in July, Douglas got two quick strikes on Rogers Hornsby. The Rajah fouled off the next two pitches. On the fifth offering Hornsby fanned. But when Douglas returned to the bench McGraw launched into a tirade, lambasting him as just plain "dumb" for throwing "too many strikes," i. e., not nibbling around the plate enough, to such a tough hitter. Douglas barked back, and the argument lasted until after the game, but the pitcher was no match for the vitriolic Little Napoleon.[6]

At the Polo Grounds on Sunday, July 30 the Pirates shelled him, scoring seven runs in seven innings.[7] The defeat earned Douglas a particularly vicious tongue-lashing from McGraw who blamed the loss on demon rum. "Where's your bottle hid?" he screamed.[8] An embittered and thirsty Douglas—with Burkett still in tow—went downtown for dinner. In Times Square he gave Burkett the slip, going on a monumental bender. The next morning police found him passed out cold at an apartment not far from his Wadsworth Avenue home. Circumstances remain controversial. Police claimed they were responding to an excessive noise complaint, but the only person arrested was an already comotose Douglas—the only noise he could be responsible for was snoring. He later contended that five detectives had burst into the room and threatened him with blackjacks.

Many felt the Giants ballclub, through the influence of its treasurer, municipal magistrate Francis Xavier McQuade, had tipped the cops off. Police hauled Douglas to the 135th Street stationhouse. When Burkett and McQuade arrived, they committed him to the private West End Sanitarium on Central Park West.

The sanitarium's regimen, consisting largely of the then-popular "Keely Cure," was hardly relaxing. Sanitarium staff immediately sedated Douglas, then subjected him to rounds of scalding hot baths and stomach-pumping.

All the while no one bothered informing Douglas' wife of his whereabouts. Not until Wednesday was she notified. The next day she visited him; on Friday he was sedated again. The next morning, Saturday, August 5, a still very wobbly Douglas left for home.

Two days later McGraw ordered the still heavily medicated Douglas to the Polo Grounds. He was barely alert. "He was more or less in a daze," recalled teammate George "Highpockets" Kelly. "He was starry eyed. You could see in his eyes he didn't know what the hell was going on, with the kind of torture they'd put him through. Whatever it was . . . the man wasn't himself. He wasn't right." Not helping his condition was alcohol. He had started drinking heavily again right after leaving the sanitarium.[9]

On reaching the Giants' locker room Douglas learned he had been personally charged $224.30 for his incarceration and even for his cab fare to the sanitarium. Still clutching the bills, he was summoned to McGraw's office where the Little Napoleon subjected him to a 20-minute closed-door tirade so loud it could be clearly heard by the rest of the team. "Don't bother to dress!" concluded a screaming McGraw. "Go home and sleep it off, you big bum! But be here tomorrow, or I'll fix you so you'll never pitch for anybody again!"[10] For good measure McGraw docked Douglas $187.85 for missing five days' work and topped that off with a $100 fine.

Discouraged, embittered, and still groggy, Douglas sat down in a corner of the clubhouse and began writing to Cardinals outfielder Les Mann, an old teammate from the 1918 National League champion Cubs. The Cards, then in Boston and staying at that city's Brunswick Hotel, were neck-and-neck with the Giants for first. Reaching for some Giants stationary, the Shuffler scratched out the following:

New York, N.Y.

Aug. 7

Dear Leslie:

I want to leave here but I want some inducement. I don't want this guy [McGraw] to win the pennant and I feel if I stay here I will win it for him. You know I can pitch and win. So you see the fellows, and if you want to, send a man over here with the goods, and I will leave home on the next train. Send him to my home on the next train. Send him to my house so nobody will know, and send him at night. I am living at 145 Wadsworth Avenue, Apartment 1R. Nobody will ever know I will go down to fishing camp and stay there. I am asking you this so there won't be any trouble to anyone. Call me up if you are sending a man. Wadsworth 3210. Do this right away. Let me know. Regards to all.

Phil Douglas[11]

Douglas summoned the Giants' clubhouse attendant, handed him the letter, and told him to mail it special delivery.

Les Mann was the oddest of candidates to fix a pennant race or for that matter to do anything illegal. He enjoyed a reputation as one of the game's more upstanding individuals. A Springfield College graduate, Mann neither smoked nor drank, was active in the YMCA movement, and in the off-season served as assistant director of athletics at Indiana University. That Douglas believed Mann would abet such dishonesty either attests to his addled state of mind, his innate stupidity, or both. As baseball historian Lee Allen once observed, Douglas might as well as have sent the letter to Landis himself.[12]

The next day Douglas, if it were possible, was digging himself into an even deeper hole. Giants club secretary Jim Tierney had tipped off the *New York Evening Telegram*'s Fred Lieb that Douglas "was in real trouble with McGraw."

"Mac is very angry with him," explained Tierney. "This time, it isn't only his drinking. Phil is really in McGraw's doghouse; he says he doesn't give a damn whether Phil pitches another game for him."

The next day, Lieb wrote: "Phil Douglas is in McGraw's doghouse, and this time it may take more than . . . Jesse Burkett to get Phil out of it. The manager has lost all patience . . . It isn't entirely Phil's drinking problems. This time he is in deeper trouble."

The article infuriated Douglas. That afternoon he and Burkett were leaving the park when they saw Lieb through the chickenwire that separated the passageway from the press box.

"I don't like what you wrote about me today," Douglas screamed. "They were a pack of damned lies. I want to warn you—don't ever put my name in your paper again. Whether I win or lose, I don't ever want to see my name in your paper again. If I see it, there will be trouble."

"I ought to punch you in the nose," Douglas continued. Just then, press box attendant Perry Grogan arrived and grabbed him. "What are you so damn mad about?" Grogan wanted to know, "Isn't the story true?" Douglas evidently hadn't considered that. After thinking about it, he silently trundled out of the park.[13]

Douglas remained home for the rest of the homestand. On Saturday, Sunday, and Monday, August 12-14, the Giants' team physician, the appropriately named Dr. William Bender, visited Douglas to administer additional sedation. On Monday Douglas, Burkett, and fading outfielder Dave Robertson worked out at the Polo Grounds before traveling to Pittsburgh to join the team.

Douglas meanwhile had regained his cockiness. At Penn Station he bragged to the *New York Sun*'s Frank Graham that his latest "vacation" would be his last: "No, sir, you don't have to worry about Doug no more."[14]

Aboard the same train was John McGraw. For whatever reasons, whether his longstanding policy of avoiding his players off the field or because he suspected—or *knew*—trouble was brewing regarding Douglas, he traveled in a separate car from the rest of the Giants.[15]

Douglas' career, indeed his life, was about to come undone. Mann, scared silly at the thought of becoming another Buck Weaver, had immediately contacted his manager, Branch Rickey. Rickey, like Mann, was a highly religious college man. He was *also* a sharp competitor, who by informing on Douglas could strip a competing team of its ace pitcher.

Furthermore, Rickey was angry at the Giants. On July 30 New York had acquired pitcher Hugh "Red" McQuillan[16] from Braves owner George Washington Grant for $100,000, fading righthander Fred Toney and two rookies. Many accused McGraw of controlling the Braves through his old friend Grant. Rickey protested to Landis and to National League president John Heydler that McGraw was trying to "buy a pennant." Even some elements of the New York press agreed that if the Giants captured the championship there would "be a blot on it."

Much the same was going on in the American League. The Yankees, in a nip-and-tuck battle with the Browns, had just raided Harry Frazee's near-bankrupt Red Sox for third baseman "Jumping Joe" Dugan and outfielder Elmer Smith. St. Louisans were outraged. That city's Rotary Club even wrote a lengthy missive to Landis, contending the practice "will militate against the future of baseball."

"What chance," echoed Rickey, "have we ever to win a pennant in St. Louis if such conditions are permitted to go on?" Both Landis and Heydler turned Rickey down, but (except waiver transactions) within the fortnight Organized Baseball banned such exchanges after June 15.[17]

So there was no reason for Rickey to remain silent and every reason for him to turn Douglas in. He told Mann the letter was a "hot potato, in fact, dynamite" and ordered him to write Landis at once.[18][19]

Ardent Cubs fan Landis must have been familiar with how personally pathetic Douglas was. But in the highly suspicious atmosphere following the Black Sox scandal, there was little room for sensitivity about an alcoholic's mental state. An attempt, addled as it was, had been made to sell out a major league pennant race. Proof of the attempt existed in writing. Landis would not, in fact, he *could* not, tolerate it.

When he first learned of Douglas' letter he was at a joint major league session in Chicago. He ordered McGraw to see him in Pittsburgh. As soon as the joint meeting concluded Landis quietly boarded a train and secretly checked into the Schenley Hotel, where the Giants were staying, on Monday, August 15.

In 1918 after Christy Mathewson had accused Cincinnati Reds first baseman Hal Chase of throwing games, McGraw had nonetheless fallen all over himself to acquire arguably baseball's most corrupt player. But since exposure of the Black Sox, the Little Napoleon was no longer so cavalier. Even in a tight pennant race, he would have to throw Phil Douglas overboard.

On Tuesday morning Landis and McGraw confronted Douglas in McGraw's suite. Also present were Tierney and Heydler. The session was tense. All five men remained standing as Landis and McGraw began a summary trial of the pitcher. Douglas had almost forgotten about his letter to Mann, but when he saw Landis before him, he knew he was in trouble.

One of the most common misconceptions about the Douglas case is that Landis had banned him from the game. Actually, it was the Giants who had placed their star pitcher on the permanently ineligible list. This Landis explained to Douglas. He went on to state that the meeting's purpose was to ask the accused a few questions. If Douglas wanted to appeal the Giants' decision, he would have that right at a later date.

Perhaps attempting to find extenuating circumstances, Landis posed a series of questions to Douglas. Had the Giants ever treated him unfairly? Douglas answered no. Had they excessively fined him for his training lapses? Again, he responded negatively; all of his previous fines had been remitted. Was he underpaid? Douglas answered he now drew three times his Cubs' salary.

"Well," Landis continued, "why did you pick this player out to write to him?"

"Oh, I just knew him."[20]

Why had he done it, Landis wanted to know. "A man has to live," the spitballer answered, "and I was afraid I would be out of money and a job if Mac decided to let me go. I thought I could pick up some money from this other player and get along for a time."[21]

Then came the big question, which, in Landis' mind, was the only question.

"Did you write this, Mr. Douglas?"

Douglas sheepishly admitted, "Yes, I did."

"You know what this means, Phil Douglas; you are permanently out of Organized Baseball."[22]

Douglas, stunned beyond belief, silently left the room.[23] [24]

After Douglas departed, Landis and McGraw faced another task neither relished: informing the press.

Reporters, filing into the living room of McGraw's suite, were surprised to find Landis sitting sternly behind a desk. When he spoke, his words were tinged not with harshness or anger but with sorrow.

"Gentlemen," Landis, with some inaccuracy, began, "I have just placed the name of Phil Douglas on the permanent ineligible list."

"Why? What happened? What did he do?" they demanded of McGraw.

"Ask the Judge," he muttered.

"I called Douglas in and asked him if he had written this," Landis responded as he brandished and explained, but did not actually reveal, Douglas' letter to Mann. "He confessed that he had. . . ." Landis added, "There was nothing else for me to do. . . ."[25]

"There is nothing I can say. Mr. McGraw has told you everything . . . . There is no excuse to be offered for Douglas. He is the victim of his own folly. It is tragic and deplorable. I might use even more forceful terms if so many people hadn't already criticized me for using strong language."[26]

Just about all Landis had by way of further comment was that Douglas was "caught with the goods."[27]

Realizing they would get nothing further from either Landis or McGraw, reporters rushed to Douglas' room. He bitterly denied he had ever "thrown a game in [his] life."

Douglas said, "What makes me so mad is that Mac won't even give me my pay. I don't know how I'm going to get out of here unless I get some money, and I'm ashamed to wire my wife.

"I knew all along he was going to throw me out. Here I am without a cent with everybody spotting me as a traitor and a deserter and all that sort of bunk. I'm as innocent as a child."[28]

An hour later, shortstop Dave Bancroft entered McGraw's room. "I've got Doug in my room," he informed McGraw. "He's crying. He wants to know if you'll see him."

"No," McGraw responded. "It wouldn't do him any good, or me either. I feel sorry for him but there is nothing I can do to help him." He instructed Bancroft to tell Douglas he had arranged for his transportation back to New York. "And give him this," he added, handing Bancroft an envelope with $100 in it.

Despite his flaws Douglas was well liked by his teammates. In the Schenley lobby most of the Giants met him and shook his hand as he left. As this scene unfolded, Landis, with two porters in tow, entered the lobby. He was on his way to Forbes Field. Douglas confronted him, hoping to hear some word that maybe this nightmare really wasn't happening.

"Is this all true, Judge," he asked, "that I am through with baseball?"

"Yes. Douglas, it is."

"Do you mean that I can never play baseball again?"

"Yes, Phil, I am afraid that is just what it means."[29]

That ended the Judge's conversation with Douglas, but reporters soon surrounded Landis. He brushed off their questions, saying he would only be available following that afternoon's contest.

Tierney and Burkett accompanied the banished player to the train station. Douglas was still crying. Burkett, who boarded the train with him, was only slightly less forlorn; the big pitcher's banishment meant his "coaching" job was at an end. "The Crab" now left the big leagues to earn his keep as a Giants' scout.[30]

By now McGraw was feeling less sympathy for Douglas, saying he was "heartily glad to be rid of him." "Without exception," McGraw swore, Douglas was "the dirtiest ballplayer" in his recollection.

Considering McGraw's experiences with such crooks as Chase and Heinie Zimmerman that was quite an indictment.

McGraw continued bitterly, "I have worried more over Douglas than over any player I have ever had, and have had more trouble with him, without any return on his part."[31]

At Forbes Field McGraw and Landis officially informed the assembled Giants of Douglas' addled treason. McGraw spoke first, then Landis told the club, "You don't look to me like players who would fight any the less hard to win the pennant. I can't, in my position, wish you success for the pennant. I can't wish any team success, but I can wish you courage."[32]

Landis had promised to speak with reporters, but as soon as the game concluded, he announced, "I'm going back to Chicago tonight," and left for home. John Heydler also hurriedly left town, heading for Cincinnati to investigate a rumor that the National League race had been fixed in favor of Pittsburgh.[33]

When Douglas reached New York, reporters followed him to his home. Still sobbing, he advanced new lines of defense. Pathetically and not very convincingly he pointed out that his letter didn't mention the Giants and that he never mentioned money, only "inducements."

"I may never get back in the game," he protested, "but I'll force them to admit I was guilty of no crookedness."

His main rationalization, however, was that he had written the letter *before* McGraw had fined him and assaulted him "with the most vile names." Douglas now stated that on leaving the hospital he believed he had been released from the club; only after meeting McGraw did he learn he remained a Giant. "I then realized that I was still to be retained on the club," he told reporters, "and that night I phoned Mann . . . and begged him to tear up the letter." Mann, contended Douglas, promised to destroy the document. Instead he turned it over to Rickey.[34]

The flaw in Douglas's story, of course, is why would he need an inducement to leave a club he no longer belonged to. Either he had been so confused as he wrote the letter that this elemental logic escaped him, or he was lying again.

Meanwhile, McGraw grew angrier, rebutting the pitcher's tales of harsh treatment. Douglas, McGraw charged, knew "if he would get in condition every cent would be remitted. He had already overdrawn his account by $200 and said he was dead broke. So I ordered that $200 be sent to Mrs. Douglas, along with a $90 check for the rent."[35]

Some elements of the press refused to believe that the simple-minded Douglas had acted alone. A wild story briefly circulated that gamblers forced him to write the incriminating letter and then "double-crossed" him. Some theorized that Arnold Rothstein or, as Joe Vila put it in *The Sporting News*, other "long-nosed gamblers," had manipulated Douglas. In his *New York Sun* column Vila flatly stated that Douglas "didn't originate the plan" and questioned the very integrity of post-season play. Frank Graham, while admitting he was dealing in "pure conjecture," also wondered aloud about the existence of a conspiracy.[36]

In response to such rumblings, Landis, now back in Chicago, emerged from his silence, facing rumors not only fueled by Douglas himself, stating that Douglas had not initiated the bribe attempt but also that Landis was in fact responding to an earlier letter. If either scenario was true, yet another game-throwing conspiracy existed—bad news for baseball and for Landis. If Douglas acted alone the damage could be contained.

"After asking him every conceivable question," Landis told reporters in Chicago, "to find out whether there were any gamblers or anybody else in it with him, I came away with a pretty firm conviction in my own mind that there was nobody else."[37]

Landis had previously refused to release Douglas' letter to reporters. On Wednesday, August 18, he did: "When you read this letter," he pointed out,

> I want you to examine it very carefully. If you see the same things in it that I see, you will be convinced that it was written by a man who was making, not answering, an offer to desert his team for money. It was written by Douglas to a man who had never heard of the proposition before. The tone of the letter indicates that Douglas was taking the initiative. There is nothing pointing to an earlier letter to Douglas. . . .[38]
>
> In regard to the player who received the letter as absolutely innocent to my way of thinking. The wording of the Douglas letter to him is not such as would be used if there had been any dealings between the two, and this player, within fifteen minutes of receiving the letter, had shown it to others of his team at the hotel or clubhouse, whichever it was, in the town where they were.[39]

Public sentiment solidly backed banning Douglas and was particularly complimentary to McGraw. The *Cleveland Press* remarked that Douglas "got off pretty light." The *St. Louis Star* likened McGraw to a "plumed knight." *The Sporting News* derided Douglas as "sub-normal, at his best, from which you may guess his mentality after a two-weeks' debauch. . . ." The *Reach Guide* labeled him as potentially "a future menace to base ball." Frank Graham remarked that like Cicotte and Jackson and Felsch, Douglas had "stretched forth his hand for thirty pieces of silver."

Landis had once again masterly read public opinion.[40]

Yet, how much credit *did* McGraw deserve for purging Douglas? Circumstantial evidence exists that he may have known of Douglas' treachery *prior* to Landis' action, and that he was fully prepared to cover up the incident and retain Douglas on his staff. Reports floated that Douglas' call to Mann had been overheard. And Jim Tierney's words to Fred Lieb ("This time, it isn't only his drinking") hinted that McGraw knew of the abortive plot before Landis did—and did nothing about it.[41]

In Pittsburgh Landis had informed Douglas of his right to appeal. And on Sunday, August 20, the pitcher engaged Yonkers attorney Edward J. Lauterbach to secure a new hearing. Two days later Landis curtly dismissed Douglas' pleas. "The guilty party has been found and punished," he responded, "and so far as our office is concerned the matter is a closed incident."

Lauterbach responded with a two-pronged strategy. First, he threatened to sue the Giants for $100,000. Then he alleged Douglas had received a letter offering $15,000 to help throw the 1921 World Series. Douglas supposedly had shown it to his wife before destroying it. Presumably, this was designed to illustrate Douglas' fundamental honesty; i.e., that he would never actually be involved in fixing a game. More likely, all Landis saw was further "guilty knowledge" on Douglas' part, but the threat of a lawsuit gets anyone's attention, and Landis became far more circumspect. "I wrote to Mr. Lauterbach," he told reporters, "telling him that if he would have the evidence presented in the form of an affidavit. I would give the matter my attention, and if the evidence is sufficient will reopen the case."[42]

Meanwhile Douglas had traveled to Saratoga on "vacation," compounding matters by losing heavily at the resort city's track and casinos. To return home he needed a handout from *New York American* sportswriter Damon Runyon, who was at Saratoga covering the racing meet.

Back in New York Douglas met once more with Lauterbach to

determine his next step. During the session he broke down into wild sobbing. Lauterbach soon dropped the case.[43]

Douglas, however, continued to lobby for reinstatement. An April 6, 1922, letter from Landis to the Reds' Garry Herrmann indicates that Douglas had been corresponding with the Cincinnati owner on the subject. Landis wrote cryptically to Herrmann that "inasmuch as it appears that the player's contract covered the year 1921-1922, his present position makes it impossible to put him anywhere except on the ineligible list." Douglas remained banned from the game.[44]

Douglas returned to the South, performing in various independent and semipro leagues. As his talents faded he found work driving a laundry truck and even working in a factory making baseballs. By 1936 he was on relief. That year he wrote to *Birmingham News* sportswriter Zipp Newman, begging for his help in gaining reinstatement in baseball.

"I think I have been treated unfair," he wrote to Newman, "but I have not the means to fight it. It has worked many hardships and caused me many heartaches, this hanging over my good name. I love baseball and as you know was always in there for a lot of games every year. I surely need help, and any other information I can give I'll be glad to do so. Nothing would do me more good than to have a chance to come back to life."

Newman contacted Landis and attempted to have Douglas reinstated. "Phil was weak, never bad," contended Newman. Douglas, now 46, was far too old to pitch anywhere but the lowest minors, but Newman thought the gesture might help his damaged morale. Landis rejected the plea but sent Douglas a personal check to help tide him over.[45]

In poor health for some time, Douglas died of a stroke in July 1952. One last attempt to reinstate Douglas came in 1990. Commissioner Fay Vincent turned it down.[46]

# CHAPTER 17

# "BASEBALL IS O.K."

Reminders of the Black Sox scandal kept haunting Landis.

Dickey Kerr had been one of the so-called "Clean Sox"—White Sox players who had not taken part in the fix. Despite the disadvantage of having half the team playing behind him of dubious loyalty, Kerr, nonetheless, won two games during the 1919 Series. In 1920 his record soared to 21-9, and even in 1921 when the Sox skidded to seventh place, the 5'7" southpaw posted a very respectable 19-17 mark.

Harry Grabiner offered Kerr either $4,500 or $6,500 (accounts vary) for the upcoming season—but whatever the amount, it did not include the $500 raise Kerr desired. Instead the pitcher accepted a $5,000 contract to play with Texas semipros. There he performed against some of the banned Black Sox, and Landis suspended him. Not until August 1925 would Kerr be reinstated.[1]

Far less innocent—but far less punished—was former Giants pitcher Rube Benton.

Benton had been one of the earliest witnesses in Charles McDonald's grand jury investigation of baseball gambling. Benton initially testified that the only game-fixing incident he knew of was an offer made to him in September 1917 by teammates Buck Herzog and Hal Chase to throw a contest to the Cubs for $800. Benton further claimed he had promptly informed Giants captain Art Fletcher of the plot.

Yet, Benton soon changed that story. Two Boston Braves, third baseman Norman Boeckel[2] and catcher Art Wilson, provided affidavits regarding Benton's knowledge of the 1919 Series fix. Recalled to the grand jury, Benton now admitted that he had been present when Giants pitcher Jean Dubuc received a telegram from Sleepy Bill Burns telling him of the fix. Benton also revealed how Chase had won $40,000 betting on the Reds to win the Series, but he denied the charge that he himself had won $3,800 on the Fall Classic.[3]

Nonetheless, when the 1921 season began Benton remained on

the Giants' active roster. On August 1 he was breezing along with a
5-2 record and a 2.87 ERA when his past finally caught up with him,
and the Giants released him as an "undesirable." He, nonetheless,
remained in Organized Baseball, catching on with Minneapolis in
the American Association, where in 1922 he posted a 22-11 record.
Suddenly, Benton's moral lapses no longer seemed so important.

The Browns purchased his contract, but Ban Johnson prohibited
the deal, arguing that Benton was "barred" from his circuit for "guilty
knowledge of the Black Sox scandal."[4]

In the National League, Cincinnati had finished second in 1922
and was looking for the one player to put them over the top. The Reds
could not resist the temptation Benton presented. League president
John Heydler at first diplomatically tried to dissuade the Reds from
acquiring Benton, but Garry Herrmann, a longtime rival of Heydler,
pointed out with some logic that if Benton was an "undesirable" in
the majors, he should be equally undesirable in the minors and refused to back down. In February 1923, National League owners voted
6-2 to support Heydler and ban Benton, but they left themselves
some wiggle room, saying they would be "wholly guided" in the matter by whatever decision Landis might make.[5]

Here they miscalculated. At the request of Minneapolis president John Norton, Landis was already examining Benton's eligibility
to play in the majors. "If the Judge adheres to his expressions given
me," said Norton, "he will admit Benton and clear him of all taint."[6]

On March 8, 1923, just before leaving for his winter home at
Florida's Bell-Air Hotel, Landis issued his ruling: Benton was eligible to play for Cincinnati.

Despite his previous rulings that Buck Weaver and Joe Gedeon
be banned from the game for "guilty knowledge," the Squire found
that no problem regarding Benton.

"This is at war with every conception of justice and fair play,"
Landis thundered regarding Benton's blacklisting. "Certainly the
time to present and act upon charges which seek to permanently
deprive a man of his chief means of livelihood is at the time the matters alleged become known, not at the objectors' discretion upwards
of two years later.[7]

"I have carefully analyzed Benton's case, and I find him as clean
as any man in baseball," Landis informed reporters. "I have given out
a definite ruling on the subject and it will stand. No league official or
club can bar such a player from advancing in his own profession.

Benton is eligible to play with the Cincinnati club and no one is going to keep him from doing so if that club wants him."[8]

John Heydler had clearly not expected Landis to rule as he had. From his southern California vacation Heydler wired Herrmann that no matter what Landis ruled Benton would *not* play in the National League. "It is our judgment that Benton is not the type of character of player we want," he commented, "and therefore I will not sanction his return to our organization."[9]

Landis, meanwhile, was heading by train toward Florida. His first stop would be at the Brooklyn Robins' training camp at Clearwater. Near Jacksonville he made the acquaintance of Reds first baseman Frank Harding and of a Cincinnati fan named Charley Comello. They informed Landis of Heydler's actions.

"The judge at first refused to believe Heydler had made such a ruling," Harding later told reporters. "It was all new to him. But after we assured him we believed it to be the truth he said no one was going to overrule his decision . . ."

"No one is going to keep Rube Benton out of baseball or the National League," the Squire stormed. "I said he was eligible to play in organized baseball, and I'd like to see anybody try to stop him."[10]

He maintained that position as the days went on. After watching the Reds play Washington at Tampa he cockily remarked, "That case is absolutely settled. I have decided that Benton is eligible to play anywhere and so he is."

Reporters wanted to know what he would do if Heydler resisted. "I do not think he will do so," Landis smugly responded, "but, if he does, you will see something quite interesting. My decision in this case will stand."[11]

As spring training wound down Landis summoned Heydler to a closed-door session in Chicago. Heydler began backpedaling furiously. From the Cubs' spring base at Catalina Island, California, he now said the choice was clearly one for Cincinnati, but after meeting with Landis in Chicago he meekly said no more about the case. "Commissioner Landis has decided that the Cincinnati club is at liberty to sign and play Benton," was all Heydler would say, "and as far as I am concerned that ends the incident."

Even Ban Johnson—perhaps knowing that public opinion[12] was with Landis—pulled in his horns. Asked in August 1923 if he would protest Benton's presence if the Reds saw World Series action, Johnson blandly commented Benton was a National League issue.[13]

Landis had triumphed once again, but it was a puzzling victory. Why had the man who had established—and brutally enforced—the principle of "guilty knowledge" gone easy so on Benton?

Richard Nardinelli in a scholarly article in the journal *Baseball History* argues that the true issue in the Benton case was neither "guilty knowledge" or a statute of limitations—it was Landis' own authority, what Nardinelli calls "the cartel manager hypothesis" of Landis' commissionership. "Landis wanted to make it clear that only he had the authority to ban players from the game," Nardinelli observed, pointing out that in reinstating Benton Landis was overruling Heydler. True enough, but he was also overruling Ban Johnson who had earlier banned Benton. Landis would revisit the same principle four years later in the Cobb-Speaker case and treat it in very much the same way.[14]

The most similar case to Benton's was Joe Gedeon's. Both players had "guilty knowledge" of the Series fix, although in comparison to Buck Weaver's "guilty knowledge" theirs was mere hearsay.[15] The Browns had suspended Gedeon immediately following his grand jury testimony, and when Landis' tenure began, Gedeon was effectively out of Organized Baseball. Benton on the other hand was not. To repeat Bill Veeck's analysis: "[Landis] simply drew a line between the present and the past, granting an amnesty—if not necessarily immunity—to all who had sinned under the previous regime." Landis' overriding criteria was clearly that he *would not* deal with issues left over from the old administration. He would not allow *his* baseball to be tarnished by the sins of what had gone before. Obviously, in Landis' mind that "line between past and present" was very real, and he rarely—if ever— dared dredge up *anything* or punish anyone on the other side of it.[16]

On August 18, 1923, yet another gambling scandal appeared on Landis' horizon—but this one at least had the comfort of *not* being related to the Black Sox. *Collyer's Eye*, despite having accurately broached rumors of the 1919 Series fix, was a Chicago sporting weekly of somewhat dubious reputation. An article bylined by *Collyer's Eye* staffer Frank O. Klein charged that "two and possible three" Cincinnati players had been approached by New York gamblers to help throw a crucial recent five-game series against the Giants, a series the Giants had in fact swept. Klein's key points, however, were based on sheer insinuation. Arnold Rothstein *might* be involved, but there was no proof. Second baseman Sam Bohne (née

Sammy Cohen) and left fielder Pat Duncan (who in 1921 became the first player to hit a fair ball out of Redlands Field—a decade after it had opened!) had been "approached by the agent of the gamblers" and offered $15,000 each, but again there was "no direct evidence" they had accepted the cash.

A skeptical Landis wired the Reds' Garry Herrmann: "The character of the paper rather refutes any assertion made in its columns. However, any suggestion, even from such a source, will receive thorough investigation."[17]

Landis, however, maintained an atypical low profile and passed off the primary investigation to National League president Heydler. He, nonetheless, kept in constant contact with Heydler, who summoned Bohne and Duncan, along with Cincinnati sportswriters Tom Swope, Jack Ryder, Bill Phelon, and Bob Newhall, to New York for questioning. *Collyer's Eye* had smeared Bohne and Duncan with these words, "Their friends maintain their poor performances during the series were only attributal to such relapses as any player is likely to have, even in an important series." But the writers told Heydler they had seen nothing suspicious in the duo's play. Bohne batted .286 in the series, while committing two miscues. Duncan hit .350.[18]

Heydler immediately cleared the players and urged them to sue *Collyer's Eye*. From a sickbed in a Toronto spa Bert E. Collyer telegraphed Landis, urging "an immediate and thorough inquiry" and that Landis meet with one of Collyer's allies, former Illinois lieutenant governor, Major Barret O'Hara. Landis refused to respond to Collyer's wire.[19]

Public opinion easily accepted Heydler's verdict and had little interest in a further investigation. The *New York Times* spoke for many when it labeled the case a "dud."[20] *Collyer's Eye* began backing away from its original story. True, even Colonel O'Hara admitted, though while "a sudden flood" of money had been wagered on the Reds-Giants series, there was no doubt Bohne and Duncan were "fine young gentlemen . . . highly rated both as ball players and honorable individuals."[21]

From New Orleans Landis issued his own judgment:

> There never was any question in my mind as to Bohne and Duncan being implicated with gamblers in an effort to throw the Cincinnati games in Cincinnati with the Giants, as I know and believe both men are hard players, conscientious and above reproach,

and that as a result they would not stoop to the level of even considering a conference with gamblers which would hurt the chances of the Reds for the pennant and themselves of a nice little part of the world's series money.

The publication which brought the charges should be prosecuted by both Bohne and Duncan, for their own vindication and for the good of the game. Such tirades against players should be stopped and the sooner the editors of such publications are brought to the bar of justice and made to state on what grounds they publish such unfounded charges as those brought against Bohne and Duncan, the better for the game.

To reporters Landis went further, evincing his believe that *Collyer's Eye* had acted maliciously, making up its "facts" out of whole cloth.

"Baseball is O.K.," he declared. "It is being run straight. There is nothing crooked about it. The races in the big leagues show this. The strongest clubs are up at the top, and the weakest at the bottom. McGraw's pitchers are bad and he has faltered. Cincinnati and Pittsburgh are charging fast, but they have been stopped by clubs that seem to be easy for the others in the league."[22]

On September 7 Bohne and Duncan did just as Heydler and Landis "suggested." They filed suit in United States District court for $50,000 in damages apiece from the Collyer Publishing Co.

Their case, however, dragged on until February 1928. When the matter finally came to trial, Collyer alleged that he could not fully defend himself in court because his sources, gamblers fearful of public scrutiny, would never testify in public. Federal judge Walter C. Lindley instructed the jury to find the original article libelous, and they did. At that point Collyer agreed to settle out of court, paying $100 in damages ($50 to each player) plus court costs.

Yet as Collyer was making peace, *Collyer's Eye* ran yet another inflammatory piece. Landis caught sight of it and brought it to the attention of Bohne and Duncan's attorney, Walter H. Jacobs. Collyer assured Jacobs the article had been prepared before the settlement was reached, and Jacobs convinced the enraged Landis this should not derail the long-postponed settlement.

Landis was pleased. "Both the game," he crowed, "and the players, Bohne and Duncan, have been vindicated before the American public." John Heydler was even happier—so happy he had the National League pick up the entire $3,313.84 cost of the case.[23]

Just as the *Collyer's Eye* case began to wind down, a more vexatious one appeared.

Charles Stoneham had purchased the Giants from John T. Brush's estate in 1919 for an estimated $1.3 million. That was just a small portion of the Jersey City-born Stoneham's holdings. The pudgy, bug-eyed Stoneham had begun life as a humble office boy but by the early 1920s had accumulated a personal fortune of $10 million. He had gotten rich in a particularly disreputable way. His brokerage houses were actually "bucket shops," cut-rate, low-commission operations in which brokers never actually purchased stock for their clients but gambled on being able to buy or sell at a more advantageous (to them, not their clients) price later. It was legal, but in some sense it made Arnold Rothstein look like he was operating a bingo game.[24]

In 1923, a bucketshop Stoneham had supposedly divested himself of, E. M. Fuller and Company, went bankrupt. That August two of Fuller's principles, on the verge of entering prison for destroying Fuller's records, divulged to federal attorneys what their files had contained. That information—that Stoneham had supplied Fuller with $170,000 in National Entertainment Corporation (the Giants' official name) funds— led to Stoneham's August 31, 1923, indictment for perjury.[25]

Additional indictments followed. These concerned E. P. Dire and Company, of which Stoneham was also a partner. E. P. Dire had defrauded its clients to the tune of $4 million. Compounding Stoneham's embarrassment was his partner in E. P. Dire: Arnold Rothstein. The Dire partnership was not Stoneham's only connection to Rothstein. The Giants' owner gambled heavily with the "Big Bankroll," reputedly once losing $70,000 in a single night of wagering.[26]

Rumors swirled he would be ousted from the Giants. Even before his indictment, reports had fight promoter Tex Rickard, circus magnate John Ringling, John T. Brush's son-in-law Harry Hempstead, and former Browns owner Robert Hedges interested in the club. On Wednesday, September 5, Landis visited New York but was in no hurry to investigate. He was in a hurry to get to Boston and left the city after just a few hours. In Boston he officiated at an American Legion ceremony, then headed up the coast to Marblehead where the Braves and Senators met in an exhibition. The Judge returned to Manhattan that Saturday, meeting secretly with Stoneham and

Heydler at the Waldorf-Astoria and leaving for Chicago early the next morning.[27]

Frank Menke of the *The Sporting News* gleefully threw Landis' words regarding Benny Kauff's indictments and "elemental morality" back at him. "Protecting the good repute [of baseball]," jeered Menke, "based on Landis' own ideas, in the Kauff case, means ridding the game of undesirables. Stoneham is an undesirable—and something beyond."[28]

He certainly was, but another factor was at work. Said one anonymous baseball official, "The constitution of the National League does not provide any way in which a club owner can be ousted for offenses outside of baseball," Landis knew that; Heydler knew that; and most importantly Stoneham knew that. If Stoneham were to leave the game, it would be at his behest and at his asking price—rumored to be $3 million. Considering he and his partners had paid just $1.3 million for the club in January 1919, it was a steep asking price.[29]

Yet, while nothing allowed baseball to expel Stoneham from its counsels, nothing forced the National League to elect Stoneham to its board of directors, which it did while he was still under indictment.[30]

A jury acquitted Stoneham on February 27, 1925, but the verdict did little to quiet the controversy since the trial had been marked by widespread rumors of jury tampering. Charles Stoneham would remain as owner of the National League's most successful franchise.[31]

The Landis reform program was clearly slowing down.

# CHAPTER 18

# "THEY'RE MAKING A GOAT OUT OF ME"

As the 1924 season moved into its last weekend, Kenesaw Landis looked at baseball and saw that it was good. At the box office, the major leagues had finally shaken off the residue of the Black Sox affair, with a record attendance of 9,540,555—breaking the previous record of 9,120,875 set in 1920 just as the scandal broke. On the field events were equally pleasing. In the senior circuit John McGraw's Giants and Wilbert Robinson's Brooklyn Robins battled neck-and-neck for the flag. In the American League, Bucky Harris' Washington Senators barely edged out Miller Huggins' Yankees. It was Washington's first pennant, but even more gratifyingly it meant a long-delayed World Series appearance for the beloved Walter Johnson.[1]

To Landis Washington's triumph meant one more thing. In his fourth season as commissioner he would finally spend *part* of a Fall Classic outside New York. As a Chicagoan, a race innately resentful of the Big Apple, that was important.

But there was a major cloud on Landis'—and baseball's—horizon. Before that cloud moved on, it would expose deep divisions, even hatreds, within the game and dredge up still more ugly incidents from baseball's past.

The autumn calm would blow apart thanks to a young Giants' part-timer named Jimmy O'Connell.

James Joseph O'Connell was an expensive benchwarmer. In 1919 the 19-year-old had signed with the Pacific Coast League's San Francisco Seals. He batted a modest .262, but by 1921 his average had soared to .337. In the process, the kindly but unsophisticated youngster not only established himself as one of the Bay Area's most popular players but also attracted covetous major league eyes. Before the 1922 season began John McGraw would outbid the Yankees for

O'Connell's services, literally sending Seals owner Charles Graham a blank check. Graham filled in "seventy-five thousand dollars," then the highest price ever paid for a minor leaguer. McGraw, however, allowed the Seals to keep O'Connell for another year, and the youngster responded with a .335 average and 39 stolen bases, earning the somewhat overblown title of "The Babe Ruth of the Pacific Coast." Graham, taking no chances that O'Connell wouldn't arrive safely in John McGraw's hands before the check cleared, insured him for $75,000.[2]

Fame was particularly fleeting for O'Connell. Even before the 1923 season began, his record price tag was eclipsed when teammate Willie Kamm (.342, 20 HR, 124 RBI) fetched $100,000 from the White Sox. And McGraw, sitting on a wealth of talent, decided against rushing his young prospect. "You will be with us a long time," he reassured the kid, " . . . we will get our money out of you. So just relax . . . " O'Connell needed encouragement. He hit just .250 in 1923 and although he improved to a healthy .317 the following year, he batted just 104 times.[3]

On Saturday, September 27, 1924, John McGraw stood on the verge of his fourth straight championship, something no big league manager had yet accomplished. At the Polo Grounds his Giants had just swept three games from Bill McKechnie's Pirates, eliminating them from the race. Only Wilbert Robinson's Robins remained in contention. McGraw and Robinson had once been the closest of friends, but that was way in the past. Now they despised each other with a hatred that only *former* friends can share. With three days left in the regular season, any combination of two Giant victories and Robin losses would give McGraw the pennant.

New York's odds were good, but for at least one Giant, not good enough.

That Saturday the club played seventh-place Philadelphia. Before the game Jimmy O'Connell walked across the Polo Grounds diamond toward three Phillies, shortstop John Henry "Heinie" Sand, journeyman righthander Johnny Couch, and former 20-game-winner Joe Oeschger, casually striking up a conversation about off-season exhibition games on the coast. Sand said he was staying east that winter. As Couch and Oeschger moved away, O'Connell remained.

It was Sand who O'Connell really wanted to talk to, although except for his position, Sand was hardly a key Phillie—if it can

indeed be said there are any key players on a next-to-last-place team.
He had arrived in the majors just the previous season, batting a mere
.228. In 1924 he hit .245 with a propensity for strikeouts. In fact, his
weak stickwork inspired baseball's shortest poem. It read:

Sand
fanned.

But like O'Connell, Sand was a San Francisco boy, and while
Jimmy had played with the Seals, Sand performed in the Coast
League with Salt Lake City, establishing himself in September 1921
when one afternoon he not only homered twice but executed an un-
assisted triple play. Sand had also fetched a good price from a major
league club: $40,000 from the penurious Phillies.[4] O'Connell felt he
could do business with Sand.

O'Connell wanted to know how Sand felt about the pennant race.
He replied that since O'Connell was a friend, he was pulling for the
Giants, but still wanted his own club to win their two remaining
games against New York and for last-place Boston to beat Brooklyn
twice, thus forcing a tie for the pennant.

Then O'Connell asked: "Would $500 change your mind?"

The proposition disgusted Sand. He made a face to register his
displeasure. "Jimmy," he responded, "I am not interested."

"All right, Heinie," O'Connell said, as he guiltily edged away, "this
is just between you and I. It needn't go no further."

But it did. Almost immediately a shaken Sand confided in both
Oeschger and second baseman Horace "Hod" Ford.[5]

The Giants won that game anyway, with southpaw Jack Bentley
defeating righthander Jimmy Ring, 5-1. Sand went 0-for-3, but
walked, scored the Phils only run, and handled three chances without an error. In Boston, young Johnny Cooney beat Brooklyn, 3-2.[6]

The Giants had won the pennant.

Sand tried to pretend O'Connell's foolish proposition had never
taken place, but Ford argued with him to report O'Connell. Both remembered how Landis had banned Buck Weaver for life for his "guilty
knowledge" of the 1919 fix; they thought of Les Mann turning in
Shufflin' Phil Douglas and avoiding Landis' wrath. Sand was convinced. He sought out Phils manager Art Fletcher, finally finding him
asleep in his room. Nervously, he told Fletcher what had happened.

"I don't know what's behind this," Fletcher responded, "but now that I know something's up, I can protect you. And I'll find out what's behind it."[7]

Art Fletcher had long known McGraw. From 1909 through 1920 he was the Little Napoleon's regular shortstop, enjoying his best performance (.319) in the Giants' pennant-winning 1911 season. Again, luck was against O'Connell. Fletcher hated to lose. That he would countenance losing *on purpose* was inconceivable.

Despite the late hour Fletcher phoned National League president John Heydler at his Long Island home: "I've got something important to tell you, but I do not wish to discuss it on the telephone. Where can I meet you?"

At a New York hotel, the three men talked over breakfast the next morning, Sunday, September 28. Once Heydler heard Sand's story he immediately left the table to telephone Landis. On returning he swore both Fletcher and Sand to secrecy.

In Chicago Landis was preparing to travel, but not to New York. The Squire, Winifred Landis, and Leslie O'Connor were headed for Washington where the World Series would begin on Saturday, October 4. Now, Landis and O'Connor hastily changed plans, arriving in New York's Penn Station the following morning, with the Judge secretly checked into Room 670 at the Waldorf-Astoria. The Phils were still at the Polo Grounds, scheduled to play the season's now meaningless last game.

Landis met first with Heydler; then with Sand. "Were," Landis demanded, "any other Philadelphia players approached—as far as you know?"

"I did not hear of any, Judge," Sand responded.

"Have you any idea why O'Connell should have picked you—as he apparently did—as the only Philadelphia player he might safely approach with a proposition such as this?"

"No."

"Is he a friend of yours?"

"Not particularly. I've known him quite a while and I've always liked him."[8]

Landis now summoned McGraw and Giants owner Charles Stoneham. Both were surprised that Landis was in town and professed shock and bewilderment at Sand's charges. But their attitude soon changed to anger at Heydler, who they felt should have contacted them before running to Landis.

"Why didn't you advise us of this matter before?" McGraw snarled.

"I considered it to be a matter for the Commissioner," Heydler answered.

"But whose ballplayer is it that's being accused?" McGraw shot back, "It's our ballplayer and we have a right to know about this—about any of it."

Then he turned his fire at Landis. "How do you know Sand isn't lying," he wanted to know.

"I don't know," said Landis. "But I propose to find out. Get hold of O'Connell and tell him I want to see him.... I want to see him alone, by the way, gentlemen."[9]

O'Connell found Landis alone in his sitting room. As he entered it he thought how ordinary the scene looked. Landis sat at a small davenport with a table beside it. O'Connell stood uncomfortably. Before long he would be even more uneasy.

When the questioning began, O'Connell, much to Landis' surprise, admitted everything. "I've been asked why I didn't lie ... ," O'Connell later explained. "It never occurred to me. I never have been a liar, and it never entered my mind to lie. I just told him what happened and let it go at that."

O'Connell's honesty sealed his doom. "When he said yes, there was nothing I could do but dismiss him from baseball," Landis once told Charlie Graham. "If he had said no it would have been his word against the accusing player and I probably would have had to ignore the whole matter."[10]

Landis now had no choice but to say, "Do you understand that as a result of what you are saying, you will be expelled from baseball?"

"Yes, sir," O'Connell responded.[11]

But there was a bigger game afoot. Landis asked, "Who put you up to it?" Jimmy responded just as easily, "Why Cozy Dolan. That was on Saturday morning before the game. He said the whole team would chip in to make up the $500. Frankie Frisch, Pep Youngs, and George Kelly all knew about it. When I told Pep what Dolan had said about the money, Youngs said, 'Go for it!' Then, I told Frisch, and Frank said to me, 'Give Sand anything he wants.' "[12]

Suddenly here was information that could destroy the New York franchise. Second baseman Frankie Frisch (7 HR, 69 RBI, .328), right fielder Ross "Pep" Youngs (10 HR, 74 RBI, .356), and first baseman George Lange "Highpockets" Kelly (21 HR, a league-leading 136 RBI, and a .356 average)[13] were the heart of the club's offense. All were future Hall-of-Famers.

Giants first base coach Albert J. "Cozy" Dolan was another matter. Dolan had begun his major league career in 1909 as a Cincinnati third baseman, going to the Giants in time to play on the 1911-1912 pennant winners. No one ever accused him of being a great player or a genius—even a genius of the baseball variety.[14]

After a stint of minor league managing in 1920, he returned to the majors as a coach. As *The Sporting News* put it:

> Good ol' Coz, champion pie eater of baseball, comes back as a member of the Chicago Cubs. [Manager] Fred Mitchell figured Dolan would put life into his somewhat dead team . . . As Coz puts it himself, he will play the role of goat. If a base-runner gets caught off base, they will blame Coz. If the runner by some accident advances, the runner will get the glory, but it's all the same to Coz. In whatever position he is put he will add to the gaiety of nations, to the joy of the fans. There is only one Dolan, although there are many counterfeits.[15]

The following year he joined the Giants, where he specialized in snitching on players to McGraw and guffawing uproariously at his jokes. "Not only was Cozy the first to laugh . . . ," noted an unimpressed sportswriter Joe Williams, "but the last to stop." Williams coldly dismissed Cozy as McGraw's "yes man."[16]

"His functions on the team," the *Herald-Tribune* added, "were those of a superannuated errand boy. He scarcely dared to breathe in the clubhouse without permission."[17]

Dolan was the first of the accused quartet Landis interrogated.[18] He had been working at the Giants' ticket office, when he received word Landis wanted to see him. "I suspected nothing," he claimed. "I had always been friendly with the Judge, often had brought him a mess of ducks to Chicago from my home . . . in the off season." With O'Connell still in the room, Dolan refused to categorically deny his allegations, repeatedly resorting to such answers as "I cannot recall it," "I cannot remember it," "I don't remember it," and "Not that I can remember."

A frustrated and angry Landis had no doubt—reasonable or otherwise—that with so much at stake Dolan should easily remember

a conversation of such overwhelming import a mere three days previously. Cozy had just written himself a one-way ticket to baseball
oblivion.

Next came Youngs, Frisch, and Kelly. Each denied O'Connell's
story, although Youngs' and Frisch's testimony contained some disquieting hedging.

Youngs told Landis: "I have heard talking around and such
things mentioning it, but I don't remember who by. You hear fellows
talking around that boys are offering money and something like that.
I never heard anything like this, offering money here. This is the first
I heard of it. . . . Cozy might have been talking or something like
that, but so far as offering money, or something like that, no."[19]

Yet Landis—either buying into the idea that talk like this was
mere horseplay or fearing to pursue it fully for fear of where it would
go—failed to follow up.

Frankie Frisch also denied urging O'Connell to give Sand "anything he wants," but like Dolan he too initially professed not to "remember" any clubhouse talk of O'Connell's bribe offer. Suspiciously he
conceded there was "always a lot of kidding going on on every bench."[20]

Landis found Frisch's comments somewhat disturbing but not
enough to prevent clearing him along with Kelly and Youngs.

The Judge was in no hurry to let the public know about this latest
scandal. Would these embarrassments never cease? he wondered.
And why had this one erupted at such a particularly inopportune
time? He was looking forward to a "ripping" World Series that would
finally take place outside New York City, and, like so many fans, relished the prospect of seeing Walter Johnson showcased in post-season
play. Now, not only was the sheen being removed from this particular
World Series but, for all he knew, perhaps from all to follow.

On Wednesday October 1—just three days before the Series
would commence at Griffith Stadium—100,000 overjoyed Washington fans thronged Pennsylvania Avenue, celebrating their first pennant. "As the head of an enterprise which transacts some business in
this town," President Calvin Coolidge twanged before presenting
Nats manager Bucky Harris with a ceremonial loving cup. "I have
the double satisfaction in welcoming the victorious ball team." Such
was the spirit of jubilation on the Potomac that Coolidge actually
smiled as he spoke.[21]

That day Landis—still in New York, but leaving *very* quickly for
Washington—dropped a three paragraph bombshell, exposing the

scandal. He banned not only O'Connell but also Dolan, whose testimony he derided as "of such a character as to be unacceptable." Frisch, Youngs, and Kelly were cleared. "Their testimony . . . ," he concluded with some lack of total candor, "was a clear refutation of [O'Connell's] charge, which, standing alone, was exceedingly unreasonable."[22]

There was one little-noted reason, however, why Landis did not believe O'Connell's allegations regarding his teammates. O'Connell told Landis that immediately after talking with Sand, he informed George Kelly of Sand's response, and then took batting practice. Sand branded that a lie. "I was curious to see if he would approach one of our other players," Sand noted. "I stood near the grandstand and watched him. However, he did not approach anyone else, but walked back to the bench. He sat down on the bench alone. I did not see him speak to any one." Fred Lieb, no doubt referring to this incident, wrote in the *Telegram* that Landis told him, "No court in the world would convict Frisch, Kelly and Youngs on the evidence which was furnished me."[23]

Beyond saying the incident was "deplorable" and of deep personal "regret," Landis refused further comment. Reporters noted that his tiny frame seemed a little more bent and his face more lined than usual. Gamely, he put a positive spin on events, noting how "the majority of players are honest" and commending Sand for his actions.[24]

Meanwhile a stunned O'Connell was visiting the Giants' clubhouse. Sitting on a rubbing table, he muttered to reporters, "They're making a goat out of me. I've been a damned fool. They were all in on it and they deserted me when they found I was caught." Except for outfielder Irish Meusel who gave him a pat on the back, his former teammates ignored him. He waited in vain "to have it out" with Dolan and call him a liar "to his face." Dolan never showed.[25]

John McGraw maintained an air of puzzlement over the affair, deriding O'Connell's and Dolan's intelligence. O'Connell, McGraw scoffed, was "never a quick thinker on the ball field."[26]

When asked whether Dolan possessed "more judgment," McGraw snapped: "You haven't known Cozy as long as I have."[27]

"I can't understand why these men did what they did," McGraw told reporters, "when the chances were 100 to 1 that New York would win the pennant. The only explanation I can give is that they are a couple of saps. If you search the country over, you probably couldn't find two bigger ones."[28]

In Washington McGraw remained bitter. In the lobby of the Hotel

Raleigh, he remarked, "It is to laugh. Why should we pay one of the guys [from the Phillies] to lose a ball game? They get paid for losing games all year."[29]

The scandal, nonetheless, had one positive effect. Before it surfaced, labor unrest filled the air, with Giants players seriously discussing striking to obtain not only their Series' gate share but also their normal salary prorated for the duration of the post-season. They were preparing to approach the Senators with this scheme.

Also mulling over a strike were the umpires scheduled to work the Fall Classic. Bill Klem, Tommy Connolly, Bill Dineen, and Ernie Quigley wanted compensation equivalent to the players' World Series shares. But when the O'Connell-Dolan affair broke, both the umpires and the Giants thought better of their ideas.[30]

O'Connell still maintained he was telling the truth about his fellow players as well as about Dolan. "I've given out the whole truth," he said. "There is not any reason I should lie about it, is there?"[31] There *was* no good reason for him to lie. And in actuality, perhaps he had confessed so rapidly because so many others had known of his actions.

Adding to Landis' problems were his fellow executives. Predictably Ban Johnson, incensed by Landis' failure to notify him of events but no doubt motivated more by his violent residual hatreds for both Landis and McGraw, was there to knife the Judge in the back. By Friday Johnson had charged there was "an astonishing lot of scandal" in baseball's ranks and called for a federal investigation into "rotten influences" at work in the game. While United States Attorney General Harlan Fiske Stone found no jurisdictional grounds for a probe, Congressman Sol Bloom (D-NY) supported Johnson, introducing legislation for the sport's federal regulation. "Baseball magnates recognized the demand for some sort of super-regulation when Judge Landis was chosen as Czar," contended Bloom, "but the game is too big for one man to control."[32]

The American League's jowly president continued his outbursts, demanding that second-place Brooklyn represent the National League in the Series. "And if Brooklyn isn't permitted to play," Johnson stormed, "there should be no World's Series at all." Childishly he announced he would not attend the Series and would instead be vacationing at Excelsior Springs, Missouri.[33]

But there was still more in Johnson's bag of tricks, as he seemed intent not only on destroying Landis, McGraw, and the National

League, but baseball itself. He made unsupported allegations that other Phillies had been approached to throw games. Gleefully he produced a February 1923 affidavit from former Boston catcher Lou Criger, swearing that back in 1903 at Pittsburgh's Monongahela Hotel a gambler named Anderson offered Criger $12,000 to throw the very first modern World Series.[34] The document had no particular relevance to the present case, but Johnson took pains to point out a portion of the old catcher's tale— that when Criger was introduced to Anderson in 1901, it was in the presence of McGraw and Robinson.[35]

Reports even circulated that Johnson publicly threatened to drive Landis, McGraw, and Stoneham out of baseball. He denied such remarks but was hardly conciliatory. "Landis," he charged from Chicago, "was on the bench for seventeen years here and got away with insulting a lot of lawyers who appeared before him. He has insulted me and my umpires. He is off the bench now and down among men and should act like a man."[36]

If Landis did not already mortally despise Ban Johnson, he had every excuse to now.

Also pouring petrol on the flames was Pirates owner Barney Dreyfuss, who broadly hinted that McGraw himself was at the heart of a conspiracy. It was ludicrous, he contended, "to ask people to believe that two rather obscure [Giants] would go and offer to pay somebody five hundred dollars, solely of their own money, to have something crooked done that would benefit many other persons besides themselves.

"The New York players change," Dreyfuss added, in case anyone missed his point, "but the manager remains the same."[37]

Dreyfuss was more than eager to join Johnson in curbing Landis' unlimited powers. He also wanted the World Series canceled, calling it a "growing menace to the best interests of the game."

Dreyfuss, again like Johnson, planned to boycott the Series. But at the last minute he and Bill McKechnie traveled to Washington, allegedly to provide Landis with information about the scandal—or perhaps on other scandals involving McGraw. Landis didn't want to hear any of it. He "shut the door in my face," charged Dreyfuss.[38]

Later Dreyfuss and McKechnie came upon the Judge in his hotel lobby. "When will you be in?" Dreyfuss demanded. "I came all the way from Pittsburgh to talk to you."

"I *will not* be in," Landis spat out.

"Why won't you be in?" McKechnie asked.

Landis now virtually unhinged, shouted at him, "Who are you? I have nothing to do with you."

A disgusted Dreyfuss returned home, vowing that if Landis wanted any information from him "he will have to ask for it."[39]

What evidence was Dreyfuss so eager to reveal? Most likely it did not revolve around the rumors, which McKechnie had already denied, that his own club had been approached to toss games to the Giants. Actually Dreyfuss was agitated over reports that the 1921 Giants—specifically Dolan—had bribed Brooklyn players to throw games, thus giving New York the pennant over Pittsburgh. Dolan had also allegedly "tampered" with Pie Traynor. Adding to Dreyfuss' chagrin, of course, was the fact that in anticipation of a Pirates' 1921 World Series appearance he spent a small fortune needlessly increasing Forbes Field's capacity.[40]

A boiling Landis curtly informed reporters: "All I will say to you at this time is that, in view of these statements, it seems to me a pretty good time for gentlemen who are not clothed with responsibility to keep their shirts on."[41]

Criticism also greeted the Judge in the press. In *The Sporting News* veteran sportswriter Francis Richter scalded Landis' performance in the case and charged him with some severe character flaws. "Commissioner Landis," he contended, ". . . exhibited the same arrogance which has estranged nearly everyone from support and cooperation, an astonishing incapacity or unwillingness to probe the case to the bottom." The *New York Herald-Tribune* found it inconceivable that the Judge, with "his knowledge of human nature and the law," could believe O'Connell and Dolan had concocted this scheme on their own—nor could it see how he could expect anyone else to accept it. Grantland Rice wrote that "the vast baseball public refuses to believe that O'Connell and Dolan acted alone."[42]

But Landis was not without his defenders. John Heydler gave Landis his full backing. So did Phillies owner William F. Baker. The *New York Times* editorial page praised Landis' "high degree of moral courage" and argued that "again he has vindicated the wisdom of his appointment as arbiter of the national game." And the *Herald-Tribune*—despite its doubts—expressed confidence that Landis would nonetheless get to the bottom of the case with both "courage and enthusiasm."[43]

Not surprisingly McGraw dismissed Dreyfuss as a "crack pot," sneering he was bitter about not being able to fill the extra seats he had built. Dreyfuss shot back: "McGraw says I am still sore about the Pirate defeat in 1921. If all that happened in 1921 had been exposed, McGraw might not look very good. McGraw should be the last person to refer to 1921. . . . He is not in my class."[44]

Washington's Clark Griffith was an old friend and supporter of Ban Johnson. But the nation's capital was now delirious over the Senators, with scalpers fetching $1,000 for tickets to Game One. Obviously "The Old Fox" knew it was in his own interest to foil Johnson's plans to crash the Series. He defended the game's integrity and Landis' swift handing of the case and accused Johnson of "playing baseball politics."[45]

Fred Lieb quoted one unnamed magnate who compared Landis' methods to those of the old National Commission, contending that under the old system the scandal would never have been made public—and certainly not soon enough to jeopardize an upcoming World Series. "Landis has no property interests in baseball," he summarized, "and property rights with him are a secondary consideration. He regards himself as the public's steward in baseball and is jealous of that trust."[46]

All the while the Series' fate hung in doubt. Landis made his decision. "The series," he decreed, "will be played."[47]

In Washington on the morning of the first game of the Series, Hearst columnist Damon Runyon cornered Landis and grilled him about the scandal. Landis' mood switched from sadness to anger. He jumped to his feet and pointed a bony finger. "The appalling stupidity of it!" Landis exclaimed to Runyon. "It left me dazed." He dismissed O'Connell as not "a particularly keen sort" but reserved his real bile for Dolan and his inept stonewalling. For Runyon, Landis staged an elaborate recreation of Dolan's performance at the Waldorf, first looking down, then up, then running his fingers through his hair and rubbing his chin, before mimicking Cozy's pathetic response, "I don't remember."

He then fixed a long, almost hostile stare at Runyon, before continuing, confessing he "was absolutely dumbfounded" at Dolan's response.[48]

Once Calvin Coolidge threw out the first pitch of the Series, however, scandal took second place to the excitement of an exceedingly well-played Fall Classic. In Game One, Walter Johnson suffered a heartbreaking 12-inning, 4-3 loss. Game Two was even better, although Silent Cal, unwilling to offend foes of Sunday baseball, did not bother to attend. In his absence, the Giants in the top of the ninth scored twice to tie the game, but in the bottom of the inning the Senators tallied the winning run to even the Series.[49]

Game Three would be played in New York. By Monday morning, October 6, Landis had returned to the Waldorf-Astoria, and Jimmy O'Connell, despite reports that he was leaving for California, was there to see him. O'Connell, clearly grasping at straws, claimed he had received no official notice of his banishment. When Landis pointed out he had mailed it, O'Connell admitted receiving something, but that since it wasn't signed, contended it couldn't be valid. Landis had no problem in obliging him with a signature.

O'Connell then asked why Landis believed his story regarding Dolan but not about Frisch, Youngs, and Kelly. Landis carefully led him through Dolan's testimony. He got O'Connell to admit Dolan was "lying," then told the young man he could not "find these [other] men guilty" based on available evidence. He assured O'Connell, however, that the case was not closed and virtually begged for more evidence: "On your question as to whether this is ended, I tell you that it is not ended, that if anything happens, if there is anything in the world that suggests further inquiry, it will be followed up, that it is never ended."[50]

O'Connell had nothing new to offer.

He did, however, ask Landis about an article appearing in that morning's tabloid *New York Daily Mirror*. Entitled "Broadway Gamblers at Bottom of Bribe Scandal," it alleged that gamblers, out to protect $100,000 in bets on the National League pennant race, had approached Dolan at Times Square's Gaiety Billiard Parlor and paid him $5,000. It further contended Landis had possession of a letter signed just "Jimmy" to that effect. Landis denied knowing of any such missive until he read about it in the *Mirror*. For his part Dolan not only denied the story, he claimed he *never* set foot in any New York City pool hall.[51]

That afternoon it was mercifully back to baseball. At the Polo Grounds Landis had 15-year-old Julian Dubosky as his guest. Dubosky, an Ebbets Field scorecard vendor, had taken the train to Washington for the first two games of the Series. There Senators reserve first baseman Mule Shirley befriended him and admitted him into the park for free. Inside Landis tendered the lad an invitation to be his guest when the Series returned to New York. But that solved just one of the urchin's problems. He had money enough to reach only as far as Baltimore on his return trip, so a kind conductor let him ride home free.[52]

On the field the Senators struggled to a 6-4 win, pulling ahead of New York two games to one. Fans taunted McGraw with cries of "Where's Jimmy O'Connell?" and "Put Cozy Dolan on the coaching line."[53]

Dolan, meanwhile, had phoned Landis in Washington and requested another hearing. He got one on Tuesday morning, October 7, at Landis' 11th-floor Waldorf-Astoria suite. The two men got nowhere and the session quickly degenerated into a shouting match, with the 57-year-old, 130-pound Landis more than willing to mix it up with the 34-year-old, 160-pound coach, shaking his fist in Dolan's face and shouting: "You are standing here and telling me in that belligerent attitude and manner what you won't stand for. I haven't any interest in that. Maybe you could get me in a physical combat. You are a younger man than me."

"Judge," Dolan responded, "I don't want you to think that. I am not that kind of a man."

Landis continued, "Although maybe I could put up some sort of a defense if you want to try."

Even Cozy Dolan was smart enough to realize wrestling baseball's High Commissioner to the floor was counterproductive. "Judge," he pleaded, "I don't come down here to look for a fight."

"What is this demonstration for?" Landis wanted to know.

"You ran over at me," Dolan explained. "I just want to tell you I don't know anything about it."[54]

That was about as productive as the meeting got.

As dominating and vexatious a topic as the O'Connell scandal was, a World Series *was* taking place—and a damned good one at that. New York took the final two games at home, gaining a 3-2 edge. When play returned to Griffith Stadium, Landis, seated on the third-base side, assumed his customary pose, chin planted firmly upon the concrete wall in front of him. So intent was he on maintaining this posture, he moved only to take a seventh-inning stretch.[55]

Washington captured Game Six to even the Series. Then came one of the great contests in World Series annals. Down 3-1 going into the bottom of the eighth, the Nats tied the score on Bucky Harris' two-out, two-run single. Just two days before, Walter Johnson had pitched eight innings and was still looking for his first Fall Classic win, but Harris—managing perhaps more with his heart than his head—brought the Big Train in to relieve. The game went into extra innings, and Johnson put runners on in the ninth, 10th, 11th, and 12th innings, but Harris stuck with him.

In the bottom of the 12th catcher Muddy Ruel led off and hit a pop foul to his counterpart Hank Gowdy. Gowdy tripped over his mask, dropped the ball, and gave Ruel another chance. He made the best of it, doubling down the third-base line. Then Walter Johnson was due up. Harris let him hit. Shortstop Stonewall Jackson bobbled the ball, and Johnson reached first with Ruel holding second. Up came center fielder Earl McNeely who grounded routinely to third baseman Freddie Lindstrom. It was an easy out, perhaps even a double—or triple—play. But the ball hit a pebble, bouncing crazily over Lindstrom's head. Walter Johnson had his World Series victory, and a sentimental nation cheered.

Kenesaw Mountain Landis marveled to Fred Lieb, "You have just watched the greatest world's series that you, I or any one else has ever looked at. You have just seen the most remarkable baseball game that was ever played anywhere."[56]

Washington went baseball mad that night, and as Landis watched the jubilation from his hotel balcony, half in joy and half in fear, he turned to Lieb, asking: "I wonder whether we are looking at the high tide of this thing we love. Greece and Rome had their sports; they must have reached a peak, and then receded. Are we looking at such a peak tonight?"[57]

The Squire could not get Washington's exhilaration out of his mind. He remarked, "That demonstration was the most impressive thing I ever saw during my connection with baseball. If a world's championship can give an entire city such joy, then surely the world's series is worth preservation as an American institution."[58]

But the O'Connell scandal would not go away. Landis had planned a month's vacation in Asheville, North Carolina, but now scrapped his itinerary. He then returned to New York, where between a lot of golf and a lot of reporters' questions he continued the investigation. "A man making an investigation doesn't shout it from the housetops," he snapped to reporters.[59]

Cozy Dolan was again in the limelight, barking at Landis' door and asking for forgiveness. But now the case had a new and additionally troublesome twist. Aiding Dolan was one of the great criminal lawyers of his era, William J. Fallon, known as "The Great Mouthpiece."

Fallon carried the stench of corruption with him. Often retained by gamblers such as Nicky Arnstein and Arnold Rothstein, who used him to circumvent justice in the Black Sox case, Fallon had also previously represented both Stoneham and McGraw. Fallon defended McGraw after an unpleasant August 1920 incident in front of New York's Lambs' Club when McGraw fought with a fellow member, was suspected of fracturing another's skull, and was formally charged with violating the Volstead Act. "I never fight," McGraw curiously explained, "unless I am drunk." The Lambs expelled the Little Napoleon, but Fallon kept him out of jail.[60]

In August 1923 Stoneham, a shady Wall Street type, was indicted for perjury. Fallon represented him and for his efforts was himself indicted for bribing a juror. He went into hiding. Just a few weeks before taking Dolan's case, Fallon emerged and beat the rap. Now he was ready to aid the Giants—and the cause of baseball corruption—once more.[61]

Fallon began by spreading a patina of lies over the case, saying he had a "complete record" of Landis' interrogations of Dolan. He did not and proved that by later demanding that Landis release those stenographic records. He repeated his client's contention that "I don't remember" was actually a "badly rattled" way of denying O'Connell's charges. He amazingly claimed that Dolan had *not* been banned from baseball—only from the proceeding World Series.[62]

On Thursday, October 23, Fallon trotted Dolan out for reporters. Cozy provided a somewhat inaccurate version of his two interviews with Landis.[63] Suspicions, of course, arose as to how a nonentity like Dolan could afford a high-powered attorney such as Fallon. Finally, the Great Mouthpiece admitted to the *New York Sun*'s Frank Graham that it was, indeed, as many had suspected, McGraw himself who had secured his services.

"If you had a man working for you for years, and he had been faithful to you, and then got into a jam," asked Fallon in explaining McGraw's actions, "would you try to help him or would you run out on him?"[64]

By late October Fallon was brazenly contending that Dolan had categorically denied O'Connell's charges. He now threatened to sue Landis, Heydler, and possibly even Leslie O'Connor for Dolan's forfeited World Series share as well as for $100,000 in damages for

defamation of character. When Dolan had first engaged Fallon, Ban
Johnson sniffed, "It looks like a repetition of 1921." But when Fallon
announced Johnson might also be a defendant, he whimpered he
had nothing to do with Landis' actions and should not be included in
the suit.[65]

But just as suddenly Dolan dropped the case. "My client backed
off," Fallon told Frank Graham. "He has an idea Landis is going to
reinstate him. You know he isn't and so do I, but Cozy was here a
week or so ago mumbling about a promise he'd got from Landis and
doesn't want to antagonize him. He also said there was a lawyer
friend of his back in Oshkosh who, he thought, could help him, so I
gave him all the papers I had prepared and told him to take them to
his friend."

Fallon had his reasons for wanting to pursue *Dolan v. Landis et
al*. "When Landis was a Federal judge I was in his courtroom in Chicago one day when he sentenced a bootlegger to three years in Atlanta," he recounted. "I never forgave him for that. I vowed I would
get even with him some day and I would have when I got him under
cross-examination in Dolan's case."[66]

Fallon's concern for bootleggers was genuine. At just 41, he would
die of alcoholism. Just as genuine was his love of baseball. In April
1927 he was defending McGraw in a minor civil case, when he collapsed in court. Two days after being carried home, he told his wife,
"Do you think for a minute I'm going to lie here when I can go see the
baseball game?"

With that he got out of bed and promptly dropped dead.[67]

Actually, the Dolan camp's reason for abandoning the lawsuit
may have been far different that the story Fallon provided Graham.
In *The National League Story*, Lee Allen, one of baseball's most
knowledgeable historians, hinted that Landis threatened Stoneham:
if the owner did not drop the matter, Landis would resume his investigation with a vengeance, possibly wrecking baseball—and certainly
the Giants—in the process.[68]

Earlier Landis had promised to release his evidence in the case,
most notably the transcripts of his interrogations, but by late December he still had not done so. Suspicions festered he was hiding something or protecting someone. On December 27 six New York
sportswriters wrote Landis, begging for release of his transcripts,
pointing out that "a lot of earnest, well-meaning and good friends of
baseball firmly believe there is something [being] held back . . . "

In early January Landis wrote the following letter to one of these writers, the *Herald-Tribune*'s John Kieran:

> The day after my visit with you gentlemen here [in Chicago] some kind of a bug laid me low, with the result that I am only now getting back into the harness.
>
> I have again read your letter . . . which you and Messrs Cain, McGeehan, Daley, Bulger, Harrison and Hunt sent to me and have not the slightest doubt of the accuracy of what you say, namely "a lot of earnest, well-meaning and good friends of yourself and baseball firmly believe that there is something held back in the O'Connell-Dolan matter." Of course, to me personally this is not entirely agreeable, because if anything is being held back, I am the fellow that is doing the holding. However, although I had expected to give out that testimony for publication long before this and will not postpone such action much longer, I must withhold it at least for a few more days in what I conceive to be the discharge of my obligation in the matter.
>
> Will you be good enough to inform your colleagues who joined with you . . . of the above?
>
> Your and their taking the trouble to write to me is certainly appreciated.
>
> With all good wishes.
>
> Very truly yours,
> KENESAW M. LANDIS[69]

While Landis stalled, baseball fans were presented with fresh evidence—if any was needed beyond Phil Douglas, Jimmy O'Connell, and Cozy Dolan—that serving under John McGraw seemed a positive detriment to common sense. Out in California, O'Connell was trying to salvage his life, picking up a few dollars playing basketball in a Bay Area semi-pro league. Among O'Connell's new teammates, however, were former Tiger pitcher Bert Cole, Vernon righthander "Wee Willie" Ludolph, Texas Leaguer Ran Kelly, and former Reds' prospect "Imp" Begley.[70] That was bad enough, but also on the roster were two current major leaguers, Sammy Bohne (of *Collyer's Eye* fame) and, most remarkably, George Kelly.

The news hit John Heydler "right between the eyes," and he expected Landis to take action. But on what grounds? If management agreed, a big leaguer could play as much football or basketball as he wished in the off-season. John McGraw had banned Frankie Frisch from off-season football but saw no problem with Kelly playing hoop—even alongside the banned O'Connell. "As far as the O'Connell end of it goes," said McGraw, "that's up to Judge Landis." The Reds' Garry Herrmann was similarly unconcerned and doubted a league official had any jurisdiction in the affair. Nonetheless, he soon changed his tune and ordered Bohne off the team.

O'Connell, himself, solved the problem by voluntarily resigning from the team. His attitude was diametrically opposed to Dolan's. "I have no hard feelings for Judge Landis," he wrote in a February 1925 syndicated series on his life. "I think he did what he thought was fair and right, and I believe that he honestly wants to find out all that he can about the affair."[71]

As if Kelly, Johnson, Dreyfuss, and Fallon were not enough, Landis was soon facing a new wrinkle: criminal prosecutions.

In January 1925 the *New York Sun* questioned whether O'Connell and Dolan had violated a 1920 New York State law passed in the wake of the Black Sox scandal regarding bribing ballplayers and calling for penalties of not less than one year or more than five years in prison, and up to $10,000 in fines.

Manhattan district attorney Joab H. Banton rose to the bait and vowed he would prosecute if Landis provided the necessary evidence. John Heydler candidly admitted that in the initial furor over the case no one in baseball's hierarchy—not even a certain former federal judge—had even considered the possible legal ramifications. Ban Johnson "heartily endorsed" the probe, while a no doubt chagrined Landis had no public comment.[72]

Within a fortnight the case had taken on still more facets. A Rockford, Illinois, newspaper reported one fan's allegation that rookie Pirates southpaw Emil Yde had confided that other Phillies besides Sand had been approached. Yde, who had led the league in winning percentage, immediately denied all, but Landis spent an hour grilling him nonetheless. "This disposes of another flock of base-less rumors," said Landis, obviously pleased to be so easily "scotch-ing" another bothersome and potentially dangerous report.[73]

Another published report had Braves center fielder Bill Cunningham, a former Giant, alleging that Ross Youngs indeed knew of O'Connell's offer to Sand but thought it mere harmless "kid-ding." Cunningham called the story "a pack of lies" just before being admitted to a San Francisco hospital for an operation.

Landis, on his way to a mid-winter vacation, sent his transcripts to Banton's office but took pains to remind the prosecutor that a conviction could not be obtained on the uncorroborated testimony of an accomplice, a situation that applied not only to Frisch, Youngs, and Kelly but also to Dolan. On January 21 Landis sailed from New Orleans to Havana. No doubt he felt he had earned a rest, although the district attorney's office thought justice would be better served if he remained stateside and assisted in the probe rather than golfing in the Caribbean. With the Squire was Winifred who was in poor health. It was thought the trip would do her well.[74]

From Balboa in the Canal Zone on January 26 Landis wired Banton:

> In view of O'Connell's refusal [to come to New York] and Cunningham's illness will gladly defray expenses your representatives visiting California to interview them. Appreciation.
> LANDIS, Commissioner.[75]

Banton's office interrogated not only Dolan, Sand, and a number of his Phillie teammates but also the Frisch-Youngs-Kelly trio. When Kelly reached New York a telegram was waiting for him. Back in San Francisco his brother had passed away. The district attorney never did grill O'Connell since he refused to grant the ex-player immunity. Without such protection O'Connell, now relying on advice of counsel, wanted no part of a New York visit. In any case, Banton's office contended that having Landis' transcript of O'Connell's testimony made his personal appearance unnecessary. Nor did Banton's office interview Heydler, Dreyfuss, or any Giants officials.[76]

In early February Banton issued his report. Despite Johnson and Dreyfuss' bleatings, Landis was vindicated. O'Connell, it held, may have been guilty of violating the bribery statute, but it found "no legal evidence to justify the belief that Kelly, Frisch, and Young had anything to do with this alleged bribe." The same might also be said for Dolan, but he had "brought suspicion on himself" by his evasive answers to Landis. The district attorney's investigation had not "removed" those doubts.[77]

Despite the prosecutor's brave words of just a few weeks before, there was no indictment of O'Connell and never would be.

On February 16 Landis, just back from the Caribbean, met with Banton's office. He assured the prosecutors of baseball's continued cooperation. "Commissioner Landis says that the baseball authorities will pay all expenses," Assistant District Attorney George N. Brothers told the press, "and that we may send for any men needed in the examinations." But nothing more came of the case.[78]

Both O'Connell and Dolan made periodic attempts to return to the game. In 1925 Dolan appealed to Landis, saying: "You know, Judge, there is no evidence that I did anything wrong." Landis coldly responded, "Nothing has happened to change my opinion as to your status in baseball."[79]

At first Dolan made ends meet by selling Florida real estate. By 1928 he had found work as a stage comedian. Soon afterward he opened a nightclub on Chicago's Gold Coast. His final appearance in the public eye came in July 1930 when federal agents raided the club and seized large amounts of illegal alcohol. Oddly enough, his last employment was as a bailiff in the Chicago Municipal Courts.[80]

The public, however, had far more sympathy for O'Connell. After leaving his basketball team, he played baseball briefly in the outlaw Copper Frontier League, performing alongside such other pariahs as Chick Gandil, Hal Chase, Swede Risberg, Lefty Williams, and Tom Seaton.[81]

O'Connell returned to the coast and found work as a longshoreman, hauling 100-pound sacks of Hawaiian coffee. Once Damon Runyon approached Landis, arguing for O'Connell's reinstatement. "Don't you think this boy has been punished enough, Judge?" he asked. "I believe the public would be with you if you reinstated him."

"Damon," Landis responded, "I'm just as sorry for that young fellow as you are. But what can I do? O'Connell confessed his guilt, namely that he tried to bribe another player to throw a game. I couldn't let him back. You know that. Every ball player we expelled would be in my office demanding reinstatement. As for the great bulk of other players, what would they think? They know now that any action seeking to throw, or otherwise tamper with a game, means expulsion. And it has to stay that way. Damn, no, I can't do it."[82]

The case had one final mysterious gasp, when in 1929, Stoneham, McGraw, and former Giants treasurer Judge Francis X. McQuade tangled in court over club finances. McQuade, accused by his former partners of various drunken improprieties, including insulting McGraw's wife and physically assaulting his successor, Leo Bondy, retaliated by threatening to reopen the now largely forgotten incident.[83]

"At the proper time," McQuade's lawyer warned, "McGraw will be asked to explain some of the scandals of organized baseball, particularly the expulsion of two Giant players [sic] by Judge Landis about the time of the 1924 World Series."

But although the case went to trial,[84] nothing came of the threat.[85]

The great riddle of the O'Connell-Dolan scandal is why it ever happened in the first place. Its abysmal stupidity is the rock upon which all rational explanations of it still founder. Was it just the work of the dimwitted Dolan and O'Connell? Had Youngs, Frisch, and Kelly abetted the scheme? Were McGraw and Stoneham the actual "masterminds" of this harebrained plot? Or was Jimmy O'Connell lying about his teammates, just as he had lied about his own activities immediately after approaching Sand? Had O'Connell tried to twist reality just as he had pretended Landis had not really banished him? Is that the reason why he never criticized Landis' motives? Or had Landis stopped short of a thorough investigation for fear of wrecking one of baseball's premier franchises?

Perhaps, the best rationale was advanced by Giants teammate Freddie Lindstrom. "You know," he hypothesized decades later, "the whole story has never ceased to mystify me. Why would O'Connell try to bribe Sand? That was the thing I could never understand. The only explanation I can think of is that O'Connell was, as I said, a naive sort of fellow. And a youngster on that ball club, he was kidded and booted around quite a bit. There was always a lot of foolery and horseplay in the clubhouse. It's quite possible that somebody might have made a facetious remark and O'Connell picked up on it. I think that's what it finally amounted to, O'Connell taking seriously something said in jest and actually going ahead with it, trying to pull a fast one."[86]

It was as good a guess as any.

CHAPTER 19

# "THIS IS THE
# COBB-SPEAKER CASE"

Landis' handling of the Weaver, Kauff, Douglas, and O'Connell cases may not have put the fear of God into potentially crooked ballplayers, but it did instill a healthy fear of *Landis*. Following the O'Connell case new instances of game-fixing stopped, but whispers of *pre*-Landis scandals kept emerging.

The biggest of these materialized following the 1926 season and involved not just merely two of the game's grandest names, Ty Cobb and Tris Speaker, but also a subplot involving Landis' rival, Ban Johnson. The accused players would survive the episode. The now pathetically erratic Johnson would not.

Both Cobb and Speaker were now player-managers on the downside of spectacular careers. In 1926 Cobb's Tigers had finished sixth, Speaker's Indians, second, just three games behind the Yankees. In early November Cobb, who had never seemed at ease in the managerial role, handed in his resignation to Detroit owner Frank Navin. Three weeks later, in a much more surprising move, Speaker resigned from his $35,000-per-year position—supposedly to enter private business.

Their exits had nothing to do with how their clubs finished and everything to do with nearly decade-old charges of gambling and game-fixing.

As the 1919 season drew to a close, Speaker's Indians had clinched second place behind the now-infamous White Sox. The Tigers (not yet managed by Cobb) were battling the Yankees for third place and a share of World Series money. It was the first time first-division teams would receive any post-season share.

After a September 24, 1919, contest, Cobb and Speaker met with two other players under the stands at Navin Field: Indians righthander Smoky Joe Wood and Detroit southpaw Hubert "Dutch"

Leonard. Wood and Leonard had been Speaker's teammates on the Red Sox. Both were pitchers of some ability. In 1912 Wood had gone 34-5 with a 1.91 ERA. Soon afterward his arm went dead, but he remained in the majors, converting to the outfield. With the 1914 Red Sox Leonard posted a 0.96 ERA, the lowest in baseball history. He followed that up with no-hitters in 1916 and 1918.

According to Leonard, Speaker commented that the Tigers, particularly with righthander Bernie Boland pitching for them against the Indians, were sure to win the following day. Overall, Boland was mediocre but against Cleveland he was deadly. Cobb, Speaker, Leonard, and Wood thought they might as well make some money on such a sure thing. Cobb would bet $2,000, Speaker $1,500, and Wood and Leonard $1,000 each. Cobb suggested that a Navin Field attendant named Fred O. West place the bets for them. Betting on games by players was not then illegal.[1]

Detroit did indeed win, 9-5, in the one-hour-and-six-minute contest. If the game were fixed, it was difficult to tell it from anyone's performance. Speaker went 3-for-5 (including triples to center in the fifth and seventh) and recorded six putouts. Cobb, on the other hand, went just 1-for-5, grounding out three times. Neither Wood nor Leonard appeared in the contest. If the game were fixed, Cobb would argue in his autobiography, "would not Tris have gone easy with his bat and wouldn't I have been fed some easy pitches?"[2]

Speaker had indeed fielded his best team—with the exception of shortstop Ray Chapman who had returned to Cleveland to prepare for his forthcoming marriage. Chapman's replacement, light-hitting Harry Lunte, committed two errors.[3]

Even before the game, Leonard had left Detroit for his home in California. On October 23, Cobb wrote him from his Augusta, Georgia, home, informing him that not all had gone as planned:

Augusta, Ga., October 23, '19
Dear Dutch:

Well, old boy, guess you are out in old California by this time and enjoying life.

I arrived home and found Mrs. Cobb only fair, but the baby girl was fine, and at this time Mrs. Cobb is very well, but I have been very busy getting acquainted with my family and have not tried to do any correspondence, hence my delay.

Wood and myself are considerably disappointed in our business proposition, as we had $2,000 to put into it and the other side quoted us $1,400, and when we finally secured that much money it was about 2 o'clock and they refused to deal with us, as they had men in Chicago to take the matter up with and they had no time, so we completely fell down and of course we felt badly over it.

Everything was open to Wood and he can tell you about it when we get together. It was quite a responsibility and I don't care for it again, I can assure you.

Well, I hope you found everything in fine shape at home and all your troubles will be little ones. I made this year's winner's share of World's Series on cotton since I came home, and expect to make more.

I thought the White Sox should have won, but am satisfied they were too confident. Well, old scout, drop me a line when you can.

We have had fine weather here, in fact, quite warm, and have had some dandy fishing since I arrived home.

With kindest regards to Mrs. Leonard, I remain, sincerely

TY

Shortly, thereafter Leonard received the following letter from Wood:

Cleveland, O., Friday.

Enclosed please find certified check for sixteen hundred and thirty dollars ($1,630).

Dear Friend "Dutch":

The only bet West could get up was $600 against $420 (10 to 7). Cobb did not get up a cent. He told us that and I believe him. Cobb would have put some at 5 to 2 on Detroit, but did not, as that would make us put up $1,000 to win $400.

We won the $420. I gave West $30, leaving $390, or $130 for each of us. Would not have cashed your check at all, but West thought he could get it up to 10-7, and I was going to put it all up at these odds. We would have won $1,750 for the $2,500 if we could have placed it.

If we ever have another chance like this we will know enough to try to get it down early.

Let me hear from you, "Dutch."
With all good wishes to yourself and Mrs. Leonard, I am always

JOE WOOD[4]

Leonard remained with Detroit through 1921, but his friendship with Cobb deteriorated, which was not a surprising development as Cobb's greatest failing as a manager was his poor handling of pitchers. After the 1921 season Leonard jumped Detroit to play semi-pro ball on the West Coast, but in August 1924 won reinstatement from Landis and returned to Detroit. Nonetheless, his already poor relationship with Cobb (who termed him a "bolshevik") was quickly eroding even further. By mid-season 1925 Leonard compiled an 11-4 mark, but Detroit nonetheless traded him to Vernon in the Pacific Coast League. No other big league club, including Speaker's Indians, wanted him. A bitter Leonard retired from the game.

Leonard believed he had been railroaded out of baseball. He felt betrayed first by Cobb and then by Speaker, his old Red Sox teammate. He had kept his correspondence from Cobb and Wood and determined to now put those letters to good use.[5]

Traveling to Chicago in June 1926 Leonard tracked down Ban Johnson and received $20,000 for the letters. He later claimed to have been reluctant to reveal their contents and did so only because "by so doing, I was lending assistance in clearing up certain existing conditions which were detrimental to the good of baseball." That was his *official* explanation. In a less guarded moment he chortled to writer Damon Runyon, "I've had my revenge."

By early September 1926 Leonard forwarded the letters to Ban Johnson who—still thinking he could operate as he had before Landis—quickly investigated the matter and called a secret session of the AL's board of directors. On September 9 it decided Cobb and Speaker should be quietly eased out of the game.[6]

But as John Heydler had in the Benton case, the American League then decided to kick the matter upstairs—to Landis for what they assumed would be his rubber stamp. They guessed just as wrong as Heydler had.

Landis launched his own investigation and summoned Leonard to Chicago. But Leonard refused to go, so on October 29 the Judge visited him at his ranch near Sanger, California. On returning home, the Squire again attempted to secure the pitcher's presence at a hearing. Leonard once more refused. "They got guys in Chicago who bump people off for a price," he noted. Leonard, a very successful wine and grape producer,[7] also alibied that business requirements made his absence from home impossible. The truth may have been that he was afraid of a physical attack by the always fierce Cobb.[8]

After Cobb's resignation on November 3, manager John McGraw took an interest in signing the fiery Georgian for the Giants, a match that is fascinating to contemplate. Having heard "rumors" however, McGraw instructed club secretary Jim Tierney to inquire to Landis about Cobb. The Judge sent back a terse message: "You have asked me a direct question and I must reply in the same way: Lay off Cobb."

"Of course," McGraw later commented, "that closed the incident with me."[9]

In late November Landis interviewed Cobb, Speaker, Wood, and Fred West. Highlights of his interviews included these exchanges between the Judge and the Georgia Peach:

*Landis*: Mr. Cobb, I hand you a document dated Augusta, Ga., Oct. 23, 1919 addressed to "Dear Dutch" and signed, "Sincerely, Ty," which will be marked Exhibit One. And I ask you to look at that document and tell me if you wrote that letter.
*Cobb*: It is my letter.
*Landis*: I call your attention to the letter which you have just identified as having been written by you and ask you if you recall the occasion of having written that letter.
*Cobb*: Yes, I wrote that letter.
*Landis*: And what was it about?
*Cobb*: It was in response to a request by Leonard that I ascertain from Wood the amount of money that was wagered on this game in question.
*Landis*: The amount of money that was wagered on what?
*Cobb*: On the game in question.
*Landis*: That is the game of September 25, 1919?
*Cobb*: Yes, sir. He stated that he was leaving and wanted to check up on the amount that had been wagered.

\*\*\*

*Landis*: Give me the conversation, as near as you can remember it, just what was said.

*Cobb*: Well, [Leonard] was leaving, could not be there after the game, and he wanted to find out as quickly after the game as possible—he wanted me to ascertain from Wood, the amount that was paid. That is, to the best of my ability. That is, to the best to my knowledge.

*Landis*: When did you first hear that a bet was to be put on the ball game?

*Cobb*: Leonard came to me and wanted to know who would be a man they could trust, and that is where I figured the —

*Landis*: What was your answer to him?

*Cobb*: I told him I would get a man for him.

*Landis*: And what did you do along that line?

*Cobb*: I pointed out West, a man that was employed at the park.

*Landis*: Where was West, a man that was employed at the park?

*Cobb*: Well, to the best of my knowledge, he was either close to the edge of the playing field or was inside the field.

*** 

*Landis*: What did you understand Leonard to mean when he asked you the name of somebody he could trust, or you could trust, whichever it was?

*Cobb*: Well, I figured that he wanted to bet on the game.

*Landis*: What made you think so?

*Cobb*: Well, that is the only inference that I could gather from what he said.

*Landis*: Had you any conversations with him before about betting on ball games?

*Cobb*: No, sir.

*Landis*: Was there anything else in his inquiry to you that you have not mentioned here that would indicate to you the kind of trust he wished to repose in somebody?

*Cobb*: Well, there might have been other conversations. I am only relating what I can remember—away back there. And there might have been other things. For instance, he talked about a certain amount of money that would be put up by Wood, see? He wanted me to inquire.

*Landis*: Did you have any conversation with Wood about this bet?

*Cobb*: I did not. I did not until after the game. That is—wait a minute. I did not until I asked him concerning the amount of money bet.

*Landis*: Did you have any conversations with Speaker about this game?

*Cobb*: None whatever.

*Landis*: Betting on the game?

*Cobb*: No.

*Landis*: Did you bet any money on the game?

*Cobb*: Positively did not.

*Landis*: Did you intend to?

*Cobb*: I did not.

*Landis*: Did you have any conversation with anybody whatever about betting on a game?

*Cobb*: I did not.

*Landis*: You played in that game?

*Cobb*: I must have. I have never seen the box score yet.

*Landis*: I now hand you the box score, taken from a paper of Sept. 26. Does that box score refresh your memory as to whether you played in that game?

*Cobb*: It indicates I must have played in that game.

*Landis*: Well, after this conversation with Leonard, if you had not played in the game, you probably would remember you had not been in the game, wouldn't you?

*Cobb*: At this time, I would not. I don't know anything about it; I don't remember any of the details concerning the game.

*Landis*: You have no recollection of the game?

*Cobb*: No.

*Landis*: How it was played?

*Cobb*: No.

*Landis*: It appears from this box score that Detroit won 9-5.

*Cobb*: Yes.

*Landis*: I wish you would look at your letter, and calling your attention to the language of that part starting with "Wood and I."

*Cobb*: Yes, "Wood and myself."

*Landis*: Now, make any statement you desire to make respecting the language which you used in that letter to Leonard.

*Cobb*: In writing this letter to Leonard, it is apparent that I, in a way, tried to veil the betting end of it as a betting proposition. I stated to Leonard just what Wood had told me. The amounts of $2,000 to $1,400 quoted by the other side was entirely different from the information that Wood conveyed to Leonard in his letter, which indicated

I was not in on the betting proposition, that Wood merely put off by giving me the wrong information and a fictitious amount.

*Landis*: Now, in this statement that Leonard made to me in California and which I have read into this record, he tells of a conversation under the stands after the game played the preceding day. Was there any such conversation between you, Wood, Speaker and Leonard?

*Cobb*: Positively, no. If such a frameup were true, why should we stop for a few minutes under the stands and arrange such an important matter? The players—both sides—come to the field through a dugout from their respective club houses. Where would we have the time and where could we go for just a few minutes, as Leonard has stated, to frame up such an important matter?

*Landis*: Do you remember what the position of the Detroit club in the pennant race was at the time?

*Cobb*: From memory, no. Indications were that it was in third place.

*Landis*: Yes, that is the indication. I don't remember the details.

\*\*\*

*Landis*: Why was it you mentioned West to Leonard as a man he could trust?

*Cobb*: He is the only man that I knew of that was handy, and I figured he could be trusted. No other reason in the world except as I have stated.

*Landis*: Had you ever had West place any bets for you on anything?

*Cobb*: No, sir.[10]

Such was the nature of the evidence presented to Landis. In the midst of the investigation both Landis and Johnson received respective votes of confidence. At the annual American League session on December 15, owners (by a 7-0 vote with Charles Comiskey abstaining) restored Johnson to his position on the Major League Advisory Board,[11] a post they had removed him from two years earlier. Prior to the meeting Landis had been at home, laid up with his usual autumn cold, and not in full communication with the AL magnates. Somehow they had gotten the mistaken idea Landis supported the concept. Only after it was too late did they learn he did not. Suddenly they were filled with fear he would refuse a new term if he had to put up with Johnson in any more of an elevated position than Johnson already enjoyed. The

Squire merely laughed off the incident. He had no intention of working with Johnson no matter what titles he held.[12]

The following day American and National League owners met in a joint session. Unlike previous meetings, little controversy was on tap. The main item on everyone's mind was Landis' contract. His original pact would not expire until November 12, 1927, but since this was the last regularly scheduled joint meeting prior to that date, speculation floated for weeks on his future. As usual he kept silent, but it was clear no meaningful opposition remained.[13] At the National Association's winter meetings in Asheville, while Landis busied himself at golf, minor league executives virtually clamored for the honor of paying part of his salary, something they had not previously done. At the American League session, owners unanimously endorsed his retention. Johnson-loyalist Phil Ball not only *voted* for the resolution, he *proposed* it.[14]

The magnates went beyond bestowing a new seven-year contract upon Landis, they rewarded him with a $15,000 a year raise, bringing his annual salary up to $65,000. The move came as a complete surprise to virtually everybody in the room. As a way of demonstrating AL support for Landis, Colonel Ruppert had made the formal motion renominating him. Protocol called for the seconding motion to come from a National Leaguer, but carried away with enthusiasm, the A's Ben Shibe leapt to his feet and seconded Ruppert's motion. Ruppert quickly chided Shibe, who hastily withdrew his second. William Veeck then stood up to second, but as he did he offered an amendment raising Landis' salary. The American Leaguers knew nothing of the proposal, and the National Leaguers had already discussed a Christmas bonus for the Judge and rejected the idea. Yet, the atmosphere in the room was now so confused that Ruppert quickly accepted the amendment, and just as quickly his fellow owners unanimously approved the huge raise. The Squire was now the highest paid man in baseball, earning far more than Babe Ruth's $52,000 annual salary.[15]

Such was the emotion at the gathering, that at its conclusion Ban Johnson was the first to propel himself toward the Squire to pump his hand in congratulations.

The next day Landis went to his office and found a stack of congratulatory telegrams a foot deep. Johnson had a stack nearly as high, and he continued in his unusually sanguine mood. "Landis is all right." he chirped, "There are lots worse people than the Judge. I'm glad everybody wishes him well. I do."[16]

For his part, Landis had turned 60 the previous month and now had a full seven years to run on his commissionership. He must have felt confident that the job was his for life.

Meanwhile Cobb and Speaker were regaining their naturally combative natures and demanding Landis take action. Leonard still refused to come east, but on December 20 Cobb and Speaker, nervous because of increasing gossip surrounding their circumstances, demanded the Judge release details of the case to the public. Rumors spread in the press regarding the situation, and reporters demanded to know what was going on. "I'm sorry, mighty sorry," Landis responded as he shook a forefinger at reporters. "I'm sorry I cannot discuss that now." He fairly shouted the last word, then calmed down and promised he would release the necessary information at four o'clock the next afternoon.

He did exactly that, handing out copies of Leonard's correspondence and transcripts of the players' testimony, but otherwise he gave off mixed messages. While he decried the "gossip, rumors, innuendoes, and distorted, garbled accounts of the case," he also indicated he would be doing nothing further. "These men being out of baseball," he announced, "no decision will be made, unless changed circumstances in the future require it."[17]

Ban Johnson was incensed that Landis had let the cat out of the bag. Johnson had naively hoped that the entire operation could have been carried out quietly. Publicly he professed sympathy for Cobb and Speaker, glossing over the fact it was he who had banned them from the game on particularly flimsy evidence. "I feel deeply sorry for [their] families . . .," he stated. "It is a terrible blow to them. Cobb and Speaker evidently saw the 'crash' coming and stepped out before the scandal became a public byword. While it shocked me beyond expression, it simply goes to show that ballplayers cannot bet on ball games and escape the results that are bound to come."[18]

Cobb had gotten what he wanted in release of the record, but he wanted more: vindication and re-instatement. "Is there any decency left on earth?" he moaned. "I am beginning to doubt it. I know there is no gratitude. Here I am, after a lifetime in the game of hard, desperate and honest work forced to stand accused without ever having a chance to face my accuser. It is enough to try one's faith.

"I am branded a gambler on a ball game in which my club took part. I have never in the 22 years I have been in baseball made a single bet on an American League game."[19]

Public opinion was clearly on the side of the accused. "I want the world to know that I stand with Ty and Tris," drawled Will Rogers — and he spoke for many. "I've known them 15 years. If they are crooked, it shouldn't have taken them 20 years of hard work to get enough to retire on. If they had been selling out all these years, I would like to have seen them play when they weren't selling."[20]

Even Babe Ruth defended his not always friendly rival Cobb (most of the unfriendliness it must be admitted came from the surly Cobb). "This is a lot of bull," he snorted from a San Francisco vaudeville stage. "I've never known squarer men than Cobb and Speaker. Cobb doesn't like me and he's as mean as—. But he's as clean as they come."[21]

Some not only defended Cobb. They attacked Landis for making the matter public. "Judge Landis' act in publishing this story is indefensible and in line with his history of hypocritical sensationalism," charged Detroit municipal judge Guy A. Miller. Another Detroit jurist, E. L. Jeffries concurred, "Landis has fouled his own nest in his desire for sensationalism. He has unnecessarily gone out of his way to destroy two of the greatest idols of the day." In the Motor City a petition circulated to censure Landis, who remained publicly unflappable. "Thanks for the information," he responded to reporters' queries on the subject. "Not a word to say about it."[22]

Local jurists, rope-twirling comics, and Sultans of Swat were the least of Landis' problems if he wished to ban Cobb and Speaker. Arguably the cagiest of ballplayers, the ornery Cobb had also parlayed a brilliant business sense into a personal fortune. If he was not a millionaire by 1927, he soon would be. Such wealth gave Cobb entree to circles not normally frequented by mere ballplayers. In Washington he visited with former Supreme Court Justice Charles Evans Hughes who advised him to sue baseball for "defamation of character." United States senator Hoke Smith, Democrat of Georgia, stood by his constituent. "Evidently he is in a position to blow the top off a game already riddled with knavery," Smith charged. In Augusta a massive pro-Cobb, anti-Landis rally featured three bands and hung the Squire in effigy.[23]

Tris Speaker also had his support. The *Cleveland Press* printed ballots asking:

Here is my opinion of Tris Speaker and Ty Cobb, baseball stars on the face of the evidence published in the present baseball scandal:

Are Speaker and Cobb innocent? . . . . . . . . . . . . . . . . . . . . . . . . . . .

Are they guilty? . . . . . . . . . . . . . . . . . . . . . . . . . . . . . . . . . . . . . . .

Should they be reinstated in baseball? . . . . . . . . . . . . . . . . . . . . .

Should they be returned to the big leagues? . . . . . . . . . . . . . . . .

Cleveland fans, no doubt swayed by pro-Speaker sentiment, voted 35-to-1 (1,430 to 41) in favor of the accused. Out-of-town ballots, with responses coming from as far away as Denver, Houston, and Albuquerque, ran 1,400 to 76 in their favor. Youthful fans were particularly supportive of their heroes.[24]

And the rival *Plain-Dealer* did its part to buck up support for Speaker. When New Years' Eve approached it printed front page greetings from the local hero:

**Tris Wishes Fans**
**Happy New Year**

I wish everyone a Happy New Year. As 1927 is about to greet us, baseball is uppermost in my mind. May no scandal ever interfere with the greatest of all American sports.

To all my friends, to all the baseball fans and particularly to the hundreds of thousands of baseball kids, I send my honest, loyal greetings.

*Tris Speaker*[25]

Both Cobb and Speaker employed powerful counsel in their behalf. Speaker retained William H. Boyd, a prestigious Cleveland lawyer. Cobb engaged James O. Murfin, a former Michigan circuit court judge and a current regent of the University of Michigan who claimed a long history of experience in baseball litigation. Both attorneys exuded confidence. "It's a cinch," Murfin crowed in early January. Boyd echoed his buoyancy: "If Murfin thinks Cobb's case is a cinch, you can get a fair idea of what I think about Tris Speaker's case. For Tris is only implicated . . . through Leonard's charges. He wrote no letters and is not referred to in the letters written by Cobb and Wood."²⁶

And if those were not enough weapons in the Cobb-Speaker arsenal, there was still another: the threat of jumping to a new league. Prominent sportsmen were said to be behind a new circuit intent on placing franchises in Cleveland, Pittsburgh, Cincinnati, Detroit, Milwaukee, Kansas City, and either Minneapolis or Indianapolis. It was rumored that its backers had approached the University of Pittsburgh in regard to renting or even purchasing its new $2 million, 70,000-seat stadium.

Cobb had batted .339 in 1926; Speaker, .306. Both were still viable stars, and would certainly shine in any new circuit. Either one was a bigger name than any player that had jumped to the Federal League. And the new circuit was also said to be interested in Rogers Hornsby, who was involved in a messy trade from St. Louis.²⁷

Landis had his reasons for the delay, however. The longer he waited the longer the public could mull over how Johnson had expelled two of the game's greatest stars on flimsy evidence—and in total secrecy. Landis would wait for the pressure to build to reinstate Speaker and Cobb—and the pressure might very well serve to rid himself of his most nettlesome problem.

But while Landis waited, another crisis exploded in his face. Since the Black Sox scandal, Swede Risberg had been living on a small dairy farm outside Rochester, Minnesota. The December 30, 1926, *Chicago Tribune* now quoted him as saying: "I can give baseball's bosses information that will implicate 20 big leaguers who never before have been mentioned in connection with crookedness. . . Landis will never ask me to tell him what I know. The facts are there, but they don't want to know them."²⁸

The gist of his story concerned two doubleheaders played between the White Sox and Detroit on September 2 and 3, 1917. Chicago was fighting hard for the pennant, but Detroit was out of the race. The Sox took all four games—by scores of 7-2, 6-5, 7-5, and 14-8. As Risberg told it the series was fixed and the entire Detroit club was in on the "slough." Risberg also claimed that the entire White Sox team, including manager Clarence "Pants" Rowland, knew of the arrangement. The Sox contributed $45 each to a purse to reward the Tigers for their cooperation.

For good measure, Risberg added a tale of yet another Tiger-

White Sox fix. In late September 1919 Chicago again had the pennant wrapped up, but Detroit was now battling for third-place money. "We paid Detroit by sloughing off two games to the Tigers," Risberg professed. "I know I played out of position, and Jackson, Gandil, and Felsch also played out of position."

The broad hint of revenge clung to Risberg's account—revenge against those White Sox who had not participated in the Black Sox fix, those teammates who became public heroes while the Black Sox slunk off to obscurity and disgrace. "They pushed Ty Cobb and Tris Speaker out on a piker bet," Risberg fumed. "I think it's only fair that the 'white lilies' get the same treatment."[29]

Landis called Risberg's bluff, wiring him: "Papers print statement purporting to come from you to the effect that you can give 'information that will implicate 20 big leaguers who never before have been mentioned in connection with crookedness.' Assuming that you made the statement, I earnestly request you come here with the facts. Fair compensation for your time and expenses guaranteed. Wire collect when you may be expected, the earlier the better."[30]

"Today's story not true," Risberg wired back. "Will come to Chicago as soon as I can make arrangements to leave farm."[31]

Landis' public stance was that the entire matter was news to him. It was not. Rumors of the 1917 fix had long floated about in baseball circles.

In October 1920 Ban Johnson had informed District Attorney Maclay Hoyne about the fix. And in February 1921 Landis himself learned of the allegations from White Sox catcher Ray Schalk. Nor was the matter simply "inside baseball." Reports of the allegations occasionally surfaced in the press as in the case of a Joe Vila column written in the wake of the Shufflin' Phil Douglas scandal.[32]

Landis, nonetheless, reacted quickly—and publicly—regarding Risberg's accusation, interrogating Risberg privately on New Year's Day 1927 and beginning open hearings just a few days later.

He had scheduled the hearing for his offices in the People's Gas Building, for 10 o'clock on the morning of Wednesday, January 5. A hundred reporters jammed the place. Hundreds of news-hungry sensation seekers congregated outside on Michigan Avenue. But Risberg phoned the Commissioner that he would not be able to arrive until 1:30, and in fact the hearing did not even begin until 20 minutes after that. Prior to Risberg's testimony, a long parade of witnesses preceded him to the stand including former White Sox managers

Rowland and William "Kid" Gleason; former Sox players second baseman Eddie Collins, pitchers Red Faber and Dickie Kerr; and former Tigers Cobb, shortstop Owen "Donie" Bush, outfielder Harry Heilman, catcher Oscar Stanage, and pitchers George Dauss and Howard Ehmke.

In his search for the truth Landis left no stone unturned. In several cases his call for witnesses led to profound embarrassment—his own. Among those summoned to Chicago was former A's catcher Jack Lapp. Why Lapp was beckoned was a mystery particularly in view of his death from pneumonia in February 1920. But that wasn't Landis' only snafu. Four players whom he summoned—and who dared not to appear—weren't on either team in 1917.[33]

Cobb was a particularly bitter presence in the courtroom. He wanted Landis to clear him and couldn't understand why he wasn't doing it—and doing it *now*. "You could see by the expression on Cobb's face he was very bitter at Landis," noted Chicago sportswriter Irving Vaughn. Called to the stand, Cobb virtually spat out the words "Want to swear me in?" at the Squire. As soon as his testimony was over, he headed back home to Georgia. On arriving he wired Landis, demanding he ask each witness if he had ever known Cobb to be involved in any fix. The Judge obliged. Each witness answered in the negative.[34]

In fact, each witness—with the exception of Chick Gandil, who had traveled from Arizona where he was managing a semi-pro team denied Risberg's charges. "Nobody seems to have given thought to the fact that if I was in on any kind of a deal, as Risberg declares, I certainly would not have used about every good pitcher I possessed. If the games were fixed and I had knowledge of it I could very easily have bluffed my way through by working some of the second-raters."[35]

One-thirty came and Risberg had still not arrived. "Does anybody know where Mr. Risberg is?" Landis demanded.

"Downstairs trying to sneak into the building without causing a riot," came a response.

Risberg finally arrived at 2 PM. Hatred for him filled the room. For his part, the Black Sox ringleader evinced a contempt for the entire process.

After Risberg finished testifying, Landis ordered him to take a seat just in back of the witness box, literally in a corner of the room. From that vantage point he could see only each succeeding witnesses' back, Landis, and a stuffed fish on the wall. To amuse himself,

Risberg flicked ashes on a nearby bust of Abraham Lincoln. Landis didn't like that, but had too much on his hands to take issue.[36]

A particularly tense moment came after Bernie Boland testified: "As far as I know those 1917 games were on the square. I don't believe this story that they were 'sloughed.'"

At that point, Risberg whispered to Landis that Donie Bush was nodding to Boland. Boland swiveled around. He and Boland were almost face-to-face, and Boland spat out: "You're still a pig!"

"I am not a pig," Risberg retorted.[37]

Bush would have no more of Risberg's accusations and moved his chair so he now sat in back of the witness stand.

More witnesses appeared. All denied that the purse was a payoff. Former third baseman Buck Weaver (banned with the rest of the Black Sox) came to the stand. It was rumored Weaver had encouraged Risberg to make his charges and that he had even helped him make the trip down to Chicago. Surely, he would verify Risberg's charges, charges Risberg *was* making despite his original denial.[38]

But he didn't. Regarding events of 1917, Weaver told how he had broken his finger that August and was not even with the team on September 2 or 3. He claimed that as far as he knew, the four games in question were honestly played, as were the contests of September 27 and 28, 1919. He had no recollection of any of his teammates playing out of position in the latter series. Weaver further stated that although he had been asked to contribute $45 to the pool, he had refused.

But he had more on his mind than that. "As far as baseball is concerned, Your Honor, I do not owe baseball a thing, but I think baseball owes me something," he went on. "As I told you before I knew nothing about the 1919 world's series, and therefore, I am asking you today to be reinstated. That is all I have to say, Judge."

The plea took everyone aback. Even Landis seemed surprised. He paused before responding: "Well, drop me a line to that effect and I will take the matter up."[39]

Weaver wasn't the only player demanding reinstatement. On Friday, January 7, Chick Gandil finally appeared in Landis' office. "Have you received any money for coming here, other than that I promised, for expenses?" Landis asked.

"The *Chicago Tribune* gave me $500 for expenses," Gandil responded. "It didn't take all that for my expenses. I promised to pay them back. I want to ask you, Mr. Landis, why, after I was dragged

through a court trial and acquitted in the 1919 Series, I was blacklisted?"

"Do you want to be reinstated?" Landis answered.

"No, I don't, but I want to know why I was blacklisted."

"I couldn't pass on that unless I could ask you some questions
about the 1919 World Series."

"I don't want to go back to that Series."

"Well, if you want an answer right now, you have just testified
that you played out of position in two games in 1919. That would
cause you to be placed on the ineligible list."[40]

When the hearings concluded, Landis was left to ponder the
whole affair. While he mulled his options, Risberg and Gandil continued making news. From Risberg's Minnesota farm came puzzling
news that Risberg, now professing no hard feelings against his
former colleagues, had expressed hope that the "whole affair might
be whitewashed."[41]

Gandil meanwhile had decided to remain for a few days more in
Chicago, filling out expense vouchers in the amount of $278.12 (in-
cluding $90 as lost wages from his new occupation as a plumber), and
stewing over Pants Rowland's remarks that he had actually traveled
to Philadelphia in September 1917 not to pay off a bribe but to "meet
a couple of friends."

"Rowland lied," Gandil sneered. "I never had any friends."[42]

And as the Squire contemplated the fate of over two dozen players, he also pondered over what two days of hearings had done to his
office. "Isn't this room a sight?" he muttered.[43]

Reports spread he would reinstate Buck Weaver. On January 8
the *Chicago Daily News* speculated Weaver's reinstatement would be
a "by-product" of the affair, noting he had emerged from the hearings
with "flying colors." Two days later Weaver did as Landis had asked,
filing a formal request for reinstatement.[44 45]

Landis released his verdict on January 12. Placing heavy empha-
sis on the sequence of events, he exonerated every player Risberg and
Gandil had accused:

> The Chicago players' salaries were paid August 31 [1917]; they
> had funds, yet there was no discussion about raising money to pay
> Detroit for "sloughing" that Risberg claimed was "common talk" on
> the Chicago team. Again, on September 12, Chicago players re-
> ceived checks, and two days later they played 3 games in Detroit. Al-

though Gandil and Risberg and [Bill] James and the other pitchers were all there, and that was the last time these teams would meet all year, still not a word [was said] about the "bribe" money, and no inquiry or promise as to when payments would be made.

If the Gandil story . . . were true he and James entered into a corrupt bargain for throwing the games, certainly those who were to receive the bribe would have been demanding their money. On the other hand, Detroit had not yet played Boston, so the Chicago players did not know how many games Detroit would win from Boston, or that any fund would be necessary. Then when those games had been played, the Chicago players raised the fund, notwithstanding it was shortly before another pay day and several of them had no money and Gandil and Risberg traveled to Philadelphia to deliver it. These facts discredit the testimony of Gandil and Risberg that it was payment for "sloughing" the games on September 2 and 3, and corroborate the testimony of all the others that it was for Detroit's work against Boston.

It is the finding of the Commissioner that the fund raised by the Chicago players about September 28, 1917, was not collected or paid the Detroit players for "sloughing" the Chicago games of September 2 and 3, 1917, but was paid because of Detroit's beating Boston; and there was no "sloughing" of the September 26, 27, 28, 1919 games, except possibly by Risberg and Gandil. . . .

If the Risberg-Gandil version be correct, it was an act of criminality. If the other versions be true, it was an act of impropriety, reprehensible and censurable, but not corrupt.[46]

Most observers were satisfied with the verdict. "I fully expected such a decision," commented Barney Dreyfuss, "on the face of the evidence and testimony presented."[47]

On the other hand the *New York Herald-Tribune* editorialized: "Professional baseball has been whitewashed once more. We hope Judge Landis will not have to rule again soon in a similar case."[48]

Of course, there was no pleasing Ban Johnson. "This is the same case that was tried by the Commissioner six years ago," he revealed. "These same players appeared before the Commissioner when he first was inducted into office and all were exonerated. This is just a retrial on those same charges. At that time, Eddie Collins, Faber, Schalk and the rest of them were absolved from all wrong doing." But even Johnson admitted it was "simply a reward for a player to use

extra effort against a rival. . . . of course, it was wrong doing . . . . yet
it was not a criminal act."[49]

For his own reasons, Landis was equally unhappy. "Won't these
God damn things that happened before I came into baseball ever stop
coming up?" he fumed to friends. Publicly, he finally proposed closing
the books on pre-Landis scandals, advancing the following program:

> 1—A statute of limitations with respect to alleged baseball offenses,
> as in our state and national statutes with regard to criminal of-
> fenses.
> 2—Ineligibility for one year for offering or giving any gift or reward
> by the players or management of one club to the players or manage-
> ment of another club for services rendered or supposed to be, or
> have been rendered, in defeating a competing club.
> 3—Ineligibility for one year for betting any sum whatsoever upon
> any ball game in connection with which the bettor had no duty to
> perform.
> 4—Permanent ineligibility for betting any sum whatsoever upon
> any ball game in connection with which the bettor has any duty to
> perform.[50]

All of this, had, of course, distracted Landis from the Cobb-
Speaker case. While the full force of public opinion was pulling Landis
in the direction of leniency, Ban Johnson was following his own drum-
mer and marching off in the other direction. The *Chicago Tribune*
quoted "a leader in organized baseball" as saying neither Cobb nor
Speaker "ever again will play or manage on an American League
club." The article set off a chain reaction. Landis was at French Lick,
Indiana, for a joint major-minor league meeting on draft issues.
Cobb's attorney, Judge Murfin, tracked the Squire down, demanding
to know what was happening. Landis, suspecting Johnson was the
mysterious figure in back of the quote, called a special meeting of AL
owners for Monday, January 24, "for the purpose of ascertaining what
basis, if any, there was for the publication of the article." Beyond that
he had nothing to say, but his manner betrayed deep anger.

Johnson, oblivious to how little support he had with the public-
at-large or with his own owners, called a special league meeting for
the day before—and admitted he was the baseball "leader" in question. "The American League is a business," he snapped. "When our

directors found two employees who they didn't think were serving them right, they had to let them go. Now isn't that enough? As long as I am president of the American League, neither one of them will manage or play on our teams.

"I don't believe Ty Cobb ever played a dishonest game in his life. If that is the exoneration he seeks, I gladly give it to him. But it is from Landis Cobb should demand an explanation. The American League ousted Cobb, but it was Landis who broadcast the story of his mistakes.

"I love Ty Cobb. I never knew a finer player. I don't think he has been a good manager and I have to strap him as a father would strap an unruly boy. But I know Ty Cobb's not a crooked ballplayer," he continued. "We let him go because he had written a peculiar letter about a better deal that he couldn't explain and because I felt that he violated a position of trust." Johnson showed little sympathy for Speaker, however. The Gray Eagle, he noted, was "a different sort of fellow, cute"—the type who consorted with gamblers and permitted his players to do the same.[51]

Then, mad with rage and fueling his own destruction, he tore into Landis as he never had before:

> This data belongs to me, and not to Landis. The American League gave Landis enough to show why Cobb and Speaker were no longer wanted by us. That's all we needed to give him. I have reports on Speaker which Landis will never get unless we go to court. . . .
>
> I only hope he holds an open meeting. I want the public to know what the American League did and what Landis did. . . .
>
> When Landis released that testimony and those letters I was amazed. I couldn't fathom his motive. The only thing I could see behind that move was a desire for personal publicity. I'll tell him that when I take the witness stand. . . .
>
> When I take the stand Monday I may tell the whole story of my relationship with the Judge. If he wants to know when I lost faith in him tell him this:
>
> When the Black Sox scandal broke the American League voted to prosecute the crooked players. Landis received the job. After several months had passed I asked him what he was doing and he replied: "Nothing."
>
> I took the case away from him, prosecuted it with the funds of

the American League and never asked him for help. I had decided he didn't want to cooperate.

My second break with Landis came over a financial matter. I do not care to discuss it now, but I will tell about it Monday, if he wants me to.

This statement of mine probably means a new fight with Landis. But he has chosen to make the public think the American League passed the buck to him on the Speaker and Cobb case. That's not true, and I don't intend to let the public keep on thinking that way.[52]

The outburst was in character. Johnson could not see that circumstances had changed in baseball and that his word was no longer law. It was more often a harbinger of his own undoing as he carelessly unburdened himself to seemingly friendly reporters only eager to broadcast his rantings. "Ban was a rich mine for scribes," noted Earl Obershain, a friendly chronicler of his career. "They would trap him into a statement which would be played up gleefully as something to feed the forces of war."[53]

Obershain advanced the theory that not only Johnson may have been manipulated by others. Landis' collision course with Johnson, he theorized, may have been originally designed by anti-Johnson owners. "That idea," Obershain wrote in *Collyer's Eye*, "cleverly conveyed to Landis that Johnson had to be curbed, may have had some effect on the relations between and attitude toward each of the two men. Mr. [William Howard] Taft and other great men had seen through the screen, the impulsive Landis seemingly did not."[54]

A showdown between Landis and Johnson had been brewing ever since the Judge had assumed the commissionership. After a stormy beginning the Landis-Johnson relationship had publicly quieted down, but under the surface problems remained, and in 1923 Landis urged owners to rein Johnson in. They did nothing.

Johnson's aspersions during the O'Connell-Dolan matter once more brought old hatreds to the surface. Then Johnson launched his own investigation of gambling in the Pacific Coast League, stepping not only on National Association turf but also on Landis'. Landis, not about to share his role as guardian of baseball morals, was infuriated.

So was Pacific Coast League president Harry A. Williams and Salt Lake City owner Bill Lane. At that December's minor league meetings at Hartford they blasted Johnson for his interference. Keeping the matter from coming to a head was Landis' absence. His sister-in-law had just died, and Winifred was hospitalized at the Mayo Clinic for a jaw condition. The Squire missed the session but fumed nonetheless and threatened to quit unless Johnson was muzzled.

American League owners hoped to patch the problem over although Charles Comiskey bluntly told Johnson to "shape up or ship out." At 11 o'clock on the morning of December 17, 1924, a committee consisting of Jacob Ruppert, Thomas Shibe, and Ernest Barnard met with Landis at New York's Commodore Hotel, bringing with them a statement concerning the situation. The Squire was in no mood for compromise. "Ruppert," he snapped, "you people have got to make up your minds whether you want me or Ban Johnson." He ordered them to rewrite their statement. "You must rewrite this," he ordered and then dictated what he wanted in the document.

At one o'clock the owners returned with their revised declaration. Landis had the victory he wanted.

At 3:30 American and National league owners met jointly. They emerged after three hours of discussion, and Landis, smiling broadly, ordered Leslie O'Connor to read what had just been passed:

> We recognize that conditions have arisen that are gravely harmful to baseball and that must be intolerable to you [Landis] and that these conditions have been created by the activities of the president of the American League.
>
> While you were dealing promptly and efficiently with a most deplorable exception to baseball's honorable record, our president sought to discredit your action and to cast suspicion on the 1924 World Series.
>
> One year ago you made known to us, in his presence, various of his activities, and that it was our expectation and hope that the unanimous action then taken certainly would operate as a corrective, but in this expectation and hope we have been disappointed.
>
> We do not extenuate these things or question their harmful effect on baseball. However, he has been president of our league since its inception and we ask you again to overlook his conduct and accept from us these guarantees:
>
> 1. That his misconduct will cease or his immediate removal from office will follow.
> 2. That legislation will be adopted that will limit his activity to the internal affairs of the American League.

3. That any and all measures which you may deem advisable to the above will be adopted.

As expressing our attitude toward your administration of the Commissioner's office, we tender you herewith a copy of the resolution unanimously adopted at its annual meeting in New York, December 10, 1924.

(signed)           Thomas S. Shibe, Philadelphia
                   Clark C. Griffith, Washington
                   Robert Quinn, Boston
                   Charles A. Comiskey, Chicago
                   E. S. Barnard, Cleveland
                   Jacob Ruppert, New York
                   Frank J. Navin, Detroit[55]

Not signing was Phil Ball who bitterly commented that "the biggest figure in the national game has been a victim of men whose gratitude had bowed to the dollar sign."[56]

Yet the wrangling did not stop. In January 1925 Johnson called for federal control of the game—a clear slap at Landis' stewardship. "It is my firm conviction," he proclaimed, "that we can only secure adequate and satisfactory results through the medium of a commission created by the government."[57]

In the final game of the 1925 World Series Bucky Harris started Walter Johnson, and Johnson, surrendering nine runs (five earned) and 15 hits in eight innings, lost, 9-7. Ban Johnson, still fuming over the O'Connell-Dolan incident and boycotting the Series, wired Harris: "You sacrificed a World's Championship for the American League through your display of sentiment." The telegram soon became public knowledge.

"That was a lousy thing to do," Landis snapped.[58]

In December 1925 the joint major league rules commission authorized the use of resin by a pitcher to dry his hands during any portion of a game. Johnson, however, thought it could become the basis of a new "trick pitch," and the following February, the AL voted to ban the substance. In April Landis overruled it, saying not only that pitchers in either major league could use resin if they desired but also that umpires must carry a resin bag with them and provide it to a pitcher on his request. "It does not sound," noted *New York Herald Tribune* sports editor W. O. McGeehan, "as though the issue had been raised for any other purpose than to question the authority of Judge Landis."[59]

The AL voted 6-2 to ratify Landis' decision, but to mollify Johnson ordered its managers not to request the substance. Phil Ball, faithful to the end, groused, "Landis should not be allowed to dictate to the American League even in such a trivial matter as a use of resin."[60]

The Judge had no intention of losing the Battle of the Resin Bag. On April 21, 1926 he wrote to his ally Frank Navin that the American League's failure to comply with the new resin rule might breach: "(1) the players' contracts, (2) the Major League Agreement and Rules, and (3) the Major-Minor League Agreement and Rules."[61]

The dispute marked yet another notch down in Johnson's declining influence. "Mr. Johnson has," columnist Westbrook Pegler noted, "at a liberal estimate, about as much authority in baseball as the guest of honor has at a thirty-six hack funeral."[62]

Such was the situation for Johnson as first the Cobb-Speaker and then the Risberg-Gandil controversies detonated between December 1926 and January 1927.

In January 1927 Johnson compounded his problems by being quoted, either accurately or inaccurately, as making a series of inflammatory charges: the 1922 World Series had been fixed; Cleveland players had bet on horse races and baseball games; and that he had hired private detectives to spy on them. Within a week he had denied making all of them. All the while Landis kept a public silence.[63]

On Sunday, January 23, 1927, American League owners (minus Comiskey) entered the spacious Rose Room of Chicago's Congress Hotel. There sat Johnson, barely functioning. Almost immediately after calling the meeting to order, he found himself savagely confronted by Jake Ruppert who demanded to know if Johnson had indeed told a Chicago morning newspaper that the Yankees had thrown the 1922 World Series. Johnson could barely utter a reply. In a trembling voice he denied any such action. His actions appeared "pitiable." He shuffled out of the room, and wandered around the lobby in a semi-dazed condition, barely aware of what was transpiring about him.[64]

With Johnson temporarily out of the picture, the owners set to work on trimming his powers one last time. They drafted a new resolution of allegiance to Landis and dispatched a delegation led by Jacob Ruppert to his office to invite the Judge to their meeting. He arrived at 5:00 PM, and was handed a copy of a resolution they had adopted prior to his arrival. It read:

> The members of the league unanimously repudiate any and all criticism appearing in the public press as emanating from Mr. Johnson reflecting in any way upon Judge Landis or his handling of the several investigations concerning the integrity of ballplayers in the American League, and commend Judge Landis for his efforts in clearing baseball of any insinuations of dishonesty. . . .
>
> Dr. Robert G. Drury, Mr. Johnson's personal attending physician, certified to the meeting that Mr. Johnson's health was such that he should immediately take a much-needed rest. Thereupon the duties of the President were entrusted for the time to Mr. Frank J. Navin of Detroit. . . .[65]

Landis was greatly pleased. Sincerely or insincerely, he remarked "it would have been an act of inexcusable brutality" to have forced Johnson's resignation. "As soon as I learned [of] the doctor's report I realized that it would be impossible to ask Johnson to resign," he commented. "At no time during the afternoon meeting did I attempt to force his resignation. Such a thing would have been inhuman."[66]

Most observers now expected that after a decent interval a broken Johnson would finally submit his resignation. Instead, he retired to Hot Springs, Arkansas, recovered a semblance of health and by Opening Day 1928 seemed ready to resume his normal duties.

Two seemingly trivial disputes between Johnson and Connie Mack's A's marked the last straws of the league's patience for its founder. On Friday, July 8 AL owners called a meeting at New York's Belmont Hotel to discuss modification of the league constitution. The pretext fooled no one: this was the end of the line for Byron Bancroft Johnson.

Johnson refused to attend, remaining in his room just down the hall. Three times groups of owners visited him, urging his resignation. Finally, he gave in. To the end he maintained his fierce pride, rejecting any of the $320,000 salary remaining on the eight years left to his contract.

Johnson refused to leave his room or to permit anyone to enter it. Finally, he slipped his resignation under the door. It read, "After 34 years of service as your president, I tender my resignation as president, treasurer, and secretary, to be effective November 1 or earlier should I desire, compensation to end immediately on my retirement."[67]

Johnson had been disposed of, but there remained the Cobb-Speaker case. On January 27, 1927, Landis released his decision:

Cobb, Speaker, and Wood were available, but Leonard, a retired player, residing in California, declined to attend a hearing. Therefore, his statement was taken in California and in substance was that this game (September 25, 1919) had been fixed. Cobb, Speaker and Wood branded this charge as false. A wager had been made, but they vigorously denied that the game had been fixed and they insisted upon an opportunity to face their accuser. Leonard, however, persisted in his refusal to come, and despite the fact that his attendance could not be forced, the hearing was finally set for November 29, and all parties, including Leonard and the American League president and directors, duly notified. Leonard replied that he would not be present.

Cobb and Speaker appeared on November 27 and were informed of Leonard's attitude, whereupon they canvassed the whole situation with the Commissioner and reached the conclusion that they would rather quit baseball than have a hearing with their accuser absent. Their reason was: The mere announcement of charges of this character, whatever the personality or motives of the accuser, or the scarcity even absence of evidence supporting the charges, would be harmful to the accused persons, experience having shown that a vindication by baseball authority, based upon a manifest insufficiency or even a total failure of supporting proof, has been labeled a "whitewash." While they insisted they had no doubt of their ability to answer the charges, they were concerned about the possible effect upon themselves and others in whom they were deeply interested. They appeared to be particularly disturbed respecting the situation of Joe Wood.

These considerations, as Cobb and Speaker represented the matter to me, brought about their desire to quit baseball, despite their appreciation of the fact that such action might be misconstrued.

Inasmuch, therefore, as Leonard's attendance could neither be induced or enforced, the Commissioner consented that the hearing be put over indefinitely, and it was understood that would be the end of the matter, unless conditions thereafter should so require a different course. It was pointed out at the time that a number of people knew or had heard of the Leonard charges and of the Cobb and Wood letters and the likelihood of suspicion and rumor resulting from a retirement in these circumstances of two players of such prominence was discussed. And it was definitely understood that the interests of all concerned might thereafter require a public statement setting forth the charges and answers.

The American League directors were informed of the status of affairs and that Cobb and Speaker desired to leave baseball for the reasons stated. Accordingly, the Detroit and Cleveland clubs granted releases and the American League directors rescinded their resolution calling for a hearing, with the same understanding that this ended the matter unless subsequent developments should necessitate a hearing and publication.

Shortly thereafter, gossip and rumor got busy. As usually transpires when these two kindly, sympathetic agencies are at work, they left in their wake a variety of progeny infinitely more harmful to the individuals concerned than the truth could possibly be. Many press accusations and scores of newspapers were persistently demanding the facts. Thereafter, Cobb and Speaker and Wood were called to Chicago and the situation laid before them. They all realized that untrue, distorted and garbled accounts were being innuendoed and agreed that a hearing had become desirable, even with Leonard persisting in staying away.

Accordingly, a final effort was made to induce Leonard to attend, but again he refused. The hearing was held, and the Commissioner at once issued the record for publication in accordance with his definite understanding with Cobb, Speaker and Wood.

This is the Cobb-Speaker case. These players have not been, nor are they now, found guilty of fixing a ball game. By no decent system of justice could such finding be made. Thereafter, they were not placed on the ineligible list.

As they desire to rescind their withdrawal from baseball, the releases which the Detroit and Cleveland clubs granted at their requests, in the circumstances detailed above are canceled and the players' names are restored to the reserve lists of those clubs.[68]

Modern historians have advanced a number of theories to explain Landis' verdict. Fred Lieb agreed with Landis "That to expel these superstars . . . on less than conclusive evidence might have given professional baseball a blow from which it could not recover."

Many contend the entire case was a mere pretext to humiliate Ban Johnson. David Quintin Voigt, in his *American Baseball: from the Commissioners to Continental Expansion*, makes the point that in the early years of his commissionership Landis had to expel players in virtual wholesale fashion to restore public confidence in the game. By 1927, the Black Sox scandal was receding into historical status. The fans no longer feared crookedness in the game. "Sensing this," noted Voigt, "Landis pragmatically abandoned his punitive role and became the efficient priest. As priest-judge, he evolved [a more flexible] operational code that spelled out his notion of 'conduct detrimental to baseball.' "[69]

Publicly Cobb professed to be "well pleased" with Landis' verdict, but the episode won the Judge little gratitude from the Georgia Peach.[70] "Very decent of the judge," Cobb sneered in his autobiography. "For weeks, I had been agonized by the scandal, sick of heart and convinced that my baseball bow-out would always be tainted with a question. I'll reveal something here never before told. That famous Landis 'verdict' was dictated to him by attorneys representing Speaker and myself."[71]

There was one final twist to the affair. Landis, who had shown such solicitude for Johnson's feelings just a few days before, insisted on dictating where Cobb and Speaker could now play. He would not allow them to return to their original clubs—although there was little chance they would choose to anyway. But Landis also mandated that they could only sign with American League clubs. This was Landis putting his heel once more on Johnson's throat. He would force Johnson to tolerate the presence in *his* league of the two men he had hoped to expel from baseball.

Landis' scenario worked out far better than even he could have hoped. One of the controversies precipitating Johnson's resignation involved Ty Cobb. In early May Johnson indefinitely suspended the Georgia Peach for "accidentally" bumping umpire Red Ormsby. The suspension came just six days before Ty Cobb Day at Detroit's Navin Field and would have meant cancellation of the affair. Johnson quickly backed down, but the incident angered both Connie Mack and Detroit's Frank Navin who then joined in demanding Johnson's scalp.

Landis had planted a time bomb named Ty Cobb back in the American League. When it went off, the only casualty was Byron Bancroft Johnson, forced out less than two months after this otherwise pedestrian affair had transpired.[72]

CHAPTER 20

# "THERE IS NO GAMBLING CONNECTED WITH BASEBALL"

Until now we have looked at Kenesaw Landis' career in largely chronological terms. But there were many issues such as gambling, the farm system, racial integration, or even his very style of governance that defy such an approach. To force these accounts into narratives of other incidents, such as his battle with Babe Ruth or his handling of the Cobb-Speaker embroglio, would prove counterproductive. Accordingly, we must now break from strict chronology to a more topical handling of his career—starting with life-long antipathy toward baseball gambling.

Landis' inflexible hatred of gambling helped provide baseball with the strength it needed to surmount the Black Sox scandal. It was a hostility he possessed long before 1919. In 1909 when he had traveled to Milwaukee to address Marquette University law students, he carefully laid out his thoughts on the subject. "I have been going to baseball games for thirty years," he told his audience. "I never saw a game or heard of one where somebody did not call the umpire a robber or a thief, and yet no intelligent man doubts the integrity of baseball. . . .

"It is a great game this baseball—a great game. I have just been thinking about it. It is remarkable for the hold it has on the people, and equally remarkable for its cleanness. You know what happened to horse racing. Gambling killed it. Boxing, wrestling and almost all games of professional sports have unpleasant features connected with them. It is different with baseball, the managers realize it, and they keep it clean. There is no gambling connected with baseball, and I am glad of it, for it is certainly a wholesome sport. It is a compliment to the nation to love such a clean and thoroughly wholesome sport."[1]

"He was an absolute fanatic when it came to gambling," Leo Durocher once observed. "As far as Judge Landis was concerned, it was a gambler who had undoubtedly set Sodom and Gomorrah on the road to ruin."[2]

"You know, I don't know if it was because of him or what," recalled his granddaughter Susanne, "but I never even *went* to a race track until after he died."[3]

His most visible pre-baseball assault on Chicago's gamblers came in 1916 when he had investigated Mont Tennes' bookmaking ring. His war on baseball gambling began as soon as he assumed the commissionership. In a visit to St. Louis in December 1920, the Squire spoke to reporters about the importance of restoring confidence in baseball:

> If more stringent laws are needed to prevent gambling in baseball, they can be had through either state or federal statutes. I don't believe there would be any difficulty in having such legislation introduced in Washington for decent people are too fond of the game to pass up an opportunity to do what they can for its good. To help the game we must not only get rid of evil, but every appearance of evil. I think one highly important matter for baseball men to ponder is the betting which goes on in the stands between friends. For instance, two friends make a bet on the game. Somebody sees the money pass when the bet is paid. He recalls then that in a certain inning some player made a boner or struck out at a critical time. "Uh-huh!" says this fan to himself, "so it's that way, eh?" Then, having in mind what happened at the world's series of 1919, his suspicion grows.
>
> To eliminate this sort of thing, and I think it is highly important that it be eliminated, I have great faith in the loyalty of the fan for one thing and such influences as can be devised.[4]

The depth of his hostility was shown in February 1921, when he wrote to a Massachusetts' state legislator, Holyoke representative Hugh J. Lacey. Lacey had introduced a bill mandating a year's prison sentence, a $500 fine or both for players who had thrown games. Landis not only supported increasing the crime to a felony, with penalties of two to five years imprisonment, but making it applicable to betting on games at ballparks, no matter how small the bet. If there was no betting, Landis reasoned, there would be no bribery.[5]

In June 1921 the Judge rolled into Pittsburgh and was aghast to find civil authorities had failed to cooperate in his holy war against ballpark wagering.

"Politics or no politics, we'll put a stop to this gambling," he thundered to reporters in the lobby of Pittsburgh's Schenley Hotel once Barney Dreyfuss informed him that after the Pirates' private detectives apprehended gamblers in Forbes Field, local police magistrates released them as quickly as possible.

"Mr. Dreyfuss has explained the whole situation to me," the Squire continued. "The Pittsburgh Club has the ground thoroughly covered by police officers whom it pays $5 a day. Crooks caught violating the anti-gambling law have been taken to the police station, a block from the park, and there discharged by whoever is authorized by Pennsylvania law or city ordinance to turn criminals loose.

"Mr. Dreyfuss will have all the support I can give him. . . .

"I haven't decided whether I shall call upon Mayor E.V. Babcock myself, but baseball can get rid of undesirable elements in its ranks or around its ball parks whether the police aid it or not."

Having gotten that off his chest, Landis headed to the ballpark with Dreyfuss to watch Pittsburgh's Chief Moses Yellowhorse, a full-blooded Pawnee, pitch. "Mr. Dreyfuss and I will hold our annual meeting," he concluded. "We shall reminisce, watch the baseball game and be happy."[6]

Within a month, Landis' vigilant eye was fixed upon the West Coast. The PCL's Seattle Raniers had barred suspected gambler James L. Finnerty from their grounds, and Finnerty responded with a lawsuit. Landis wrote league president William H. McCarthy, praising his circuit's efforts and reassuring him of his support in regard to any potential litigation.

"I never had the slightest doubt that the exclusion of these gentry might result in damages suits," Landis declared. "But it is one thing to bring the suit and quite another to establish the right to damages."

While confident that no jury "outside of the penitentiaries" could be found to side with a gambler against Organized Baseball, Landis was preparing a contingency plan if they did and—in a move that to modern ears smacks of jury tampering—wanted the names and addresses of any jurymen that would find in favor of such gamblers.[7]

It would be a mistake to see Landis' tirades against mere gambling (as opposed to game-fixing) as insignificant or frivolous. They had a significant impact on players' consciousness. As early as 1921 that effect was taking hold. That year newly-appointed Tigers player-manager Ty Cobb walked past a Detroit pool-selling establishment and spied three of his men emerging. Cobb warned them to "get the hell away" from such places, but they protested they were "just looking around."

"Get away now and don't come back," the Georgia Peach snarled, "or I'll turn you over to [Frank] Navin's cop. Or would you rather talk to Landis?" It is interesting to consider that so fearsome a figure as Ty Cobb thought he had scare players with the specter of Kenesaw Landis.[8]

As the 1923 season began the Squire implored the nation's press to forego printing weekly runs scored totals, as that was a significant component of baseball wagering. "This form of gambling," Landis noted, "by which large sums are taken in by the swindlers, comes from small bettors. You seldom hear of the big man interested in a baseball pool. It is mostly the little fellow. This kind of gambling is most dangerous to baseball and should be eliminated."[9]

"It's not a gamble," Landis told local Elks in Albany, New York, where he traveled to open the Eastern League season alongside Governor Alfred E. Smith, "it's a swindle. If the people only knew that less than 30 per cent of the money received is ever paid out the baseball pool gambling would soon stop."

Albany—a wide open city—was the center of a huge baseball pool, taking in as much as $50,000 per week. As Landis watched the season opener from his box at the city's Chadwick Park he could not take his mind off the subject. On seeing a Texas Leaguer drop over the second baseman's head, he remarked, "I often wonder why they don't hit more of those." Then he continued with his Elks Club sermon, "They look so easy. I suppose that's what some folks think about their chances in a baseball pool. They look easy. But they aren't. The poor sucker hasn't a thing to do with what's happening."[10]

One of Landis' easier gambling "scandals" occurred immediately following the 1928 Yankees-Cards World Series. A Brooklyn clergyman, Father Belford, raised some hackles by alleging that pennant races were fixed on the orders of ownership. He specifically charged that in 1916 the fourth-place Giants had thrown the pennant to Brooklyn, reminding the public of John McGraw's stewing that his club wasn't trying hard enough—charges that had long been floating in the baseball world, having been reported for example in Joe Vila's

*New York Sun* column in the aftermath of the Shufflin' Phil Douglas affair. And not only were the Giants' actions in that year suspect. Brooklyn had supposedly raised a purse to reward Boston for defeating the Phils in a crucial series.

John Heydler immediately brought Father Belford's charges to Landis' attention. The Squire quietly traveled to Brooklyn, grilled Belford, and forced him to admit that he had nothing to back up his allegations. Furthermore, the Reverend confessed that even though he was a close personal friend of Brooklyn vice president Steve McKeever and was on the ballclub's pass list, he hadn't even *been* to a major league game in five or six years. The Judge exacted a formal retraction from Belford and returned to Chicago as quickly as he came.[11]

A particular Landis *bête noir* was Hall-of-Famer Rogers Hornsby.

Hornsby was the greatest right-handed hitter the game has ever seen—boasting a .358 lifetime average and three times bettering the .400 mark. He, however, was also the greatest right-handed *horse player* baseball had ever seen—not a trait to endear him to Landis.

One day in the 1920s, while Hornsby was still with the Cardinals, Landis summoned him to Chicago. "His office looked like a federal court," Hornsby once recalled. "Some guy was taking a transcript."

"Mr. Hornsby," Landis started out, "I've received varied reports and strong rumors that you bet on race horses."

"Well, Judge Landis, they aren't just rumors. I bet on horses. That's my only recreation."

"Then I'm ordering you to stop. It's gambling."

"I know it's gambling, and baseball and gambling don't mix. That's why I never play cards in the clubhouse with the other players. They're playing for money. I wait till later and maybe pick out a horse."

"That's some excuse. And you're going to stop."

"Look at it this way. I don't drink, smoke or go to movies. Don't even read anything but the baseball boxscores. Don't even go to the races over once or twice a year. I can relax by betting a horse now and then."

"It's gambling," responded Landis, waving his bony finger at Hornsby. "It's gambling."[12]

But Hornsby kept on gambling, and Landis kept on fuming. In 1927 Cincinnati bookmaker Frank Moore actually sued the ballplayer to recover $92,000 in gambling debts he claimed the second baseman owed him. Hornsby won in court, but Landis was not amused.[13]

While a star of his magnitude normally remained with one team for most of his career, the ornery Rajah bounced from team to team—from the Cards to the Giants to the Braves to the Cubs. By 1932 Hornsby was player-manager for Chicago. The Cubs were in second place on August 4, but management finally had enough and fired Hornsby anyway.

Rumors swirled that Hornsby's gambling figured in his dismissal—and further rumors circulated of a Landis probe. The Squire, as usual, was coy. "I am always investigating something . . . ," he told reporters, "draw your own conclusions."[14]

Cubs GM William Veeck was incensed that such an inquiry was taking place, arguing that it was an "outrageous" impediment to a club in the thick of a pennant race. Hornsby had been fired for just one reason, Veeck swore, the club was not winning—but, of course, it was, with a 53-46 record when Hornsby was dismissed. "If [Hornsby] gambled on the horses," Veeck said, putting his credibility at even graver risk, "I know nothing of it."[15]

For his part Hornsby countered that if every ballplayer who gambled was disciplined "it would disrupt the whole league."[16]

At this point Landis publicly entered the controversy. On August 11, 1932 he arrived in Pittsburgh to interrogate members of the Cubs, returning quickly to Chicago without issuing any public comment.

But two days after leaving Pittsburgh he popped up in St. Louis where, with Leslie O'Connor and a court stenographer in tow, he grilled Hornsby, infielder Woody English, pitchers Guy Bush and Pat Malone, and coach Charley O'Leary in open session.

At one point Landis questioned Hornsby regarding when he had last bet on a horse:

*Hornsby*: Well, about 1929, I guess; 1930, something like that.
*Landis*: This is 1932. Have you made a bet on a race horse since 1930?
*Hornsby*: Well, I am not going to say whether I have or not.
*Landis*: Or last year?
*Hornsby*: Put in my position, I am not going to say. I refuse to answer that question.
*Landis*: I am not so much interested in an answer to that question from your standpoint as I am from the standpoint of these boys here—Guy Bush, and Charley O'Leary and Woody English and Pat Malone—some of whose names have been badgered about in the

last few weeks as having been interested with you in betting on the races.

*Hornsby*: These fellows, Judge, as I have said before, have never been interested with me in any way of betting.[17]

Hornsby it turned out had been borrowing huge sums from his fellow Cubs to cover his gambling debts. From English he obtained $1,860, of which he repaid just $745, and from Malone $500, all of which had been repaid. From O'Leary he had borrowed $2,000. Guy Bush had co-signed a note for an additional $2,000 late in Hornsby's Chicago tenure—and in 1929 had co-signed for a $5,000 note.[18]

Bush was particularly upset by being drawn into the affair. He denied printed reports that he owed a bookie $35,000 and that he and Hornsby had associated with "two ladies known as blondes" in order to obtain gambling information.

Bush protested: "Don't you think this attack has been unfair to me?"

"If you are innocent, yes," Landis responded.

"I am innocent."

"But I am trying to find out. You know why I am here don't you?"

"Yes, but you know it is bad for them to accuse me of something I am not guilty of."

"Well, Guy, they have been accusing me for sixty years."

"Why did the *Chicago Daily News* pick me out in Chicago?"

"I don't know anything about that," Landis responded in avuncular fashion. "No matter what anybody accuses you of, or has ever accused you of, or may accuse you of hereafter, if the whole world believes this accusation, but you know it is not true that will carry you along, won't it?"

The Squire chose not to issue an official finding on the Hornsby case. Instead he merely released 36 pages of transcripts of his grilling of Hornsby, English, Bush, O'Leary, and Malone. "There will be no formal decision," he told the press, "the transcript speaks for itself." Some saw the move as vindication for the Rajah—they were wrong. Landis would keep a suspicious eye on Hornsby.[19]

"That fellow will never learn," Landis once fumed. "His betting has got him into one scrape after another, cost him a fortune and several jobs, and still he hasn't enough sense to stop it."[20]

Landis had the opportunity to rule against Hornsby once more in

1932. The Cubs went on to win the National League pennant but refused to vote their former manager a World Series share. A livid Hornsby appealed to Landis. "I do not know what the rules on the subject say —," he fumed in his letter to the Judge, "I did not read them. But I do feel that I deserve a share more than some of those who will receive full portions."[21]

Landis, deliberate as ever, waited two weeks before responding. He cited a then-current rule that no player ineligible to play in the World Series could receive a post-season share unless "all the players entitled to receive a full share" voluntarily agreed to it. Accordingly, the Squire refused to overturn the Cubs' decision, although he informed the Rajah he would be happy to do so if Hornsby would provide him with any supporting material. He knew there was none.

"He can overrule the votes of the players anytime," Hornsby complained, alleging that several Cubs had been "ordered" by someone (presumably Veeck) not to vote to give him a share.[22]

According to baseball historian Daniel Ginsburg, an expert on baseball gambling, "precedent and public opinion were with Hornsby" but Landis was "technically" correct in his decision. No doubt he was happy to have that technicality on his side."[23]

Hornby quickly found another job in baseball. Branch Rickey signed him to a Cardinals' contract, planning to employ him as a pinch hitter and spare infielder. Landis tried to block the signing, informing Rickey, "The demoralizer Hornsby has been in baseball too long. He's a bad influence."

"I will write a contract," Rickey countered, "and I will describe the gambling that Hornsby will not do, and he will sign it. Will you then deny this man the right to earn a living as a baseball player?"[24]

Landis surrendered. But Hornsby didn't last long with the Cardinals. In July 1933 he became manager of the rival Browns. Hornsby's prickly personality soon wore out his Browns welcome, but management had made the mistake of signing him to a multi-year contract. If the club fired Hornsby, they would have to pay him anyway — and the threadbare club could barely afford to pay current employees, let alone ex-employees. It retained Hornsby but made his life as miserable as he made life for his players. They hired detectives to investigate his gambling and brought the information to Landis. He already knew all he needed to know about Hornsby and gambling. The Judge blandly informed the Browns they should have known about Hornsby before they hired him. He was *their* problem—not his.[25]

Yet Landis had his own detectives trailing Hornsby, and he found out that Hornsby was placing bets through a clubhouse man named "Alabam." "Alabam" revealed that not only was he carrying wagers for Hornsby but also for umpires Bill Dinneen, Lou Kolls, and Cal Hubbard, who had received a tip on a race from Hornsby.

When the umpiring crew reached Chicago, Landis summoned it to his office. "Young man," Landis scolded Hubbard, "don't you know it's wrong to be gambling on horses?"

Hubbard should have taken the path of least resistance. Instead he responded, "Well, Judge, it's legal." That was not the right answer. Landis exploded and began a 10-minute tirade. In retribution he kept Hubbard out of that fall's World Series.[26]

Hornsby's luck finally ran out when the Browns were sold to loan magnate Donald Barnes. Barnes *could* afford to fire the Rajah. In July 1937 Browns business manager Bill DeWitt confronted Hornsby on the gambling issue. "Have you been playing the horses again?" he demanded.

"I have," the Rajah spat out. "What about it?"

"You're through," DeWitt informed him.[27]

"I'm thinking of the day the Browns fired me...," Hornsby once recalled. "Three horses won that day. I was on 'em. So was Buck [Bobo] Newsom, the Red Sox pitcher. He won as much as I did, and two weeks later the Browns traded for him. I guess it's who bets what."[28]

After Hornsby's dismissal from the Browns, Landis summoned him to Chicago. No reason was given for the command, but logically the Rajah would be grilled regarding his firing. When the Rajah arrived, only Leslie O'Connor was present. O'Connor explained that Landis had ordered him to take testimony from Hornsby. Hornsby refused, saying he'd talk to Landis or nobody. "The Judge didn't send no word to me," Hornsby later related, "so after a few minutes I left his office, and from that day on I never talked to him." Perhaps in response, Hornsby was effectively blacklisted from the majors as long as Landis lived.[29]

For a while the Rajah was reduced to playing for the semi-pro Denver Bay Refinery Club. Then in 1938 he returned to Organized Baseball as player-manager at Baltimore. By that July, however, he had once more worn out his welcome. He then found work in the Southern Association as player-manager of Joe Engel's Chattanooga

Lookouts. In honor of the occasion, the colorful Engel had a jockey present him with a swaybacked nag. Landis was not amused.

"I do not think your latest stunt a bit funny," the Judge telegraphed Engel. "If anything like that happens again, you will be in big trouble."[30]

Hornsby finished out the season with Chattanooga. That October he journeyed to Wrigley Field to watch his old mates, the Cubs, oppose the Yankees in the World Series. He had a pass, guaranteeing him access to the park's press box, but Landis barred him from using it. "Maybe the Judge thought I was trying to chisel my way in," said Hornsby, "but he's wrong . . . I don't know if Landis was trying to block me because I bet on the horses."

Denying there was any "hidden significance" to his highly unusual action, Landis, who had jurisdiction of the press boxes as well as all other aspects of the Series, blandly said he was merely trying to clean up an ongoing abuse of the facilities.

"I ordered the pass taken up," he contended, "for no other reason than that the issuance of the pass to Hornsby did not conform with the purpose for which it is designed. We have ordered others taken up too.

"I am simply trying to help better conditions for the baseball writers, who have work to do in those press boxes. For a number of years I have been watching them drag horses, oxen and everything else over you fellows trying to do your work, and so decided the time had come to take action. No one is entitled to enter the working press section except those actually engaged in work, and I'm merely putting an end to an abuse."[31]

For his part, Hornsby never apologized for his gambling. "No one has ever accused me of a thing in baseball," he once said in his own defense. "As a player I hustled with the best of them, and as a manager I made every effort to win. I don't drink or smoke, never did, and racing is my recreation. I enjoy it and get a kick out of it. Racing, and betting on races, is permitted by law in many of the states, so I was doing nothing illegal. Some of the best people in the country, including Cabinet ministers, attend races and bet on races. I always give full time to my baseball jobs, and if I bet money on races, it was my own, honestly earned. I could see no difference from betting a horse would win and a lot of club owners playing the market and betting a stock would go up or down."[32]

The last remark was a carefully aimed dig at Landis who had lost money for Organized Baseball in the 1929 stock market crash.[33] As long as Landis lived, the acerbic Hornsby (1940 Texas League Manager of the Year) was never again able to obtain another major league managing or coaching job. By 1944, the only baseball job he could find was with last-place Veracruz in Jorge Pasquel's Mexican League. Not until seven years after the Judge's death was the Rajah able to return to the majors, if one could call Bill Veeck's St. Louis Browns a major league club.[34]

In dealing with gambling *owners*, however, Landis had only a mixed record. He, of course, had forced Charles Stoneham and John McGraw to divest themselves of their Cuban racetrack and casino holdings. In 1934 Braves president Judge Emil Fuchs announced he would be operating dog racing at Braves Field. Landis vowed he would quit if that came to pass and stopped the scheme in its tracks.

He has less luck against Emil Fuchs' partner, Charles F. Adams. In 1927 Adams, a Boston businessmen, bought into the Braves. Shortly thereafter when Massachusetts legalized horse racing, Adams became a partner in Suffolk Downs.

Landis didn't like the situation but did nothing to force Adams to choose between baseball and racing. By 1935 Adams owned 65 percent of Boston stock. All Landis could effectively do was to prevent Adams from serving as a Braves' officer or to be formally listed as a stockholder. But Adams effectively controlled the club anyway; by 1941 his share of team stock had risen to 73 percent. Landis now finally increased his pressure on Adams, and in January 1944 he sold his Boston stock to Lou Perini's "Three Little Steamshovels" syndicate.[35]

Landis was far less successful against Detroit's Frank Navin who owned six racehorses and who allegedly placed $1,000 horse race bets on a daily basis—but superstitiously would never make a single wager if he spied a cross-eyed person at the track. Some said Landis was clearly playing favorites as the quiet but intelligent Navin was one of the Judge's closest friends among the owners and often furnished him with invaluable advice. Others said Landis did try cracking down on Navin, but he threatened to sue.[36]

A ballclub that presented recurring problems for Landis was Brooklyn. "The Dodger clubhouse," noted Arthur Mann, "reeked with gamblers, bookmakers, racing handicappers, fast 'friends,' and ticket scalpers. They had long enjoyed access to Ebbets Field and scurried from dugout to locker room like happy, squealing vermin in the rat runs of an aging barn."

In New York City prior to the 1941 World Series Landis warned Dodger general manager Larry MacPhail and manager Leo Durocher about Durocher's providing actor George Raft with four tickets to his private box. Raft was no ordinary actor. He had a long history of associating with racketeers including Joe Adonis, Meyer Lansky, and Bugsy Siegel. Landis warned MacPhail and Durocher that Raft had won a $100,000 betting on baseball games and to therefore stay away from him.

Durocher and Raft were close friends. Durocher spent a month each winter at Raft's California mansion. He told Landis he wasn't about to repay Raft's hospitality by taking back the tickets. "I gave the man the four seats and he's going to keep the four seats," Leo insisted. Landis countered that if he didn't obey he'd never put on his uniform again.

The Squire finally led Durocher back to the privacy of his bedroom. "Now this isn't the first conversation we've had in here, son" he told Durocher. "You will get those tickets back...." Even Landis' soft sell failed. Durocher still refused to give in.

When Durocher and MacPhail left Landis' suite, MacPhail fumed to his manager: "What are you blind or something? Couldn't you see me giving you the sign to tell him Yes? I'll give him four seats in a box as good as yours. What difference does it make to him?" But Durocher refused to give in. Not helping matters was Raft, who threatened to sue Landis for defamation of character.

In February 1943 when Branch Rickey took over the Brooklyn franchise, Landis summoned him to Chicago and ordered him to "clean house."

"You must break up that nest of horseplayers and card sharks," he ordered. The biggest casualty of the cleanup was Dodger coach Charlie Dressen who was fired for associating with gambler "Memphis" Engleberg.[37]

In 1944 Landis and Durocher tangled again over the issue of the Durocher-Raft relationship. While the Dodgers were training that spring at Bear Mountain, New York, Raft ensconced himself at Durocher's New York apartment. On one occasion Raft hosted a party at which a guest was allegedly cheated out of $12,000 by the use of loaded dice. Once again, Landis futilely warned Durocher to steer clear of the actor.[38]

In 1931 Chicago Cub catcher Gabby Hartnett, a Landis favorite, was not only photographed at Al Capone's private box at Comiskey

Park but gladly provided an autograph for the mobster's 12-year-old boy Sonny. Landis hit the ceiling.

"I go to his place of business," Hartnett explained regarding Capone. "Why shouldn't he come to mine?"[39][40]

Yet another answer Landis did not want to hear.

Landis ordered both NL president John Heydler and AL president Will Harridge to issue instructions banning players from talking with *any* fan, before, during or after a game. The penalty: a $500 fine.

At about the same time the Squire even forbade managers from announcing their starting pitchers in advance of gametime. He wanted to keep gamblers from gaining an edge, but all he accomplished was to prevent ballclubs from announcing such box-office matchups as Dean vs. Hubbell or Grove vs. Ruffing. Club owners groused that he was needlessly costing them money—and with nothing at all to show for it. The media sided with ownership.

Landis ignored the criticism. "I'm battling to keep this game clean," he contended, "and away from gamblers, and some of these writing fellows are trying to make it harder for me."[41]

The Squire was forever checking into gambling activities at ballparks. In April 1940 he wrote to Connie Mack detailing widespread gambling at Shibe Park. "There is only one thing we can do (and that much we must)," he wrote Mack, "with these rats, and that is to everlastingly keep after them..."[42]

But the problem persisted. In August 1944 he wrote Mack again, complaining over the use of the park's pay phones by gamblers ("at least tear out those damned telephones") and giving Mack his philosophy on gamblers in the parks:

> I wish you would give me your conclusions as to what you can do, or propose to do. Of course, I prefer local clubs handle it, rather than have the public know the Commissioner had dipped into it. As to the fellows that bet among themselves inside the park, there is nothing to be added to what has been sent to you in the past. Those fellows pester and bedevil honest men and women who come out to the park to see a ball game, and it would not be unreasonable should their activities result in persons annoyed by them getting the notion that it was all right with the club to have gambling operations carried on. If you can't get them in jail, you can at least get them thrown out of the ball park on their heads—which would be some satisfaction.

Many of Landis' antigambling investigations involved the lower minors. One case involved Texan Bob Tarleton. In the 1937-38 seasons Tarleton, then business manager of the Texas League's Dallas Steers, "officially certified" a known bookmaker to scout for his club. The following year Tarleton found himself with Longview in the Class C East Texas League. Again Tarleton retained this same gambler to scout. By season's end Landis had finally caught wind of the situation. He placed Tarleton on the ineligible list.[43]

Yet Landis could also show leniency—and not only to superstars such as Cobb and Speaker. In 1941 Fort Pierce hurler Lefty "The Great" Covington had been charged with throwing the last game of the Florida East Coast League season. From his spring headquarters, Landis grilled not only Covington and his accusers, but even Covington's shoemaker father-in-law, Antonio Pugliese. Covington's accusers were rich on comments on his general character, such as "The most terrible trouble maker to any team . . . It is a wonder . . . that the man came through the season without having his head busted open."

Landis wanted to know everything about Covington—how much he earned and how much he owed; how much he paid for rent and what sort of second-hand furniture he bought. The Judge—who by now hadn't banned anyone from the game for gambling on games in nearly two full decades, reinstated Covington. Covington, however, learned little from the experience—and never really would. In 1943 he pitched a perfect game at Scranton, earning him a promotion the following year to the talent-depleted Phillies. He lasted there long enough to refuse his manager's orders to walk Stan Musial. "Imagine telling a guy with my stuff to walk Musial," Covington grumbled. Philadelphia management imagined something even more unimaginable—shipping Covington and his attitude all the way down to Utica in the Eastern League.[44]

Once again, Covington found himself drawing Landis' attention. As the season drew to a close, teammate Freddie Daniels accused him of indifferent pitching. He retaliated by slugging Daniels and by hitting at least other one player with a bat.

Landis, just weeks from death, dispatched Leslie O'Connor to Utica to investigate this obstreperous pitcher. Once again, he cleared Covington.

Four decades after Landis' death, Elden Auker, Tigers starting pitcher in the 1934 World Series, provided this insight into Landis and into a typical—but little known—Landis tilt against gambling:

> We were even afraid to go to the racetrack. If we had anything to do with gambling whatsoever we were suspect.
>
> I was pitching a ballgame. I was with the St. Louis Browns, and I was pitching a game against the White Sox one day on Sunday. In Chicago's old Comiskey Park, the box seats were even with the dugout. The dugout didn't stick out away from there. We had a second baseman named Don Heffner, and he was injured. So he was out of the ballgame and he came over during the ballgame and he sat down at the edge of the dugout and right behind him in the boxseat was Barney Ross.
>
> Well, we all knew Barney. He was a fighter, and we knew him just as a fighter.[45] He sat there during the whole game. Well, Landis always sat on the White Sox dugout side about halfway down between home plate and the dugout. He was there that particular day. So the game was over, and we all went back to the hotel. When we got back Fred Haney, who was the manager of our team at that time, got a call from the Judge's office. The secretary said, "Judge Landis wants you in his office tomorrow morning at 9:30, downtown Chicago. And he wants your player Don Heffner to be with you." Everybody was suspicious as to what was going to happen. So Fred and Don go down to his office, and they walk into his office. And after the greetings and everything the Judge said, "Mr. Heffner, I want to ask you a question, and I want an answer, and I want an honest answer." He said, "What were you talking to Barney Ross about yesterday?"
>
> Well Don said, "So help me, I couldn't think of one single thing we'd even talked about. We were just talking you know."
>
> Landis said, "I know you were talking. I want to know what you were talking about. I want to know exactly what you were saying to Barney Ross."
>
> Don said he couldn't think of a single word he'd even talked about. Well, after he'd convinced the Judge that he really wasn't talking about anything, Landis said, "'Well, I want to tell you something. Barney Ross is affiliated with the mobs in Chicago, and if I ever hear of you ever speaking to Barney Ross again, I'll kick you out of baseball." And he said "Mr. Haney, I want you to tell your players I never want any of your players ever to speak to Barney Ross again. And I want you to tell the rest of the American League, the rest of the

teams, that Barney Ross has no business talking to one of our base-ball players in the American League or the National League. Make sure you never violate that. If I ever hear of it, you're gone."

And that was the old judge, and boy the word went around fast. We had a meeting. Fred and Don came out to the clubhouse and sat down and Don was still white from the conversation. But the Judge wasn't fooling, and that's the way it was. And he would have done it. He would have done it without a question or a doubt. But he was a great man.

He frowned on gambling. Nobody ever questioned the Judge. He was the Judge, and he had our respect. The best thing that happened to baseball. I wish we had him today.[46]

# CHAPTER 21

# "DARKNESS IN THE MIDDLE OF THE AFTERNOON"

A crooked World Series catapulted Kenesaw Landis into the newly created commissionership. As commissioner, Landis would do all he could not only to ensure the survival of the Series but to firmly imprint the stamp of his character upon the Fall Classic.

The modern World Series began in 1903 as a best-of-nine challenge but quickly went to the best-of-seven format now familiar to most fans. In 1919, however, it reverted to best-of-nine, with the Reds obtaining a tainted victory in eight games, the Indians winning in seven in 1920, and the Giants beating the Yankees in eight games in 1921.

Landis thought the longer Series a blunder. "That 1921 Series stretched out too long," he complained. "This should be the greatest sports event of the year, but if it drags out two weeks, the public loses interest."[1]

Not everyone agreed. At the major league meetings held at New York's Hotel Commodore in December 1921 the NL opposed shortening the Series, but the AL sided with Landis. That was enough for him to have his way.[2]

This was all the public knew of Landis and the 1921 World Series. But beneath the surface rumors of baseball corruption continued to swirl. In the eighth inning of Game Four the Yankees, enjoying their first post-season ever, held a 1-0 lead. Suddenly Giants hitters pounded Yanks star lefthander Carl Mays, collecting four hits and scoring three runs to take the lead—and ultimately the game.

That evening a well-known Broadway actor approached newsman George Perry with this story: in that fateful eighth inning, Mays' wife, sitting in the stands, had signaled her husband by wiping her face with a white handkerchief. The actor alleged that motion

328

was the cue that a bribe had been handed over and Mays should now throw the game.

Perry conveyed the actor's story to the man in charge of that Series' press arrangements, the *New York Telegram*'s Fred Lieb. Lieb headed for Yankee owner T. L. Huston's suite at Manhattan's Hotel Martinique. There Lieb found Huston and Red Sox owner Harry Frazee passed out from Prohibition-era booze.

Lieb, Perry, the unidentified actor, and the revived Huston piled into a cab and—without calling in advance—rushed to Landis' suite at East 42nd Street's Commodore Hotel. Arriving after midnight, they rapped vigorously on his door. Landis, clad in a flannel nightshirt, appeared even more offputting than usual. "What in hell do you fellows want at this hour of the night?" he grumbled.

"Judge," Lieb stammered, "here's a man who thinks the game yesterday wasn't entirely on the up-and-up. He thinks Mays let up in the last two innings."

With that Landis left Perry, Lieb, and Huston in the sitting room and took the actor into a bedroom. Emerging half an hour later, he announced, "I am making a full investigation of this man's story. I have already called up the detective agency that my office employs from time to time, and they will keep their eyes on Mays for the remainder of the Series."

Turning to Lieb the Judge warned, "Freddy, don't you use this in your paper until there are further developments."

Lieb followed orders—even after Mays lost the deciding eighth game of the Series. Landis informed Lieb that his detectives had turned up nothing on Mays.

That, however, was not the end of the story. In 1928 Lieb visited Huston's Georgia hunting lodge. Once again the Yankee co-owner was in his cups and—after everyone else had dozed off—he confided to Lieb, "I wanted to tell you that some of our pitchers threw World Series games on us in both 1921 and 1922."

"You mean that Mays matter of the 1921 World Series?" Lieb wanted to know.

"Yes," the barely functioning Huston slurred, "but there were others—other times, other pitchers." With that he lurched off to bed.

Lieb didn't bother to follow up on this revelation for a year. When he did, Huston wouldn't provided further details—but he wouldn't retract his story either.

A few years later Lieb received what he regarded as a clue

regarding who the other pitcher might have been. Yankee manager Miller Huggins was telling Lieb how he would financially help virtually any player he had ever managed. "I made only two exceptions," Huggins revealed, "Carl Mays and Joe Bush. If they were in the gutter, I'd kick them." Bullet Joe Bush had blown leads to the Giants in both Game One and Game Five of the 1922 World Series.[3]

That 1922 World Series continued to haunt Landis for some time. In January 1927 a sportswriter phoned, wanting to know if Landis had surreptitiously investigated "irregularities" in that Fall Classic. "There's nothing to it," Landis exploded. "These stories are now being cooked up by the newspapers. They print the story in one edition and deny it in the next.

"I'm getting tired spending all my time making denials to these silly stories.

"Some of these reporters get themselves filled with stale beer, mince pie, and, oh, well . . . " By that time he had worked himself into such a frenzy he slammed down the phone.[4]

The 1922 Series also saw Landis personally involved in a very public controversy. After 10 innings Game Two was deadlocked at 3-3. Over a decade remained before a major league club first installed lights, and umpire George Hildebrand called the contest on account of darkness. Deadlocked World Series contests were nothing new. Dating back to 1884 four previous Fall Classic games had been recorded as tied (the last being in 1912), but there was a problem with this one: it was only 4:46 PM and 45 minutes of daylight remained.

Halting the contest had not been Landis' idea and had barely been Hildebrand's. Hildebrand always claimed that fellow ump Bill Klem had put him up to it. "Sure, it's light now," Klem argued, "but will it still be light by the time both sides complete their turn at bat? Suppose one team has a big inning, and scores six or seven runs, and the inning takes three-quarters of an hour? What then?"

The crowd had not particularly noticed Hildebrand conversing with Klem, but they *had* seen Hildebrand talking with Landis shortly before the game had been called. They assumed Landis had made the decision. They also assumed the decision hinged less on "big innings" than on "big profits." A tie game would create the need for another game, and another game would translate into bigger profits for ownership.

While all this was happening, Landis was blissfully chatting with Lord Louis Mountbatten. The 22-year-old Mountbatten, a great-grandson of Queen Victoria, had been enjoying a grand time, devouring six ice cream cones, four sodas, and two bags of peanuts, cheering Babe Ruth and grousing like his American cousins at umpires' decisions. He had just been introduced to Landis when Hildebrand called the game.

Reporters furiously rushed to Landis' box, wanting to know what had happened. "I stand by the umpire's decision," the Judge stated succinctly. The crowd, meanwhile, was reacting to events by turning furiously and viciously on him. Boos, insults, and threats filled the Polo Grounds, "thief" and "robber" being two of the kinder epithets. "My goodness, Judge," Mountbatten exclaimed, "but they are giving you the bird!" As Kenesaw and Winifred left their seats, a menacing crowd surrounded them, and a police escort proved necessary. "The mob," noted sportswriter Henry Farrell, "need[ed] but one stroke of leadership to do something serious."[5]

Landis was furious. "You're all cowards," he roared as he neared the right-field exit. He was accustomed to public acclaim, not catcalls and boos and fumed: "I never saw such a damned thing in my life. And those darned fools thinking I called that game to make a little more money for the club owners. As for that blankety-blank umpire, what was he thinking about? I may not be the smartest person in the world, but I've got sense enough not to call a ball game on account of darkness in the middle of the afternoon."

He would have to reclaim the crowd's favor—and fast. Despite the stress of events he had not lost his skill for deploying a dramatic master stroke. Without consulting anyone, he issued the following statement:

> Under baseball laws umpires are charged with the sole authority of calling a game on account of darkness. In the exercise of this authority to-day's game was called at the end of the tenth inning.
>
> Many of the spectators were of the opinion that the game could have continued. Of course, the umpires on the field are in much better position to judge conditions and their effects on play. But regardless of any question whether this decision was erroneous, the two New York clubs, acting for themselves and their teams, have decided, with the approval of the commissioner, that the entire receipts of to-day's game shall be turned over to the funds for the benefit of disabled soldiers and to the charities of New York.

Landis had thus given away $120,554, and when he appeared at the Polo Grounds the following day the fans cheered him. He also made sure his relations with the players remained secure. The Giants' Dave Bancroft and the Yankees' Babe Ruth approached him after hearing rumors that players would now receive revenues from only three games. Landis reassured them they had nothing to worry about.

Landis had less respect for ownership's concerns.[6] The *Reach Guide* bluntly accused him of a "mistake" for not obtaining the "knowledge or assent" of the Advisory Board under "whose auspices the World Series is supposed to be conducted, simply because an unreasoning mob doubted the motive for calling the tie game." Ownership may have grumbled quietly, but they were still too cowed to criticize him publicly.[7]

In 1923 yet another Giants-Yankees World Series took place, and the Chicago-based commissioner was growing tired of the experience. "Isn't this World's Series job ever going to get me out of New York?" he groused. "It looks as though I can keep in a standing hotel reservation there at World's Series time."[8]

In comparison with 1922, however, post-season 1923 was positively placid, marked only by two minor squabbles. The first involved the Yankees' proposed roster substitution of rookie Lou Gehrig for the injured Wally Pipp. "It's all right with me," Landis stated, "but McGraw must give his consent."

John McGraw, however, remained as combative as ever and as resentful of the Yankees, even forbidding his Giants to dress at new Yankee Stadium (he made them change at the Polo Grounds and ride in taxis to the Bronx). "The rule is there," McGraw stated, "and if the Yankees have an injury to a regular, it's their bad luck." The hobbled Pipp stayed in the Yankee lineup and batted just .250.[9]

In Game Three, before a record crowd of 62,450, Giants outfielder Casey Stengel created further controversy. Stengel's dramatic ninth-inning inside-the-park home run had won Game One. In Game Three he spared himself the exertion by depositing one of Sad Sam Jones' pitches into the Yankee Stadium's right-field stands. When Stengel had approached the plate, the Yankee bench had ridden him unmercifully. Now circling the bases, Stengel had his revenge, and to rub it in he gleefully thumbed his nose at his tormentors. "I made like a bee or fly was bothering me," he later explained, "so I kept rubbing the end of my nose, with my fingers pointing toward the Yankee dugout."[10]

Yankee owner Jake Ruppert was beside himself, particularly

when Stengel's blast proved to be the difference in the 1-0 contest. He wanted Landis to discipline the veteran outfielder. "No, I don't think I will," the Squire responded, "A fellow who wins two games with home runs may feel a little playful, especially if he's a Stengel." Casey Stengel, for his part, later told his audiences in varying versions of the Stengel legend that Landis had either tongue-lashed him ("If you do that again, I promise you one thing: You won't receive a dollar of your World Series share") or fined him $50. But it wasn't so.[11][12]

The 1924 Senators-Giants Fall Classic had, of course, been preceded by the exceedingly messy O'Connell-Dolan scandal, but once the Series started there was little controversy and much glory for baseball. The 1925 Washington-Pittsburgh Series, however, was far less successful. The Senators failed to repeat, in part because of shortstop Roger Peckinpaugh's record eight errors, many of which came in key situations. Ironically, before the Series began the Pirates had discussed trying to avoid hitting the ball to Peckinpaugh, the 1925 AL MVP. Landis, still nervous about gambling scandals, had Peckinpaugh trailed by detectives but found nothing to indicate more than mere incompetence and nervousness on Peckinpaugh's part.[13][14]

In 1925 Landis was still smarting from the uproar over George Hildebrant's calling off Game Two of the 1922 World Series. A torrential rainstorm delayed the start of 1925's Game Seven and turned Forbes Field into a swamp. Shortly after the contest started, the downpour began again. With the game tied, 7-7, in the seventh, the game could, and probably should, have been stopped.

But Landis, fearing a repeat of 1922, refused to allow a rainout. Each inning a wheelbarrow full of sawdust was dumped on the mound to help provide some added footing. It was no use; the mound became a slippery slope of mud. The situation was so bad Walter Johnson carried sawdust out to the diamond in his cap to help. But Landis saw to it that, come hell or high water (particularly high water), play would continue. The contest ended as a 9-7 Pittsburgh triumph.[15]

Nineteen twenty-eight saw another Landis rule change—one made before the Series began—which effected the outcome of Game Four. There had not been much drama in that fall's Cardinals-Yankees Series prior to the seventh inning of that game. New York had captured the first three contests but trailed 2-1 as St. Louis' 21-game winner Willie Sherdel faced Babe Ruth.

Sherdel got two quick strikes on Ruth. Then the Babe stopped to jaw with Cardinals catcher Earl Smith. Sherdel quick-pitched and deposited a waist high fastball right down the middle of the plate. Quick pitches, illegal in the American League, were permitted in the National, and the Sportsman's Park crowd of 37,331 cheered in appreciation. But Ruth and homeplate umpire Cy Phirman thought otherwise. "What the—kind of strike is that?" Ruth demanded. "That don't count! That's a quick pitch!" Phirman agreed.

Before the Fall Classic Landis had banned such deliveries in the Series. The Cardinals surged around Phirman, but his decision stood. All the while Ruth remained aloof, a picture of innocence and detachment.

But when the ruckus ended, Sherdel put the next two pitches outside homeplate. Ruth watched each go by, and the count even at 2-2. Then the Babe called out to Sherdel: "The National League is a hell of a league."

Sherdel couldn't disagree much with that statement, so Ruth bore in with, "Put one right here and I'll knock it out of the park for you."

Sherdel's next offering was a strike. Ruth swung and the ball went into the right-field stands—for an *undisputed* World Series called-shot home run.[16]

In 1929 Landis finally saw a Chicago team participate in postseason play, Joe McCarthy's Cubs. That Series included Howard Ehmke's surprise start in Game One and Philadelphia's 10-run comeback in Game Four. But it was also a Series marked by vicious bench-jockeying. Before Game Five began, Landis finally had enough and summoned McCarthy and A's manager Connie Mack. "I have stood for all of this monkey business that I intend to," he warned. "The boys have been going entirely too far. From now on, any player guilty of offensive language will be fined a full share. Often it is difficult to tell exactly which player is yelling some of these objectionable things. In that case, I will fine the manager."

Mack, not wishing to test Landis' patience, called his team together, ordering them, "From now on, all jockeying is off. I'll not hear another word of it." The A's, however, were a pretty tough bunch, with catcher Mickey Cochrane being one of the toughest. "After this game," Cochrane sneered sarcastically, "we'll serve tea in the clubhouse."

"Do you want this to cost you money, Mickey?" Mack shot back.

Cochrane cut out the swearing, but before the game, he called out to the Cub bench, "Come on out boys? Put on your bib and tucker. We're serving tea and cookies today." Not far away from Cochrane was Landis, sitting in his private box. "He never by the slightest movement betrayed that he heard my wisecrack," Cochrane later recalled. "He did not even lift his chin off the rail."

But he did hear it.

After the game—a 3-2 Philadelphia victory that nailed down the world championship—the Squire visited the A's clubhouse to offer congratulations. He moved from player to player, extending felicitations to all, that is, except Cochrane. "He never gave me a tumble, sitting over in a corner . . . ," said Cochrane. "I thought he was sore and was going to pass right over me."

Finally as Landis was leaving, he approached Cochrane and shot out his right hand. Suddenly he put on a mock scowl and growled, "Hello, sweetheart. I came in after my tea and cookies."

"Did you hear me?" the surprised catcher gasped.

"You said it loud enough," Landis responded, but that was the end of the matter.[17]

Landis did not cotton to rivals in the baseball firmament—whether it was Ban Johnson, Branch Rickey, J. G. Taylor Spink—or umpire Bill "Catfish" Klem. Klem was often as imperious as Landis. He was, as fellow ump Beans Reardon undiplomatically put it, "an arrogant little guy." Landis first called Klem on the carpet during the 1924 World Series when Klem had been unable to control his temper and had several squabbles with Washington outfielder Goose Goslin.

Seven years later Klem complained to Landis about criticism John McGraw had launched at the umpire for his work during the 1931 Cardinals-A's World Series. McGraw, in a newspaper column, charged Klem with blowing a particular call.

This incensed Klem who wanted Landis to discipline the Little Napoleon. With fellow arbiter Dolly Stark in tow, he visited the Squire in the living room of his suite at Philadelphia's Bellevue-Stratford Hotel. Klem, brandishing a copy of the offending article, did all he could to influence Landis. The Judge barely noticed him, looking out a window most of the time.

Finally Klem finished. Landis, who had been behind a writing desk, arose. He stalked back and forth. Then suddenly he halted dramatically in front of Stark, a rather high-strung young fellow.

"How old are you?" he wanted to know.

"Thirty-three, sir."

"Thirty-three, eh?" Landis responded. "Well, go get a job, young man. At least be among respectability."

That was it. "The Judge never spoke a word to me from my entrance to my exit, and he never told me what his decision was," Klem later recalled. "I still don't know what it was all about."[18]

The 1932 World Series—remembered today for Babe Ruth's disputed "called-shot" off Cubs pitcher Charlie Root—was a public relations disaster for Landis. Tickets had been sold in sets for each of the games to be played at Yankee Stadium. This being perhaps the worst year of the Depression, advance sales were slow. Yankee management wanted to sell seats on an individual game basis, but Landis refused and over 20,000 tickets remained unsold before the first game. Compounding the problem, a steady downpour blanketed New York that morning. Many fans felt the contest would be postponed, and there was virtually no walk-up trade for the many tickets that remained available.

The Yankees wanted the game halted, ostensibly because of wet grounds but actually on account of empty seats. Only 41,459 fans partially filled the 65,000-seat capacity stadium. Landis, however, refused to accede to the Yankees' wishes—no matter how much money was lost or how bad the empty seats looked. "The schedule called for the Series to open in New York on a Wednesday, September 28," he declared. "That meant that Saturday and Sunday games were scheduled for Chicago, even if the Series ran to only four games. I wanted nothing to interfere with that arrangement. Many of the Chicago fans purchased their three-game strip tickets to see these week-end games, and I wanted to play fair with them, even though some New Yorkers had to sit on wet seats."

That 1932 Series again saw a Bill Klem-centered complaint reaching Landis. But this time it was a player complaining against Klem. The unlikely whiner was normally mild-mannered Lou Gehrig, who had engaged Klem in a running battle over ball-and-strike calls, a skill Klem was particularly vain about. Finally, Klem—now umpiring at second—even refused to move out of the way when the Iron Horse was at bat. Gehrig followed up his words by rifling a shot right at Klem—so near that Old Catfish had to jump to get out of the ball's way. Klem's refusal to budge was all Gehrig could stand. He approached Landis to complain about the incident and about an epithet Klem had launched in his direction. "He called me something that wasn't called for," Gehrig complained, "and I won't take it."

But he would have to take it. Landis thought the episode merely amusing—although he did bring it to Klem's attention.

The Squire, however, did not find the Yankees-Cubs bench-jock-eying amusing. "The language was getting brutal," recalled Yankee shortstop Joe Sewell. "Mrs. Sewell told me they could hear it in the stands, and it was embarrassing." After Game Three (the "called-shot" game) Landis dispatched a letter to managers Joe McCarthy and Charlie Grimm warning them that any player caught using foul language would be fined $500. "And do you know," Sewell remembered, "you could have heard a pin drop?

"We sat there like a bunch of mummies. But our bats made a lot of noise. We won 13-6 for a four-game sweep."[19]

Other controversies remained in the Series' wake, specifically involving division of the Cubs' World Series shares. The first issue involved the cut for deposed-manager Rogers Hornsby (see Chapter 14: "Baseball is O.K."), but another centered on shortstop Mark Koenig's World Series share. Koenig, a one-time Yankee, had joined the Cubs on August 5, 1932, and proved crucial in their pennant chase, batting .353 and driving in 17 runs. His new teammates rewarded his efforts with a half-share.

The Cubs' "cheapness" incensed Koenig's old friends in New York—and the Yankees' anger boiled over during the Series. Much of the baseball public, including Landis, was also outraged. He called Charlie Grimm to his office and fumed, "You can tell your boys that everybody feels bad about them voting Koenig only a one-half share and that they won't get their World Series checks until next January."[20]

But his anger soon cooled. Two weeks after the Series concluded, Landis had his secretary Elinor Donohue call Cubs team captain and third baseman Woody English. She summoned English from his Newark, Ohio, home to Chicago for an interview with the Commissioner. The topic: Mark Koenig.

Instead of meeting Landis at his Michigan Avenue offices, however, English headed straight for Landis' home, where the Commissioner was laid up with the flu. Winifred Landis led English up to the Squire's room where he lay in bed. "Before you sit down, would you mind getting me a glass of water and one of those pills in the bottle on the stand there," he requested before beginning the interview.

Landis then put English through an odd set of paces. "Woody," he asked, "I want you to call the Cub office and ask them when Mark Koenig reported to the club." English did, noting it was in early August. Then Landis asked, "Now call them again and ask how many games he played in and how many games you played in." Koenig had played in 33; English in 127.

"Now," pronounced Landis, "Koenig's got half a World Series share and you got a full share. If he had gotten a full share that would have cut down on your share. Now you played in 125 [sic] games and he played in 30 [sic]. I don't think he's entitled to a full share."

Landis had clearly changed his mind, but, nonetheless, English seemed defensive. "Judge," he explained, "I never voted against Koenig to get a full share. Only two of the players voted against a full share for him and the vote had to be unanimous. I'll never reveal who those two were because it was a secret vote. The manager and the coaches were not allowed in the meeting. Being captain I had to conduct the meeting."

That was the end of the matter. The Cubs' "cheapskate" decision would stand.[21]

In the fourth game of the 1933 Giants-Senators World Series, umpire Charley Moran banished Senators left fielder Heinie Manush after Manush and several of his teammates questioned a close call at first base. Landis never publicly criticized the fiery Moran for his actions (the Giants finally won the game, 2-1, in 11 innings) and even fined Manush $50. But before Game Five began, Landis called the entire umpiring crew together and informed them that fans had paid top dollar to see the brightest stars in the World Series and that henceforth they were not to banish *any* players from the Fall Classic without his approval. That December he formalized his decision and kept the rule in effect until his death.[22][23]

Nineteen thirty-four's World Series between the Tigers and the Cardinals was an eventful one for Landis—too eventful. It started out positively enough. In September 1934 the Judge engineered the first sponsorship of World Series broadcasts. Remarkably, though the Series had been broadcast since 1921, this was the first time broadcasts would have sponsorship.

The Squire cajoled Henry Ford to part with an unprecedented $400,000 for a four-year radio contract. Annually players would receive $42,000—or almost $1,000 per man on the winning club ($600 extra for each loser). "The Judge is jubilant," wrote Dan Daniel in the *New York World-Telegram*, "the club owners are glad, though slightly sour over Landis' lavish provision for the hired men, and the players are more than elated."[24]

Landis also took charge of the artistic aspects of the broadcasts, banning Ty Tyson from Detroit's WWJ from broadcasting the Series for being "too excessively partisan." Instead, he appointed France Laux, Ted Husing, and Pat Flanagan for CBS and Tom Manning, Ford Bond, and Graham McNamee for NBC. But Tyson's popularity was such that 600,000 protesting fans wrote Landis, and he was forced to reverse his decision.[25]

The Tigers captured Game Five by a score of 3-1. A particularly frustrated Cardinal was catcher Bill Delancey who struck out three times, the last instance coming in the ninth with the tying runs aboard. When umpire Brick Owens called Delancey out, the catcher exploded with profanity. Owens dutifully reported the incident to the Judge, who the next morning summoned Delancey to his hotel room to get his side of the story. Later an amused Landis conveyed results of the session to his closer friends among the press. "I asked Bill what he had said to Brick," the Squire narrated. "He told me this: 'When Owens called that first strike on me, I called him a dirty so and so. When he called the second on me, I said he was a dirty — — — so and so, and believe me, Judge, when he called the third one, I just had to say he was a dirty — — — — — so and so."

With that the Judge convulsed with laughter, finally admitting, "You know that boy was so honest, I just had to let him off with a $50 fine."[26]

But the real fireworks of the 1934 Series occurred in Game Seven. In the sixth inning Cards left fielder Joe Medwick tripled to right-center, driving in a run and making the score 9-0 in favor of St. Louis.

When Medwick had slid into third, he spiked Tiger third baseman Marv Owen, who then fell to the ground. "You, Hunky — — — —, who are you trying to cut down?" Owen screamed.

"I'll ram that ball down your throat if you ever try to tag me like that again," Medwick responded.

With that the two traded blows, a brief battle that Bill Klem, umpiring at third, soon broke up. Medwick calmed down and stuck out his hand. Owen refused to shake it. When the inning ended, Medwick trotted out to left field, but the frustrated Navin Field crowd didn't want him there. They showered Medwick not only with verbal abuse but with every sort of projectile they could lay their hands on—apples, oranges, vegetables, rolled-up newspapers, half-eaten hot dogs, pop bottles, beer bottles, milk bottles. Whenever their rage seemed about to subside, a new avalanche descended upon Medwick. "I watched the crowd and Medwick and the pelting missiles through field glasses," wrote Paul Gallico in the *New York Daily News*, "and it was a terrifying sight. Every face in the crowd, women and men, was distorted with rage. Mouths were torn wide, open eyes glistened and shone in the sun. All fists were clenched."

"Take him out," the mob chanted over and over again, "Take him out!"

While this frenzy transpired, Landis had moved a few rows up from his box. There he carried on a conversation—but while everyone thought he must be discussing the near-riot going on around him, the Judge was doing nothing of the sort. Later Landis' confidant revealed what the tête-à-tête was actually about. "Well," he recounted, "I'll tell you. The Judge was quite proud. He told me for years he had been trying to spit tobacco juice the way Pepper Martin lets it squirt from his lips and teeth, and had just acquired the knack."[27]

Having finished his dialogue Landis returned to his seat and beckoned Medwick and Owen, the game's four umpires, and Frankie Frisch and Mickey Cochrane. Owen walked very, very slowly down the third-base line to Landis' box and gamely flashing a smile at the Judge. Landis was unresponsive—"like a piece of concrete" as Owen put it.

"Is there any reason at all why this man Medwick should have taken a kick at you?" Landis wanted to know from Owen.

"No, sir," came the response.

Accounts vary wildly on what happened next. Landis may then have just nodded and turned to Medwick to order him out. Or he may have asked the Cardinal outfielder, "Did you kick Owen?" At that point Medwick either answered "Yes" or denied it, saying "No, I was just trying to protect myself, but if I did I didn't mean to, Judge. I ain't mad at him."

In any case Landis gave the order: "Mr. Medwick, you're out of the game—to prevent bodily harm from the fans."

The unprecedented decision stunned Cards manager Frankie Frisch. If Detroit fans rioted, why should *his* team be penalized? If any penalty was to be exacted it should be in the form of a forfeit—in St. Louis' favor.

Turning to Frisch, the Squire ordered: "Take him out and resume play."

"Why should I take him out?" Frisch screamed as he lunged at Landis. Bill Klem grabbed Frisch by the shoulders and pulled him back.

"Because I say so," Landis shot back, knowing that a forfeit would mean a full-scale riot. "We want to go on with this game, and it wouldn't look so good if a World Series game had to be forfeited. So get it over with."

The answer hardly mollified Frisch. "That old son of a bitch. I'm going to take him," he fumed to umpire Beans Reardon. Reardon told him to let it ride; with a 9-0 lead it wasn't worth it.

"Before the Series," Landis explained after the game, "the umpires are instructed not to put any player off the field unless the provocation is very extreme. I saw as well as everyone what Medwick did, but when Umpire Klem took no action and the players quieted down I hoped the matter was ended. But when it became apparent that the demonstration of the crowd would never terminate I decided to take action." In other words, in Landis' mind he had not really given in to mob rule, he had merely done what the umpires should have done but feared doing to avoid displeasing him. His explanation, however, did not rationally deal with why he not acted until *after* the mob had showered Medwick with garbage.

Not everyone bought Landis' explanation. Not everyone thought he had made the right decision. Even the Judge admitted he probably wouldn't have bounced Medwick if the game had been closer. Yet he had his admirers. "Landis did the sane and reasonable thing," argued Paul Gallico. "Flames were creeping toward a powder mine. He extinguished that flame..."[28]

"I sincerely believe Judge Landis saved the day," praised American League umpire George Moriarty. "It is a crowning achievement because it has set a precedent and it makes Judge Landis loom across the baseball horizon as a keen, forceful and fearless head of the game."

Landis put it simpler that evening: "We had a ball game to continue."[29]

Another incident—less famous, of course, than the Medwick affair—also marred the 1934 Series. In one game Detroit outfielder Goose Goslin was trotting back to his position in left field when he sneered to Bill Klem (with whom Goslin had been feuding during the Series), "Klem, you are an old bastard."

Few had ever dared take such liberties with Klem. However, Catfish knew Landis would not allow him to toss Goslin, so he kept his rage within himself. But that night he came upon Goslin in the lobby of Detroit's Book-Cadillac Hotel. Goslin stuck out his hand and cheerily said, "Hello, Bill."

Klem unhinged. He shouted whatever names he could think of at Goslin. The press reported the incident, and Landis called both in for an explanation. Each gave their side, and Landis reserved his decision.

When the Series ended, the Squire requested both men to appear once more. Klem decided returning home for a scheduled hunting trip was more important and left Detroit without meeting Landis.

Landis responded by deducting $50 from Klem's World Series' paycheck.

"The Judge was a ham," Klem fumed, "and when you were summoned to be an audience for him he didn't like to be ignored. That's why I was fined for ignoring him—not for what I said to Goslin. I was fined for *lèse maiesté*; that's what it was: the old Arbitrator was fined for *lèse maiesté*."

But the fine was the least of Klem's problems. The going rate for *lese majesté* in Landis' court was considerably more than $50. He made the imperious Klem wait until 1940 before he worked another World Series.

In 1935 the brand-new Mutual Network wanted to broadcast the Series, but as it consisted of just three stations, Landis said no. *Unless*, that is, it could cajole NBC-affiliate WLW in Cincinnati to switch to it. WLW would switch but only if its crack announcer Red Barber could broadcast the Series. Mutual had no problem with that. Barber began his World Series career in the company of Quin Ryan and Bob Elson.

Landis was also throwing his weight around at CBS. At CBS Landis barred Ted Husing entirely. During the 1934 Series, Husing had blasted the umpiring as "some of the worst I've ever seen." Landis wouldn't take that kind of editorializing.[30]

It may have been of Husing that Landis once spoke: "For five years I tried to teach this fellow the difference between a home run and a bunt. When he couldn't learn that simple difference in five years, I went to his sponsors and told them he could not be used in broadcasting either a World Series or an All-Star game."[31]

Before the 1935 Series Landis gathered that year's broadcasting team together and provided them with instructions on how to call a baseball game:

Gentlemen, I congratulate you. You are the best in your business, or you wouldn't be here in this room at this time. . . . You are the very best in your business. I am very aware of who you are.

But, gentlemen, this afternoon on the playing field there will be two ballclubs that for this year are the best in their business. They know how to play baseball and they know it very well. They have demonstrated their abilities over the full season.

Gentlemen, in the dugouts this afternoon will be two managers, who for this year are the best in their business. . . . they are the two winning managers, and they know how to manage.

And, gentleman, there will be four men in blue suits on the field this afternoon . . . the umpires . . . and for this year, and for this Series, they are the best in their business.

Gentlemen, I wouldn't presume to tell you how to conduct your business. But I will tell you to let the ballplayers play—they don't need your help. Let the managers manage. And above everything else, you let the umpires umpire.

When you arrive in your radio boxes today, I want you to know that the full power of the Commissioner's Office will see to it—that you will not be disturbed in your prerogatives. I promise you that not a single ballplayer will interfere with you at your microphone . . . not a manager will try to tell you anything . . . and, certainly, not one of those umpires will come up there and tell you how to broadcast.

Gentlemen, you report. Report everything you can see. Report what the ballplayers do, but don't feel sorry for them or rejoice for them. Report what they do. That's all the listeners want to hear—what the ballplayers do.

Report what the managers do. Report each move each manager makes, but just report it. He knows more about what he is doing than you can know . . . and what he does—or why he does it—is none of your business.

Report what the umpire does. Report what he calls the pitch—not what you think he should have called. In fact, you are in the stands . . . he is right behind the plate. You can't see what it is, and it isn't your business to think you can see what it is. It is his business to see what it is and to call it what it is . . . and he, gentlemen, will call it what it is. You report what he calls it.

By report, I mean you have the right to say what is going on, no matter what is going on, or where it is going on. But don't voice your opinions. Don't editorialize. Report . . .

That is what I mean by reporting. Suppose a ballplayer goes to the dugout and fills his mouth with water. Suppose he also has a chew of tobacco in his mouth. And he walks over to where I'm sitting in a rail box, he leans in to me, and he spits right in my face.

Report each step the player makes. Report how much spit hits me in the face. If you can see it, report how much tobacco gets on my face. Report my reaction, if any. Report what happens thereafter. Report but don't feel disturbed about the Commissioner. That will be my affair after I have been spit upon. Your job is simply to report the event.

And, gentlemen, one more thing. . . . There are a lot of motion-picture actors who show up at the World Series every year, taking bows and getting their pictures taken. They haven't been around all year, but now they're here. Gentlemen, I don't want any of those Hollywood characters named on the radio. The World Series is for baseball people.

Gentlemen, good day.[32]

There is no doubt they followed his instructions to the letter.

That 1935 World Series saw yet another round of vicious bench-jockeying. The unpleasantness began in the first game when the Cubs went after Detroit slugger Hank Greenberg with a tirade of anti-Semitic name-calling. It was "Jew this and Jew that," Greenberg later recalled.

"I'll be the last to deny that the great Hank Greenberg was our main target," admitted Charlie Grimm. "Do you heckle a substitute or a star?"[33]

In the Series' third game the vitriol continued, and umpire George Moriarty ejected three Cubs: Grimm, shortstop Woody English, and outfielder George "Tuck" Stainback. In the course of his ejection Moriarty gave as good as he got.

Landis called a meeting before he issued penalties—on both sides. At the appointed time, however, Moriarty was not present. "Did you notify Mr. Moriarty that this meeting was called for nine o'clock?" Landis grumbled to Leslie O'Connor.

"Yes, sir."

Landis and the Cubs waited another 10 minutes for Moriarty to arrive. "Mr. Moriarty," Landis wanted to know, "what time was this meeting called for?"

"Nine o'clock, Judge, but I had trouble in the coffee shop at the hotel. I'm sorry."

Then Landis wanted each Cub to recount what happened. "What did you call Moriarty?" Landis asked Billy Herman.

"I don't want to say," he muttered back.

"Go ahead. This room has been filled with blue smoke before."[34]

Years later Landis, noted for his own profane language, would confide, "In my time in this world I have always prided myself on a command of lurid expressions. I must confess that I learned from these young men some variations of the language even I didn't know existed."[35]

Landis had no problem in fining Moriarty $500 and English, Herman, and Billy Jurges $400 each "for vile, unprintable language," the largest fines yet levied during a World Series.

Actually Landis needed no hearings to fine the Cubs or Moriarty. Both he and National League president Ford Frick had easily heard the combatants go at it. "Moriarty had no complaints," said Grimm.[36]

After the Series, Greenberg, however, complained to reporters about Moriarty's fine. An incensed Landis wrote Greenberg on October 30, 1935: ". . . you are requested to forward to me, in affidavit form, your testimony respecting the subject matter, and specifically, the language used between players Herman, Jurges and English and umpire Moriarty. That language was the occasion of the fines. . . ."

Greenberg backed down. "I wish to state," he wrote Landis, "that I did not overhear any part of the argument between Moriarty and players. Therefore I could not be more explicit . . ."

Landis nonetheless summoned Greenberg to Chicago. "Landis got on me like a district attorney," he wrote in his autobiography. "I said I didn't hear anything, but I just assumed. He told me not to assume anything. If I had anything to say, back it up, or keep my mouth shut. But that's the way he ran baseball, with an iron fist, and that's the reason baseball prospered at the time."[37]

The Judge created one last innovation in the 1938 Cubs-Yankees World Series. In Game Three umpire Charley Moran suffered a broken nose and some loosened teeth when he was hit by an errant throw from the otherwise steady Joe Gordon. Had Moran not decided to tough it out and stay in the contest, Landis would have continued the game and the Series with three umpires. He didn't have to resort to that contingency, but the incident left him thinking, and in the off-season, he deigned that henceforth six arbiters would work every Fall Classic.[38]

Yet while Landis had no compunction about dictating to owners or umpires or broadcasters during the Fall Classic, he drew the line at interfering with official scorers. Once, one scorer asked him if he had any special instructions. "No," the Judge responded, "just go ahead and score the game in your usual damned incompetent fashion."[39]

CHAPTER 22

# "BIG AS A HOUSE, ISN'T IT?"

In the early 1920s Branch Rickey began the modern farm system and Landis began trying to tear it down.

The Judge's very first decision as commissioner, the February 1921 Phil Todt case, saw him ruling that Rickey and the Browns had "covered up" the slick-fielding first baseman. In 1928 Landis hit Rickey again, this time stripping his new team, the Cardinals, of a future Hall-of-Famer, outfielder Chuck Klein. That year the young Klein had torn up the Class B Central League, batting .331 (with 26 homers in just 88 contests). However, Klein's club, the Fort Wayne Chiefs, was not the only Cardinal farm in that circuit. In violation of baseball law, St. Louis also owned the rival Dayton Aviators outright. Landis ordered Rickey to sell off the Cards' Fort Wayne holdings.[1]

By the late 1920s the Cardinals' farm system remained relatively small, but the popularity of the idea was spreading, and Landis was not the only person worrying about its growth. In December 1927, the American Association—in the wake of Cincinnati's acquisition of its Columbus franchise—adopted a rule prohibiting the sale of any of its clubs to a big league team. The following year National Association president Mike Sexton wondered aloud about how long it would take before the major leagues would control enough minor league teams to influence National Association policy.[2]

A week later Landis must have been pondering the same thing. The agreement which created his commissionership was, after all, based upon the existence of the minors as a separate, independent entity. The Squire had no intention of seeing that autonomous force being gobbled up by big league interests. At the close of a very tepid joint major league session, Landis startled owners by demanding each reveal their minor league interests. They may have been startled but were not cowed. Shortly after the meeting the Giants acquired Bridgeport in the Eastern League.[3]

In March 1929 Landis went from asking questions to taking action, freeing 10 major and minor league players from Pirate, Senator, Tiger, and Athletic clutches, including Washington's Guy Cantrell and Mel Simons; the A's' Ernest Wingard; and the Browns' Bubber Jonnard. All of these illegally signed players were now free to sign with any club they wished. The aforementioned players were spare parts at best, but Landis also emancipated Tigers' catching prospect Rick Ferrell, a .300 hitter with Columbus. The Browns' Phil Ball signed the future Hall-of-Famer backstop for a $12,500 salary plus a $25,000 signing bonus.[4]

By December 1929 at the National Association meetings at Chattanooga, Landis had launched a public attack on the farm system, sparing neither major nor minor leaguers in his denunciation.[5]

The following year's session, held at Montreal's Mount Royal Hotel, Branch Rickey lashed back. With the Judge just a few feet away, he launched into an aggressive defense of his practices and a not-very-veiled attack on Landis himself:

> The farm system is not an ideal system, and nobody is talking about whether it is ideal or not. When people are hungry, they eat food which may or may not be ideally cooked and served. No questions asked because it is not an issuable point. The point is, do we have food and can we live on it? Is there sustenance in it? Yes. Then eat it and don't complain too much about where it came from, who cooked it, how it is served.
>
> It is all right to have a physician who will feel your pulse and look at you and say 'You are a sick man, I think you are going to die.' He offers you no medicine, none at all. He gives you no change of climate. He says you are just sick, he's awfully sorry. Then along comes somebody else who says you've got epizootic and he can cure epizootic and he doesn't have to cut out the epi. He doesn't have to take out an eye. He can make you live. Here's pill number one and here's pill number two and when you get through with one you can take number two.
>
> I claim that such a doctor in a hopeless case should be acceptable both to the patient and to the helpless doctor who has had the case. In no way should it be said, in my judgment, that anyone should say to the new physician who is offering assurance of a cure, if, in a rational hope a thousand held interest, 'You can't give him those pills! You can't give him anything!'

... Golf, motoring, economic conditions and bad management have played havoc with our minor league operations. Our farm clubs have been hurt, of course, but we have not suffered at all in comparison with those who are unable to continue, and those champions of local interest who may fail in midseason. I deplore the philosophy of indifference to what is going on. For without the minor leagues, baseball can get nowhere. When the majors get to the point where they think they do have to consider the status of the minors, then a great danger exists to the structure of baseball.

Baseball is bigger than any one club. I owe much to this game. It is bigger than I am. It is bigger than any one man.[6]

Rickey's blunt words no doubt outraged Landis. If he had any fondness left for the Mahatma it vanished in December 1930.

But even prior to Rickey's salvo, Landis had been caught in a more direct challenge to his authority. It also came from St. Louis, from Browns owner Phil Ball.

The fracas originated in early April 1930 when Ball attempted to send outfielder Fred Bennett to the Milwaukee Brewers of the American Association, a club under his financial control. This made the third season Bennett would be with a minor league club owned by St. Louis, the previous two being spent at Tulsa (Western League) and Wichita Falls (Texas League). Such conduct was illegal under current rules prohibiting long-term farming of individuals.

Beginning on April 9, 1930, Ball and Landis launched into a heated flurry of correspondence regarding Bennett. On that date the Judge wrote Ball inquiring when he assumed ownership of the Wichita Falls ballclub. Four days later Ball responded, wanting to know what authorized Landis to inquire about his or anyone's personal finances.

On April 16 a quite restrained Landis returned Ball's missive, explaining he had no personal interest in what Ball owned or didn't own, but as the matter related to baseball it was certainly within his jurisdiction. Two days later, Ball wrote back, repeated his earlier question regarding Landis' authority, to which Landis responded by quoting the rules in question.

On April 23 Ball concluded by writing that "since you are so technical I will refer the matter to my counsel." He then proceeded to send Bennett to Milwaukee. When the Squire moved to block the transfer, Ball checkmated him, having the Brewers obtain an injunction against his action. Landis then retreated, letting Bennett play all year in Milwaukee.

At season's end Ball attempted to send Bennett back to Milwaukee. This time Ball would have to expose Bennett to waivers and any club willing to spend $7,500 could own the outfielder. When both the Pirates and the Yankees claimed the outfielder, Ball withdrew waivers and sent Bennett once more to Milwaukee. Now it was Bennett's turn to act. Tired of being buried in the Browns' system, he petitioned Landis for free agency.

The Judge granted it, and the Browns sued "to restrain the Commissioner of Baseball from interfering with the relation between Bennett and the plaintiffs or either of them, or with Bennett's contract with the St. Louis club and any assignments thereof previously or subsequently made."[7]

"As long as Mr. Landis is commissioner of Organized Baseball, those clubs belonging to the organization known as the National Association of Professional Baseball Leagues must abide by his edicts, right or wrong," George W. Miller, now Landis' attorney, informed the court. "The commissioner doesn't have to wait for any complaints. If he suspects anything detrimental to the best interests of baseball, it is not only his right, but also his duty to investigate and take whatever remedial or punitive action he deems necessary."[8]

In April 1931 Judge Walter C. Lindley ruled in favor of Landis:

> The various agreements and rules . . . of Organized Baseball . . . describe a clear intent . . . to endow the Commissioner with all the attributes of a benevolent but absolute despot and all the disciplinary powers of the proverbial pater familias.
>
> The commissioner rightfully found that the common control of St. Louis and the named Minor Clubs by one person made it possible to create a situation whereby the clear intent of the adopted code that the players under the control of a Major club shall not be kept with a Minor club more than two successive seasons without giving other Major clubs the right to claim him was clearly violated, and a result achieved highly detrimental to the national game of baseball.
>
> No agreement is to be made between a Major club and a Minor club for the purpose or with the effect of covering up a player from selection.

The decision, however, was hardly a clear-cut Landis victory.

Lindley, although voiding what he called "secret absolute control" of players, also upheld the Squire's *bête noir*, the farm system.[9]

Ball, however, in June 1931 appealed Lindley's decision. A furious Landis summoned American League owners (including Ball) to his office. He reminded them that they had signed an agreement to refrain from public criticism of his actions. Even with Ban Johnson gone, Ball was not living up to it. What were Ball's fellow magnates going to do about it, the Squire demanded.

Ball remained unswayed. On the way out of the building, he turned to Cleveland's Alva Bradley and asked, "Did you ever see a more stubborn man than Landis?"

"Yes, I have," Bradley, a friend of Landis, answered as he glared straight at Ball.

"You don't mean me do you?" asked a surprised Ball.

"I don't mean anyone else," Bradley shot back. Ball paused and responded, "Well, if I am more stubborn than Landis, I must be the most stubborn man in the United States. If that is so, I'd better call my lawyers and tell them to drop the appeal."

Yet, once free from Bradley's icy stare, Ball made *no* move to withdraw his appeal. Only on December 28, 1931, when Clark Griffith and Red Sox president Bob Quinn, a former Ball employee, pointed out that if Ball did not back down, Landis would resign and place baseball in a very embarrassing situation, did Ball kill his appeal, pointedly remarking he had acted only at his fellow owners' request.[10]

Even with the Depression deepening and with entire minor leagues folding, Landis refused to acknowledge pleas that the minors needed big league support to survive. He once told the Associated Press' Paul Mickelson: "Yes, yes, I know the minor leagues, especially those of lower classification, are having their financial worries. But what can I or the major leagues do? It would take an act of Congress and the United States treasury to pull them out. Baseball is suffering just like all other business. It just seems that it can't be helped. They'll get along all right in time. Five B and C leagues already have suspended, while a lot of others, A leagues included, are caught in the general depression and a lot of business houses are in a whole lot worse shape than some of the weakest and sickest minor leagues."

"What about the big surplus the major leagues have stored up for a rainy day," Mickelson asked Landis. "It has been suggested that the majors turn over some of that money over to the minors to tide them over the bumps?"

"Surplus? Surplus?" Landis responded. "Now, I know you're talking foolish. Sometimes I don't know who's in the craziest profession
. . . you or I. Goodbye."[11]

Landis was testy because his battle was already lost. In December 1932 the majors adopted a new rule on options that effectively
voided his actions in the Bennett case. Instead of only being able to
option a player before he earned his freedom, their new rules still
permitted only three options, but on the fourth the player could now
be released outright to a big league club's farms. Landis bitterly
opposed the new rule and argued it could not take effect until the
National Association's Executive Committee ratified it. But the minors were no longer composed of independent operators. They were
now largely vassals of major league owners. In February 1933 the
National Association approved the new rule.[12]

As the Depression worsened, more and more minor leagues
folded. By 1932 the National Association was down to just 19 circuits
and forlornly announced it would make no efforts to recruit new
leagues, but would concentrate on propping up what survivors remained. Even that strategy didn't work. Four leagues disbanded in
mid-season. Only fourteen started the 1933 season.[13]

But that was the low point. Thanks in equal parts to improving
economic conditions; badly needed structural reforms; the election of
William Bramham as National Association president; the introduction of night baseball; and the Shaughnessy playoff plan (which created post-season play for the top four teams in each league); and, of
course, the farm system, the minors rebounded. Twenty leagues
began the 1934 season, and the number would steadily grow, reaching 44 by 1940.

Landis, however, continued fighting his rear-guard action
against major league control of the minors—freeing minor leaguers
on a case-by-case basis, either individually or by the carload. In 1936
Landis would deal with his most famous minor league case, that of
Indians phenom Bob Feller.

The Indians' Cy Slapnicka, the new assistant to Cleveland president Alva Bradley, had signed Feller off the Iowa sandlots. Slapnicka
confidently informed club directors that Feller "will be the greatest
pitcher the world has ever known."[14]

Technically, Fargo-Moorhead of the Class D Northern League
had signed the 17-year-old Feller, but this was a charade. Feller was
Cleveland's property, and Slapnicka had no intention of letting any-

one else near him. Instead of sending the pitcher to Fargo-Moorhead, Slapnicka, on the pretext of Feller having a sore arm, brought him directly to Cleveland.

As Feller's arm "healed" Slapnicka arranged for him to pitch for the city's best semi-pro club, the Rosenblums, against Akron. But on July 6 Slapnicka had a bigger assignment for him—for Cleveland in an exhibition against the St. Louis Cardinals.

Feller fanned eight of the nine Cardinals he faced. After the game a photographer asked Dizzy Dean to pose with the youngster. "Why ask?" Dean rejoined. "You'd better ask *him* if he'll pose with me."[15]

Feller then returned to the Rosenblums for another game and struck out 15. Slapnicka arranged for Fargo-Moorhead to "transfer" his contract to New Orleans, which accommodatingly "transferred" it to Cleveland. Bob Feller was now an Indian.

He made his first American League start on August 24, 1936, in one of the most spectacular debuts in big league history, striking out 15 St. Louis Browns, one short of Rube Waddell's modern AL record and two shy of Dizzy Dean's major league mark. Three weeks later he struck out 17 A's and tied Dean's effort.

The Indians had clearly "covered up" Feller, in violation of the Major-Minor League Agreement prohibiting a major league club from directly signing a player off the sandlots. Yet Landis did nothing, and would do nothing until being forced into action by Des Moines (Western League) owner E. Lee Keyser, who filed a formal complaint against the Tribe. Even Feller would later admit Keyser's charge was "substantially true" but contended that "covering up" was common practice and that only his sore arm prevented him from playing for Fargo-Moorhead as planned. On September 23, 1936, the *Cleveland News* revealed Landis was investigating Keyser's complaint.[16]

Yet unlike Fred Bennett, Feller did not *want* to be freed. On the last day of the 1936 season Feller walked into Slapnicka's office, wanting to know, "If I am declared a free agent, can I sign again with Cleveland? That's what I will want to do."

Slapnicka informed him that normally emancipated players could not sign with their previous teams.

"That will be too bad," the teenager tersely responded.[17]

Shortly thereafter, Feller and his father, W. H. "Bill" Feller, met with Landis in his Chicago headquarters. Over the years, Feller's recollections of the experience have varied.

"As my father and I walked into his office . . . ," he wrote in 1947, in his first autobiography, *Strikeout Story*, "I felt exactly as I did when I was a kid and had been called into the office of my school principal.

". . . I now know that [Landis] was a just and kindly man who always was interested in the protection of ball players. That day he seemed a menacing figure."[18]

Four decades later, in his second autobiography *Now Pitching: Bob Feller*, the young Feller appeared a little more composed. "He [Landis] was an impressive sight to a kid, but not an intimidating one to me," Rapid Robert now contended. "He asked what I thought were reasonable questions, and I gave him straight-from-the-shoulders answers."[19]

In any case Landis was on his best behavior. "He was very pleasant, very sociable, very nice and polite," Feller related in a 1995 interview. "He wasn't bullying. He wasn't a bully. Some say may have said he was a big bully. It didn't appear that way to me. Not to me he wasn't or my father either."[20]

After an initial exchange of pleasantries, the Judge got to the point. "There seem to be a number of discrepancies in this case," he informed the Fellers, obviously referring to whether or not Robert had a sore arm. "I intend to get to the bottom of it. . . I intend to get the complete truth."[21]

At one point Landis indicated he might issue a ruling separating the youngster from the Indians—actually the *only* ruling he could make *if* his decision was based on baseball law. On hearing this, Feller blurted out: "I don't want to play anyplace else. I want to play for Cleveland."[22]

Bill Feller backed up his son with a threat the Judge could respect. "The Cleveland club has treated us fair," he commented. "It's our intention for him to play for Cleveland, if they want him, and they want him. And if you don't permit that, then we're going to sue you in civil court, because we have a civil law contract and we want to test it to see if baseball law supersedes civil law."[23]

Landis had something else to worry about. If he freed Feller, it would ignite an unprecedented bidding war. The Yankees and Red Sox reportedly would pay $100,000 to sign Feller. "My father didn't want it," Feller later wrote, "and this sacrifice of so much money for his loyalty to the bargain he had made is another factor in the case which should not be overlooked."[24]

While Landis pondered the Feller case,[25] he acted to free two Cincinnati farmhands, speedy outfielder Lee "Jeep" Handley and catcher Johnny Peacock, a former University of North Carolina quarterback. Handley signed with Pittsburgh for $20,000; Peacock with the Red Sox for a reported $15,000.[26]

The Indians professed to be unconcerned at the ruling. "As I understand the Cincinnati case," Alva Bradley commented, "the Cincinnati club was accused of hindering the progress of the two players through the minors and into the National League. We certainly can't be similarly accused in Feller's case. Our rights to his services probably never would have been challenged if we had kept him in the minors instead of rushing him straight to the big leagues."[27]

It was expected that Landis would finally issue his decision at the annual National Association meeting, commencing in Montreal the first week of December. While major and minor league clubs assembled, however, Landis remained in Chicago. There he met with Slapnicka, ostensibly in town to shepherd Feller to a 4-H club meeting. Neither would publicly comment on their session.[28]

Landis, however, had laid the groundwork for a decision favoring Cleveland. On Friday, December 4, 1936, the gathering in Montreal passed legislation nullifying the rule the Indians had violated in signing Feller—and others had violated in obtaining many, many other prospects. "They had to change the rule," Feller would observe decades later, "because everybody was cheating. It was no secret, no secret at all."[29]

That same day—Friday, December 4, 1936—Landis lost the first major vote of his tenure when the minors rejected his proposal that all information on sandlot players be filed with himself and the league presidents. At first the minors voted with Landis, then after pressure from the majors, they reversed themselves and repealed what they had just enacted.

"When you come right down to it," observed syndicated columnist Joe Williams, "the judge, though he is called the czar of baseball, is no more than a hired hand who owes his office to the club owners and draws his salary from them. In the final analysis then, he does not boss them; they boss him. At least they have the power to do so.

"His alternative is to resign."

Rumors circulated that Landis *was* about to resign his commissionership. Other reports circulated that if he ruled against Cleveland, he would be fired. Most observers, however, discounted such whispers. In fact, despite Joe Williams' theories, most owners remained terrified of the old man. "I'd as soon slap the judge in the face as ask him when he'll announce the Feller decision," confided one magnate.[30]

That same day the minor league meetings concluded. Regarding the Feller case, Landis maintained his usual discretion, telling reporters the next day, "You'll get ample notice of any decision."[31]

The major league meetings opened on Tuesday, December 8, at New York's Roosevelt Hotel. There, Landis and the 16 big league owners conferred over such mundane issues as the liveliness of the ball and assistance for down-on-their-luck former players. Reporters gave up hope that Landis would issue a decision regarding Feller. Suddenly on Thursday, December 10, Leslie O'Connor ordered all reporters in the building to gather in the press room. "Gentleman, I have the decision in the Feller case," he said as he handed out mimeographed copies of it. Landis had promised that no one would be scooped, and he kept his word.

"A handout," grumbled one reporter. "The judge ain't even here."

"This is the decision in the Feller case," O'Connor responded, "but if you want to know in a hurry what happened, the judge awarded the pitcher to Cleveland and Cleveland pays Des Moines $7,500 damages." Scribes writing for evening papers rushed to their phones. Those on morning ones calmly headed for the bar.[32]

Landis had already read his decision to ownership. As he rumbled through it, Jake Ruppert turned to Alva Bradley and smugly whispered, "You've lost that ball player." But Ruppert had spoken too soon.[33]

"The case has been thoroughly investigated," Landis' official report noted:

> It turns out, in reality, Fargo-Moorhead had nothing whatsoever to do with the signing of Feller, which was done by the Cleveland club, its agent, Cyril Slapnicka, using for that purpose a minor league contract because he could not sign him to a Cleveland contract.
>
> This legislation must be regarded as construing the covenant of the majors not to sign sandlotters as fulfilled if the player first signs a minor league contract notwithstanding he was in fact signed by or for a major league club.
>
> When Cleveland officially acquired Feller on July 13, 1936, he had previously contracted with a minor club (Fargo-Moorhead).

Consequently, the commissioner is precluded from entering an order invalidating the Cleveland-Feller contract.

Further, so far as Des Moines, the complaining club, is concerned invalidation of the Cleveland Feller contract would be futile, as its only result would be to re-create precisely the same situation through Feller's signing a new contract in the name of some other minor league club acting for some other major club.

Under this rule, had Cleveland taken the precaution to become the owner of the Fargo-Moorhead club, and to have Slapnicka designated as vice president of the Fargo-Moorhead club, but had signed Feller, there would never have been a Feller case, because the minors adopted the foregoing rule with full knowledge that it enabled major league clubs to sign sandlot players if they merely had them signed to contracts of their own minor clubs by persons designated as officials of such clubs.

The natural, inevitable consequence was that other major league clubs assumed that, to compete with their farm system associates, it was necessary that they likewise secure sandlotters by signing them in the name of or by minor clubs with which they were "working" or friendly.

This was done by a process which is euphemistically termed "recommendation"—a major league club, through its officials and scouts, recommending to a friendly minor club that the sandlotter be signed, and subsequently "recommending" that he be transferred to the major club or to some other club it designates.

This was the procedure followed in the Feller Case, wherein Cleveland "recommended" that Fargo-Moorhead contract Feller, "recommended" that New Orleans offer and Fargo-Moorhead accept $200 for the contract, "recommended" that Feller "retire," "recommended" that he go to Cleveland where he was given employment by Cleveland in its concession department and "recommended" for semi-pro ball in that vicinity, "recommended" that he be gotten off the retired list (after Cleveland used him—ostensibly a New Orleans player "retired" from baseball—in the exhibition game with the Cardinals), and finally "recommended" that New Orleans transfer him to Cleveland for $1,500, the $200 New Orleans-Fargo-Moorhead and the $1,500 Cleveland-New Orleans transfer considerations being mere functions of the player's contract.

However, the minor leagues on December 4, 1936 legislated that no major-minor rules shall be construed as prohibiting "recommendation" of players and acquisition of such players by the "recommending" club.

This legislation must be regarded as construing the covenant of the majors not to sign sandlotters as fulfilled if the player first signs a minor contract. That construction of the covenant by beneficiary, binds the commissioner. Consequently the commissioner is precluded from entering an order invalidating the Cleveland-Feller contract.[34]

In Iowa, Rapid Robert applauded the decision,[35] and suddenly displayed increased interest in pecuniary matters. The now 18-year old high school student told reporters that "judging from salaries paid other pitchers in the big leagues, I believe I ought to be worth $20,000 to Cleveland next year." On hearing this Cy Slapnicka suddenly realized that Feller wasn't quite as valuable as he had been cracked up to be. Feller, Slapnicka contended, was "way out of line" but he anticipated no trouble once Rapid Robert "soberly reflect[ed] on the value of an 18-year-old to a major league club." Feller ended up signing for $10,000—in a ceremony broadcast live on Cleveland radio.[36]

In Des Moines, Lee Keyser, publicly placed the best face possible on the decision and professed to be satisfied with the token $7,500 settlement he received. "It was a fair and wise decision," Keyser contended. "I've always felt Cleveland violated the major-minor rule against signing sandlot players when they obtained Feller's contract."[37]

Not surprisingly Landis' decision was greeted wildly in Cleveland. Manager Steve O'Neill said he was "tickled to death." The News' Ed McCauley defended the Judge against charges that he was afraid or had been pressured. McCauley theorized Landis had based his ruling on "two homely but irrefutable tenets of common sense. First, there is such a thing as abstract justice, transcending the letter of every law. Secondly, a penal law that is generally violated is not a good law—as witnessed by the late prohibition amendment."[38]

Or as fellow News columnist Tommy Tucker penned:

So ends the case of Feller.
All's well that ends weller.[39]

And in New York, even Joe Williams, while admitting that technically speaking the Judge's decision was "farcical," found it "excellent" in voiding the effects of a rule that "border[ed] on the ridiculous."[40]

Other cases involving Cleveland's control of promising minor leaguers followed. The first came in the spring of 1937. The player in question was outfielder Tommy Henrich, who in 1934 had been signed by Tribe scout Bill Bradley and assigned to the Indians' farm club at Zanesville in the Middle Atlantic League. After a stop at Monessen in the Pennsylvania State Association, Henrich arrived at New Orleans. With the Pelicans in 1936, he hit .346, driving in 100 runs and scoring 117. At season's end his contract was transferred to Milwaukee, another club associated with Cleveland. He was clearly a hot prospect.

During the off-season he discovered articles about himself in the *Cleveland Plain Dealer*. One article informed readers that Milwaukee would sell Henrich to the Red Sox, but another contended Cleveland was going to trade him and former All-Star outfielder Joe Vosmik to the Browns. The stories raised a disquieting question: who *really* owned him? Milwaukee? Or Cleveland?

"The way I figured it," he later recalled, "was that if you find there's something wrong with the transactions involving Cleveland, Milwaukee, and New Orleans, I wouldn't belong to any of them anyway, so the contract with Milwaukee wouldn't be binding."[41]

One night Henrich informed his father, "Dad, I'm thinking about writing to Judge Landis." His father wanted to know why. Henrich explained the situation, adding "There's only one guy I trust on this—Judge Landis. . . . if there's anyone at all on the side of the players, it's Landis. It's certainly not the owners."[42]

Henrich Sr., who favorably recalled Landis' decisions in a case involving Chicago plasterers, admired the Judge and gave his assent.

Henrich's first experience was unpleasant. Leslie O'Connor wrote back, tersely explaining that the Judge was vacationing in Florida and that "Our records show you are the property of the Milwaukee Brewers."

Henrich wrote again, demanding that his original complaint be forwarded to Landis. "Well, I got a telegram back from him," recalled Henrich, "about fourteen lines deep, the biggest telegram I ever saw in my life. I wish I could remember his exact words, but it went along like this: 'You say so-and-so, Prove it. You say so-and-so. Prove it. You say this and that. Can you prove it?' And on and on like that."[43]

While Henrich waited to appear before Landis, he received advice on how to handle his command performance. "Don't let Landis scare you with his blustering," he was told. "Don't be afraid to speak up."

"I've got nothing to speak up about," he responded. "I asked the judge a question and I'm just going to wait for an answer."[44]

The answer he got was highly pleasing. Landis' official ruling read:

> In re: player Tom Henrich:
>
> Investigation of the status of the player, instigated at his own request, discloses that he has been "covered up" for the benefit of the Cleveland club and that his transfer by New Orleans to Milwaukee was directed by the Cleveland club and prevented his advancement to a major league club under the selection clause. Because of the violation of the player's rights under his contract and the major-minor league rules, he is thereby declared a free agent.[45]

"The judge could have let it go," Henrich later observed, "but because he didn't like Slapnicka, and because I think he got a kick out of me writing to him and standing up for my rights, he declared me a free agent."[46]

As part of his decision, Landis barred the Indians from bidding for Henrich's services. Nine clubs joined the fray: the Yankees, Giants, Browns, Red Sox, Bees, Reds, Cubs, Tigers, and A's. The Giants offered $20,000, but when the Yankees went to $25,000, Henrich signed with them.[47]

On one of the Yankees' first trips to Comiskey Park, an usher walked up to Henrich, asking "Are you Henrich?"

"That's right," he responded.

"Well, the Commissioner wants to see you," he was informed.

Henrich wasn't sure this was good news; in fact, he was sure it was bad news, although he couldn't quite figure out what he had done wrong.

Trying to act as nonchalant as possible, he asked, "How are you, Mr. Commissioner?"

Landis just glared at him, then asked, "How are they treating you?"

"Just fine," Henrich responded.

"Well," grumbled Landis, "they'd better."[48]

If Landis had evened up with the Tribe by freeing Henrich,[49] he should have stopped right there. But he struck against Cleveland again the following spring. In March 1938 he ruled the Indians had "covered up" pitcher Charles Stanceu and outfielder-first baseman Myron McCormick at Buffalo. The supposed sale of the duo the previous September from Buffalo to Cleveland was a hoax, Landis ruled, and "the alleged payments by Cleveland to Buffalo were secretly refunded by Buffalo to Cleveland." He further decreed that neither Stanceu and McCormick could sign with either Cleveland, Buffalo, or any club affiliated with them for a full three years.[50]

Ironically, Cleveland owner Alva Bradley shared many of Landis' feelings on the farm system. When Browns owner Don Barnes defended farming in November of 1937, Bradley took issue with Barnes' statement, and that provided Landis with the chance to unburden himself to Bradley in a November 20, 1937 letter:

> What you say about the farm system and its effect on the sport is absolutely true. I have been opposing that thing since before you came into baseball and have been licked to a frazzle, as you know. A very real objection to the whole thing is the hypocrisy that characterizes the operation. The Major League gentlemen not only are raping the Minor League organization, but during the actual process, they talk about ethics and ideals and morals and how they are "saving" the Minors; whereas, the truth is, that down to this blessed minute, not one of them has let go of a thin dime to any Minor League interest without extorting from the victim a mortgage on his past, present and future baseball assets.[51]

While the Feller and Henrich case had provided Landis with a stage upon which to embarrass Cleveland's personnel machinations, he had never quite relaxed his gaze from his prime target—Branch Rickey's huge Cardinal system.

Aside from ideological differences with the St. Louis general manager, Landis' skin crawled at the very thought of the sanctimonious Rickey and his moralistic weeping on the one hand and his penurious chicanery on the other. "That hypocritical preacher," and "that Protestant bastard [who's] always masquerading with a minister's robe" were two of the Judge's kinder epithets for the Mahatma.[52]

His hostility stemmed in part from a sense of frustration. When Rickey began building his minor league empire, Landis (influenced by veteran owners Dreyfuss and Navin) believed his system would collapse of its own weight: that no major league club could support a chain of minor league affiliations. When Rickey proved Dreyfuss' theory wrong in spectacular fashion, it was too late for Landis to do much about it. But he never withdrew his hostility to the system Rickey had created.[53]

Landis had good reason to be suspicious of Rickey and Rickey's often unethical business practices. Aside from controlling more than one club in several minor leagues, Rickey often signed prospects to unfiled contracts in order to tie up huge quantities of talent. "By the late 1930s," historian Neil Sullivan has observed, "the farm system had failed any reasonable moral test."[54]

Rickeyism at its worst seemed revealed in the so-called Cedar Rapids case of 1938, in which Landis revealed the Cards were in fact running two separate farm systems, one above-board and legitimate; the other—under the aegis of the Class A Western League's Cedar Rapids Raiders—surreptitious and highly illegal. Because of St. Louis' Cedar Rapids connection, in four separate Class D leagues, the Nebraska State, the Arkansas-Missouri, the Northern, and the Northeast Arkansas, the Cardinals possessed multiple farm teams in each circuit.[55] To Landis this was a clear violation of the game's integrity.

He also discovered that Cedar Rapids had dealt with the Cards' Monett farmclub of the Arkansas-Missouri League, supposedly for itself but actually as a front for St. Louis. A similar "gentleman's agreement" for illicit player transaction existed between Cedar Rapids' Newport farm and St. Louis' PCL farmclub at Sacramento. The Rickey web was indeed a tangled one.

Additionally Landis found that back in 1932 in the Three-I League, the Cardinals, while owning the circuit's Danville franchise, had an agreement with the rival Springfield Cardinals to purchase any one of its players for $25,000.

In early 1938 the Judge called on Rickey to explain his Three-I League dealings. The preserved exchange between the two is a rare glimpse of the interaction between the two rivals:

*Landis*: You have this arrangement which obligates Springfield to take optional players only from the owner of the Danville club, its competitor. The same principle is involved as if the agreement provided that they look to you for all their players. It is only a difference of degree, because one recognized source of supply for minor league players is optioned players, and another source is players they get outright; those two kinds of players make up every club. Your ownership of Danville, in the same league, with that limitation they [Springfield] impose upon themselves that they will take optional players only from you, involves that principle.

*Rickey*: I cannot assume that there is any violation of any rule, that the whole underlying structure of good sportsmanship which must be preserved in professional baseball is infringed upon, when you take a club in one league and own it and then say to another club in the same league you shall not take optioned players. What can happen when it is done? Is there a hazard in the games? . . . Is there any overlapping of interest? . . .

*Landis*: Suppose Springfield and Danville are in first and second positions, making a fight, and that Springfield can get an optional player who will strengthen Springfield? Have you a right under this agreement to say to Springfield, "You shall not take that player"?

*Rickey*: I think we have.

*Landis*: Is that good?

*Rickey*: It is not good for Springfield.

*Landis*: Is it good for that league? Is it good for the whole institution?

*Rickey*: Many a club makes an agreement that is bad for itself. It is entirely a question of can a man make a deal for himself.

*Landis*: I am not dealing with the question of the selfish interest of Springfield in the deal. I am dealing with this question: Here is a pennant race in the Three-I League that is, as far as the principle is concerned, just as important as if it were a pennant race in the National or American leagues. They are fighting your club. You have the power to say to them: "The avenue of strength to your club we shut off." It is pretty plain that would be bad for the league, wouldn't it? Not merely the club that was thus deprived of strengthening itself by its own acts with its eyes open, but that would not be good for the league. Springfield has agreed with the owner and operator of Danville that Springfield will not strengthen its club from this source.

*Rickey*: I get your point. Danville and Springfield are contending for the pennant in the same league. All right. Suppose they have left as the only avenue that they can take optional players from St. Louis and then we withhold the benevolent hand and say, "You can't have any optional players from us, and other sources of supply are

stopped; therefore, that will leave you in second place and Danville
will win, because you cannot contend with us and we will not give
you any players?" Yes, that is in it; you are right.
*Landis*: That is in this [agreement with Springfield]; isn't it?
*Rickey*: Yes, that is in there.
*Landis*: Big as a house, isn't it?
*Rickey*: It is not big as a house.
*Landis*: I think it is as big as the universe. This is just as important
in the Three-I League as it would be in the National or American
leagues. You two fellows are in a fight for the pennant and Springfield says: "Here I have a chance of getting a player." You have the
power to say: "You can't do it."[56]

Landis' interrogation of Rickey had transpired in secret. Six
weeks later, in Belleaire, Florida at 10:30 AM on Wednesday, March
23, 1938, Leslie O'Connor handed reporters copies of Landis' nine-
page, 5,000-word decision, his longest yet. The Squire watched as
Leslie O'Connor distributed copies, but barked at reporters, "I can't
talk to you about it. It's all set forth in that statement."[57]

While Landis declined comment, O'Connor took pains to deny
any claims that the decision was aimed not at specific incidents but
rather at the farm system concept. "That is not the case," O'Connor
explained. "What this decision intends to do is to prevent one organization from operating or controlling two clubs in one league."[58]

Landis' ruling freed 74 Cardinal players, valued at $200,000 in-
cluding slick-fielding infielder Skeeter Webb (he had been with
Springfield in 1932 and Cedar Rapids in 1935-36) and a very young
outfielder named Pete Reiser. Players from the Mitchell, Fayetteville,
and Newport clubs could sign with any club they chose, including
their old clubs, but for a full three years could not sign or later be
transferred to Cedar Rapids or any club in the Cardinal chain. The
17 Monett players freed were barred from signing with that club.

As spectacular as Landis' action in the Cedar Rapids case was, it
was hardly significant at all. In terms of talent, while Landis
stripped the Cards' system of quantity, he hardly stripped it of quality. Of the 74 players emancipated, only Webb and Reiser were worth
mentioning. And to such a huge chain as St. Louis', 70-some low minor leaguers hardly mattered. After all, just two years later the
Cards would boast ownership of 32 farmclubs and working agreements with eight more, translating into 600 players under contract.[59]

Webb quickly signed with Cleveland, but the big fish that got away was Pete Reiser. Rickey had signed Reiser out of the St. Louis Municipal League when the outfielder was just 15 years old. He kept the boy carefully hidden away, not ever playing him, but having him travel and work out with various Class D and C clubs. Finally, in 1937 the 17-year-old "Pistol Pete" got to perform for New Iberia and Newport. At that point Landis discovered Reiser's situation and set him free. The Dodgers signed him for $100. "I didn't care about the money then," he later recalled. "I just wanted to play."

Reiser's signing was in fact yet another Rickey subterfuge. He had asked Brooklyn's Larry MacPhail to "hide" Reiser for him, but when Reiser accumulated 14 straight hits in spring training, the deal was off. Reiser remained a Dodger.[60]

Not every emancipated player thought kindly of Landis. Some baseball "slaves" longed for the security of the Rickey "plantation." Former Monett player-manager Joe Davis complained loudly. "Where does that put me?" he wailed. "I don't want to be a free agent. I had a job and I liked it. I've got to start all over again."[61]

Cedar Rapids' president Harry Johnson denied he had any sort of formal agreement, written or unwritten, with St. Louis. Rickey claimed he was guilty merely of friendship with Johnson. "I don't see how you can legislate against friendship...," the Mahatma argued. "I have many friendships in baseball; they have often proved valuable..."[62]

Rickey, of course, was hardly amused by Landis' costliest swipe at him to date. He was not stupid and had known it was coming. Rumor had it that he had been consulting with a prominent St. Louis attorney for weeks. As Rickey—at his own Florida cottage—read over the nine pages of the final decision, the waves of the Gulf of Mexico lapped just a few yards from him. They brought no peace. "Maybe my reply will be even longer than this decision," Rickey snapped to reporters. Having just barely waded through Landis' decision they groaned at the thought of the Mahatma's response.[63]

In the days following the Cedar Rapids decision, both sides left Florida. On Friday, March 25 Cards owner Sam Breadon cut short his spring training stay at Madeira Beach by 10 days for a two-day drive to St. Louis—as Rickey put in, "to look at a few records." The Squire departed for Chicago the next morning.[64]

In St. Louis Rickey urged Breadon to appeal Landis' ruling. Breadon had publicly praised Rickey as one who had helped the game more than "any man or officiated connected with [it]" *despite* "the constant opposition of the Commissioner's office." But Breadon smarted at the public humiliation Rickey's actions had caused him and refused to further battle Landis.[65]

"To whom would we appeal?" Breadon wondered aloud after his grueling 1,180-mile drive home. "Landis is the last word. He has the authority to do whatever he thinks is right for the good of the game."[66]

St. Louis sportswriter J. Roy Stockton was present at the tense meeting that followed between Breadon and Rickey. "Breadon was a proud man," Stockton later recalled, "a man of integrity. He was ashamed the Cardinals had been caught cheating.... He recalled that he had told Rickey the Cedar Rapids situation was wrong and urged that it be cleared up." The incident triggered an irreparable breach between Rickey and Breadon and eventually led to Rickey's departure from St. Louis.[67]

Another factor in Breadon's reticence may have been the sense, widespread throughout baseball, that Rickey and Breadon had gotten off easy. "So," one anonymous National League official theorized, "why should Branch stick his neck out any further? The judge is letting him off light. At least, he hasn't called him up for a hearing or demanded any promises or apologies from him or the Cardinals. The Cardinals cue now is to keep discreetly quiet and leave the judge alone because you can't beat him."[68]

Landis himself hinted at such sentiments in his decision: "Notwithstanding this investigation resulted in disclosure of misconduct meriting the imposition of severe penalties, none are imposed, for the reason that it is desired to take only the 'remedial and preventive action' inescapably required to terminate this situation... it is the commissioner's hope and belief that this will suffice, without 'punitive action' to forestall the possibility of these or any other baseball organizations hereafter entering into any arrangement for the control of more than one club in a league."[69]

Landis, however, later had second thoughts about letting Rickey off so gently. Years later Larry MacPhail revealed, "Judge Landis told me his one mistake as baseball commissioner was in not barring Rickey from the game as a result of that Cedar Rapids deal where he was covering up players. Landis told me he never encountered anything equal to this case for brazen contempt of baseball law."[70]

For his part Rickey's smoldering animus for Landis only increased—and Landis gave him more reason for hatred.

That May, the *Cleveland Plain Dealer*'s Gordon Cobbledick reported Rickey was rounding up opposition to a new Landis term when his present one expired in December 1941. He supposedly had support from the Reds, Dodgers, Pirates, and Browns. Landis, however, kept up the pressure on Rickey's often cut-rate tactics, prohibiting clubs from signing prospects and not filing their contracts, a Rickey trick designed to corral huge numbers of players for a minimal outlay of cash. At one time, it was said, Rickey had 150 of these so-called unpromulgated contracts stuffed away in his St. Louis office. Each other big league club supposedly had at least 50 apiece.[71]

Landis struck again in January 1940 but this time chose a new target, freeing five players on Detroit's major league roster: pitchers Dizzy Trout, Lloyd Dietz, and Steve Rachunok, and second baseman Benny McCoy, along with 87 Tiger farmhands, including George Metkovich, Danny and Al Gardella, Johnny Sain, and Roy Cullenbine. The Tiger organization, unlike the Cardinals, was decimated. Just 78 players remained under contract to the Detroit organization, including 35 on the major league roster. Only one player remained with the Tigers' Hot Springs Cotton States League farm. The Tigers lost an estimated $500,000 in talent.[72]

Landis also ordered the Tigers to pay $47,250 to 15 other players. He rebuked league presidents J. Alvin Gardner of the Texas League, Tom Fairweather of the Class C Western Association, Walter Morris of the Class C East Texas League, and Milton Price of the Class D West Texas–New Mexico League for allowing the Tigers to operate in the fashion they did.[73]

"I have had no less than one thousand players go through my hands at Beaumont [in the Texas League]," grumbled Detroit general manager Jake Zeller, "and not one has complained to Landis or any one else of the treatment they received from me. It is a 'witch hunt.'"[74]

Tigers owner Walter O. "Spike" Briggs was more conciliatory. "I have received Commissioner Landis' recent decision," he remarked from his winter home at Miami Beach. "We have surely been fully penalized for any mistakes or wrongdoings within the organization. The cost of this is mine and will be properly taken care of."

"This decision," Briggs continued with some prescience, "will affect our minor league operations but I do not think it will handicap the Tigers this season." It was an understatement. The major league club not only suffered no damage, it won its first pennant since 1935.[75]

The Tigers caught a long-term break when Landis reconsidered on Trout, finding that Trout's Toledo contact had, in fact, been "duly filed." Had Trout entered the free agent market, he would have fetched an estimated $20,000. Trout contributed little to Detroit's 1940 pennant, but later twice won 20 games for the Tigers.[76]

Dietz and Rachunok were ciphers, but a furious bidding war erupted for McCoy and Cullenbine. The 22-year-old McCoy's emancipation voided a trade the Tigers had just completed with the A's sending him to Philadelphia for outfielder Wally Moses. Connie Mack still wanted McCoy badly and outbid the Senators, Reds, Dodgers, Pirates, and Giants for him. The normally parsimonious Mack expended $45,000 to sign McCoy. Bidding was also fierce for Cullenbine, with Brooklyn's Larry MacPhail landing him for $25,000.[77]

Landis followed up his Detroit thunderbolt by issuing another blast at the farm system concept. On January 16, 1940, he delivered the following commentary:

> From the beginning, the commissioner has regarded the farm system as evil; evil not because ownership of several non-competing clubs is bad in itself—although it unquestionably is preferable that every club be independently owned and operated—but evil because such ownerships are operated to control great numbers of players, imperiling their essential rights, if the rules do not prevent such operation, and also because it reduces minor clubs to subservience....
>
> Instead of being free to advance as rapidly as their ability merits, and to advance to and through any and every club in baseball, players are unjustly restricted to "grooved" advancement through the one system which controls them and solely as that system may conceive to be in its interests.
>
> To this there is but one exception—the remote possibility that a player may be drafted.[78]

National League president Ford Frick was among the unconvinced. "Good or bad," he retorted, "you can't throw baseball's farm system out the window unless you've got something to take its place."[79]

Actually, Landis *did* have a plan to replace the farm system. On January 26, 1940, he dispatched a 3,000-word letter to all club owners, outlining a bold new plan to cripple chain gang baseball. His plan involved: 1) creating centralized schools for the development of baseball talent; 2) eliminating option agreements; and 3) granting subsidies to B, C, and D circuits.[80]

The scheme outraged many. One anonymous club official charged, "His idea seems to be toward socializing baseball, but it's too fantastic to survive."[81]

"In the matter of Judge Landis versus the farm system he sits as prosecutor, judge and jury, and there is no appeal," complained Brooklyn's Larry MacPhail. "Either he is dealing out justice or he is engaging in 'witch hunts' in which the innocent will burn along with the guilty."[82]

While denying he was "leading any fight against Landis," MacPhail refused to back down and predicted that the Judge's plan would destroy between 10 and 15 minor leagues. "The trouble with most of the club owners is they're so afraid of Landis they don't dare say 'Boo!' let alone get up and tell him frankly where he is slightly in error."[83]

Clark Griffith was among those outraged by Landis' proposals. "Landis might be able to out-think me, but Landis can't out-think me in a baseball way. I say again that he didn't realize the far-reaching effects of that recommendation."[84]

Yet it would be a mistake to believe Landis was without his supporters. He had clearly miscalculated the amount of support he could garner, but he did have some. Among the majors the Cubs, White Sox, Red Sox, A's, Indians, Phillies, and Browns backed him. So did Pacific Coast League president W. C. Tuttle, who proudly aligned himself with Landis in "breaking up the chains." In the International League, both Buffalo and Baltimore came out in support, as did Elmer Daly of the shaky Middle Atlantic League. American League president Will Harridge grandly claimed Landis' plan "eliminated most of baseball's problems."[85]

But the proposal went nowhere.

That was the last big case involving Landis and the topic of farm systems, but he never mellowed on either the topic itself—or regarding Branch Rickey.

In January 1944, Rickey issued a statement on a now long-forgotten controversy. Landis—10 months from death—was incensed.

"I suppose you saw the recent pronouncement by that L.L.D of all assistant pismires, Branch Rickey," Landis wrote to John Heydler. "Had you been obliged to contact that sort of garbage atmosphere, any step you would have taken would have been forgivable. That fellow is a perfect photograph of the inferiority complex victim. I have heard men say that Rickey was over-egoed, but they are mistaken. The poor fellow has the other thing, and everything he does fits in with that diagnosis—constantly on the alert for something to 'jump up' about. If you will take a little time out and go to the book, you will be able to classify the case."[86]

CHAPTER 23

# "THE COMMISSIONER OF ALL TIME"

Before the Judge became the Commissioner, he was a fan, and as such always retained a fan's interest in those who played the game. Throughout his tenure Landis cultivated an image as the "player's commissioner" and—aside from his not negligible defense of the legality of the reserve clause—the reputation was largely deserved.

The players in turn adored him. "I loved Judge Landis," recalled Tommy Henrich. "He was quite a man. I've always said that the two greatest names in baseball are Babe Ruth and Judge Landis. Landis cleaned it up and Babe Ruth glorified it."[1]

Players had no fear in approaching Landis with their complaints. In 1940 infielder Marv Owen wanted his release from the Red Sox but couldn't obtain it. "I called Judge Landis at his hotel," Owen recalled, "and told him I was benched. He said, 'Come see me at my hotel.' After I had told him the circumstances, he said I had a case. He then got in touch with the management and said give this man a job or give him free agency. I received a wire from management asking if I would accept free agency. I sent back a one word response, 'Yes.' I signed with Portland, three years as a player, and three years as a player/manager, winning the Coast League title in 1945. The Judge was the ball player's best friend! He didn't give a snap of his fingers who the involved parties were. He'd go to bat for a minor league player as quickly as for an outstanding big-timer."[2]

"He was the commissioner of all time," advanced Giants outfielder Jo-Jo Moore, "and when he said it he meant it. He got results by being stern. If anything was wrong he straightened it out. He was the best one that we've had that I know of.

"He led you right up to what he was going to tell you quick. He didn't fool around. He'd tell you just like it is... Mr. Landis, whenever

371

he said something, it meant something. I respected him and I think everybody else did."³

"He was always on the side of the ballplayer;" claimed Leo Durocher, "he had no use for the owners at all. 'Don't worry about them,' he would tell me, 'They're not out to help you. You know where your friend is. Right here, *I'm* your man... The only way a player could lose with him was to be daft."⁴

But there was, of course, also the element of fear. "When he came around, the players jumped," recounted Whitey Kurowski, "When they heard he was coming to town, they straightened up. They were afraid of him. And the owners were afraid too. He didn't take any stuff."⁵

Said Elden Auker in 1995:

> We all knew the Judge. He was in our clubhouse, when he'd come to Detroit, he'd always come in our clubhouse. We all knew him, and we all respected him. I think we all feared him...
>
> But he was a great man. He always called you by your last name, Mr. Auker, you know, and Mr. Fox, Mr. Greenberg, Mr. Gehringer, you know. Just a regular common old shoe. Always had his hat on. Old. Grey hair sticking out. Kinda grumpy guy but had a great sense of humor, great sense of humor. He loved baseball, and he was a protector, and we knew it.
>
> He frowned on gambling. Nobody ever questioned the Judge. He was the Judge, and he had our respect. The best thing that happened to baseball. I wish we had him today...
>
> He was a very quiet old gentleman, always at a ball game, he'd always sit at a box seat with his chin on his hands overlooking the field. But he was always around. He was in the game. And he might appear at most any game. You never knew. He might be at Yankee Stadium. He might be at Comiskey Park, be at Fenway Park. He used to come to Detroit regularly. He was affiliated with the game, and he kept his eye on it.⁶

Landis advanced the players' cause with his vigorous fight to extend the major league draft. He believed that the draft helped ameliorate the basic illegality and unfairness of the reserve clause,⁷ the clause that tied players to their clubs in perpetuity. If that clause, of dubious legality to begin with, had any validity, an individual player must have the chance to advance as far as his talent would carry him and not be left trapped in the minors. The draft (a "strictly fair American system" in Landis' words) helped give players that chance; exemption from the draft could and did bury players deep within the minors.[8]

"A situation," Landis snapped, "where a group of ballplayers can be boxed into a minor league, and can advance only at the whim of their employer is intolerable and un-American. So long as I am in this job, I will fight for full restoration of the draft."[9]

The draft was also of significant interest to major league owners. The major and minor leagues had long existed in an uneasy symbiosis. The majors needed fresh talent from the minors; the minors required infusions of cash from big league coffers to keep going. How those transfers would be accomplished created the conflict: would the minors be free to sell their best players to the majors for whatever the market would bear (a thought the majors did not relish) or would the majors have relatively free (and cheap) access to talent through a draft?

By January 1919 the disagreement had grown so large that the minor leagues broke with the majors, withdrawing outright from the National Agreement.

Landis' election healed the breach—at least superficially. A new National Agreement restored a form of the draft but only in a highly weakened fashion. Only one player in each Double-A (what we now know as Triple-A) club could be drafted, and entire leagues could opt out from the process. Five did: the three Double-A circuits (the International League, the American Association, and the Pacific Coast League), the Class A Western League, and the Class B Three-I League.[10]

The agreement did little to please either Landis *or* the major leagues. Double-A clubs, now free to hoard as much talent as they wished, could dispose of it at record prices. Baltimore's Jack Dunn was best at this game. Not only did Dunn create an International League dynasty that from 1919 through 1925 won seven consecutive pennants, he also netted over $1 million from player sales during the decade.

Following the 1922 season the majors unilaterally altered their system, cutting back on the number of players allowed on option and declaring that players sent out after January 23, 1923, would be draft eligible. The action incensed Pacific Coast League (PCL) president William H. McCarthy. The minors, McCarthy declared, had been "humbugged, deluded, deceived and cheated by the two major leagues . . . with the knowledge, consent and approval of the new Moses [Judge Landis]."[11]

Yet December 1923 saw the draft extended and McCarthy's league voluntarily a part of it. In what became known as the "modified draft," the majors, with Landis' backing, agreed to option players to any of the draft-exempt leagues if they would allow certain players to be drafted. The Western and Three-I Leagues quickly agreed, with the AA and PCL doing so by the end of the 1923 season, leaving only the International League (IL) as a holdout. Landis blasted its recalcitrance, contending that IL players who could advance "only by the purchase route were in virtual peonage." By 1924, however, even that circuit had finally fallen into line. Landis—and major league owners—had triumphed.[12]

In 1928 Landis was given an opportunity to rule on the issue of women in baseball. The occasion was Blanford, Indiana's Margaret Gisolo's presence in a regional American Legion tournament. Her eligibility was questioned, and no one in the Legion wished to handle the issue. Eventually tournament officials turned the matter over to Landis—who, of course, again had no real jurisdiction in the matter. Nonetheless, he ruled on it: Margaret Gisolo could play Legion ball. The Squire even sent her an autographed ball reading "To Margaret Gisolo, With my very good wishes."

The following season, the American Legion clarified its rules on the issue and barred all females from play.[13]

But while in Landis' eyes women may have qualified for amateur play, they did *not* meet professional standards. In April 1932 Chattanooga owner Joe Engel signed distaff pitcher Jackie Mitchell to appear in an exhibition against the barnstorming New York Yankees. She struck out Babe Ruth and Lou Gehrig,[14] but when Engel announced he would use Mitchell in official Southern Association contests, Landis overturned her contract. Professional baseball was "too strenuous" for a woman, he explained.[15]

In September 1930 Landis voided a far less significant transaction. The Texas League's San Antonio owner Homer Hammond traded slick-fielding second baseman Leonard Dondero to the Dallas Steers for 12 frycakes—which were promptly eaten by Hammond and Dallas owners George and Julius Schepps. Landis disallowed the deal.[16]

Landis' reach—if he felt like exercising it—could extend to the most distant branches of the game. In the late 1930s he forced Honus Wagner, then commissioner of the National Semi-Pro Baseball Congress (NSPBC), into banning "outlaw" players from NSPBC tournaments. And he could even intervene in remote town team affairs. A dispute between two such teams, Newville and London, in Jefferson County, Wisconsin, was resolved by local Judge Jesse Earle in favor of London. Newville then took the case all the way to Landis who upheld the umpire's decision in the case.[17]

But Landis' most famous minor league decision involved ex-con Edwin Collins "Alabama" Pitts. In June 1935 Pitts, serving time for a New York City grocery store holdup, was due to be paroled from Sing Sing. In prison he had compiled an impressive baseball record, batting .500 in 21 games with eight homers while playing center field. Manager Johnny Evers of the International League's Albany Senators offered Pitts a $200-a-month contract, but other minor league officials derided Albany's move as a cheap publicity stunt. When both minor league czar William G. Bramham and the National Association's Executive Committee ruled against Albany, the club had but one recourse: Landis.

The nation's fans did not know that Bramham had first conferred with Landis before issuing his controversial decision. He thought he had Landis' backing. "I wanted to get the commissioner's viewpoint before making any decision," Bramham later recounted to close friends, "and thought I was expressing it when I ruled against Pitts."

But public pressure favoring Pitts had reached floodgate levels. Even the man Pitts robbed, John Costello, came to his defense. Costello wired Albany: "If the parole commissioner thinks it safe to send Pitts out it ought to be safe for baseball players. My sympathies are entirely with Alabama in this controversy."

Letters and telegrams poured into the commissioner's office. Newspapermen badgered the Squire for comment, and he took to ducking them altogether. Finally, one reporter cornered Landis and showed him proofs of a forthcoming *Saturday Evening Post* editorial. It assumed Landis had ruled in favor of Bramham and blasted him mercilessly. That was it; he would rule in favor of Pitts. "The sentiment for Pitts was so strong, and those wishing to give him a chance in baseball were so unanimous, that no one could resist this tide," the Judge confided to Bramham.[18]

Landis allowed Pitts to play but displayed no bleeding heart for him. He took pains to spell out that despite press accounts to the contrary the ballplayer was no choir boy led astray, explaining that Pitts was armed while his accomplice merely acted as lookout on the fateful night of the Costello robbery, that Pitts had been "involved in at least five other similar robberies," and that despite subsequent sympathetic media reports there was nothing in the record to indicate extenuating circumstances.

"In the course of the considerable publicity in this case there have been created erroneous impressions which require correction," wrote Landis:

> It has been represented that the offense committed, which is the basis of the National Association ruling, grew out of an "escapade" wherein Pitts, "drunk" and "hungry," was misled into accompanying "an older man" (or "a tough guy") into a store, only to discover that his companion's purpose was robbery, which the companion accomplished by using a gun, while Pitts, unarmed and merely obeying his companion's orders, took "$5 or $10" from the cash register; that this was the only offense in which Pitts ever was involved; and that Pitts pleaded guilty out of consideration for his companion's wife and children and to lessen his companion's punishment by "taking the rap" for him.
>
> The official record, certified by the court which sentenced Pitts, establishes that it was Pitts who entered the store, held up the clerk with his loaded revolver, and took $76.25 from the cash register. (The amount is not important—it depended upon what the cash register contents happened to be—but $5 or $10 is more consistent with the "drunk" and "hungry" and "escapade" representations.) Pitts' accomplice (one year older than Pitts) acted as "lookout" and was unarmed.

Landis also took pains to quote from Morris Koenig, the trial judge who sentenced Pitts. Koenig had written: "There is no evidence before me that he [the lookout] was in any other robbery than this, while Pitts has been in at least five other robberies. . .

"I should think Pitts was very fortunate that he was not compelled to plead guilty to robbery in the first degree, where the mandatory sentence would have been twenty years."

In his conclusion, Landis revealed his sympathy for Bramham

and basically admitted that it was only public pressure that forced him to reverse his fellow czar:

> As originally presented to the President and Executive Committee of the National Association, this case involved only a general question [involving the hiring of felons], which they decided properly, as their duty required, and as the commissioner would have been obliged to rule. Since then, however, a new situation has arisen. Conditions have been created as the result of which there can not be much doubt as to the destructive effect, upon Pitts' effort toward rehabilitation, of not permitting him to enter baseball employment. This was not contemplated by, nor is it due to, the ruling of the President of the National Association. And in this situation, reputable people have expressed to me their belief that there has been a complete reformation in Pitts' character, and their confidence in his earnest intent to regain an honorable position in society. Solely for these reasons, Pitts will be allowed to play . . .[19]

But Pitts' publicity outmatched his talent. He batted just .233 for Albany and soon washed out of professional baseball. In June 1941 he visited a North Carolina dancehall. When Pitts cut in on a couple, the man, Newland LeFevres, pulled out a knife, fatally severing an artery in Pitts' shoulder.[20]

Baseball's most colorful star of the 1930s was the Cardinals unpredictable loudmouth, Jay Hanna "Dizzy" Dean. Almost from the very beginning Dean got into Landis' hair. Had the Judge's mane not been snow-white already, Dean would have single-handedly turned it that color.

Dizzy arrived to stay in the majors in 1932 and before long declared that the Cardinals had signed him illegally—that he was underage when he had signed his contract and that he would petition Landis for emancipation. Landis never needed much prodding to tangle with St. Louis' Branch Rickey, but this time Rickey clearly had right on his side. At a hearing the Mahatma produced Dean's marriage certificate, signed by Dean and proving conclusively that the young prospect was not only of age but 22 when he signed his Cardinal pact.

"You got me, Mr. Rickey, you got me," Dean guffawed, but Landis wasn't laughing. He didn't like having his time wasted, and he didn't like liars. He gave Dean what one Rickey associate called "the tongue lashing of the century."[21]

Despite this stunt, Dean won 18 games his rookie year, 20 the following season, and 30 in 1934 as the Cardinals captured the World Championship. But the 1934 season was hardly without its share of controversy.

In August, Dean and his brother Paul ("Daffy") cavalierly absented themselves from a Cardinals' exhibition in Detroit. Cards manager Frankie Frisch, already tired of the Deans' antics, fined Dizzy $100 and Paul $50.

Dizzy went berserk. He ripped off his Cardinal uniform, announced he'd never pay the fine, and warned that he and Daffy were heading to Florida to go "fishing."

The Cards, enjoying the backing of their players and their fans, indefinitely suspended both Deans. Dizzy was intelligent enough to know he was out on a limb. Daffy was even smarter and surrendered unconditionally, leaving his older brother alone on that limb.

But Diz also knew that Major League Rule 13 stated: "A player suspended by a club has the right to appeal to Commissioner Landis, who has authority to order his reinstatement and afford him adequate redress if he holds that the punishment is excessive or not merited."

Dean exercised that right.

On Thursday, August 16 he phoned Landis and arranged for a meeting. Landis agreed, and Dean drove seven hours to make a 10 o'clock session the following morning.

"Sit down, young man," said Landis.

Dean, who complained of "being persecuted by the Cardinals' management," told Landis, "I want to get back to pitching baseball. And I'm willing to do anything necessary to straighten this thing out."[22] Landis wasn't about to take action merely on Dean's word. "Well, we'll straighten out this whole matter," he responded. "You go back to St. Louis and be at the Park Plaza Hotel at 10 o'clock on Monday morning. And when I say '10 o'clock' I don't mean 'one minute after 10.'"

The Squire also got on the phone to St. Louis, ordering Rickey, Frisch and Cards owner Sam Breadon to appear at the session.[23]

By Sunday, Dizzy was willing to forget the whole thing, but Breadon, confident that Landis would rule in the club's favor, told him to wait until the hearing.

Landis flew into St. Louis and headed straight for his $45-a-night Park Plaza suite. Over Dean's objections no sportswriters were allowed into the hearing, but Landis was not about to alienate the press. "The first thing he did when he entered was open the vent above the door," noted sportswriter Ray Gillespie. "We heard the whole shebang."[24]

Quite a shebang it was, lasting for four hours and five minutes. Not only were Frisch, Rickey, and the Dean brothers present, but so were two coaches, the team physician, its trainer, pitcher Jesse Haines, and shortstop Leo Durocher.

Landis generally maintained his silence as Dizzy Dean lambasted the Cardinal organization for cheapness; Paul Dean made excuses as to why he had missed the exhibition; and the Cardinals fired back about the Deans' ingratitude. Landis, for his part, wanted it known that he was only involved because he had to be, because there existed the question of whether an "indefinite" suspension was "excessive."

"What I do in my position as Commissioner with this organization [the Cardinals]," he barked at Branch Rickey, "is in the exercise of authority conferred and the discharge of a duty that devolves on me, and not because of reaching out to get something that doesn't accrue to me. I have got enough without doing that."[25]

Finally, after both sides had talked (or in some cases screamed) each other out, Landis announced his decision.

The "players' commissioner" would rule in favor of the ballclub.

"Ballplayers owe their public a certain obligation, and you two boys owed the City of Detroit, the management of the Tigers, and the management of the Cardinals something important in their lives," said Landis,

> You should have done everything possible to accompany your team. But you didn't, did you?
>
> You were disgusted, Dizzy, you said, because you lost a game to the Cubs and thought you might have a sore arm. Paul, you said you were worried about your ankle and that you sat at your hotel waiting for Dizzy to pick you up and drive you to the station but that he never showed up. That's too deep for me and it's difficult for me to accept your statements.
>
> You boys owe it to your profession to show yourselves on the ballfield at all times. People go out there, pay their money to see you, and you threw baseball down in this instance. Then when you

were informed of your fines by the Cardinals, you got huffy and wanted to quit. You wouldn't go to the field. You were not going to do this, you were not going to do that.

I do not feel the Cardinals were unreasonable, either in their fine or their suspension of ten days for you, Dizzy. I support them fully.[26]

Landis' decision shocked Dizzy. Martin J. Haley wrote in the *St. Louis Globe-Democrat*, "His facial expression indicated he could not believe what he heard. . . . It seemed as if he felt that his best friend had turned against him."[27]

Dean, however, was soon appealing to the Squire once more, and this time with better results. In 1933 Dean had signed a contract with St. Louis Browns business manager Bill DeWitt to act as his agent for non-baseball income. DeWitt did very well by Dean. From May 28, 1933 to December 1934 he obtained $68,911.93 in income for Dean—an amazing total considering Diz earned only $21,389 (including a $5,389 World Series share in 1934) from the Cardinals for that time period.

There was a catch, however. Dean's contract called for him to deliver one-third of outside income earned through October 1934 back to DeWitt. Then DeWitt's commission fell to a more reasonable 10 percent. Landis ordered DeWitt's percentage slashed to 10 percent for the entire length of the agreement.[28]

Perhaps exhausted from his dealings with Dean and the Cardinals, Landis announced he was heading to Arizona for a two-month vacation, resulting in a crack made at the January 1935 New York Baseball Writers Dinner: "How does Landis know when he's on vacation?"[29]

The answer was when Landis had no dealings with Dizzy Dean. The following April he summoned Diz into the woodshed once more, after news circulated that Dean and Browns righthander Bobo Newsom had each accepted bonuses from East St. Louis furniture dealer Dick Slack. The Judge demanded to know if handsome fees given the duo were for advertising Slack's merchandise or bonuses for onfield production. If the latter, they were a clear violation of baseball law.

"What's all this about?" Landis demanded.

"Nothing to it, Judge," Dean replied, "as far as I know. I got a contract with Slack for $5,000 this season for radio work and personal appearances at his store. That's all. He's a pretty nice guy, Judge. And he's got plenty of dough."

Landis still wanted to make sure nothing was amiss: "Just answer my question, Dizzy. Does it interest you to know where 'lots of dough' comes from?

"What about this one hundred dollars per game for every game you won last year?" Landis continued, telling Dean he "must accept no money from anyone except your ballclub for your performance on the ballfield. If anyone offers you money, I want you to promise me that you will kick him in the teeth. Will you do that?"

"Yes sir. Yes sir, yes, sir, but if someone offers me three thousand dollars, can't I take it?"

"Not if you don't know what it's for. If it's for your activities on the field I want you to take a baseball bat and hit the man over the head that offers it to you. Is that clear?"

"Yes sir, Judge. It sure is."[30]

Not all observers thought Landis' concerns were valid. Columnist Westbrook Pegler raked him over the coals for the incident. "This was strictly the old Chamber of Commerce routine," Pegler replied, ". . . the sort of thing that Landis is paid for at a much higher rate than Dizzy Dean is paid for winning pennants. It was intended to impress baseball customers with the piety of the baseball industry and to obscure the tyrannical guise of sport. Baseball lives on the sporting illusions of its customers and hires a resounding mane of an old-time news-maker of the U.S. District Court to endorse its habits."[31]

The 1935 season saw no further Landis-Dean run-ins, but as soon as the campaign was over Dean found himself once more in trouble. Diz had signed on to a barnstorming tour, but his box-office appeal was clearly sagging. Crowds proved scarce, and when only 200 customers showed up at Engel Stadium, home of the Southern Association's Chattanooga Lookouts, he petulantly refused to suit up. "Hellfire," he stormed, "I can pick up more money playin' poker on the train."

Similarly poor attendance greeted him at New Orleans the next day. Meanwhile back in Tennessee, flamboyant Lookouts owner Joe Engel challenged Diz to a prize fight for a $15,000 purse. That sounded pretty interesting to Dean, but he gave no immediate answer to Engel.[32]

Dean was attracting negative publicity nationwide for the incidents. In both Chattanooga and New Orleans, charities were to have benefitted from Dean's appearances. In Depression-era America he looked particularly selfish.

Nonetheless, Dean tried putting the best spin on events. "As far as the New Orleans benefit was concerned," he explained, "I wasn't goin' to take a chance on ruinin' my arm for just a few fans, so I went back to the hotel and wrote 'em outta check for $25 for their charity. I'm not goin' to be made a goat outta this and if they wanna take it up with Judge Landis, I'm ready."

Landis was *just* as ready. The first thing he did was prohibit any Engel-Dean pugilistic exhibition. The second was to make Dean sweat for five months before letting him know what his penalty would be. Finally, he let Dean off lightly, with a mere $100 fine.[33]

In June 1937 Diz was on the warpath again, lambasting National League president Ford Frick and umpire George Barr as "the two biggest crooks in baseball." Frick suspended Dean indefinitely "for conduct detrimental to the best interests of baseball."

Dean threatened to appeal to Landis—and more importantly to sue baseball for $250,000. Frick blinked and allowed Dean back on the active roster. Dean would have been better off suspended. Pitching in that year's All-Star Game he suffered the broken toe that ended his pitching dominance.[34]

Later he would threaten to sue the Cardinals for $250,000— this time for rushing him back into action too soon and damaging his arm. Landis talked him out of it, arguing the suit would be bad for baseball.[35]

Surprisingly Landis, however, could look the other way at Dean's indiscretions, particularly when one considers their nature—gambling.

"Dizzy was always betting the horses but Commissioner Landis was real good about letting it go," recalled Clay Bryant, a Dean teammate on the 1937 Cubs. "At the time we were not supposed to bet on horses but Dizzy never paid much mind to that. [Landis] could have stepped in if it got out of hand, but he was real good to Dizzy."[36]

Yet Landis' tolerance had its limits. In 1944 Landis prohibited Dean, that season's *Sporting News* Broadcaster of the Year, from announcing the Browns-Cardinals World Series. It was not the first time Landis had banned broadcasters he found objectionable. Back in 1935 he had declared Ted Husing *persona non grata* not only from that season's Fall Classic (he had worked each one from 1928 on) or from post-season play, but from all baseball broadcasting. Husing's crime: during the 1934 he had condemned the umpiring as "some of the worst I've ever seen."[37]

In 1944 the Judge accused Dean of "oral atrocities" and of grammar "unfit for a national broadcaster." It was a long-standing Landis opinion. Twice before he had blocked Dean from obtaining national broadcasting engagements.[38]

"How can that commissar say I ain't eligible to broadcast?" retorted Dean, doing little to rebut Landis' point. "I ain't never met anybody that didn't know what 'ain't' means."[39]

Actually, Landis' actions to safeguard America's grammatical purity were unnecessary. Gillette, the Series' sponsor, had their own stable of announcers—Don Dunphy, Bill Slater, and Bill Corum—that they wanted to use. Landis was so relieved to be rid of Dean he had no reservations about employing announcers who would have once derided for their lack of baseball experience.[40]

Players' bad checks were another problem Landis had to deal with. A past master of rubber checks was shortstop Leo Durocher. When Durocher joined the Cardinals in 1933, he finally sapped the Judge's patience. Landis ordered him not to write another check—good or bad—to *anyone*. If he had to pay any bill, he should have the ballclub write the check. Period. Case closed.

Within the season, however, the fiery Durocher—not surprisingly—became engaged in an altercation with an umpire and ended up earning a fine. The rules stated, and still state, that such a fine must be paid by the ballplayer himself and not by the ballclub, although as a matter of course the ballclub almost always does pay the fine.

Durocher for once followed instructions to the letter—and the Cardinals wrote out the check covering his fine. When Landis received it, he hit the ceiling.

He called Durocher into his office, berating him: "You of all people should know the proper procedure for paying a fine. How dare you let the club send it in for you."

"Because," Leo replied innocently, *"you* told me never write another check."

"You do it!" Landis stormed. "I didn't mean *me.*"[41]

Actually, Durocher was a terrific booster of the Judge—and of his collecting methods. In his autobiography he wrote, "Let me tell you something. If a ballplayer owes you money, all you have to do is write a letter to the Commissioner, and I guarantee that you'll get paid right now."

After calling a player into his office Landis, noted Durocher, would search about his cluttered desk and miraculously find whatever bills were in question. "Now why haven't you paid these bills?" he might say. "You're short of money, aren't you? You'd be only too happy to pay these bills if you had the wherewithal, isn't that right?"

Then he'd get less friendly and more censorious, but before long he'd put his arm around the player and say, "Now when you run short and need some money, what are you worried about? Come to me. I'm the place to come, that's what I'm here for. I'm your man."[42]

One major leaguer who could vouch for Landis' bill-collecting effectiveness was Hank Greenberg. In May 1941 Greenberg entered the air corps and lent a teammate $1,000. When by 1943 the player had made no effort to repay the debt and ignored Greenberg's letters on the subject, Greenberg contacted Landis. After first writing the player, Landis turned to the Tigers, saying "$500 is to be subtracted from the player's contract immediately and next payday another $500 is to be subtracted from his contract. Such $1,000 is to be forwarded to me so I can forward it to player Greenberg." Greenberg got his money.[43]

One of the relatively few surviving pieces of Landis' baseball-related correspondence involves another instance of a ballplayer getting in deeper than he should have. The case involved minor league manager John Fitzpatrick, who co-signed a note for $125 with the Muskogee Industrial Finance Co. When they couldn't collect, they went to Landis. The Commissioner straightened the matter out, but not without offering Fitzpatrick some Dutch-uncle advice, via his new employer, Spencer Harris, president of Olean's PONY League club:

> Dear Mr. Harris:
>
> Herewith canceled note of John Fitzpatrick to the Muskogee Industrial Finance Corp. Please deliver it to Mr. Fitzpatrick, with the perhaps gratuitous advice that he ought not to tie himself up on any document of this character in the future. It evidently carries an excessive rate of interest and very onerous terms, and it is not only an ill-advised document for anyone to execute, but it is particularly censurable for anybody to ask a friend to sign it as a co-maker. In the present instance, he has been fortunate in only being required

to pay $125 principal and $2.71 interest, which is less than he
should have paid on an equitable basis. It would be a mistake for
him to assume that he can always get out as easy as that.

> Very truly yours,
> Commissioner.[44]

Dizzy Dean was not the only player to appeal a suspension. Another Durocher visit to 333 North Michigan involved Brooklyn
catcher Babe "Blimp" Phelps. In 1941 Phelps, who had a history of
missing team travel, skipped the Dodgers' first western trip, informing his roommate, third baseman Lew Riggs, that he didn't feel well.
Larry MacPhail fined Phelps $1,000 and suspended him. Phelps ap-
pealed to Landis.

Durocher, then the Dodger manager, wanted the suspension lifted
and hinted to Landis that Phelps was concerned about his heart.

Landis took the bait and began to solicitously lead the witness.
"Were you sick, Babe? Was your heart bothering you?" he asked. "Is
that the reason you didn't make the trip? Did you feel you were having
a slight heart attack? Was that it, that your heart was bothering you?"

"No," Phelps densely responded.

Landis started in again, "Well, I was told, Babe . . . you heard
your manager, Mr. Durocher, tell me that you had got in a cab with
Lew Riggs and told him that you didn't feel well and couldn't make
the trip. That you didn't feel well and went back to the hotel and got
into bed because *you didn't feel well* and that's why nobody could get
in touch with you."

"That's not so," Phelps averred. "I didn't get into any cab with
Lew Riggs."

At that point the Judge ordered Leslie O'Connor to get Lew Riggs
on the phone. Riggs repeated his story that Phelps had said he was
not feeling well.

"Well, do you think Mr. Riggs is lying?" Landis asked Phelps. "Do
you care to answer that? You don't have to if you don't want to, but I'd
be interested in anything you have to say."

Phelps wouldn't say Riggs was lying, and Landis started in
again, attempting to lay the groundwork for exonerating Phelps:
"Well, then, your heart was bothering you . . . You didn't feel well and
as far as you were concerned your health came first. . . You decided it

would be very dangerous to your future well being to make this trip because of your heart condition."

*None* of which Phelps would admit to—even though he was *notoriously* nervous about his heart. A frustrated Landis had to let the fine and suspension stand. Phelps, incensed that Landis had not ruled in his favor, sat out the rest of the season at his Odenton, Maryland, home.[45]

Sometimes Landis' duties involved protecting retired ballplayers from themselves. Such was the case after the alcoholic Grover Cleveland Alexander left the majors and was touring with the a barnstorming team, that of the Michigan-based religious sect, the House of David. One night in Harrisburg, Pennsylvania, he was too inebriated to play and "just lay on the bench drunk." Former major league first baseman Eddie Onslow wired Landis, asking him to do something about the situation. Landis wired back, wanting to know where the House of David was stopping next. When the Squire learned it was Lancaster, he dispatched a scout to that city to retrieve Alexander and bring him safely back home.[46]

Protecting the dignity of the game also meant banning such players as Cubs outfielder Hack Wilson and White Sox first baseman Art "The Great" Shires from pursuing careers in professional boxing. Shortly after Shires' initial bout (in which he stopped opponent Dan Daly in 21 seconds of the first round), Daly alleged he had thrown the fight. Ring authorities immediately banned Daly for life, and Shires was banned in 32 states. When Landis also banished Shires from the ring, an independent promoter offered "Art the Great" $10,000 to fight *Landis.* [47]

Just about any matter could come before Landis, and usually did, including who paid the damages when a Miss Marie Kaeser of Cleveland got whacked on the head by a Rick Farrell foul ball in May of 1936. The entire affair was a comedy of errors, with Farrell, who had been with the Red Sox when the incident occurred but was later traded to Washington, threatened with arrest if he returned to Cleveland. Nobody wanted Farrell arrested (except Miss Kaeser if she didn't receive $327.61 in damages)—but nobody would admit responsibility for payment. Not Farrell. Not the Indians. Not the Red Sox. And not the Senators.

Into Landis' lap the case fell, and over this paltry amount he grilled Ferrell at Philadelphia's Bellevue-Stratford Hotel and BoSox owner Tom Yawkey in Cleveland.

The Squire's patience must have been wearing thin as he asked multimillionaire Yawkey: "I have got to go under the theory [that] as a practical operation of our business, a club has got to take care of that ball player's rights in that lawsuit, haven't I?"

Yawkey was well known as a "players' owner"—but evidently not when the player in question was now with another team. He still wouldn't pay Miss Kaeser's claim.

Finally, Landis ordered the Boston club to reimburse Miss Kaeser for $327.61 plus five percent interest. And he ordered them to do one more thing: "return this communication to the Commissioner for the Commissioner's files, there being no clerical help today."[48]

As anyone who has ever had to deal with secretarial help knows, there are limits even to a czar's powers.

All of which also serves to illustrate that the reverse of the coin from Landis' benevolent despotism over players was his often just plain surly despotism over owners. A good portion of his power ironically derived from his threat to walk away from that power—*if* he didn't get his way. "Phil Piton, who worked in the Commissioner's office," former sportswriter Carl Lundquist has recounted, "told me that Landis carried a letter of resignation with him at all times. About six times he pulled it out and was ready to use it."[49]

Ford Frick, a former sportswriter turned owner-friendly league president, viewed Landis with some displeasure. "He was intolerant of opposition, suspicious of reform and reformers and skeptical of compromise," Frick contended. "He ruled the game as if baseball were a courtroom and the players and officials were culprits awaiting sentencing for their misdoings."[50]

Those misdoings often involved player contracts. "A player," noted Bill Veeck, "in trouble might tremble when called to Landis' office but he would leave with his problem solved and the final Landis admonition: 'Don't go to those owners if you get into trouble, come to me. I'm you're friend; they're no good.' The happiest times in his life seemed to come when he was setting players free from their contracts."[51]

Landis had his close friends among ownership, most notably Philip K. Wrigley, Frank Navin, and Alva Bradley, but he could also take pleasure in ordering owners about. Clark Griffith's nephew Calvin Griffith once recalled: "My uncle didn't feel well and didn't want to go to Chicago. But Landis demanded he come, and Clark Griffith went to Chicago and had his appendix burst on him. He was in the hospital over two weeks . . . " A horrified Landis realized he had gone too far. "You talk about a man apologizing," Calvin Griffith added. "Landis was all over himself apologizing."[52]

For all of his power and all his bluff, Landis did not always get his way in baseball. Repeatedly he found himself on the losing end of arguments regarding the shape of the minors, and he had no use for night baseball. "MacPhail," he barked at Larry MacPhail when the Cincinnati executive wanted to install the first lights in the majors, "what's your hurry? Young man, you can write this down. Not in my lifetime or yours will you ever see a baseball game played at night in the majors."[53]

Landis also exhibited very early concern regarding revenue disparity, but again was powerless (or too unimaginative) to do anything about it. Shortly after taking office in 1921 he commented on the trend toward big, new parks: "The danger of the situation may be merely theoretical but advance fears are seemingly justified when one side is capable of sending seventy-five thousand fans to a ball game while another is restricted to crowds of twenty thousand." He pledged to offer plans to equalize resources but nothing came of it. He simply had no ideas or suggestions to present.[54]

Many times Landis retreated into a reactive mood, acting less like an administrator than like a, well, *judge*. "Do it and I'll rule on it," he would bark at owners and officials. The habit failed to endear him to owners and front office personnel. "He failed to advise beyond the rules to the same extent and vigor that he criticized," noted Branch Rickey's aide and biographer Arthur Mann.[55]

One time Landis clearly met his match with ownership involved the then-threadbare Brooklyn franchise. In December 1929 factionalism divided the club's board of directors, with Steve McKeever and team attorney Frank B. York on one side and Joe Gilleaudeau and manager Wilbert Robinson on the other. Robinson had been holding both the position of field manager and of club president, and McKeever wanted him out.

John Heydler cajoled Landis into mediating the dispute, and both sides met with Landis at his suite at New York's Roosevelt Hotel. A half an hour of Brooklyn wrangling was more than enough for the Squire, and he emerged mopping his forehead and muttering, "In all my experience on earth I've never seen anything like it." It was left for Heydler to finally work out an acceptable compromise.[56]

The commissionership involved the full range of ceremonial

duties and often arduous travel, travel that aggravated his tendency toward respiratory problems. "He couldn't stand air-conditioned trains," recalled his granddaughter Cathy. "He always said they made him sick and gave him troubles."

Some of Landis' duties involved an occasional funeral, such as that of Brooklyn owner Charlie Ebbets for whom he served as a honorary pallbearer for Philadelphia's William F. Baker whom he graciously—if not truthfully —praised as "a pillar of the baseball community." When he returned from Jake Ruppert's services, he regaled relatives with his impression of the clergyman's prayers.[57]

Another portion of his ceremonial duties involved opening ballparks—at practically any level whatsoever—from million-dollar Wrigley Field[58] in Los Angeles (where he dedicated its impressive clock tower as a memorial to World War I dead) to Delorimier Downs in Montreal to Redbirds Stadium in Columbus to Memorial Stadium in Terre Haute ("the finest of its kind for a city of this size"), to massive Municipal Stadium in Cleveland. In June 1939 he traveled to Cooperstown to dedicate baseball's new $100,000 Hall of Fame. "I would like to dedicate this museum to all America...," he told a nationwide radio audience, "to lovers of good sportsmanship ... healthy bodies ... and keen minds. It is to them ... that I propose to dedicate this shrine of sportsmanship." Despite his displeasure at the concept, he was even on hand at baseball's first successful night game, in Des Moines in May 1930.[59]

The job may not have been as easy as Landis made it look. Leslie O'Connor, who had a closer look at the Landis commissionership than anyone, was widely rumored to be his successor. "I have a short life to live," he responded to such reports, "and I want none of that job. It's a killer."[60]

# CHAPTER 24

# "A BUNDLE OF NERVES AND BLOOD VESSELS"

History remembers Kenesaw Mountain Landis as either snarling at club owners or sitting immobile at a ballgame, with his chin propped up on the rail of his private box. It has transformed him into a caricature of the public persona he himself created.

But what was he like away from the spotlight, away from the courtroom or the commissioner's office? At home? With his family? Around friends?

He was certainly not a handy man around the house. In fact, despite his farm origins, he was remarkably awkward at performing physical tasks. "I don't think I ever saw him carry anything or pick up anything or change a tire, anything like that," recalled his granddaughter Cathy. He never learned how to drive a car, and his attempts at carving the family turkey were uniformly disastrous. So was his try at pruning an apple tree at his summer camp. "He killed it dead," reminisced Cathy, "pruning it to smithereens . . ."

His golf game was truly abysmal. "A terrible golfer!" exclaimed another granddaughter, Nancy Landis Smith Lucas. "I have pictures of him—just terrible—hacking away."[1]

Landis had strengths, though, on the course: concentration, accuracy, and an unusually cheerful attitude. He would study each shot as if it were the Standard Oil decision, step up to the tee, and hit the ball fairly straight (if not far). He maintained that concentration even though he would continue to jabber away as he swung. Almost oblivious to the score he seemed happy just to be outside, walking about the links. One surprised partner described him as "one of the most companionable golf partners that could be found."[2]

As bad a golfer as he was, however, he was certainly game. In the spring of 1923 he journeyed from Belleaire to the Indians' spring training base at Lakewood, not only to catch an A's-Indians exhibition but also to officiate at an American Legion ceremony. Sitting in the stands before the Indians' contest, he spied two Cleveland sportswriters named Powers and Williams who were obviously either coming or going to the links, golf attire being no more muted then than now.

"You fellows are dressed like golfers and I suppose you think you can play," the Judge joshed. "Well, I'll tell you just what I'll do. When I come to Cleveland in April to address the Ad Club, I will play you fellows and beat you too." Landis' reputation had preceded him, so his challenge was eagerly taken up. Another sportswriter named Bill Becker joined in the foursome, with the *Plain Dealer*'s Francis J. Powers pairing with Landis.

Powers may have been even worse than Landis, but the Squire did his best to buck up his spirits. "Be of strong heart, partner," he advanced after Powers dumped a drive into a bunker, "the jeers are but a lot of wise remarks from Messrs. Becker and Williams; the jeers are but the chattering of jealous rivals. We will take them now."

Bill Becker's putting ability amazed the jurist. "But how can we beat this man Becker," he marveled after the fifth hole. "He neither looks at the ball or the hole, yet the darn balls go down every time. His putting is a gift."

When the Judge took the sixth hole, a mere 95 yards from tee to green, he was ecstatic. "At last, I've found one green I can reach with my drive," he chortled.

On the next hole, it was, alas, back to normal. After whacking his first drive out of bounds, he topped his second attempt. Not until his fifth stroke did he reach the green. "And the Scotch fiends call this a sport," he harrumphed. "Bah! It's a curse."

But with a speech coming up at noon, the foursome, which had completed just seven holes by half past 11, was compelled to call it a day. Still the Squire kept up the conversational stream. He could not get his mind off the sixth hole. "You fellows took the long holes," the Squire admitted, "But that short 100-yard sixth that the old boy won, a three—that was the real test of golf. A lot of fellows can play the long ones, but where accuracy and deftness of touch is required—I am asking you, who won the short hole?

"I will be back in July and we are going to continue this battle at that time. Six holes and the short time we had today does not decide the matter. I want a thirty-six hole contest and that's what we will have."[3]

Winifred Landis hardly shared her husband's passion for the game. "I hate golf!" was her actual position, and her attitude only worsened one day at the Landis home in September 1937 when she tripped over the Squire's golf clubs—and broke her arm. "Hereafter," she quipped, "I will have to keep a caddy around the house. Of all things to fall over!"[4]

As quiet as the Judge was at ballgames, outside the ballyard he dominated every room he entered. "He was wiry," observes grandson Keehn Landis. "He was a bundle of nerves and blood vessels and very little meat on his bones. Slim and wiry, but he had some muscle. He was *active*. He was never still."

To prospective in-laws he could be somewhat intimidating. When a fellow named Burt Smith was first courting Landis' granddaughter Nancy—whom he eventually married—he was invited over for dinner to meet the rest of the Landis tribe. At one point a silence fell over the table and the Squire awkwardly tried to get the conversation moving again. "Grandpappy turned to [Burt]," recalled Nancy's sister Cathy, "and said, 'How high is Niagara Falls?' "

"Burt didn't know at all," added Nancy.[5]

Landis himself had opinions on any number of topics, including that of health. In 1907 Landis provided a reporter for the *Cincinnati Post* with what he considered the key to good health, sleep:

> Some folks are saying you can spit away your life in tobacco juice, others say drinking or smoking will kill any one who does them, but to my mind sleep is the most important thing in one's life. Give one plenty of sleep and the other things—provided, of course, one doesn't fall in the gutter—won't hurt much.
>
> For many years I have been getting on an average of six hours in the 24. But only my mind gets tired. My body never does. I believe I have thirty-five years more of life ahead of me, if I get plenty of sleep.[6] I believe all of us ought to have eight hours sleep, and the fact that six hours suffices me leads me to suspect the tissues of what I fondly term my brain are built up at the expense of something else. Who knows—maybe we shall not live thirty-five years more.
>
> I never smoke after dinner or drink coffee during that meal, for if I do I can't sleep until two or three o'clock the next morning.[7] I walk two-thirds of the way home every day in Chicago, and I live six miles from the courtroom. That is practically all the exercise I get, for I take my lunch at my chambers.[8]

He was not exaggerating about being an avid walker, being well-known throughout Chicago for striding as briskly as his legs could carry him.[9] All the time he walked to and from his office, his black chauffeur, Leonard Edwards, slowly trailed him in the family limousine.[10]

In November 1916 Landis' popularity had grown to such an extent that the *Chicago Tribune* interviewed him on the occasion of his 50th birthday, providing *Tribune* readers with some rare insight regarding how a judge who ruled his courtroom like a tyrant exercised far less control over his own home life:

> Every member of this family does exactly as he or she wants to do. Each one is his or her supreme court. Anything for the common good of the family is decided according to the wishes of the whole family. Each one knows what is right and each one can do whatever he thinks is best. It is purely democratic. I have nothing to say and consequently I say nothing.

Even the question of a family photo he left open to the judgment of his brood. "Now, I knew you would want that [photo]," he informed the *Tribune*'s photographer, "but I don't know whether Mrs. Landis and the children will stand for it.

"If she says 'No,' then it's 'No.' If the children say 'No,' there is no appeal. Ask me for my own and I say 'May as well,' but as for the others, ask 'em. I can say this, though: I'll do my best to hold my dog, John, for a pose whether he wants it or not."[11]

Landis may not have been guilty of overstatement when he claimed "every member of this family does exactly as he or she wants to do." When daughter Susanne was a young girl, the Judge received the followed imperious instructions from his crown princess:

> Father
> Will you please send lennie [chauffeur Leonard Edwards] to Marshel [sic] Shields [sic] and Co. and tell him to get me a snake You can get them on the 8th floor at the favor counter. and bring it home to night and don't forget.
>
> Susanne[12]

A number of authors have pointed out that while Landis sentenced bootleggers to long prison sentences, he himself was known to take a Prohibition nip. The most famous occurrence was at a party thrown in 1922 by George Weiss in New Haven. Liquor was all over the place, but most of the partygoers were ill at ease at the thought of drinking in the fearsome Landis' presence. The Squire sensed this and taking cocktail in hand, raised his glass and shouted: "Gentlemen, before we begin, I want to propose a toast. I want to drink a toast to the Eighteenth Amendment." With that he let out a mischievous smile and swigged down his drink.

After that everyone had a great time, including Landis, whether he was regaling listeners with the story of the Scandinavian who got off the trolley in search of an outhouse or prompting a would-be orator in the recitation of "The Shooting of Dan McGrew"—prompting purposely designed to sabotage the narration.

One reveler was so inebriated he thought "Judge" Landis was "George" Landis. "That George Landis is all right," he'd bellow. "Here's to George Landis."

For years thereafter New York sportswriters who had attended the affair would greet the Squire with a jovial "How's good old George Landis?"

"Wasn't that a great party in New Haven?" the Squire would invariably respond.[13]

Yet that must have been one of the few instances that Landis drank.[14] "Our families when they used to drink they used to drink Old Fashioneds," recalled grandson Keehn, "but I don't think I ever saw him drink."[15]

The older Landis generation, noted nephew Lincoln Landis, were "very strong Prohibitionists. Abraham [Landis] for the most part didn't touch the stuff and tried to instill that in his kids.

"And on one occasion Kenesaw, as a child of nine or ten, maybe eleven, having accompanied Abraham to a reunion, wondered why there was so much drinking going on. And he was putting his father on the spot: 'How come there's all this drinking going on here when you've told us it's a sure way of going to hell?' (I'm embellishing a little bit there). And his father said, 'Well, you know, it would be a shame if these fellows could not have their memories improved a little bit by these spirits on these occasions.' I think his father was a quick thinker.

"It's true there was a very strong prohibition, abstemious attitude toward booze. A lot of it had to do with a very strong influence of church, the United Brethren Church—that was mainly on the Kumler side."[16]

Kenesaw did, however, smoke—in his younger days an inveterate cigarette smoker. One day, America's most famous antismoking advocate, Lucy Page Gaston, dropped in for a visit. No one ever dared to smoke in her presence—except for Landis. "Miss Gaston," he lectured her, "unless you've tramped through the woods until you're tired, and then sat down to inhale the fragrance of a good cigarette, you've never known what a real friend a roll of paper and tobacco can be."

In his later life, though, he restricted his smoking to cigars. "But he chewed 'em as much as he smoked," recalled grandson Keehn. "But he did smoke. He smoked black, crooked Cuban cigars, terrible looking. I don't know if he ever quit, seems to me he always did."[17]

During the 1923 World Series Jimmy Carroll, brother of Broadway producer Earl Carroll, invited a number of baseball people to see the "Earl Carroll Vanities," a particularly risqué show for the time. Kenesaw and Winifred went along, and Landis was no worse the wear for comedian Joe Cook's jibes regarding the controversial calling of Game Two in the 1922 Series, but Mrs. Landis had her problems with the chorus girls. "Well, Joe Cook certainly was very funny," she commented, "but I must say I would have preferred it if the young ladies had worn more underwear."

The Judge had his own thoughts. "Bully! Bully!" he exclaimed, "Wouldn't have missed it for anything." Then in his very best stage whisper, he confided to the rest of the party, "They had enough clothes on for me."[18]

Kenesaw's relationship with Winifred seemed to be a strong one. "Deeply attached to his wife," was the way Keehn Landis described his grandfather. But in some ways they were an odd couple. She, a Democrat, born to very comfortable circumstances. He, a Republican, who had to claw his way up in the world. He comported himself as the Hoosier rube and courted the favor of the masses. She dressed to the nines and limited her socializing to the most proper of clubs. "To us nephews and nieces Winifred was just very loving and gracious," recalled nephew Lincoln Landis, "but we could tell that we were from Logansport, a small town, and we could tell that aunt Winifred was from the city, and she dressed I'm sure in the latest fashion. I had the general impression that she was always very fashionable .... A person of great dignity. She had a presence, yet she was warm."

She was *not* a great cook. In fact, she was not a cook at all. The Landises usually lived in hotels, such as the Chicago Beach Hotel or the elegant Ambassador East, and Winifred *never* cooked, always ordering from room service. "She never even made tea," Keehn recalled. "She always ordered it."

"She gave the impression that she didn't do much housework," adds Lincoln Landis. "Zero."[19]

Though Landis played the rube, he, nonetheless, clearly moved among Chicago's rich and famous. From Walter Gresham to Edwin Uhl to Frank Lowden to Charles Dawes he hobnobbed with those who could advance his career and social status and belonged to such prestigious local entities as the Chicago, Washington, and Mid-Day clubs.[20]

But even more important factors to Landis in choosing his associates than their wealth or influence was where they came from. If you were a Hoosier, Kenesaw Mountain Landis had a soft spot in his heart for you. His circle of close friends included a number of fellow former Indianans, including *Chicago Tribune* cartoonist John T. McCutcheon, McCutcheon's sometime collaborator humorist George Ade, and stockbroker Orson C. "Ort" Wells. Landis' grandchildren knew Wells as "Uncle Ort." When he died in December 1939, Ort Wells left Landis $50,000 of his multi-million dollar estate.[21][22]

Wells was known as "Circumnavigation" Wells for his predilection for traveling. Supposedly, the parents of movie *wunderkind* Orson Welles had met Ade and Wells on a Caribbean voyage just before his birth and decided to name him for Wells.

Wells and Ade were noteworthy in another aspect. Author Simon Callow characterized them as homosexual lovers who often traveled together. Nonetheless, they maintained a certain discretion about their relationship, and that discretion may explain Landis' tolerance of their sexual preference.[23]

Landis spent part of each summer and fall at a camp he owned at Burt Lake in the far-northern reaches of Michigan's lower peninsula. As in Chicago, at Burt Lake Landis surrounded himself with fellow Hoosiers.[24] Sometime around 1905 the Landises had first visited the area at the invitation of federal judge Albert B. Anderson of Indianapolis. They enjoyed the area so much ("Dad and Mom fell in love with the place," noted daughter Susanne) that after completing their stay at the Anderson cottage they moved down the road into the local hotel, the Buckeye House, for a few more weeks. For between $10.50 and $12.00 per week a family could have a room, maid service, and all meals at the Buckeye.

The following year the Landises rented a nearby cabin, but the next year they bought their own lot and began constructing a cottage.[25] The first thing built, however, was not the cottage. It was a boat house, and the family lived there all summer. Not until the following year was their summer home constructed.

Nonetheless, the Landises, like other Burt Lake cottagers, continued taking meals at the Buckeye House, enjoying its large helpings and complimentary sugar cookies—and dodging its cad flies. Not until Susanne's son William was born in 1921, and the Landises had added on to their cottage, did the family cease eating at the hotel.

The Squire exhibited an unexpected facility on Burt Lake's often frigid waters. "He was very skilled in boatmanship," recollected Lincoln Landis, "but [Reed and Susanne] were terrified with the idea that he would drive a car."

There was not much else to do at Burt Lake besides boating, fishing, and hiking, but its summer residents professed not to mind. "Well, it's this…" theorized Judge Anderson, "The Profs came because the fish were obliging. The food at the Buckeye was tolerable and firewood was free for picking up. But most of us came just to sit and think and some of us just came to sit." The fishing was good, with pickerel, walleye, perch, and bass plentiful.

"I never saw anything easier to look at," the Squire wrote regarding Burt Lake after spending eight or nine days there in the summer of 1943.

Talking politics was a good part of Burt Lake's charms. "I loved to listen to the men talk —Judge Anderson, Judge Landis [and two or three others] . . . ," recalled a woman who had eavesdropped while a girl. "We were fascinated by the male conversation—sometimes they went out to the middle of the lake to 'cuss out' the government but the things they said on dry land were fascinating enough."

The Buckeye House's food may have been tolerable, but Kenesaw had his doubts about its coffee. One day he came tromping into the Buckeye's dining room, wielding a steaming pot of coffee. Stopping in front of his family's table he spoke loud enough for all to hear: "I've drunk that black poison of Laura's [the cook] for the last time. Now I'll have my own." Turning to Winifred, he exclaimed without warning, "And another thing madam, don't criticize my clothes." With that he lifted up his galluses to reveal his trousers were held up by four large safety pins. His wife laughed along with the rest of the diners. But Reed and Susanne were painfully embarrassed.[26]

This was not the only time Landis dressed particularly shabbily on vacation. Once he traveled to the nearby town of Petoskey and while there visited a men's store. A clerk took one look and mistaking him for a beggar ordered him out of the place. That was fine with the Squire, and he promptly headed for the street.

By now the shop's proprietor had seen how his help had tossed one of America's most famous celebrities out of his establishment. He rushed outside to smother the Squire with apologies and welcome him back into his stove.

Landis' sartorial shabbiness was not restricted to vacations. He bought good clothes but then simply wore the hell out of them. "He would just grab a hat with his fist and jam it on his head," noted Lincoln Landis. "My father had the same habit. They liked to wear hats but didn't particularly care what they looked like once they were on their heads."[27]

Dishabille was not restricted merely to Landis' wardrobe. A visit to Landis' chambers might not just reveal Reed Landis' now-famous airplane propeller and the Judge's perpetually cluttered desktop, but also a number of mementos designed to either reveal the Landis character or totally confuse visitors.

Atop his desk was a rusted cannonball, which upon further examination proved to be a shell of Civil War vintage. "This shell," Landis would explain, "was found on Kennesaw Mountain in Georgia . . . A few years ago, three Georgians were walking along Kennesaw Mountain one Sunday afternoon and they came across this shell. It had been washed out by the rains of fifty years. They sent it to me."

That was perhaps the most straightforward object in the room. On one wall hung an immense muskellunge—which one might surmise the Judge had caught.

It was, said Landis, caught by Mrs. Landis.

"We were fishing in Wisconsin," Landis once informed the *Detroit News*'s H. D. Salsinger. "We had the baby with us. Mrs. Landis was holding the baby asleep on her lap, while fishing. There was a sudden jerk on the line. It awoke the baby. She called and asked me to take the line. You know how it is when you try to pull in some other person's fish; if it should happen to get away . . . . So I said, 'I'll take the baby and you look after the fish.' I took the baby and she finally landed the fish, a twenty-one-pounder. It was a long, hard struggle, but Mrs. Landis got him."[28]

Salsinger thought Landis had said the 38-inch muskie weighed 26 pounds.

"No," snapped Landis, "It weighed twenty-one pounds. A twenty-one pound fish is large enough, as you see."[29]

Landis regarded much of organized religion as a fish story. "Some considered him an atheist,"[30] J. G. Taylor Spink noted, and his was not alone in this observation.[31]

But such a characterization would be an oversimplification. "He was not in the traditional sense religious," nephew Lincoln observed. "However—and I find this one of the strong points that I'm going to make—he had reverence for the Almighty and he would frequently take liberties speaking about God, the Almighty or the 'Big Feller.' But in a way, he had, as I read him, he showed respect and reverence. My father I would say may have had a very similar reverence. Again, my father never went to church to my knowledge but he was quite a speaker, an orator, and he was quite often moved to speak about God the Almighty. He had a reverence but it was certainly never expressed in any outward fashion, and Kenesaw was certainly not to do that either."[32]

Skeptic that he was, the Squire could be surprisingly sensitive to the religious feelings of others. When his former court clerk Joseph O'Sullivan's wife died in the summer of 1943, he wrote a highly respectful letter to O'Sullivan's parish priest purchasing "high masses for her, one at an early date and others annually on the anniversary of her death:

> If, as I understand, you send a card to Mr. O'Sullivan, I hope you can arrange it so that a card will be sent to him preceding each mass. If any announcement of these masses is made from the pulpit, please just say they are at the request of a friend.[33]

In his scrapbook, Landis pasted a typewritten poem that may have given some clue to his religious feelings:

MY CREED

I think that many a soul has God within,
Yet knows no church nor creed, no word of prayer,
No law of life save that which seems most fair
And true and just, and helpful to its kin
And kind; and holds that act alone as sin
That lays upon another soul its share

Of human pain, or sorrow, or of care,
Or plants a doubt where faith has ever been.
The heart that seeks with zealous joy the best
In every heart it meets, the way
Has found to make its own condition blessed.
To love God is to strive through life's short day
To comfort grief, to give the weary rest.
To hope and love—that, surely, is to pray.

- Alice Stead Binney[34]

The Squire was a voluminous reader. It was perhaps his favorite indoor recreation. "No hobbies that I know of," he wrote to Henry Pringle in November 1926, "as to books, biography, and plays, mystery."[35]

"He had standing orders at all the bookstores because he just read constantly," recalled granddaughter Nancy, "The books were always piled up next to his bed, and he read at night, you see, a lot. He just didn't sleep a lot."[36]

The Judge was a strong family man and fiercely loyal, sometimes too loyal. When Reed and his wife, Marion Shipman Keehn,[37] divorced in 1942, Landis turned with some vehemence on his ex-daughter-in-law, blaming her for holding Reed's business career back. The Judge's attitude helped drive a wedge not only between her and Landis but between him and his grandchildren.

"You see, Buzzie [Keehn Landis' grandson] had one thing he used to say about our grandparents," reminisced Nancy Landis Smith Lucas. "One was the Old Testament, and the other grandfather was the New Testament. One grandfather was fierce; the other grandfather was loving kindness. And we had both kinds of grandfathers, really. We were very close to the other grandparents."

"It was real fierce there, but I call it justice and righteous wrath," explained Keehn. "He could turn it on when he had to. He did when I was at the [1932 World Series] game and I was harassing the umpires. He turned it on, then he could turn it off. I'm sure it was the same way in court. He could make you quake in court. Some lawyers were afraid to appear before him. He could be fierce, but it was a tool in his bag of tricks to accomplish a purpose. I never saw him, I never even heard of him, losing control, losing his temper. Maybe he did, but I never heard of it or saw it."[38]

Yet Landis could worry about his grandchildren, particularly that they could be used to settle old—or even new—scores against him. "We were not to be conspicuous," recalled granddaughter Cathy. "We were only told not to go off in cars with people," added her sister Nancy. "They were never sure that somebody he put in the can or something would retaliate, with some kidnappings."[39][40]

Landis was highly supportive of his brothers' families. "He was an important part of our lives," recollected Frederick's son Lincoln. "I don't know how much he realized that. I was twelve when my father died. He was, of course, the younger brother of Kenesaw. That must have been quite a shocker to Kenesaw. He was very kind to my mother in years following that. He displayed an interest in how we were doing. He was always very encouraging to her and she responded and thought that he was a rather marvelous individual, very warm and very loyal and helpful."[41]

At times his interest extended to financial matters. In 1928 his namesake, Frederick's son Kenesaw M. Landis II, entered his senior year at Columbia and wrote "Uncle Squire" for a $1,000 loan. "Sure," Landis instantly wrote back in his tersest manner, "And it is not a loan."[42]

In 1923 former *New York Mail* sports editor Warren W. Brown moved to Chicago, assuming the same post with the local *Herald-Examiner*. One day shortly thereafter he looked up from his desk to see a tiny but fierce figure advancing upon him.

"My name is Landis," the Commissioner thought to announce.

Brown, of course, knew that, nodded nervously and wished to know the nature of the visit.

"I was in New York a few days ago," he explained. "I met up with one of your confraternity who used to work here and, as I was given to understand, drank himself out of his job. He has pulled himself together. I want to help him. I want to send him some money. I don't want him to know, in my lifetime, that it came from me. I will leave it to your good judgment how best to get it to him."

Brown protested that Landis should not place such confidence—not to mention responsibility—in a man he was meeting for the very first time.

"Never mind that," Landis ordered. "Just remember if he ever finds out the money came from me, there'll be the greatest gut-letting this community has known since there were Indians around Fort Dearborn [in Illinois]. And they'll be your guts. Good day, sir."

With that he turned toward the door, dropped the pretense of his fierce mein, twirled his cane, and grinned as wide as he could.

Brown became a great admirer of Landis, one who felt that his bluster was coldly calculated but warmly motivated. "I knew," he later wrote, "that he acted seldom, if at all, upon impulse. For all his theatrical mannerisms, no kindlier soul and no more sincere person has ever found his way into baseball."[43]

But while Landis may have been generous to some, he had his limits, and those limits sometimes involved lending money to strangers.

In October 1940 Landis bitterly complained to one such alms seeker:

> I have just received your letter of October 7. I wish I could send you that money, but I can't. They got me skinned clean down to the bone. I should be able to retire and live in a little decent comfort because I have been at work for sixty-four years, but the human race appears to have gotten together and agreed that this is not for me, that my job is to be played for a sucker by the aforementioned human race and the millions and billions that compose it. Preachers give me hell because I won't rebuild their churches after God Almighty has stricken them with lightning and burned them up because of their no accountness. I congratulate you upon evidently being in a situation where at least you are not made the kind of a target I'm talking about. . . . I wish I could do it, but I can't.[44]

He seemed to be in a particularly foul mood that month. The day before he had written to a poor woman asking the Squire to aid her church: "In view of the competition among churches to get money from non-members, I suggest these church organizations get together and thereby not only reduce the overhead but probably do a better job flogging the devil. This is only a suggestion."[45]

Yet, despite this temporary bout of misogyny, he continued lending money to strangers. In early 1943 he fell for the story of a Canadian who wished to visit his son in New Jersey before going off to fight overseas and lent him a considerable sum for that purpose.

Instead, Landis' beneficiary took a defense plant job and promised to repay the loan at the rate of $25 per month. Four months passed, and the Judge received nothing in the mail. Patience at an end, Landis took time to write him. "I am reminding you of this," he concluded sarcastically, "not on the theory that you have forgotten it or overlooked it, but that for some reason you have just concluded not to pay the money back, else you would have written me a statement before this."[46]

Landis may have loved Chicago, but even when he was not at Burt Lake he spent a lot of time away from the Windy City, with the commissionership providing him with an excuse to flee to Florida for spring training each year. His commissioner's salary also enabled him to spend winters in Arizona. His usual haunt was the San Marcos Hotel in Chandler, Arizona, where he would rent one of the bungalows adjacent the hotel's main structure. The San Marcos was not for those on a strict budget. The Spanish colonial-style resort was winter home to a host of other celebrities, including Gene Tunney, Herbert Hoover, John Masefield, Margaret Sanger, and Gloria Swanson. Frank Lowden even announced his abortive 1928 presidential bid from the San Marcos. The hotel lured visitors not only with arid Arizona's first grass golf course but with polo, sunken gardens, a shopping arcade, and formal teas.[47]

The Squire had come a long way from Logansport.

Another perk awaited Landis at the San Marcos—nearby fields of alfalfa. For some reason he was fascinated by the crop and even kept a photo of an alfalfa field on the wall of his commissioner's office. "There, before you," he would explain, "you see the finest photograph ever taken of alfalfa. You see how they got it—dug a trench until they got below the roots. Notice those roots, longer than the alfalfa, roots thrust straight down, deep into the earth. That picture explains why alfalfa can be grown in arid places where people believe no vegetation can survive. The roots are long enough to get between the barren layers."

Just after assuming the commissionership Landis even confided: "Some day I am going to have an alfalfa farm.

"I am going to have acres and acres of alfalfa. But we will have to clear up this base ball tangle first. After that we can get into the alfalfa business."[48]

Landis' tastes in flora were distinctly unorthodox. Once while visiting his brother John in Cincinnati he treated another reporter to a lecture on dandelions.

"Dandelions," he snapped as he inserted one into the button hole of his salt-and-pepper cutaway coat, "I think they are pretty. To think that the rich employ a small army of men to root them up. Why, if they didn't want to grow so badly that they do it all by themselves, the same rich folks would pay thousands of dollars setting them out in their yards."[49]

To most observers there did not seem to be a private Landis. Babe Ruth may indeed have been the "most photographed man in America" but Landis was a close second and probably enjoyed it more—even if he didn't look it.

His appetite for the limelight was hardly a secret, as witnessed by this 1927 poem:

> Ah, there, Jedge. Just hold that pose
> 'Till camera men go to it.
> Classy poser, goodness knows—
> Thanks! We knew you'd do it.
> Seems to us you've missed a bet.
> Say, you'd simply kill 'em
> If in movies you would get
> And bust out in film.
>
> Kinda tough on others, true,
> 'Course they'd all grow leary
> What would Conrad Nagle do,
> Will Hays, and Wallace Beery?
>
> Watch the birdie! We've a hunch
> You're right in your glory!
> Pep and vigor, vim and punch—
> What a repertory![50]

# CHAPTER 25

# "YOU FELLOWS SAY
# I AM RESPONSIBLE"

Kenesaw Landis' America was largely segregated. Most schools, most neighborhoods, and the entire United States Army were separated either *de facto* or *de jure* by race.

So was America's national pastime.

The game had once been integrated. In the 19th century Organized Baseball had featured literally dozens of blacks. Two of them, catcher Moses Fleetwood Walker and his brother Weldy, had even performed briefly at the major league level—with Toledo of the American Association in 1884. But the Walkers were hardly welcomed with open arms. "Walker," noted pitcher Tony Mullane, "was the best catcher I ever worked with, but I disliked a Negro and whenever I had to pitch to him I used to pitch anything I wanted without looking at his signals."

The Walker brothers, however, would be the last black major leaguers for nearly three quarters of a century. In the minors, African-Americans remained but endured fierce hostility. Cap Anson's Chicago White Stockings threatened to walk away from an exhibition with the International League's Newark team if Newark's star pitcher, a black named George Washington Stovey, played. Newark benched Stovey. Frank Grant, described as "the greatest Negro baseball player of the 19th century," found his Buffalo teammates refusing to sit with him for a team picture. He and fellow black Bud Fowler had to fashion primitive shinguards to protect them from hostile white baserunners. By the turn of the century, blacks had disappeared from Organized Baseball.[1]

They had vanished, but racist attitudes remained. In 1913 Ban Johnson forbade barnstorming by American League teams. The reason: race. "We want no makeshift club calling themselves the Athletics to go to Cuba to be beaten by colored teams." In 1914 when the

Browns refused to grant first baseman George Stovall his release, he fumed, "No white man ought to bartered like a broken down plow horse." Brooklyn owner Charles Ebbets derided Baltimore as a prospective big league city because "it had too many colored population to start. They are a cheap population when it gets down to paying their money at the gate." Southern minor league ballparks were uniformly segregated. St. Louis' Sportsman's Park retained Jim Crow seating until May 1944.[2]

Such was the situation Landis inherited in December 1920.

So much of the modern consideration of Landis revolves around the question of his responsibility for maintaining that situation. Landis was the dictator of baseball, numerous critics contend. While he lived he stood in the way of the game's integration. It is no coincidence, none at all, they argue, that the barriers tumbled so soon after his November 1944 death.

As the decades have progressed Landis has bore an increasingly greater share of the burden for the national pastime's Jim Crow status. The allegations have continued to grow—often with little consideration for accuracy. With no evidence, Ken Sobol in *Babe Ruth & The American Dream* called him "openly biased" against "nonwhites."[3] James Bankes in *The Pittsburgh Crawfords* similarly—and inaccurately—stated that he "made little effort to disguise his racial prejudice during his twenty-five years in office" and even mistakenly termed him as a "man of the South." Another historian termed the midwestern Landis a "hard-bitten Carolinian." One highly respected and knowledgeable author claimed that Landis pronounced heavyweight champion Jack Johnson guilty of white slavery when he married a white woman. Actually he had merely arraigned him on violating the Mann Act.[4] Janet Bruce in her otherwise excellent *The Kansas City Monarchs* claimed that Landis had "banned" the 1946 Paige/Feller barnstorming tour until the World Series had concluded. Landis had been dead for nearly two years.[5]

What share of the responsibility for baseball's Jim Crow status *did* Landis bear? What were his attitudes on race and how did he handle racial matters—both as arbiter of baseball and on the federal bench? The answers may never be really known, but the picture of Landis as an "openly biased" individual who almost single-handedly blocked baseball's integration clearly distorts the actual events, America's racial attitudes, and perhaps even the man himself. Landis certainly bears some responsibility for baseball's segregation.

However, to imply that it was he—and he alone—who created or prolonged the situation whitewashes the attitudes and actions of much, if not most, of baseball's establishment.

The Judge's political ideology was formed by the liberal Republicanism that developed into Theodore Roosevelt's progressivism. But just as Landis' (and Roosevelt's) World War I jingoism seems at variance with a liberal philosophy, so do many progressives' attitudes towards race. Seeing the politics of a hundred years ago through late 20th century eyes is not always a productive process.

Economic liberals were often among the most illiberal on racial issues. Former Populist presidential candidate Tom Watson was violently anti-black, anti-Semitic and anti-Catholic and wrote that "Lynch law is a good sign. It shows that a sense of justice lives among the people." William Jennings Bryan openly supported racial separation. Woodrow Wilson segregated what black federal employees he did not fire and publicly praised D. W. Griffith's *The Birth of a Nation*. A more middle-class progressive such as William Allen White wrote of America's "race life" and the need for protection of "clean Aryan blood."

Of course, not only progressives expressed such sentiments. Socialist Victor L. Berger was particularly virulent on the racial issue, showing little sympathy and often open hostility toward blacks. In the May 31, 1902, issue of his *Social Democratic Herald*, Berger wrote, "There can be no doubt that the negroes and mulattoes constitute a lower race—and that the Caucasians and indeed the Mongolians have the start on them in civilization by many thousand years—so that negroes will find it difficult to overtake them. . . . free contact with the whites has led to the further degradation of the negro." [6]

Racism was indeed pervasive among whites in general. But as historian George Mowry noted "neither conservative nor radical was as specific in his racism as the reformer." [7]

Yet to say with confidence to what extent Landis shared the racism of his day is difficult. We possess at best some highly fragmentary evidence.

In the highly charged racial atmosphere of the late 19th century, Landis' mentor, Walter Q. Gresham, could be categorized as moderate to liberal,[8] described in one contemporary account as "opposed to unlimited Negro suffrage [but] demanded equal protection for the Negro under the law." In this latter regard he was highly influential in the Cleveland administration in preventing southerners from repealing Reconstruction Era civil rights statutes.[9]

The Republican Party Kenesaw Landis grew up in was by the standards of the day relatively tolerant on matters of race. Still living in the shadows of the Civil War, it was an age in which blacks voted Republican, and Democrats did what they could—which in the South was considerable—to disenfranchise freedmen. Blacks may not have gotten much from the Grand Old Party beyond oratory and a little patronage, but it was more than they received from the opposition.

The Landis family was probably typical of late 19th-century and early 20th-century Republicans—particularly when it came to campaign oratory. At a 1901 Washington Day dinner in Peoria, Kenesaw managed to stray from Washington to Illinois' Lincoln and to offer his own comments on racial matters. Lincoln, the Squire proclaimed, had not merely "learned the Union could not exist 'half slave, half free,' he also knew that in fair proportion as men enslave their fellowmen, they themselves would be weighed down in the march of progress as with a millstone hung about their necks."[10]

Racial themes were often present in Frederick Landis' stump speeches—and his slant was similarly liberal. We have seen how the great Booker T. Washington was in attendance when Frederick first unleashed his oratorical skills and moved the black leader to tears. Elected to Congress Frederick held to his views. After a series of violent anti-black outbursts in Indiana, not only did Landis bluntly inform a campfire gathering that the state now stood in "shame and tears" over "this monstrous outrage," he went further (egregiously mixing metaphors, however): "Contemplate the shocking, sickening story of the lash [of slavery] and you will agree with me that from the seed that has been sown, we have not reaped the whirlwind; only the summer breeze.

"All discussion worth the while must proceed from the assumption: The colored man is here to stay."[11]

After Walter Gresham, Kenesaw Landis' second political hero was the Rough Rider, Theodore Roosevelt, whose record on racial issues was decidedly mixed. TR opposed lynching, had drawn a firestorm of criticism when he invited Booker T. Washington to the White House (and determined never to invite a black again) and had appointed blacks outside the South to federal patronage positions. Yet TR also outraged the black community by his actions in the infamous Brownsville affair of August 1906, by cashiering virtually three entire companies of black infantrymen including six Medal of Honor winners.[12] And when William Howard Taft's renomination resulted in part from the manipulation of the black rotten-borough vote in the South (i.e. blacks were far more represented in the GOP convention than their voting strength could actual justify), Roosevelt noted bitterly that these black Taft delegates, "represent[ed] nothing but their own greed for money or office" and were "overwhelmingly antiprogressive." A bitter TR determined he would not build up the Progressive Party "by appealing to the negroes or to the men in the past who have derived their sole standing from leading and manipulating the negroes" and barred southern blacks from serving as Progressive Party delegates. Blacks, led by Booker T. Washington, responded by deserting Roosevelt in droves.[13]

In 1917 Landis found himself nearly dragged into one of America's most violent racial incidents. Trouble had slowly been brewing in East St. Louis, Illinois. From 1900 the number of blacks there had doubled as opportunities opened in the aluminum and packing industries. Many local whites feared blacks would take their jobs. Political apprehensions soon joined the economic and social ones. In 1916 local Democrats charged Republicans with bringing blacks up from the South ("colonizing") to swing local elections. President Wilson gave credence to these unlikely charges when he ordered the federal government to investigate.

Following a union meeting on May 28, 1917, a rumor circulated that a black man had shot a white man during a holdup. Local whites rampaged, and Governor Lowden dispatched the National Guard. Lowden erred, however, by withdrawing troops too quickly, and a bloodbath resulted. Accounts of the violence vary widely, but at least eight whites (including two police officers) and 39 blacks died. A white reporter witnessed six black corpses at one street corner, and remarked, "I think every one I saw killed had both hands above his head begging for mercy." A two-year-old African-American child was shot and then thrown into a burning building.[14]

Lowden now ordered 12 companies of state militia back into East St. Louis, but they were ineffective and seemed to favor the rioting whites. In response he personally led a cavalry troop and seven infantry companies back to the city.

Some thought that federal law had been violated, specifically Section Nineteen of the United States Penal code and the 1866 Civil Rights Act. United States Attorney Karch believed that "if evidence can be procured showing that either the State, the county, or the municipal authorities failed to perform the duties required of them

. . . in relation to these people because they were Negroes, there is a basis for [federal] grand jury investigation . . . "

Karch also believed Kenesaw Mountain Landis was the man to head that investigation. So did a host of prominent Illinois politicians.

Karch, however, had no authority on his own to commence such activity. That was up to President Wilson and Attorney General Thomas W. Gregory. Both were southern-born and in no mood to look into civil rights violations.

Karch himself, soon began to backtrack. In a confidential letter to Gregory, he noted that former House Speaker "Uncle Joe" Cannon detested Landis and had vowed the jurist would never again oversee a case in that congressional district.

Gregory was all too eager to rule that no federal jurisdiction existed, and Landis—despite earlier private musings to the contrary—was soon echoing that opinion.[15]

In the following decade, the Landis family showed itself to be no friend of the resurgent Ku Klux Klan. The last two surviving Landis brothers shared the Klan's Prohibitionist sentiments, but there was no way they could countenance its vigilantism—either to enforce the Volstead Act, harass blacks, Catholics, and Jews, or to horsewhip those offending the Invisible Empire's version of sexual morality. In 1928, when Frederick sought the Republican nomination for governor of Indiana ("LANDIS *in May Will* LAND US *in November*"), he spoke out harshly against politicians associated with powerful Indiana Klan leader David C. "Steve" Stephenson. Indiana was a KKK stronghold. A 100,000 Klansmen had once gathered in Kokomo, and the Invisible Empire had briefly ruled state government. In 1922 when Frederick Landis' mentor, Albert Beveridge, angered the Klan, it ended his comeback bid and helped elect Democrat Samuel M. Ralston to the United States Senate. A sexual scandal brought "Steve" Stephenson down in 1925, but the Klansmen remained influential in the state and Frederick continued to battle them. At Indianapolis in 1928 Frederick had his 18-year-old son Kenesaw II denounce Klan politicians thusly: "We can not elect any man who was ever selected by Steve to help put his program of piracy across upon the people of Indiana."[16]

The depth of Frederick Landis' opposition to the Klan[17] may best be gauged by the recollections of his son Lincoln. "In 1934 he ran for Congress," Lincoln noted, "and in campaigning during that summer he regularly carried a gun in the car. Sometimes he would have an officer of the law accompany him but other times I think he drove by himself and had the gun on the floor of the car because of Klan-related concerns that he had... He was known as very intolerant of the Klan and its activities ... I have no reason to think that Kenesaw's attitudes would have been any different."[18]

But while Kenesaw echoed Frederick's views on the Klan, he did not always follow his brother's willingness to openly attack it. Either out of fear or out of strategy (i.e., let the KKK's own outrages sink it) the Judge's reticence was hardly unique. From President Coolidge to the 1924 Democratic convention, many politicians drew back from attacking the Klan by name. In April 1922 an old friend from the Cleveland administration, the *Dallas News'* Colonel William Greene Sterrett, wired Kenesaw, begging him to "say what you think" about the Klan. Landis, however, claimed that "several rather sensible public officials, who are going to the mat with the Klan," advised him not to.[19]

Yet he would not always be so careful. In the midst of one ornery civics lesson-style speech, Landis paused for what the *Chicago Tribune* called "a characteristic crack at the Ku Klux Klan": "There are a good many of those who call themselves 'one hundred percent American' among those who fail to vote on election day. To my way of thinking, theirs is the cheapest, shabbiest, shoddiest kind of Americanism we have in this country."[20]

On assuming the commissionership, Landis enjoyed a fairly liberal reputation on the race issue. In 1922 one Chicago columnist wrote of him:

> Negroes and poor white people of Chicago ought to put his picture on walls where children can look at that face of understanding. Poor whites he judged easily because of their condition; negroes he judged mercifully because he understood.
>
> "I will stand with God and time; they alone are the Negro's friends," he would say.[21]

Respect for Landis ran so high in Chicago's black community that when congressional forces leveled impeachment charges against him for retaining his judgeship after becoming baseball's czar, the black *Chicago Advocate* editorialized:

> The Chicago Advocate, speaking for the entire race, wishes to

extend to Judge Landis their appreciation for his fair and impartial justice, handed out regardless of color or creed, paying no attention to such men as Senator Dial of North [sic, South] Carolina. . .

We the Negroes of this portion of the country, are thoroughly satisfied with the decision[s] of Judge Landis, and have no fault whatever to find with them. All of the Negroes ever convicted by him have been proven guilty beyond all reasonable doubts.[22]

Another black paper, the *Chicago Defender*, while saying "it is not our purpose to defend Judge Landis; he needs no defense at our hands," left no doubt where it stood in the controversy, flaying Dial for conflict of interest and for representing a segregationist state. "To say the least," it argued, "there is a cloud upon Senator Dial's right to a seat in the Senate."[23]

The Judge evidently was also more familiar with black baseball than the average white fan. Shortly after Landis became commissioner, Negro Leagues organizer Rube Foster visited him in order to gain permission to use big league ballparks. Landis called out, "Why I know you: You're Rube Foster."[24]

Many blacks even dared hope that Landis would end baseball's Jim Crow status. The *Baltimore Afro-American*, for example, editorialized that he was "eminently fair and if it were left to him, there would be colored major league baseball clubs tomorrow." Shortly after becoming commissioner, Landis received a letter on the subject from Billy Matthews, a black former Assistant U.S. Attorney and one-time star Harvard shortstop, begging him to do something:

> You will note that every other class of people are counted eligible to play in the big leagues. Why keep the Negro out if he can play the same grade of baseball demanded of the other groups? Are the big leagues more exclusive than the best colleges and athletic clubs in the land? Does an attitude on the part of the National Commission square with your plea of injustice to Afro-Americans? If baseball leaders would adopt the open door policy toward the Negro player, don't you think it would be another guarantee on their part that baseball in the future is to be on the level?[25]

There is no record of any Landis response.

A oft-repeated criticism of Landis involves the allegation that he banned white teams from barnstorming against Negro League teams.

As persistent as this claim, is, however, it is extremely difficult to find evidence as to when Landis implemented the ban. Obviously, barnstorming limitations were something he had to deal with regardless of racial issues, as he had in facing off against Babe Ruth in October 1921. Interestingly enough, that same month, at St. Louis' Sportsman's Park, Cardinals third baseman Milt Stock had scheduled an exhibition series against the Negro National League's St. Louis Giants. Local papers derided the exhibition as "bad stuff" and "the grand African show." Attendance (segregated, with whites on the third-base side and blacks on the first-base side) for a Sunday doubleheader was poor, and Browns business manager Bob Quinn pulled the plug on the series. Landis, however, appears to have played no part in the Browns' decision.[26]

Yet it remains extremely murky as to exactly when—if ever—Landis clamped down fully on integrated play. In the 1920s Rube Foster's Chicago American Giants were playing an all-star team headed by Harry Heilman.[27] One day Foster received a call from Heilman, informing them that the series was canceled; Judge Landis had ordered it stopped. Foster supposedly confronted Landis face-to-face. "The very idea, Judge, that you can cancel this game," he exclaimed. "This is a chance that we have every year to play against your fellows, make a little extra money. Why do you do this?"

Landis responded: "Mr. Foster, when you beat our teams it gives us a black eye."[28]

James A. Riley, perhaps the most knowledgeable of Negro Leagues historians, indicates that Landis' action was more restricted; that is, on any given barnstorming outfit Landis limited the number of players from any one major league team, thus preventing the embarrassment of having a "big league" team beaten by a squad of Negro Leaguers.

It is alleged that in 1922 after the black Philadelphia Hilldales had played the Detroit Tigers to a standstill and swept the St. Louis Browns, 3-0, Landis barred major league clubs from barnstorming as units. In the future, they would have to bill themselves as All-Stars.[29]

Former Hilldales shortstop Paul "Jake" Stephens provided a variation on that theme—that after the Hilldales had beaten the Philadelphia A's three straight times, "that's when Judge Landis made a ruling that never would a big league club play a negro baseball club intact again." However, Cool Papa Bell told James Bankes that Landis had clamped down after *his* St. Louis Stars had beaten the Tigers two out of three in 1922.[30]

Others have also alleged that Landis went further than that. Negro Leaguer Ernest "Willie" Powell charged that after the Chicago American Giants beat the Babe Ruth All-Stars in six out of seven contests "the Commissioner broke that up, cut down on the number of games they could play us." Later in the same interview he claimed that after playing Tris Speaker's team in 1925 "Landis made them cut it out."[31]

Negro Leaguer Gene Benson fancifully claimed that after Satchel Paige's club had toured with Bob Feller's, "Landis stopped us from playing them because we were winning too many games." Willie Wells and "Sug" Cornelius (who indicated Landis flew to California to personally clamp down) put the date of Landis' ban on interracial barnstorming as 1935.[32 33]

Obviously, Landis could not have stopped integrated barnstorming in all these cases. He could not have logically halted a practice virtually year after year. In fact, as late as the spring of both 1941 and 1942 Landis did not interfere when the Dodgers, training in Cuba, played against mixed-race Cuban teams.[34] In 1941 Brooklyn split four games against such competition. It was no secret that the Cuban teams featured black players. In March 1942 the *Daily Worker* headlined, "Dodgers Play Cuban-Negro Stars Today."

In 1942, however, we do have solid evidence of the Judge banning interracial play, prohibiting in-season games at major league parks (see below). His stated rationale: these games were outdrawing big league games in the same cities.[35 36]

During the 1938 season the racial issue arose in a most unexpected way. Landis dealt with it quickly and forcefully.

Yankee outfielder Jake Powell was a ballplayer of fair talents, but his violent and bigoted nature overshadowed his accomplishments on the diamond. He traded punches with the Senators' Joe Kuhel and the Red Sox' Joe Cronin, and once crashed into Hank Greenberg at first base and broke his wrist. Powell offered no apology, and many suspected him of anti-Semitism.[37]

Before a Yankee game at Comiskey Park on July 29, 1938, White Sox radio announcer Bob Elson interviewed Powell over a live mike.[38 39]

When Elson asked Powell what he did in the off-season, he responded, "I'm a cop in southern Illinois and I get a lot of pleasure beating up niggers and then throwing them in jail." A shocked Elson halted the interview. Back at the station an announcer nervously explained that it was not responsible for guests' remarks.

Chicago's large black community (living largely in the area near Comiskey Park) was rightfully incensed. The followed morning they bombarded Landis' office with protests, and before that afternoon's contest a community delegation presented umpire-in-chief Harry Giesel with a petition demanding that Powell "be asked to apologize and be barred from professional baseball." They went out to state that they would shortly be formally petitioning the Judge to take action.

What they did not know is that Landis already had, summoning Powell and Yankee manager Joe McCarthy to his office for an interrogation. Powell denied making any objectionable comments, later telling reporters, "I don't remember saying anything like that at all, and I certainly would never mean to say anything offensive to the Negroes of Dayton, Chicago or anything else.

"I have some very good friends among the Negroes in Dayton," he added.

But Landis wasn't buying Powell's explanation and issued the following terse statement: "Over the radio in his so-called dugout interview . . . Player Powell made an uncomplimentary reference to a portion of the population. POWELL HAS BEEN SUSPENDED FOR TEN DAYS."[40]

Landis' prompt and forceful action is puzzling on two counts. The first, of course, being his less-than-progressive reputation on racial issues. But the second involves his attitude toward the commissionership. Landis could be perfectly willing to leave most matters to club and league officials. After suspending Babe Ruth for barnstorming violations, he almost gladly left the issue of his assaulting an umpire to Ban Johnson. After Ford Frick took over the National League presidency in 1934, he visited Landis. The phone rang, and the caller clearly wanted Landis to intervene in some matter. Landis exploded, saying that while he was the commissioner, he was "not a personal nursemaid." He pointedly instructed the caller to deal with American League president Will Harridge. Then he turned to Frick and gave him two pieces of advice: "Never go looking for trouble. Let 'em come to you. And don't start bothering me with your own league problems. They're your babies. I've got problems of my own."[41]

Yet in the Powell case Landis—with little prodding from the white press (who virtually ignored the incident)—jumped in feet first. He may have acted because the Yankees themselves seemed disinclined to punish Powell. Joe McCarthy expressed no outrage at all over his player's remarks, passing them off as a "joke" and contending he "sure meant no harm." McCarthy reserved his real wrath for radio announcers, whom he said were always "pester[ing]" players for interviews.[42]

Despite Landis' imposition of a 10-day suspension, black protests against Powell only increased.[43] At Washington's Griffith Stadium he was pelted with soda bottles. Six thousand New York fans submitted a petition demanding that he be banned from the game for life. In response, Powell embarked on a unique pilgrimage of public contrition, going from bar to bar in Harlem, "despite the fact," as Harlem's black paper *The New York Age*, pointed out, "that various groups of Harlemites had said they would beat him up, etc., if they caught him away from the ballpark." Powell's first stop was at the Mimo Club where he met up with a Colonel Hubert Julian, who, impressed by Powell's sincerity (or perhaps by his courage), volunteered to act as his "bodyguard and protector" for his tour. Along the way Powell bought drinks and asked Harlemites for forgiveness.[44]

Until his death, Landis maintained an almost sphinxlike pose on the issue of integration. The Landis who could fulminate on the farm system or the veterans' bonus would not comment on the subject unless backed into a corner.

In the 1920s few persons—black or white—were advocating baseball's integration, but beginning in the 1930s the agitation would increase slowly but surely. In 1931 columnist Westbrook Pegler (an unlikely crusader—he later became notorious for his anti-Semitism and briefly belonged to the John Birch Society) and the *New York Daily News'* Jimmy Powers began lobbying for integration.

Mal Goode, the first black to become a network news correspondent, recounted a 1938 incident directly involving Landis. "The two managing editors of the *Pittsburgh Courier*, the largest black newspaper in the world, met with ... Landis," Goode related. "He said that the time wasn't right for blacks in baseball. 'You do whatever you want,' he told them. In those days, they would say to you, 'Boycott if you want, we don't care.' There weren't that many blacks going to major league games."[45]

Pressure from blacks counted for little in those days. In 1936, however, the Communist *Daily Worker*, whose sports editor was "both a Communist and a Dodger fan," initiated a campaign against baseball's color-bar. In the 1940s white-led unions joined in. At the New York World's Fair in 1940 the New York Trade Union Athletic Association challenged baseball's "Jim Crow" stance. Two years later the Congress of Industrial Organizations (CIO) organized a "Citizens Committee to End Jim Crow in Baseball."

That same year, blacks finally recorded some modest progress: a major league tryout. On March 18, 1942, former UCLA football star Jackie Robinson and Baltimore Elite Giant pitcher Nate Moreland were given a tryout with the White Sox at Pasadena. Chicago manager Jimmy Dykes claimed he had no problem with the idea of integration. " 'Get After Landis, We'd Welcome You,' Sox Manager Tells Negro Stars," the *Daily Worker* headlined, but nothing resulted from the event. [46]

Meanwhile, interracial barnstorming continued. On May 28, 1942 Satchel Paige and the Kansas City Monarchs drew 29,000 at Wrigley Field against the "Dizzy Dean All-Stars," beating them, 3-1. Two days later the two teams drew 22,000 at Griffith Stadium, as the Monarchs again won, this time by a score of 13-3. At Pittsburgh on June 5 Paige (now on loan to the Homestead Grays) beat the Dean All-Stars again, by an 8-1 margin before 22,000 fans—the largest Forbes Field crowd of the season. In response Landis banned a projected July 4 contest. His stated reason: the first two games had outdrawn major league contests.[47]

That same summer the *Daily Worker* ran yet another story demanding major league integration, this time quoting several major leaguers to that effect.[48] The article also quoted Dodger manager Leo Durocher as saying he'd be only too happy to sign a black if he could. "I'll play the colored boys on my team if the big shots give the O.K.," Durocher was quoted as saying. "Hell, I've seen a million good ones." He further charged there was a "grapevine understanding or subterranean rule" in force barring blacks.[49]

On July 15, 1942, an angry Landis summoned Durocher to Chicago for a closed-door meeting. When Durocher emerged, he contended he was misquoted, while Landis protested:

Certain managers in organized baseball have been quoted as saying the reason Negroes are not playing organized baseball is [that the] commissioner would not permit them to do so. Negroes are not barred from organized baseball by the commissioner and never have been in the 21 years I have served. There is no rule in organized baseball prohibiting their participation and never has been to my knowledge. If Durocher, or any other manager, or all of them, want to sign one, or twenty-five, Negro players, it is all right with me. That is the business of the managers and the club owners. The business of the commissioner is to interpret the rules of baseball and enforce them.[50]

Segments of the black press took Landis at his word and reacted with undisguised glee. The *Washington Afro-American* headlined LANDIS CLEARS WAY FOR OWNERS TO HIRE COLORED. The *Pittsburgh Courier* was less definite, asking WAS THE JUDGE JIVING? The *Chicago Defender*'s Fay Young declared his statements "Bosh" and compared him unfavorably to golf's George S. Mays who had forced the $15,000 Tam O'Shanter Open to allow blacks. "Landis," wrote Young, "isn't going to take the 'hell' Mays took because there aren't many George Mayses in the world."[51]

That July Landis found himself visited by the *Daily Worker*'s Conrad Komorowski who endeavored to secure some answers on where Landis actually stood on the subject.

Landis would not cooperate.

Komorowski began the interview by asking the Judge his thoughts on a resolution sent him by an 80,000-member auto workers union. "No comment," came the response to that question and to several that followed it.

"Why do you refuse to comment?" Komorowski finally asked.

"You fellows say I am responsible," Landis cryptically responded.

"Aren't you?"

"You fellows say I am."

"If you are not, why don't you defend yourself?"

The Judge would not even provide even a "no comment" on that one but eventually began to hint that ownership was the responsible party. "Why don't you put them on the spot?" he demanded.[52]

Landis then began to open up slightly, admitting the power of the campaign to open baseball up to blacks and that he keenly felt its pressure. He realized the interview was going badly and that his "no comments" would be read in Harlem and across black America, and that blacks would hold him responsible for their ostracism.

"There is no man living," Landis claimed, "who wants the friendship of the Negro people more than I." Komorowski advanced that Landis could gain their friendship by lifting the racial bar. Once more Landis lamely fell back on "no comment."[53]

The following month, however, saw dramatic evidence of what Landis was hinting at regarding ownership's attitudes.

The *Pittsburgh Courier* had approached Pirates owner Ben Benswager about signing blacks. Benswager virtually echoed Landis, averring there was "no rule of any sort, written or unwritten" against blacks performing in the majors. But then he went further than he probably wished to, saying while he was not opposed to the possibility of black major leaguers, no one had yet "approached" him on the subject. Reports also quoted Benswager as saying he had invited three Negro Leaguers, catcher Roy Campanella, second baseman Sammy T. Hughes, and fireballing righthander Dave Barnhill to Forbes Field for a tryout on August 4.

The *Daily Worker* jumped into the fray once more, wiring the three players that it was, in fact, they who had arranged the audition. On July 30 Benswager denied making any invitation and wrote to *Daily Worker* sports editor Nat Lowe canceling the tryout.[54]

That same day Leo Durocher's boss at Brooklyn, Larry MacPhail, raked Landis over the coals for leaving the door open to blacks. He stormed:

> First, there is no real demand for Negro baseball players.
> Second, how many of the best players in the Negro circuit do you suppose would make the National or American Leagues? Very few.
> Third, why should we raid those circuits and ruin their games?
> Fourth, I have talked with some of the leading Negroes. Ask them what they think of breaking down the custom.
> Judge Landis was not speaking for baseball when he said there is no barrier: there has been an unwritten law tantamount to an agreement between major league clubs on the subject of the racial issue.[55]

*The Sporting News* obviously saw nothing wrong with MacPhail's comments.[56] In its August 6 issue it editorialized on the subject in a piece entitled "No Good from Raising Race Issue."

Members of both the black and the white race, the paper advanced, "prefer to draw their talents from their own ranks and both groups know their own psychology and do not care to run the risk of damaging their own game."

*The Sporting News* condemned "agitators, ever ready to seize an issue that will not redound to their profit and self-aggrandizement." They should stop making "an issue of a question on which both sides would prefer to be left alone."[57]

Oddly enough that summer some Negro League voices echoed those sentiments. Barnstorming in Albany, New York, Satchel Paige contended he wasn't in favor of integrating the game. On August 8 Homestead Grays manager Vic Harris also came out against lowering the color bar. "If they [Organized Baseball] take our best boys," Harris prophesied, "we will be but a hollow shell of what we are today. No, let us build up our own league and . . . then challenge the best white team in the majors and play them."

Not surprisingly heavy criticism greeted both men. Paige had to publicly retract his remarks before taking the mound at that summer's East-West Game, the Negro Leagues's version of the All-Star Game.[58]

During the 1942 season the wolves were gathering at the door of embattled Phillies owner Gerry Nugent. The franchise (the only National League team ever to lose 100 or more games for five straight years) was a disaster. It had dropped 109 games in 1942 and was now $256,000 in debt.

Looking to purchase the woebegone Phils was future major league impresario, Bill Veeck, Jr., then the owner of the minor league Milwaukee Brewers. In his 1962 autobiography *Veeck As In Wreck*, he revealed that part of his plan to revitalize the ailing franchise involved the wholesale stocking of it with Negro League stars.[59]

Somewhere in his travels between Milwaukee and Philadelphia, Veeck, according to his story, stopped off at Chicago to inform Landis of his plans. "Out of long respect" for the Judge, Veeck revealed his plans—including the idea to obliterate baseball's color bar. Landis, wrote Veeck, "wasn't exactly shocked but he wasn't exactly overjoyed either. His first reaction, in fact, was that I was kidding him."[60]

Veeck then boarded the Broadway Limited for Philadelphia. When he arrived, Nugent had a surprise for him—the club had been turned over to the National League. Veeck was aghast, but Nugent held firm. "What are you going to do, sue me?" he jeered.

For once Veeck was nonplussed. "I don't know," was all he could mutter.[61]

Veeck then visited National League president Ford Frick who informed him that the club had already been sold to a syndicate headed by 33-year-old New York lumber dealer William D. Cox. Ironically, Cox was a friend of the man who would eventually integrate the game, Branch Rickey.

That was Veeck's tale, but actual events were somewhat more complicated. In fact, serious doubts exist about Veeck's account.

Frick clearly had desired for Cox to take over the Phillies for some time. He had also planned for ownership to be transferred to Cox and his partners (including Captain G. Herbert Walker, namesake of George Herbert Walker Bush, and also a close friend of Rickey) as quickly as possible. But some snags developed, and soon three other groups were bidding for the club, one of which was led by Grace Kelly's father, Philadelphia contractor John B. "Jack" Kelly, Sr.[62]

We do not know if Veeck remained in the hunt at this point. We do know that Veeck claimed that he had promises of financial backing from two separate sources, the Congress of Industrial Organizations (CIO), which was interested in promoting an integrated team, and Phillies Cigars, which presumably was simply concerned about profits and the advertising possibilities of a team with the same name as their product.

However, a careful reading of Veeck's account reveals that his financial backing was hardly solid. The CIO insisted Veeck always place a "mixed team" on the field, an assurance he was unwilling to provide. The "willingness" of the cigar company to back Veeck could only be described as "potential."

Veeck may or may not have also been working with another group. Eddie Gottleib, a veteran Negro League promoter, one-time secretary of the Negro National League, and officer of the black Philadelphia Stars, and Ike and Dr. Leon Levy, owner of a Philadelphia radio station, also wanted to acquire the Phillies from Nugent. They too were looking to integrate the game, with Gottleib serving as the team's general manager and presumably recruiting black talent for the club.

Author Bruce Kuklick relates a story about Gottleib and Levy, similar to Veeck's. According to Kuklick, Frick was referring to Gottleib, Levy, and their operation when he "made it clear he wanted neither Jews nor blacks in the majors."[63] [64] Frick, however, may also have not wanted underworld figures in the majors. Gottleib's partner in the Stars was Ed Bolden, about whom significant controversy still exists. While Negro Leagues historian James Riley characterizes Bolden as a "gentlemanly . . . postal worker," author Donn Rogosin identifies him as one of "the most powerful black gangsters in the nation."[65]

Yet if the situation did largely transpire as Veeck alleges, questions still remain as to what role—if any—Landis played in the affair—and if he had, why? In the decades that have followed, Landis has taken an increased share of the blame for the incident—but with very little actual evidence.

In *Veeck As In Wreck*, Frick, not Landis, is the target of Veeck's ire. "Word reached me soon enough," wrote Veeck, "that Frick was bragging all over the baseball world—strictly off the record, of course—about how he had stopped me from contaminating the league."[66]

Later, however, Veeck began shifting more and more of the blame to the Judge ("I realize now that it was a mistake to tell him")[67] and even broadly hinted to an unsuspecting *Washington Post* sports columnist that Landis was a southerner: "After all, a man who is named Kenesaw Mountain was not born and raised in the state of Maine." In the years that have followed *Veeck As In Wreck*'s publication, the story became an unquestioned article of baseball history that Landis had acted to prevent Veeck from integrating the game.[68]

Yet when pressed on the matter by author Jules Tygiel, the best Veeck could say of Landis' culpability was "I have no proof of that. I can only surmise." For his part, Tygiel, while positing that Veeck's story had credibility because Veeck "named names, [i.e.,] accusing Ford Frick, who was still commissioner," later expressed serious doubt regarding Veeck's tale. "Most of us," Tygiel noted in August 1996, "who have worked in the field of baseball integration have always naively, and even unprofessionally, taken Veeck at his word although his report was totally unsubstantiated by any supporting evidence."[69] By March 1997 Tygiel was even more skeptical regarding the tale. "I think most people today," he told the *Chicago Tribune*, "believe that [Veeck's story] was never the case."[70]

There is a more puzzling, very basic, question about Veeck's account. If Veeck had indeed planned on hiring the cream of black talent, he did not have to own the Phillies to do it. He could have signed Negro League stars for the American Association's Milwaukee Brew-

ers and once they proved their worth, Veeck could easily have for resold them to major league clubs for huge profits. Yet Veeck's Brewers
never signed one black player. As Veeck himself admitted, "the only
way the Commissioner could bar me from using Negroes would be to
rule, officially and publicly, that they were 'detrimental to baseball.'
With Negroes fighting in the war, such a ruling was unthinkable."[71]

Baseball historian David Jordan has explored the Veeck/Nugent
negotiations in detail and found "many problems" with Veeck's claim.
Jordan discovered that the entire episode started as a false newspaper report that Veeck was interested in buying the Phils. Veeck actually *wasn't* interested, but the account put the idea into his head.
Following the 1942 World Series, Veeck and his right-hand man Rudy
Schaffer met with Nugent. "We talked about his club," Veeck was
quoted in the October 18, 1942, *Milwaukee Journal*, "[Nugent]
quoted some large figures, of course, but that was all." The meeting
"wasn't a productive one," Schaffer revealed to Jordan, basically
because Veeck was not willing to pay Nugent's asking price.
"[Schaffer] and Veeck went back to Milwaukee," noted Jordan, "and
Schaffer knew of no further contacts between Veeck and Nugent."
Jordan also notes that Veeck's October meeting with Nugent does not
fit into the time-frame of November-to-February negotiations that
actually saw the Phillies transferred from Nugent.

"There was no acceptance of an offer by Nugent, and there was
no interference in a Veeck deal by either Landis or Frick," Jordan
concludes. "Veeck, nothing if not a storyteller, seems to have added
these embellishments, sticking in some guys in black hats, simply to
juice up his tale."[72]

Also casting doubt on Veeck's account is surviving correspondence from Veeck to Landis. Writing on May 22, 1944, from "Somewhere in the Pacific" Veeck's handwritten letter contains no
reference to the supposed incident and no hint of acrimony. In fact,
Veeck notes that his Marine Corps experiences are "somewhat different from the last time I saw you, and, I can't say nearly as interesting
or enjoyable." This is not the sort of correspondence that would exist
if the account in *Veeck As In Wreck* was correct.[73]

One can only wonder whether the liberal Veeck was trying to
explain away why his rival, the more conservative Rickey, and not
Veeck himself had broken down the color bar—either in the minors
at Milwaukee or in the majors (after Landis was dead) after June
1946 when he owned the Cleveland Indians. Of course, while in this

realm of the highly theoretical, one can also ask: did Branch Rickey help block Veeck, so *he* could be first to integrate the game? Or if Landis—and/or Frick—had acted to block Veeck were they actually concerned with whether Veeck was underfinanced rather than with any racial schemes he may or may not have had?

While Veeck faded from the scene, the issue of integration remained. At the major league meetings held that December in Chicago, a committee from the Chicago Council of the CIO including longshoremen and auto workers (all but one of whom was white) had approached Landis demanding that the owners conduct a study of integration. The Squire refused to allow the discussion to take place, ruling that it was not on the agenda and that it violated baseball rules to schedule it at such a late date.[74]

In the spring of 1943 another tryout of Negro Leaguers was announced. The PCL's Los Angeles Angels promised to look at Nate Moreland, Cleveland Buckeyes righthander Chet Brewer, and Homestead Grays third baseman Howard Easterling. Pressure from other league clubs caused club president Clarence "Pants" Rowland to cancel the offer.[75]

In November 1943 *Chicago Defender* sportswriter Sam Lacy secured Landis' approval to make their case at the major league meeting to be held in December at New York's Hotel Roosevelt.

Both Landis and Lacy, however, were soon double-crossed. To garner increased publicity, instead of sending Lacy, other delegation members replaced the sportswriter with black singer Paul Robeson.[76]

Robeson was perhaps the most accomplished black in America. In an era where few African-Americans attended college, in 1917 he had been named to the All-American football team as an end at Rutgers. The following year, he was elected to Phi Beta Kappa; in 1923 he earned a law degree from Columbia. While still at law school Robeson began dabbling in stage work and quickly found himself starring on Broadway. Despite never taking voice instruction, his powerful bass voice established him as a major singing talent, starring in such hits as *Show Boat*. Soon his fame spread beyond Broadway, as he starred on the London stage and toured Europe with a series of recitals.

But Robeson was also a highly controversial figure. Among his European venues was Stalin's Soviet Union, and his support for the Loyalist cause in the Spanish Civil War caused many to wonder about his political sympathies. By 1942 he was widely regarded as a Communist sympathizer, if not an actual party member. Even when allied to the Soviets in fighting Hitler, most Americans—and most major league club owners—wanted nothing to do with the Reds.

Neither did most blacks. Lacy himself was incensed—both on a personal and on a tactical level. His boiling anger caused him to resign from the *Chicago Defender* in protest. Wendell Smith was equally perturbed. "The Communists did more to delay the entrance of Negroes in big league baseball than any other single factor," Smith later claimed.[77]

"Wendell and I both knew [the Communists] were involved," added Lacy, "but we didn't want their help. We wanted to be completely divorced from any communist influence. That's the reason I knew Paul Robeson was going to be rejected when he went out there—we knew it and didn't want it to happen."[78]

He was right. To send a man of Robeson's reputation to plead your case before the scourge of the IWW seemed damned foolhardy.[79]

Foolhardy or not, Robeson, accompanied by Ira F. Lewis of the *Pittsburgh Courier*, John Sengstaike of the *Chicago Defender,* and Howard Murphy of the *Baltimore Afro-American,* nonetheless appeared before Landis and baseball owners.

The press was formally barred from the session, but, as Landis had done in the past, he failed to close the transom door to the room. Listening outside was the *Daily Worker*'s correspondent. Landis began the meeting graciously. "It is unnecessary to introduce Paul Robeson," he began. "Everybody knows him for what he has done as an athlete and an artist. I want to introduce him to you as a man of great common sense."

Then he added, "I want to make it clear that there is not, never has been and, as long as I am connected with baseball, there never will be any agreement among the teams or between any two teams preventing Negroes from participating in organized baseball. Each manager is free to choose players regardless of race, color, or any other condition."

"Now, Paul Robeson will speak to us."[80]

Robeson addressed the gathering for between 15 and 20 minutes. He told of playing football at Rutgers and how a black man's presence on a collegiate team was then a rarity but now it was accepted as commonplace. He went on to talk about how the same tolerance now greeted a black in a white stage cast, pointing to his recent smashing success on Broadway as Othello. "They said that America would never stand for my playing Othello with a white cast," said Robeson, "but it is the triumph of my life."[81]

Baseball's magnates had no questions for Robeson or his companions. In this they follow Landis' lead. Just before the session, he cautioned them: "Don't interrupt Robeson. Let's not get into any discussion with him."[82]

The owners probably needed little urging in that regard. Most had little sympathy for integration. The one man in the room who most certainly did, the Dodgers' Branch Rickey, had his own reasons for keeping silent. He was already actively plotting to break baseball's color bar, but he would do it at his own pace and would not allow Robeson or anyone to upset his carefully laid out timetable and strategy. During the meeting, he scribbled away, trying to settle his own thoughts.

Rickey carefully laid out the pluses and minuses of allowing blacks into the big leagues. In the negative column, the first entry was "Robeson a Communist?" a question that would be clearly answered in the affirmative in the years to come. The second was the word "South," a reference not only to southern fans and to the problems of training in the south, but also of the large numbers of white southerners playing professional baseball. They would surely be unsympathetic to integration. The third such entry was "Negro leagues." Would those circuits, among the largest black-owned enterprises in the nation, allow their players to walk away from contracts and perform in the white majors?

But outweighing those factors were three items sacred to Rickey: "Attendance," "Jesus," and "America."

When Robeson had finished and the three blacks had walked out of the room, Landis spoke to the owners, "The gentlemen asked for an opportunity to address the joint meeting. They were given an opportunity. What's next on the agenda?"[83]

Not only were Landis and baseball's ruling executives not particularly interested in the issues Robeson raised, but the great majority of the white press was equally blasé. The *New York Times*' John Drebinger probably spoke for most when he doubted anything would come of the incident but allowed that Landis had handled the matter "tactfully."[84]

That was Landis' last known consideration of the issue,[85] although the major leagues took a very concrete measure against segregation, ending Jim Crow seating at Sportsman's Park in May 1944.[86]

What motivated Landis in his actions—or more precisely in his clear lack of action—regarding integration?

First off, it is extremely unlikely that Landis or any commissioner would have had to exert much effort to thwart efforts to integrate baseball. If Landis blocked integration, the question arises: whose actions was he blocking? What major league—or minor league—owners chomped at the bit to integrate the game and could only be restrained by Landis' icy stare?

Aside from Branch Rickey, the probable answer is none. When Landis was gone and baseball was integrated, he served as a convenient scapegoat for the actions and attitudes of most of baseball. Larry MacPhail's attitudes may have stood out only in their frankness. Connie Mack, for example, contended that he could not buck Landis on the race issue, but Mack's actions belied his pious words. The Tall Tactician's neighbors recalled his strenuous efforts to bar blacks from his Germantown neighborhood. In the early 1940s local black newspapers reported that Mack was among the "most bitter" opponents of baseball integration. When the American League finally integrated, Mack's A's encouraged a particularly obnoxious fan to heckle Larry Doby and even paid him to follow the player about the circuit.[87]

There was certainly no mad rush to integrate following Landis' death. Most big league clubs waited years following not only Landis' passing, but also Jackie Robinson's signing, before securing their own black players—and then only placed blacks on big league rosters in limited numbers. Certainly Landis did nothing from his grave to prevent the Boston Red Sox from not featuring their first black player until 1959.

Yet the Squire certainly did nothing to hasten integration and most likely feared it. Perhaps the most direct word of his motivation came from Cubs owner Phil Wrigley who once revealed that Landis was reticent to integrate because of a fear of rioting at ballparks. To modern day observers, that seems like a mere excuse. To someone of Landis' era and age, it was a very real fear. The East St. Louis race riot was not the first of the young century. Anti-black violence in New York (1900); Springfield, Ohio (1904); Atlanta (1906); Greensburg, Indiana (1906); and Springfield, Illinois (1908) had preceded it. In

1919 more rioting occurred in Charleston, South Carolina; Longview, Texas; and Washington, D.C.

In July 1919 Landis could see racial turmoil firsthand as Chicago erupted into five days of violence. The carnage started at a place of recreation, a Lake Michigan beach, and before it was over Chicago police had shot and killed seven African-Americans. Sixteen other blacks and 15 whites had died at the hands of mobs and individuals. Over 500 suffered injuries, and Frank Lowden again had to call out Illinois national guardsmen to restore order. Within the next 10 months more rioting occurred in Knoxville, Omaha, and Elaine, Arkansas—where after a white deputy sheriff was shot 12 blacks were given death sentences and 67 other were given lengthy prison sentences. All were later overturned by the Supreme Court.

In 1943 riots erupted in both Harlem and Detroit. In Detroit that June 25 blacks and nine whites were killed. Rioting did not end until President Roosevelt dispatched 6,000 troops to the city. Three hundred and fifty armed guards patrolled Briggs Stadium to maintain order. In the middle of this chaos, Landis received a letter from Detroit: "These hospitable shores have been in a bit of turmoil lately due to race riots . . . The parkway out in front of the [Detroit Athletic] Club is still full of soldiers and armored trucks. We have been under what practically amounted to martial law."[88]

In the often racially-charged atmosphere of the times, the mind of Kenesaw Mountain Landis could envision big league ballparks torn by riots or even going up in smoke if black men were to play against whites in them. That was in *northern* parks. In *southern* minor league parks, it was not even possible for him to conceive the basic premise of that scenario.[89]

One solid reason existed for Landis to be wary of the Negro Leagues: gambling. Many of the Negro Leagues most prominent owners—Gus Greenlee, Abe Manley, Alex Pompez, Ed Semler, Ed Bolden, Robert Cole, Tom Wilson, Dick Kent —were notorious gamblers and racketeers. "Under Greenlee's leadership," contended Negro Leagues historian Donn Rogosin, "Negro National League meetings were conclaves of the most powerful black gangsters in the land."[90]

"If Greenlee had been white," admitted historian John Holway, "he would never have passed the scrutiny of Kenesaw Mountain Landis and been allowed to buy a big league franchise. His financial sources were, frankly, unsavory."[91]

To keep an eye on gambling, Landis—without any authority whatsoever—once intervened in Negro League administration. In a game between Greenlee's Pittsburgh Crawfords and the white semi-pro Brooklyn Bushwicks, catcher Josh Gibson dropped a pop fly with two out in the bottom of the ninth, giving the Bushwicks the win. Recalled Crawfords pitcher Theolic Smith, "the big wheels and the gangsters too would bet heavily on the black teams that came in. When Josh dropped that pop-up the fans threatened us, and they said there was a bomb placed in our bus, and we had two or three squad cars escort us back to New York City. We was afraid."

The controversy was so great that Landis' hatred of gambling overrode his aversion to the Negro Leagues and he summoned Gibson for questioning. He cleared the slugger.[92]

One of the least known but most original theories explaining Landis' failure to integrate the game relies on purely economic motives: Richard Nardinelli's view of baseball as a "monopsony," a labor market dominated by a single employer. Nardinelli's reasoning goes like this: Organized Baseball had long maintained a tight control over player movements and salaries. If the decision was made to sign blacks, a bidding war might very well have erupted for their services. If that occurred, there is no reason to believe that white players would not have wanted their own salaries to substantially increase, thus creating an upward wage spiral.

Nardinelli admits that when integration finally occurred after 1946, the process was so slow and grudging that no such bidding war erupted. "The owners of the 1930s," says Nardinelli, "however, could not have known that integration would not threaten their position. Landis made sure that they did not have to find out."[93]

Virtually throughout his commissionership Landis was in daily contact with blacks—although technically the relationship was that of master and servants. Kenesaw and Winifred Landis employed two longtime black domestics, Leonard and Elsie Edwards. Leonard was Landis' chauffeur, although often that meant simply following Landis in his car, while the Judge, a great walker, would traverse the distance from the Ambassador East Hotel to his office on foot.[94]

Landis' relationship with Leonard Edwards was actually quite close. "They were friends," Landis' granddaughter Nancy explained with some force. "He left money to [the Edwardses] and not to any of us [grandchildren], not to our father, but he left money to them."

Nancy's sister Cathy, who has a less favorable view of her grandfather than her sister does, agrees: "He sure was good to Leonard. He liked Leonard. I think he was his friend, sort of."

"He was very closely tied to Leonard and very helpful to Leonard," confirms nephew Lincoln Landis, "and I can recall seeing Leonard and being so happy, myself being a kid of thirteen or fourteen, to talk with Leonard when he would drive the Judge down to Logansport. He was such a wonderful, warm fellow himself and he was very happy in his work and proud to serve the Judge and Mrs. Landis. . . . the Judge took very good care of Leonard even in Leonard's later years. . . . he was generous to Leonard. He was kind and did his utmost for Leonard after Leonard got pretty old and was no longer his chauffeur."[95]

Leonard and Kenesaw often traveled together, and their travels included trips to the segregated South. The situation deeply disturbed the supposedly segregationist Landis. "He used to get irritated because Leonard had so much trouble driving through the South," Nancy Landis Smith Lucas recalled, "where he could stay and where he couldn't stay. Sometimes Elsie went down too, so Leonard had a vacation. [Grandfather] used to get upset about that. Grandfather thought a great deal about not letting the blacks in. You have to think in the terms of the times, I think."[96]

Landis deserves no praise for his leadership or lack thereof in racial policies. But to pretend he was the single or even the major roadblock to integration or to ascribe to him actions he never took whitewashes the attitudes of an entire generation of baseball leadership.

CHAPTER 26

# "PIECES WERE DROPPING OFF OF ME"

Baseball had changed since Kenesaw Landis first assumed the commissionership in January of 1921. It had become a cleaner sport, rightly perceived by the general public as more honest than before, which had always been the Judge's primary mission. But the game had also altered in ways of which Landis had little approved. The farm system and night baseball, for example, rankled the Squire to no end.

Yet the national pastime itself remained substantially static during the Judge's tenure: 16 big league teams stayed in the same cities he had found them in; no consequential rule modifications were made; there were hardly any changes in the major league parks in which the sport was played.[1] And, of course, the sport remained lily-white.

America itself had changed far more in the years of the Squire's commissionership. The 1920s had roared, and the Stock Market had crashed. Harding and Coolidge's conservatism had been junked in favor of the activism of Franklin Roosevelt's New Deal, an administration former-progressive Landis viewed as dangerously radical.

The nation was also moving once again toward war, and that could and would impact baseball mightily. During the First World War the game had been declared nonessential to the war effort and seemed about to disappear for its duration. The 1918 major league season prematurely ended on Labor Day. Big league attendance plummeted from over five million in 1917 to a mere 3,080,126 in that truncated campaign. Crowds proved so poor at 1918's Cubs-Red Sox World Series that Boston's winning share amounted to just $1,102. Chicago's losing share was a pitiful $671. Only nine minor leagues started the 1918 season, and only one, the International, completed it. At one point Ban Johnson announced that the game would shut down until war's end.[2]

431

After Pearl Harbor, baseball faced similarly bleak prospects. Would it be consigned once more to "nonessential" status and fade away after a season or two? Not helping matters was the Squire's attitude toward Franklin Roosevelt. Aside from his antipathy to FDR's domestic policies, he also blamed Roosevelt for what he felt was America's insufficient preparation for war.

Early on the morning of December 8, 1941, *Sporting News* publisher J. G. Taylor Spink was waiting for the Judge at Landis' 333 North Michigan office. When Landis arrived, tears of "anger and mortification" could be seen in his eyes. After struggling to remove a huge overcoat from his 129-pound frame, the Squire walked over to a window and for a long time stared silently at Lake Michigan's frigid waters. Finally, he bounded toward Spink. Poking a finger into his guest's frame he barked bitterly, "Do you realize, Spink, that we now are a secondary power in the Pacific?"

For that, he blamed Roosevelt as much as he blamed the Japanese. "Landis," Spink noted, "was no pacifist or appeaser. His criticism of the Roosevelt Administration was that it didn't come to grips earlier with Hitler and the Japs, and for not being better prepared when the big blow came."

The Squire went on to cryptically castigate a "colleague" of Spink's for Pearl Harbor. It took a while for the comment to sink in, but Spink eventually discerned Landis was referring to Secretary of War Frank Knox, owner of the *Chicago Daily News* and an erstwhile Republican vice-presidential candidate.[3]

Animosity between Roosevelt and Landis was clearly mutual. "Landis," Washington's Clark Griffith once confided to sportswriter Shirley Povich, "wasn't much more welcome at the White House than the Japanese ambassador."[4] Nonetheless, on January 14, 1942, the Judge—at Griffith's urging—penned a letter for Griffith's delivery to FDR. "Baseball is about to adopt schedules, sign players, make vast commitments, go to training camps," Landis wrote Roosevelt, dropping the issue squarely in the presidential lap. "What do you want it to do? If you believe we ought to close down for the duration of the war, we are ready to do so immediately. If you feel we ought to continue, we would be delighted to do so. We await your order."

The shrewd Roosevelt was not about to take the blame for even the temporary demise of the national pastime. He responded immediately with his famous "Green Light" letter, giving baseball the O.K. to continue:

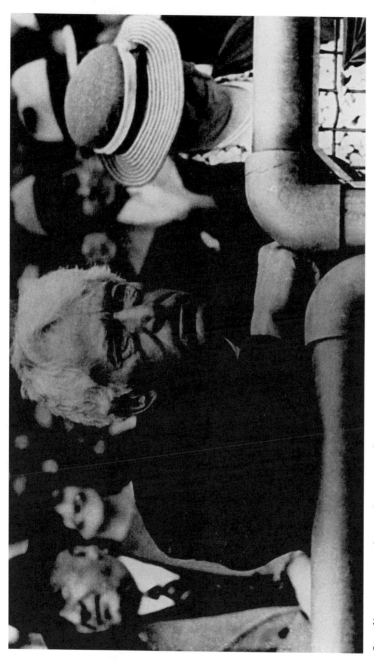

Landis was a man in motion everywhere except *at the ballpark*. There he would sit motionless for hours, leaning against a rail. (*Photo credit: National Baseball Hall of Fame Library and Archive, Cooperstown, New York*)

TELESCOPE

DAYTON, OHIO, JANUARY 29, 1908.

JUDGE KENESAW MOUNTAIN LANDIS
CONGRESSMAN CHARLES B. LANDIS
Ex CONGRESSMAN FREDERICK LANDIS
POSTMASTER WALTER KUMLER LANDIS
DOCTOR JOHN HOWARD LANDIS

A QUINTETTE OF
MASTER MINDS

*All* the Landis brothers evidently enjoyed posing for the camera.
*(Courtesy: Lincoln Landis)*

Kenesaw Mountain Landis—before the bench turned his hair white.

Standard Oil magnate John D. Rockefeller evaded the summons to Landis' court—but finally took the stand.

The *Chicago Tribune*'s John McCutcheon's opinion was colored by his friendship with Landis, but this cartoon, nonetheless, accurately reflected popular opinion.

## THE TERROR OF THE CROOKS

This *New York Press* cartoon of August 6, 1907 precisely predicted the outcome of the Standard Oil case.

The newspapers had a field day with the historic battle between Landis and Rockefeller.

In the teens the federal government filmed its most colorful judge at work. Here's Judge Landis in a scene from that movie, *The Immigrant. (Photo credit: Chicago Historical Society, G1980.0211.3.2.)*

Many of Landis' duties were ceremonial, including this visit to Los Angeles on September 29, 1925 to dedicate Wrigley Field, then known as Cubs Park. (*Courtesy Dick Beverage*)

Reed Gresham Landis was the apple of his father's eye.

A rare Landis grin is seen as the Judge poses with wife Winifred and son Reed.

Contemporaries regarded Judge Landis' decision regarding the Chicago
building trades as having national importance.

American League president Byron "Ban" Johnson ruled baseball—until
Kenesaw Landis became its commissioner.

The Judge frowned on ballplayers associating with gamblers and racketeers. Cub Gabby Hartnett tempted Landis' wrath by posing with Al Capone and Capone's son Sonny.

Landis enjoyed a day on the links, even though his score was usually nothing to brag about. Here he is seen at Pinehurst, New Jersey, in 1931. *(Courtesy: Lincoln Landis)*

Landis ardently supported America's efforts in the First World War. Here the Judge is seen visiting some wounded servicemen.

The Judge loved an audience, and throwing out the first ball always provided one. *(Photo credit: National Baseball Hall of Fame Library and Archive, Cooperstown, New York)*

THE WHITE HOUSE
WASHINGTON

January 15, 1942

My dear Judge—
Thank you for yours of January fourteenth. As you will, of course, realize, the final decision about the baseball season must rest with you and the Baseball Club owners—so what I am going to say is solely a personal and not an official point of view.

I honestly feel that it would be best for the country to keep baseball going. There will be fewer people unemployed and everybody will work longer hours and harder than ever before.

And that means that they ought to have a chance for recreation and for taking their minds off their work even more than before.

Baseball provides a recreation which does not last over two hours or two hours and a half, and which can be got for very little cost. And, incidentally, I hope that night baseball can be extended because it gives an excellent opportunity to the day shift to see a game occasionally.

As to the players themselves, I know you agree with me that individual players who are of active military or naval age should go, without question, into the services. Even if the actual quality of the teams is lowered by the greater use of older players, this will not dampen the popularity of the sport. Of course, if any individual has some particular aptitude in a trade or a profession, he ought to serve the Government. That, however, is a matter which I know you can handle with complete justice.

Here is another way of looking at it—if three hundred teams use five thousand or six thousand players, these players are a definite recreational asset to at least twenty million of their fellow citizens—and that in my judgment is thoroughly worthwhile.

With every best wish,
Very truly yours,
Franklin D. Roosevelt

Landis' responded in low-key fashion. "I hope our performance would be such as to justify the president's faith," he told reporters. He must have been relieved to see baseball continue, but not happy that permission had to hinge on "That Man in the White House."

The Squire must also have been displeased by Roosevelt's advocacy of increased night play—a trend he was still resisting. The clause must have also been the work of Griffith, once among the harshest critics of evening baseball, but now one of its staunchest advocates.

Griffith would continue to work against Landis on this issue. In March 1943 he would write to presidential aide, Stephen Early: "Steve, . . . please don't fail to make mention of the fact that weekend ball and night baseball would be in the best interests of war workers in Washington and throughout the country." The Old Fox went on to pointedly add: "I have a hard time convincing Commissioner Landis that everyone is supposed to stay on the job in the daytime."[5]

As early as December 1941 Griffith and the Browns' Don Barnes had lobbied to increase their clubs' yearly night schedules to 28 contests each. Landis, in conjunction with the National League, blocked their bid and retained the existing seven-night contest limit per club.

In February 1942, however, baseball had reconsidered Roosevelt's words on the benefits of night play. Big league owners voted to allow each club 14 night contests per year—with one exception. Griffith's Senators could schedule 21.

Landis and Griffith continued sparring over night play. In July 1942 the Washington owner sought permission to convert all games remaining on his home schedule (except for Sunday and holiday contests) to evening contests. The AL ratified Griffith's plan, but once more Landis and the NL blocked his plans. "After all," the Squire stated with not a little sarcasm, "there still must be some fans in Washington who would like to see a ball game in the afternoon."

Landis won again that December, but in July 1943 he finally relented, admitting that "wartime conditions in Washington make it worthwhile to have more night games." Griffith had worn the Squire down by producing Washington's attendance figures. Senators' night games drew an average of 14,000 fans—a huge figure by Washington standards.[6]

Baseball also faced a serious curb on wartime travel. The question "Is this trip necessary?" applied as much to baseball as to any civilian enterprise. Following the 1942 season, Office of Defense Transportation head Joseph B. Eastman requested of Landis that the national pastime seriously economize on its travel.

The Judge's response exceeded Eastman's expectations. Traveling to Washington,[7] Landis presented Eastman with a two-pronged idea designed to save five million "man miles" per year on the nation's railroads. Eastman was thrilled, and on January 5, 1943, Landis publicly announced the plan. First, while maintaining the traditional 154-game schedule, the majors would decrease in-season travel by having each club visit its rivals three rather than four times annually.

Then came the Landis-Eastman Line—formulated by Landis without the owners' approval and basically dictated to them. It demarcated where big league teams could train and largely paralleled the Mason-Dixon Line. Landis limited spring training to north of the Ohio River and east of the Mississippi, except in the case of the Browns and Cards who could train anywhere in Missouri that they wished. Major league clubs moved from such balmy climes as Miami and Catalina Island and Havana to such inhospitable spring venues as Muncie, Indiana, and Wallingford, Connecticut. With professional teams also training in French Lick, Evansville, Bloomington, Purdue, and Terre Haute, the Limestone League replaced the Grapefruit League.

The Squire reaped a public relations bonanza for his patriotic moves. "Judge Landis came to us with certain proposals which I approve," Eastman said. "I approve of baseball's cooperation with the war effort, and I'd say baseball's cooperation with us might serve as a pattern for the nation."[8]

It would also serve as a pattern for Landis, who announced he'd forgo his usual trips to Belleaire for the duration. "I'll freeze up north with them," he said referring to his shivering ballplayers.[9]

Charity work was another integral portion of the war effort. In April 1943 Landis led a delegation of baseball officials to a meeting with the Army Emergency Relief Fund and the Navy Relief Society. To aid the servicemen's families, major league clubs would annually donate the proceeds of one regular season game. Minor league clubs would also pitch in and do what they could. In Louisville that translated into a "Waste Fat Night," in which fans donated 2,587 pounds of grease.

Some major league owners wished to improve on Landis' brand of patriotism. In December 1941 Larry MacPhail advanced an ambitious proposal for baseball's support of the war effort. Ownership adopted most of MacPhail's program, but failed to act on his most flamboyant suggestion—that they pay for an army bomber "to carry our compliments overseas." It was to have been named the "Kenesaw Mountain Landis."[10]

Meanwhile, Landis skillfully lobbied for baseball's existence. In January 1943 he informed the New York Baseball Writers' Association:

> We do not want baseball exempt from the liabilities of common life in America. We want the same rules applied and enforced on us as on everyone else. When I give thought to the statutes ruling our lives in war, I think of those fellows in New Guinea crawling in trenches and those fellows in Africa. They have complied with those statutes.
>
> This is baseball's position and I take full responsibility for it. I don't want any man in the stands to think that any man on the field is exempt from any law or statute. On the question of going to Washington, I didn't want a story to come out of Washington that would justify the inference that we were seeking any better treatment of exemptions from the conditions of war. I think baseball is strong enough and that we don't need to send a lobby and can leave the situation to the sixty million fans. And about the question of whether baseball is going to die or is going to live, I've formed the habit of living.[11]

A year later he told the same organization: "Before I left Chicago, I received a letter signed by five men in the army. They wanted to be sure that they would be at the next World Series. I am not given to prophesying, but this is my conviction. These boys away from home, they want this thing called baseball to continue."[12]

He had not changed his basic attitudes towards America's enemies. The man who wanted to hang the Kaiser and his sons thought similar punishment was appropriate for Axis leaders. Peace, he wrote in September 1943, "is the sort of thing we are not going to be able to figure on until there is a lot of gutletting—thinking of Hitler, Himmler, Hirohito and about fifteen thousand little Hitlers, Himmlers and Hirohitos. Then we can all make plans to live again."[13]

Landis' plans for a post-war world, however, did not include the United Nations. In August 1943 a journalist wrote the Squire regarding the question of world government. He didn't want to publicly enter the fray, but, nonetheless, confidentially advanced his "notion" that it was "all bull to talk about a United States of the World."

"If I were younger," he concluded, "had more vitality and all the et ceteras that go to put a man in shape for the kind of fight I would be getting into, I would not put this to you in confidence."[14]

As in the First World War Landis had highly personal reasons for being concerned about the conflict. First and foremost, Reed (who in March 1940 had become a regional vice president of American Airlines) had re-enlisted in the Air Corps, although in a nonflying capacity. Reed, the aging Squire wrote to Frank Lowden, "is in his best humor since he got out twenty years ago.

"These fellows," Landis continued with some puzzlement, "regard it as a fine war. I really think he has got that in his head."[15]

There were also other Landises for him to worry about. Reed's son Keehn had earned his fighter wings in the Army Air Corps. Daughter Susanne's son Richie (in the Navy); brother Frederick's sons Lincoln (at West Point for most of the war), Frederick (in the Navy), and Charles (also in the Navy); brother Charles' son John and grandson Charles also were in the service. So were Frederick's daughters, Betsy and Frances, both WAVES (Women Accepted for Volunteer Emergency Services) ensigns. Betsy's husband, Chicago newsman Richard L. Cullen, was also a Navy officer.

The war was not without its close calls. The Squire's nephew John was wounded overseas and John's son Charles was wounded in France. In October 1943 Kenesaw's nephew Charles survived the sinking of the *U.S.S. Bristol* off the coast of Sicily. When the *Bristol* went down, Charles' fate was not immediately known, and his Uncle Squire wrote the Navy Department to ascertain events. "Can you give me anything about it?" he meekly asked. "If under Naval procedure you are not at liberty to do this, I will understand."

When the Judge discovered Charles had survived, he quickly wrote him, enclosing an early Christmas present and commenting "it is a grief to think of [the Bristol's] fate, but a great joy to reflect upon your present status."[16]

The Squire had not forgotten how to wage war domestically.

Nineteen forty-three saw a long-simmering feud between him and J. G. Taylor Spink break out into the open. In 1942 Spink's *Sporting News* had taken over publication of baseball's official guidebook, receiving in the process a $10,000 subsidy from Organized Baseball.

Spink, as irritable and imperious a figure as was the Judge, had sided with Ban Johnson against Landis, and the Squire took a very long time to forgive the publisher for the transgression. Not until 1935, Spink claimed, did the two even have even the briefest of conversations. Finally, at that year's Joe Louis-Battling Levinsky title bout at Comiskey Park, the two broke the ice.[17]

In June 1942 the *Saturday Evening Post* ran a long profile by journalist (and *Sporting News* contributor) Stanley Frank on Spink. Several times in the course of the article Frank referred to Spink as "Mr. Baseball." Landis thought *he* was "Mr. Baseball," and this set his bushy hair on end.

The situation only worsened when a week later *The Sporting News* ran a Dan Daniel piece claiming that while Landis and Spink had once been mortal enemies "now they are pals."

"If you catch Spink in a weak moment . . . ," Daniels went on, "he will confide to you that this man Landis stands out EVEN ABOVE JOHNSON. Spink will whisper this, so Ban can't hear it."

That last observation should have made Landis proud. It did not. He did not like sharing the title "Mr. Baseball" with Spink, and he did not relish the thought that the game needed any other watchdog than him. And above all he did *not* want to be counted as J. G. Taylor Spink's "pal," particularly after granting him a $10,000 subsidy.

Daniel caught wind of Landis' displeasure and reached him by phone. "There are a lot of things in that article that should have never been written," the Judge warned. "How about: 'Now we [Landis and Spink] are chummy.' Don't you put me in bed with that kind of company."

And he continued: "Since when is it necessary to have a watchdog for baseball?"

"Well," Daniel explained, "I think Spink does a great job in the field that he operates in."

"Wherin does he do such a wonderful job?"

"What I mean is that he hollers out against bad practices, wherever they occur in baseball."

"A man with a paper can put in whatever he likes if he thinks he can holler about bad practices."

"That's the way I look at it."

"Well, we just don't see eye to eye," Landis concluded.

Spink—perhaps more concerned about the continuance of the $10,000 subsidy than about Landis' personal feelings—determined to patch things up. One afternoon in August 1942 he dropped in on

Landis who greeted him with an intense and undisguised hostility, repeatedly referring to him as "Mr. Baseball" and at one point advising an employee: "Be very careful what you do. That's Mr. Baseball; he'll watch everything you do."

Landis then proceeded to berate Spink and to accuse him of having given editorial approval on Frank's *Saturday Evening Post* article and of having the power to censor Daniel's *Sporting News* piece, which according to Landis should *never* have included any reference to the publisher and the Commissioner being friends. Spink pointed out that he previously promised Daniel he would never edit his prose. Landis, recalled Spink, "brushed that aside."

Spink then got to his real point: could the *Sporting News* again print an "official" guide? "No," Landis snapped, adding that if it did, it might confirm Daniels' article, i.e., that the two were friends—this Landis would not allow. With that he threw on his coat and stormed out of his own office, leaving Spink to commiserate with future National Association head Phil Piton, then a Landis employee.

Piton promptly reported details of the conversation to Landis. The next morning Spink called American League president Will Harridge, attempting to get another meeting with the Judge. He got one, but it was not what he was counting on. Landis put him through a literal interrogation, complete with a court reporter transcribing his every word. He asked Spink four questions concerning his conversation with Piton. Inquisition over, Landis opened a door. Behind it was a sink, and he proceeded to wash his hands.

"Well," a nonplussed Spink asked, "where does this put us now? Am I still a friend of yours, or am I not a friend?"

"I have no friends," Landis shot back, "and you're just the same as you were before."

Spink then wanted to know if Landis would shake hands with him. The Judge had no problem with that and as he did, remarked to Spink, "Remember me to the lady," a reference to Mrs. Spink, with whom Landis had always gotten along quite nicely.

Landis proceeded to put out his own official 1943 guide, but the result was a disaster, coming out far too late to be useful to writers or fans, and being discontinued after just one year. When he was preparing it for publication, Landis met with statistician John S. Phillips. The meeting was to be highly confidential, but the next night, Phillips received a call from Spink, demanding to know what was going on and accusing Phillips of treason. Phillips rushed to report the call to Landis.

Phillips arrived at Landis' office before he did. Before the Squire could even remove his raccoon coat, the nervous Phillips narrated his tale. "Why," Landis sighed, "did God ever create a son of a bitch like Spink?"[18]

Landis' last significant case involved Phillies owner William D. Cox. The brash Cox came from a well-to-do background. Born on New York's posh Riverside Drive, he attended New York University and Yale before leaving the latter school in his senior year to take a position with a New York bank. He later worked for an investment house and a lumber company, becoming its president at just age 26.

Cox' entry into professional sports came in 1941 when he purchased a share of the New York Americans of the American Football League. Professional football was hardly the hunt club. It was hardly anything, and the American Football League was even less. But Cox managed to sully even its nondescript reputation by rushing onto the gridiron one day to protest a call, earning a 15-yard penalty.

After the impecunious Jerry Nugent finally lost control of the threadbare Phillies in 1943, Cox headed a 30-man group which purchased the club. The sale price: just $190,000 in cash and a note for an additional $50,000.

The Phillies were a dreadful team, had been dreadful for a long time, and looked like they might very well be dreadful forever. They had finished dead last every season since 1938, and had not emerged above seventh since 1933.

The 1943 Phillies had only 14 players in camp when spring training opened in Hershey, Pennsylvania, so eighth place might actually have been an accomplishment. Cox hired the veteran Bucky Harris to manage the club, and the Phils saw some improvement, even threatening to emerge from the second division before ultimately finishing seventh.

The club's unexpected (if modest) performance and Cox' promotional abilities doubled attendance in 1943, but trouble was brewing. Cox could not refrain from interfering in Harris' business. The two men fought, and one of them would have to go. It would not be Cox—at least, not yet.

Ninety games into the 1944 season, Cox fired Harris, telling newspapers of the fact before he told Harris. Harris' players were outraged and threatened to walk out before a Sportman's Park Red

Cross benefit game unless Cox apologized to his former manager. "We feel," the players explained, "that because of his background and experience, he is entitled to that decency."

Cox did apologize ("The ouster is not intended in any way to reflect on your ability as a baseball manager"), narrowly averting a player strike, and the Phils responded by breaking an 11-game Cardinal winning streak. Harris, for his part, informed his former players in the backward syntax of a *Time* magazine article: "The stand you have taken on my behalf flatters me no little."

But Cox could not let well enough alone and soon alleged that Harris had called his loyal players "those jerks."

Harris responded that Cox was "an All-American jerk."

To which Cox replied, "He calls me an All-American jerk. Doesn't he know what league he's in?"

But there was more transpiring than insults and feeble witticisms. Offhandedly Harris grumbled to reporters about one of Cox' habits: betting on the Phils.[19]

Now the fact that Cox was betting *on* his team made no difference as far as baseball's rules were concerned. Ever since the Cobb-Speaker fracas of 1927 Rule 21 (d) 2 prohibited such actions, clearly stating: "Any player, umpire, or club or league official or employee who shall bet any sum whatsoever upon any baseball game in connection with which the bettor had a duty to perform shall be declared permanently ineligible."[20]

Cox denied Harris' charges, informing Landis that he had not placed any bets. It had been a lumber business associate of his actually placing them. He further claimed that when in May 1943 he first heard of these wagers he asked his friend to stop and that the associate complied immediately.

Landis wasn't about to let Cox escape on his own word. He kept up the investigation. All the while Cox himself was prying to find out what, if anything, Landis was uncovering.

In mid-October a Phillies' minority stockholder named Nathan Alexander informed the Phillies' board of directors that back in May Cox admitted placing bets on the team. Cox had to know the tale would find its way back to Landis. Such information always did.

Finally, in New York City on November 3 Landis got Cox to crack. Cox admitted placing "approximately fifteen to twenty bets" of "from twenty-five to one hundred dollars per game on Philadelphia to win."

He contended that once he learned of Rule 21 (d) in May 1944, he stopped the practice.

The Judge met again with Cox in Chicago. Once more, the owner admitted wagering on his own team. On November 15, 1944 Landis wrote Cox directing him to appear in New York City on December 4 to answer charges and present a defense.

"You are also requested," Landis demanded, "to mail to me a complete statement of bets made by you upon baseball games in the 1943 season, as stated to me by you, including as to each bet the amount, the date of the game, the teams involved, the name of the team and address of the person with whom the bet was placed."

Landis also told Cox one more thing: pending the outcome of the investigation he was not "to participate in any baseball meeting or transaction." In other words, he was suspended from the operation of the club.

Three days later, Cox responded, surrendering completely but, nonetheless, trying to save some face in the process. He informed Landis he was resigning as Phils chairman and president and even from the club's board of directors. He would sell the team as soon as he could find a "satisfactory purchaser."

But he also begged out of any hearing, claiming his appearance would "serve no useful purpose ... in view of my resignations, and the full statements which I have heretofore made to you ..."

Cox' statement hardly impressed Landis. In fact, it incensed him. "These were not 'full' statements," he shot back to Cox in a November 22 letter, recounting both Cox' statements to him in Chicago and New York and his own unfulfilled demand for a written bet-by-bet account of the affair.

Landis was perhaps most outraged that his plans for a hearing were being shortcircuited. The proposed December 4 hearing, he concluded, was meant "to develop full statements of the facts by yourself and others, and to give you an opportunity to present anything you might want to have considered. Therefore, I am not in accord with your view that such a hearing would serve no useful purpose. However, you decline to attend such hearing and to answer fully in this matter." Cox was now informed he was *permanently* banned from all of baseball.[21]

Cox took to the airwaves. Over New York's powerful radio station WOR, he confessed that had made "a few comparatively small and sentimental bets" on his team and bid "good luck and goodbye" to all of baseball.[22] Within days he would be out as Phillies owner, his interest sold to 28-year-old Robert R. M. "Ruly" Carpenter, Jr., a scion of the DuPont family. Carpenter was now the youngest club owner in major league history.

Landis had gone up to New York's Hotel Roosevelt anyway for his annual meeting with the owners. The meeting should have been relatively routine, but it wasn't. Negro journalists (who had become more visible through Paul Robeson's efforts) petitioned Landis that he integrate the game. He tersely said there was no rule against integrating, then provided sportswriters with another surprise story: the Cox hearing would proceed the next day as originally scheduled.

For over six hours the next day Landis held public court. Basically it was Harris and Nathan Alexander against Cox and several Philadelphia employees, with Cox' attorney implying something sinister about the sale of the club to the ultrarespectable Carpenter family, focusing on Alexander's role in that sale.

Incredibly, Cox now denied betting on his own club, but he did not deny *telling* Alexander he had. Why had he done so? Because he had wished to "test" Alexander's "loyalty." He further testified that while he had not bet on whether the Phillies would win or lose a specific game, he had bet on where they would be in the standings.

To Landis it was a distinction without a difference.

Landis grilled him in depth about his apologia on WOR. "Just what did you have in mind when you made that statement?" Landis wanted to know about his now-recanted admission he *had* bet on games, "Did you consider that a true statement of the facts to be made to the public?"

Cox responded that at the time he just wanted to put the whole episode behind him, but that he could not. The day after the broadcast, newspaper reports linked him to "racketeers and gamblers" and he "decided to come forth with the truth," saying that the truth was that he was innocent of gambling as his Phils were of a World Championship—"I only made those statements of betting to a man I had considered my friend."

Finally, the parade of witnesses ended, and it was Landis' turn to pronounce judgment. For over a half hour he went on, reading the text of all pertinent correspondence, reciting *en total* Cox' farewell over WOR. The audience wearied of the proceedings, but *he* seemed to gain strength. It was as if he sensed this would be the last great public performance of his life. The *Times*' John Drebinger marveled at how "tireless" this 77-year-old could be.

Then with a cloud of tobacco smoke choking the air out of the room, Landis came to his conclusion.

"I see no reason," he squawked, "with such intelligence as I am endowed or inflicted with to draw the conclusion that Cox came to me with any such thing in mind as his statement today that his admissions of betting were all part of a plan to smoke somebody out of his organization.

"The rules on gambling are obligatory on me as on other baseball men and the order will have to be that I do not put out a new order."[23]

William D. Cox was out of baseball.

Landis' health had long been bothersome. As early as 1928 he was frail enough to be lain extremely low by a malady as simple as the flu. "The flu makes a fellow's knees awfully wobbly," he wrote Frank Lowden. "The strange thing to me about it all has been my complete willingness to keep lying here in bed."[24]

In January 1936 it was reported that the 69-year-old commissioner had entered a Chicago hospital for what was innocently termed as "bronchial ailment." Some sort of throat operation was said to be involved, and his recovery was described as a "stormy convalescence." It took two weeks for him to leave the hospital.[25]

But the whole story was a lie. Actually on January 4 doctors operated on Landis for a cancerous prostate. Some thought he was near death. "Don't ever let anything get wrong with your prostates," he later informed one sportswriter, "that's the damnest thing that can happen to a man."

But the operation was a success—a "perfect job of trimming" as he termed it, which not only took care of his prostate problem but in the process lowered his blood pressure (previously up to a high of "220 above God knows what") back to normal. "He was a new man . . . ," noted Taylor Spink.[26]

Landis also suffered from numerous bronchial difficulties. "He really just had a lot of respiratory problems, all his life," recalled granddaughter Nancy. In early October 1941 the Squire was vacationing at his Burt Lake camp. After a lengthy hike, Landis—now close to 75—took ill, and checked into the Little Traverse Hospital in nearby Petoskey. At first, his doctor downplayed the illness as "a very severe cold," but by the next day the Judge had been diagnosed with bronchial pneumonia, a situation dangerous enough to require treatment in an oxygen tent. He remained in Little Traverse until November 5, signing checks for the 1941 Yankees-Dodgers World Series (the "Mickey Owen" Series) from his bed.[27]

"It wasn't difficult," observed Taylor Spink, "to see he had been through an ordeal."[28]

While Landis was hospitalized at Petoskey, his old friend Frank Lowden offered "to take care of" him if he would move to Lowden's farm "Sinnissippi."

"Here Nature," Lowden wrote, "presents a kindly face, notwithstanding all the evil man can do. My cattle are still good company and maintain their serenity."

Landis thought better of the idea, opting instead for his usual winter accommodations at the Bell-Air, but didn't close the door on the invitation. "I'm thinking Old boy," he telegraphed Lowden that Christmas Eve, "of the time when I move my quarters to that farm. Meanwhile you are authorized to continue as trustee."[29]

Landis, however, never took up the offer. Lowden, long in worse health than Landis and now beset with cancer, himself died of pneumonia in March 1943.[30]

In January 1942 the Judge was strong enough to leave Chicago for Florida, but he was not strong enough to be very ambitious about what he would do once he got there. "The old doc says it will help me to lie around in the sun," he wrote to a friend in Wisconsin, "and I am book-wormish enough to be able to obey that prescription."

Meanwhile Landis' prostate continued to bother him, and he was not shy about writing to his friends about it, often in graphic detail. In July 1941 he complained to John Heydler that his "prostate has to be spoonaddled out every twenty minutes after I go bed. Funny thing about it is I can go all day while I am up and around at work without any trouble. Just as soon as things come around so I can do without bothering anything, I am going to the hospital and have the damn thing bored out again."[31]

He took his time about that operation, waiting until December 1942 before checking into Chicago's Presbyterian Hospital. "You have observed, traveling through the country," he wrote Heydler, "the operations performed by a great big drainage machine constructing a ditch for the draining off of water. Well, that's what they did to me—

went up through my old outlet and opened up drainage by boring a great big whole [sic] through the prostate gland. I will tell you that is one heluva way for a feller to spend his vacation."

That was Landis, showing he could tough it out with the best of them, but elsewhere in the letter was the clear sense he was wearying of the struggle.

"Apparently," he wrote to the 73-year-old Heydler (three years Landis' junior and retired since 1934), "you and I have hung on a time when, as Ben Franklin said a couple of centuries ago—'I have hung on to a time when I should long ago have been asleep.' "[32]

Thoughts of mortality increasingly dogged him. At about the same time he informed *Chicago Times* sports editor Gene Kessler, "I feel like an old, old tree. You've seen dead limbs drop off an old, old tree, haven't you? Well, that's how I feel. Like pieces were dropping off of me—and will continue to do so until there isn't anything left." To Judge William Bramham he expressed the same fatalistic sense. "Just a line," he wrote in December 1943 (At Christmastime Landis would send out very brief letters to friends in lieu of cards), "we have traveled a long way since our roads crossed in 1920. In the very nature of things it can't go much farther. Whether it is short or far, whatever there is worthwhile to you and yours."[33]

Kenesaw was by now now the last of the Landis siblings and feeling very mortal. The clan had been shrinking for some time. In November 1917 Walter died at Logansport of complications of a hookworm infection contracted while he lived in Puerto Rico. In August 1918 John passed away after overexerting himself while at golf. Catherine died in November 1921. Charles followed them in April 1922 while in Asheville, North Carolina. He was in Asheville less than a week when he began to fail dramatically. Kenesaw sped to be at his side, but Charles died before his arrival.[34]

Only Frederick, Frances, and Kenesaw remained. Frederick continued to lecture profitably, and his delivery was likened to that of Will Rogers. In 1923 he relocated to New York City, taking a position as an editorial editor with the Hearst chain's *New York American*. In October 1926 he returned once more to Logansport ("I would rather renew notes in Indiana than pay dividends in New York"), becoming editor of the *Pharos-Tribune*, writing a popular syndicated column ("Reason: A National Column for Those Who Think") and eventually founded a monthly anti-New Deal journal modestly titled the *Hoo-*

*sier Editor*. And periodically, he attempted a political comeback. In 1928 and 1932 Frederick unsuccessfully sought the Republican gubernatorial nomination.

His opportunity finally came in 1934. Frederick defeated two opponents in the primary and despite that being the year of the GOP's lowest ebb, went on to defeat a Democrat incumbent to reclaim his old Congressional seat—28 years after he had lost it—thus becoming the only Republican member of the Indiana House delegation. He even harbored hopes of challenging Franklin Roosevelt in 1936.[35]

Toward the end of the campaign a burst of exertion brought on pneumonia and made Frederick unable to function. His condition deteriorated and Kenesaw rushed to Logansport, taking a room at the hospital and refusing to leave the building. The Squire even brought doctors from Chicago with him, but one heart attack followed another and in the early morning of November 16, 1934, Frederick expired.[36][37]

Sister Frank ("my little sister") died in March 1939. She was 85 and had not been in good health. Aside from the normal infirmities of age she had suffered, in the Squire's words, from "various falls, fractures, and pneumonia." Kenesaw was "very sure that for the last two or three years her uppermost interest was to have the thing ended" but her passing still left him shaken and feeling alone.

"I am, as you suggest, the lone survivor," he wrote to Frank Lowden, "but a rather impressive fact stands out in connection with the Landis family and the Kumler family . . . In 1891 I attended a reunion of [the Kumler] family at Hamilton, Ohio. There were present over 700 blood relatives. Should an effort be now made to get the family together, the result would show that in two generations the family had practically 'run out.' At that time there were big families of children. Now there are one or two or no children."[38]

Landis celebrated his 77th birthday in 1943—and despite all his problems and worries was momentarily in reasonably good health and spirits, telling reporters he felt as good as he had when he had reached the half-century mark, and perhaps a little better. "That worried me," Landis remarked, "getting as old as 50. I thought it would be terrible. But I got over it. I feel great."[39]

Nonetheless, he was shortly confiding to a friend: "The only adventure left to me is death, and I look forward to it."[40]

He was certainly strong enough to throw a roadblock—albeit only temporarily—in Larry MacPhail's plans to purchase the Yankees in the spring of 1944. MacPhail did not have the money to purchase the club himself. But he put together a consortium of over a dozen money men, the most important of whom was John Hertz, a Chicago taxi cab magnate—but Hertz was also involved in horse racing, and that made him anathema to Landis, who bluntly ordered MacPhail to find himself another backer.

MacPhail, however, was scheduled to sign the papers with the Ruppert estate. Landis' order would have stopped most men; it hardly slowed MacPhail down. With barely a cent behind him, MacPhail bought the most fabled franchise in sports and only then set about trying to find the money to pay for it. He found one buyer at the "21" Club—Brooklyn Dodgers football owner Dan Topping. The other was Arizona developer Del Webb. Before signing on, Webb— who knew Landis—asked him for advice. The Squire was typically acerbic: "If, when you're making a putt, you want to worry; if, when you're having your dinner, you want to worry; if, before going to bed, you want to worry, well, go ahead and buy the Yankees."[41 42]

In 1944 the Judge faced yet another unwelcome change in his life. For years he had enjoyed living at the swank Ambassador East Hotel. Now, he and that establishment faced off in an argument over increased rent. For once, Landis lost, and he and Winifred moved not only out of the hotel, but out of Chicago, to Glencoe, Illinois, about a block away from daughter Susanne, her husband Richard and daughter Jodie. Glencoe had also been home to Reed Landis' family for some time.

To Susanne's son, Richie (now in the Navy), Landis wrote, trying a reasonably positive spin on events, claiming he should have moved "onto a farm about seven or eight years ago, or whenever it was that farms were available at what now appears to have been reasonable prices. But I didn't. Fellows that did are sitting on top of the world."[43]

That summer nephew Lincoln Landis visited. "It was rather modest," Lincoln recalled decades later, "typical of neighborhood homes. It may have been a bungalow. Not a pretentious home. Just another home in a row of homes, all of which were individualistic but at that time were considered strong middle class homes. . . . It was a kind of ordinary and comfortable middle class home."

Uncle Squire did his best to radiate pleasure at his new suburban surroundings. "He took me out to his garden," Lincoln recollected. "How proud he was of the onions and radishes and the various vegetables he had planted. He showed them to me—how well they were getting along—how proud he was of his garden. I was most impressed by that. I think that's the deepest memory I can carry with me, his happiness with his garden."[44]

Actually the Squire was miserable. To a friend in Wisconsin, he wrote: "Confidentially I put it to you that a man who doesn't submit to any kind of blackmail attempted on him by hotel people is a plain damned fool, and would be so adjudged by any jury of Eau Claire County lumber-jacks. This is in confidence to you. I am still making a valiant effort to keep up a front, to create the illusion that all is well."[45]

On September 1, 1944 Landis was writing to a friend from Florida's Bell-Air Hotel. "Time has been running against most of (at least the undersigned)," he admitted, "with the result that I have gotten to the point where I am almost obliged to count it up in centuries, instead of decades. I will be 78 in November, if I live that long, and already I have begun to wobble about on my pins."[46]

A little over a month later, on October 2, Landis entered Chicago's St. Luke's Hospital with what was described as a severe cold contracted after working in his Glencoe garden. That same day, Winifred Landis also entered St. Luke's with a broken wrist. For a few days the Squire's hospitalization was kept secret. When it was finally announced, a typically bland explanation was provided: the Commissioner was in for tests and perhaps a rest, that was all. "It is nothing serious," explained Leslie O'Connor, "The Judge had quite a heavy cold, and needed a rest. He thought he would play it safe, and go to the hospital. A few weeks there will fix him up fine. When he comes out, he'll be better than ever."[47]

But all was not well. In addition to his respiratory problems the Judge had also suffered a heart attack. He failed to attend the 1944 Browns-Cardinals World Series (the first Fall Classic he had missed since becoming commissioner; O'Connor filled in for him) and had to satisfy himself with listening to it on the radio—and berating doctors and nurses for any unseemly reports on his condition. He read all newspaper accounts of his illness and would blast hospital staff for allowing such "drivel" to circulate in the public press.

He received visitors and seemed grumpy enough to be on the road to recovery. He carved up the World Series proceeds. It was anticipated he would chair that December's major league meetings—

and they were even moved from New York to Chicago to accommodate him. But there was one very serious straw in the wind: he had
hoped to leave the hospital in order to vote against Franklin
Roosevelt on Election Day, November 7. But his condition worsened,
and he remained at St. Luke's.[48]

As Landis lay in his hospital room the press displayed little sense
of urgency—or any great interest—regarding his illness. After all, he
had been in and out of hospitals for a decade and though he was approaching 78, it was hard to believe he would ever leave the
commissionership, let alone die.

One anonymous *Chicago Tribune* staffer, however, did remember
the old jurist and had this bit of doggerel inserted in the paper's editorial page:

### Nosegay For Judge Landis

With crinkly smile and mane of snow-white hair
Shocked up like corn against the frost of years,
You formerly came in to greet the dears
Who worked across the hall. With blossoms fair
You'd nonchalantly wander over there,
Bestow a dandelion to win their cheers
And leave them, more than likely close to tears,
Touched by your kindliness, your will to share.
Today in dreary hospital confines,
With vehemence you probably protest
Restriction in that evil-smelling gloom,
And one old-timer pens these limping lines
To wish you all of everything that's best
And bring a bit of brightness to your room.[49]

Also thinking of Landis was Washington's Clark Griffith, celebrating his 75th birthday on November 20—the same day as
Landis' 78th. "Judge," Griffith wired Landis, whose condition was
now officially described as "continued satisfactory," "I feel sure you
are going to be okay soon and that you will be with all of us old fellows for a long time to come."[50]

Newsmen were not the only ones trusting in the Judge's immortality—so were baseball's owners. Not only did they calculate he

would chair their December meetings, they calculated he would lead them into the 1950s. His contract expired on January 21, 1946, and while there had been grumbling against him that summer, on November 17, 1944, a joint major league committee voted to extend the Squire's contract (with no diminution in powers) for another term, to January 1953—when he would be 86 years old. "Members of the committee," wrote J. G. Taylor Spink, "seemed to have no doubt the Judge would go on."[51]

In the very early morning of Saturday, November 25, however, it was apparent life was running out very quickly for the weakened commissioner. The night before St. Luke's Hospital announced his condition as "low." Gathering about his bed were wife Winifred, Leslie O'Connor, son Reed, daughter Susanne, and her husband Richard W. Phillips, Sr. Also present were a niece and nephew, Mr. and Mrs. John Stephenson. He was still able to speak to those gathered around him, but around 4:30 AM doctors placed an oxygen tent around him. As late as a half hour later the hospital was still telling reporters his condition was unchanged, but at 5:35 AM he was dead. Winifred Landis collapsed when doctors announced it was all over.

Morticians from C. H. Jordan undertakers immediately removed his body. Per his wishes, the body of Kenesaw Landis was immediately cremated.[52]

It was left to Leslie O'Connor to read the official announcement of his passing. O'Connor wept as he read out the brief message:

> Judge Kenesaw Mountain Landis died at 5:35 with his family at his bedside.
> In compliance with his wishes no funeral services will be held. Also in accord with his desires cremation will take place privately and friends have been asked not to send flowers.[53]

Nothing more than a modest headstone marked Landis' Chicago resting place, but just two weeks later a special committee named him to baseball's Hall of Fame. "KENESAW MOUNTAIN LANDIS," his plaque in Cooperstown reads,

> Baseball's First Commissioner, Elected, 1920—Died in Office, 1944. His Integrity and Leadership Established Baseball in the Respect, Esteem and Affection of the American People.

And that *was* his legacy. Restoring and maintaining the public's faith in baseball was what the owners had hired their new commissioner to do when they crowded into the back of his courtroom in December 1920. It was no easy task. The Squire may have been arbitrary, capricious, old-fashioned, vindictive, and more than occasionally profane, but no one could deny Kenesaw Mountain Landis had accomplished what he had been hired to do.

# NOTES

## Chapter 1 Notes

1. *Washington Times*, October 15, 1994, p. B3; Undated Clipping, KML Scrapbooks, Chicago Historical Society.
2. *The Sporting News*, August 12, 1940.
3. At Chickamauga in September 1863 Dr. Landis had unsuccessfully treated West Point graduate Captain William G. Jones. Before Landis buried him he removed Jones' watch, epaulets, and two $1 gold pieces, intending to return them to the dead man's family. During Landis' captivity, he kept with him the personal effects taken from Jones' body. He meant to retain them no matter what so he might return them at war's end to the officer's family. Luckily for Landis he was freed after six weeks and after leaving the service managed to return Captain Jones' possessions to the dead man's brother.
4. *The Sporting News*, August 12, 1940.
5. Ed Fitzgerald, "Judge Landis, Baseball's High Commissioner," *Sport*, June 1950, p. 51.
6. J. G. Taylor Spink, *Judge Landis and Twenty-Five Years of Baseball*, p. 1.
7. Ed Fitzgerald, "Judge Landis, Baseball's High Commissioner," *Sport*, June 1950, p. 51.
8. *Baltimore News*, July 9, 1907.
9. Maj. Gen. Oliver O. Howard, *Battles and Leaders of the Civil War, passim*; James P. Boyd, *The Life of General William T. Sherman, passim*; Benson J. Lossing, *Our Country, passim*.
10. *Revolutionary Ancestors of Indiana*, Vol. I, p. 370; Interview with Lincoln Landis, February 12, 1996.
11. Dr. George D. Miller, *A Biographical Sketch of the Deceased Physicians of Cass County*, p. 22; *Cincinnati Post*, August 23, 1918.
12. The home, built in the 1830s, still stands today. Appropriately, it overlooks a ballfield.
13. Joy Kay, "Kenesaw Mountain Landis: Ohio Town Takes Pride in Being the Birthplace of First Baseball Commissioner," *Logansport Pharos-Tribune*, November 20, 1994; KML to Otto J. W. Witte, December 12, 1930, KML papers, Chicago Historical Society.
14. For Daniel Flickinger, who in 1885 would also reach the rank of bishop, this was the first of his 11 missionary visits to Africa, including one in which he was shipwrecked.
15. *Dictionary of American Biography*, Vol. X, pp. 511-512; *Dictionary of American Biography*, Vol. VI, p. 470; *The Twentieth Century Biographical Dictionary of*

Notable Americans; Dayton Telescope, January 29, 1908, p. 9; Interview with Keehn Landis, July 27, 1995.

16. Dr. George D. Miller, *A Biographical Sketch of the Deceased Physicians of Cass County*, p. 22.

17. J. G. Taylor Spink, *Judge Landis and Twenty-Five Years of Baseball*, p. 2; Interview with Lincoln Landis, February 15, 1996.

18. Undated Clipping, KML Scrapbooks, Microfilm Volume II, Chicago Historical Society.

19. *Indianapolis Star*, May 21, 1922.

20. *Indianapolis Star*, May 21, 1922.

21. J. G. Taylor Spink, *Judge Landis and Twenty-Five Years of Baseball*, p. 3; *Dayton Telescope*, January 29, 1908, p. 17; *Cincinnati Commercial Tribune*, August 24, 1918; *Cincinnati Post*, August 23, 1918.

22. *St. Louis Post-Dispatch*, June 8, 1902; *Dayton Telescope*, January 29, 1908, p. 17; Dr. Jehu Z. Powell, *History of Cass County Indiana*, p. 123; *Indianapolis Star*, May 21, 1922.

23. Logansport, the seat of Cass County, then numbered 15,000 souls. Located on the Wabash River at the mouth of the Eel River (the "City of Bridges"), its white settlers acquired the site from the Miami and Potawatomi Indians in October 1826, but named it after a Shawnee chief, Captain Logan, who was considerably more friendly toward whites.

24. J. G. Taylor Spink, *Judge Landis and Twenty-Five Years of Baseball*, p. 9.

25. A century later this hospital tangentially again featured in baseball history when California Angels outfielder Lyman Bostock's murderer, Leonard Smith, was committed there. On June 20, 1980, less than two years after Bostock's June 23, 1978 slaying Smith was released from the Logansport State Hospital, as it was then known. He was pronounced cured.

26. *Cincinnati Post*, September 18, 1907.

27. Interview with Lincoln Landis, February 12, 1996.

28. *Indianapolis Star*, May 21, 1922.

29. *Logansport Pharos-Journal*, October 17, 1883.

30. Eliot Asinof, *Eight Men Out*, p. 253.

31. Taylor Spink says Kenesaw was atop "Buckskin" before Frederick got his hands on him; local sources seriously doubted that. Spink also contended that Landis was hawking the *Chicago Tribune*. "We are sure that Judge Landis never passed the *Chicago Tribune* —," jibed a childhood associate of Landis, "except, perhaps, on the way to his Chicago offices."

32. Graham Taber, *History of Logansport and Cass County*, p. 52.

33. J. G. Taylor Spink, *Judge Landis and Twenty-Five Years of Baseball*, p. 6.

34. F. C. Lane, "Baseball's Dictator," *Baseball Magazine*, February 1920, p. 415.

35. *Logansport Leader*, August 4, 1907, p. 1; *Logansport Press*, November 26, 1944, p. 6; KML to E. S. Shaffer, December 19, 1924, KML papers, Chicago Historical Society.

36. *1944 Current Biography*, p. 373; *New York Tribune*, November 13, 1920, p. 13; *Cincinnati Post*, November 21, 1920, p. 1.
37. Andrew Ritchie, *Major Taylor: The Extraordinary Career of a Champion Bicycle Racer*, p. 13.
38. *The* [Logansport] *Sunday Critic*, July 6, 1884.
39. John T. McCutcheon, "Kenesaw Mountain Landis, Judge," *Appleton's Magazine*, October 1907; *Chicago Record-Herald*, August 4, 1907, p. 2; Richard S. Simons, "Indiana's Baseball Magnates," *Indianapolis Star*, October 9, 1977, p. 8; *The* [Logansport] *Sunday Critic*, November 21, 1886; Dr. Jehu Z. Powell, *History of Cass County*, pp. 111, 123.
40. *Logansport Leader*, August 4, 1907.
41. John T. McCutcheon, "Kenesaw Mountain Landis, Judge," *Appleton's Magazine*, October 1907.
42. Eliot Asinof, *Eight Men Out*, p. 254.
43. J. G. Taylor Spink, *Judge Landis and Twenty-Five Years of Baseball*, p. 8.
44. John T. McCutcheon, "Kenesaw Mountain Landis, Judge" *Appleton's Magazine*, October 1907.
45. Ray Ginger, *Altgeld's America*, p. 248.

# Chapter 2 Notes

1. *New York Times*, April 28, 1995, p. 2.
2. Charles W. Calhoun, *Gilded Age Cato: The Life of Walter Q. Gresham*, pp. 116, 118-120.
3. *Encyclopedia Britannica*, 1958 edition, Vol. 10, p. 878; Walter LaFeber, *The New Empire*, pp. 197-199; Charles W. Calhoun, *Gilded Age Cato*, pp. 123-124; Horace Samuel Merrill, *Bourbon Leader*, p. 168.
4. James E. Watson, *As I Knew Them*, p. 44; Charles W. Calhoun, *Gilded Age Cato*, p. 124.
5. Matilda Gresham, *Life of Walter Quintin Gresham*, p. 580; John Braeman, *Albert J. Beveridge*, p. 30.
6. Ed Fitzgerald, "Judge Landis, Baseball's High Commissioner," *Sport*, June 1950, p. 52; *Logansport Press*, November 26, 1944, p. 6.
7. Walter LaFeber, *The New Empire*, pp. 200-218, 242-255, 285.
8. *New York Herald*, February 27, 1921, p. 6; *The Literary Digest*, March 12, 1921, p. 44; *Chicago Daily Journal*, February 18, 1922, p. 2.
9. J. G. Taylor Spink, *Judge Landis and Twenty-Five Years of Baseball*, p. 12.
10. Alfred Henry Lewis, "Judge Landis," *Human Life*, October 1907, p. 6; Alfred Henry Lewis, "Cloak Room Tales," *New York American*, January 3, 1909.
11. Alfred Henry Lewis, "Judge Landis," *Human Life*, October 1907, p. 5.
12. Yet Landis was not alone in sartorial foibles. Secretary Gresham had one of his own, preferring to pore over papers at his desk with his hat firmly fixed upon his head. Puffing on a huge cigar, he must have been quite the sight.

13. *The Indianapolis Star Magazine*, October 9, 1977, p. 9.
14. *New York Times*, March 26, 1905, p. 4.
15. Alfred Henry Lewis, "Judge Landis," *Human Life*, October 1907, p. 6.
16. Alfred Henry Lewis, "Judge Landis," *Human Life*, October 1906, p. 6.
17. Alfred Henry Lewis, "Cloak Room Tales," *New York American*, January 3, 1909; Alfred Henry Lewis, "Judge Landis," *Human Life*, October 1907, p. 6.
18. Matilda Gresham, *Life of Walter Quintin Gresham*, pp. 780-781.
19. *Chicago Evening Post*, January 5, 1907.
20. *Cincinnati Post*, June 28, 1907, p. 1.
21. J. G. Taylor Spink, *Judge Landis and Twenty-Five Years of Baseball*, p. 12
22. *Washington Post*, July 8, 1907.
23. John T. McCutcheon, "Kenesaw Mountain Landis, Judge," *Appleton's Magazine*, October 1907.
24. *New York Times*, February 21, 1893, p. 1; Earl D. Babst and Lewis G. Vander Velde, *Michigan and the Cleveland Era*, p. 257.
25. Alfred Henry Lewis, "Judge Landis," *Human Life*, October 1907, pp. 6-7.
26. Matilda Gresham, *Life of Walter Quintin Gresham*, p. 760.
27. When Cleveland arrived in Chicago, he led a parade of 620,000 to the Exposition.
28. Charles W. Calhoun, *Gilded Age Cato*, p. 126; Matilda Gresham, *Charles Quintin Gresham*, p. 699.
29. Donald Barr Chidsey, *The Spanish-American War*, New York: Crown, 1971, pp. 23-24.
30. *New York Times*, March 16, 1895, p. 1.
31. *Washington Post*, July 8, 1908; John T. McCutcheon, "Judge Landis, Judge" *Appleton's Magazine*, October 1907; *New York Times*, March 16, 1895, p. 1; Charles W. Calhoun, *Gilded Age Cato*, p. 214.
32. *The National Cyclopaedia of Biography*, Volume XXIV, p. 330.
33. Interview with Nancy Landis Smith Lucas, July 27, 1995; Charles W. Calhoun, *Gilded Age Cato: The Life of Walter Q. Gresham*, p. 131.
34. Interviews with Nancy Landis Smith Lucas and Keehn Landis, January 17, 1995.
35. Charles W. Calhoun, *Gilded Age Cato*, p. 125; Alan Nevins, *Grover Cleveland*, p. 633.
36. Alan Nevins, *Grover Cleveland*, p. 632; *Chicago Evening Post*, January 5, 1907.
37. Alfred Henry Lewis, "Judge Landis," *Human Life*, October 7, 1907, p. 6.

# Chapter 3 Notes

1. *New York Times*, August 11, 1907, Part V, p. 3.
2. Actually, Uhl was in ill health. He was all too happy to dissolve his Chicago holdings to return home to Michigan.

3.  *New York Times*, August 11, 1907, Part V, p. 3; *Washington Post*, July 8, 1907, page unknown; Earl D. Babst and Lewis Vander Velde, *Michigan and the Cleveland Era*, p. 285.

4.  *The National Cyclopaedia of Biography*, Volume XXI, pp. 355-356; *New York Times*, April 15, 1907, p. 7; *New York Times*, December 2, 1924, p. 25; *Chicago Tribune*, April 15, 1907, p. 2; Horace Samuel Merrill, *Bourbon Leader*, p. 174.

5.  F. C. Lane, "Baseball's Dictator," *Baseball Magazine*, February 1920, p. 416.

6.  *New York Times*, March 26, 1905, p. 4.

7.  *Chicago Evening Post*, July 26, 1915.

8.  Kennedy, Lawrence, *Biographical Dictionary of the American Congress 1774-1971*, Washington: U. S. Government Printing Office, 1971, p. 1259; *Dayton Daily News*, September 20, 1907; *New York Tribune*, January 14, 1897, p. 1; *New York Tribune*, April 28, 1901, p. 1; *New York Times*, January 25, 1922, p. 17; *Washington Times*, October 15, 1994, p. B3; Charles B. Landis to Kenesaw Mountain Landis, January 2, 1900, KML Papers, Chicago Historical Society.

9.  *St. Louis Post-Dispatch*, June 8, 1902; *Havana Daily Post*, July 30, 1907.

10. *New York Tribune*, November 16, 1903, p. 3.

11. Associated Press Dispatch, November 15, 1934.

12. *New York Tribune*, May 23, 1902, p. 2; Dr. Jehu Z. Powell, *History of Cass County*, Vol. 1, p. 285; Undated Clipping, *Logansport Pharos*, files of the Logansport Public Library; John Braeman, *Albert J. Beveridge*, pp. 31-34; Claude Bowers; *Beveridge and the Progressive Era*, p. 82.

13. *Logansport Pharos-Tribune*, November 17, 1934, p. 1.

14. *Havana Daily Post*, July 30, 1907.

15. Geneological information, KML Collection, Chicago Historical Society; Spink, *Judge Landis and Twenty-Five Years of Baseball*, p. 2; Interview with Lincoln Landis, February 15, 1996.

16. Interview with Keehn Landis, January 17, 1995.

17. Interview with Keehn Landis, January 17, 1995; *Logansport Pharos-Journal*, Undated clipping, 1902, KML Scrapbooks, Chicago Historical Society.

18. George E. Mowry, *The Era of Theodore Roosevelt and the Birth of Modern America 1900-12*, pp. 85-105.

19. *Harper's Monthly Magazine*, April 1927, p. 619.

20. Joseph G. Gannon to KML, August 26, 1902, KML papers, Chicago Historical Society.

21. *Washington Post*, July 8, 1907.

22. Joel Arthur Tarr, *A Study in Boss Politics*, pp. 131-132.

23. William T. Hutchinson, *Lowden of Illinois*, p. 122.

24. Joel Arthur Tarr, *A Study in Boss Politics*, p. 134 fn.

25. William T. Hutchinson, *Lowden of Illinois*, p. 123.

26. Joel Arthur Tarr, *A Study in Boss Politics*, p. 135; *The National Cyclopedia of Biography*, Volume XXIV, p. 330.

27. William T. Hutchinson, *Lowden of Illinois*, p. 130.
28. *Washington Post*, undated clipping, KML Scrapbooks, Chicago Historical Society.
29. Charles W. Fairbanks to Kenesaw M. Landis, March 16, 1905.
30. *The Cincinnati Post*, September 18, 1907.
31. William Hard, "Kenesaw Mountain Landis and His Altitudinous Fine," *Saturday Evening Post*, September 14, 1907, p. 9.
32. Peter Carlson, *Roughneck*, p. 265; David Garrard Lowe, *Chicago Interiors*, pp. 111-112; Granville Hicks, *John Reed*, p. 310.
33. William Hard, "Kenesaw Mountain Landis and His Altitudinous Fine," *Saturday Evening Post*, September 14, 1907, p. 1.
34. Interstate Commerce Commission v. Reichmann, *145 Federal Reporter 235; Saturday Evening Post*, September 14, 1907, p. 1.
35. March 6, 1906 letter of Charles Beary Landis to KML, KML Scrapbooks, Chicago Historical Society.
36. George Murray, *The Madhouse on Madison Street*, pp. 4-15.
37. William J. Jackson et al, *History of the American Nation*, Vol. 5, p. 1463-1465; Edward Wagenknecht, *American Profile 1900-1909*, p. 187; J. Gordon Melton, *Encyclopedia of American Religions*, p. 1692; Samuel Macauley Jackson, *The New Schaff-Herzog Encyclopedia of Religious Knowledge*, Volume III, pp. 40, 498; *Chicago Tribune*, March 10, 1907, p. 3.
38. *Holmes v. Dowie*, 148 Federal Reporter 640-641; *Chicago Daily News*, July 27, 1906, p. 1.
39. *Chicago Daily News*, July 27, 1906.
40. *Chicago Tribune*, March 10, 1907, p. 3; *Chicago Tribune*, March 11, 1907, p. 5.

# Chapter 4 Notes

1. Matthew Josephson, *The Robber Barons*, pp. 109-120; *Chicago Tribune*, August 4, 1907, p. 2; Gabriel Kolko, *The Triumph of Conservatism*, pp. 11-56, 113-138.
2. C. P. Connolly, "Big Business and the Bench," *Everyone's Magazine*, May 1912, p. 660.
3. Mortimer J. Adler (ed.), *The Annals of American History*, Volume 12, p. 540; A. E. Swanberg, *Citizen Hearst*, p. 219, 240; Edward Wagenknecht, *American Profile 1900-1909*, p. 201.
4. Mortimer J. Adler (ed.), *The Annals of American History*, Vol. 13, pp. 129-132; *Chicago Tribune*, August 4, 1907, p. 2; *Chicago Tribune*, August 16, 1907, p. 5; *New York Times*, August 20, 1907, p. 2; Gabriel Kolko, *The Triumph of Conservatism*, p. 123.
5. *Saturday Evening Post*, September 14, 1907, p. 1.
6. The day before Landis had excused himself from a trial resulting from the failure of the Chicago National Bank, pleading a "relationship during the last fifteen or twenty years" with bank personnel.

Notes 459

7. *United States v. Standard Oil, 148 Federal Reporter 719; New York Times,* January 4, 1907, p. 4; *Chicago Tribune,* January 4, 1907, p. 3; *Chicago Tribune,* January 5, 1907, p. 7; *Chicago Examiner,* January 4, 1907, pp. 1, 2; *Chicago Record-Herald,* January 4, 1907, pp. 1, 2; *Chicago Tribune,* January 4, 1907, pp. 1, 2.

8. *Chicago Tribune,* March 5, 1907, p. 3; *Chicago Tribune,* April 13, 1907, p. 2.

9. *Chicago Tribune,* August 4, 1907, p. 1; *Chicago Examiner,* January 4, 1907, p. 2.

10. *Chicago Tribune,* March 7, 1907, p. 3; *Chicago Tribune,* March 10, 1907, p. 1; *Chicago Tribune,* March 14, 1907, p. 6.

11. *Chicago Tribune,* March 12, 1907, p. 7.

12. *New York Times,* April 10, 1907, p. 1; *New York Times,* April 11, 1907, p. 5.

13. *New York Times,* August 14, 1907, p. 1.

14. *Chicago Tribune,* April 14, 1907, pp. 1, 2; *New York Times,* April 14, 1907, p. 1.

15. *Chicago Tribune,* April 15, 1907, pp. 1, 2; *New York Times,* April 15, 1907, p. 7.

16. *New York Times,* June 20, 1907, p. 1.

17. While Rockefeller had claimed infirmity to avoid testifying, within a month his physicians would reveal that he was in perfect health and should live another quarter century.

18. *Chicago Tribune,* July 7, 1907, pp. 1,3; *Chicago Tribune,* July 9, 1907, p. 3; *Chicago Tribune,* August 4, 1907, p. 3; *Cleveland Plain Dealer,* July 8, 1907, pp. 1, 2; *New York Press,* August 5, 1907, p. 4.

19. *Chicago Tribune,* June 28, 1907, p. 3; *New York Times,* June 27, 1907, p. 8; *New York Times,* June 29, 1907, p. 4; *New York Times,* June 30, 1907, Part I, p. 2; *Cincinnati Post,* June 28, 1907, p. 1; *Chicago Daily Journal,* July 6, 1907, p. 3.

20. *New York Times,* July 1, 1907, p. 2; *Cleveland Plain Dealer,* July 2, 1907, p. 1; *Cleveland Plain Dealer,* July 3, 1907, pp. 1, 2; *Chicago Tribune,* July 3, 1907, p. 1; *Albany Times-Union,* July 3, 1907, p. 1; *New York Sun,* July 3, 1907, p. 1.

21. *Chicago Tribune,* June 29, 1907, p. 4; *Berkshire Evening Eagle,* June 28, 1907, p. 2; *Berkshire Evening Eagle,* July 2, 1907, p. 2; *Cleveland Plain Dealer,* July 3, 1907, p. 2.; Peter Collier and David Horowitz, *The Rockefellers,* pp. 73, 159 fn., 651-652.

22. *Chicago Tribune,* June 29, 1907, p. 4; *Cleveland Plain Dealer,* July 4, 1907, pp. 1, 2; *New York Times,* June 30, 1907, Part I, p. 2; *Chicago Tribune,* July 3, 1907, pp. 1-2; *New York Tribune,* July 4, 1907, p. 1; *Chicago Tribune,* July 5, 1907, p. 1; *Knickerbocker-Press & Albany Morning Express,* July 4, 1907, p. 5; *New York Sun,* July 4, 1907, p. 1; *Albany Argus,* July 4, 1907, p. 1; *New York Press,* July 4, 1907, pp. 1, 2; *Berkshire Evening Eagle,* June 29, 1907, p. 2; *Berkshire Evening Eagle,* July 1, 1907, p. 1; *Berkshire Evening Eagle,* July 2, 1907, p. 2; *Berkshire Evening Eagle,* July 3, 1908, p. 1.

23. *Chicago Tribune,* July 5, 1907, p. 1; New York Sun, July 7, 1907, p. 2; *New York Press,* July 5, 1907, p. 1; *Berkshire Evening Eagle,* July 5, 1907, p. 1; *Berkshire Evening Eagle,* July 6, 1907, pp. 1, 2.

24. Edith Rockefeller McCormick was the wife of Harold Fowler McCormick, heir

to the McCormick farm machinery fortune and cousin of future *Chicago Tribune* publisher, Colonel Robert McCormick. She was the most ostentatious member of this rather stolid Baptist family, wearing $2-million strings of pearls and $1-million strands of emeralds and diamonds, and eating off solid gold plates. But Edith's flamboyance went far beyond mere conspicuous consumption. She studied psychology with Carl Jung, claimed to be reincarnated from the pharaohs of Egypt, committed adultery, and eventually divorced her unfortunate husband. Mr. McCormick, for his part, remarried and charged up his batteries with glands transplanted from an accommodating blacksmith. Such surgery inspired poetry:

Underneath the spreading chestnut tree
the village smithy stands;
The smith a gloomy man is he.
McCormick has his glands.

25. *Chicago Tribune*, July 6, 1907, pp. 1-2; Peter Collier and David Horowitz, *The Rockefellers*, p. 73; Joseph Gies, *The Colonel of Chicago*, p. 23.
26. *New York Tribune*, July 7, 1907, p. 1; *Chicago Tribune*, July 7, 1907, p. 3.
27. *Chicago Tribune*, July 7, 1907, pp. 2, 3; *New York Sun*, July 7, 1907, pp. 1, 2; *Albany Times-Union*, p. 1; *New York Press*, July 7, 1907, pp. 1, 2; *Chicago Tribune*, July 6, 1907.
28. *Chicago Tribune*, July 7, 1907, p. 2; *Chicago Examiner*, July 7, 1907, p. 3; *Chicago Daily Journal*, July 6, 1907; *Chicago Evening Post*, July 9, 1907.
29. *New York Sun*, July 7, 1907, p. 2; *Chicago Tribune*, July 7, 1907, p. 2; *Cleveland Plain Dealer*, July 7, 1907, p. 1; *New York Tribune*, July 7, 1907, p. 2; *Chicago Record-Herald*, July 7, 1907, p. 2.
30. *Chicago Tribune*, July 7, 1907, pp. 2, 3; *New York Press*, July 7, 1907, p. 2; *Chicago Evening American*, July 7, 1907, p. 3.
31. *Chicago Record-Herald*, July 7, 1907, p. 3.
32. Elsewhere in his speech Bryan advocated tariff reform and recommended the Christianization of Japan.
33. *New York Press*, July 7, 1907, pp. 2, 4; *Albany Times-Union*, July 6, 1907, p. 1; *Albany Journal*, July 8, 1907, p. 3.
34. *Chicago Evening Post*, July 9, 1907.
35. *Chicago Evening Post*, July 9, 1907, *Highland Park News Letter*, July 20, 1907.
36. *Chicago Evening Post*, July 9, 1907; *Indianapolis News*, July 11, 1907.
37. *Chicago Daily News*, August 3, 1907, p. 2; *New York Press*, August 4, 1907, p. 1; *New York Sun*, August 4, 1907, p. 1.
38. *Chicago Tribune*, August 4, 1907, p. 1, 2; *Chicago Daily News*, August 3, 1907, p. 2; *Schenectady Evening Star*, August 3, 1907, p. 1.
39. *Chicago Tribune*, August 4, 1907, p. 2.
40. *Chicago Tribune*, August 4, 1907, pp. 1, 2, 3; *New York Times*, August 4, 1907, pp. 1, 2; *New York Tribune*, August 4, 1907, pp. 1, 2, 4; *Schenectady Evening Star*, August 3, 1907, p. 1.

41. *Albany Argus*, August 4, 1907, p. 2.
42. *Chicago Tribune*, August 4, 1907, p. 2.
43. *Chicago Tribune*, August 4, 1907, p. 2; *Chicago Record-Herald*, August 3, 1907, p. 2.

## Chapter 5 Notes

1. George E. Mowry, *The Era of Theodore Roosevelt and the Birth of Modern America*, pp. 43, 265.
2. *Chicago Examiner*, July 8, 1907.
3. *New York Tribune*, August 4, 1907, p. 4.
4. *Chicago Tribune*, August 4, 1907, Part I, p. 3, Part III, p. 4; *New York Times*, August 4, 1907, Part II, pp. 1, 2; *New York Press*, August 4, 1907, p. 4; *New York Press*, August 5, 1907, pp. 3, 4; *Knickerbocker Press and Albany Morning Express*, August 3, 1907; *Schenectady Evening Star*, August 4, 1907, p. 1; *Harper's Monthly Magazine*, April 1927, p. 619; *Chicago Tribune*, August 5, 1907, p. 2; *Wall Street Journal*, August 5, 1907, p. 1; *Wall Street Journal*, August 6, 1907, p. 3; *Wall Street Journal*, August 9, 1907, p. 6; *Albany Argus*, August 6, 1907, p. 4; *St. Louis Globe-Democrat*, August 5, 1907; Frank D. Pavey, "The Standard-Oil Fine," *The North American Review*, September 1907, p. 114; *New York Tribune*, August 4, 1907, p. 4.
5. *Chicago Tribune*, August 4, 1907, p. 3; *Chicago Tribune*, August 5, 1907, pp. 2, 3; *New York Times*, August 4, 1907, Part II, p. 2, Mark Sullivan, *Our Times*, Vol. III, p. 495; *New York Herald*, August 5, 1907, p. 2; Peter Collier and David Horowitz, *The Rockefellers*, p. 58; *New York Press*, August 4, 1907, p. 2; *New York Press*, August 6, 1907, p. 4; *Albany Argus*, August 4, 1907, p. 2; *Chicago Examiner*, August 5, 1907, p. 1; *Chicago Record-Herald*, August 5, 1907, p. 1.
6. Handwritten notation, KML scrapbooks, Chicago Historical Society; *New York Sun*, August 5, 1907, p. 4.
7. *New York Times*, August 21, 1907, pp. 1, 2; Noel Busch, *T.R. – The Story of Theodore Roosevelt and His Influence on Our Times*, p. 199; Edward Wagenknecht, *American Profile 1900-1909*, pp. 340-341.
8. *Chicago Tribune*, March 13, 1907, p. 9; *Chicago Tribune*, August 5, 1907, p. 2; *New York Herald*, August 6, 1907, p. 4; *New York Times*, August 6, 1907, p. 2; *Chicago Evening Post*, August 5, 1907, p. 1; *Chicago Daily News*, August 5, 1907, p. 1; *Saturday Evening Post*, September 14, 1907, p. 1.
9. *Chicago Examiner*, May 21, 1907; *Chicago Tribune*, May 21, 1907.
10. *Chicago Tribune*, August 4, 1907, pp. 1, 3; *Chicago Daily News*, August 3, 1907, p. 2; *New York Times*, August 21, 1907, p. 2.
11. Unidentified Logansport Newspaper, August 10, 1907, Files of Logansport Public Library.
12. *New York Times*, August 14, 1907, p. 4.

13. *New York Times*, August 4, 1907, p. 2; *Wall Street Journal*, August 6, 1907, p. 3; *New York Times*, August 5, 1907, p. 3; *Chicago Tribune*, August 5, 1907, pp. 1-2; *New York Press*, August 5, 1907, p. 3.
14. *Chicago Tribune*, August 4, 1907, pp. 1,7; *Chicago Tribune*, August 6, 1907, p. 1; *New York Times*, August 13, 1907, p. 4; *New York Sun*, August 4, 1907, p. 2; *Chicago Evening Post*, August 3, 1907, p. 1.
15. *New York Herald*, August 6, 1907, p. 4; *New York Times*, August 13, 1907, p. 4; *New York Times*, August 14, 1907, p. 4.
16. *New York Times*, August 13, 1907, p. 4; *New York Times*, August 14, 1907, p. 4; *New York Times*, August 15, 1907, p. 6; *Chicago Tribune*, August 5, 1907, p. 2.
17. *New York Times*, August 14, 1907, p. 4.
18. *Webster's American Biographies*, p. 115; *New York Times*, August 8, 1907, p. 2; *New York Times*, August 16, 1907, p. 4.
19. *New York Times*, August 15, 1907, p. 6; *New York Press*, August 15, 1907, p. 1; *Chicago Tribune*, August 15, 1907, p. 3.
20. *Webster's American Biographies*, p. 732.
21. *Chicago Tribune*, August 16, 1907, p. 5; *New York Times*, August 20, 1907, p. 3.
22. *Quincy Daily Whig*, September 3, 1907, p. 1.
23. *New York Times*, September 3, 1907, p. 8; *New York Times*, September 5, 1907, p. 2; *Chicago Tribune*, September 5, 1907, p. 3; *Inter-Ocean*, September 3, 1907.
24. *Chicago Tribune*, September 4, 1907, p. 3.
25. *New York Sun*, September 6, 1907.
26. *Chicago Tribune*, September 6, 1907, p. 4; *New York Herald*, September 7, 1907; *New York World*, September 6, 1907; *New York Sun*, September 6, 1907.
27. Telegram from William Loeb to KML, September 4, 1907, KML papers, Chicago Historical Society.
28. *The Bay City Times*, September 16, 1907.
29. *Cincinnati Times-Star*, September 18, 1907; *Cincinnati Commercial Tribune*, September 18, 1907; *Cincinnati Commercial Tribune*, September 19, 1907; *Dayton Daily News*, September 19, 1907.
30. *Cincinnati Times-Star*, September 18, 1907.
31. *Dayton Daily News*, September 20, 1907.
32. Charles J. Bonaparte to Edwin W. Sims, September 20, 1907, KML Collection, Chicago Historical Society; *Chicago Tribune*, September 25, 1907, p. 2.
33. *New York Times*, August 4, 1907, Part II, p. 2; *New York Times*, August 21, 1907, p. 2; *Chicago Tribune*, September 25, 1907, p. 2; *New York Times*, September 25, 1907, p. 5; *Chicago Examiner*, September 25, 1907, p. 1; *Chicago Daily News*, September 30, 1907; *Chicago Tribune*, December 30, 1907, pp. 1, 5.
34. *Zanesville News*, July 7, 1907; *Boerne Texas Star*, undated clipping in KML Scrapbooks, Chicago Historical Society.
35. *Schenectady Daily Union*, August 16, 1907, p. 7.
36. *Washington Times*, September 15, 1907; *Memphis News Scimitar*, September 15, 1907.

37. William T. Hutchinson, *Lowden of Illinois*, pp. 177-178; *Washington Herald*, August 6, 1907; *Inter-Ocean*, August 5, 1907, p. 1; *Chicago Record-Herald*, August 6, 1907.

38. *Saturday Evening Post*, September 14, 1907; *Review of Reviews*, October 1907, pp. 498-499; *American Mercury*, December 1907, p. 120; John T. McCutcheon, "Kenesaw Mountain Landis, Judge," *Appleton's Magazine*, October 1907; Alfred Henry Lewis, "Judge Landis," *Human Life*, October 1907.

39. *Chicago Daily Journal*, July 6, 1907, p. 3.

40. *New York Herald*, July 7, 1907.

41. KML Scrapbooks, Chicago Historical Society.

42. Henry Pringle, "Portrait of a Bench Warmer," *Harper's Monthly Magazine*, April 1927, p. 619; *Davenport Democrat*, September 29, 1907.

43. *Schenectady Daily Union*, August 16, 1907, p. 7.

44. William T. Hutchinson, *Lowden of Illinois*, p. 177-178.

45. *Chicago Tribune*, June 11, 1908; *Chicago Examiner*, June 17, 1908.

46. *Cleveland Plain Dealer*, July 7, 1907, p. 1; *Chicago Daily Journal*, June 12, 1908; *Chicago Record-Herald*, June 13, 1908; *Chicago Evening Post*, June 12, 1908; *Chicago Tribune*, July 4, 1907, p. 2; *Chicago Tribune*, July 6, 1907, p. 4; *Chicago Tribune*, July 9, 1907, p. 6; *Chicago Tribune*, July 10, 1907, p. 5; July 12, 1907, p. 7; *Chicago Tribune*, July 14, 1907, Part I, p. 8; *Chicago Tribune*, July 16, 1907, p. 4; *Chicago Tribune*, July 17, 1907, p. 5; *Chicago Tribune*, July 19, 1907, p. 1.

47. *Chicago Tribune*, December 5, 1907, p. 1; *Chicago Record-Herald*, June 13, 1908, p. 1; *Chicago American*, June 12, 1908; Herbert Asbury, *Gem of the Prairie*, pp. 196- 201.

48. *Chicago Record-Herald*, June 13, 1908, p. 1; *Chicago Evening Post*, June 12, 1908.

49. *Chicago Daily Journal*, June 12, 1906; *Chicago Record-Herald*, June 13, 1908, p. 1; *Inter-Ocean*, June 13, 1908; *Chicago Daily News*, June 12, 1908; *Chicago Evening Post*, June 12, 1908.

50. Herbert Asbury, *Gem of the Prairie*, p. 166.

51. *Chicago Daily News*, June 30, 1908; *Inter-Ocean*, May 25, 1909; *Chicago Tribune*, May 25, 1909.

# Chapter 6 Notes

1. *An Appeal to Reason*, January 8, 1910, p. 1.

2. *An Appeal To Reason*, January 15, 1910, p. 1.

3. Ray Ginger, *The Bending Cross: A Biography of Eugene Victor Debs*, pp. 129-167; Nick Salvatore, *Eugene V. Debs: Citizen and Socialist*, pp. 131, 136-137.

4. *New York Times*, April 15, 1907, p. 8.

5. The world of Chicago's court system was a small one, and Landis had long

known Grosscup. Upon the death of Landis's brother-in-law, James Eckels, Grosscup had commented that after he "had come to admire him as a man I came to love him as a man." Eckels, like Sampsell, had also served as a Union Traction receiver.

6. *Chicago Tribune*, September 7, 1907, p. 2; *Chicago Tribune*, September 22, 1921, p. 3; *An Appeal To Reason*, January 5, 1910, p. 1.

7. *The National Encyclopeaedia of American Biography*, Volume VX, p. 253; *The Dictionary of American Biography*, Volume 4, Part 2, p. 21; Richard Hofstadter, *The Age of Reform*, pp. 223-224; *New York Times*, January 17, 1908, p. 1; *New York Times*, October 2, 1921, p. 16; *Chicago Tribune*, September 20, 1911, p. 2; *Chicago Tribune*, October 2, 1921, pp. 1-2.

8. *Chicago Tribune*, September 20, 1911, p. 2; *Chicago Tribune*, October 2, 1921, Part 1, page 2.

9. *Chicago Tribune*, August 31, 1907, pp. 1, 5; *Chicago Tribune*, October 27, 1907, p. 1.

10. *Chicago Tribune*, August 31, 1907, p. 5.

11. *New York Times*, October 29, 1907, p. 1; *New York Times*, October 30, 1907, p. 1; *New York Times*, October 31, 1907, p. 1; *Chicago Tribune*, October 27, 1907, p. 1; *Chicago Tribune*, October 30, 1907, p. 4.

12. *New York Times*, October 29, 1907, p. 1; *New York Times*, October 29, 1907, p. 1.

13. *Chicago Evening American*, December 3, 1907; *Chicago Evening Post*, December 3, 1907; *Fort Wayne Labor Times-Herald*, July 24, 1908, p. 1.

14. *Chicago Examiner*, June 1, 1907, p. 1; *Cincinnati Post*, July 24, 1908, p. 1; Gabriel Kolko, *The Triumph of Conservatism*, p. 125.

15. *Wall Street Journal*, August 9, 1907, p. 6.

16. *Chicago Tribune*, July 22, 1907, p. 1; *Chicago American*, July 22, 1907; *Inter-Ocean*, July 22, 1907; *United States v. Standard Oil, 148 Federal Reporter 719*.

17. *Standard Oil of Indiana v. United States, 164 Federal Reporter 376; New York Times*, July 23, 1908, p. 2.

18. *New York Times*, July 24, 1908, p. 1; *Chicago Tribune*, July 24, 1908, p. 2.

19. *Standard Oil Co. of Indiana v. United States, 164 Federal Reporter 276; Chicago Tribune*, July 24, 1908, p. 2.

20. *Chicago Tribune*, April 15, 1907, p. 1; *Chicago Tribune*, June 24, 1908, p. 1; *Chicago Evening Post*, September 19, 1907.

21. Charles G. Little, "Punishment of the Corporations," *Illinois Law Review*, pp. 446-453; *St. Louis Post-Dispatch*, August 17, 1908; *Chicago Record-Herald*, August 22, 1908, p. 1; *Chicago Tribune*, August 1, 1908, p. 1.

22. Henry W. Pringle, *Theodore Roosevelt*, p. 306; *New York Times*, July 23, 1908, p. 2; *New York Times*, July 24, 1908, p. 1; *New York Times*, July 28, 1908, p. 4; *New York Evening Call*, July 23, 1907, p. 6; *Chicago Tribune*, July 24, 1908, p. 1; *Chicago Tribune*, July 23, 1908, p. 8; *Chicago Tribune*, July 26, 1908, p. 1; *New York Sun*, July 28, 1907, p. 2; *New York Call*, July 25, 1908, p. 2; William Allen White, *The Autobiography of William Allen White*, p. 440.

23. *New York Times*, July 23, 1908, pp. 2, 6; *New York Sun*, July 24, 1907, p. 4; *New York Tribune*, July 23, 1908, p. 6.

24. *New York Call*, July 25, 1908, p. 2.

25. Bruce Bringhurst, *Antitrust and the Oil Monopoly: The Standard Oil Cases, 1890-1911*, pp. 138-139; *New York Times*, September 22, 1911, p. 3; *Chicago Tribune*, July 17, 1908; *Chicago Tribune*, July 23, 1908, p. 1; *Chicago Tribune*, July 26, 1908, p. 1; *New York Sun*, July 25, 1908, p. 9; *New York Times*, July 26, 1907, p. 1; *Berkshire Evening Eagle*, July 27, 1908; *Berkshire Evening Eagle*, July 30, 1908, p. 1; *Inter-Ocean*, July 30, 1908; *New York Times*, September 22, 1911, p. 3; Gabriel Kolko, *The Triumph of Conservatism*, p. 125.

26. *New York Times*, July 23, 1908, p. 2.

27. Peter Collier and David Horowitz, *The Rockefellers*, p. 58.

28. *New York Herald*, August 6, 1907, p. 4; *Chicago Tribune*, July 24, 1908, p. 1; *New York Times*, July 24, 1908; *New York Sun*, July 25, 1907, p. 9; *Chicago Record-Herald*, August 22, 1908; *Chicago Tribune*, January 5, 1909, pp. 1, 5.

29. *Chicago Record-Herald*, January 5, 1909.

30. *Chicago Record-Herald*, January 5, 1909; *Chicago Record-Herald*, March 1, 1909, pp. 1-2; *Inter-Ocean*, March 1, 1909, p. 1; *Chicago Tribune*, January 7, 1909, p. 9; *Chicago Tribune*, March 10, 1909, p. 1; *Chicago Tribune*, March 11, 1909, pp. 1, 2; Interview with Nancy Landis Smith Lucas, July 27, 1995.

31. *Chicago Record-Herald*, March 11, 1909, p. 2.

32. *Chicago Tribune*, January 23, 1908, p. 3; *Webster's American Biographies*, p. 1132.

33. *Chicago Tribune*, February 16, 1908, p. 1; *Chicago Tribune*, February 17, 1908, pp. 1, 7; *Chicago News*, January 14, 1909; *Chicago Examiner*, January 15, 1909; *Chicago Tribune*, January 15, 1909, p. 11.

34. *Chicago Examiner*, February 13, 1908; *Chicago Examiner*, February 16, 1908; *Chicago Tribune*, February 16, 1908, p. 1; *Guthrie Capital*, April 24, 1908.

35. *Chicago Examiner*, February 6, 1908.

36. In Milwaukee, as he had in Cincinnati, Landis exhibited his keen, almost fanatical, interest in the National Pastime. He simply could not keep from talking baseball. "How is your ball team?" he asked. "In the lead? Fine, I am glad to hear it. In the lead by a safe margin, eh? Did you hear what the Cubs did yesterday? By gosh, they broke the hoodoo, eight scores in the eighth inning." Even his address at Marquette included baseball references.

37. *Milwaukee Daily News*, May 22, 1909; *Milwaukee Sentinel*, May 22, 1909; *Milwaukee Free Press*, May 22, 1909; *The Evening Wisconsin*, May 29, 1909.

38. *An Appeal To Reason*, January 8, 1910. p. 1.

39. *An Appeal To Reason*, January 8, 1910, p. 1; *An Appeal To Reason*, January 15, 1910, p. 1.

40. *Chicago Tribune*, October 2, 1921, Part 1, p. 2.

41. *New York Times*, September 20, 1911, p. 2; *New York Call*, September 20, 1911, p. 2.

42. Also allegedly on the case was Samuel Hopkins Adams, a prolific muckraking journalist whose best-known work was a short story on which the Academy Award winning film *It Happened One Night* would be based.
43. *Chicago Tribune*, September 21, 1911, p. 3; *Chicago Tribune*, September 22, 1921, p. 3.
44. *Chicago Tribune*, September 20, 1911, p. 1; *New York Call*, September 20, 1911, p. 1; *New York Times*, September 21, 1911, p. 1; *New York Times*, September 22, 1911, p. 3.
45. *New York Times*, September 20, 1911, p. 2; *New York Times*, September 21, 1911, p. 1; *New York Times* September 22, 1911, p. 3; *New York Times*, October 22, 1911, p. 10; *An Appeal to Reason*, January 15, 1910, p. 1.
46. *New York Call*, September 22, 1911, p. 3.
47. *Chicago Tribune*, October 22, 1911, p. 3; *New York Times*, October 22, 1911, p. 10.
48. *Chicago Tribune*, September 20, 1911, p. 2.
49. *New York Times*, October 2, 1921, p. 16; *Dictionary of American Biography*, Vol. 4, Pt. 2, p. 22; *New York Tribune*, December 12, 1918, p. 7; *New York Times*, December 7, 1918, pp. 1-2; *New York Times*, December 12, 1918, p. 13.
50. *Fort Wayne Labor Times-Herald*, July 24, 1908.

# Chapter 7 Notes

1. Peter Collier and David Horowitz, *The Rockefellers*, p. 59.
2. *Chicago Examiner*, September 21, 1910.
3. *New York Times*, January 15, 1909, p. 15.
4. *Cleveland Press*, March 20, 1911, p. 1.
5. KML Collection, Chicago Historical Society, Prints & Photographs Department.
6. *Chicago Tribune*, May 1, 1919, page unknown.
7. William T. Hutchinson, *Lowden of Illinois*, pp. 149, 174, 190, 227.
8. William T. Hutchinson, *Lowden of Illinois*, p. 181.
9. Ultimately, another old ally, William Lorimer, the South Side's "Blond Boss," gained the Senate seat, but he would not long retain it. Widespread rumors of bribed state legislators surfaced. The United States Senate seated Lorimer, but the gossip would not die. The *Chicago Tribune* hammered at him mercilessly. At a banquet in Chicago, ex-President Roosevelt refused to sit at the same table with the tainted office holder. A Senate committee reported Lorimer had indeed resorted to bribery, but contended that he had enough votes to win without the compromised votes and, accordingly, his election should stand. Such logic outraged reformers—and most of the public. In July 1912 the Senate finally declared, "corrupt methods and practices were employed in Lorimer's election, and that the election, therefore, was invalid." The "Blond Boss" found himself thus expelled from the Senate. The Lorimer scan-

dal provided reformers with much-needed help in passing the Seventeenth
Amendment, mandating popular election of United States senators.

10. William T. Hutchinson, *Lowden of Illinois*, p. 180; Claude Bowers, *Beveridge and the Progressive Era*, pp. 406-409; *Biographical Dictionary of the American Congress*, p. 1308.

11. *Terre Haute Post*, December 9, 1910, p. 1.

12. *Detroit Times*, January 28, 1910, p. 1.

13. *New York Times*, December 20, 1905, p. 10.

14. Frederick Landis advertising card, Archives of the Cass County Historical Society.

15. Theodore Roosevelt to Frederick Landis, June 28, 1910, Files of the Cass County Historical Society.

16. *1910 Book Review Digest*, p. 229.

17. James E. Watson, *As I Knew Them*, p. 27.

18. Kennedy, Lawrence, *Biographical Dictionary of the American Congress 1774-1971*, Washington: U. S. Government Printing Office, 1971, p. 1259; John Braeman, *Albert J. Beveridge*, pp. 149-150; *New York Times*, January 25, 1922, p. 17.

19. J. G. Taylor Spink, *Judge Landis and Twenty-Five Years of Baseball*, p. 3.

20. *Chicago American*, January 25, 1910, p. 1; *Chicago Daily Journal*, January 25, 1910, p. 1; *Chicago Tribune*, January 25, 1910, p. 1; *Chicago Record-Herald*, January 25, 1910, p. 1; Matthew Josephson, *The Robber Barons*, pp. 286-287.

21. *Chicago Examiner*, June 24, 1910, p. 1.

22. J. Ogden Armour, Louis F. Swift, Edward Morris, Edward Tilden, Arthur Meeker, Edward F. Swift, Charles F. Swift, Louis H. Heyman, Thomas J. Connors, and Francis A. Fowler.

23. Woodrow Wilson, *History of the American Nation*, Volume VI, *CD Sourcebook of American History*, Compact University, 1994; Kenesaw Mountain Landis to George W. Wickersham, June 2, 1911, KML Scrapbooks, Chicago Historical Society; George W. Wickersham to Kenesaw Mountain Landis, July 11, 1911; KML Scrapbooks, CHS.

24. George W. Wickersham to Kenesaw Mountain Landis, March 5, 1912, KML Scrapbooks, Chicago Historical Society.

25. *New York Evening Telegram*, March 19, 1912.

26. Record of Wills, Cass County Indiana, Book 7, p. 555.

27. The rift between Taft and the Landises was surprisingly brief, hardly extending beyond the 1912 election. In March 1914 Taft wrote to Landis recommending that he join the American Bar Association.

28. John Allan Gable, *The Bull Moose Years*, p. 108; Claude Bowers, *Beveridge and the Progressive Era*, p. 450.

29. Beveridge was one of the first of the Progressives, and Charles Landis had been his right-hand man in his failed bid for 1910 re-election. Charles Landis also supported Beveridge although he disagreed with him on the Payne-

Aldrich Tariff. The elections of 1914 were a disaster for the Progressives. Progressive representation dropped from nine to just three in the House of Representatives; no members of the party remained in the Senate. Beveridge finished a distant third in his race. In New York Theodore Roosevelt was making deals to regain entry into the Republican Party.

30. Claude Bower, *Beveridge and the Progressive Era*, p. 450.
31. John Braeman, *Albert J. Beveridge*, p. 238.
32. Landis did not author the play itself. A movie version followed in 1920 (again with Barrymore in the lead) but proved far less popular than the stage property.
33. 181 Fed. 427.
34. John Kobler, *Capone*, p. 64.
35. Kenna was no ordinary politician—even by Chicago standards. He and his partner, fellow alderman "Bathhouse John" Coughlin, operated any number of disreputable establishments in and around the "Levee."
36. Robert Jay Nash, *World Encyclopedia of Organized Crime*. Virgil W. Peterson, *Barbarians in Our Midst*, p. 90; Herbert Asbury, *Gem of the Prairie*, pp. 164-166.
37. Virgil W. Peterson, *Barbarians in Our Midst*, pp. 90-91; Herbert Asbury, *Gem of the Prairie*, p. 165.
38. Virgil W. Peterson, *Barbarians in Our Midst*, p. 101.
39. One such case involved Second Ward Alderman Oscar DePriest. DePriest, Chicago's first black alderman, was charged with "conspiracy to allow gambling houses and houses of ill-repute to operate and for bribery of police officers in connection with the operation of these houses." Despite the testimony of Police Chief Stephen K. Healey (indicted with DePriest), Darrow secured DePriest's acquittal.
40. Kevin Tierney, *Darrow: A Biography*. pp. 260, 280-281; William M. Tuttle, Jr., *Race Riot*, pp. 194-195; Stewart H. Holbrook, *Dreamers of the American Dream*, p. 328.
41. *Chicago Tribune*, October 4, 1916, p. 5.
42. Following Landis' death Lait would blast him as an "irascible, short-tempered, tyrannical despot. His manner of handling witnesses, lawyers—and reporters—was more arbitrary than the behavior of any jurist I have ever seen." But during the Tennes probe Lait had no problem with Landis' unorthodox tactics. "Yesterday," he wrote, "was the first time in my life that I ever saw a courtroom run as a man would run his own business—with a desire for results, the ability to get them and the courage to demand them, rather than a confused institution where private rights were so holy that public rights took a back seat. I am for Judge Landis."
43. *Chicago Herald*, October 3, 1916.
44. *The Day Book*, October 3, 1916, p. 2.
45. *Chicago Tribune*, October 3, 1916, p. 4.
46. *Chicago Examiner*, October 5, 1916; *Chicago Evening Post*, October 5, 1916, p. 1.

47. Robert Jay Nash, *World Encyclopedia of Organized Crime*; Herbert Asbury, *Gem of the Prairie*, p. 166; Virgil W. Peterson, *Barbarians in Our Midst*, pp. 110-111; W. A. Swanberg, *Citizen Hearst*, p. 641; Joseph Gies, *The Colonel of Chicago*, p. 36.
48. Files of the Prints & Photographs Department, Chicago Historical Society.
49. *Chicago Herald*, October 2, 1916.
50. Kevin Tierney, *Darrow: A Biography*, p. 281.
51. 245 U.S. 493-510; Hutchinson, *Lowden of Illinois*, pp. 331-334.

# Chapter 8 Notes

1. Robert K. Murray, *Red Scare*, pp. 13-14.
2. It is little remembered today, but remarkably similar antisedition statutes existed during World War II. On July 22, 1942, for example, federal authorities indicted 28 individuals on such charges. Even prior to that early date the FBI had arrested 9,405 persons it deemed to be Axis agents.
3. Robert K. Murray, *Red Scare*, p. 14; John Roy Carlson, *Under Cover*, pp. 409-416.
4. David Quintin Voigt, *American Baseball*, Volume II, p. 142; *Brooklyn Daily Eagle*, November 13, 1920.
5. *Chicago Daily News*, February 18, 1922; *Chicago Tribune*, May 1, 1919, p. 1.
6. Col. Edwin M. Hadley, "The Lion and the Lion's Cub," *South Shore Country Club*, date unknown, pp. 4-8; Interview with Keehn Landis, July 27, 1995.
7. *Des Moines Capital*, November 15, 1920.
8. *Chicago Daily Journal*, October 15, 1918; *Chicago Tribune*, November 13, 1918, p. 3.
9. *Chicago Tribune*, June 17, 1934.
10. A minimum of five kills qualified one as an ace.
11. *Chicago Daily Journal*, October 15, 1918; Interview with Keehn Landis, July 27, 1995; *New York Times*, April 18, 1971, p. 48; *New York Times*, September 29, 1918, p. 10.
12. *Chicago Evening American*, October 16, 1918.
13. *Chicago Tribune*, December 1, 1918, p. 9.
14. Newspaper clipping, July 11, 1917, KML Scrapbooks, Chicago Historical Society.
15. Theodore Roosevelt and William Jennings Bryan made similar requests to serve overseas. Both were also refused.
16. Newton D. Baker to Kenesaw Mountain Landis, November 3, 1917, KML Scrapbooks, Chicago Historical Society; Andrew Sinclair, *Era of Excess*, p. 133; Henry Pringle, *Theodore Roosevelt*, pp. 416-420.
17. J. G. Taylor Spink, *Judge Landis and Twenty-Five Years of Baseball*, p. 22-23.
18. *La Crosse (Wisc.) Morgen Stern*, June 5, 1917, p. 1; *Des Moines Capital*, April 28, 1917.

19. While Landis had no use for draft evaders, he had only slightly more use for those who *were* drafted. "We are a nation of cowards," he exclaimed early in the war. "The men who are exposed to conscription are those who would not volunteer for service under any circumstance."

20. Henry Pringle, "Portrait of a Bench Warmer," *Harper's Monthly Magazine*, April 1927, p. 620.

21. *Chicago Tribune*, July 6, 1917; *Chicago Tribune*, May 1, 1917; David Karsner, "The War and the I.W.W.," *The Call Magazine*, September 5, 1920, p. 1; Donald F. Tingley, *Structuring of a State*, p. 211-212; William T. Hutchinson, *Lowden of Illinois*, p. 377; Peter Carlson, *Roughneck*, p. 266.

22. *Chicago Tribune*, July 6, 1917.

23. Harold Seymour, *Baseball: The Golden Age*, p. 370.

24. Lowden was just as great a patriot as Landis and thoroughly approved of his handling of the Rockford trial.

25. Richard Norton Smith, *The Colonel: The Life and Legend of Robert R. McCormick*, p. 187.

26. Joseph Gies, *The Colonel of Chicago*, pp. 58-59, 66; Emmet Dedmon, *Fabulous Chicago: A Great City's History and People*, p. 288; William M. Tuttle, Jr., *Race Riot*, pp. 46-47.

27. *New York Times*, July 28, 1917, p. 9; *Chicago Tribune*, July 11, 1917.

28. *New York Times*, July 18, 1917, p. 9.

29. In 1919 Chicago reform Republican Harold L. Ickes asked Landis if he would run against Thompson and promised the Judge the support of publisher Victor Lawson's *Chicago Daily News* if he accepted the challenge. In Ickes' *The Autobiography of a Curmudgeon*, he wrote of visiting Landis in his chambers to make the offer. The result was a standoff. Ickes declined the offer of the dark black chewing tobacco the Squire kept on his desk to dry ("Ickes, this is the sweetest tobacco you have ever put in your mouth"), and Landis in turn declined Ickes' political proposition, saying he had been hounded by political interests since the days of the Standard Oil decision. The Judge seemed particularly irked by the rumors Standard Oil had spread about him at the time regarding his mental state. "Ickes," Landis summed up, "I would just as soon you ask me to clean a backhouse."

30. Andrew Sinclair, *Era of Excess*, pp. 119-121; John Kobler, *Ardent Spirits*, pp. 206-207.

31. Peter Hernon & Terry Ganey, *Under The Influence*, pp. 106-107.

## Chapter 9 Notes

1. Theodore Roosevelt added to the controversy when he derided the defendants and their allies as "undesirable citizens."

2. Melvyn Dubofsky, *"Big Bill Haywood,"* pp. 49, 55; Marian C. McKenna, *Borah*, pp. 48-63; Francis X. Busch, *Prisoners at the Bar*, pp. 15-50; Lowell Stillwell

Hawley, Elizabeth Gurley Flynn, *Debs, Haywood, Ruthenberg*, pp. 21-24, 26; Harrison George, *The IWW Trial*, pp. 181-182.

3. Peter Carlson, *Roughneck*, p. 158, Preston, *Aliens and Dissenters*, p. 49; David Avery and Martha Moore Goldstein, *Bolshevism: Its Cure*, p. 181.

4. Finis Farr, *Chicago: A Personal History of America's Most American City*, p. 331; Elizabeth Gurley Flynn, *Debs, Haywood, Ruthenberg*, p. 27.

5. William Preston, Jr., *Aliens and Dissenters*, p. 91. Stewart H. Holbrook, *Dreamers of the American Dream*, pp. 88-117; p. 331; Elizabeth Gurley Flynn, *Debs, Haywood, Ruthenberg*, p. 27; Joseph Conlin, *Big Bill Haywood and Radical Union Movement*, p. 179.

6. Robert K. Murray, *Red Scare*, p. 29.

7. William Preston, Jr., *Aliens and Dissenters*, p. 89; Melvyn Dubofsky, *Big Bill Haywood*, p. 99.

8. Edward Robb Ellis, *Echoes of Distant Thunder: Life in the United States 1914-1918*, p. 444.

9. *New York Times*, September 6, 1917, pp. 1-2; *New York Times,* April 1, 1918, p. 20; *New York Times*, April 2, 1918, p. 11; Lowell Stillwell Hawley, *Counsel for the Damned*, p. 227.

10. Peter Carlson, *Roughneck*, p. 255; Donald F. Tingley, *The Structuring of a State*, p. 212.

11. Russell fled Chicago. When he was apprehended, he was working in a Muskegon, Michigan, defense plant.

12. *Chicago Post*, April 6, 1918, p. 1; *Chicago Post*, April 8, 1918, p. 2; *Chicago Herald & Examiner*, August 18, 1918, p. 2; *New York Times*, April 7, 1918, p. 16; Harrison George, *The IWW Trial*, p. 13; Peter Carlson, *Roughneck*, p. 264; *Chicago Tribune*, July 9, 1918, p. 4.

13. Big Bill Haywood, *Bill Haywood's Book*, p. 322; *New York Call*, August 2, 1918, p. 3; Harrison George, *The IWW Trial*, p. 12.

14. Peter Carlson, *Roughneck*, p. 257; Lowell Stillwell Hawley, *Counsel for the Damned*, p. 227; Harrison George, *The IWW Trial*, p. 12.

15. *Chicago Herald & Examiner*, August 2, 1918, p. 13; Peter Carlson, *Roughneck*, pp. 257, 266; Stewart H. Holbrook, *Dreamers of the American Dream*, p. 332; Richard Crowder, *Carl Sandburg*, p. 62; North Callahan, *Carl Sandburg: His Life and Works*, p. 63; Penelope Nixon, *Carl Sandburg: A Biography*, p. 307; *New York Times*, June 25, 1918, p. 11; *New York Call*, June 7, 1918, p. 2; *New York Call*, August 2, 1918, p. 1. *New York Call*, June 25, 1918, p. 1; *New York Call*, August 2, 1918, pp. 1, 3; Harrison George, *The IWW Trial*, p. 181; Peter Carlson, *Roughneck*, p. 273.

16. The flamboyant Bross would tool about Chicago with a red flag flying from the back of his expensive limousine.

17. John Reed, *Adventures of a Young Man*, p. 124; Melvyn Dubofsky, *"Big Bill" Haywood*, p. 118; Stewart H. Holbrook, *Dreamers of the American Dream*, p. 334; Richard O'Connor and Dale L. Walker, *The Lost Revolutionary*, p. 231;

Joseph Conlin, *Big Bill Haywood and the Radical Union Movement*, p. 189; Peter Carlson, *Roughneck*, p. 264.

18. John Reed, *Adventures of a Young Man*, p. 122; Finis Farr, *Chicago: A Personal History of America's Most American City*, p. 333; Richard O'Connor & Dale L. Walker, *The Lost Revolutionary*, p. 231.

19. Ralph Chandler, *"Wobbly,"* p. 244.

20. Kenyon had gotten to know Landis during the Beef Trust controversy of 1910 when Kenyon was as assistant to Attorney General Wickersham.

21. *New York Call*, June 7, 1918, p. 2; *New York Call*, July 8, 1918, p. 3; *Chicago Post*, May 4, 1918, p. 1; *Chicago Examiner*, July 15, 1910, p. 1.

22. *New York Call*, July 11, 1918, p. 1.

23. David Karsner, "Kenesaw Mountain Landis," *The Call Magazine*, April 6, 1920, p. 6.

24. But Pringle, along with others, criticized Landis' failure to order a cease-and-desist notice to the bands in the rotunda of his building that blared out a ceaseless round of patriotic music as they attempted to promote war bond sales. At their loudest, these concerts would drown out testimony.

25. Melvyn Dubofsky, *Big Bill Haywood*, p. 121; Harold Seymour, *Baseball: The Golden Age*, pp. 369-370; Peter Carlson, *Roughneck*, p. 267.

26. *New York Call*, August 7, 1918, p. 1; *New York Call*, July 8, 1918, p. 2.

27. David Karsner, "Kenesaw Mountain Landis," *The Call Magazine*, April 6, 1920, p. 6.

28. There is at least one recorded instance of a defendant attempting to flee the court house. On July 8 John Baldazzi hid in a public lavatory outside Landis' chambers and then made a break down the stairways. He got as far as the second floor before being apprehended.

29. David Karsner, "The War and the IWW," *The Call Magazine*, September 5, 1920, p. 5; *Chicago Tribune*, July 9, 1919, p. 4; Peter Carlson, *Roughneck*, p. 258.

30. David Karsner, "Kenesaw Mountain Landis," *The Call Magazine*, April 6, 1920, p. 6; David Karsner, "The War and the IWW," *The Call Magazine*, September 5, 1920, p. 5.

31. David Karsner, "Kenesaw Mountain Landis," *The Call Magazine*, April 6, 1920, pp. 6-7.

32. David Karsner, "Kenesaw Mountain Landis," *The Call Magazine*, April 6, 1920, p. 6.

33. Despite Landis' allowance for such testimony, Vanderveer took his formal ruling with great disappointment and began drinking. He also faced increasing financial difficulties as his clients were not forthcoming with his fees. Back in Seattle his wife was forced to sell her diamond engagement ring to help pay their mounting bills.

34. Sometimes that case was made by prosecution witnesses. After being instructed by Landis to tell the court how long he worked his field hands, a Washington state wheat farmer contended he worked them "reasonable

hours"—which to him meant: "From four in the morning to eight in the evening—it's reasonable hours and the custom of the county."

35. Donald F. Tingley, *The Structuring of a State*, pp. 213-214; *New York Call*, July 3, 1918, p. 2; Lowell Stillwell Hawley, *Counsel for the Damned*, pp. 226, 233-235; *Peter Carlson, Roughneck*, pp. 270-271.

36. *New York Times*, May 18, 1918, p. 7; Peter Carlson, *Roughneck*, p. 269.

37. William Preston, Jr., *Aliens and Dissenters*, p. 121.

38. Harrison George, *The IWW Trial*, p. 33; *New York Call*, May 22, 1918, p. 1; William Preston, Jr., *Aliens and Dissenters*, p. 121; Lowell Stillwell Hawley, *Counsel for the Damned*, p. 236.

39. *New York Times*, May 19, 1918, p. 7; *New York Call*, July 8, 1918. p. 2.

40. Absent from the general merriment was Vanderveer. His financial troubles had worsened and his mood darkened. "His examination of prosecution witnesses became more savage and his sarcasm became more cutting than ever before," noted biographer Lowell Stillwell Hawley, "but his infectious smile which had been his most reliable weapon of the past appeared almost not at all. He seemed far more embittered than any of the defendants."

41. *New York Call*, June 29, 1918, p. 1; Lowell Stillwell Hawley, *Counsel for the Damned*, p. 235-236.

42. *Chicago Herald & Examiner*, August 6, 1918, p. 9.

43. On the eve of Haywood's testimony Landis traveled to Camp Grant in Rockford, Illinois, where he granted citizenship to 800 alien soldiers. The Judge's speech at the occasion was a short one—his audience was more interested in the card of boxing matches that followed his address.

44. In fairness to Haywood, his record on race relations was otherwise unusually liberal for the times. He refused to speak before segregated audiences, and at Alexandria, Louisiana, he forced the integration of black and white lumberjacks and millworkers in the IWW.

45. *Chicago Herald & Examiner*, August 4, 1918, p. 6; *Chicago Herald & Examiner*, August 9, 1918, p. 4; *Chicago Herald & Examiner*, August 10, 1918, p. 13; Edward Robb Ellis, *Echoes of Distant Thunder: Life in the United States 1914-1918*, p. 445; *New York Times*, August 10, 1918, p. 14; *New York Call*, August 10, 1918, pp. 1-2; Joseph Conlin, *Big Bill Haywood and the Radical Union Movement*, pp. 124-125; Harrison George, *The IWW Trial*, p. 183.

46. The only member of the IWW executive board to openly sanction draft resistance was Frank Little, who was brutally lynched near Butte, Montana, in 1917. The defendants might have chosen to distance themselves more from Little. Instead, many wore red flags in their lapels in his memory.

47. *Chicago Herald & Examiner*, August 10, 1918, p. 16; *Chicago Herald & Examiner*, August 13, 1918, p. 5; *Chicago Herald & Examiner*, August 14, 1918, p. 9; Robert K. Murray, *Red Scare*, p. 30; Stewart H. Holbrook, *Dreamers of the American Dream*, p. 331; Harrison George, *The IWW Trial*, p. 183.

48. *Chicago Herald & Examiner*, August 14, 1918, p. 9.

49. Vanderveer's foregoing of concluding remarks may have had less to do with concern for his clients or a weary jury than with spite against defense counsel Claude Porter. Porter, running for governor of Iowa, was to have followed Vanderveer's statement and had already wired advance copies of his remarks to Iowa papers. When Vanderveer chose not to address the jury, he shut the door on Porter's speech, and Porter had to scramble to head off publication of his never-delivered remarks.

50. *Chicago Daily Tribune*, August 18, 1918, p. 7; *Chicago Herald & Examiner*, August 16, 1918, p. 9; *New York Times,* August 18, 1918, p. 1; Harrison George, *The IWW Trial*, p. 204.

51. Peter Carlson, *Roughneck*, p. 280.

52. In later years Haywood expressed far less approval of Landis. In his autobiography wrote: "Pontius Pilate or Bloody Jeffreys never enjoyed themselves better than did Judge Landis when he was imposing these terrible sentences upon a group of working men for whom he had no sense of humanity, no sense of justice." For his part, Landis, despite his solicitude during the trial, would as time passed refer to the defendants as "filth," "scum," and "slimy rats."

53. *Chicago Herald & Examiner*, August 18, 1918, p. 1; Bill Haywood, *Bill Haywood's Book*, p. 324; J. G. Taylor Spink, *Judge Landis and Twenty-Five Years of Baseball*, p. 23.

54. *New York Times*, August 18, 1919, p. 1; Lowell Stillwell Hawley, *Counsel for the Damned*, p. 239; Harrison George, *The IWW Trial*, p. 207.

55. *New York Times*, August 19, 1918, p. 8.

56. *Chicago Daily Tribune*, August 18, 1918, p. 1; Lowell Stillwell Hawley, *Counsel for the Damned*, p. 239.

57. *New York Times*, August 30, 1918, p. 20.

58. *Chicago Tribune*, August 31, 1918, p. 5.

59. These included Red Doran, Harrison George, and Ray Fanning.

60. These included Ben Fletcher, John Baldazzi, and former IWW leader Vincent St. John. Fletcher had always been skeptical regarding Landis. "He's a faker," he told David Karsner. "Wait till he gets a chance; then he'll plaster it on thick." Perhaps for that reason Fletcher kept his wits about him following sentencing. "Judge Landis is using poor English today," he quipped, "his sentences are too long."

61. *New York Times*, September 2, 1918, p. 8; John Reed, *Adventures of a Young Man*, p. 123; *Chicago Tribune*, August 31, 1918, pp. 1,5; David Karsner, "Kenesaw Mountain Landis," *The Call Magazine*, April 6, 1920, p. 7; *New York Times*, August 31, 1918, p. 7; Peter Carlson, *Roughneck*, pp. 284-285.

62. *New York Times*, August 31, 1918, p. 6.

63. Robert K. Murray, *Red Scare*, p. 31.

64. Bill Haywood, *Bill Haywood's Book*, pp. 325-326.

65. Bill Haywood, *Bill Haywood's Book*, p. 328. Melvyn Dubofsky, *"Big Bill" Haywood*, p. 123.

66. Extract of letter of Lieutenant Jesse Allen Crafton to Knox College Bulletin; KML Collection; CHS.
67. Peter Carlson, *Roughneck*, p. 302.
68. *New York Times*, April 12, 1921, p. 7; *New York Times*, April 22, 1921, pp. 16, 21; Haywood, Bill Haywood's Book, p. 361; Stewart H. Holbrook, *Dreamers of the American Dream*, p. 333-334; Lowell Stillwell Hawley, *Counsel for the Damned*, p. 229.
69. *New York Times*, April 22, 1921, p. 16; *New York Times*, April 27, 1921, p. 16; Donald F. Tingley, *The Structuring of a State*, p. 212.
70. Oddly enough, working hard on the commutation was United States senator George Wharton Pepper, who in 1920 had drawn up Landis' contract as baseball commissioner.
71. Actually, Haywood was only partially interred in the Kremlin. Cremated, part of his ashes remained in Moscow. The rest returned to Chicago's Waldheim Cemetery, where they were placed alongside those of the Haymarket bombers.
72. *New York Times*, April 24, 1921, pp. 1, 6; Preston, *Aliens and Dissenters*, p. 263; Melvyn Dubofsky, *"Big Bill" Haywood*, pp. 135, 138-139; Elizabeth Gurley Flynn, *Debs, Haywood, Ruthenberg*, p. 28.
73. Peter Carlson, *Roughneck*, p. 322.

# Chapter 10 Notes

1. It was in affirming the conviction of Socialist Party General Secretary Charles T. Schenck, that Supreme Court Justice Oliver Wendell Holmes put forth the doctrine of "clear and present danger."
2. Albert Fried, *Socialism in America*, pp. 506-509; James Weinstein, *The Decline of Socialism in America*, pp. 160-161; *New York Call*, July 1, 1918, p. 1; William Preston, Jr., *Aliens and Dissenters*, pp. 89-90; Robert K. Murray, *Red Scare*, pp. 19, 22-25.
3. Approximately 2,000 persons — Socialists and non-Socialists — were ultimately found guilty of violating the Espionage Act.
4. James Weinstein, *The Decline of Socialism in America*, pp. 160-161; Albert Fried, *Socialism in America*, pp. 510-511.
5. Robert K. Murray, *Red Scare*, p. 22.
6. Albert Fried, *Socialism in America*, pp. 386, 388-389; Stewart H. Holbrook, *Dreamers of the American Dream*, p. 313.
7. Donald Young (ed.), *Adventures in Politics*, p. 55; David Goldstein and Martha Moore Avery, *Bolshevism: Its Cure*, p. 113.
8. In 1917 the People's Council had been a serious bone of contention between Chicago mayor Thompson and Illinois governor Lowden. Previously banned from Minneapolis, the Council received a permit from Thompson to meet in Chicago. Lowden, who believed the session "was designed for the purpose of bringing on draft riots and obstructing the Government," sent the National

Guard to Chicago to break up the meeting. The Chicago city council voted 42-6 to commend Lowden for his actions.

9.  *Chicago Post*, December 9, 1918, p. 2; *Chicago Herald & Examiner*, January 1, 1919, p. 1; *Chicago Daily Journal*, January 7, 1919, p. 4; William M. Tuttle, *Race Riot*, p. 205; *New York Call*, July 16, 1918, p. 3.

10.  Of the defendants in the Berger case actually only three, Berger, Germer, and Engdahl, were German. Tucker was Anglo-Saxon; Kruse of Danish descent.

11.  Landis had not always been so incensed at German-Americans. To a La Crosse, Wisconsin, audience in July 1917 he had praised the ethnic group's historic patriotism. "The German-Americans have never failed us...," he orated. "I have refused to take stock in the disloyalty of German-Americans." When the next month he attacked Big Bill Thompson's loyalty, he again declared that "The German-American is loyal. He is for America first, last and always. There may be a few who favor the Kaiser, but they are few and far between."

12.  *La Crosse (Wisc.) Morgan Stern*, June 5, 1917, p. 1; *Chicago Tribune*, July 11, 1917; *New York Call*, July 16, 1918, p. 3.

13.  Seymour Stedman, *Brief for Plaintiffs in Error. In the United States Court of Appeals for the Seventh Circuit, October term, A.D. 1918. Victor L. Berger, Adolph Germer, William F. Kruse, Irwin St. John Tucker and J. Louis Engdahl plaintiffs in error, vs. the United States of America, defendant in error. Error to the District Court of the United States for the Northern District of Illinois, Eastern Division. Honorable K. M. Landis, Judge*, pp. 39-40; *Chicago Tribune*, May 1, 1919; *Chicago Tribune*, February 1, 1921, p. 5.

14.  *Chicago Tribune*, February 21, 1919, p. 4.

15.  *Chicago Tribune*, December 4, 1918, p. 11, 5; *Chicago Tribune*, December 10, 1918, p. 9; *Chicago Tribune*, December 11, 1918, p. 11; *Chicago Tribune*, February 1, 1921, pp. 1, 5.

16.  *New York Call*, February 5, 1919, pp. 1, 3; *Chicago Tribune*, December 12, 1918; 2157 *United States v. Berger, et al* 1363-1364; Stedman, Seymour, *Brief for Plaintiffs in Error. In the United States Court of Appeals for the Seventh Circuit, October term, A.D. 1918. Victor L. Berger, Adolph Germer, William F. Kruse, Irwin St. John Tucker and J. Louis Engdahl plaintiffs in error, vs. the United States of America, defendant in error. Error to the District Court of the United States for the Northern District of Illinois, Eastern Division. Honorable K. M. Landis, Judge*, pp. 258-263.

17.  *New York Call*, January 3, 1919, p. 1; *Chicago Post*, December 30, 1918, p. 1; *New York Times*, December 25, 1918, p. 2; *New York Times*, January 9, 1919, p. 4; *Chicago Tribune*, December 23, 1918, p. 10; *Chicago Tribune*, January 3, 1919, p. 7.

18.  *New York Call*, January 19, 1919, p. 2; *Chicago Journal*, January 8, 1919, p. 1; *Chicago Journal*, January 7, 1919, p. 4.

19.  *Chicago Daily Journal*, January 9, 1919, p. 4; *Chicago Daily Journal*, January 7, 1919, p. 4; *New York Call*, January 9, 1917.

20. David Karsner, "Kenesaw Mountain Landis," *The Call Magazine*, April 6, 1920, p. 20.
21. *Chicago Herald & Examiner*, January 8, 1919, p. 1; *Chicago Herald & Examiner*, January 9, 1919, pp. 1, 4; *New York Call*, January 9, 1919, p. 2; *Chicago Tribune*, January 9, 1919, pp. 1-2.
22. *Chicago Daily Journal*, January 9, 1919, p. 4; *New York Times*, January 9, 1919, p. 1; *Chicago Tribune*, January 9, 1919, p. 2; *Chicago Tribune*, December 12, 1918, p. 13.
23. Sentence by Judge Landis, *2157 United States v. Berger, et al., 1363*.
24. *New York Times*, February 21, 1919, pp. 1, 4.
25. J.G. Taylor Spink, *Judge Landis and Twenty-Five Years of Baseball*, p. 24
26. *1945 Baseball Register*, p. 5.
27. The bombs continued after May 1, eventually blowing up the American Knitting Mills in Franklin, Massachusetts, killing four, and in July the homes of Attorney General Palmer in Washington, a congressman's in Pittsburgh and a judge's in New York City.
28. *New York Times*, May 1, 1919, p. 3; Blair Coan, *The Red Web*, pp. 31-32.
29. Paul Avrich, *Sacco and Vanzetti: The Anarchist Background*, Princeton: Princeton University Press, pp. 140-143.
30. *Chicago Evening American*, May 1, 1919, p. 1.
31. J. G. Taylor Spink, *Judge Landis and Twenty-Five Years of Baseball*, p. 24.
32. Paul Avrich, *Sacco and Vanzetti: The Anarchist Background*, pp. 156-157.
33. Of course, Landis was not the only person to feel this way. And one needn't have been a Wilsonian Democrat or a TR Progressive to share Landis' views. When the Berger-Hillquit faction of the Socialist Party condemned U.S. participation in the war, large numbers of Socialists (normally native-born members) walked out of the party. Millionaire socialist J. G. Phelps Stokes (Stokes' own wife, Rose Pastor Stokes, was herself indicted for violation of the Espionage Act), for example, presaged Landis' comments. The anti-war Socialists, Stokes declared, should "be shot at once without an hour's delay."
34. *New York Times*, December 30, 1919, p. 17; Albert Fried, *Socialism in America*, pp. 508-509; *New York Call*, May 22, 1918, p. 1.
35. Robert K. Murray, *Red Scare*, pp. 226-228.
36. *Chicago Tribune*, October 23, 1920; Harold Seymour, *Baseball: The Golden Years*, p. 371.
37. *New York Times*, June 25, 1920, p. 17.
38. McReynolds, a "Gold Democrat," was among the court's most conservative justices. He later opposed most New Deal measures, becoming known as the "Lone Dissenter."
39. *New York Times*, February 1, 1921 p. 17; *New York Herald-Tribune*, February 1, 1921, p. 1.
40. *New York Times*, February 2, 1921, pp. 10, 17.
41. *New York Times*, February 1, 1921, p. 17.

42. *Chicago Tribune*, February 1, 1921, p. 5; *New York Herald-Tribune*, February 1, 1921, p. 3.
43. *New York Times*, February 1, 1921, p.17; *Chicago Tribune*, February 1, 1921.
44. *New York Times*, February 2, 1921, p. 17; *New York Herald-Tribune*, February 1, 1921, p. 3.
45. *New York Times*, February 2, 1921, p. 10.
46. Undated clipping, KML Scrapbooks, Chicago Historical Society; *Chicago Tribune*, February 4, 1921, p. 8.
47. Francis Russell, *The Shadow of Blooming Grove: Warren G. Harding in His Times*, p. 487.

# Chapter 11 Notes

1. David Quentin Voigt, *American Baseball*, Volume II, p. 142; Richard Lindberg, *Who's on 3rd?*, p. 40; Donald Gropman, *Say It Ain't So, Joe!*, p. 197.
2. David Pietrusza, *Major Leagues*, pp. 209-235; Harold Seymour, *Baseball: The Golden Years*, pp. 196-213; Fred Lieb, *The Baseball Story*, pp. 198-203; *Washington Post*, March 14, 1915, p. 1.
3. J. G. Taylor Spink, *Judge Landis and Twenty-Five Years of Baseball*, p. 36.
4. *New York Times*, January 6, 1915, p. 14.
5. *Sporting Life*, January 16, 1915; *New York Times*, January 6, 1915, p. 14.
6. *New York Times*, January 20, 1915, p. 10; *New York Times*, January 22, 1915, p. 12.
7. *New York Times*, January 21, 1915, p. 10.
8. *New York Times*, January 21, 1915, p. 10; J. G. Taylor Spink, *Judge Landis and Twenty-Five Years of Baseball*, p. 34.
9. J. G. Taylor Spink, *Judge Landis and Twenty-Five Years of Baseball*, p. 35; Lee Lowenfish and Tony Lupien, *The Imperfect Diamond*, p. 90.
10. *Schenectady Union-Star*, January 23, 1915, p. 4.
11. *New York Times*, January 22, 1915, p. 15; *New York Times*, January 23, 1915, p. 9; *Schenectady Union-Star*, January 21, 1915, p. 1; Lee Lowenfish and Tony Lupien, *The Imperfect Diamond*, pp. 88, 106.
12. Harold Seymour, *Baseball: The Golden Age*, p. 212; Eugene Murdock, *Ban Johnson: Czar of Baseball*, p. 114; J. G. Taylor Spink, *Judge Landis and Twenty-Five Years of Baseball*, p. 34.
13. *New York Times*, February 8, 1916, p. 12; *The Reach Official American League Guide for 1916*, pp. 54-58; *Sporting Life*, October 23, 1915, p. 8; *Sporting Life*, December 25, 1915, p. 8; David Pietrusza, *Major Leagues*, p. 238.
14. Harold Seymour, *Baseball: The Golden Years*, pp. 247-253; John Thorn, Pete Palmer, and Michael Gershman, *Total Baseball* (4th edition), pp. 106, 533, 543.
15. Daniel E. Ginsburg, *The Fix Is In*, p. 84.
16. Harold Seymour, *Baseball: The Golden Age*, p. 296.

17. *Chicago Evening American*, November 8, 1919.
18. *Associated Advertising*, January 1920, pp. 8-10, 38-40; Associated Advertising Clubs of the World, *Special Bulletin of the National Vigilance Committee*, December 12, 1919; *Chicago Tribune*, October 30, 1919; *Chicago Evening American*, November 8, 1919; *Chicago Herald-Examiner*, November 9, 1919; *Chicago Daily News* undated clipping.
19. Chicago released Hendrix, and he never pitched professionally again. Three other Cubs—Fred Merkle, Buck Herzog, and Paul Carter—were also under suspicion, but no proof was produced. Nonetheless, none ever played big league ball again.
20. The jury did not learn that during the World Series Tennes had also tipped off Comiskey.
21. Eliot Asinof, *Eight Men Out, passim*; Harold Seymour, *Baseball: The Golden Age*, pp. 294-310; Bill Veeck, *The Hustler's Handbook*, p. 258-260; Irving M. Stein, *The Ginger Kid*, p. 217; Daniel E. Ginsburg, *The Fix Is In*, pp. 133-136.
22. Eugene Murdock, *Ban Johnson, passim*; Harold Seymour, *Baseball: The Early Years*, pp. 307-324; David Q. Voigt, *American Baseball: From the Gentleman's Sport to the Commissioner's System*, pp. 313-317; *Harold Seymour, Baseball: The Golden Age*, pp. 259-272; George Wharton Pepper, *Philadelphia Lawyer*, p. 358.
23. *New York Evening Telegram*, September 17, 1919; *Chicago Herald*, November 3, 1916; *The Sporting News*, January 5, 1920, p. 1; *The Sporting News*, November 25, 1920, pp. 3, 4; *Brooklyn Daily Eagle*, January 11, 1920; *New York World*, January 11, 1920; *New York Sun*, January 11, 1920; *Cleveland Plain Dealer*, January 10, 1920.
24. *Chicago Evening Post*, January 7, 1920; Irving M. Stein, *The Ginger Kid*, p. 208.
25. Harold Seymour, *Baseball: The Golden Age*, pp. 311-312; *Detroit News*, November 29, 1920; *The Sporting News*, October 7, 1920, p. 4.
26. *The Sporting News*, March 14, 1951.
27. Comiskey had actually known of the fix as long as Johnson had. Browns second baseman Joe Gedeon, a friend of Swede Risberg, and St. Louis gambler Harry Redmon both provided details to Comiskey. Joe Jackson had tried to confess on several occasions, but Comiskey rebuffed him. It was clearly in the Noble Roman's interest to prevent exposure.
28. Bill Veeck, *The Hustler's Handbook*, pp. 273-274.
29. There were games within games. Johnson was also promising the commissionership to *Chicago Tribune* sports editor Harvey Woodruff.
30. Bill Veeck, *The Hustler's Handbook*, pp. 269, 285.
31. Johnson had lived in Chicago since the mid-1890s.
32. Eugene Murdock, *Ban Johnson: Czar of Baseball*, p. 148.
33. Eugene Murdock, *Ban Johnson: Czar of Baseball*, p. 190.
34. J. G. Taylor Spink, *Judge Landis and Twenty-Five Years of Baseball*, pp. 66-67; Harold Seymour, *Baseball: The Golden Age*, pp. 313-314; *New York Times*, November 9, 1920, p. 1.

35. Bill Veeck, *The Hustler's Handbook*, p. 282.
36. Bill Veeck, *The Hustler's Handbook*, p. 287.
37. Harold Seymour, *Baseball: The Golden Age*, pp. 317-318.
38. Undated clipping, KML Scrapbooks, Chicago Historical Society.
39. *Chicago Tribune*, November 10, 1920, page 1; Harold Seymour, *Baseball: The Golden Age*, pp. 318-319; *Kansas City Journal*, November 9, 1920.
40. *Kansas City Journal*, November 10, 1920.
41. F. C. Lane, "How Judge Landis Became Baseball's Sole Commissioner," *Baseball Magazine*, pp. 499, 501-502.
42. Harold Seymour, *Baseball: The Golden Age*, p. 319.
43. Bill Veeck, *The Hustler's Handbook*, p. 291; *Chicago Herald and Examiner*, November 13, 1920; *Chicago Tribune*, November 13, 1920, p. 2; *New York Times*, November 13, 1920, p. 12.
44. Bill Veeck, *The Hustler's Handbook*, p. 292.
45. Leading contenders for the other positions on the committee were McDonald, Big Bill Edwards, and a representative of the minor leagues. With Edwards favoring the National League and Johnson's coup to take over the minors having failed precipitously, there was little percentage for Johnson in staffing the whole commission or even a majority of it.
46. Bill Veeck, *The Hustler's Handbook*, p. 292; *Chicago Tribune*, November 13, 1920, p. 2; *Chicago American*, November 12, 1920, p. 26; *Chicago Daily Journal*, November 11, 1920, p. 1.
47. *The 1945 Baseball Register*, p. 19.
48. Universal Service wire report, November 13, 1920; *Chicago Herald & Examiner*, November 13, 1920; *Chicago Tribune*, November 13, 1920, p. 1.
49. *Chicago Herald & Examiner*, November 13, 1920; *Literary Digest*, December 4, 1920.
50. *Boston Herald*, November 13, 1920; *Des Moines Capital*, November 15, 1920.
51. *Chicago Herald & Examiner*, November 13, 1920.
52. *New York Times*, November 13, 1920, p. 1; Ed Fitzgerald, "Judge Landis, Baseball's High Commissioner," *Sport Magazine*, June 1950, p. 55.
53. *Chicago Herald & Examiner*, November 13, 1920.
54. J. G. Taylor Spink, *Judge Landis and Twenty-Five Years of Baseball*, p. 72.
55. *Boston Herald*, November 13, 1920.
56. *Chicago Herald & Examiner*, November 14, 1920.
57. *Boston Herald*, November 13, 1920.
58. *New York Times*, November 13, 1920.
59. *Detroit News*, November 29, 1920.

# Chapter 12 Notes

1. Harold Seymour, *Baseball: The Golden Age*, p. 323; Donald Gropman, *Say It Ain't So, Joe!*, p. 198.

2. Bill Veeck, *The Hustler's Handbook*, p. 293.
3. *Spalding's Official Base Ball Record for 1921*, p. 61; Harold Seymour, *Baseball: The Golden Age*, pp. 321-322.
4. George Wharton Pepper, *Philadelphia Lawyer*, p. 358.
5. Bill Veeck, *The Hustler's Handbook*, pp. 296-297.
6. Major league attendance dropped from 5,080,300 in 1920 to 4,620,328 in 1921, but this seems to be the start of a trend that began even before the scandal broke since attendance had already fallen off from 6,532,439 in 1919.
7. *New York Sun*, June 3, 1921, p. 18.
8. Bill Veeck, *The Hustler's Handbook*, p. 293.
9. J. G. Taylor Spink, *Judge Landis and Twenty-Five Years of Baseball*, p. 78
10. Years later O'Connor was rooming at the minor league meetings with veteran Texas baseball man Howard Green. Green asked him what he would have done had he not taken the job with Landis. "I would have become one of the outstanding attorneys in Chicago," O'Connor replied.
11. *Chicago Tribune*, February 5, 1921, p. 11; *New York Times*, February 5, 1921, p. 12; Interview with Howard Green, August 13, 1995; *Reach American League Guide for 1922*, p. 52.
12. J. G. Taylor Spink, *Judge Landis and Twenty-Five Years of Baseball*, p. 90; *Reach Official American League Guide for 1922*, p. 48; *New York Times*, February 21, 1921, p. 17.
13. *Reach Official American League Guide for 1922*, p. 28; Irving M. Stein, *The Ginger Kid*, pp. 261-262; Eliot Asinof, *Eight Men Out*, p. 262; Harold Seymour, *Baseball: The Golden Age*, pp. 324-325.
14. *Reach Official American League Guide for 1922*, p. 50; Harold Seymour, *Baseball: The Golden Age*, pp. 372-373; Daniel Ginsburg, *The Fix Is In*, p. 164.
15. Daniel Ginsburg, *The Fix Is In*, p. 164; Harold Seymour, *Baseball: The Golden Age*, pp. 372-373; Fred Lieb, *The Baseball Story*, p. 230; *New York Times*, March 25, 1921, p. 20.
16. Donald J. Proctor, "The Blacklisting of Ray Fisher," *1981 Baseball Research Journal*, pp. 34-45, 182-188; Richard Nardinelli, "Judge Kenesaw Mountain Landis and the Art of Cartel Enforcement," *Baseball History*, 1989, p. 103.
17. *Reach Official American League Guide for 1922*, p. 51; Dan Ginsburg, *The Fix Is In*, p. 165-166; *Harold Seymour, Baseball: The Golden Age*, p. 374; J. G. Taylor Spink, *Judge Landis and Twenty-Five Years of Baseball*, p. 98.
18. *New York Times*, May 11, 1921; *New York Times*, May 12, 1921.
19. *Chicago Tribune*, March 9, 1921, p. 15; *Chicago Tribune*, March 12, 1921, p. 11; *Sports Collectors Digest*, April 30, 1993, p. 71; Robert Smith, *Baseball*, p. 239.
20. *New York Times*, April 8, 1921, p. 14; *Sports Collectors Digest*, p. 71.
21. *Reach Official American League Base Ball Guide for 1922*, p. 51; Charles Alexander, *John McGraw*, p. 229; *Sports Collectors Digest*, April 30, 1993, p. 72; *New York Times*, February 22, 1921; *New York Sun*, May 11, 1921, p. 2. *New York Sun*, May 12, 1921, p. 2.

482    JUDGE & JURY: The Life and Times of Judge Kenesaw Mountain Landis

22. Some might infer that Landis reacted against Kauff because Kauff was Jewish. Recent scholarship (by David Spaner in the fifth edition of *Total Baseball*) reveals that Kauff was *not* Jewish. Whether Landis, knew that is, of course, open to question.

23. Spink, *Judge Landis and Twenty-Five Years of Baseball*, p. 91; Daniel Ginsburg, *The Fix Is In*, p. 168.

24. Fred Lieb, *The Baseball Story*, p. 229.

25. *New York Times*, September 13, 1921, p. 14; *Sports Collector's Digest*, April 30, 1993, p. 72.

26. *New York Times*, January 18, 1922, p. 15.

27. *Sports Collector's Digest*, April 30, 1993, p. 72.

28. *New York Times*, September 12, 1922, p. 17.

29. Harold Seymour, *Baseball: The Golden Age*, pp. 391-392; *Reach Official American League Base Ball Guide for 1922*, p. 49; *New York Times*, April 25, 1921, p. 12; *Baseball Magazine*, August 1921, p. 431; Lee Allen, *The Cincinnati Reds*, p. 156; *New York Sun*, May 4, 1921, p. 16.

30. Johnson's decision was overturned in New York State Supreme Court by future U.S. senator Robert F. Wagner.

31. Eugene Murdock, *Ban Johnson*, pp. 167-171; *New York Times*, June 13, 1921, p. 11.

32. Kenesaw M. Landis, "In re: Application of Player Henry K. Groh for Reinstatement to the Active List," June 9, 1921, KML Scrapbooks, Chicago Historical Society; *New York Tribune*, June 10, 1921, p. 18.

33. *New York Times*, June 10, 1921, p. 10.

34. *Chicago Tribune*, June 12, 1921, Part 2, p. 2.

35. Robert Creamer, *Stengel: His Life and Times*, p. 144.

36. Groh, as if to spite Landis, spent his post-baseball career as a cashier in a Cincinnati racetrack.

37. *Chicago Tribune*, June 12, 1921, Part 2, p. 2; *New York Times*, June 14, 1921, p. 11; Robert Creamer, *Stengel: His Life and Times*, p. 144; Gene Karst and Martin J. Jones, Jr., *Who's Who in Professional Baseball*, p. 390.

38. *Reach Official American League Base Ball Guide for 1922*, p. 49; *New York Times*, June 13, 1921, p. 11.

39. F. C. Lane, "The Famous Landis-Groh Decision," *Baseball Magazine*, August 1921, pp. 414, 432.

40. Frank Graham, *McGraw of the Giants*, p. 131; Charles Alexander, *John McGraw*, pp. 216-217, 229; Fred Lieb, *The Baseball Story*, p. 229; Harold Seymour, *Baseball: The Golden Age*, p. 389.

41. J. G. Taylor, Spink, *Judge Landis and Twenty-Five Years of Baseball*, pp. 93-96; Rich Westcott and Frank Bilovsky, *The New Phillies Encyclopedia*, pp. 297-298; Damon Rice, *Seasons Past*, pp. 173-174; Frederick G. Lieb, *The Pittsburgh Pirates*, pp. 189-191.

42. Fifty-five years later Friend would drop dead while listening to a White Sox-Indians game on the radio.

43. J. G. Taylor Spink, *Judge Landis and Twenty-Five Years of Baseball*, pp. 80-83; Irving M. Stein, *The Ginger Kid*, pp. 263-271; Harold Seymour, *Baseball: The Golden Age*, pp. 324-339, Daniel E. Ginsburg, *The Fix Is In*, pp. 142-144.

44. Eliot Asinof, *Eight Men Out*, pp. 271-304; Irving M. Stein, *The Ginger Kid*, pp. 263-273; Harold Seymour, *Baseball: The Golden Years*, p. 324; *Reach Official American League Guide for 1922*, p. 32.

45. *New York Times*, August 4, 1921, p. 1.

46. Calvin Coolidge, *Have Faith in Massachusetts*, p. 223; *New York Times*, August 14, 1921, p. 14.

47. Branch Rickey with Robert Riger, *The American Diamond*, p. 34.

48. *Chicago Tribune*, August 1, 1921, p. 19; *Chicago Tribune*, August 10, 1921, p. 19; *Chicago Tribune*, August 11, 1921, p. 10; *New York Times*, August 10, 1921, p. 10; *New York Times*, December 29, 1921, p. 12; *The Sporting News*, November 13, 1930.

49. *Chicago Tribune*, June 11, 1921, p. 1; *Chicago Tribune*, June 12, 1921, pp. 1, 3; *Chicago Tribune*, June 15, 1921, p. 5; *New York Times*, August 13, 1921, p. 1; *Chicago Tribune*, September 2, 1921, p. 1; *Chicago Tribune*, September 8, 1921, pp. 1, 3; *New York Times*, September 8, 1921, pp. 1, 2; *Chicago Tribune*, September 9, 1921, p. 8; *New York Times*, September 9, 1921, pp. 14, 17; *Chicago Tribune*, September 10, 1921, pp. 1, 4; *Chicago Tribune*, September 13, 1921, p. 1; *New York Times*, December 4, 1921, Section X, p. 19; *Literary Digest*, September 24, 1921, pp. 13-14.

50. *Reach Official American League Base Ball Guide for 1922*, p. 51; James Charlton, *The Baseball Chronology*, p. 213.

51. *Reach Official American League Guide for 1922*, p. 49; *Sacramento Bee*, October 27, 1921; *Sacramento Bee*, November 4, 1921; *Sacramento Bee*, November 5, 1921; *Sacramento Bee*, September 17, 1971, Section E, p. 2.

52. Evidence in Harry Grabiner's diary indicates this may not be true—that Weaver was aware of a plot as early as mid-summer 1919.

53. *New York Tribune*, January 14, 1922; Bill Veeck, *Veeck As In Wreck*, pp. 283-284.

54. Harvey Frommer, *Shoeless Joe and Ragtime Baseball*, p. 176.

55. *Reach Official American League Base Ball Guide for 1923*, pp. 32-33; Irving M. Stein, *The Ginger Kid*, p. 275; Eliot Asinof, *Eight Men Out*, pp. 314-315.

56. Landis's eldest nephew, John, son of Charles Landis, was a graduate of West Point's Class of 1910.

57. *Washington Post*, October 6, 1988.

# Chapter 13 Notes

1. *Chicago Tribune*, March 3, 1921, p. 1; Harold Seymour, *Baseball: The Golden Age*, p. 372.

2. *Collyer's Eye*, November 29, 1932.

3. *Chicago Daily News*, January 12, 1921; Harold Seymour, *Baseball: The Golden Age*, p. 322; *Chicago Tribune*, December 29, 1920.
4. *New York Times*, January 16, 1921, p. 10; Harold Seymour, *Baseball: The Golden Age*, p. 371.
5. *New York Globe*, January 18, 1920.
6. *New York Times*, January 16, 1921, p. 10; Harold Seymour, *Baseball: The Golden Age*, p. 371.
7. *New York Times*, February 3, 1921, p. 5.
8. Landis, of course, acted as an arbitrator not only for baseball; in 1921 he also acted to arbitrate problems in Chicago's construction industry. Fellow federal judge Samuel Alschuler performed in a similar capacity for wage rates in the local beef industry.
9. *New York Times*, February 12, 1921. p. 3.
10. *Chicago Tribune*, February 12, 1921, p. 11; *New York Times*, February 12, p. 3; Paul Eaton, "Impeaching Judge Landis," *Baseball Magazine*, May 1920, p. 563.
11. *New York Times*, February 12, 1921, p. 13.
12. *New York Times*, April 29, 1920, p. 1.
13. Paul Eaton, "Impeaching Judge Landis," *Baseball Magazine*, May 1920, p. 563; Ed Fitzgerald, "Judge Landis, Baseball's High Commissioner," *Sport*, June, 1950, p. 56.
14. Ed Fitzgerald, "Judge Landis, Baseball's High Commissioner, *Sport*, June 1950, p. 56.
15. Gene Brown, *The Complete Book of Baseball*, p. 31.
16. Thomas, Welty, and Dial were all Democrats. They could not only see that Landis was a practicing Republican but that almost all other candidates for baseball's new commissionership—Wood, Pershing, and Taft—were also all Republicans. Organized Baseball, under the guidance of Albert Lasker, was clearly a preserve of the GOP.
17. *New York Post*, February 14, 1921.
18. *The Sporting News*, February 17, 1921, p. 1; *The Sporting News*, February 24, 1921, p. 4; *Chicago Tribune*, February 22, 1921, p. 2.
19. *Literary Digest*, March 12, 1921, p. 44.
20. *Chicago Tribune*, February 15, 1921, p. 2.
21. *New York Times*, February 13, 1921, p. 1.
22. *Chicago Tribune*, February 14, 1921, p. 2.
23. *Literary Digest*, March 12, 1921, p. 42.
24. *Chicago Tribune*, February 15, 1921, p. 2.
25. *Chicago Tribune*, February 16, 1921, p. 7.
26. *Chicago Tribune*, February 15, 1921, p. 2.
27. Paul Eaton, "Impeaching Judge Landis," *Baseball Magazine*, May 1920, *op cit*, p. 564.
28. Paul Eaton, "Impeaching Judge Landis," *Baseball Magazine*, May 1920, *op cit*, p. 564.
29. *Chicago Tribune*, March 3, 1921, p.1; Eaton, *op cit*, p. 564.

30. *The Sporting News*, February 24, 1921, p. 4; *Collyer's Eye*, November 29, 1932.
31. *New York Times*, February 16, 1917, p. 5.
32. One of the most bizarre incidents in Landis' judicial career—in fact of *anyone's* judicial career—involved Prohibition. It was not of his own making. After the advent of the Volstead Act and Landis' energetic efforts to enforce it, a Chicago resident named Frank Beiswanger got it into his head to pose as Landis and shake down foreign-born bootleggers. Aiding Beiswanger were three Chicago policemen who in their free time would variously pose not only as the police but also as representatives of the Prohibition Enforcement Bureau or the Secret Service. If their victims failed to immediately offer a bribe to drop all "charges," they would haul them to a Clybourne Avenue address where Beiswanger operated his own version of Federal Court, snarling from the bench and levying heavy fines on his "defendants." Oddly enough, Beiswanger looked nothing at all like the by-then well-known Landis.
33. John Kobler, *Ardent Spirits*, p. 223; *New York Times*, February 15, 1923, p. 15.
34. *Chicago Tribune*, January 8, 1921, p. 17.
35. *Literary Digest*, March 21, 1921, p. 42.
36. J. G. Taylor Spink, *Judge Landis and Twenty-Five Years of Baseball*, p. 107.
37. *Chicago Tribune*, March 3, 1921, p. 1.
38. *New York Times*, July 19, 1921, p. 17.
39. Defending Landis was former United States senator James Hamilton Lewis, whose long political career was, if not the most distinguished in Congressional annals, at least among the more distinct. Lewis, a Democrat, had originally been elected to the House of Representatives from Washington State. After losing a bid for the United States Senate at the turn of the century, he moved to Illinois and in 1908 lost there for governor. In the Wilson sweep of 1912 the bewhiskered, floridly oratorical Lewis was finally elected to the Senate but was defeated in the 1918 Democratic primary. In 1930 he made one final comeback, returning to the Senate where he served until his death in 1939.
40. Howland, like Welty, was a Spanish-American War veteran but a Republican and was experienced in judicial conduct, having served on a panel examining impeachment charges against a federal judge, Robert W. Archbald, in 1912.
41. Harold Seymour, *Baseball: The Golden Age*, p. 372; T. L. Huston to KML, November 15, 1921, KML Scrapbooks, Chicago Historical Society; Lawrence Kennedy, *Biographical Dictionary of the American Congress 1774-1971*. p. 1,151.
42. J. W. Heintzman to T. L. Huston, November 1, 1921, KML Scrapbooks, Chicago Historical Society.
43. *Chicago Daily Journal*, February 18, 1922, p. 1; *Chicago Daily News*, February 18, 1922, p. 1; *Chicago Evening Post*, February 18, 1922, p. 1.
44. Undated clipping, KML Scrapbooks, Chicago Historical Society.
45. *New York World*, March 1, 1922.
46. *Columbus Dispatch*, March 1, 1922; Ed Fitzgerald, "Judge Landis, Baseball's High Commissioner," *Sport*, June 1950, p. 56.
47. *New York Sun*, August 28, 1924.

48. *The National Tribune*, April 16, 1925; Undated clipping, KML Scrapbooks, Chicago Historical Society.

# Chapter 14 Notes

1. *Evanston News-Index*, January 31, 1921.
2. Andrew Sinclair, *The Available Man*, pp. 260, 264; William Allen White, *A Puritan in Babylon*, p. 252; William Leuchtenburg, *The Perils of Prosperity 1914-32*, p. 92.
3. *New York Times*, May 3, 1924, p. 3.
4. *Chicago Herald and Examiner*, May 3, 1924. p. 1.
5. Actual ownership or consumption of alcohol was never prohibited under the Eighteenth Amendment. The public was permitted to retain all alcohol it possessed prior to Prohibition going into effect. And with a one-year grace period before the law took hold, Americans—particularly wealthy Americans—had plenty of time to stock up.
6. *Chicago Herald and Examiner*, May 3, 1924, p. 1; *New York Times*; May 3, 1924, p. 3.
7. *Chicago Tribune*, May 7, 1924; *New York Times*, May 7, 1924, p. 4.
8. *New York Times*, May 16, 1924, p. 2;1 Fed.2d 941; *Ex Parte Grossman*, 267 U.S. 87.
9. *Tripoli* (Iowa) *Leader*, February 19, 1920; *Grand Rapids Herald*, June 26, 1919; *Chicago Times*, November 25, 1944, p. 4; John Kobler, *Ardent Spirits*, p. 197.
10. Undated Clipping, KML Scrapbooks, Chicago Historical Society.
11. *Chicago Tribune*, January 11, 1919, p. 13; Francis Russell, *The Shadow of Blooming Grove*, pp. 355-396; Andrew Sinclair, *The Available Man*, pp. 136-151; James Watson, *As I Knew Them*, p. 219.
12. *Cincinnati Tribune*, April 20, 1921; *Hamilton* (Ohio) *Journal* April 26, 1921; *Lincoln Evening Courier*, July 30, 1921, p. 4.
13. *Chicago Tribune*, February 25, 1922.
14. Kenesaw Mountain Landis to Arthur H. Vandenberg, August 2, 1923, KML Scrapbooks, Chicago Historical Society.
15. Hadrian Baker to Kenesaw Mountain Landis, May 18, 1924, KML Scrapbooks, Chicago Historical Society.
16. John H. Lally to William Wrigley, Jr., May 27, 1924, KML Scrapbooks, Chicago Historical Society.
17. Yet *another* friend, William S. Kenyon, by this time a federal judge, finished third in GOP vice-presidential balloting.
18. William Allen White, *A Puritan in Babylon*, pp. 301-305, 311, 322.
19. *Houston Chronicle*, August 23, 1923.
20. R. P. Martin to Kenesaw Mountain Landis, January 18, 1924; Kenesaw Mountain Landis to R. P. Martin, January, 1924, KML Scrapbooks, Chicago Historical Society.
21. Miss Gladys Brown to Kenesaw Mountain Landis, February 20, 1924; Kenesaw Mountain Landis to Miss Gladys Brown, February 23, 1924, KML Scrapbooks, Chicago Historical Society.

22. Clipping, Unknown Philadelphia newspaper, January 25, 1924, KML Scrapbooks, Chicago Historical Society.

23. *Chicago Daily Journal*, Undated Clipping, KML Scrapbooks, Chicago Historical Society.

24. *Cleveland News*, February 19, 1924; *Cleveland Times*, February 19, 1924; *Cleveland Plain Dealer*, February 19, 1924; *Cleveland Times*, February 19, 1924; *Chicago Herald and Examiner*, February 20, 1924.

25. *Houston Post*, August 30, 1930.

26. *Chicago Tribune*, October 18, 1924, p. 1.

27. *New York Times*, October 1923.

28. KML to William G. Bramham, January 20, 1928, KML Collection, Chicago Historical Society; James E. Watson, *As I Knew Them*, p. 257.

29. KML to Lew Wallace, Jr., May 2, 1930, KML Collection, Chicago Historical Society.

# Chapter 15 Notes

1. *New York Times*, October 18, 1921, p. 13; *New York Sun*, October 18, 1921, p. 20.

2. *New York Tribune*, October 15, 1921, p. 14; *Reach Official American League Guide for 1922*, p. 35; *Downtown Athletic Club News*, June 1922.

3. Robert Creamer, *Babe: The Legend Comes To Life*, p. 244.

4. J. G. Taylor Spink, *Judge Landis and Twenty-Five Years of Baseball*, pp. 103-104.

5. Fred Lieb, *Baseball As I Have Known It*, p. 131.

6. J. G. Taylor Spink, *Judge Landis and Twenty-Five Years of Baseball*, p. 106.

7. Robert Creamer, *Babe: The Legend Comes To Life*, p. 245.

8. Robert Creamer, *Babe: The Legend Comes To Life*, p. 245.

9. *1945 Baseball Register*, p. 9.

10. Robert Creamer, *Babe: The Legend Comes To Life*, p. 245.

11. *New York Times*, October 16, 1921, Section 8, p. 2.

12. *New York Times*, October 18, 1921, p. 13; *New York Sun*, October 18, 1921, p. 20; *New York Tribune*, October 18, 1921, p. 14; *New York Daily News*, October 17, 1921, p. 20.

13. *New York Tribune*, October 19, 1921, p. 13.

14. *New York Tribune*, October 17, 1921, p. 10; *New York Times*, October 18, 1921, p. 13; *New York Tribune*, October 19, 1921, p. 13; *New York Daily News*, October 17, 1921, p. 20.

15. *New York Times*, October 19, 1921, p. 13.

16. *New York Sun*, October 18, 1921, p. 20.

17. *New York Tribune*, October 17, 1921, p. 10.

18. *New York Sun*, October 18, 1921, p. 20.

19. *New York Sun*, October 18, 1921, p. 20; *New York Tribune*, October 18, 1921, p. 14; *New York Tribune*, October 19 1921, p. 13.

20. *New York Sun*, October 19, 1921, p. 18; *Schenectady Gazette*, October 20, 1921, p. 16.
21. *The Sporting News*, October 24, 1921, p. 1.
22. *New York Tribune*, October 22, 1921, p. 13.
23. Babe Ruth, *The Babe Ruth Story*, p. 97.
24. *New York Times*, October 24, 1921, p. 20.
25. *The Sporting News*, November 2, 1921, p. 4.
26. *Reach Official American League Guide for 1922*, p. 37.
27. *New York Times*, October 22, 1921, p. 16.
28. Ed Barrow, *My Fifty Years in Baseball*, p. 135.
29. T. L. Huston to KML, November 15, 1921, KML Scrapbooks, Chicago Historical Society.
30. *Official Reach American League Guide for 1922*, pp. 37-38; *New York Tribune*, December 6, 1921, p. 14.
31. *New York Times*, December 7, 1921, p. 20.
32. *Reach Official American League Guide for 1922*, p. 52.
33. Kal Wagenheim, *Babe Ruth: His Life and Legend*, p. 99.
34. *The Sporting News*, January 19, 1922, p. 1.
35. *The Sporting News*, March 30, 1922, p. 1; Robert Creamer, *Babe: The Legend Comes To Life*, p. 255.
36. *New York Times*, August 15, 1922, p. 21; Harold Seymour, *Baseball: The Golden Age*, p. 393.
37. Kenneth L. Briggs, "Barnstorming Days: The Babe & Bob Came To My Hometown!," *Oldtyme Baseball News*, Volume 6, Issue No. 6, p. 21.
38. *The Sporting News*, January 19, 1922, p. 1, *The Sporting News*, January 26, 1922, p. 4.
39. Roger A. Godin, *The 1922 St. Louis Browns*, p. 57.

# Chapter 16 Notes

1. *Reach Official American League Guide for 1923*, p. 32.
2. Tom Clark, *One Last Round for the Shuffler*, p. 44.
3. John Lardner, "That Was Baseball: The Crime of Shufflin' Phil Douglas," *The New Yorker*, May 12, 1956, p. 132.
4. *Albany Times-Union*, August 18, 1924, p. 11.
5. John Lardner, "That Was Baseball: The Crime of Shufflin' Phil Douglas," *The New Yorker*, May 12, 1956, p. 132.
6. Tom Clark, *One Last Round for the Shuffler*, p. 76.
7. *New York Times*, July 31, 1922, p. 8.
8. Tom Clark, *One Last Round for the Shuffler*, p. 79.
9. Tom Clark, *One Last Round for the Shuffler*, p. 83.
10. Frank Graham, *The New York Giants*, p. 136.

11. *New York Tribune*, August 19, 1922, p. 8; John Lardner, "That Was Baseball: The Crime of Shufflin' Phil Douglas," *The New Yorker*, May 12, 1956, p. 136.

12. *New York Tribune*, August 20, 1922, p. 14; Lee Allen, *The National League Story*, p. 218.

13. *New York Times*, August 9, 1922, p. 21; John Lardner, "That Was Baseball: The Crime of Shufflin' Phil Douglas," *The New Yorker, May 12, 1956*, pp. 136-137; Tom Clark, *One Last Round for the Shuffler*, p. 88; *St. Petersburg Times*, January 9, 1977, p. 10C.

14. Frank Graham, *McGraw of the Giants*, pp. 158-159.

15. Tom Clark, *One Last Round for the Shuffler*, p. 91.

16. While with Boston, McQuillan paid hefty alimony payments to his ex-wife, a New York resident, and when in arrears was always nervous about visiting Manhattan. "There's the sheriff," his teammates would say as McQuillan walked down city streets. "Nope," the pitcher would exhale, "he's not one. I know 'em all."

17. Fred Lieb, *The St. Louis Cardinals*, p. 96; Frank Graham, *The New York Giants*, p. 135; Charles Alexander, *John McGraw*, p. 241; Arthur Mann, *Branch Rickey*, p. 119; Harold Kaese, *The Boston Braves*, p. 181; Ed Linn, *The Great Rivalry*, pp. 85-86; Donald Dewey and Nicholas Acocella, *Encyclopedia of Major League Baseball Teams*, p. 56; *Reach Official American League Baseball Guide for 1923*, p. 24; Roger Godin, *The 1922 St. Louis Browns*, pp. 111-113; *New York Times*, August 15, 1922, p. 21.

18. Another version of this story has Rickey turning the letter over to Jim Tierney and Tierney presenting it to Landis at the joint major league meeting in Chicago.

19. John Lardner, "That Was Baseball: The Crime of Shufflin' Phil Douglas," *The New Yorker*, May 12, 1956, p. 136; Arthur Mann, *Branch Rickey*, pp. 119-120.

20. *New York Sun*, August 19, 1922, p. 8; Tom Clark, *One Last Round for the Shuffler*, p. 96.

21. *New York Times*, August 17, 1922, p. 9.

22. J. G. Taylor Spink, *Judge Landis and Twenty-Five Years of Baseball*, p. 111.

23. During his interrogation, Douglas had sullenly and stubbornly provided Landis with little reason for leniency. George Kelly, generally sympathetic to Douglas, nonetheless, thought he understood why Landis acted as he had: "Landis was in a tough spot," Kelly later explained with perhaps more optimism than realism, "because after that 1919 scandal baseball had a terrible name. But if Phil had talked to Landis—this is my observation—Landis would have given him a chance to come back. Landis wasn't that tough. He'd have put him out maybe for a month, or maybe for the rest of the season."

24. Tom Clark, *One Last Round for the Shuffler*, p. 98.

25. Frank Graham, *McGraw of the Giants*, p. 159.

26. *New York Times*, August 17, 1922, p. 1; Tom Clark, *One Last Round for the Shuffler*, pp. 100-101; Harold Seymour, *Baseball: The Golden Age*, p. 376.

27. *New York Times*, August 17, 1922, p. 9.

28. *New York Sun*, August 17, 1922, p. 18; *Schenectady Union-Star*, August 17, 1922, p. 10.

29. *New York Times*, August 17, 1922, p. 1.

30. Frank Graham, *The New York Giants*, p. 138.

31. *New York Times*, August 17, 1922, p. 9.

32. *New York Tribune*, August 17, 1922, p. 13.

33. Tom Clark, *One Last Round for the Shuffler*, p. 103; *New York Times*, August 18, 1922, p. 10.

34. Virtue had its reward. In December 1929 the major leagues funded one of Mann's youth baseball programs to the tune of $10,000.

35. *New York Times*, August 19, 1922, p. 8; *New York Times*, August 20, 1922, p. 22; *New York Sun*, August 19, 1922, p. 8.

36. *New York Times*, August 18, 1922, p. 10; *New York Sun*, August 17, 1922, p. 18; *New York Sun*, August 18, 1922, p. 8; Tom Clark, *One Last Round for the Shuffler*, pp. 101-102; *The Sporting News*, August 24, 1922, p. 1.

37. *New York Times*, August 17, 1922, p. 1; *New York Tribune*, August 19, 1922, p. 8.

38. *New York Times*, August 19, 1922, p. 8.

39. *New York Tribune*, August 19, 1922, p. 8.

40. *Schenectady Union-Star*, August 18, 1922, p. 10; *The Sporting News*, August 24, 1922, p. 3; *Reach Official American League Guide for 1923*, p. 32; *New York Sun*, August 17, 1922, p. 18.

41. *St. Petersburg Times*, January 9, 1977, p. 10C.

42. *New York Sun*, August 24, 1922, p. 12; *The Sporting News*, August 24, 1922, p. 1; *New York Times*, August 24, 1922, p. 12.

43. John Lardner, "That Was Baseball: The Crime of Shufflin' Phil Douglas," *The New Yorker*, May 12, 1956, p. 143.

44. Kenesaw Mountain Landis to August Herrmann, April 6, 1922.

45. *The Sporting News*, undated clipping; Tom Clark, *One Last Round for the Shuffler*, pp. 137-138; Harold Seymour, *Baseball: The Golden Age*, p. 376.

46. Daniel E. Ginsburg, *The Fix Is In*, p. 178.

# Chapter 17 Notes

1. Lee Lowenfish and Tony Lupien, *The Imperfect Diamond*, p. 104; Eliot Asinof, *Eight Men Out*, p. 318; Richard Lindberg, *Who's on 3rd?*, p. 47; Gene Karst and Martin J. Jones, Jr., *Who's Who in Professional Baseball*, p. 516.

2. Boeckel's other claim to fame centers on his demise. He is the first known major leaguer to be killed in an automobile accident.

3. Steve Boren, "The Bizarre Career of Rube Benton," *1983 Baseball Research Journal*, pp. 180-183; Daniel E. Ginsburg, *The Fix Is In*, pp. 135-136, 179; Eliot Asinof, *Eight Men Out*, pp. 177, 179-180.

4. Daniel Ginsburg, *The Fix Is In*, p. 180; Eugene C. Murdock, *Ban Johnson*, p. 206.

5. *New York Times*, February 14, 1923, p. 14; The 1983 *Baseball Research Journal*, p. 182; Harold Seymour, *Baseball: The Golden Age*, pp. 376-377; Eugene C. Murdock, *Ban Johnson*, p. 206.
6. *New York Times*, February 25, 1923, p. 15.
7. Kenesaw Mountain Landis, "In re: Player J. C. Benton," March 8, 1923, KML Scrapbooks, Chicago Historical Society; *New York Times*, March 9, 1923, p. 11.
8. *Pittsburgh Press*, March 13, 1923.
9. *New York Times*, March 10, 1923, p. 11; Harold Seymour, *Baseball: The Golden Age*, p. 377; *Albany Times-Union*, March 10, 1923, p. 12; *Albany Times-Union*, March 12, 1923, p. 13.
10. *Chicago Herald & Examiner*, March 13, 1923; *New York Times*, March 13, 1923, p. 25.
11. *New York Times*, March 28, 1923, p. 15.
12. "Landis . . . can hang Heydler and the National League on the limb of public opinion and he knows it," noted David J. Walsh of William Randolph Hearst's International News Service.
13. *New York Times*, March 15, 1923, p. 22; Daniel E. Ginsburg, *The Fix Is In*, p. 180; *New York Sun*, August 1, 1923, p. 20; *Albany Times-Union*, March 10, 1923, p. 12.
14. Richard Nardinelli, "Judge Kenesaw Mountain Landis and the Art of Cartel Enforcement," *Baseball History*, 1989, p. 110.
15. One of Landis' few modern defenders in the Benton Case is historian Bill James. "The evidence against the Black Sox, while not convincing enough to send them to jail, was about a hundred times stronger than the evidence against Rube Benton, who was alleged to *have known about* crimes that the White Sox *perpetrated* . . . ," James noted. "Too many of [Landis'] critics have confused 'leniency' with a finding of 'not guilty.'"
16. Bill Veeck, *The Hustler's Handbook*, pp. 296-297.
17. Lee Allen, *The Cincinnati Reds*, pp. 156, 165; *New York Times*, August 24, 1923, p. 7; *New York Sun*, September 1, 1923, p. 10; *New York Tribune*, August 24, 1923, p. 11.
18. J. G. Taylor Spink, *Judge Landis and Twenty-Five Years of Baseball*, pp. 124-125.
19. *New York Times*, August 25, 1923, p. 8; *New York Times*, August 27, 1923, p. 9; J. G. Taylor Spink, *Judge Landis and Twenty-Five Years of Baseball*, pp. 124-125; *Albany Times-Union*, August 25, 1923, p. 13.
20. *New York Times*, August 23, 1923, p. 9.
21. *New York Times*, September 8, 1923.
22. *New York Times*, August 31, 1923, p. 11.
23. Daniel Ginsburg, *The Fix Is In*, p. 183; J. G. Taylor Spink, *Judge Landis and Twenty-Five Years of Baseball*, pp. 125-126; Walter H. Jacobs to C. J. McDiarmid, February 21, 1928; Garry Herrmann Papers, National Baseball Library; John Heydler to C. W. Danziger, February 24, 1928; Garry Herrmann Papers, National Baseball Library; John Heydler to C. J. McDiarmid, January 20, 1928; Garry Herrmann Papers, National Baseball Library; C. J.

McDiarmid to John Heydler, August 24, 1928; Garry Herrmann Papers, National Baseball Library; John Heydler to C. J. McDiarmid, August 29, 1928; Garry Herrmann Papers, National Baseball Library.
24. Charles Alexander, *John McGraw*, p. 210; Harold Seymour, *Baseball: the Golden Age*, p. 390.
25. *New York Times*, September 1, 1923, pp. 1, 6.
26. Daniel E. Ginsburg, *The Fix Is In*, pp. 181-182.
27. *New York Sun*, June 3, 1921, p. 18; *New York Times*, September 11, 1923, p. 11.
28. *The Sporting News*, November 15, 1923.
29. *New York Times*, September 5, 1923, p. 19; *New York Times*, September 1, 1923, p. 1.
30. Harold Seymour, *Baseball: The Golden Age*, p. 390.
31. Daniel E. Ginsburg, *The Fix Is In*, p. 182.

# Chapter 18 Notes

1. John Thorn, Michael Gershman, and Pete Palmer, *Total Baseball* (4th Edition), p. 107.
2. *New York Times*, December 8, 1921, p. 22; *New York Times*, December 12, 1921, p. 16; *New York Tribune*, December 9, 1921, p. 16.
3. Bill O'Neal, *The Pacific Coast League 1903-1988*, pp. 275-276; Frank Graham, *McGraw of the Giants*, p. 165.
4. Rich Westcott and Frank Bilovsky, *The New Phillies Encyclopedia*, p. 330; Lloyd Johnson and Miles Wolff, *The Encyclopedia of Minor League Baseball*, p. 155.
5. *New York Times*, January 11, 1925, p. 2; *New York Times*, February 5, 1925, p. 21; *New York World*, January 22, 1925.
6. *Albany Times-Union*, October 3, 1924, p. 12.
7. Frank Graham, *McGraw of the Giants*, p. 183; *New York Telegraph and Evening Mail*, October 2, 1924, pp. 1, 17; *New York World*, January 28, 1925.
8. Frank Graham, *McGraw of the Giants*, p. 184.
9. Frank Graham, *McGraw of the Giants*, p. 184.
10. *New York World-Telegraph*, December 18, 1938.
11. Frank Graham, *McGraw of the Giants*, p. 185; Frank Graham, *The New York Giants*, p. 153; *Pittsburgh Post*, February 21, 1925.
12. Damon Rice, *Seasons Past*, p. 195.
13. Kelly was the nephew of former major leaguer Bill Lange, whom McGraw used to scout O'Connell.
14. Dolan was the second "Cozy" Dolan in the majors. The first, Patrick Henry Dolan, was a Braves outfielder who died of typhoid fever in spring training of 1905. The outbreak—and Dolan's death—caused the end of Boston's spring camp.

15.  Daniel E. Ginsburg, *The Fix Is In*, p. 188.

16.  *Schenectady Union-Star*, October 4, 1924, p. 7; Daniel E. Ginsburg, *The Fix Is In*, pp. 186, 188-189.

17.  *New York Herald-Tribune*, October 3, 1924, p. 14.

18.  Somewhere in the middle of Dolan's testimony a court stenographer arrived late to record the proceedings. All quotes of Landis' investigation from this point on reflect that official record.

19.  *New York Telegraph and Evening Mail*, October 24, 1924, p. 21; Harold Seymour, *Baseball: The Golden Years*, p. 379; *New York Times*, January 11, 1925, Section 9, p. 2.

20.  *New York Times*, January 11, 1925, Section IX, p. 2.

21.  *New York Herald-Tribune*, October 2, 1924, p. 17; *Schenectady Gazette*, October 2, 1924, p. 13; William B. Mead and Paul Dickson, *Baseball: The President's Game*, pp. 50-51.

22.  *New York Times*, October 2, 1924, p. 1; *Schenectady Gazette*, October 2, 1924, p. 13.

23.  *New York Telegraph and Evening Mail*, October 14, 1924, p. 18; *New York Telegraph and Evening Mail*, October 15, 1924, p. 18.

24.  *New York Times*, October 2, 1924. p. 10; *Albany Times-Union*, October 2, 1924, p. 18.

25.  Charles Alexander, *John McGraw*, pp. 257-258; *Albany Times-Union*, October 2, 1924, pp. 1, 3.

26.  *Schenectady Union-Star*, October 3, 1927, p. 16.

27.  *Schenectady Union-Star*, October 3, 1927, p. 16.

28.  Damon Rice, *Season's Past*, p. 196; Charles Alexander, *John McGraw*. p. 258.

29.  *Schenectady Union-Star*, October 4, 1924, p. 7.

30.  *Albany Times-Union*, October 3, 1924, p. 2; Jack Kavanagh, *Walter Johnson: A Life*, pp. 181-182.

31.  *Schenectady Union-Star*, October 3, 1924, p. 16.

32.  *New York Herald-Tribune*, October 3, 1924, p. 18; *Schenectady Union-Star*, October 3, 1924, p. 17; *Schenectady Gazette*, October 3, 1924, p. 23; *Albany Knickerbocker-Press*, October 3, 1924, p. 2; *New York Times*, October 10, 1924, p. 15; *New York Times*, October 7, 1924, p. 17.

33.  *New York Herald-Tribune*, October 4, 1924, p. 13; *New York Times*, October 5, 1924, Section X, p. 1; J. G. Spink, *Judge Landis and Twenty-Five Years of Baseball*, p. 134; Eugene C. Murdock, *Ban Johnson: Czar of Baseball*, p. 209; *Albany Times-Union*, October 3, 1924, p. 2; *Albany Times-Union*, October 4, 1924, p. 9.

34.  Also coming forward with a tale of fixes and Giants was Charles "Red" Dooin, a one-time Phillies' manager and vaudevillian known for performing an Irish comedy act called "His Last Night Out." Dooin, who had once managed Dolan, vouched for his honesty and blamed "one higher up." He revealed how in 1908 a Giants' catcher offered him $40,000 in cash, an unlikely amount, to absent himself from the Phillies in a crucial late-season series against New York. Whether

Johnson had a hand in Dooin's revelations is not known. The otherwise obscure Dooin achieved an immortality of sorts by being portrayed by actor Billy Wayne in the Ronald Reagan film *The Winning Team*.

35.  *New York Herald-Tribune*, October 4, 1924, p. 13; *New York Times*, October 4, 1924, p. 8; *Albany Times-Union*, October 4, 1924, p. 9; Harold Seymour, *Baseball: The Golden Age*, p. 379; Rob Edelman, *Great Baseball Films*, p. 79.

36.  *New York Times*, October 5, 1920, Section X, p. 1.

37.  Harold Seymour, *Baseball: The Golden Age*, p. 380.

38.  *New York Herald-Tribune*, October 4, 1924, p. 13; *Albany Times-Union*, October 5, 1924, p. 13; *New York American*, October 12, 1924; Fred Lieb, *The Baseball Story*, p. 237.

39.  Frederick G. Lieb, *The Pittsburgh Pirates*, p. 201; *Albany Times-Union*, October 5, 1924, p. 13.

40.  *Schenectady Union-Star*, October 2, 1924, p. 12; *New York Telegraph and Evening Mail*, October 2, 1924, p. 1; *New York Telegraph and Evening Mail*, October 14, 1924, p. 18; *New York Times*, October 14, 1924, p. 26; Eugene Murdock, *Ban Johnson: Czar of Baseball*, p. 209; *New York Times*, October 4, 1924, p. 8; *The Sporting News*, January 13, 1927, p. 1.

41.  Lee Allen, *The National League Story*, p. 176; *Albany Times-Union*, October 4, 1924, p. 1.

42.  Eugene C. Murdock, *Ban Johnson: Czar of Baseball*, pp. 208-209; *New York Tribune*, October 3, 1924, p. 10; *Albany Knickerbocker-Press*, October 4, 1924, p. 1.

43.  *New York Times*, October 3, 1924, p. 20; *New York Times*, October 4, 1924, p. 8; *New York Tribune*, October 3, 1924, p. 14; *New York Telegraph and Evening Mail*, October 2, 1924, p. 17.

44.  *New York Times*, October 24, 1924, p. 7; *New York Herald-Tribune*, October 4, 1924, p. 13; *Schenectady Union-Star*, October 4, 1924, p. 7; *New York Telegraph and Evening Mail*, October 3, 1924, p. 1.

45.  *New York Times*, October 4, 1924, p. 8; *Albany Times-Union*, October 4, 1924, p. 9; *New York Telegraph and Mail*, October 3, 1924, p. 22.

46.  *New York Telegraph and Evening Mail*, October 3, 1924, p. 22.

47.  Frank Graham, *McGraw of the Giants*, p. 186.

48.  *Albany Times-Union*, October 4, 1924, p. 9.

49.  William B. Mead and Paul Dickson, *Baseball: The President's Game*, p. 52.

50.  *New York Telegraph and Evening Mail*, October 8, 1924, p. 18; *New York Times*, January 11, 1925, Section IX, p. 2.

51.  *New York Times*, January 11, 1925, p. 2; *New York World*, October 7, 1924.

52.  *Albany Times-Union*, October 6, 1924, p. 13.

53.  Charles Alexander, *John McGraw*, p. 259.

54.  *New York Times*, January 11, 1925, Section IX, p. 3.

55.  *New York Times*, October 7, 1924, p. 17.

56.  *New York Telegraph and Evening Mail*, October 13, 1924, p. 13.

57. J.G. Taylor Spink, *Judge Landis and Twenty-Five Years of Baseball*, p. 138.
58. *New York Telegraph and Evening Mail*, October 24, 1924, p. 18.
59. *New York Telegraph and Evening Mail*, October 14, 1924, p. 18.
60. Frank Graham, *McGraw of the Giants*, pp. 136-139; Charles Alexander, *John McGraw*, pp. 221-223, 234; Damon Rice, *Seasons Past*, pp. 163-164.
61. Charles Alexander, *John McGraw*, pp. 250, 263.
62. *New York Times*, October 22, 1924, p. 24.
63. J. G. Taylor Spink's *Judge Landis and Twenty-Five Years of Baseball* uses Dolan's version rather than the official stenographic version of events.
64. J. G. Taylor Spink, *Judge Landis and Twenty-Five Years of Baseball*, p. 139.
65. *New York Times*, October 22, 1924, p. 24; *New York Times*, October 23, 1924, p. 24; *New York Times*, October 29, 1924, p. 25; *New York Telegraph and Evening Mail*, October 23, 1924, p. 18.
66. Frank Graham, "How Fallon, Ace Lawyer, Missed Landis Hassle," *Baseball Digest*, April 1964, p. 72.
67. Charles Alexander, *John McGraw*, p. 277; Joseph Durso, *The Days of Mr. McGraw*, pp. 128-129.
68. Lee Allen, *The National League Story*, p. 222.
69. *New York Times*, January 7, 1925, p. 9.; *New York World*, January 11, 1925.
70. Both Ludolph and Kelly—all 5'6" of him—later made the majors.
71. *New York Times*, January 6, 1925, p. 28; *New York Times*, January 7, 1925, p. 29; *Pittsburgh Post*, February 21, 1925; Harold Seymour, *Baseball: The Golden Age*, pp. 380-381.
72. *New York Times*, January 16, 1925, p. 11; *New York World*, January 21, 1925.
73. *New York Times*, October 17, 1924, p. 25; *New York Times*, October 18, 1924, p. 11; *New York Telegraph and Evening Mail*, October 22, 1924, p. 19; *New York World*, January 27, 1925; Daniel E. Ginsburg, *The Fix Is In*, p. 191.
74. *New York Times*, January 6, 1925, p. 28; *New York World*, January 30, 1925; Harold Seymour, *Baseball: The Golden Age*, p. 381.
75. *New York Times*, February 3, 1925, p. 7.
76. *New York World*, January 22, 1925; *New York World*, January 27, 1925; *New York World*, January 28, 1925; *New York World*, January 30, 1925; *New York Times*, January 30, 1925; *New York Times*, February 3, 1925, p. 7; Harold Seymour, *Baseball: The Golden Age*, p. 381.
77. *New York Times*, February 5, 1925, p. 21.
78. *New York World*, January 27, 1925.
79. J. G. Taylor Spink, *Judge Landis and Twenty-Five Years of Baseball*, p. 149.
80. *New York Telegraph and Evening Mail*, July 31, 1930; *The Sporting News*, March 29, 1958; Daniel E. Ginsburg, *The Fix Is In*, pp. 194-195.
81. *New York Evening Telegraph and Evening Mail*, August 13, 1928; Daniel E. Ginsburg, *The Fix Is In*, p. 194.
82. J. G. Taylor Spink, *Judge Landis and Twenty-Five Years of Baseball*, p. 136-137.

83.  Charles McGraw, *John McGraw*, pp. 297, 298, 302-303; Joseph Durso, *The Days of Mr. McGraw*, p. 211; Frank Graham, *The New York Giants*, pp. 188-190; Frank Graham, *McGraw of the Giants*, pp. 244-247.

84.  McQuade won against Stoneham and McGraw in trial court and on appeal, but lost in New York's highest court, the Court of Appeals, which unanimously held that he had violated a law barring outside employment for magistrates and hence his holding the Giants' treasurer's post had been illegal. In 1931 the Seabury Commission, investigating municipal corruption, forced McQuade off the bench.

85.  *New York Telegraph and Evening Mail*, December 11, 1929.

86.  Donald Honig, *The October Heroes*, p. 270.

# Chapter 19 Notes

1.  *New York Times*, December 22, 1926, p. 17; J. G. Taylor Spink, *Judge Landis and Twenty-Five Years of Baseball*, pp. 154-155; Charles Alexander, *Ty Cobb*, p. 185.

2.  *New York Times*, September 26, 1919, p. 8; Ty Cobb, *My Life In Baseball*, p. 243.

3.  *New York Times*, December 12, 1926, p. 17.

4.  *New York Times*, December 22, 1926, p. 17; Franklin Lewis, *The Cleveland Indians*, p. 149.

5.  Eugene Murdock, *Ban Johnson: Czar of Baseball*, p. 215; Charles Alexander, *Ty Cobb*, pp. 186-187.

6.  *New York Times*, December 23, 1926, p. 1; Eugene Murdock, *Ban Johnson: Czar of Baseball*, p. 215-216; Daniel E. Ginsburg, *The Fix Is In*, p. 205; Charles Alexander, *Ty Cobb*, p. 187-188.

7.  Leonard left a $2 million estate on his death.

8.  *New York Times*, December 22, 1926, p. 17; Charles Alexander, *Ty Cobb*, p. 188; Al Stump, *Cobb*, p. 371; Fred Lieb, *Baseball As I Have known It*, p. 62.

9.  *New York Times*, December 22, 1926, p. 17.

10.  *New York Times*, December 24, 1926, p. 12; Al Stump, *Ty Cobb*, pp. 377-378.

11.  AL owners also named a three-person committee (Ruppert, Ball, and Barnard) to meet with Landis and discuss the board's powers and to urge that he consult it more frequently.

12.  *New York Times*, December 19, 1926, Section IX, p. 1; Eugene Murdock, *Ban Johnson: Czar of Baseball*, p. 214-215; *New York Times*, December 16, 1926, p. 31.

13.  The only dissent came from the Texas League's Tulsa club. No one, in or out of baseball, followed their lead.

14.  *New York Times*, December 4, 1926, p. 21; *New York Times*, December 5, 1926, Section X, 1; *New York Times*, December 16, 1926, p. 31.

15.  *New York Times*, December 19, 1926, Section IX, pp. 1, 2; *New York Times*, December 18, 1923, p. 13.

16. *New York Times*, December 18, 1923, p. 13.

17. *New York Times*, December 21, 1926, p. 26; *New York Times*, December 22, 1926, p. 1; Eugene Murdock, *Ban Johnson: Czar of Baseball*, p. 217.

18. Eugene Murdock, *Ban Johnson: Czar of Baseball*, p. 217.

19. Ty Cobb, *My Life In Baseball*, p. 244; Daniel E. Ginsburg, *The Fix Is In*, p. 205.

20. Ty Cobb, *My Life in Baseball*, p. 245; Daniel E. Ginsburg, *The Fix Is In*, p. 205.

21. Al Stump, *Ty Cobb*, p. 382.

22. *New York Times*, December 23, 1926, p. 16; *New York Times*, December 26, 1926, p. 1.

23. *New York Times*, December 24, 1924, p. 1; Al Stump, *Ty Cobb*, pp. 382-384; Franklin Lewis, *The Cleveland Indians*, p. 151.

24. *Cleveland Press*, January 1, 1927, p. 1; *Cleveland Press*, January 4, 1927, p. 1.

25. *Cleveland Plain Dealer*, January 1, 1928, p. 1.

26. *Cleveland Press*, January 1, 1927, p. 1; *Cleveland Plain Dealer*, January 2, 1927, p. 4B; Charles Alexander, *Ty Cobb*, p. 191.

27. *New York Times*, December 24, 1926, p. 12; *New York Times*, December 26, 1926, Section IX, p. 1.

28. *New York Times*, December 30, 1926, p. 16; *New York Times*, December 31, 1926, p. 9; *The Sporting News*, January 20, 1927, p. 5; Daniel E. Ginsburg, *The Fix Is In*, p. 208.

29. Daniel E. Ginsburg, *The Fix Is In*, pp. 208-209; Harold Seymour, *Baseball: The Golden Years*, p. 384.

30. *The Sporting News*, January 20, 1927, p. 5; *New York Herald Tribune*, January 13, 1927.

31. *The Sporting News*, January 20, 1927, p. 5; *New York Herald Tribune*, January 13, 1927.

32. Bill Veeck, *The Hustler's Handbook*, pp. 274, 298; Harold Seymour, *Baseball: The Golden Age*, p. 385; *Reach Official American League Baseball Guide for 1923*, pp. 30-31; *New York Sun*, August 17, 1922, p. 18.

33. *The Sporting News*, January 13, 1927, p. 1; *The Sporting News*, January 20, 1927, p. 4; Irving M. Stein, *The Ginger Kid*, p. 286.

34. Charles Alexander, *Ty Cobb*, p. 193.

35. *New York Times*, January 5, 1927, p. 16.

36. *Chicago American*, undated clipping; Irving M. Stein, *The Ginger Kid*, p. 286.

37. *The Sporting News*, January 13, 1927, p. 5.

38. *The Sporting News*, January 13, 1927, p. 1.

39. *New York Times*, January 6, 1927, p. 1; *Schenectady Union-Star*, January 6, 1927.

40. *The Sporting News*, January 13, 1927, p. 7.

41. *New York Times*, January 11, 1927, p. 29.

42. *New York Times*, January 9, 1927, Section X, p. 1.

43. *New York Times*, January 9, 1927, Section X, p. 1.

44. Once again Landis rejected Weaver's appeal. In March 1927 he ruled: "I regret it is not possible for me to arrive at any other conclusion than that set forth in

the decision of December 11, 1922, that your own admissions and actions in the circumstances forbid your reinstatement. . . .The world's series then was played and so played that even during the series, your manager, at a meeting of the players, stated something was wrong. You knew your club officials were seeking to ascertain the facts, but you kept still."

45. Irving M. Stein, *The Ginger Kid*, p. 292; *New York Times*, March 14, 1927, p. 23.
46. *The Sporting News*, January 20, 1927, p. 5; *New York Herald Tribune*, January 13, 1927; Daniel E. Ginsburg, *The Fix Is In*, pp. 210-212.
47. Undated clipping, Kenesaw Mountain Landis Scrapbooks, Chicago Historical Society.
48. *New York Herald Tribune*, January 14, 1927.
49. *The Sporting News*, January 20, 1927, p. 5; Harold Seymour, *Baseball: The Golden Age*, p. 386.
50. *The Sporting News*, January 20, 1927, p. 5; Daniel E. Ginsburg, *The Fix Is In*, p. 212.
51. *New York Times*, January 16, 1927, Sect IX, p. 3; *New York Times*, January 19, 1926, p. 18; *New York Times*, January 20, 1927, p. 17; Fred Lieb, *The Detroit Tigers*, p. 181-182; Daniel E. Ginsburg, *The Fix Is In*, p. 205; Charles Alexander, *Ty Cobb*, p. 190.
52. *New York Times*, January 20, 1927, p. 17; Eugene Murdock, *Ban Johnson*, p. 218.
53. Eugene C. Murdock, *Ban Johnson*, p. 210.
54. *Collyer's Eye*, November 28, 1932.
55. *New York Times*, January 22, 1927, p. 17; J. G. Taylor Spink, *Judge Landis and Twenty-Five Years of Baseball*, pp. 141-144; Harold Seymour, *Baseball: The Golden Age*, pp. 396-397; Eugene Murdock, *Ban Johnson*, pp. 210-211.
56. Eugene C. Murdock, *Ban Johnson*, p. 211.
57. *New York Times*, January 15, 1925, p. 17.
58. Jack Kavanagh, *Walter Johnson: A Life*, p. 228.
59. *New York Herald Tribune*, May 1, 1926.
60. Eugene C. Murdock, *Ban Johnson*, p. 213.
61. Kenesaw Mountain Landis to Frank J. Navin, April 21, 1926, KML Scrapbooks, Chicago Historical Society.
62. Westbrook Pegler column, "The Sporting Goods," April 18, 1926.
63. *Cleveland Press*, January 24, 1927, p. 1; *New York Times*, January 23, 1927, Section IX, pp. 1,2.
64. *Cleveland Press*, January 24, 1927, p. 1; *New York Times*, January 23, 1927, Section IX, p. 2; Eugene Murdock, *Ban Johnson*, p. 219.
65. Eugene C. Murdock, *Ban Johnson*, p. 239.
66. *New York Times*, January 25, 1927, p. 16; Eugene Murdock, *Ban Johnson*, p. 219.
67. Eugene Murdock, *Ban Johnson*, p. 222.
68. *New York Times*, January 28, 1927, p. 11; *The Sporting News*, February 3, 1927, p. 3.
69. Fred Lieb, *Baseball As I Have Known It*, p. 63; David Quintin Voigt, *American Baseball: From the Commissioners to Continental Expansion*, p. 145.

70. Smokey Joe Wood saw things differently. "Very little did I hear from Dad," recalled Wood's son Robert. "I got the sense, however, that there was an element of betting on the game but as far as throwing the ballgame certainly not. Dad saw Judge Landis in New York at a World Series game and his thought was 'How are things going at Yale, Joe?' And Dad says, 'As far as I know fine.' And Landis says, 'Well, if there's any trouble up there, I'll come up and straighten them up.' "

71. *New York Times*, January 28, 1927, p. 11; Ty Cobb, *My Life In Baseball*, p. 246; Interview with Robert Wood, April 29, 1995.

72. Eugene Murdock, *Ban Johnson*, pp. 220-221; Charles Alexander, *Ty Cobb*, pp. 199-200.

# Chapter 20 Notes

1. *Milwaukee Sentinel*, May 22, 1909; *Milwaukee Free Press*, May 22, 1909.

2. Leo Durocher, *Nice Guys Finish Last*, p. 71.

3. Interview with Susanne Landis Huddleson, July 27, 1995.

4. *Chicago Herald*, October 3, 1916, p. 1; *St. Louis Star*, December 4, 1920.

5. *Chicago Tribune*, February 24, 1921, p. 1.

6. *New York Times*, June 21, 1921, p. 4.

7. *New York Times*, July 13, 1921, p. 10.

8. Al Stump, *Ty Cobb*, pp. 317-318.

9. *New York Times*, April 24, 1923, p.18.

10. *New York Times*, April 26, 1923, p. 14; *Albany Knickerbocker Press*, April 26, 1923, p. 3.

11. *The Sporting News*, October 25, 1928, p. 1; *The Sporting News*, November 15, 1928, p. 1; *New York Sun*, August 18, 1922, p. 8.

12. Rogers Hornsby, *My War With Baseball*, pp. 24-25.

13. Daniel Ginsburg, *The Fix Is In*, p. 214.

14. *New York Times*, August 12, 1932, p. 20.

15. *New York Times*, August 12, 1932, p. 20.

16. Charles Alexander, *Rogers Hornsby*, p. 179.

17. Charlie Grimm, *Grimm's Baseball Tales*, p. 86.

18. *The Sporting News*, August 18, 1932, p. 1; Charles Alexander, *Rogers Hornsby*, p. 178.

19. *The Sporting News*, August 18, 1932, p. 5; Charles Alexander, *Rogers Hornsby*, p. 179.

20. J. G. Taylor Spink, *Judge Landis and Twenty-Five Years of Baseball*, pp. 208-209; Charles Alexander, *Rogers Hornsby*, p. 180.

21. Charles Alexander, *Rogers Hornsby*, p. 180.

22. Charles Alexander, *Rogers Hornsby*, p. 181.

23. *New York Times*, October 15, 1932, p. 21; J. G. Taylor Spink, *Judge Landis and Twenty-Five Years of Baseball*, p. 208; Daniel Ginsburg, *The Fix Is In*, p. 215.

24. Arthur Mann, *Branch Rickey*, p. 176.
25. Charles Alexander, *Rogers Hornsby*, pp. 205-207.
26. William B. Mead, *Even the Browns*, pp. 59-60.
27. Tom Murray (ed.), *Sport Magazine's All-Time All Stars*, p. 269.
28. Tom Murray (ed.), *Sport Magazine's All-Time All Stars*, p. 270.
29. Charles Alexander, *Rogers Hornsby*, p. 218.
30. David Pietrusza, *Minor Miracles*, p. 182; Charles Alexander, *Rogers Hornsby*, p. 221.
31. *New York Times*, October 8, 1938, p. 11; Charles Alexander, *Rogers Hornsby*, p. 221.
32. J. G. Taylor Spink, *Judge Landis and Twenty-Five Years of Baseball*, p. 209.
33. In response to losing $29,000 of baseball's funds, Landis voluntarily took a $25,000-per-year pay cut for four years to make amends for the loss. The stock market loss was fairly well known in baseball circles. Landis never publicized his pay cut.
34. Daniel E. Ginsburg, *The Fix Is In*, p. 215; J. G. Taylor Spink, *Judge Landis and Twenty-Five Years of Baseball*, pp. 209-210.
35. *The Sporting News*, February 1, 1964; Harold Kaese, *The Boston Braves*, pp. 232-233, 235, 254.
36. Michael Betzold and Ethan Casey, *Queen of Diamonds*, p. 43; Joe Falls, *The Detroit Tigers*, pp. 58-59; Harold Seymour, *Baseball: The Golden Age*, p. 391.
37. Leo Durocher, *Nice Guys Finish Last*, pp. 238-240; Arthur Mann, *Branch Rickey*, pp. 244-245; Peter Golenbock, *Bums*, p. 107.
38. Daniel E. Ginsburg, *The Fix Is In*, p. 223.
39. Oddly enough in April 1934 it was reported in the *New York Herald-Tribune* that half the Yankee ballclub went to visit Capone—in Atlanta Penitentiary.
40. John Kobler, *Capone*, photo insert; William B. Mead, *Two Spectacular Seasons*. p. 75; G. H. Fleming, *The Dizziest Season*, p. 56; Robert S. Boone and Gerald Grunska, *Hack*, p. 102.
41. J. G. Taylor Spink, *Judge Landis and Twenty-Five years of Baseball*, pp. 201-202.
42. Kenesaw Mountain Landis to Connie Mack, April 27, 1940, KML Papers, National Baseball Library.
43. *In re ROBERT TARLETON, December 2, 1939*, KML files, National Baseball Library.
44. *The Sporting News*, July 31, 1976.
45. Ross was welterweight champion of the world briefly in 1934 and again from 1935 through 1938.
46. Interview with Elden Auker, April 30, 1995.

# Chapter 21 Notes

1. J. G. Taylor Spink, *Judge Landis and Twenty-Five Years of Baseball*, pp. 111-112.

2.  *New York Times*, December 12, 1921, p. 16; *The Reach Official American League Base Ball Guide for 1922*, p. 24; Damon Rice, *Seasons Past*, pp. 176-177.

3.  Fred Lieb, *Baseball As I Have Known It*, pp. 142-145; Mike Sowell, *The Pitch That Killed*, pp. 300-301.

4.  *The Sporting News*, January 20, 1927, p. 5.

5.  This was not the only time a crowd booed Landis. The other instance we know about also involved an umpire. On July 26, 1936, Landis was attending a contest at Comiskey Park. Umpire Bill Summers had been knocked unconscious by a thrown pop bottle. Landis marched to the public address system mike and announced a $5,000 reward for the culprit. The crowd responded with another chorus of boos.

6.  Landis also unilaterally moved up World Series starting times to 1:30.

7.  James M. Kahn, *The Umpire Story*, p. 134; J. G. Taylor Spink, *Judge Landis and Twenty-Five Years of Baseball*, p. 113; Damon Rice, *Seasons Past*, p. 183; Frank Graham, *The New York Giants*, pp. 139-140; Lee Allen, *The World Series*, p. 105; Joseph Durso, *DiMaggio: The Last American Knight*, pp. 56-57; *New York Tribune*, October 6, 1922, pp. 1, 13; *New York Tribune*, October 9, 1922, p. 13; *New York Tribune*, October 7, 1922, pp. 8, 10; *Albany Times-Union*, October 6, 1922, p. 13; *The Reach Official American League Guide 1923*, p. 18.

8.  J. G. Spink, *Judge Landis and Twenty-Five Years of Baseball*, pp. 126-127.

9.  Joseph Durso, *The Days of Mr. McGraw*, p. 161; Frank Graham, *The Giants*, pp. 145-146.

10.  Joseph Durso, *Casey*, p. 77.

11.  Landis wasn't always so patient with Stengel's hijinks. He drew a firm line at dealing with umpires. Once when Stengel precipitated a riot in Toledo after he had caused a scene with future AL umpire Joe Rue. Landis summoned Rue and Stengel to Chicago for a hearing and stormed at Stengel: "If you ever behave again like you did toward these umpires, I'm going to throw you out of baseball for the rest of your life. Now *get out!*"

12.  Robert Creamer, *Stengel: His Life and Times*, pp. 168-169; Joseph Durso, *Casey*, p. 77.

13.  Peckinpaugh had his own take on things, claiming that many of his errors were caused by Pittsburgh's official scorers who wanted to erase Honus Wagner's old record of six errors in a Series. For the record, four of his errors took place in Pittsburgh, four in Washington.

14.  J. G. Taylor Spink, *Judge Landis and Twenty-Five Years of Baseball*, p. 148; Jack Kavanagh, *Walter Johnson: A Life*, p. 222; Frederick Lieb, *The Pittsburgh Pirates*, pp. 205, 219; Eugene Murdock, *Baseball Between the Wars*, p. 15.

15.  Jack Kavanagh, *Walter Johnson: A Life*, pp. 227-228; Frederick Lieb, *The Pittsburgh Pirates*, pp. 216-219.

16.  Robert W. Creamer, *Babe: The Legend Comes To Life*, pp. 312-313; Ken Sobol, *Babe Ruth & The American Dream*, p. 221; Kal Wagenheim, *Babe Ruth: His Life and Legend*, pp. 178-179; Frederick G. Lieb, *The St. Louis Cardinals*, p. 138; Dave Anderson, Murray Chass, Robert Creamer, and Harold Rosenthal,

*The Yankees: The Four Fabulous Eras of Baseball's Most Famous Team*, p. 44; Babe Ruth (as told to Bob Considine), *The Babe Ruth Story*, pp. 161-162.

17. Frederick G. Lieb, *Connie Mack: Grand Old Man of Baseball*, p. 230; Donald Honig, *The Man in the Dugout*, p. 281; Anthony J. O'Connor, *Baseball For The Love Of It*, p. 194.

18. James M. Kahn, *The Umpires*, pp. 131-132; Larry Gerlach, *The Men in Blue*, pp. 10, 35, 62.

19. J. G. Taylor Spink, *Judge Landis and Twenty-Five Years of Baseball*, p. 205-207; Anthony J. O'Connor, *Baseball For The Love Of It*, p. 195.

20. Charlie Grimm, *Grimm's Baseball Tales*, pp. 87-88.

21. Eugene Murdock, *Baseball Players and their Times*, pp. 289-292.

22. Landis was, nonetheless, highly supportive of umpires in the Fall Classic. Umpire George Pipgras once recalled to historian Larry Gerlach: "They were easy to umpire because of discipline. I remember when we met with . . . Landis before the World Series, he said, 'I want this to be clean and damn clean.' Landis was tough. If ballplayers cursed the umpires or in any way got rough with them, they lost their whole Series check. Landis wouldn't allow any of that stuff."

23. James M. Kahn, *The Umpires*, pp. 126-128; *Baseball Guide and Record Book 1945*, p. 119.

24. G. H. Fleming, *The Dizziest Season*, pp. 251-252; Curt Smith, *Voices of The Game*, pp. 36, 549.

25. Curt Smith, *Voices of The Game*, p. 34; Richard Bak, *Cobb Would Have Caught It*, pp. 39-40.

26. Frederick G. Lieb, *The Detroit Tigers*, p. 210.

27. Martin was a particular favorite of Landis. They had first met in St. Louis during the 1931 World Series. "Well, Mr. Pepper Martin," the Squire beamed as he shook hands with the Wild Horse of the Osage, "what I wouldn't give to be in your shoes." Martin eyed him and responded, "I'd be happy to make the switch Judge, I'd trade my sixty-five hundred a year for your sixty-five thousand any day." "We all laughed," recalled pitcher Wild Bill Hallahan, "the Judge the loudest."

28. *Detroit News*, October 10, 1934, p. 19; Robert Gregory, *Diz,* pp. 236-237; Frederick G. Lieb, *The St. Louis Cardinals*, p. 174; Robert Gregory, *Diz.* pp. 236-237; Frederick G. Lieb, *The St. Louis Cardinals*, p. 174; Richard Bak, *Cobb Would Have Caught It*, pp. 69, 232-234; Joe Falls, *The Detroit Tigers*, p. 82; Larry R. Gerlach, *The Men In Blue*, p. 21; G. H. Fleming, *The Dizziest Season*, p. 307-309; Donald Honig, *The October Heroes*, pp. 199-200; Charles Einstein (ed.), *The Second Fireside Book of Baseball*, pp. 101-103; Vi Owen, *The Adventures of a Quiet Soul*, pp. 68-77.

29. *Detroit News*, October 10, 1934, p. 19; Robert Gregory, *Diz,* pp. 236-237; Frederick G. Lieb, *The St. Louis Cardinals*, p. 174; Richard Bak, *Cobb Would Have Caught It*, pp. 69, 232-234; Joe Falls, *The Detroit Tigers*, p. 82; Larry R.

Gerlach, *The Men In Blue*, p. 21; G. H. Fleming, *The Dizziest Season*, p. 307-309; Curt Smith, *America's Dizzy Dean*, pp. 79-80.

30. Curt Smith, *Voices of The Game*, pp. 36-37; Red Barber, *The Broadcasters*, p. 27.
31. *Baseball Guide and Record Book 1945*, p. 120.
32. Red Barber, *The Broadcasters*, pp. 81-83.
33. Hank Greenberg, *The Story of My Life*, p. 83; Charlie Grimm, *Grimm's Baseball Tales*, p. 112.
34. Dick Bartell, *Rowdy Richard*, p. 227.
35. Warren Brown, *The Chicago Cubs*, pp. 145-146.
36. *New York Times*, October 25, 1935, p. 27; Charlie Grimm, *Grimm's Baseball Tales*, p. 113.
37. Hank Greenberg, *The Story of My Life*, p. 84.
38. James M. Kahn, *The Umpires*, p. 126.
39. *Baseball Guide and Record Book 1945*, p. 120.

# Chapter 22 Notes

1. The Yankees wanted Klein and his Fort Wayne teammates but were outmaneuvered by the Phillies, who obtained all concerned for a bargain $7,500.
2. *Spalding's Official Base Ball Guide for 1928*, p. 335; *Spalding's Official Base Ball Guide for 1929*, p. 335.
3. *Spalding's Official Base Ball Guide for 1928*, p. 335; *Spalding's Official Base Ball Guide for 1929*, p. 335.
4. *New York Times*, March 17, 1929, Section V, p. 5; Lee Lowenfish and Tony Lupien, *The Imperfect Diamond*, pp. 117-118; Gene Karst and Martin L. Jones, Jr., *Who's Who in Professional Baseball*, p. 301.
5. *Reach Official American League Guide for 1930*, p. 157.
6. Arthur Mann, *Branch Rickey*, pp. 165-167.
7. J. G. Taylor Spink, *Judge Landis and Twenty-Five Years of Baseball*, pp. 198-199.
8. *The Sporting News*, February 12, 1931, p. 2.
9. 49 F.2d 298; *New York Times*, April 22, 1931, p. 31.
10. *New York Times*, December 29, 1932, p. 29; J. G. Taylor Spink, *Judge Landis and Twenty-Five Years of Baseball*, p. 200.
11. *The Sporting News*, July 28, 1932, p. 4.
12. *New York Times*, February 28, 1933, p. 22.
13. *Spalding's Official Base Ball Guide for 1932*, p. 101.
14. Franklin Lewis, *The Cleveland Indians*, p. 190.
15. Franklin Lewis, *The Cleveland Indians*, pp. 192-193.
16. Bob Feller, *Strikeout Story*, p. 62; *Cleveland News*, December 10, 1936, p. 14.
17. *Cleveland Press*, December 11, 1936, p. 56.
18. Bob Feller, *Strikeout Story*, p. 63.
19. Bob Feller, *Now Pitching: Bob Feller*, p. 42.

20. Interview with Bob Feller, May 29, 1995.
21. Bob Feller, *Strikeout Story*, p. 63.
22. Franklin Lewis, *The Cleveland Indians*, p. 196.
23. Don Honig, *Baseball When The Grass Was Real*, p. 268.
24. Bob Feller, *Strikeout Story*, p. 66.
25. While the Feller case was proceeding, Landis turned 70. Writers wired him congratulations and Landis, pretending their well wishes were feigned, cabled back, "Thanks for your welcome perjury."
26. *Cleveland News*, December 10, 1936; *Cleveland Plain Dealer*, December 15, 1937, p. 18; Mike Shatzkin, *The Ballplayers*, pp. 438, 849; *Cleveland Press*, December 2, 1936, p. 22.
27. *Cleveland Plain Dealer*, December 1, 1936, p. 18.
28. *Cleveland Plain Dealer*, December 2, 1936, p. 22.
29. *Cleveland Press*, December 4, 1936, p. 54; Interview with Bob Feller, May 29, 1995.
30. *Cleveland Plain Dealer*, December 7, 1936, p. 17; *Cleveland News*, February 4, p. 18; *Cleveland Press*, December 7, 1936, p. 25; *Cleveland Press*, December 9, 1936, p. 24; *Cleveland Press*, December 10, 1936, p. 34.
31. *Cleveland Plain Dealer*, December 6, 1936, Section B, p. 2.
32. *Cleveland Plain Dealer*, December 11, 1936, p. 22; *Cleveland News*, December 10, 1936, p. 14.
33. Dick Bartell, *Rowdy Richard*, p. 193.
34. J. G. Taylor Spink, *Judge Landis and Twenty-Five Years of Baseball*, pp. 228-229; *Cleveland News*, December 10, 1936, p. 14; *Cleveland Plain Dealer*, December 10, 1936, p. 22; Bob Feller, *Strikeout Story*, p. 67.
35. "The Commissioner was no fool," Feller would comment nearly six decades later, "he knew we'd win... My father just told him he would sue him, and the judge knew he would and so did the Cleveland ballclub know I would do it."
36. *Cleveland Press*, December 11, 1936, p. 52; Bob Feller, *Strikeout Story*, pp. 66, 71; Bob Feller, *Now Pitching: Bob Feller*, p. 42; Interview with Bob Feller, May 29, 1995.
37. *New York Times*, December 11, 1936, p. 36.
38. *Cleveland News*, December 10, 1936, p. 14; *Cleveland News*, December 11, 1936, p. 24.
39. *Cleveland News*, December 11, 1936, p. 24.
40. *Cleveland Press*, December 11, 1936, pp. 52, 56.
41. Tommy Henrich, *Five O'Clock Lightning*, p. 10.
42. Tommy Henrich, *Five O'Clock Lightning*, p. 8.
43. Don Honig, *Baseball Between the Lines*, p. 26.
44. *Cleveland Plain Dealer*, April 1, 1937, p. 15.
45. *Cleveland Plain Dealer*, December 15, 1937, p. 18.
46. Don Honig, *Baseball Between the Lines*, p. 2.
47. *Cleveland Plain Dealer*, April 19, 1937, p. 14.

48. Don Honig, *Baseball Between the Lines*, p. 27.
49. "I don't think he liked Slapnicka, anyway," Henrich once remarked of Landis.
50. *Cleveland Plain Dealer*, April 1, 1938, p. 16; *New York Times*, April 1, 1938, p. 18; *Cleveland Plain Dealer*, May 28, 1938, p. 15.
51. Kenesaw Mountain Landis to Alva Bradley, November 20, 1937, KML Collection, Chicago Historical Society.
52. Murray Polner, *Branch Rickey*, p. 149.
53. Harold Seymour, *Baseball: The Golden Age*, p. 417.
54. Neil Sullivan, *The Minors*, p. 112.
55. Cedar Rapids' four farms teams were the Nebraska State League's Mitchell Kernels, the Arkansas-Missouri League's Fayetteville Angels, the Northern League's Crookston Pirates, and the suspiciously named Northeast Arkansas League's Newport Cardinals.
56. J. G. Taylor Spink, *Judge Landis and Twenty-Five Years of Baseball*, pp. 234-235.
57. *St. Louis Post-Dispatch*, March 23, 1938, p. 2B.
58. *St. Louis Globe-Democrat*, March 25, 1938, p. 8A.
59. Neil Sullivan, *The Minors*, p. 113.
60. Charles Einstein, *The Second Fireside Book of Baseball*, pp. 190-191; *1994 Microsoft Complete Baseball*.
61. *St. Louis Post-Dispatch*, p. 2A.
62. *St. Louis Post-Dispatch*, March 23, 1938, p. 2B; *St. Louis Globe-Democrat*, March 24, 1938; p. 12A.
63. *St. Louis Globe-Democrat*, March 24, 1938, pp. 10A, 12A.
64. *St. Louis Globe-Democrat*, March 26, 1938, p. 8A; *St. Louis Post-Dispatch*, March 27, 1938, p. 11A.
65. *New York Times*, March 30, 1938, p. 26.
66. *St. Louis Post-Dispatch*, March 27, 1938, p. 11A.
67. Murray Polner, *Branch Rickey: A Biography*, p. 116; Arthur Mann, *Branch Rickey: American In Action*, p. 208.
68. *New York Times*, March 25, 1938, p. 24.
69. *St. Louis Globe-Democrat*, March 24, 1938, p. 12A.
70. Murray Polner, *Branch Rickey*, p. 139.
71. *Cleveland Plain Dealer*, May 28, 1938, p. 2; *New York Times*, May 28, 1938, p. 11; *Cleveland Plain Dealer*, May 29, 1938, p. 2B.
72. In the aftermath of the Tiger decision, Detroit pitcher Bobo Newsom went from being a 21-game winner to a 20-game loser in 1941, prompting Zeller to propose cutting his salary from $30,000 to $12,500. "Hell, Curly," Bobo postulated the bald-headed Zeller, "you lost ninety players, and I don't see you takin' no cut." Zeller sold him to Washington.
73. *In re DETROIT CLUB "WORKING AGREEMENTS,"* January 13, 1940, KML Papers, National Baseball Library.
74. *New York Times*, January 16, 1940, p. 26.

75. *New York Times*, January 17, 1940, p. 26.
76. *In re DETROIT CLUB "WORKING AGREEMENTS,"* January 15, 1940, KML Papers, National Baseball Library; *New York Times*, January 16, 1940, p. 26.
77. *New York Times*, January 28, 1940, Section V, p. 1; J. G. Taylor Spink, *Judge Landis and Twenty-Five Years of Baseball*, pp. 237-238; Leo Durocher, *The Dodgers and Me*, 49.
78. *New York Times*, January 17, 1940, p. 26.
79. *New York Times*, January 17, 1940, p. 26.
80. *New York Times*, January 27, 1940, p. 17.
81. *New York Times*, January 28, 1940, Section V, p. 1.
82. *New York Times*, February 2, 1940, p. 20.
83. *New York Times*, February 3, 1940, p. 17.
84. *New York Times*, February 6, 1940, p. 25.
85. *New York Times*, January 28, 1940, p. 5; *New York Times*, January 29, 1940, p. 20.
86. Kenesaw Mountain Landis to John A. Heydler, January 25, 1944, KML Collection, Chicago Historical Society.

# Chapter 23 Notes

1. Don Honig, *Baseball Between the Lines*, p. 27.
2. Vi Owen, *The Adventures of a Quiet Soul*, p. 97.
3. Interview with Jo-Jo Moore, April 30, 1995.
4. Leo Durocher, *Nice Guys Finish Last*, pp. 70-71, 76.
5. Bill Gilbert, *They Also Served*, p. 72.
6. Interview with Elden Auker, April 30, 1995.
7. In the early 1940s Bill Veeck wrote to Landis diplomatically suggesting that the reserve clause was legally untenable and that some concessions were in order before the entire system collapsed. "So I didn't hear anything back from Landis for six weeks, maybe longer," Veeck recalled decades later. "Les O'Connor. . . eventually wrote me a letter which I can quote verbatim. 'Dear Bill: Some very bright fellow once said a little knowledge is a very dangerous thing, and you've just proven him to be a wizard!' "
8. J. G. Taylor Spink, *Judge Landis and Twenty-Five Years of Baseball*, p. 98; Richard C. Lindberg, *Stealing First in a Two-Team Town*, p. 170.
9. David Pietrusza, *Minor Miracles*, p. 7; Harold Seymour, *Baseball: The Golden Age*, p. 407.
10. Harold Seymour, *Baseball: The Golden Age*, pp. 404-407.
11. Harold Seymour, *Baseball: The Golden Age*, p. 408.
12. Harold Seymour, *Baseball: The Golden Age*, pp. 408-409; J. G. Taylor Spink, *Judge Landis and Twenty-Five Years of Baseball*, p. 126.
13. Harold Seymour, *Baseball: The People's Game*, p.88; Barbara Gregorich, *Women at Play*, pp. 61-62.

14. Film of the event raises serious questions as to just how much the Yankee duo was trying.

15. David Pietrusza, *Minor Miracles*, p. 178; Barbara Gregorich, *Women at Play*, pp. 66-70.

16. David Pietrusza, *Minor Miracles*, p. 24; Bill O'Neal, *The Texas League*, p. 72.

17. Dennis De Valeria and Jeanne Burke De Valeria, *Honus Wagner*, pp. 292-293; Harold Seymour, *Baseball: The People's Game*, p. 211.

18. David Pietrusza, *Minor Miracles*, pp. 91-95.

19. *Albany Evening News*, June 18, 1935; Robert S. Boone and Gerald Grunska, *Hack*, pp. 116-117.

20. David Pietrusza, *Minor Miracles*, pp. 96-97; Robert S. Boone and Gerald Grunska, *Hack*, pp. 117-118.

21. Vince Staten, *Ol' Diz*, pp. 80-82.

22. *Before K. M. Landis, Commissioner in the Matter of Appeal of Jerome H. Dean, relative to fine and suspension on or about August 14th, 1934 at St. Louis, Missouri*, p. 4; Curt Smith, *America's Dizzy Dean*, p. 61.

23. G. H. Fleming, *The Dizziest Season*, p. 211; Curt Smith, *America's Dizzy Dean*, p. 61; Robert Gregory, *Diz*, pp. 171-172.

24. Curt Smith, *America's Dizzy Dean*, p. 61; Robert Gregory, *Diz*, p. 173.

25. *Before K. M. Landis, Commissioner in the Matter of Appeal of Jerome H. Dean, relative to fine and suspension on or about August 14th, 1934 at St. Louis, Missouri*, p. 8.

26. Robert Gregory, *Diz*, p. 176.

27. G. H. Fleming, *The Dizziest Season*, p. 231.

28. Vince Staten, *Ol' Diz*, pp. 157-158.

29. Robert Gregory, *Diz*, p. 247.

30. *New York Times*, April 11, 1935, p. 28; Curt Smith, *America's Dizzy Dean*, p. 90.

31. Curt Smith, *America's Dizzy Dean*, p. 90.

32. Bill O'Neal, *The Southern League*, p. 57; Robert Gregory, *Diz*, p. 278.

33. Robert Gregory, *Diz*, p. 278.

34. Robert Gregory, *Diz*, p. 329; Curt Smith, *America's Dizzy Dean*, p. 103; Fred Lieb, *The St. Louis Cardinals*, pp. 181-182.

35. Robert Gregory, *Diz*, p. 347.

36. Vince Staten, *Ol' Diz*, pp. 233-234.

37. Curt Smith, *Voices of The Game*, p. 36-37.

38. Robert Gregory, *Diz*, p. 369.

39. Vince Staten, *Ol' Diz*, p. 218; Curt Smith, *Voices of The Game*, p. 104.

40. Robert Gregory, *Diz*, p. 369.

41. Leo Durocher, *Nice Guys Finish Last*, p. 72.

42. Leo Durocher, *Nice Guys Finish Last*, p. 71.

43. Hank Greenberg, *The Story of My Life*, pp. 149-150.

44. Kenesaw Mountain Landis to Spencer F. Harris, July 26, 1944, KML Papers, National Baseball Library.

45. Leo Durocher, *Nice Guys Finish Last*, pp. 71-76; Leo Durocher, *The Dodgers and Me*, pp. 74-75.

46. Eugene Murdock, *Baseball Between the Wars*, p. 109.

47. Charles Einstein (ed.), *The Third Fireside Book of Baseball*, p. 251; Lee Allen, *Cooperstown Corner*, p. 64; Robert S. Boone and Gerald Grunska, *Hack*, p. 90.

48. Richard Ferrell to Kenesaw Mountain Landis, June 9, 1938; Kenesaw Mountain Landis to Boston American League Club November 19, 1938; Transcript of Kenesaw Mountain Landis interrogation of Boston officials, August 2, 1938, p. 26.

49. Interview with Carl Lundquist, December 18, 1996.

50. Richard S. Simons, "Indiana's Baseball Magnates," *Indianapolis Star*, October 9, 1977, p. 8.

51. Bill Veeck, *The Hustler's Handbook*, p. 297.

52. Jon Kerr, *Calvin: Baseball's Last Dinosaur*, p. 33.

53. Don Warfield, *The Roaring Redhead*, p. 57-58; Michael Gershman, *Diamonds*, p. 155; David Pietrusza, *Lights On!*, p. 105.

54. *Cleveland News*, April 21, 1921, page unknown.

55. Arthur Mann, *Branch Rickey*, p. 189.

56. *Reach Official American League Guide for 1930*, p. 116; Richard Goldstein, *Superstars and Screwballs*, p. 161; Frank Graham, *The Brooklyn Dodgers*, p. 119.

57. Richard Goldstein, *Superstars and Screwballs*, p. 147; Rich Westcott and Frank Bilovsky, *The New Phillies Encyclopedia*, p. 473; Interview with Nancy Landis Smith Lucas, July 25, 1995.

58. Wrigley Field was home to the Pacific Coast League's Los Angeles Angels from 1925 to 1957 and the Hollywood Stars from 1926 to 1935. It was named for Chicago Cubs owner William Wrigley (father of Philip K. Wrigley) who owned both the Cubs and the Angels.

59. Michael Gershman, *Diamonds*, p. 186; Lawrence Ritter, *Lost Ballparks*, p. 122; Michael Benson, *Ballparks of North America*, pp. 121-122, 190; Franklin Lewis, *The Cleveland Indians*, p. 172; Talmadge Boston, *1939: Baseball's Pivotal Year*, pp. 229-230; Dennis De Valeria and Jeanne Burke De Valeria, *Honus Wagner*, pp. 2-4; David Pietrusza, *Lights On!*, p. 57.

60. David Quintin Voigt, *American Baseball: From the Commissioners to Continental Expansion*, Volume II, p. 144.

# Chapter 24 Notes

1. Interview with Nancy Landis Smith Lucas, July 27, 1995.

2. *Cleveland Plain Dealer*, April 21, 1923, p. 17.

3. *Cleveland Plain Dealer*, April 21, 1923, p. 17; *Cleveland News*, April 21, 1923.

4. *New York Times*, September 5, 1937, p. 8.

5. Interviews with Cathy Landis Huddleson and Nancy Landis Smith Lucas, June 27, 1995.

6.  A remarkable prediction. He actually lived 37 years more.

7.  Each morning, regardless of the season, Landis invariably enjoyed the same thing for breakfast—soup.

8.  *Cincinnati Post*, September 18, 1907.

9.  "Did you ever see his legs?" granddaughter Nancy once asked, "He had skinny little legs."

10. Interviews with Keehn Landis and Nancy Landis Smith Lucas, July 25, 1995.

11. *Chicago Tribune*, November 20, 1916, p. 13.

12. Susanne Landis to Kenesaw Mountain Landis, date unknown, KML Collection, Chicago Historical Society.

13. J. G. Taylor Spink, *Judge Landis and Twenty-Five Years of Baseball*, pp. 114-115.

14. His wife Winifred shared his largely teetotaling habits, although they were not averse to supplying liquor to guests. Ford Frick, then still a sportswriter, and fellow New York writer Frank Graham would often visit the Landises. "Let's walk over and see the Judge," Frick would say. "It was always pleasant." Graham once recalled, "The Judge and Mrs. Landis were wonderful hosts and the Judge, while breaking out a bottle of bourbon, would say, 'It's nice of you to come over. Mother and I get a little lonesome in the evening.' "

15. Interviews with Keehn Landis and Nancy Landis Smith Lucas, July 27, 1995.

16. Interview with Lincoln Landis, , February 12, 1996.

17. *Chicago Daily News*, February 18, 1922; Interview with Keehn Landis, July 27, 1995.

18. J. G. Taylor Spink, *Judge Landis and Twenty-Five Years of Baseball*, p. 128.

19. Interview with Keehn Landis, July 27, 1995; Interviews with Lincoln Landis, February 12, 1996, September 27, 1996.

20. *Chicago Record-Herald*, July 7, 1907, p. 3.

21. Frank Brady, *Citizen Welles*, p. 1; Barbara Learing, *Orson Welles: A Biography*, p. 8; Interview with Nancy Landis Smith Lucas, July 27, 1995.

22. Aside from Wells' nurse, a Mrs. Nini Callahan Shores (who also received $50,000), the rest of Wells' estate (estimated to be approximately $1.5 million) was left either to relatives or to Chicago hospitals and clinics.

23. Simon Callow, *Orson Welles: The Road to Xanadu*, pp. 10-11.

24. Fellow Burt Lake residents included the president of, and two professors from, Wabash College, a newspaper publisher from Fort Wayne, and Lew Wallace, Jr.

25. The deed contained a restricted covenant—not on race as might be presumed—but on liquor. The owner, the deed read, shall "not use said premises for sale or manufacture of intoxicating liquors."

26. A contemporary at Burt Lake saw Reed and Susanne as "dear, slender, affectionate, wild little things, awfully attractive."

27. Helen Boyd Higgins, *Our Burt Lake Story*, pp. 27, 30-33, 59, 61, 63-65; Interview with Keehn Landis, July 27, 1995; Kenesaw Mountain Landis to Fred Lesh, September 1, 1943, KML Collection, Chicago Historical Society; Interview with Lincoln Landis, September 27, 1996.

28. *Detroit News*, November 29, 1920.
29. Decades later when hearing this story not one of Reed Landis' children could picture their prim and proper grandmother ever catching as much as a minnow.
30. Landis' idol Walter Gresham was also considered a "skeptic" and was closely allied with Robert G. Ingersoll, the 19th century's most prominent agnostic.
31. J. G. Taylor Spink, *Judge Landis and Twenty-Five Years of Baseball*, p. 292; Charles W. Calhoun, *Gilded Age Cato: The Life of Walter Q. Gresham*, p. 9.
32. Interview with Lincoln Landis, February 12, 1996.
33. Kenesaw Mountain Landis to Pastor of St. James Roman Catholic Church, Maywood, Illinois, August 28, 1943, KML Collection, Chicago Historical Society.
34. KML Scrapbooks, Chicago Historical Society.
35. Kenesaw Mountain Landis to Henry F. Pringle, November 30, 1926, KML Collection, Chicago Historical Society.
36. Interview with Nancy Landis Smith Lucas, July 27, 1995.
37. Reed had married Marion in 1919. A graduate of the Emma Willard finishing school, she had served with the Motor Corps at Ford Sheridan during the First World War. She was the daughter of George Washington Keehn, a lumber industry executive and brilliant mathematician.
38. Interviews With Keehn Landis and Nancy Landis Smith Lucas, July 27, 1995; Lincoln Landis to author, September 27, 1996.
39. Landis was not the only Chicago baseball figure to fear kidnapping. To protect Hack Wilson's son Bobby, Al Capone dispatched a bodyguard who walked the boy to and from school and sat with him at Wrigley Field.
40. Interview with Cathy Landis Huddleson and Nancy Landis Smith Lucas, July 25, 1995; Robert S. Boone and Gerald Grunska, *Hack*, pp. 102-103.
41. Interview with Lincoln Landis, February 12, 1996.
42. Kenesaw Mountain Landis II to Kenesaw Mountain Landis, September 13, 1928, KML Collection, Chicago Historical Society; Kenesaw Mountain Landis to Kenesaw Mountain Landis II, September 14, 1928, KML Collection, Chicago Historical Society; Kenesaw Mountain Landis to Kenesaw Mountain Landis II, November 21, 1928, KML Collection, Chicago Historical Society.
43. Warren W. Brown, "Down Memory Lane: Landis had a sense of humor, but he protected rights of the players," *Baseball Digest*, September 1970, pp. 52-53.
44. Kenesaw Mountain Landis to Arthur Hoyt Bogne, October 23, 1940, KML, Chicago Historical Society.
45. Kenesaw Mountain Landis to Laura Shanklin Dennis, October 22, 1940, KML Collection, Chicago Historical Society.
46. Kenesaw Mountain Landis to Charles S. Perkins, August 12, 1943, KML Collection, Chicago Historical Society.
47. *San Marcos ... Over 80 Years of History* (pamphlet published by the Sheraton San Marcos; Chandler, Arizona).
48. *Detroit News*, November 29, 1920.
49. *Cincinnati Post*, September 18, 1907.
50. *Schenectady Union-Star*, January 5, 1927, p. 13.

# Chapter 25 Notes

1. David Pietrusza, *Minor Miracles*, pp. 127-133.
2. Jules Tygiel, *Baseball's Great Experiment*, p. 27; David Pietrusza, *Major Leagues*, pp. 220-221, 250; Michael Benson, *Ballparks of North America*, p. 349; Lawrence Ritter, *Lost Ballparks*, p. 190.
3. Ken Sobol, *Babe Ruth & The American Dream*, p. 134.
4. Shortly after the suicide of Jack Johnson's first wife in September 1912, he found himself accused of kidnapping a young white woman, Lucille Cameron. The accuser was Lucille's mother. Federal authorities then attempted to prove Johnson guilty of violating the Mann Act (which prohibited transporting a woman across state lines for immoral purposes) with Miss Cameron. Lucille, however, refused to implicate Johnson and, in fact, shortly thereafter married him. Nothing became of either the kidnapping nor the Mann Act charge. That November, however, a federal grand jury presided over by Landis did indict Johnson on 11 counts of violating the Mann Act with a known prostitute, Belle Schreiber. Landis demanded $30,000 in bail from Johnson for him to go free but refused to accept Johnson's money for this purpose. "I will not accept a cash bond in this case," said Landis. "There is a human cry in this case that cannot be overlooked in consideration of a bond." After the heavyweight champion spent four days in prison, Landis consented to accept $32,000 in property from Johnson's mother as bail.

    After a 12-hour trial (and an hour-and-45 minutes of jury deliberation) under federal judge George A. Carpenter, Johnson was found guilty, fined him $1,000, and sentenced him to a year and a day in Joliet. He soon skipped the bail Landis had freed him on, posing as black baseball pioneer Rube Foster (to whom be bore a striking resemblance) and escaped to Canada and ultimately to Europe.
5. James Bankes, *The Pittsburgh Crawfords*, pp. 138-139; John B. Holway, *Voices from the Great Black Baseball Leagues*, p. 7; Jack Kavanagh, *Walter Johnson: A Life*, p. 147; J. G. Taylor Spink, *Judge Landis and Twenty-Five Years of Baseball*, p. 36; Janet Bruce, *The Kansas City Monarchs: Champions of Black Baseball*, p. 105.
6. Albert Fried, *Socialism in America*, p. 386; Nathaniel Weyl and William Marina, *American Statesmen on Slavery and the Negro*, p. 295.
7. Nathaniel Weyl and William Marina, *American Statesmen on Slavery and the Negro*, pp. 280-286, 325-337; George E. Mowry, *The Era of Theodore Roosevelt*, p. 93.
8. Running for Congress in the 1860s, however, Gresham was considerably less moderate, terming whites the "superior race" and claiming that his party had "no disposition to make the negro equal to the white man."
9. *The National Cyclopaedia of Biography*, Volume XXIV, p. 330.
10. *Peoria Herald-Transcript*, February 23, 1901.

11.  Associated Press Dispatch, November 15, 1934; Undated clipping, KML Scrapbooks, Chicago Historical Society.
12.  On the evening of August 13, 1906, 15 to 20 black infantrymen from Fort Brown, Texas, rioted and shot up the town of Brownsville, Texas, resulting in the death of one individual. When the guilty soldiers' compatriots refused to testify against them, a frustrated TR discharged virtually every black serving at the fort, cashiering a total of 167 soldiers. TR's action set off a political firestorm. All 167 were reinstated in 1972.
13.  Nathaniel Weyl and William Marina, *American Statesmen and the Negro*, pp. 319-320.
14.  German propagandists took careful note of the East St. Louis riots and of the still common practice of lynching to urge Americans not to support the war. Their efforts, however, had little effect.
15.  Elliot Rudwick, *Race Riot at East St. Louis*, passim; William T. Hutchinson, *Lowden of Illinois*, pp. 338-339; Donald F. Tingley, *The Structuring of a State*, pp. 296-300; William M. Tuttle, Jr., *Race Riot: Chicago in the Red Summer of 1919*, pp. 12-13; *Chicago Tribune*, July 7, 1918, p. 5; John Hope Franklin, *From Slavery to Freedom*, pp. 474-475.
16.  David M. Chalmers, *Hooded Americanism*, pp. 162-174; "Frederick Landis for Governor" (political pamphlet), files of the Logansport Public Library.
17.  Frederick Landis wrote in the Memorial Day 1925 edition of the *New York American*: "Let Prejudice Stand Without the Gate this Day as We Go in with Flowers for All Who Fought and fell for Us. For they Are Not Protestants, Catholics, Jews, Jews Nor Gentiles Now—Nor Whites Nor Blacks—Only Old Glory's Silent Brotherhood."
18.  Interview with Lincoln Landis, February 12, 1996; Lincoln Landis, *The Washington Times*, October 14, 1994, p. B3.
19.  William G. Sterrett to KML (telegram), March 29, 1922; KML to William G. Sterrett, April 6, 1922; *Dallas News*, undated clipping 1922.
20.  *Chicago Tribune*, October 18, 1924, p. 1.
21.  *Chicago Defender*, February 25, 1922.
22.  *Chicago Advocate*, February 19, 1921.
23.  *Chicago Defender*, March 5, 1921, p. 12.
24.  John B. Holway, *Black Diamonds*, p. 28.
25.  Neil Lanctot, *Fair Dealing and Clean Playing*, p. 179.
26.  Charles Alexander, *Rogers Hornsby*, pp. 68-69.
27.  Cool Papa Bell, however, once told interviewers that when his St. Louis Stars played the Detroit Tigers, Heilmann (and the racist Ty Cobb) refused to play. He did, however, contend that Landis refused to allow major leaguers to barnstorm under their team names after that.
28.  Donn Rogosin, *Invisible Men*, p. 184; John Holway, *Voices from the Great Black Baseball Leagues*, p. 55, 117; James Bankes, *The Pittsburgh Crawfords*, p. 63.
29.  Interview with James A. Riley, September 20, 1996; John B. Holway, *Voices from the Great Black Baseball Leagues*, pp. 6-7.

30. John B. Holway, *Black Diamonds*, p. 10; Bankes, *The Pittsburgh Crawfords*, p. 63.
31. John B. Holway, *Black Diamonds*, pp. 41, 45.
32. There are problems with many of these accounts. Landis could not have affected the Feller-Paige tour of 1946. He died in November, 1944. In regard to the 1935 incident Wells claimed Landis acted after the Negro Leaguers won 21 straight; Cornelius put the number at a more modest seven.
33. John Holway, *Black Diamonds*, p. 72; John Holway, *Voices from the Great Black Baseball Leagues*, pp. 225, 237.
34. Landis himself personally attended integrated games in Cuba. In 1925 he witnessed the last game of the Cuban League season and saw a black team beat a white one, 1-0, on Oscar Charleston's homer off major leaguer Dolf Luque.
35. Yet even this does not end the chronology. In May 1944 we read of the Homestead Grays being allowed to play the Fall River Shipyard team of the New England Industrial League at Fenway Park.
36. David Falkner, *Great Time Coming*, p. 96; John B. Holway, *Black Diamonds*, pp. 110-111; James Charlton, *The Baseball Chronology*, pp. 320, 331.
37. Gene Karst and Martin J. Jones, Jr., *Who's Who in Professional Baseball*, p. 772.
38. It was Elson who just a few years before had conducted the first live on-field interview. It was Landis who had granted permission for it.
39. Interview with Bob Broeg, June 18, 1995.
40. *New York Times*, July 31, 1938, Part V, pp. 1,3; *The Pittsburgh Courier*, August 6, 1938, p. 1; Art Rust, Jr., *"Get That Nigger Off The Field,"* p. 130.
41. Ford Frick, *Games, Asterisks, and People*, p. 216.
42. *New York Times*, July 31, 1938, Part V, p. 3; Richard Crepeau, "The Jake Powell Incident and the Press: A Study in Black and White," *Baseball History*, Summer 1986, pp. 32-46.
43. Landis received little appreciation for banning Powell. While *Pittsburgh Courier* columnist Chet Washington praised him, the *Philadelphia Afro-American* and the *Chicago Defender* thought the whole incident merely reflected the racism prevalent in baseball under Landis. The few white columnists who took notice of the controversy—the *New York Daily News'* Westbrook Pegler and the *New York Post's* Hugh Bradley—both damned Landis for doing nothing to lift the color bar. Pegler accused Landis of attempting to "placate the colored clientele of a business which trades under the name of the national game, but which has always treated the Negroes as Adolf Hitler treats the Jews."
44. *New York Age*, August 20, 1938, p. 8; Phil Dixon and Patrick J. Hannigan, *The Negro Baseball Leagues: A Photographic History*, pp. 252-253.
45. David Faulkner, *Great Time Coming*, p. 95; Harvey Frommer, *Rickey and Robinson*, p. 98.
46. David Faulkner, *Great Time Coming*, pp. 68-69, 95-96; James Overmyer, *Effa Manley and the Newark Eagles*, p. 215; Jules Tygiel, *Baseball's Great Experiment*, p. 34.

47. *Pittsburgh Courier*, May 30, 1942, p. 16; *Pittsburgh Courier*, June 6, 1942, p. 16; Mark Ribowsky, *Don't Look Back*, pp. 207-208; Jim Charlton, *The Baseball Chronology*, p. 320.

48. Actually, the paper had not conducted the interviews at all but was reprinting interviews performed by the *Pittsburgh Courier*'s Wendell Smith.

49. John Holway, *Josh and Satch*, p. 150; Peter Golenbock, *Bums*, p. 122; Joseph Thomas Moore, *Pride Against Prejudice*, p. 20.

50. Donn Rogosin, *Invisible Men*, p. 193; Robert Peterson, *Only The Ball Was White*, p. 177-178.

51. John Holway, *Josh and Satch*, p. 151; *Chicago Defender*, July 25, 1942, p. 24; *Chicago Defender*, August 1, 1942, p. 24.

52. Landis' grandson Keehn provides further evidence of this: "I had the feeling from some stuff I heard from granddad that the owners of the clubs were not anxious to [integrate] . . . It wasn't just granddaddy."

53. *The Daily Worker*, June 24, 1942.

54. Thomas Moore, *Pride Against Prejudice*, p. 21; Jules Tygiel, *Baseball's Great Experiment*, p. 40; Jim Charlton, *The Baseball Chronology*, p. 321; John B. Holway, *Black Diamonds*, pp. 131-132.

55. Thomas Moore, *Pride Against Prejudice*, pp.21-22.

56. MacPhail continued his racist attitudes after Landis' death. In 1945 he wrote to Landis' successor, A. B. "Happy" Chandler, "we can't stick our heads in the sand and ignore the problem. If we do, we will have colored players in the major leagues in 1945 and in the major leagues thereafter."

57. Jim Charlton, *The Baseball Chronology*, p. 321.

58. Mark Ribowsky, *Don't Look Back*, pp. 211-215.

59. Veeck's story, however, had been circulating for some time. A. S. Young's 1954 book, *Great Negro Baseball Stories*, noted the tale in passing but referred to it as "unsubstantiated."

60. Bill Veeck, *Veeck As In Wreck*, p. 171.

61. Thomas Moore, *Pride Against Prejudice*, p. 23; William Barry Furlong, "This Morning," *Washington Post*, February 9, 1976.

62. *New York Times*, February 11, 1943, p. 26; *New York Times*, February 16, 1943, p. 24; *New York Times*, February 12, 1943, p. 26; *New York Times*, February 19, 1943, p. 25; Rich Westcott and Frank Bilovsky, *The New Phillies Encyclopedia*, p. 478.

63. Frick's supposed remarks about Jews in the majors is somewhat puzzling in view of the many Jewish players in the game's history as well as the Dreyfuss family's control of the Pirates when Frick's alleged statements were made.

64. Bruce Kuklick, *To Every Thing A Season*, p.146; James A. Riley, *The Biographical Encyclopedia of the Negro Baseball Leagues*, p. 328; James Overmyer, *Effa Manley and the Newark Eagles*, pp. 135-136.

65. Donn Rogosin, *Invisible Men*, p. 107; James A. Riley, *The Biographical Encyclopedia of the Negro Leagues*, p. 91; Interview with James A. Riley, September 20, 1996.

66. Bill Veeck, *Veeck As In Wreck*, pp. 171-172.
67. Harvey Frommer, *Rickey & Robinson*, p. 98.
68. William Barry Furlong, "This Morning," *Washington Post*, February 9, 1976.
69. Jules Tygiel, *Baseball's Great Experiment*, p. 41, SABR-L (list server of the Society for American Baseball Research), August 29-30, 1996.
70. William Hageman, "Chicago's 55-Year-Old Secret Jackie Robinson's Tryout With the White Sox," *Chicago Tribune*, March 26, 1997.
71. Bill Veeck, *Veeck As In Wreck*, p. 171.
72. David Jordan to the author, April 24, 1996.
73. Bill Veeck to Kenesaw Mountain Landis, May 22, 1944, KML Collection, Chicago Historical Society.
74. Thomas Moore, *Pride Against Prejudice*, p. 23.
75. David Faulkner, *Great Time Coming*, p. 97; James A. Riley, *The Biographical Encyclopedia of the Negro Baseball Leagues*, p. 567.
76. Jules Tygiel, *Baseball's Great Experiment*, p. 41.
77. Janet Bruce, *The Kansas City Monarchs*, p. 109.
78. David Faulkner, *Great Time Coming*, p. 100.
79. The delegation's tactics were also askew on another level: timing. Landis had other things on his mind. The following day he would toss Phillies owner William D. Cox out of baseball.
80. David Faulkner, *Great Time Coming*, p. 99.
81. Jules Tygiel, *Baseball's Great Experiment*, p. 41.
82. Murray Polner, *Branch Rickey*, p. 149.
83. Jules Tygiel, *Baseball's Great Experiment*, p. 31.
84. *New York Times*, December 4, 1943, p. 17.
85. Ironically, at the same time the Judge was taking no action on integrating baseball, his namesake Kenesaw Mountain Landis II—an ardent integrationist—was authoring a groundbreaking study, "Segregation in Washington," about race relations in the nation's capital. "I was nine months writing it, and it damned near killed me," he complained, and he wasn't exaggerating. Kenesaw II barely outlived his aged uncle.
86. *Logansport Pharos-Tribune*, July 6, 1946, pp. 1, 13; *The Sun* (Springfield, O.), August 6, 1949.
87. Bruce Kuklick, *To Every Thing A Season*, pp. 146-147.
88. Paul M. Angle, *Philip K. Wrigley, A Memoir of a Modest Man*, p. 122; William A. Tuttle, Jr., *Race Riot: Chicago in the Red Summer of 1919*, passim; Charles A. Hughes to KML, June 24, 1943, KML Collection, Chicago Historical Society; John Hope Franklin, *From Slavery to Freedom*, pp. 474-475, 481-483, 597-598.
89. While such images of racial violence were easy for Landis and his contemporaries to conjure up, it should be noted that such outrages were not, however, endemic in American sporting events. College football and early professional football both featured black players (including Paul Robeson). Black boxing champions Jack Johnson, Joe Walcott, Henry Armstrong, and Joe Louis fought without having arenas burnt down around them.

Yet, resistance to blacks in sports other than baseball was clearly evident. In 1914 federal legislation prohibited interstate transportation of prize fight films, for fear that the sight of an African-American defeating a white could provoke rioting. Even in relatively-liberal New York, the state athletic commission banned inter-racial bouts. The National Football League segregated itself in the 1930s not allowing blacks to return to the gridiron until 1946. The National Basketball Association did not integrate until 1951.

90.  Donn Rogosin, *Invisible Men*, p. 107.
91.  John B. Holway, *Black Diamonds*, p. 308.
92.  Donn Rogosin, *Invisible Men*, pp. 114-115.
93.  Richard Nardinelli, "Judge Kenesaw Mountain Landis and the Art of Cartel Enforcement, *Baseball History*, p. 111.
94.  Interview with Keehn Landis, July 27, 1995.
95.  Interview with Lincoln Landis, February 12, 1996.
96.  Interviews with Nancy Lucas Smith Landis, and Susanne Landis Huddleson, July 27, 1995.

# Chapter 26 Notes

1.  Only two new major league parks opened in Landis' quarter-century rule: Yankee Stadium in 1923 and Cleveland's Municipal Stadium in 1932. And Municipal Stadium was used only for night, weekend, and holiday games until 1947. The rest of the Tribe's schedule remaining at old League Park.
2.  Harold Seymour, *Baseball: The Golden Age*, pp. 244-255; James Charlton, *The Baseball Chronology*, p. 198; David Q. Voigt, *American Baseball: From the Commissioners to Continental Expansion*, pp. 120-124; David Pietrusza, *Baseball's Canadian-American League*, p. 151.
3.  J. G. Taylor Spink, *Judge Landis and Twenty-Five Years of Baseball*, pp. 240-241.
4.  Bill Gilbert, *They Also Served*, p. 42.
5.  Richard Goldstein, *Spartan Seasons*, p. 20; William B. Mead and Paul Dickson, *Baseball: The President's Game*, pp. 78-79.
6.  David Pietrusza, *Lights On!*, pp. 163-165.
7.  This was Landis' only wartime trip to Washington to meet with government officials. "I'll not go to Washington," he explained, "nor will I ask a favor for baseball for anyone."
8.  Lee Allen, *The National League Story*, p. 233; Bill Gilbert, *They Also Served*, pp. 80-81; William B. Mead, *Even The Browns*, pp. 73-74; *Baseball Guide and Record Book 1945*, p. 118; J. G. Taylor Spink, *Judge Landis and Twenty-Five Years of Baseball*, p. 280.
9.  *Baseball Guide and Record Book 1945*, p. 122-123; KML to Mrs. Theodore Peters, September 1, 1944, KML Collection, Chicago Historical Society.
10.  Richard Goldstein, *Spartan Seasons*, pp. 64-65; David Pietrusza, *Baseball's Canadian-American League*, p. 151, 156.

11. *Baseball Guide and Record Book 1945*, pp. 123-124.
12. Richard Goldstein, *Spartan Seasons*, p. 40.
13. Kenesaw Mountain Landis to Fred Lesh, September 1, 1943, KML Collection, Chicago Historical Society.
14. Kenesaw Mountain Landis to Paul Egan, August 17, 1943, KML Collection, Chicago Historical Society.
15. Kenesaw Mountain Landis to Frank Lowden, March 28, 1942, KML Collection, Chicago Historical Society; *New York Times*, March 6, 1940, p. 21.
16. *Cleveland Plain Dealer*, May 30, 1943; *New York Times*, January 8, 1944, p. 8; Interview with Lincoln Landis, September 10, 1996; Kenesaw Mountain Landis to Commander Edward A. Hayes, October 14, 1943; Kenesaw Mountain Landis to Ensign Charles W. Landis, October 28, 1943.
17. Photographer Robert Artega, however, claimed that Landis, Will Rogers, and Spink shared a box at the 1934 World Series. At one point Spink, a big tipper, gave a vendor a $20 bill for some hot dogs. When the boy said he'd be back with Spink's change, Spink cheerfully yelled out, "Stick the change up your behind," meaning the lad should keep it. The next day Spink paid the same vendor with another $20 bill. The boy thought Spink would continue his largess, pocketed the bill, and walked away. "Hey," Spink bellowed, "you sonafabitch, where the hell is my change?" "I'd never seen Judge Landis laugh before," Artega recalled, "but this time he roared."
18. *Taylor Spink . . . The Legend and the Man; J. G. Taylor Spink, Judge Landis and Twenty-Five Years of Baseball*, pp. 250-275.
19. Rich Westcott and Frank Bilovsky, *The New Phillies Encyclopedia*, p. 441; Richard Goldstein, *Spartan Seasons*, p. 74.
20. J. G. Spink, *Judge Landis and Twenty-Five Years of Baseball*, p. 281
21. Untitled Decision regarding William D. Cox, November 23, 1943, KML Papers, National Baseball Library; *New York Times*, December 5, 1943, Section III, p. 3.
22. *New York Times*, November 24, 1943, p. 24.
23. *New York Times*, December 5, 1943, Section III, p. 1.
24. Kenesaw Mountain Landis to Frank Lowden, August 24, 1928, KML Collection, Chicago Historical Society.
25. *New York Times*, January 7, 1936, p. 27; *New York Times*, January 8, 1936, p. 27; *New York Times*, January 21, 1936, p. 30; *New York Times*, January 29, 1936, p. 16.
26. Kenesaw Mountain Landis to Alva Bradley, January 6, 1936, KML Collection, Chicago Historical Society; Kenesaw Mountain Landis to Alva Bradley, January 21, 1936, KML Collection, Chicago Historical Society; J. G. Taylor Spink, *Judge Landis and Twenty-Five Years of Baseball*, p. 276.
27. Interview with Nancy Landis Smith Lucas and Susanne Landis Huddleson, July 27, 1995; *Petoskey (MI)Evening News*, October 11, 1941, p. 1; *New York Times*, October 11, 1941, p. 12; *New York Times*, October 12, 1941; Section V, p. 10; *New York Times*, October 13, 1941, p. 26; *New York Times*, October 18,

1941, p. 31; *New York Times*, November 4, 1941, p. 32; *New York Times*, November 6, 1941, p. 26; J. G. Taylor Spink, *Judge Landis and Twenty-Five Years of Baseball*, pp. 276-277.

28. Kenesaw Mountain Landis to Roy B. Wilcox, December 16, 1941, KML Collection, Chicago Historical Society; J. G. Taylor Spink, *Judge Landis and Twenty-Five Years of Baseball*, pp. 277.

29. William T. Hutchinson, *Lowden of Illinois*, pp. 743-744.

30. Landis long nursed a belief that Lowden might finally become president. In 1935 he heard reports that the New Deal was "on the slide." But as much as he wanted to believe such theories—and he wanted mightily to believe them—he was shrewd enough to know voters rarely cast their ballots against Santa Claus. "I still have my doubts that they can beat that campaign fund," he wrote of New Deal relief measures. "I think too many of us are for sale." He thought Lowden might be the party's candidate in 1936, but once again the idea fizzed. By 1940 Lowden was too infirm to even be considered for the presidency. Nonetheless, Landis kept a suspicious eye cocked toward the GOP's eventual standard bearer, New York corporate attorney Wendell Willkie. When that spring someone sent him material on the candidate, Landis performed some basic research: "I looked up Wendell Willkie in Who's Who and find him registered as a Democrat as late as 1937. We sure seem to be in a heluva fix for somebody to put up for the 1940 crucifixion."

31. Kenesaw Mountain Landis to John A. Heydler, July 9, 1941, KML Collection, Chicago Historical Society.

32. Kenesaw Mountain Landis to John A. Heydler, December 28, 1942, KML Collection, Chicago Historical Society.

33. *Chicago Times*, November 25, 1944, p. 25; KML to William G. Bramham, KML Collection, Chicago Historical Society.

34. Family Correspondence File, Biographical Information Folder, KML Collection, Chicago Historical Society; *New York Times*, April 25, 1922, p. 17; Interview with Lincoln Landis, September 10, 1996.

35. The Squire definitely had mixed feelings about the GOP's eventual candidate, Kansas governor Alf Landon. That year he talked about the election with NL president Ford Frick. "He always called me 'Mr. Fo'd, Mr. Fo'd,'" Ford once recalled. "He said, 'Mr. Fo'd, who's the lousiest President the United States ever had'? I said, 'A lot of people. Lots of different opinion. Harding was no bargain. And Andrew Johnson.' 'Andrew Johnson, hell!' he roared. 'The lousiest President of the United States ever had was Calvin Coolidge. Did you ever hear the man talk? Ever read anything he wrote? 'Course he was the lousiest President we ever had. And now they're calling this man Landon "The Kansas Coolidge." You know what I think of Landon? I think he's a beer-bellied, pinch-pennied Presbyterian sonafabitch. But I've going to vote for him anyway, 'cause he's the kind of man this country needs.'"

36. Frederick's widow Bessie and his son Frederick both made attempts to fill the

vacancy, but the nod went instead to Charles Halleck, future House Minority Leader. Kenesaw II (1910-1949) carried on his father's work, obtaining a law degree and writing his own syndicated column, "Corn on the Cob," that appeared in the *Chicago Times* and from 1941 until his death in the *Chicago Sun-Times*. Frederick Jr. later became a prosecuting attorney, state representative, state senator, and Indiana Supreme Court judge, capping his career in 1969 with an appointment to the United States Customs Court in New York City. In both 1938 and 1940 he made unsuccessful attempts to wrest his father's old house seat from Halleck.

37. Lawrence Kennedy, *Biographical Dictionary of the American Congress, 1774-1971*, p. 1259; *New York Times*, November 15, 1934; *New York Times*, November 16, 1934; *Logansport Pharos-Tribune*, November 9, 1967, p. 1; *Logansport Pharos-Tribune*, November 16, 1934, p. 1; *Logansport Pharos-Tribune*, November 17, 1934, p. 1; Interview with Lincoln Landis, February 12, 1996.

38. Kenesaw Mountain Landis to Frank Lowden, April 13, 1939, KML Collection, Chicago Historical Society.

39. *New York Times*, November 21, 1943, Section III, p. 1.

40. *Baseball Guide and Record Book 1945*, p. 122.

41. Somewhat before the MacPhail incident Landis had supposedly stopped Bing Crosby from buying into the Pirates. The reason: Crosby's ownership of a racing stable and his prospective purchase of a track.

42. Don Warfield, *The Roaring Redhead*, pp. 155-163; Lee MacPhail, *My 9 Innings*, p. 38.

43. Kenesaw Mountain Landis to R. W. Phillips, Jr., April 1, 1944, KML Collection, Chicago Historical Society.

44. Interview with Lincoln Landis, February 12, 1996.

45. Kenesaw Mountain Landis to Hon. Roy P. Wilcox, August 8, 1944, KML Collection, Chicago Historical Society.

46. Kenesaw Mountain Landis to Mrs. Theodore Peters, September 1, 1944, KML Collection, Chicago Historical Society.

47. *Chicago Sun*, November 26, 1944, p. 1; J. G. Taylor Spink, *Judge Landis and Twenty-Five Years of Baseball*, pp. 288-289.

48. *Chicago Times*, November 25, 1944, p. 4; *Chicago Daily News*, November 25, 1944, p. 1; J. G. Taylor Spink, *Judge Landis and Twenty-Five Years of Baseball*, p. 289; *Baseball Guide and Record Book 1945*, p. 123.

49. *Chicago Tribune*, November 23, 1944, p. 20.

50. *New York Times*, November 21, 1944, p. 18.

51. J. G. Taylor Spink, *Judge Landis and Twenty-Five Years of Baseball*, pp. 289-290.

52. *Chicago Tribune*, November 26, 1944, Section I, p. 13; *Chicago Times*, November 25, 1944, p. 3; *Chicago Daily News*, November 25, Section II, p. 1; *Chicago Sun*, November 26, 1944, p. 1.

53. *Chicago Daily News*, November 25, 1944, Section 2, p. 1.

# BIBLIOGRAPHY

## Books

Adler, Mortimer J., *The Annals of America*. Chicago: Encyclopaedia Brittanica, 1968.

Alexander, Charles, *John McGraw*. New York: Viking, 1988.

Alexander, Charles, *Rogers Hornsby*. New York: Henry Holt & Co., 1995.

Alexander, Charles, *Ty Cobb*. New York: Oxford University Press, 1984.

Allen, Lee, *The Cincinnati Reds*. New York: G. P. Putnam's & Sons, 1948.

Allen, Lee, *Cooperstown Corner*. Cleveland: Society for American Baseball Research, 1990.

Allen, Lee, *The National League Story*. New York: Hill & Wang, 1961.

Allsop, Kenneth, *The Bootleggers: The Story of Prohibition*. New Rochelle (NY): Arlington House, 1968.

Anderson, Dave; Chass, Murray; Creamer, Robert; and Rosenthal, Harold, *The Yankees: The Four Fabulous Eras of Baseball's Most Famous Team*. New York: Random House, 1979.

Angle, Paul M., *Philip K. Wrigley: A Memoir of a Modest Man*. Chicago: Rand McNally & Co., 1975.

Asbury, Herbert, *Gem of the Prairie*. New York: Alfred A. Knopf, 1940.

Avery, Martha Moore and Goldstein, David, *Bolshevism: Its Cure*. Boston School of Political Economy, 1919.

Avrich, Paul, *Sacco and Vanzetti: The Anarchist Background*. Princeton: Princeton University Press, 1991.

Babst, Earl D. and Vander Velde, Lewis G., *Michigan and the Cleveland Administration*. Ann Arbor: University of Michigan Press, 1948.

Bak, Richard, *Cobb Would Have Caught It*. Detroit: Wayne State University Press, 1991.

Bankes, James, *The Pittsburgh Crawfords: The Lives & Times of Black Baseball's Most Exciting Team!* Dubuque: William C. Brown, 1991.

Barber, Red, *The Broadcasters*. New York: Dial Press, 1970.

Barrow, Edward and Kahn, James M., *My 50 Years in Baseball*. New York: Coward-McCann, 1951.

Bartell, Dick (with Macht, Norman), *Rowdy Richard*. Berkeley: North Atlantic Books, 1987.

Benson, Michael, *Ballparks of North America*. Jefferson (NC): McFarland & Co., 1989.

Betzold, Michael and Casey, Ethan, *Queen of Diamonds: The Tiger Stadium Story*. West Bloomfield: A&M Publishing, 1992.

Boone, Robert S. and Grunska, Gerald, *Hack: The Meteoric Life of One of Baseball's First Superstars: Hack Wilson*, Highland Park (IL): Highland Press, 1978.

Boston, Talmage, *1939: Baseball's Pivotal Year*. Fort Worth: The Summit Group, 1994.

Boyd, James P., *The Life of General William T. Sherman*. Publishers Union, 1891.

Brady, Frank, *Citizen Welles: A Biography of Orson Welles*. New York: Charles Scriber's Sons, 1989.

Braeman, John, *Albert J. Beveridge: American Nationalist*. Chicago: University of Chicago Press, 1971.

Brown, Gene, *The Complete Book of Baseball*. New York: Arno Press, 1979.

Bringhurst, Bruce, *Antitrust and the Oil Monopoly: The Standard Oil Cases, 1890-1911*. Westport (CT): Greenwood Press, 1979.

Busch, Francis X., *Prisoners at the Bar: An Account of the William Haywood Case, the Sacco-Vanzetti Case, the Loeb-Leopold Case, the Bruno Hauptmann Case*. Indianapolis: Bobbs-Merrill, 1952.

Busch, Noel F., *T.R. — The Story of Theodore Roosevelt and His Influence on Our Time*. New York: Reynal & Co., 1963.

Calhoun, Charles W., *Gilded Age Cato: The Life of Walter Q. Gresham*. Lexington: University Press of Kentucky, 1882.

Callahan, North, *Carl Sandburg: His Life and Works*. University Park: Pennsylvania State University Press, 1987.

Callow, Simon, *Orson Welles: The Road to Xanadu*. New York: Viking, 1995.

Carlson, Peter, *Roughneck: The Life and Times of Big Bill Haywood*. New York: W. W. Norton & Co., 1983.

Chalmers, David M., *Hooded Americanism: The History of the Ku Klux Klan*. New York: Doubleday & Co., 1965.

Chandler, Happy (with Vance Trimble), *Heroes, Plain Folks, and Skunks: The Life and Times of Happy Chandler*. Chicago: Bonus Books, 1989.

Chaplin, Ralph, *"Wobbly": The Rough-and-Tumble Story of an American Radical*. Chicago: University of Chicago Press, 1948.

Chidsey, Donald Barr, *The Spanish American War*. New York: Crown, 1971.

Clark, Tom, *One Last Round for the Shuffler*. New York: Truck Press, 1979.

Cobb, Ty (with Al Stump), *My Life in Baseball: The True Record*. Lincoln (NE): University of Nebraska Press, 1993.

Collier, Peter and Horowitz, David, *The Rockefellers: An American Dynasty*. New York: Summit Books, 1976.

Conlin, Joseph Robert, *Big Bill Haywood and the Radical Union Movement*. Syracuse (NY): Syracuse University Press, 1969.

Costello, James and Santa Maria, Michael, *In the Shadows of the Diamond: Hard Times in the National Pastime*. Dubuque: Elysian Fields Press, 1992.

Creamer, Robert W., *Babe: The Legend Comes to Life*. New York: Pocket Books, 1976.

Creamer, Robert W., *Stengel: His Life and Times*. New York: Simon and Schuster, 1984.

Crowder, Richard, *Carl Sandburg*. New York: Twayne, 1964.

Curran, William, *Big Sticks: The Batting Revolution of the Twenties*. New York: William Morrow & Co., 1990.

D'Antonio, Dave, *Invincible Summer: Traveling America in Search of Yesterday's Baseball Greats*. South Bend (IN): Diamond Communications, 1997.

De Valeria, Dennis, and De Valeria, Jeanne Burke, *Honus Wagner: A Biography*. New York: Henry Holt, 1995.

Dedmon, Emmet, *Fabulous Chicago: A Great City's History and People*. New York: Atheneum, 1981.

Dewey, Donald and Acocella, Nicholas, *Encyclopedia of Major League Baseball Teams*. New York: HarperCollins, 1993.

Dixon, Phil and Hannigan, Patrick J., *The Negro Baseball Leagues*. Mattituck (NY): Amereon House, 1992.

Dubofsky, Melvyn, *"Big Bill" Haywood*. New York: St. Martin's Press, 1987.

Durocher, Leo (with Ed Linn), *Nice Guys Finish Last*. New York: Simon & Schuster, 1975.

Durso, Joseph, *Casey: The Life and Legend of Charles Dillon Stengel*. Englewood Cliffs: Prentice-Hall, 1967.

Durso, Joseph, *The Days of Mr. McGraw*. Englewood Cliffs: Prentice-Hall, 1969.

Durso, Joseph, *DiMaggio: The Last American Knight*. New York: Little, Brown & Co., 1995.

Edelman, Rob, *Great Baseball Movies: From Right Off The Bat to A League of Their Own*. New York: Citadel, 1994.

Einstein, Charles (ed.), *The Second Fireside Book of Baseball*. New York: Simon & Schuster, 1958.

Einstein, Charles (ed.), *The Third Fireside Book of Baseball*. New York: Simon & Schuster, 1968.

Ellis, Edward Robb, *Echoes of Distant Thunder: Life in the United States 1914-1918*. New York: Coward, McCann & Geoghegan, 1975.

Falkner, David, *Great Time Coming: The Life of Jackie Robinson from Baseball to Birmingham*. New York: Simon & Schuster, 1995.

Falls, Joe, *The Detroit Tigers: An Illustrated History*. New York: Prentice Hall Press, 1989.

Farr, Finis, *Chicago: A Personal History of America's Most American City*. New Rochelle: Arlington House, 1973.

Feller, Bob (with Bill Gilbert), *Now Pitching: Bob Feller*. New York: Birch Lane Press, 1990.

Feller, Bob, *Strikeout Story*. New York: A. S. Barnes and Co., 1947.

Fleming, G. H., *The Dizziest Season*. New York: William Morrow & Co., 1984.

Flynn, Elizabeth Gurley, *Debs, Haywood, Ruthenberg*. New York: Workers Library Publishers, 1939.

Frick, Ford C., *Games, Asterisks, and People: Memoirs of a Lucky Fan*. New York: Crown Publishers, 1973.

Franklin, John Hope, *From Slavery to Freedom: A History of American Negros* (3rd edition). New York: Vintage, 1969.

Fried, Albert, *Socialism in America: From the Shakers to the Third International*. Garden City (NY): Doubleday, 1970.

Frommer, Harvey, *Rickey and Robinson: The Men Who Broke Baseball's Color Barrier*. New York: Macmillan, 1982.

Frommer, Harvey, *Shoeless Joe and Ragtime Baseball*. Dallas: Taylor, 1992.

Gable, John Allan, *The Bull Moose Years: Theodore Roosevelt and the Progressive Party*. Port Washington (NY): Kennikat Press, 1978.

George, Harrison, *The I.W.W. Trial*. New York: Arno Press, 1969.

Gerlach, Larry R., *The Men In Blue: Conversations with Umpires*. New York: Viking, 1980.

Gilbert, Bill, *They Also Served: Baseball and the Home Front, 1941-1945*. New York: Crown, 1992.

Ginger, Ray, *Altgeld's America 1890-1905: The Lincoln Ideal Versus Changing Realities*. New York: Quadrangle, 1965.

Ginger, Ray, *The Bending Cross: A Biography of Eugene Victor Debs*. New York: Russell & Russell, 1969.

Ginsburg, Daniel E., *The Fix Is In: A History of Baseball Gambling and Game Fixing Scandals*. Jefferson(NC): MacFarland & Co., 1995.

Godin, Roger A., *The 1922 St. Louis Browns: Best of the American League's Worst*. Jefferson (NC): McFarland & Co., 1991.

Goldberg, Harvey (ed.), *American Radicals: Some Problems and Personalities*. Monthly Review Press, 1957.

Goldstein, Richard, *Spartan Seasons: How Baseball Survived the Second World War*. New York: Macmillan, 1980.

Goldstein, Richard, *Superstars and Screwballs: 100 Years of Brooklyn Baseball*. New York: Dutton, 1991.

Golenbock, *Bums: An Oral History of the Brooklyn Dodgers*. New York: G. P. Putnam's Sons, 1984.

Graham, Frank, *McGraw of the Giants*. New York: G. P. Putnam's Sons, 1944.

Graham, Frank, *The New York Giants*. New York: G. P. Putnam's Sons, 1952.

Greenberg, Hank, *The Story of My Life*, New York Times Books, 1989.

Gregorich, Margaret, *Women at Play: The Story of Women in Baseball*. San Diego: Harcourt Brace, 1993.

Gregory, Robert, *Diz*. New York: Viking, 1992.

Gresham, Matilda, *Life of Walter Quintin Gresham*. Chicago: Rand McNally & Co., 1919.

Grimm, Charlie (with Prell, Ed), *Grimm's Baseball Tales*. South Bend: Diamond Communications, 1983.

Gropman, Donald, *Say It Ain't So, Joe!: The True Story of Shoeless Joe Jackson*. New York: Citadel, 1992.

Hawley, Lowell Stillwell, *Counsel for the Damned: A Biography of George Francis Vanderveer*. Philadelphia: Lippincott, 1953.

Haywood, William Dudley, *Bill Haywood's Book: The Autobiography of Big Bill Haywood*. New York: International Publishers, 1929.

Hecht, Ben, *A Child of the Century*. New York: Ballantine Books, 1970.

Henrich, Tommy (with Bill Gilbert), *Five O'Clock Lightning: Ruth, Gehrig, DiMaggio, Mantle and the Glory Days of the NY Yankees*. New York: Birch Lane Press, 1992.

Hernon, Peter and Ganey, Terry, *Under The Influence: The Unauthorized Story of the Anheuser-Busch Dynasty*. New York: Simon & Schuster, 1991.

Hicks, Granvile, *John Reed: The Making of a Revolutionary*. New York: Macmillan, 1936.

Higgins, Helen Boyd, *Our Burt Lake Story*. Burt Lake (MI): Helen Boyd Higgins Memorial Library, Burt Lake Christian Church, 1974.

Holbrook, Stewart H., *Dreamers of the American Dream*. Garden City (NY): Doubleday, 1957.

Holtzman, Jerome, *The Commissioners*. New York: Total Sports, 1998.

Holway, John, *Black Diamonds: Life in the Negro Leagues from the Men Who Lived It*. Westport (Ct.): Meckler, 1989.

Holway, John, *Josh and Satch*. Westport (CT): Meckler, 1991.

Honig, Don, *Baseball Between the Lines: Baseball in the '40s and '50s*. New York: Coward, McGann & Geoghegan, Inc., 1976.

Honig, Don, *Baseball When The Grass Was Real*. New York: Coward, McGann & Geoghegan, Inc., 1975.

Honig, Donald, *The Man in the Dugout*. Chicago: Follett, 1977.

Howard, Major General Oliver O. Howard, *Battles and Leaders of the Civil War*. New York: The Century Co., 1884-1888.

Hornsby, Rogers, *My War With Baseball*. New York: Coward-McCann, 1962.

Hutchinson, William T., *Lowden of Illinois: The Life Story of Frank O. Lowden*. Chicago University of Chicago Press, 1957.

Ickes, Harold, *The Autobriography of a Curmudgeon*. New York: Reynal & Hitchcock, 1943.

Jackson, William J. et al, *History of the American Nation*. CD Sourcebook of American History, Compact University, 1994.

Johnson, Lloyd and Wolf, Miles, *The Encyclopedia of Minor League Baseball*. Durham: Baseball America, Inc., 1993.

Johnson, Rossiter (editor-in-chief), *The Twentieth Century Biographical Dictionary of Notable Americans*. Boston: The Biographical Society, 1904.

Kaese, Harold, *The Boston Braves*. New York: G. P. Putnam's Sons, 1948.

Kahn, James M., *The Umpire Story*. New York: G. P. Putnam's Sons, 1953.

Karst, Gene and Jones, Martin, J., Jr., *Who's Who in Professional Baseball*. New Rochelle (NY): Arlington House, 1973.

Kavanagh, Jack, *Walter Johnson: A Life*. South Bend: Diamond Communications, 1995.

Kennedy, Lawrence, *Biographical Dictionary of the American Congress 1774-1971*. Washington: U.S. Government Printing Office, 1971.

Kerr, Jon, *Calvin: Baseball's Last Dinosaur*. Madison: William C. Brown Publishers, 1990.

Kobler, John, *Ardent Spirits: The Rise and Fall of Prohibition*. New York: G. P. Putnam's Sons, 1973.

Kobler, John, *Capone*. New York: G. P. Putnam's Sons, 1971.

Kolko, Gabriel, *The Triumph of Conservatism: A Reinterpretism of American History, 1900-1916*. New York: The Free Press, 1963.

Kuklick, Bruce, *To Every Thing a Season: Shibe Park and Urban Philadelphia 1909-1976*. Princeton: Princeton University Press, 1991.

LaFever, Walter, *The New Empire: An Interpretation of American Expansion 1860-1898*. Ithaca: Cornell University Press, 1963.

Lanctot, Neil, *Fair Dealing and Clean Playing: The Hilldale Club and the Development of Black Professional Baseball, 1910-1932*. Jefferson (NC): McFarland & Co., 1994.

Landis, D. B., *The Landis Family of Lancaster County. Pa*. Lancaster: Published and Printed by the Author, 1888.

Learing, Barbara, *Orson Welles: A Biography*. New York: Viking, 1984.

Leuchtenburg, William E., *The Perils of Prosperity 1914-32*. University of Chicago Press, 1958.

Lieb, Fred, *Baseball As I Have Known It*. New York: Coward, McCann & Geoghegan, 1977.

Lieb, Fred, *The Baseball Story*. New York: G. P. Putnam's Sons, 1950.

Lieb, Frederick G., *Connie Mack: Grand Old Man of Baseball*. New York: G. P. Putnam's Sons, 1945.

Lieb, Frederick G., *The Detroit Tigers*. New York: G. P. Putnam's Sons, 1946.

Lieb, Frederick G., *The Pittsburgh Pirates*. New York: G. P. Putnam's Sons, 1948.

Lindberg, Richard C., *Stealing First in a Two-Team Town: The White Sox from Comiskey to Reinsdorf*. Champaign: Sagamore Publishing, 1994.

Lindberg, Richard, *Who's on 3rd?: The Chicago White Sox Story*. South Bend: Icarus Press, 1983.

Linn, Ed, *The Great Rivalry: The Yankees and the Red Sox 1901-1990*. New York: Ticknor & Fields, 1991.

Lewis, Franklin, *The Cleveland Indians*. New York: G. P. Putnam's Sons, 1949.

Loessing, Benson J., *Our Country*, 1905.

Lowe, David Garrard, *Chicago Interiors*. New York: Wing Books, 1995.

Lowenfish, Lee and Lupien, Tony, *The Imperfect Diamond: The Story of Baseball's Reserve System and the Men Who Fought To Change It*. New York: Stein and Day, 1980.

Lyle, Judge John H., *The Dry and Lawless Years: The Crusade Against Public Enemies and Corrupt Officials in Chicago*. Englewood Cliffs (NJ): Prentice-Hall, 1961.

MacPhail, Lee, *My 9 Innings: An Autobiography of 50 Years in Baseball*. Meckler Books, Westport (CT): Meckler Books, 1989.

Mann, Arthur, *Branch Rickey: American In Action*. Boston: Houghton Mifflin Co., 1957.

McGraw, John, *My Thirty Years in Baseball*. Lincoln: University of Nebraska Press, 1995.

McKenna, Marian C., *Borah*. Ann Arbor: University of Michigan Press, 1961.

McPhaul, John J., *Deadlines & Monkeyshines*. Englewood Cliffs, (NJ): Prentice-Hall, 1962.

Mead, Frank S., *Handbook of Denominations in the United States*. New York: Abingdon-Cokesbury Press, 1951.

Mead, William B., *Two Spectacular Seasons*. New York: Macmillan, 1990.

Merrill, Horace Samuel, *Bourbon Leader: Grover Cleveland and the Democratic Party*. Boston: Little Brown and Company, 1957.

Miller, Dr. George D., *A Biographical Sketch of the Deceased Physicians of Cass County*. Logansport: Privately Printed, 1920.

Moore, Joseph Thomas, *Pride Against Prejudice: The Biography of Larry Doby*. New York: Praeger, 1988.

Mowry, George E., *The Era of Theodore Roosevelt and the Birth of Modern America 1900-1912*. New York: Harper & Brothers, 1958.

Murdock, Eugene, *Ban Johnson: Czar of Baseball*. Westport (CT): Greenwood Press, 1982.

Murdock, Eugene, *Baseball Between the Wars: Memories of the Game By The Men Who Played It*. 1920-1940, Westport (CT): Meckler, 1992.

Murdock, Eugene, *Baseball Players and Their Times: Oral Histories of the Game, 1920-1940*. Westport (CT): Meckler, 1991.

Murray, George, *The Madhouse on Madison Street*. Chicago: Follett Publishing Co., 1965.

Murray, Robert K., *Red Scare: A Study in National Hysteria, 1919-20*. New York: McGraw-Hill Paperbacks, 1955.

Murray, Tom (ed.), *Sport Magazine's All-Time All Stars*. New York: Signet, 1977.

Nash, Jay Robert, *The Encyclopedia of Organized Crime*. Dallas: ZCI Publishing, Inc., 1994.

Nevins, Alan, *Grover Cleveland: A Study in Courage*. New York: Dodd, Mead & Co., 1966.

Nixon, Penelope, *Carl Sandburg: A Biography*. New York: Charles Scribner's Sons, 1991.

O'Connor, Anthony J., *Baseball for the Love of It: Hall of Famers Tell It Like It Was*. New York: Macmillan, 1982.

O'Connor, Richard and Walker, Dale L., *The Lost Revolutionary: A Biography of John Reed*. New York: Harcourt, Brace & World, 1967.

O'Neal, Bill, *The Pacific Coast League*. Austin: Eakin Press, 1990.

O'Neal, Bill, *The Southern League*. Austin: Eakin Press, 1994.

O'Neal, Bill, *The Texas League*. Austin: Eakin Press, 1987.

Overmyer, James, *Effa Manley and the Newark Eagles*. Metuchen (NJ): Scarecrow Press, 1993.

Owen, Vi, *The Adventures of a Quiet Soul; A Scrapbook of Memories*, San Jose: Rosicrucian Press, 1996.

Pepper, George Wharton, *Philadelphia Lawyer: An Autobiography*. Philadelphia: J. P. Lippincott, 1944.

Peterson, Robert, *Only The Ball Was White*. New York: McGraw-Hill, 1970.

Peterson, Virgil W., *Barbarians in Our Midst: A History of Chicago Crime and Politics*. Boston: Little, Brown & Co., 1952.

Pietrusza, *Baseball's Canadian-American League: A History of Its Inception, Franchises, Participants, Locales, Statistics, Demise and Legacy, 1936-1951*. Jefferson (NC): McFarland & Co., 1990.

Pietrusza, David, *Lights On! The Wild Century-Long Saga of Night Baseball*. Lanham (MD): Scarecrow Press, 1997.

Pietrusza, David, *Major Leagues: The Formation, Sometimes Absorption and Mostly Inevitable Demise of 18 Professional Baseball Organizations, 1871 to Present*. Jefferson (NC): McFarland & Co., 1991.

Pietrusza, David, *Minor Miracles: The Legend & Lure of Minor League Baseball*. South Bend: Diamond Communications, 1995.

Pietrusza, David, *The Roaring Twenties*. San Diego: Lucent, 1997.

Polner, Murray, *Branch Rickey: A Biography*. New York: Signet Books, 1982.

Powell, Dr. Jehu Z., *History of Cass County Indiana*. Chicago: Lewis Publishing Co., 1913.

Preston, William, Jr., *Aliens and Dissenters: Federal Suppression of Radicals. 1903-1933*. New York: Harper Torchbooks, 1963.

Pringle, Henry W., *Big Frogs*. New York: Macy-Masius, the Vanguard Press, 1928.

Pringle, Henry W., *Theodore Roosevelt*. New York: Smithmark, 1995.

Reed, John, *Adventures of a Young Man*. San Francisco: City Lights, 1975.

Reichler, Joe, *The World Series*. New York: Simon & Schuster, 1979.

Reisler, Jim, *Black Writers / Black Baseball: An Anthology of Articles from Black Sportswriters Who Covered the Negro Leagues*. Jefferson (NC): McFarland, 1994.

Ribowsky, Mark, *A Complete History of the Negro Leagues 1884 to 1955*. New York: Birch Lane, 1995.

Ribowsky, Mark, *Don't Look Back: Satchel Paige in the Shadows of Baseball*. New York: Simon & Schuster, 1994.

Rickey, Branch (with Robert Riger), *The American Diamond: A Documentary of the Game of Baseball*. New York: Simon & Schuster, 1965.

Riley, James A., *The Biographical Encyclopedia of the Negro Baseball Leagues*. 1994.

Ritchie, Andrew, *Major Taylor: The Extraordinary Career of a Champion Bicycle Racer*. San Francisco: Bicycle Books, 1988.

Ritter, Lawrence S., *Lost Ballparks: A Celebration of Baseball's Legendary Fields*. New York: Viking, 1992.

Rogosin, Donn, *Invisible Men: Life in Baseball's Negro Leagues*. New York: Atheneum, 1985.

Rudwick, Elliot, *Race Riot at East St. Louis*. Urbana: University of Illinois Press, 1982.

Russell, Francis, *The Shadow of Blooming Grove: Warren G. Harding in His Times*. New York: McGraw-Hill, 1968.

Rust, Art, Jr., *"Get That Nigger Off The Field!"* New York: Delacorte, 1976.

Ruth, Babe (as told to Bob Considine), *The Babe Ruth Story*. Winston-Salem: Starstream Products, 1980.

Salvatore, Nick, *Eugene V. Debs: Citizen and Socialist*. Urbana: University Press of Illinois, 1982.

Seymour, Harold, *Baseball: The Golden Age*. New York: Oxford, 1971.

Sinclair, Andrew, *The Available Man*. New York: The Macmillan Co., 1965.

Sobol, Ken, *Babe Ruth & The American Dream*. New York: Ballantine Books, 1974.

Smith, Curt, *America's Dizzy Dean*. St. Louis: The Bethany Press, 1978.

Smith, Curt, *Voices of The Game: The First Full-Scale Overview of Baseball Broadcasting, 1921 to the Present*. South Bend: Diamond Communications, 1987.

Smith, Robert, *Baseball*. New York: Simon and Schuster, 1947.

Smith, Robert, *Baseball in the Afternoon: Tales from a Bygone Era*. New York: Simon & Schuster, 1993.

Smith, Robert Norton, *The Colonel: The Life and Legend of Robert R. McCormick*. Boston: Houghton Mifflin, 1997.

Spink, J.G. Taylor, *Judge Landis and Twenty-Five Years of Baseball*. New York: Thomas Y. Crowell, 1947.

Staten, Vince, *Ol' Diz*. New York: Harper, Collins, 1992.

Stedman, Seymour, *Brief for Plaintiffs in Error. In the United States Court of Appeals for the Seventh Circuit, October term, A.D. 1918. Victor L. Berger,*

*Adolph Germer, William F. Kruse, Irwin St. John Tucker and J. Louis Engdahl plaintiffs in error, vs. the United States of America, defendant in error. Error to the District Court of the United States for the Northern District of Illinois, Eastern Division. Honorable K. M. Landis, Judge.*

Stein, Irving M., *The Ginger Kid: The Buck Weaver Story*. Elysian Fields Press, 1992.

Stump, Al, *Cobb: A Biography*. Chapel Hill (NC): Algonquin Books of Chapel Hill, 1994.

Sullivan, Mark, *Our Times, Volume III: Pre-War America*. New York: Charles Scribner's Sons, 1971.

Swanberg, W. A., *Citizen Hearst*. New York: Charles Scribner's Sons, 1961.

Taber, Graham, *History of Logansport and Cass County*. Logansport (IN): Pharos-Tribune.

Tarr, Arthur Joel, *A Study in Boss Politics: William Lorimer of Chicago*. Urbana: University Press of Illinois, 1971.

Thorn, John and Holway, John, *The Pitcher*. New York: Prentice Hall Press, 1987.

Thorn, John; Gershman, Michael; and Palmer, Pete, (editors), *Total Baseball* (4th edition). New York: Viking, 1995.

Thorn, John; Gershman, Michael; Palmer, Pete; and Pietrusza, David (editors), *Total Baseball* (5th edition). New York: Viking, 1997.

Tierney, Kevin, *Darrow: A Biography*. New York: Thomas Y. Crowell, 1979.

Tingley, Donald F., *The Structure of a State: The History of Illinois 1899 to 1928*. Urbana: University of Illinois, 1980.

Tuttle, Willam M., Jr., *Race Riot: Chicago in the Red Summer of 1919*. New York: Atheneum, 1982.

Tygiel, Jules, *Baseball's Great Experiment*. New York: Oxford University Press, 1983.

Van Doren, Charles (ed.), *Webster's American Biographies*. Springfield (MA): Charles Merriam Co., 1974.

Veeck, Bill (with Ed Linn) *The Hustler's Handbook*. New York: G. P. Putnam's Sons, 1965.

Veeck, Bill (with Ed Linn), *Veeck — As In Wreck*. New York: G. P. Putnam's Sons, 1962.

Voigt, David Quintin, *American Baseball: from the Commissioners to Continental Expansion*. University Park (PA): Penn State University Press, 1983.

Wagenheim, Kal, *Babe Ruth: His Life and Legend*. New York: Henry Holt, 1992.

Wagenknecht, Edward, *American Profile 1900-1909*. University of Massachusetts Press, 1982.

Warfield, Don, *The Roaring Redhead: Larry MacPhail — Baseball's Great Innovator*. South Bend, Diamond Communications, Inc., 1987.

Watson, James E., *As I Knew Them: Memoirs of James E. Watson*. Indianapolis: Bobbs-Merrill, 1936.

Watts, Richard M., *The Kings Depart: The Tragedy of Germany, Versailles and the German Revolution*, London: Weidenfeld & Nicholson, 1968.

Weinstein, James, *The Decline of Socialism in America: 1912-1925*. New York: Monthly Review Press, 1967.

Westcott, Rich and Bilovsky, Frank, *The New Phillies Encyclopedia*. Philadelphia: Temple University Press, 1993.

Weyl, Nathaniel and Marina, William, *American Statesmen on Slavery and the Negro*. New Rochelle (NY): Arlington House, 1971.

White, William Allen, *The Autobiography of William Allen White*. New York: Macmillan, 1946.

White, William Allen, *A Puritan in Babylon: The Story of Calvin Coolidge*. New York: Macmillan & Co., 1939.

Wilson, Woodrow, *History of the American People, CD Sourcebook of American History*, Compact University, 1994.

Young, A. S., *Great Negro Baseball Stories*. New York: A. S. Barnes & Co., 1953.

# Journals

*Illinois Law Review*

# Magazines

| | |
|---|---|
| *Appleton's Magazine* | *The Literary Digest* |
| *Baseball Digest* | *The Minneapolis Review of Baseball* |
| *Baseball History* | *The National Pastime* |
| *Baseball Research Journal* | *The New Yorker* |
| *Baseball Magazine* | *The North American Review* |
| *D.A.C. News* | *Outlook* |
| *Everyone's Magazine* | *Review of Reviews* |
| *Harper's* | *Saturday Evening Post* |

# Newspapers

Albany Argus
Albany Journal
Albany Times-Union
An Appeal To Reason
Baltimore News
Bay City Times
Berkshire Evening Eagle
Boehne Texas Star
Chicago Daily Journal
Chicago Daily News
Chicago Defender
Chicago Evening Post
Chicago Examiner
Chicago Record-Herald
Chicago Tribune
Cincinnati Post
Cincinnati Times-Star
Cincinnati Tribune
Cleveland Plain Dealer
Collyer's Eye
Davenport Democrat
Day Book (Chicago)
Dayton Daily News
Detroit News
Detroit Times
Fort Wayne Labor
    Times-Herald
Guthrie Capital
Havana Daily Post
Houston Post
Indianapolis Star
Knickerbocker-Press & Albany
    Morning Express
La Crosse (WI) Morgen
    Stern (Morning Star)
Logansport Pharos-Journal
[Logansport] Sunday Critic
New York Age

New York American
New York Daily News
New York Evening Call
New York Herald
New York Herald-Tribune
New York Press
New York Sun
New York Telegraph and
    Evening Mail
New York Times
New York Tribune
New York World
New York World-Telegraph
Oldtyme Baseball News
Peoria Herald-Transcript
Petoskey (MI) Evening News
Pittsburgh Courier
Pittsburgh Post
Quincy (IL) Daily Whig
Sacramento Bee
St. Louis Globe-Democrat
St. Petersburg Times
Schenectady Daily Union
Schenectady Evening Star
Schenectady Gazette
Schenectady Union-Star
Sporting Life
The Sporting News
Wall Street Journal
Washington Herald
Washington Post
Washington Times
Zanesville (OH) News

# INDEX

## A

Adams, Charles F. 322
Adams, Samuel Hopkins 466
Addington, Keene 156
Ade, George 97, 396
Adonis, Joe 323
Aeolian Company 225
Agnosticism 510
"Alabam" 320
Albany (NY) 72, 233, 315, 420
*Albany Argus* 65
Albany Senators (IL) 375-377
Albee, E. F. 230, 235
Albuquerque (NM) 295
Aldee, Alvey 25
Aldrich, Charles H. 221
Aldrich-Vreeland Act 34
Alexander, Grover Cleveland 159, 174, 386
Alexander, Nathan 441, 443
Alexandria (LA) 473
Alfalfa 403
*Aliens and Dissenters: Federal Suppression of Radicals, 1903-1933* 128
Allen, Lee 179, 245, 278
*Alliancia* 25
Allis-Chalmers Company 41
Alongi, Gianni 95
Alphonse and Gaston" 48
Alsace 3
Alschuler, Judge Samuel 146, 484
Altgeld, Peter 80
Ambassador East Hotel (Chicago) 395, 448
American Aero Squadron 25, 111
American Airlines 436
American Association (major league) 405

American Association (minor league) 254, 347, 373, 374, 422
American Association of Advertising Agencies 227
American Bar Association 207, 467
*American Baseball: from the Commissioners to Continental Expansion* 311
American Civil Liberties Union 136
American Communist Party 136
American Federation of Labor 91, 116, 121, 139
American Football League 440
American Knitting Mills 477
American League xiii 73, 154, 156, 160-161, 162, 166, 167, 169, 173, 231, 287, 291, 292, 294, 302, 303, 305-306, 307, 309-311, 324, 326-327, 334, 341, 351, 364, 369, 405, 415, 419, 427, 434, 439, 496, 501
American Legion 136, 149, 200, 212, 221, 224, 226-227, 374, 391
*American Mercury* 75
American Railway Union 26, 80
American Seating Company 68
*American Socialist* 140
American Tobacco Company 47
American Tobacco Company 48
American Tribunal 221
Amoco Standard Oil of California 47
*An Appeal To Reason* 91, 92
Anderson (gambler) 271
Anderson, Judge Albert B. 89, 91, 396-397
Andreytchine, George 134-135
*Angel of the Lonesome Hill: A Story of a President* 97
Anheuser-Busch Brewery 115

535

# E

# H

Hammond (IN) 125
Hammond, Homer 374
Handley, Lee "Jeep" 355
Haney, Fred 326-327
Hanly, James Franklin 31
Hanna, Sen. Marcus A. 34, 37
Hanson, Mayor Ole 147, 219
"Happy Hooligan" 48
Harding, Frank 256
Harding, Warrren G. 149, 152, 169,
    197, 209, 214, 215, 219, 220, 431,
    518
Hardwick, Sen. Thomas W. 147
Harlem 416, 419, 428
Haroun-Al-Raschid 188
Harridge, Will 324, 369, 416, 439
Harris, Bucky 262, 275, 276, 306,
    440-441, 443
Harris, Spencer 384-385
Harris, Vic 420
Harrisburg (PA) 386
Harrison (sportswriter) 279
Harrison, Benjamin 15, 80
Hartford (CT) 304
Hartnett, Gabby 323
Harvard Law School 65
Harvard University 126, 412
Hately, John 46
Havana (Cuba) 184-185, 281
Hawaii 18, 22, 25
Hawley, Lowell Stillwell 128, 473
Haymarket Riot 475
Hays, Will 165, 174, 404
Haywood, William Dudley "Big Bill"
    vii, 116-117, 121, 124, 128, 129-
    131, 132, 133, 134, 135, 136-137,
    213, 473, 475
Healey, Stephen K. 468
Hearst, William Randolph 42, 48, 65,
    83, 106, 114, 273, 446, 491
Heath, Mrs. Frank 130
Hecht, Ben 148
Hedges, Robert 260

Heffner, Don 326-327
Heilman, Harry 298, 413, 512
Heintzman, J. W. 208
Heitler, Coleman 100
Hempstead, Harry 260
Hendee, A. L. 144
Henderson (gambler) 180
Hendrix, Claude 159, 479
Henrich, Tommy 359-361, 371, 505
Hepburn Act 34
Herman, Billy 344
Herrmann, Garry160, 162, 167, 168,
    169, 178, 179, 183-184, 253, 258,
    280
Hershey (PA) 440
Hertz, John 448
Herzog, Buck 160, 254, 479
Hessians 223
Heydler, John 162, 164, 175, 176,
    246-247, 250, 255, 256, 257, 258,
    261, 265, 272, 277, 279, 280, 281,
    287, 316, 324, 370, 388, 445-446,
    491
Hickory Flats (OH) 4
Hildebrand, George 330, 333
Hill, Joe 116
Hillquit, Morris 139, 477
Himmler, Heinrich 436
Hirohito 436
"His Last Night Out" 493
History of the American Nation 100
Hitler, Adolf 34, 425, 436, 513
Hitt, Rep. Robert L. 38
Hoan, Mayor Daniel W. 141
Hoard (editor) 219
Hoch, Johann 42, 43
Hollands, F. S. 71
Hollywood, Edwin L. 95
Holmes, Justice Oliver Wendell 147,
    150, 475
Holway, John 428
Holyoke (MA) 313
Home Trust Company 199

Lucas, Nancy Landis Smith (grand-
daughter) 26, 171, 390, 392, 400,
429, 430, 444
Ludolph, "Wee Willie" 279, 495
Lundquist, Carl 387
Lunte, Harry 285
Luque, Dolph 513
*Lusitania* 93, 108

# M

MacArthur, Charles 148
MacBeth, W. J. 234
Mack, Connie 169, 171, 308, 324, 334,
368, 427
MacPhail, Larry 323, 365, 366, 368,
369, 385, 387, 419, 427, 435-436,
448, 514, 519
Madeira Beach (FL) 365
Madison Square Garden 44
Magee, Lee 157
Magna Carta 41
Maharg, Billy 160, 181
Major League Advisory Board 291
Malone, Pat 317, 318
Manley, Abe 428
Mann Act 511
Mann, Arthur 322
Mann, Les 193, 244-245, 246, 247,
250, 252, 264, 490
Mann, Louis 123
Manning, Tom 339
Manush, Heinie 191, 338
Maranville, "Rabbit" 174
Marblehead (MA) 260
Marine Corps 423
Marine Transport Union 128
Marion (IN) 11
*Marion Chronicle* 5, 10
Marlatt, Norval 125, 133
Marquard, "Rube" 153
Marquette University 91, 312, 465
Marsans, Armando 153, 154
Marshall, Charles R. 98

Martin, "Pepper" 340, 502
Martin, R. P. 223
Martinique Hotel (NYC) 231, 329
Masefield, John 403
Mathewson, Christy 247
Matthews, William Clarence "Billy" 412
Mattoon and Charleston Interurban
Railway 82, 92
Mayer, Edward 200
Mayer, Levy 43
Mayer, Meyer, Austrian & Platt 93
Mayo Clinic 305
Mays, Carl 162, 232, 233, 241, 242,
328-330
Mays, George S. 418
McAdoo, William Gibbs 162
McAleer, Jimmy 164
McCaffrey, John 60
McCarthy, Joe 334, 337, 415, 416
McCarthy, William H. 191, 314, 374
McCauley, Ed 358
McCormick Reaper Strike 13
McCormick, Col. Robert 460
McCormick, Edith Rockefeller 459-460
McCormick, Harold Fowler 459-460
McCormick, Sen. Medill 215
McCormick, Myron 361
McCoy, Benny 367, 368
McCutcheon, John T. 85, 396
McDonald, Judge Charles A. 160,
162-164, 165, 169, 172, 173, 186,
254, 480
McGeehan, W. O. 279, 306
McGovern, J. 205
McGovern, W. 205
McGraw, John 180, 181, 184-185, 230,
242-247, 249-252, 262, 263, 269,
270, 271, 273, 277, 279, 280, 282,
283, 288, 315, 322, 332, 335, 491,
496
McKechnie, Bill 263, 271-272
McKeever, Steve 316, 388
McKenna, Justice Joseph 150

# U

Weinert, Phil 180
Weisenfel, August 140-141, 151
Weiss, George 394
Welles, Orson 396
Wells, Orson C. "Ort" 396, 509
Wells, Willie 414, 513
Welty, Rep. Benjamin F. 196, 199,
    203-204, 208, 209, 212, 484
West End Sanitarium 243-244, 483
West Point 194, 436, 453
West Texas-New Mexico League 367
West, Fred O. 286, 288, 289, 291
Western Association 176, 367
Western Canada League 191
Western Federation of Miners (WFM)
    117
Western League 349, 362, 373, 374
WFI 224
Wheeler, Sen. Burton K. 216
Wheeler, Wayne 115
Whigs 4, 14
Whitaker, Supreme Court Judge
    Edward G. 182
White, Bud 102
White, Chief Justice Edward 150
White, William Allen 65, 86
"Why We Should Fight" 145
Wichita Falls (Texas League) 349
Wickersham, George Woodward 89,
    100, 472
Wilhelm II 109, 436, 476
Wilkerson, Judge James H. 218
Will, George F. 193
Williams (Cleveland sportswriter) 391
Williams, Claude "Lefty" 160, 164,
    176, 186, 193, 282
Williams, Harry A. 304
Williams, Joe 267, 355, 359
Williams, Ken 240
Willkie, Wendell 518
Wilson, Art 254
Wilson, Bobby 510
Wilson, Hack 386, 510
Wilson, Sec. of Labor William B. 147

Wilson, Tom 428
Wilson, Woodrow 48, 66, 79, 99, 108,
    147, 150, 162, 219, 226, 407, 409,
    410, 477, 485
Wiltse, Hooks 157
Wingard, Ernest 348
WLW 342
Women Accepted for Volunteer
    Emergency Services (WAVES)
    436
Wood, Gen. Leonard 162, 219, 220,
    484
Wood, Robert 499
Wood, "Smoky Joe" 284-288, 290-291,
    309-310, 499
Woodley (NJ) 27
Woodruff, Harvey 162, 479
Woods, William A. 80
WOR 442, 443
World Series (1903) 271, 328
World Series (1906) 153
World Series (1912) 330
World Series (1916) 229
World Series (1917) 153
World Series (1918) 174
World Series (1918) 158, 241, 431
World Series (1919) vii, xiv, 158, 160,
    161, 181, 191, 192-193, 254, 257,
    286, 300, 313, 328, 479, 498
World Series (1920) 328
World Series (1921) 191, 230-233,
    238, 242, 252, 272, 328-330, 338
World Series (1922) 184, 307, 330-332
World Series (1923) 184, 332-333, 395
World Series (1924) 184, 268,
    269-276, 277, 283, 333, 335
World Series (1925) 306, 333-334
World Series (1928) 315
World Series (1929 334-335
World Series (1931) 335-336, 502
World Series (1932) 318-319, 321,
    336-338, 400
World Series (1933) 338
World Series (1934) 326, 338-342, 517

# ABOUT THE AUTHOR

David Pietrusza has written extensively on the subject of baseball. He is coeditor of *Total Baseball*, the official encyclopedia of Major League Baseball, and, from 1993 through 1997 served as president of the Society for American Baseball Research (SABR).

His four other books on baseball are *Lights On: The Wild Century-Long Saga of Night Baseball*; *Minor Miracles: The Legend & Lure of Minor League Baseball* (published by Diamond Communications); *Major Leagues;* and *Baseball's Canadian-American League*. He coedited *Total Braves*, *Total Indians*, *Total Mets,* and *The Total Baseball Catalog*.

In 1994 Pietrusza served as a consultant for the PBS Learning Link system and produced the documentary *Local Heroes: Baseball On Capital Region Diamonds* for PBS affiliate WMHT, a documentary that ultimately helped lead to the election of George S. Davis to the National Baseball Hall of Fame.

He serves as editor-in-chief of Total Sports print publishing and helped produce the highly acclaimed *Total Baseball Online* (http://www.totalbaseball.com) web site.

He has also written on baseball for *The National Pastime*, *The Baseball Research Journal*, *USA Today Baseball Weekly*, *Baseball Digest*, *Nine* and *OldTyme Baseball News*.

Mr. Pietrusza is also managing editor of *Total Football,* the official encyclopedia of the NFL, and co-editor of *Total Cowboys*, *Total 49ers*, *Total Packers*, and *Total Steelers*.

His nonfiction works for young readers include *The End of the Cold War*, *The Invasion of Normandy*, *The Battle of Waterloo*, *The Chinese Cultural Revolution*, *John F. Kennedy, Smoking, The Roaring Twenties, The New York Yankees, Top 10 Baseball Managers, The Los Angeles Dodgers, Michael Jordan, The Boston Celtics,* and *The Phoenix Suns*.

Mr. Pietrusza lives in Scotia, New York with his wife, Patricia.